THE MESSIAH

Participants in the First Princeton Symposium on Judaism and Christian Origins

The First Princeton Symposium on

Judaism and Christian Origins

THE MESSIAH

Developments in Earliest

Judaism and Christianity

James H. Charlesworth, Editor

with
J. Brownson, M. T. Davis, S. J. Kraftchick, and A. F. Segal

FORTRESS PRESS **MINNEAPOLIS**

Library of Congress Cataloging-in-Publication Data

Princeton Symposiu on Judaism and Christian Origins (1st : 1987 : Princeton Theological Seminary)
    The Messi : developments in earliest Judaism and Christianity / the First Princeton Symposiu on Judaism and Christian Origins : James H. Charlesworth, editor . . . [et al.].
    p. n.
    Pr edings of a symposium held in October of 1987 at Princeton Theological Seminary.
    I udes bibliographical references and indexes.
    BN 0-8006-2563-3 (alk. paper).
    1. Messiah—History of doctrines—Congresses. 2. Messiah—Judaism—History of doctrines—Congresses. 3. Jesus Christ—Messiahship—Congresses. 4. Jesus Christ—Person and Offices—Congresses. I. Charlesworth, James H. II. Title.
BM615.P75   1987b
296.3′3—dc20   91-36381
                                                                   CIP

Manufactured in the U.S.A.   AF 1–2563

2   3   4   5   6   7   8   9   10

To the memory of
Menahem Stern of the Hebrew University
and in recognition of
Bruce Metzger of Princeton Theological Seminary

CONTENTS

Part Four
"Messianism" in Social Contexts and in Philo

PART FIVE
"THE MESSIAH" AND JESUS OF NAZARETH

PART SIX
"THE MESSIAH," "THE CHRIST," AND THE NEW TESTAMENT

CONTRIBUTORS

H. Anderson
Professor of New Testament,
  Emeritus
New College
University of Edinburgh

D. E. Aune
Professor of New Testament
Loyola University, Chicago

M. Black
Professor of New Testament,
  Emeritus
St. Andrews University

B. M. Bokser (d. 1990)
Late Professor of Rabbinic Studies
Jewish Theological Seminary
New York

P. Borgen
Professor of New Testament
University of Trondheim
Norway

F. H. Borsch
Bishop of the Episcopal Diocese of
  Los Angeles

J. Brownson
Professor of New Testament
Western Theological Seminary

J. H. Charlesworth
George L. Collord Professor of New
  Testament Language and
  Literature
Princeton Theological Seminary

W. D. Davies
George Washington Ivy Professor of
  Christian Origins, Emeritus
Duke University

J. D. G. Gunn
Professor of Divinity
University of Durham
England

N. A. Dahl
Buckingham Professor, Emeritus
Yale University

M. T. Davis
Special Research Assistant to
Professor J. H. Charlesworth
Princeton Theological Seminary

P. D. Hanson
Busey Professor of Divinity and of
    Old Testament
Harvard University

J.-G. Heintz
Professor of Old Testament and
    Ancient Semitic Languages
University of Strasbourg

M. Hengel
Professor of Early Judaism and
    Christian Origins
Tübingen University

R. A. Horsley
Professor, Study of Religion
University of Massachusetts

D. H. Juel
Professor of New Testament
Luther Northwestern
    Theological Seminary

R. G. Hamerton-Kelly
Center for International Security
    and Arms Control
Stanford University

S. J. Kraftchick
Assistant Professor of New
    Testament
Princeton Theological Seminary

B. L. Mack
Professor of New Testament
Claremont Graduate School

D. Mendels
Associate Professor of History
Hebrew University, Jerusalem

J. Priest
Professor of Old Testament and
    Classics
Florida State University

J. J. M. Roberts
William Henry Green Professor of
    Old Testament Literature
Princeton Theological Seminary

L. H. Schiffman
Professor of Jewish Studies
Skirball Department of Hebrew
    and Judaic Studies
New York University

A. F. Segal
Professor of the History of Religion
Barnard College
Columbia University

S. Talmon
J. L. Magnes Professor of Bible
    Studies
Hebrew University, Jerusalem

J. VanderKam
Professor of Old Testament
North Carolina State University

A. Yarbro Collins
Professor of New Testament
University of Chicago

PREFACE

Over the last two decades, and especially the last five years, the data available for studying Judaism and the origins of Christianity have risen phenomenally. We scholars used to talk about 7 Dead Sea Scrolls; now we struggle to comprehend over 170 Dead Sea Scrolls.[1] We began teaching advanced courses on the Old Testament Pseudepigrapha by referring to 17 writings; now we must ponder at least 65 documents,[2] sifting for early Jewish writings and the traditions in them, and, at the same time, considering the inclusion among the Pseudepigrapha documents such as the Apocalypse of Pseudo-Methodius, and the Revelation of Elchasai.[3] In addition, the vast advances in the field of archaeology and the study of ancient iconography now need to be included.

Specialists throughout the United States, Germany, Great Britain, and Israel urged me to organize an international symposium designed to answer this primary question: why and in what ways are these early Jewish and early Christian writings important for the study of Judaism and the origins of Christianity? Obviously the data are too amorphous, complex, and span too many centuries and Hellenistic cultures to be discussed fruitfully without some subquestions upon which to focus. Also, the steering committee deemed it wise not to exclude, as do the academies, the faith commitments of potential members of the symposium, so that a full discussion of the central questions can be heard by all in attendance—Jews, Christians, and others. It was decided, therefore, to provide time both for a full, honest, and nonconfessional debate, and for a discussion of the impact the results of such debates might have upon personal beliefs.

1. See the new and comprehensive edition of the Dead Sea Scrolls, organized by Princeton Theological Seminary, edited by the editor of this volume.
2. See J. H. Charlesworth, ed., *The Old Testament Pseudepigrapha*, 2 vols. (Garden City, N.Y., 1983–85).
3. See the forthcoming articles in *Journal for the Study of the Pseudepigrapha* by Stephen Gero and Gerard P. Luttikhuizen.

Professor David Dungan and I met several times and began to focus attention on a specific theological issue in one century in particular, with the recognition that contiguous centuries would also be scanned. The symposium
would examine from all perspectives—including iconographic and literary
evidence—the concept of the Messiah and related figures in first-century
Judaism and earliest Christianity, with concentration especially on Palestinian phenomena. He and I traveled to Washington, D.C., to seek advice
about funding from the National Endowment for the Humanities. A grant
from the Foundation for the Renewal of Gospel Studies covered our ex-
penses for this initial planning. Dr. Thomas Gillespie, President of Princeton
Theological Seminary, heard our request for support and further guidance.
He listened, asked some hard questions, and finally endorsed our plans and
committed a significant amount of institutional support. As a result, government funding possibilities were increased, and the success of the symposium
was enhanced.

The steering committee consisted of J. H. Charlesworth (chair), D. Dungan, J. J. M. Roberts, A. Segal, and J. Christiaan Beker. The committee set
the agenda, chose the participants, and planned the physical arrangements.

I am grateful to many for the phenomenal success of the symposium,
which was held in October 1987 at Princeton Theological Seminary. The
steering committee constantly went beyond the usual responsibilities to ensure an enjoyable as well as productive symposium. Additional grants were
received from the Foundation on Christian Origins, and especially the National Foundation for the Humanities. The Center of Theological Inquiry,
and its chancellor, the late James I. McCord, opened its doors and welcomed
us in a relaxed environment each evening. James Brownson, Steve Kraftchick,
and Alan Segal helped me edit these papers for publication. Professor Roberts
and Dr. Jin Hee Han provided significant assistance and Michelle Charlesworth helped me with the final editing. Most importantly I am indebted to
President Gillespie for his support of pure scholarly research, and to the
specialists who participated in the symposium and came from far away, including Israel, Norway, France, Germany, Scotland, and England.

On the final day of the symposium a plenary session was arranged to discern if major agreements had been reached. The consensus of the members
of the symposium was obtained by public vote and discussion.

Major disagreements. What do terms like "messianology," "eschatology,"
"apocalypticism," and "theocracy" mean, and which groups should be described by them? Scholars expressed a variety of views, many of which were
complementary. They agreed that more discussion on these terms was
needed, but that more extended discussion would probably not resolve all
the disagreements. They expressed divergent opinions about these terms,
which will require further examination and joint study. For example, the
term "son of man" (or "Son of Man") aroused considerable debate. While
there was agreement that this term was pre-Christian, there was disagree-

ment over the *influence* of this term (or title) both on the Gospels and on Jesus of Nazareth.

Experts on many sources presented fruitful papers on specific issues. They agreed that it is now necessary to discuss how these analytic studies contribute to the overall reconstruction of the period. It is time to aim at a more reliable understanding of Jews and "Christians" at the beginning of the era, and to explore those concerns, commitments, and dreams that united or separated them.

Agreements. Scholars came together from different countries and traditions to look at a common period in which streams diverge in order to gain better understandings of how they diverge and to foster understanding and overcome prejudice. They agreed that the time is propitious for sensitive and fruitful cooperation among Jews and Christians.

Christos is the title or term most frequently applied to Jesus in the New Testament. Scholars agreed that the crucial question is the following: How did this happen, since "the Messiah" is rarely found, and the functions or attributes of "the Messiah" are even less explained, in extant pre-70 Jewish documents?

The term and the title "Messiah" in the Hebrew Bible refers to a present, political and religious leader who is appointed by God. It was applied predominantly to a king, but also to a priest, and occasionally to a prophet. This carefully crafted statement was passed unanimously.

Scholars concurred that there was no single, discernible role description for a "Messiah" into which a historical figure like Jesus could be fit. Rather, each group which entertained a messianic hope interpreted "Messiah" in light of its historical experiences and reinterpreted Scripture accordingly. This position was unanimously endorsed.

It is inappropriate to speak of a single normative stream of Judaism in the postexilic period or throughout the period of the Second Temple. Diverse interpretations of common traditions were entertained by different groups. This insight was unanimously endorsed.

After this book was completed some scholars claimed that two unpublished texts among the Dead Sea Scrolls contained important references to the Messiah. One text ostensibly referred to the Messiah who will come and die for the sins of the world. The other text allegedly mentioned the Messiah will come and resurrect the dead. These claims appeared in major newspapers, like the *New York Times,* during the period from September 1991 to April 1992. In fact, in the news release by the University of Chicago of April 8, 1992, we are told that in 4Q521 "a Hebrew writer says of the coming Messiah, 'He shall heal the wounded, resurrect the dead, and proclaim glad tidings to the poor.'"

The first text is 4Q285 (photograph number 41.282). It does not contain the noun "the Messiah." And no line has the words that a person has died or will die for the sins of the world. The text seems to be an exegetical expan-

sion on Isaiah (especially chapters 10–11); it may be messianic. My response
to these claims appeared in "Sense or Sensationalism? The Dead Sea Scrolls
Controversy," *The Christian Century* 109.4 (January 29, 1992) 92–98.

The second text is 4Q521 (photograph number 43.604). S. A. Reed cata-
logued it as a text on "the resurrection."[1] There are 13 fragments. The first
line of the largest fragment has the noun *lmshyhw,* dative or accusative for
"his (i.e. God's) Messiah." On another fragment, we see *wk mshyhy,* which
means "all the Messiahs of." The document thus does not consistently refer
to one messiah; hence R. H. Eisenman's claim that this text refers to "a
single Davidic-style messiah" is misleading.[2] We need to allow for the possibility that in one place one Messiah is mentioned and in another two Messiahs as in 1QS are designated. Most importantly, the claim that the Messiah
"resurrects the dead" is inaccurate. The Lord, *adny,*[3] becomes the ruling
noun in fragment 1, line 3, and continues through line 13 in which we do
find *wmtym yhyh,* "and he will give life (to) the dead ones." As in many early
Jewish texts, including the Amidah, God is perceived as the one who resurrects the dead.[4]

1. S. A. Reed, *Dead Sea Scross Inventory Project* (Claremont: Ancient Biblical Manuscript
Center, 1992) fascicle 8, p. 10.

2. R. H. Eisenman, "A Messianic Vision," *BAR* 17 (1991) 65.

2. "Lord" is written defectively at least eight times in this document. This is the only one of
the Dead Sea Scrolls in which *adny* is always written defectively.

4. I am grateful to Loren Stuckenbruck, James VanderKam, and Larry Schiffman for discussions regarding the "unpublished messianic" passages in the Dead Sea Scrolls.

ABBREVIATIONS

I. MODERN WORKS

AB	Anchor Bible
AcOr	*Acta orientalia*
AGAJU	Arbeiten zur Geschichte des antiken Judentums und des Urchristentums
AHAW.PH	*Abhandlungen der Heidelberger Akademie der Wissenschaften—Philosophisch-historische Klasse*
AJS	Association for Jewish Studies Review
AKG	*Arbeiten zur Kirchengeschichte*
ALBO	Analecta lovaniensia biblica et orientalia
ANRW	Haase, W., and H. Temporini, eds., *Aufstieg und Niedergang der römischen Welt*. Berlin, New York, 1979–
AOAT	Alter Orient und Altes Testament
AOT	Altorientalische Texte zum Alten Testament
APAT	Kautzsch, E., ed. *Die Apokryphen und Pseudepigraphen des Alten Testaments*, 2 vols. Tübingen, phen des Alten Testaments, 2 vols. Tübingen, 1900.
APOT	Charles R. H., ed. *The Apocrypha and Pseudepigrapha of the Old Testament in English*. 2 vols. Oxford, 1913.
ARW	*Archiv für Religionswissenschaft*
ATANT	Abhandlungen zur Theologie des Alten und Neuen Testaments
ATR	*Anglican Theological Review*
BAC	*Biblioteca de autores cristianos*
BAGD	Bauer, Arndt, Gingrich, Danker, eds., *A Greek-English Lexicon of the New Testament and Other Early Christian Literature*, 2nd ed., Chicago, 1979.
BASOR	*Bulletin of the American Schools of Oriental Research*

BDB	Brown, Driver, Briggs, eds. *A Hebrew and English Lexicon of the Old Testament*. Oxford, 1907.
BETL	Bibliotheca Ephemeridum Theologicarum Lovaniensium, Paris/Gembloux
Bib	*Biblica*
BJRL, BJRULM	*Bulletin of the John Rylands Library, Bulletin of the John Rylands University Library of Manchester*
BR	*Biblical Research*
BTS	*Bible et Terre Sainte*
BWANT	Beiträge zur Wissenschaft vom Alten und Neuen Testament
BZ	*Biblische Zeitschrift*
BZNW	Beihefte zur Zeitschrift für die neutestamentliche Wissenschaft und die Kunde der älteren Kirche
BZRG	Beihefte der Zeitschrift für Religions- und Geistesgeschichte
CBQ	*Catholic Biblical Quarterly*
CBQ MS	*Catholic Biblical Quarterly* Monograph Series
CRINT	Compendia Rerum Iudaicarum ad Novum Testamentum
DACL	*Dictionnaire d'archéologie chrétienne et liturgie*
DJD	Discoveries in the Judaean Desert
EKK	Evangelisch-Katholischer Kommentar
EncBibl	Encyclopaedia Biblica, Jerusalam
EtB	*Études Bibliques*
ETL	*Ephemerides theologicae lovanienses*
EvT	*Evangelische Theologie*
ExpT	*Expository Times*
FRLANT	Forschungen zur Religion und Literatur des Alten und Neuen Testaments
GCS	Griechischen christlichen Schriftsteller derersten drei Jahrhunderte
HAT	Handbuch zum Alten Testament
HDR	Harvard Dissertations in Religion
Hist	*Historia* (Wiesbaden)
HNT	Handbuch zum Neuen Testament
HSCPh	Harvard Studies in Classical Philology
HSM	Harvard Semitic Monographs
HTR	*Harvard Theological Review*
HTS	Harvard Theological Studies
IDBS	Crim, K., et al., eds. *The Interpreter's Dictionary of the Bible, Supplementary Volume*. Nashville, Tenn., 1976.
IEJ	*Israel Exploration Journal*

Int	*Interpretation*
JAAR	*Journal of the American Academy of Religion*
JB	Jerusalem Bible
JBL	*Journal of Biblical Literature*
JJS	*Journal of Jewish Studies*
JNES	*Journal of Near Eastern Studies*
JQR	*Jewish Quarterly Review*
JR	*Journal of Religion*
JSHRZ	Kümmel, W. G., et al. *Jüdische Schriften aus hellenistischrömischer Zeit.* Gütersloh, 1973– .
JSJ	*Journal for the Study of Judaism*
JSNT	*Journal for the Study of the New Testament*
JSS	*Journal of Semitic Studies*
JSSR	*Journal for the Scientific Study of Religion*
JThC	*Journal for Theology and the Church*
JTS	*Journal of Theological Studies*
KEH	Kurzgefasstes exegetisches Handbuch
KGK	Kritisch-exegetischer Kommentar über das Neue Testament
KuD	*Kerygma und Dogma*
LSJM	Liddell, H. G., and R. Scott. *A Greek-English Lexicon,* rev. by H. S. Jones and R. McKenzie, Oxford, 1940.
MBPF	Münchener Beiträge zur Papyrusforschung und antiken Rechtsgeschichte
MNTC	Moffatt New Testament Commentary
NHS	*Nag Hammadi Studies*
NovT	*Novum Testamentum*
NTA	Neutestamentliche Abhandlungen
NTF	Neutestamentliche Forschung
NTS	*New Testament Studies*
OTP	Charlesworth, J. H., ed. *The Old Testament Pseudepigrapha.* 2 vols. Garden City, N.Y., 1983, 1985.
OTS	Oudtestamentische Studiën.
PMAAR	Papers and Monographs of the American Academy in Rome
PW	Pauly-wissowa, Real-Encyclopädie der classischen Alterthumswissenschaft
RAC	Reallexikon für Antike und Christentum
RB	*Revue biblique*
RMu	*Revue musicale*
RPh	*Revue de philologie de littérature et d'histoire anciennes*
RQ	*Revue de Qumran*
RSR	*Recherches de science religieuse*

SBLDS	Society of Biblical Literature Dissertation Series
SBLMS	Society of Biblical Literature Monograph Series
SBS	Stuttgarter Bibelstudien
SBT	Studies in Biblical Theology
SCS	Septuagint and Cognate Studies
SEÅ	*Svensk exegetisk Årsbok*
SJLA	Studies in Judaism in Late Antiquity
SJT	*Scottish Journal of Theology*
SNT	Schriften des Neuen Testament
SNTS MS	*Studiorum Novi Testamenti Societas* Monograph Series
ST	*Studia Theologica*
StNT	*Studien zum Neuen Testament*
SUNT	Studien zum Umwelt des Neuen Testaments, Göttingen
SVT	Supplements to Vetus Testamentum
SVTP	Studia in Veteris Testamenti Pseudepigrapha
TAPA	Transactions and Proceedings. American Philological Association
TDNT	Kittel G., ed. *Theological Dictionary of the New Testament*. 10 vols., trans. G. W. Bromiley. Grand Rapids, Mich., London, 1964–76.
Theoph	Theophaneia
ThRu	*Theologische Rundschau*
TLZ	*Theologische Literaturzeitung*
TRE	*Theologische Realenzyklopädie*
TSAAJR	*Texts and Studies: American Academy for Jewish Research*
TU	Texte und Untersuchungen
TWAT	Botterweck, G. J., and H. Ringgren, eds. *Theologisches Wörterbuch zum Alten Testament*. 5 vols. Stuttgart, 1973–86.
TWNT	Kittel, G., ed. *Theologisches Wörterbuch zum Neuen Testament*. 10 vols. Stuttgart, 1932–79.
TZ	*Theologische Zeitschrift*
USQR	*Union Seminary Quarterly Review*
VC	*Vigiliae christianae*
VT	*Vetus Testamentum*
WdF	Wege der Forschung
WMANT	Wissenschaftliche Monographien zum Alten und Neuen Testaments
WUNT	Wissenschaftliche Untersuchungen zum Neuen Testament
ZAW	*Zeitschrift für die alttestamentliche Wissenschaft*
ZKT	*Zeitschrift für Katholisches Theologie*

| ZNW | *Zeitschrift für die neutestamentliche Wissenschaft* |
| ZTK | *Zeitschrift für Theologie und Kirche* |

Additional Abbreviations

Ara.	Aramaic
c.	circa
cf.	compare
ch(s).	chapter(s)
col(s).	column(s)
Cop.	Coptic
esp.	especially
ET	English translation
Eth.	Ethiopic
f(f).	the following page(s)
Gk.	Greek
GNMM	Good News for Modern Man
Heb.	Hebrew
illus.	illustration
JB	Jerusalem Bible
l(l).	line(s)
Lat.	Latin
lit.	literally
LXX	Septuagint
MS(S)	Manuscript(s)
MT	Masoretic Text
n(n).	note(s)
NEB	New English Bible
NF	Neue Folge
NT	New Testament
OG	Old Greek
OT	Old Testament
p(p).	page(s)
par.	parallel
pt(s).	part(s)
RSV	Revised Standard Version
SBL	Society of Biblical Literature
Syh	Syro-Hexaplar
Syr.	Syriac
vs(s).	verse(s)
vol(s).	volume(s)

II. ANCIENT DOCUMENTS

Bible and Apocrypha

Gen	Genesis
Ex	Exodus
Lev	Leviticus
Num	Numbers
Deut	Deuteronomy
Josh	Joshua
Judg	Judges
Ruth	Ruth
1Sam	1 Samuel
2Sam	2 Samuel
1Kgs	1 Kings
2Kgs	2 Kings
1Chr	1 Chronicles
2Chr	2 Chronicles
Ezra	Ezra
Neh	Nehemiah
Esth	Esther
Job	Job
Ps(s)	Psalms
Prov	Proverbs
Eccl (Qoh)	Ecclesiastes (Qoheleth)
Song	Song of Songs
Isa	Isaiah
Jer	Jeremiah
Lam	Lamentations
Ezek	Ezekiel
Dan	Daniel
Hos	Hosea
Joel	Joel
Amos	Amos
Obad	Obadiah
Jonah	Jonah
Micah	Micah
Nah	Nahum
Hab	Habakkuk
Zeph	Zephaniah
Hag	Haggai
Zech	Zechariah
Mal	Malachi
2Ezra	2 Ezra
Tob	Tobit

Jdt	Judith
AddEsth	Additions to Esther
WisSol	Wisdom of Solomon
Sir	Sirach
1Bar	1 Baruch
LetJer	Letter of Jeremiah
PrAzar	Prayer of Azariah
Sus	Susanna
Bel	Bel and the Dragon
1Mac	1 Maccabees
2Mac	2 Maccabees
Mt	Matthew
Mk	Mark
Lk	Luke
Jn	John
Acts	Acts
Rom	Romans
1Cor	1 Corinthians
2Cor	2 Corinthians
Gal	Galatians
Eph	Ephesians
Phil	Philippians
Col	Colossians
1Thes	1 Thessalonians
2Thes	2 Thessalonians
1Tim	1 Timothy
2Tim	2 Timothy
Tit	Titus
Phlm	Philemon
Heb	Hebrews
Jas	James
1Pet	1 Peter
2Pet	2 Peter
1Jn	1 John
2Jn	2 John
3Jn	3 John
Jude	Jude
Rev	Revelation

Pseudepigrapha

ApAb	Apocalypse of Abraham
TAb	Testament of Abraham
ApAdam	Apocalypse of Adam
TAdam	Testament of Adam

LAE	Life of Adam and Eve
Ah	Ahiqar
AnonSam	An Anonymous Samaritan Text
LetAris	Letter of Aristeas
ArisEx	Aristeas the Exegete
Aristob	Aristobulus
Art	Artapanus
2Bar	2 (Syriac Apocalypse of) Baruch
3Bar	3 (Greek Apocalypse of) Baruch
4Bar	4 Baruch
CavTr	Cave of Treasures
ClMal	Cleodemus Malchus
ApDan	Apocalypse of Daniel
Dem	Demetrius
ElMod	Eldad and Modad
ApEl	Apocalypse of Elijah
HebApEl	Hebrew Apocalypse of Elijah
1En	1 (Ethiopic Apocalypse of) Enoch
2En	2 (Slavonic Apocalypse of) Enoch
3En	3 (Hebrew Apocalypse of) Enoch
Eup	Eupolemus
Ps-Eup	Pseudo-Eupolemus
ApocEzek	Apocryphon of Ezekiel
ApEzek	Apocalypse of Ezekiel
EzekTrag	Ezekiel the Tragedian
4Ezra	4 Ezra
GkApEzra	Greek Apocalypse of Ezra
QuesEzra	Questions of Ezra
RevEzra	Revelation of Ezra
VisEzra	Vision of Ezra
HecAb	Hecataeus of Abdera
Ps-Hec	Pseudo-Hecataeus
HelSynPr	Hellenistic Synagogal Prayers
THez	Testament of Hezekiah
FrgsHisWrks	Fragments of Historical Works
TIsaac	Testament of Isaac
AscenIs	Ascension of Isaiah
MartIs	Martyrdom of Isaiah
VisIs	Vision of Isaiah
LadJac	Ladder of Jacob
PrJac	Prayer of Jacob
TJac	Testament of Jacob
JanJam	Jannes and Jambres
TJob	Testament of Job
JosAsen	Joseph and Aseneth

HistJos	History of Joseph
PrJos	Prayer of Joseph
Jub	Jubilees
LAB	*Liber Antiquitatum Biblicarum*
LosTr	The Lost Tribes
3Mac	3 Maccabees
4Mac	4 Maccabees
5Mac	5 Maccabees
PrMan	Prayer of Manasseh
SyrMen	Syriac Menander
ApMos	Apocalypse of Moses
AsMos	Assumption of Moses
PrMos	Prayer of Moses
TMos	Testament of Moses
BkNoah	Book of Noah
Ps-Orph	Pseudo-Orpheus
PJ	*Paraleipomena Jeremiou*
PhEPoet	Philo the Epic Poet
Ps-Philo	Pseudo-Philo
Ps-Phoc	Pseudo-Phocylides
FrgsPoetWrks	Fragments of Poetical Works
LivPro	Lives of the Prophets
HistRech	History of the Rechabites
ApSedr	Apocalypse of Sedrach
TrShem	Treatise of Shem
SibOr	Sibylline Oracles
OdesSol	Odes of Solomon
PssSol	Psalms of Solomon
TSol	Testament of Solomon
5ApocSyrPss	Five Apocryphal Syriac Psalms
Thal	Thallus
Theod	Theodotus
T12P	Testament of the Twelve Patriarchs
TReu	Testament of Reuben
TSim	Testament of Simeon
TLevi	Testament of Levi
TJud	Testament of Judah
TIss	Testament of Issachar
TZeb	Testament of Zebulun
TDan	Testament of Dan
TNaph	Testament of Naphtali
TGad	Testament of Gad
TAsh	Testament of Asher
TJos	Testament of Joseph
TBenj	Testament of Benjamin

Vita	*Vita Adae et Evae*
ApZeph	Apocalypse of Zephaniah
ApZos	Apocalypse of Zosimus

DEAD SEA SCROLLS

*(Abbreviations from the Princeton Theological Seminary Dead Sea
Scrolls Project [only those cited])*

Rules

1QS	Rule of the Community
1QSa	Rule of the Congregation
1QSb	Collection of Blessings
4Q181	The Wicked and Holy
4QOrd	Ordinances
CD	The Damascus Document
4QMMT	Letter of Religious Rules

Hymns and Prayers

1QH	The Thanksgiving Hymns
4QPBless	Patriarchal Blessings
4QPrNab	Prayer of Nabonidus
4QShirShabb	Angelic Liturgy
1Q29	Liturgy of the Three Tongues of Fire
4Q510–11	Wisdom Canticles
8QHymn	A Hymn
4Q503	Daily Prayers

Commentaries

1QpHab	Habakkuk Pesher
1QpMic (1Q14)	Micah Pesher 1
1QpPs (1Q16)	Psalm Pesher 1
1QpZeph (1Q15)	Zephaniah Pesher 1
4QpNah (4Q169)	Nahum Pesher
4QTestim (4Q175)	Testimonies
4QFlor (4Q174)	Florilegium
4QpIsa (4Q161–165)	Isaiah Pesher 1
4QpHos (4Q166–167)	Hosea Pesher 2
4QpZeph (4Q170)	Zephaniah Pesher 2
4QCatena[a] (4Q177)	Catena A

4QCatena^b (4Q182–183)	Catena B
4QpPs^a (4Q171, 4QPs37)	Psalm Pesher 2
4QpPs^b (4Q173, 4QPs127)	Psalm Pesher 3
4QapLam (4Q179)	Pseudo-Lamentations

Apocryphal and Related Works

1QM	War Scroll
4QAgesCreat	Ages of Creation
1QJN-ar	The New Jerusalem
1QDM	Sayings of Moses
1QNoah 2	Noah Apocryphon
1QMyst	Book of the Mysteries
2QapDavid	David Apocryphon
11QTemple	Temple Scroll
1QapGen	Genesis Apocryphon
2QapProph	Prophetic Apocryphon
5QapMal	Malachi Apocryphon
6QapSam/Kgs	Samuel-Kings Apocryphon
6QProph	Prophetic Text
6QAllegory	Allegory of the Vine
6QapProph	Prophetic Apocryphon
6QApoc ar (6Q14)	Apocalyptic Text
6QPriestProph (6Q13)	Priestly Prophecy
6QCal	Calendar Text
4Q184	Dame Folly and Lady Wisdom
4QVisSamuel (4Q160)	Vision of Samuel
4Q176	Tanḥumim
4Q185	A Sapiential Testament
4Q512	Purification Ritual
1Q26	A Wisdom Apocryphon
11QMelch	Melchizedek

Other Scrolls

3Q15	The Copper Scroll
4Q186	Horoscopes

PHILO ABBREVIATIONS

Abr	*De Abrahamo*
Aet	*De Aeternitate Mundi*
Cher	*De Cherubim*

Conf	De Confusione Linguarum
Dec	De Decalogo
Ebr	De Ebrietate
Flacc	In Flaccum
Gaium	De Legatione ad Gaium
Heres	Quis Rerum Divinarum Heres
Jos	De Iosepho
Leg All	Legum Allegoriae
Migr	De Migratione Abrahami
Mut	De Mutatione Nominum
Op	De Opificio Mundi
Post	De Posteritate Caini
Praem	De Praemiis et Poenis
Quaes Ex I–II	Quaestiones et Solutiones in Exodum I–II
Quod Det	Quod Deterius Potiori insidiari solet
Quod Deus	Quod Deus immutabilis sit
Sacr	De Sacrificiis Abelis et Caini
Somn I–II	De Somniis I–II
Spec Leg I–IV	De Specialibus Legibus I–IV
Virt	De Virtutibus
Vita Mos I–II	De Vita Mosis I–II

JOSEPHUS

Ant	Jewish Antiquities
Apion	Against Apion
Life	Life of Josephus
War	Jewish Wars

NEW TESTAMENT APOCRYPHA AND PSEUDEPIGRAPHA

EBar	Epistle of Barnabas
1Clem	1 Clement
PseudClemHom	Pseudo-Clementine Homilies
PseudClemRec	Pseudo-Clementine Recognitions
GThom	Gospel of Thomas

EARLY FATHERS

AdvHaer	Epiphanius, Adversus haereses
Apol	Justin, Apologiae
CCels	Origen, Contra Celsus
DemEvang	Eusebius, Demostratio Evangelica
Did	Didache

DialTrypho	Justin, *Dialogue with Trypho*
HistEccl	Eusebius, *Ecclesiastical History*
MartPol	*Martyrdom of Polycarp*
Smyr	Ignatius, *Epistle to the Smyrnaeans*
Trall	Ignatius, *Epistle to the Trallians*

RABBINIC

ARN	Abot de-Rabbi Nathan
b. (before a rabbinic text)	Babylonian Talmud
Ber	Berakot
GenR	Bere'šit Rabbah
Ḥag	Ḥagigah
LevR	Leviticus Rabbah
m. (before a rabbinic text)	Mishnah
Meg	Megillah
Sanh	Sanhedrin
Shab	Shabbat
SifDeut	Sifre Deuteronomy
Soṭ	Soṭah
t. (before a rabbinic text)	Tosephta
Tanh	Tanhuma
Targ The	Targum on the Psalms
TargPsJon	Targum Pseudo-Jonathan
TK	Lieberman, S., ed. *Tosefta Kifshutah.* 8 vols. to date, New York, 1955–
y. (before a rabbinic text)	Jerusalem Talmud

OTHER ANCIENT WORKS

Ann	Tacitus, *Annales*
Ep.	Pliny (the Younger), *Epistulae*
LAS	*Letters from Assyrian Scholars to the Kings Esarhaddon and Assurbanipal* (AOAT 5/1; Neukirchen/ Vluyn, 1970)
Pr.A.	Akkadian Prophecies
Thuc.	Thucydides

PART ONE

INTRODUCTION

J. H. CHARLESWORTH

1

FROM MESSIANOLOGY TO CHRISTOLOGY:
Problems and Prospects

What is a "Christian"? Most people would answer: one who believes that Jesus of Nazareth was "the Christ" Jews were expecting. Many Christians, Jews, and most citizens of the modern world would tend to agree on this definition. It is, however, misleading and, indeed, inaccurate.[1] It assumes three things: (1) that the title "Christ" fully categorizes Jesus, (2) that Christians are clear and in agreement on what this title, "Christ," denotes, and (3) that all, or virtually all, Jews during the time of Jesus were looking for the coming of the Messiah or Christ. This paper reports on an examination of the sources of Jewish thought before 70 C.E., when the Temple was destroyed; the result produces a serious challenge to the third assumption and probably undermines the other two.

DEFINITION

It is helpful to define what I mean by "Messiah," "messianic," "messianology," and "christology." Scholarly publications on messianology and christology are frequently garbled by the different definitions which are used; many of which are never clarified.[2] For the most part, I am convinced, Jewish messianology developed out of the crisis and hope of the nonmessianic Maccabean wars of the second century B.C.E.[3] Palestinian Jews yearned for salva-

---

1. See Charlesworth, "From Jewish Messianology to Christian Christology: Some Caveats and Perspectives," in *Judaisms and Their Messiahs*, ed. J. Neusner, W. S. Green, and E. Frerichs (Cambridge, 1988), pp. 225–64.

2. The term "messianic" has been used loosely and incorrectly, causing confusion and distorting ancient ideologies, as S. Mowinckel stressed many decades ago in his *He That Cometh: The Messiah Concept in the Old Testament and Later Judaism*, trans. G. W. Anderson (New York, Nashville, 1954), p. 451.

3. See the important observations along this line by A. Caquot in his "Le messianisme qumrânien," in *Qumrân: Sa piété, sa théologie et son milieu*, ed. M. Delcor (Bibliotheca Ephemeridum Theologicarum Lovaniensium 46; Paris, Leuven, 1978), pp. 231–47.

tion from their pagan oppressors. For an undeterminable number of Jews the yearning centered on the future saving acts by a divinely appointed, and anointed, supernatural man: the Messiah. This eschatological figure will inaugurate the end of all normal time and history. I, therefore, use the term "Messiah" in its etymological sense, to denote God's eschatological Anointed One, the Messiah.[4] The adjective "messianic" refers to images, symbols, or concepts either explicitly or implicitly linked to ideas about the Messiah. The noun "messianology" denotes Jewish ideas or beliefs in the Messiah. The noun "christology" is used here in a narrow sense; it is reserved for reflections on Jesus as the Christ. My concern now is to discern how and why reflections about a Palestinian Jew, namely Jesus of Nazareth, could move from messianology to christology. By exploring this issue I am not implying that christology did somehow flow from the messianology.

INTRODUCTIONS

Introductions to the New Testament often imply that there was a recognizable definition of what the Messiah was to do, that there was a set concept of the Messiah, and that Jews were looking for the coming of the Messiah who would save God's people. Let me illustrate this point by quoting from three major introductions.

The most influential and celebrated Roman Catholic *New Testament Introduction* is by Professor Alfred Wikenhauser. He describes the dominant theme of Matthew as follows:

> Jesus is the Messias or Son of David who was promised in the Old Testament and earnestly awaited by the Jews; but through the fault of his people, and particularly of their leaders, he was prevented from fulfilling his mission.[5]

The paragraph ends at this point. Should not the student have been warned that Matthew does not represent a putative Jewish viewpoint, and that the Old Testament does not contain a programmed mission for "the Messiah"? The statement would also be dubbed anti-Jewish and anti-Semitic by many scholars, both Jewish and Christian, because it perpetuates the concept that Jesus was the Messiah, or Christ, who was "prevented from fulfilling his mission," or put to death, by "the Jews." Furthermore, the next paragraph be-

---

4. See Charlesworth, "Messiah," in *Illustrated Dictionary & Concordance of the Bible*, eds. G. Wigoder, S. M. Paul, B. T. Viviano, and E. Stern (New York, London, 1986), pp. 682–84 (the last fifteen lines are not by me; I am more impressed by the redactional nature of the New Testament).

5. A Wikenhauser, *New Testament Introduction*, trans. J. Cunningham (Dublin, 1958, with many reprints), p. 186.

gins with these words: "The main thesis of the Gospel is proved by showing that the Messianic prophecies are fulfilled in him; . . ." The student may erroneously assume that Matthew preserves a valid record of Jewish messianic ideas, and that Jesus should be heralded as "the Messiah" because he clearly fulfilled all messianic prophecies.

Decades ago Professor Rudolf Bultmann cogently and perceptively warned against the imposition of a messianic message onto the sayings of Jesus:

> No saying of Jesus mentions the Messiah-king who is to crush the enemies of the People . . . Jesus' message is connected with the hope of other circles. . . . [6]

Bultmann's insight is profound and needs to be stressed. The sayings of Jesus, both those which are authentic and those which were attributed to him, do not contain speculations on or prophecies concerning the coming of a Messiah who will conquer the Gentiles, namely the Romans. Hence we must ponder two possibilities: either such a messianic dimension was deleted from the teachings of Jesus, which seems improbable, or Jesus' Jewish followers refused to portray him as a teacher who was concerned with messianic predictions. Jesus' message was certainly apocalyptic and eschatological; but it was not messianic. What are the implications of this discovery?

No member of the Princeton Symposium on the Messiah holds that a critical historian can refer to a common Jewish messianic hope during the time of Jesus or in the sayings of Jesus.[7] It may not even be easy to demonstrate a common messianic hope among his earliest followers.

The most recent and erudite *Introduction to the New Testament* is by Professor Helmut Koester. Frequently he seems to assume the myth that Jews expected a Messiah and knew what functions he would perform. In describing the beliefs of the Samaritans, he states "that just like the Jews the Samaritans expected the coming of the Messiah."[8] No discussion is focused on the problem of dating the Samaritan ideas,[9] and no proof is offered to support the claim that "Jews expected the coming of a Messiah."

---

6. R. Bultmann, *Theology of the New Testament*, 2 vols., trans. K. Grobel (New York, 1951–55) vol. 1, p. 4. I have quoted Bultmann in such a way as to eliminate his invalid assumption that these "other circles" were apocalyptic—as if the concept of the Messiah does not appear in the apocalypses (see 4Ezra and 2Bar)—and the belief in a "miraculous change in historical (i.e. political and social) conditions . . . a cosmic catastrophe" cannot be messianic.

7. After the papers for the Symposium were delivered and discussed, a plenary session was devoted to a discussion of a possible consensus on such issues. See "Preface" at the beginning of this volume.

8. H. Koester, *Introduction to the New Testament* (Hermeneia; Philadelphia, Berlin, 1982), vol. 1, p. 249.

9. See the following discussion on the Samaritans, Talmon's excellent paper in this collection, and Talmon's "Types of Messianic Expectation at the Turn of the Era," *King, Cult and Calendar in Ancient Israel: Collected Studies* (Jerusalem, 1986) see esp. pp. 207–9. Professor Talmon knows the Samaritan writings and has spent considerable time with Samaritans who live today on Mt. Gerizim.

Later in the same volume, Koester describes the first great Jewish revolt against Rome in these terms: the Romans "were confronted with a movement that was inspired by revolutionary messianic ideas and that had the allegiance of large parts of the whole population" (p. 402). The next sentence also seems misleading: "Characteristic for the political messianism of the rebellion was the appearance of a group which Josephus calls the 'Zealots.'" Can we be so certain that the Jewish rebellion of 66–74 C.E. and the group called the "Zealots" were both messianic?

Surely the catalyst of the rebellion, as Josephus and Koester claim, was not Jewish messianism but "the incredible stupidity and brutality of the Roman procurator" (p. 401), who was Gessius Florus (64–66 C.E.). He robbed the Temple, desecrated Jerusalem, and wantonly offended all religious Jews. What observations allow us then to describe the revolt as "messianic"? Given Josephus' penchant to attribute apologetically the revolt of 66–74 C.E. to messianic extremists should caution us against describing it as "messianic." In contrast to the revolt of 132–135 C.E., it was not led by a heralded Messiah.

These excerpts from two of the best available introductions to the New Testament reveal a glaring problem in the study of Early Judaism and Christian Origins. There is a deeply seated and widely assumed contention that the Jews during the time of Jesus were expecting a Messiah, and that they had some agreement on the basic functions he would perform. Yet this contention is assumed; it is not researched.

CHRISTOLOGIES

Many books on christology and New Testament theology perpetuate without demonstration the following invalid assumptions: (1) One can move smoothly from Jewish messianology to Christian christology. (2) What the Jews expected was fulfilled in the life and teachings of Jesus of Nazareth, who is then transparently the Messiah, Jesus Christ. (3) Jesus' followers were convinced of his messiahship because they saw how he filled the portrait of the Messiah.

Early Jewish literature, however, cannot be mined to produce anything like a checklist of what the Messiah shall do. The proclamations and teachings in the earliest Jesus communities in Palestine may reflect the use of something like a list of testimonies about the Messiah; but these do not prove that Jews had a common messianology. They are evidence of what the earliest "Christians" created. A checklist is an objective collection of what is obvious; a testimony is one individual's or group's subjective collection of Old Testament prophecies. Jesus' earliest followers were obviously pressed to prove their claim that he was the expected Messiah. Their efforts are evident in the remnants of the old tradition that Jesus would fulfill the messianic prophecies *in the future, when he returns* as the Christ (see Acts 2:36 and

Rom 1:4), in the pneumatic exegesis of originally nonmessianic prophecies and psalms (viz. Pss 22 and 110),[10] and in the addition of messianic episodes to the story of Jesus.

Before proceeding further, it is necessary once again to illustrate the extent to which gifted and well-trained scholars have perpetuated the contention, perhaps unwittingly, that Jesus is best understood as the Messiah awaited by the Jews. Note these excerpts:

In his highly acclaimed and widely circulated *New Testament Theology*[11] Professor Ethelbert Stauffer concluded as follows:

> The first title he (namely Jesus) did accept as a valid and accurate description of his saving mission was that of "Christ" (Mark 8:29). This gives a special authenticity to the title of Messiah as a predicate to describe Jesus Christ. The early Church laid claim to all the honors that this title involved. Particularly did she stress the Messiah's vocation to suffer (Acts 17:3).

After an impressive review of the pertinent data, Professor George Eldon Ladd, in *A Theology of the New Testament*, comes to the following conclusion:

> Jesus in some way acted like the Messiah; yet a Messiah very different from contemporary Jewish hopes. It is difficult to believe that Jesus filled a role of which he was unconscious. He must have known himself to be the Messiah.[12]

I find it difficult to comprehend how the Jewish man Jesus could have thought he was the Messiah and yet one who was "very different" from the Messiah expected by the Jews. Despite knowledge of the primary and secondary sources, Ladd perpetuates two fallacies: Jesus "must have known" he was the Messiah, and there was a coherent idea of the Messiah among his fellow Jews. Also, what is meant by the statement that "Jesus in some way acted like the Messiah"? Did he or did he not?

We have numerous early Jewish sources that portray the Messiah, variously, as one who will serve as the eschatological high priest (the Dead Sea Scrolls, the T12P), or as the consummate benevolent and all-powerful king (PssSol 17). Numerous functions are sometimes attributed to the Messiah: He will judge the wicked (PssSol 17, 4Ezra 12, 2Bar 40), destroy them (PssSol 17, 18; 4Ezra 12, 2Bar 72; cf. Isa 11), deliver God's people (PssSol 17, 4Ezra 12; cf. Zech 9), and/or reign in a blessed kingdom (PssSol 17, 18; 2Bar 40; cf. Ps 2).

---

10. See D. Juel's demonstration that earliest Christian thought began as biblical exegesis and "that what stands at the beginning of that reflection and provides a focus and a direction for scriptural exegesis is the confession of Jesus as Messiah" (p. 1). D. Juel, *Messianic Exegesis: Christological Interpretation of the Old Testament in Early Christianity* (Philadelphia, 1988).

11. E. Stauffer, *New Testament Theology*, trans. J. Marsh (London, 1955), p. 112.

12. G. E. Ladd, *A Theology of the New Testament* (Grand Rapids, 1974), p. 144.

Jesus is acknowledged by Paul and the Evangelists to have performed none of these functions attributed to the Messiah. The author of Jude could not simply shift from God to Jesus a prediction about the accomplishments of the coming one in the endtime (eschaton), as described in the Books of Enoch (1En 1:9). He had to *change the prophecy* in order to have Jesus fulfill the prediction.[13]

Jesus' actions were decidedly not those often associated with the Messiah. He certainly performed miracles, as we know assuredly from studying the Evangelists' sources, Josephus, and Rabbinics; but the Messiah is not portrayed in Early Judaism as a miracle worker (even though he does perform wonders in 4Ezra 13). Jesus suffered and was crucified; and despite attempts from scholars for over one hundred years to prove otherwise from our vastly increased store of primary sources, we still have no evidence that Jews during the time of Jesus considered that God's Messiah would come and suffer.[14] The rabbinic references to two Messiahs, one of whom will die, postdate the second century C.E., and, therefore, are too late to be used to portray the messianology of the early Jews.[15] The reference to the death of the Messiah in 4 Ezra 7:29 is not a Christian interpolation into this Jewish apocalypse. But the death of the Messiah here is not efficacious and is clearly distinct from the Christian affirmation about Jesus. According to 4 Ezra 7, the Messiah's death serves to mark the end of a set period of time and history.

In his *An Introduction to the Theology of the New Testament* the former Dean of York, Alan Richardson, presents an insight that is worth quoting:

> It is truly astonishing, in view of the weight of OT prophecy concerning the Davidic Messiah, how little the NT makes of the matter. The evangelists represent Jesus as the new Moses, the new Joshua, the new Elijah, and so on; but there is perhaps only one *pericope* in the tradition which sets forth Jesus as the new David, viz. the Walking through the Cornfields on the Sabbath (Mark 2.23–28).[16]

The OT passages that Richardson has in mind as referring both to David and the Messiah refer clearly only to David. The interest in David was impres-

---

13. See my discussion in *The Old Testament Pseudepigrapha and the New Testament* (SNTS MS 54; Cambridge, 1985, repr. 1987), pp. 72–74.

14. Hengel correctly states that "in the light of all our present knowledge, the suffering and dying Messiah was not yet a familiar traditional figure in the Judaism of the first century AD" (p. 40). Hengel, *The Atonement: The Origins of the Doctrine in the New Testament*, trans. J. Bowden (Philadelphia, 1981).

15. See Charlesworth, "The Concept of the Messiah in the Pseudepigrapha," *ANRW* II.19.1, pp. 188–218; see esp. pp. 198–200; and P. Schäfer, "Die messianischen Hoffnungen des rabbinischen Judentums zwischen Naherwartung und religiösem Pragmatismus," in *Studien zur Geschichte und Theologie des Rabbinischen Judentums* (AGAJU 15; Leiden, 1978), pp. 214–43; and J. Neusner, *Messiah in Context: Israel's History and Destiny in Formative Judaism* (The Foundations of Judaism; Philadelphia, 1984), see esp. pp. 18–19.

16. A Richardson, *An Introduction to the Theology of the New Testament* (London, 1958), p. 126.

sively high during the time of Jesus, as we know more clearly now than when Richardson wrote, thanks to the recovery of compositions in the name of David—like the *More Psalms of David*—and writings which celebrate him, both among the Dead Sea Scrolls and elsewhere.[17] We now know also that there were descendants of David living in Palestine during the time of Jesus.[18]

The "truly astonishing" reaction is the key for us; the NT writings do not elevate Jesus as a type of David. Jesus was not celebrated by his earliest followers as "a" or "the" new David. And despite the movement of "Christ" from title to proper name, the confessions preserved in the NT writings celebrate Jesus as "Lord," or "Son." Conspicuously absent among the kerygmata and creeds is the confession that Jesus is the long-awaited Christ. The only true exception is Mark's account of Peter's confession.

Even if Mark accurately records Peter's words, we have no way of discerning what Peter meant by "Christ." Even if we knew exactly what he meant, we still would not be able to perceive what Jesus was thinking, since scholars throughout the world have come to agree that according to Mark Jesus did not simply accept Peter's claim that he was the Messiah (contrary to Matthew's version). If Jesus had accepted the declaration he was the Messiah, then we would be able to explain how his earliest followers came to this startling conclusion. If he did not accept the claim, as now seems obvious after years of scholars' sensitive and historical study of Mark and the Jewish literature contemporaneous with him, then we are faced with the problem of why and how his followers concluded that the title "the Messiah" was appropriate for him.[19] Research on such issues leads not to easy answers but to perplexing questions.

There was reason to be optimistic that some resolutions might be obtained by the Princeton Symposium.[20] First the problems were clarified and put into sharp focus. The two major questions seem to have been the following:

1. How and in what ways, if at all, did the Jews, in Palestine and before 70 C.E. especially, express their ideas concerning the Hebrew (and Aramaic) word "Messiah." Related to this question are others, notably these:

    a. How widespread were these concerns?

    b. Were references to "the Messiah" clustered in discernible groups, whether economic, cultic, social, synagogal, or so-called sectarian?

17. See "More Psalms of David" in *OTP*, vol. 2, pp. 609–24.

18. See D. Flusser's discussion (of the ossuary with the inscription which clarified that the bones inside belonged to a descendant of David) in *Jesus' Jewishness*, ed. Charlesworth (New York, 1991), pp. 153–76.

19. See Dahl's paper in the present collection.

20. See the resolutions of the members of the Symposium; these are presented at the beginning of this volume, p. xiii.

c. How can we be convinced we have translated מָשִׁיח or χριστός correctly as "the Messiah," rather than as "a messiah," or "the Anointed One," rather than "an anointed one"?[21]

d. How can we discern that references to "the son of David" or "David" are messianic, and how should we then define the adjective "messianic." Granted that to delimit this term only to references to "Messiah" seems myopic, but how can we avoid eisegesis and an imprecise use of this term?

e. When do nouns like *bar* and phrases like *bar nasha* move from nouns to terms, and from terms to titles, and what criteria aid us in discerning that such titles are messianic?

f. Was the title "the Messiah" an amorphous and fluid concept among the early Jews, or was it confusingly contradictory, at least to many intellectual and devout Jews?

g. Can we discern any coherence in the title "the Messiah" or are we confronted only with divisive contingencies?

The second major question is as follows:

2. If most Jews were not looking for the coming of "the Messiah," and if Jesus' life and teachings were not parallel to those often or sometimes attributed to the coming of "the Messiah" or "the Christ," then why, how, and when did Jesus' earliest followers contend that he was so clearly the promised Messiah that the title "Christ" became his proper name by at least 40 C.E., or ten years after the crucifixion? Some related questions are the following:

a. What is the relation between the post-Easter claim that Jesus is the Christ and Jesus' life before the cross?

b. What is the relation between the early kerygmatic claim that Jesus is "the Christ" and the traditions about Jesus' trial before the Sanhedrin, when according to Mk 14:61–62 he reputedly claimed to be "the Christ"?

c. What is the relation between the confession that Jesus is the Christ and Jesus' death?

d. What is the relation between the proclamation of Jesus' messiahship and either the affirmation that the resurrected Jesus had been seen or the belief that God had raised him from the dead?

---

21. The form מָשִׁיח may not even derive from the well-known root for "messiah." It may well be another noun (or form) with a prefixed *mem*. For example, E. M. Schuller wisely translates *w'ny mšyhkin* 4Q381 15 not as "and I your Messiah," but as "from Your discourse." The root is *syh*, "meditation," or "discourse." See her valuable *Non-Canonical Psalms from Qumran: A Pseudepigraphic Collection* (Harvard Semitic Studies 18; Atlanta, 186), pp. 94–97.

e. What fluidity was there in the early Palestinian Jesus Movement between the terms "Messiah" or "Christ" and its messianic content?

f. Was the author of 1 Enoch 37–71, or Jesus, or one of his followers the first Jew to link the terms "Messiah" and "Son of Man"?

g. Did the prophecy of Isaiah 53, and the concept of the suffering servant, become associated with Jesus' life in Jesus' teachings or was it a *post eventum* thought shaped only by Jesus' death on the cross?

h. At what stage did "servant" become wed with "Messiah" or obtain messianic overtones?

These two series of questions may well give the impression that I have read none of the primary or secondary literature on messianology (the term which represents the Jewish concept[s] of the Messiah), or christology (the term which specifies the Christian argument that Jesus is the Christ). Yet even after refining our nomenclature, it is frustrating to see that "Jewish" is separated from "Christian" as if Jesus and his earliest followers were not Jews and did not fit solidly and firmly within pre-70 Palestinian Judaism (or better, *Judaisms*).

These questions arise for the following reasons: the advance beyond ahistorical confessionalism by Jews and Christians alike, the ever increasing abundance of primary texts, a refined perception of the complexities of pre-70 Judaism(s) and earliest Christianity, and the development of a self-critical and sophisticated historical methodology.

The phenomenal—somewhat unparalleled—advancement in biblical research can be summarized by the following list of conclusions which is represented in a wide range of publications:

1. The term "the Messiah" simply does not appear in the Hebrew Scriptures (or Old Testament).[22] The last group of scholars to acknowledge this fact were the conservative Christians, and now the very conservative New Testament specialist [the late] Professor George Eldon Ladd states, without qualification, that "the simple term 'the Messiah' does not occur in the Old Testament at all."[23] Of course, the title "the Anointed One" denotes in the Hebrew Scriptures (or Old Testament) a prophet, a priest, and especially a king.

2. The Hebrew Scriptures (or Old Testament) certainly do contain some extremely important passages that were implicitly messianic, such as

22. See the resolutions of the members of the Symposium; these can be found at the beginning of the present work. Also, see Roberts's paper in the present collection, and W. Harrelson, "The Messianic Hope," in *Judaism, 200 B.C.–A.D. 200*, ed. J. H. Charlesworth (Evanston, Ill., 1983 [this slide series is distributed by the Religion and Ethics Institute, Inc., P.O. Box 664, Evanston, Ill. 60204]).

23. Ladd, *A Theology of the New Testament*, p. 136.

Psalm 2, 2 Samuel 7, Isaiah 7, 9 and 11, Zechariah 9, and Dan 9:26. These passages may be defined as "messianic" so long as this adjective is not used to denote the prediction of an apocalyptic, eschatological "Messiah."

3. These scriptures were interpreted with precisely this messianic connotation by Jews during the two centuries before the destruction of Jerusalem and the Temple in 70 C.E.

4. The noun, term, or title "the Messiah" appears rarely in the literature of Early Judaism or from roughly 250 B.C.E. to 200 C.E. But it is also true that in the whole history of Israel and Pre-Rabbinic Judaism "the Messiah" appears with unusual frequency and urgency only during this period, especially from the first century B.C.E. to 135 C.E.[24]

5. Jesus' sayings reveal that his message was not about the coming of the Messiah. His preaching focused on the coming of God's Kingdom, not the kingdom of the Messiah.

6. Jesus never proclaimed himself to be the Messiah. He apparently rejected Peter's confession, that he (Jesus) was the Christ, as satanic, because he did not wish for his mission and message to be judged according to human concepts of the Messiah.[25]

7. The disciples are never portrayed as asking Jesus for his views about the Messiah. Before his crucifixion in 30 C.E. they were apparently not preoccupied with speculations about the coming of a Messiah. It is far from clear what term they would have chosen to categorize him.

8. In the early Palestinian Jesus Movement, according to Acts 3:20, and in Paul's letters, "Christ" is a proper name for Jesus of Nazareth. In the gospels it is a proper name or title (Mt 1:1, Mk 1:1, Lk 2:11, Jn 1:17).

As I perceive the work of the leading specialists, these eight points reflect a broad consensus among Jewish and Christian scholars today,[26] and present

---

24. The scope of this paper does not allow for a discussion of the messianic movement related to Simon Bar Kokhba; for sources and discussion see the following: P. Schäfer, *Der Bar Kokhba-Aufstand* (Texte und Studien zum Judentum 1; Tübingen, 1981), see esp. pp. 55–67; P. Schäfer, *Geschichte der Juden in der Antike* (Stuttgart, 1983), see esp. pp. 163–65.

25. R. H. Fuller points out that Mk 8:27–33 is composed of Marcan redaction and early tradition. He concludes that Jesus' rebuke to Peter—"Get behind me, Satan"—originally followed Peter's confession, "You are the Christ." Fuller concludes: "Jesus rejects Messiahship as a merely human and even diabolical temptation." See Fuller, *The Foundation of New Testament Christology* (New York, 1965), p. 109. Fuller's insights are impressive, but it is not possible to continue to assume, as does Fuller, that "Messiah" meant "the Davidic Messiah of a religious-national kind" (p. 109). If Jesus rejected Peter's confession, it is quite possible that he did so for numerous reasons, and one of them could well be that no human or angel was empowered to make such a divine declaration. According to some Jewish documents (viz. PssSol 17, 4Ezra 13:52), only God can disclose who is the Messiah.

26. For a good bibliography on Jewish messianology, see "Messianism" in E. Schürer's *The History of the Jewish People in the Age of Jesus Christ*, ed. G. Vermes, F. Miller, M. Black, and P. Vermes (Edinburgh, 1979), vol. 2, pp. 488–92.

an enormous advance in understanding Early Judaism and Christian Origins.

Many New Testament scholars used to think the essential question was the following one: Why did the earliest followers of Jesus take the Jewish concept of the Messiah and contend that he was the one expected by the Jews? This is an incorrect question. It assumes that Jews advocated a set and coherent concept of the Messiah. It assumes that Jesus' followers were primarily interested in describing Jesus as the Messiah, and not, for example, as "the son of God," or the "Lord." The question also fails to force the thinker to ponder about what Jesus' followers may have meant by such words and whether they were terms or titles.

Another pivotal question seems to be: Why did the Jews not recognize that Jesus was the Messiah? Again this is a false question, because it assumes that there was a coherent concept of the Messiah among Jews. It also assumes that Jesus' followers had no difficulty with this acclamation, and that his life and thought were unmistakably messianic and in line with prophecy and a checklist description of the task of "the Messiah."

A major question continues to be raised but answered unsatisfactorily: If Jesus thought he was the Messiah, would he not have made that claim explicit? The common and mistaken answer is yes. In reality the answer is probably no. Jesus probably would not have proclaimed himself to be the Messiah if he had conceived himself to be the Messiah. According to some early Jewish texts, like the Psalms of Solomon 17 (and perhaps 18), only God knows the time and identity of the Messiah, and according to many other texts God is keeping the Messiah in a secret place (see 4Ezra 7:28–29, 12:31–34, 13:26; 2Bar 30:1–2; cf. OdesSol 41:15).

Another question has been disclosed to be misleading: How did Jews distinguish between the concept of "the Messiah" and other concepts, such as "the Son of Man," "the Righteous One," and "the Elect One"? It will come as a shock to many scholars that this is a very poor question. It is inappropriate because it assumes that all Jews made such a distinction. In fact, according to the Book of the Parables of Enoch (= 1En 37–71), which was composed by a Palestinian Jew before 70 C.E., these four concepts were related and at times identical.[27] There was considerable fluidity among the various titles that could be or become messianic titles.

THE LITERATURE OF EARLY JUDAISM

What shaped first-century Jewish thought? The only sources we possess for ascertaining the ideas of the Jews in Palestine before the burning of the

---

27. See my comments in *Judaisms and Their Messiahs*, see esp. pp. 236–38; and the important and convincing paper in this collection by VanderKam.

Temple in 70 C.E. are their writings. Hence we must turn to texts, acknowledging that we have only a portion of the influential literature produced by the early Jews. We are not able to demonstrate how influential are the writings which have survived; and we should recognize that perhaps the most influential thoughts came through *oral traditions* connected with the Temple cult or with socially influential groups.

The numerous Jewish writings that antedate the defeat of Bar Kokhba in 135 C.E. and the end of the period in which the New Testament documents were composed, roughly 150 C.E., cumulatively clarify three observations:

1. Most of the Jewish texts contain no reference to "a" or "the" Messiah or to "a" or "the" Christ.
2. The texts that do contain references to "the Messiah," "Christ," or "Anointed One" do not reveal a coherent picture.
3. Hence we have no evidence for the assertion that the Jews during Jesus' time were looking for the coming of "the" or "a" Messiah, and there was no paradigm, or checklist, by which to discern if a man was the Messiah. In such an ideological and social setting it was not possible for a group to point to objective proofs for its own idiosyncratic belief.

The Samaritans. The Samaritans were a splinter group with Palestinian Judaism. We have learned lately that their break with other Jews did not occur before or shortly after the Babylonian Exile; it occurred during the last few decades of the second century B.C.E. They shared with other Jews the sanctity of the Pentateuch. They heralded a very ancient Israelite holy area, namely Mount Gerizim, as the only true place for worship. They longed for the coming of the Taheb, apparently their term for "the Messiah"; but it means "restorer" and was perceived not as a new David but as a new Moses (a *Moses redivivus*). The passages in which this title appears are very late, postdating the second century C.E., and cannot be used with any reliability for assessing early Jewish messianology.[28]

Josephus. In the received Greek texts Josephus does use the noun "Christos," but the passages are suspect, prompting many scholars to conclude that they were added by a Christian scribe. I am convinced that Josephus did refer to Jesus, using the phrase *"tou legomenou Christou"* (*Ant* 20. 200); but it is far from clear what he means by these words.[29] He could be

---

28. See the definitive study of Samaritan messianism by the Professor für jüdische Religionsgeschichte am Institut für Judaistik der Universität Wien, namely F. Dexinger, *Der Taheb: Ein "messianischer" Heilsbringer der Samaritaner* (Salzburg, 1986) and Dexinger, "Die Taheb-Vorstellung als politische Utopie," *Numen* 37 (1990), 1–21.

29. See Charlesworth, *Jesus Within Judaism* (Anchor Bible Reference Library; Garden City, N.Y., 1988).

denoting "the so-called Christ," or "the proclaimed Christ." Earlier in the *Antiquities*, the Greek *ho christos houtos ēn* (*Ant* 18.63) clearly means "he was the Christ." This affirmation cannot be attributed to Josephus. The tenth-century Agabius Arabic text has "he was perhaps the Messiah." Surely neither the Greek nor the Arabic is appropriate for a Jew who was as learned and experienced as Josephus, and who had disdain for apocalyptic and messianic movements.[30] We should allow for Christian redaction in both the Greek and Arabic recensions. If Josephus did use the noun "Christ," we are far removed from what he meant by it, and even more distanced from his pre-70 fellow Palestinian Jews.[31]

The Targums. In the Targums we find a considerable number of messianic passages. One of the most militant portraits of the Messiah, for example, is found in the Targum of Pseudo-Jonathan. Note the following excerpt:

> How noble is the king, Messiah, who is going to rise from the house of Judah. He has girded his loins and come down, setting in order the order of battle with his enemies and killing kings with their rulers (and there is not a king or a ruler who shall stand before him), reddening the mountains with the blood of their slain. With his garments dipped in blood, he is like one who treads grapes in the press.   (Targum to Gen 49:11)[32]

Such passages in the Targums are too late for us to consider at the present time. In their present form they postdate 200 C.E. and often tend to reflect the historical setting of these later centuries.[33]

The Mishnah. While the Targums reflect the reintroduction of messianology into Jewish thology, the Mishnah, as compiled by Judah the Prince, reflects the discussions at Yavneh (Jamnia) and Usha, and the anatiapocalyptic and antimessianic reactions to the horrifying revolt of 66–63/4 C.E., and the clearly messianic but abortive revolt of 132–135 C.E. led by Simon Bar Kokhba, whom the greatest Rabbi of the time, Akiba, hailed as the Messiah.[34]

30. See the translations and discussions in Charlesworth, *Jesus Within Judaism*, esp. pp. 90–102.

31. Long ago A. Schlatter in *Die Theologie des Judentums nach dem Bericht des Josefus* (Gütersloh, 1932; repr. with a Stellenregister by H. Lindner: Hildesheim, New York, 1979) argued that the collapse of the Jewish revolt was for Josephus "nicht das Ende des Messianismus. . . . Aber ihre Hoffnung richtet sich nicht mehr auf den Davidssohn und Menschensohn, nicht mehr auf ein verklärtes Jerusalem und einen glänzenden Tempel, sondern flüchtet sich ins Jenseits und schaut zum Himmel empor. Die Hoffnung beschäftigt sich nur noch mit dem Schicksal des Einzelnen, mit der Erlösung seiner Seele" (p. 259).

32. J. Bowker, *The Targums and Rabbinic Literature* (Cambridge, 1969), p. 278.

33. See S. H. Levey, *The Messiah: An Aramaic Interpretation: The Messianic Exegesis of the Targum* (Monographs of the Hebrew Union College 2; New York, 1974).

34. See Schäfer, *Der Bar Kokhba-Aufstand.*

Rabbinic Judaism has no clear anti-Christian polemic, but it could not develop in ignorance of the growing strength of Christianity, which claimed to be the true religion of Israel because it was empowered by God's Messiah, Jesus Christ. Hence I have no doubt that the dearth of messianology in the Mishnah should be seen also in the context of the struggle for survival of rabbinic Judaism alongside of, and sometimes against, a messianic movement heavily indebted to Judaism, called Christianity.

Professor Jacob Neusner in *Messiah in Context* argues insightfully that "the Messiah as an eschatological figure makes no appearance in the system of the Mishnah," because the Mishnah is "a law code or a school book for philosophical jurists."[35] According to Neusner, the Mishnah fails to treat the issue of salvation, and thereby "omits all reference to its own point of origin, and thus lacks a historical account or a mythic base."[36]

Old Testament Apocrypha. The noun "Messiah" or "Christ" does not appear in the thirteen books in the Old Testament Apocrypha.[37] That fact is remarkable. It means that the Maccabean revolt, according to 1 and 2 Maccabees, was not a messianic movement, and that the revolt was organized around faithfulness to Yahweh and the Torah, and not around allegiance to some Messiah, as in the Second Great Revolt of 132–135 C.E. It also reveals that the expansions to the Hebrew scriptures, such as the Epistle of Jeremiah, the Additions to Daniel, and the Additions to Esther, were not produced by some messianic interpretation.[38]

We come now to the two main bodies of early Jewish texts that contain the most numerous and most significant messianic passages. The first is the Old Testament Pseudepigrapha. The second is the Dead Sea Scrolls.

Old Testament Pseudepigrapha. Today we know at least fifty-two documents under the category of the Old Testament Pseudepigrapha. In this collection we do indeed find some of the most impressive and significant records of Jewish messianism. As the informed Jewish scholar Joseph Klausner

---

35. Neusner, *Messiah in Context*, pp. 18–19.

36. Neusner, *Messiah in Context*, p. 19. Neusner contends that "the Mishnah presents us with a kind of Judaism that has an eschatology without the Messiah, a teleology beyond time" (p. 20). Also see Neusner, "One Theme, Two Settings: The Messiah in the Literature of the Synagogue and in the Rabbi's Canon of Late Antiquity," *Biblical Theology Bulletin* 14 (1984) 110–21.

37. See the discussion in Charlesworth, *The Pseudepigrapha and Modern Research with a Supplement* (SBL SCS 7S; Chico, Calif., 1981), p. 19.

38. J. Klausner in *The Messianic Idea in Israel* does have a section on "The Messianic Idea in the Apocrypha," but he defines "messianic idea" too broadly, including, for example, Sirach 35 as messianic, when there is no mention of the Messiah or even David. The same is true of Sirach 36, yet Klausner judged it to be "completely filled with messianic expectations . . ." (p. 253). See Klausner, *The Messianic Idea in Israel*, trans. W. F. Stinespring (London, 1956). Klausner correctly wrote, "it is proper to pay attention to one important item: *the personality of the Messiah is not mentioned in any book of the Apocrypha* (p. 250, italics his; see also pp. 254, 271).

stated long ago, "the Messianic expectations in the Apocrypha and Pseud-epigrapha are precious jewels in the crown of Judaism. . . ."[39]

Before turning to a discussion of the four documents that antedate 200 C.E. and that contain Jewish reflections on the coming of the Messiah, let me clarify why only these works will be examined. The discussion of Jewish messianology over the past one hundred years has been vitiated by loose criteria and the inclusion of passages that are now widely recognized as nonmessianic. To avoid this dilemma, only documents that actually contain the noun "Messiah" or "Christ" will be included. Each of these four documents is non-composite, hence passages linked with clearly messianic sections will also be included for examination. Restricting the following examination only to passages in which the term "Messiah" or "Christ" appears should serve for the present to clarify the complex mass of data. Hence the alleged messianic sections of the Testaments of the Twelve Patriarchs will not be examined here[40]; it is often forgotten that this document does not contain the term "Messiah" or "Christ."[41]

A more perplexing problem is confronted in the Dream Visions of Enoch (1En 83–90). This is a separate book and should not be read in light of a later work titled the Parables of Enoch (1En 37–71). Extremely important for our discussion are two alleged references to the "Messiah" in the Dream Visions of Enoch. Numerous specialists are convinced that a passage in the Dream Visions refers to the Messiah. Here are some recent translations of that passage (1En 90:38):

---

39. J. Klausner, *The Messianic Idea in Israel*, p. 386. Klausner erred in judging many of "the Apocrypha and Pseudepigrapha" as "products of the spirit of the Zealots and Sicarii in those warlike times" (p. 386, n. 1). None were probably written by the Zealots or the Sicarii. We must not attempt to align all the Apocrypha and Pseudepigrapha that were written before 70 with what we know about the groups (or sects) prior to 70. We simply are too ill-informed.

The quotations from Klausner may be misleading; he incorrectly read passages in the OT Apocrypha which referred to God's future acts as a warrior as if they were not distinguishable from the Messiah's future acts.

40. TReu 6:8 has *mechri teleiōseōs chronōn archiereōs christou;* and this phrase should be translated as "until the consummation of times; he (Levi) is the anointed high priest" (or "until the consummation of times of an [the] anointed high priest") and not "until the consummation of times of Christ the high priest." The phrase is translated correctly by H. C. Kee in *OTP*, vol. 1, and by H. M. de Jonge in *The Apocryphal Old Testament* ed. H. F. D. Sparks (Oxford, 1984). Also see the following excellent translations: ". . . jusqu'à l'achèvement des temps du grand pretre oint dont a parlé le Seigneur" (M. Philonenko, in *La Bible: Escrits intertestamentaires*, Paris, 1987); "sommo sacerdote unto indicato dal Signore" (P. Sacchi in *Apocrifi dell'Antico Testamento* [Turin, 1981]). Contrast the opinion of M. de Jonge, who defends (despite his published translation) the rendering which refers this phrase to "Christ" and explains it as a Christian statement. See M. de Jonge, ed., *Studies on the Testaments of the Twelve Patriarchs* (SVTP 3: Leiden, 1975), p. 22.

41. The two major so-called messianic passages in the T12P are TSim 7:1–2 and TJud 21:1–3. The term or title "Messiah," "the Anointed One," or "the Christ" does not appear in these verses. See Charlesworth, "The Concept of the Messiah in the Pseudepigrapha," in *ANRW*, II.19.1, pp. 188–218; see esp. p. 208. Also see M. de Jonge, *Studies on the Testaments of the Twelve Patriarchs*, pp. 223–25, 219–20.

. . . and that something became a great beast with huge black horns on its head.[42]

. . . and that buffalo became a great animal with great black horns on its head. . . . [43]

. . . and that *wild-ox* was (or became) a large animal and had big black horns on its head.[44]

. . . und dieser Stier war ein grosses Tier, und (es hatte) an seinem Kopf grosse schwarze Hörner.[45]

. . . et cette Parole devint la bête magnifique portant de grandes cornes noires.[46]

. . . e questa cosa era un grande animale con, sulla testa, grandi corna nere. . . .[47]

. . . un órix (que es un animal grande) con grandes cuernos negros en la cabeza, ... [48]

This passage is located in the famous animal allegory. Most of the translators quoted above contend that here we have a reference to the Messiah or a least a messianic passage (Uhlig, Caquot, F. Corriente and A. Piñero, and L. Fusella). I am impressed, however, by the ambiguity of the allegory, and by the absence of the noun "Messiah" in this passage and in the Dream Visions. If the beast mentioned in 1En 90:38 is to be identified as the Messiah, then who is the white bull or cow with huge horns described in 90:37? Is not the author being intentionally vague? Are there not numerous other divine mediators besides the Messiah who could possibly be considered as the "great beast with huge black horns"? Professor Matthew Black has suggested that since the "white bull" is "here clearly parallel to the white bull at 85.3 symbolising Adam, the image seems to refer to the birth of a new or second Adam, more glorious than the first, for 'his horns are large.'"[49] The image in 1En 85:3 does not necessarily represent "the Messiah." It may refer to Adam. Black's suggestion deserves serious consideration.

In my judgment 1En 90:38 is not clearly messianic, and it certainly does not contain a "description of the Messiah," as one learned scholar

---

42. Translated by E. Isaac in *OTP*, vol. 1, p. 71.

43. Translated by M. Black in *The Book of Enoch or 1 Enoch: A New English Edition with Commentary and Textual Notes* (SVTP 7; Leiden, 1985), p. 83.

44. Trans. M. Knibb in *The Apocryphal Old Testament*, p. 291.

45. Trans. S. Uhlig in *Apokalypsen: Das äthiopische Henochbuch* (JSHRZ 5.6; Gütersloh, 1984), p. 704.

46. Trans. A. Caquot in *La Bible: Écrits intertestamentaires*, edited by A. Dupont-Sommer and M. Philonenko (Paris, 1987), p. 596.

47. Trans. L. Fusella in *Apocrifi dell'Antico Testamento*, edited by P. Saachi (Turin, 1981), pp. 629–30.

48. Trans. F. Corriente and A. Piñero in *Apocrifos del Antiguo Testamento*, edited by A. Diez Macho (Madrid, 1984), vol. 4, p. 123.

49. M. Black in *The Books of Enoch*, p. 280.

claimed.[50] I am impressed by the allegory and its kaleidoscopic symbolism. Since the Enlightenment, we Western scholars have sought focused and precise language; yet phenomena are usually ambiguous. The beauty of the allegorical animal apocalypse is in its openness and comprehensiveness. As the authors of some pre-100 C.E. Jewish writings stressed, specifically the authors of the Psalms of Solomon and 4 Ezra, no sage can describe, clarify, or identify the Messiah. God has preserved the Messiah in a secret place, will reveal him at the proper time, and he alone knows the identity of the Messiah. To understand early Jewish theology our terms must be as representative as possible; we simply cannot continue to use the adjective "messianic" as if it is synonymous with "eschatological," even though an influential scholar, Professor Oscar Cullmann, encouraged us to continue such a method.[51]

We must not claim as clear what is intentionally imprecise. We must heed the words of the discerning philosophical mathematician, F. P. Ramsey, when he warns that the "chief danger" of the scholar is to treat "what is vague as if it were precise. . . ."[52] A revered New Testament scholar, Krister Stendahl, formerly Professor of New Testament at Harvard and Bishop of Stockholm, recently cautioned against the ancient and modern "authority figures . . . who claim more precision in their definitions than is good for theology."[53] In summation, the allegory in the Dream Visions may at best be allegedly messianic; but it will not influence the following synthesis of messianic ideas in the Pseudepigrapha.

We turn now to the four early Jewish documents in the Pseudepigrapha that contain the word "Messiah." In chronological order they are the Psalms of Solomon, the Parables of Enoch, 4 Ezra, and 2 Baruch. These four documents date from 50 B.C.E. to 100 C.E.,[54] were composed by Palestinian Jews in a Semitic language, and are preserved in a Semitic language. The last three are apocalypses. Let us address eleven questions to these documents.

Can the ancestry of the Messiah be discerned? The PssSol 17:21–34 and 4Ezra 12:31–34 are the only two that state he will be descended from Da-

50. The quotation is from P. G. R. de Villiers' "The Messiah and Messiahs in Jewish Apocalyptic," in *Neotestamentica* 12 (1978) 75–110; see p. 81. P. de Villiers is a gifted scholar; his research is usually outstanding and precise.

51. O. Cullmann, "Jesus the Messiah," *The Christology of the New Testament*, trans. S. C. Guthrie and C. A. M. Hall (The New Testament Library; London, 1959, 1963) pp. 111–36.

52. I have only slightly altered the quotation; Ramsey writes about the "chief danger to our philosophy. . . ." The motto is quoted from F. P. Ramsey, *The Foundations of Mathematics* (New York, 1931), p. 269. I am indebted to K. R. Popper for drawing my attention to this motto; see K. R. Popper, *Popper Selections*, ed. D. Miller (Princeton, 1985) p. 87.

53. K. Stendahl, "Foreword," in Jakob Jónsson, *Humour and Irony in the New Testament* (BZRG 28; Leiden, 1985).

54. For a discussion of the date of the Parables of Enoch, which probably are pre-70 and perhaps from the late first century B.C.E., see Charlesworth, *The Old Testament Pseudepigrapha and the New Testament*, esp. pp. 88–90, 102–10.

vid.[55] It is surprising that this part of the tradition, which we would have expected to be a set part of the lore, is found in only two of the pre-135 C.E. Jewish pseudepigrapha. It is also conceivable that the emphasis in 4 Ezra 13:22 that the Messiah is God's son is a reaction, perhaps within the Ezra cycle or group, against the claim that the Messiah must be "David's son." Messianic ideas were not necessarily Davidic. For example, the Enoch group tended to link the Messiah with Enoch, and the Samaritans believed the Taheb was to be seen in terms of Moses. Psalm 2 preserves another record of the tradition that the Lord's anointed (2:2), obviously seen in some early Jewish circles as the Messiah, is to be the son of God (2:7); but the connection of this future ideal king (2:6) with David is not made explicit. We are left with uncertain, and perhaps fluid, traditions.

Did not most Jews assume the Messiah was to be a *militant* warrior? This conclusion is assumed by many, perhaps most, New Testament specialists. They frequently argue that Jesus did not declare himself to be the Messiah, because he would have been mistaken as a political and military leader. Explicit support for this bewitching view that Jews were expecting a militant Messiah is found among the early Jewish Pseudepigrapha only in 2 Baruch 72. According to this section of 2 Baruch, the Messiah will slay Israel's enemies with the sword (Syr. *hrb*'; 2Bar 72:6). In many other passages the stress is on the *nonmilitary* means of the Messiah. Both PssSol 17:21–33[56] and 4 Ezra 13:4–11 emphasize that the Messiah will not rely on a sword, horse, or other military weapons. He will conquer not with a weapon in his hand but with what streams forth from his mouth, the word[57]: "Undergird him with the strength . . . to destroy the unlawful nations with the word of his mouth" (PssSol 17:22–24)[58]; "and whenever his voice issued from his mouth, all who heard his voice melted as wax melts when it feels the fire" (4 Ezra 13:4).[59] The Messiah's bloody confrontation—implied in 2 Baruch 72 and described in gory details in the late Targum of Pseudo-Jonathan (Gen 49:11)—is rejected by the authors of the Psalms of Solomon and 4 Ezra.

Why does the Messiah slay or defeat the nations? There is more than one documented answer. According to the Parables of Enoch, it is probably be-

---

55. 3En 45 and 48 also record the tradition that the Messiah will be a descendant of David, but the document is too late to be included here.

56. The Messiah in PssSol 17 is a political figure and he does have some military functions; but most important for understanding the messianology of this psalm is 17:33—"he (the Messiah) will not rely on horse and rider and bow, /Nor will he build up hope in a multitude for a day of war." I am convinced that this psalm was written against the belief that the Messiah will be a militant warrior. In that sense, of course, it may be taken as evidence for the existence of such a view. Was this view popular in the late or middle of the first century B.C.E.?

57. See the significant insights brought forward by Heintz regarding the iconographical background to the concept of a sword emanating from the mouth. What Heintz suggests about the biblical image should be applied also to the PssSol. See Heintz's paper in this collection.

58. See the translation of PssSol by R. B. Wright in *OTP*, vol. 2.

59. See the translation of 4Ezra by B. M. Metzger in *OTP*, vol. 1.

cause they are full of sinners who deny the Lord of the Spirits (e.g., 1En 45:2). According to PssSol 17:21 and 24, it is perhaps because they are "unlawful nations" with "unrighteous rulers." According to the PssSol 17:22 and 2 Baruch 72, it is because they rule Jerusalem or ruled over Israel. This latter concept demands the possibility that some of the nations will not be destroyed, as stated in 2Bar 72:2.

Will the Messiah not purge Jerusalem? The author and community behind the Psalms of Solomon (see PssSol 17:21–33)[60] were convinced of an affirmative answer, but most of the documents that mention the Messiah do not describe him acting on behalf of Jerusalem.[61] According to 4 Ezra 7:28–29, the Messiah will appear, inaugurate the messianic period, and then die. No active functions are given to him. He does not die in battle or in the attempt to purge Jerusalem, even though the author of 4 Ezra had lived through such a dream. He appears in history only *after* the eschatological city and land are disclosed (4Ezra 7:26).

Will the Messiah condemn sinners? This concept is found in the PssSol 17 and in 4Ezra 12:32 (cf. 1En 48, 2Bar 72). In many other texts, notably 4 Ezra 7:28–29, the ungodly are not even mentioned in connection with the Messiah.

Is he not always portrayed as a king? According to PssSol 17:21–33, he will be a king. Note this excerpt:

> See, Lord, and raise up for them their king,
>   the son of David, to rule over your servant Israel
>   in the time known to you, O God.

There could have been some dissension in the group which used these psalms liturgically in Jerusalem, because Psalm 17 is framed at the beginning and end with the affirmation that God, and not the Messiah, is the eternal king.[62] Note the beginning and end of Psalm 17:

> Lord, you are our king forevermore, . . . (17:1)
> May God dispatch his mercy to Israel;
>   may he deliver us from the pollution of profane enemies;
> The Lord himself is our king forevermore. (17:45, 46)[63]

---

60. For further discussion see Charlesworth, *Judaisms and Their Messiahs*, pp. 235–36.

61. The Parables of Enoch contain numerous ideas. 1En 56:7 does not mention the Messiah, but it does refer to the attempt of the Parthians to conquer Jerusalem.

62. TReu 6:5–12 states that the Lord will reign through Levi. It is not necessarily a contradiction to say that the Lord is King and the Messiah is King. As we know from the early traditions dating from the time of the monarchy, one stream of thought was that Yahweh is king and David and his descendants are representing God as king; hence they are kings. Likewise the early Jew saw no problem in hailing God and the Messiah as "Lord." See Ps 110 and its interpretation in the first century; most recently now see Juel, *Messianic Exegesis*.

63. See Wright's translation in *OTP*, vol. 2, pp. 665, 669.

Psalms of Solomon 17 seems to contain a polemic against the Hasmonean dynasty, which in its final years became decadent and in which the rulers, beginning with Aristobulus I (104–103) claimed the title of "king" (see PssSol 17:5–6). Hence the corruption of the Hasmonean "kings" apparently stimulated a messianology that portrayed a Messiah who was *not* a king.[64] We also observe a retransference back to God of the functions shifted in the second and first centuries B.C.E. from God to the Messiah (I shall turn to that dimension of our work at the conclusion of this paper). For now it is pertinent to point out once again the lack of a set function or status for the future Messiah.

Will the Messiah not be the eschatological judge? Leaving aside the problems with associating the messianic age with the eschatological age, which are sometimes distinguished, as in 4 Ezra, let me point out that no coherency exists here either. He shall be a judge according to most of the texts, namely PssSol 17:21–33, 4Ezra 12:31–34, and 2Bar 40:1–2. But according to 4 Ezra 7:31–44 and 7:113–14, judgment commences *only* after the Messiah dies, and after the period of primeval silence.

Did the Jews not agree that the Messiah will gather a holy people? This function is assuredly affirmed in PssSol 17:21–23, and he does "protect" them according to 2 Bar 40. According to the thrust of 4 Ezra, esp. 7:140 and 8:3, the new age will have "only a very few" in it. Moreover there are many passages, notably 4 Ezra 7:28–29 and 2 Bar 30:1–4, in which the Messiah simply performs no functions at all. Obviously it is impossible to compile a checklist of functions that the Messiah is to fulfill; some of the most significant passages that contain the word "Messiah" do not ascribe to him any function.[65]

Shall the Messiah not inaugurate a new age?[66] This dimension seems clear from Psalms of Solomon 17. But according to 4 Ezra 7, the Messiah does not begin a new age, he simply seems sandwiched between two eras, following one and dying before the next begins. His death has no efficacious dimensions.[67] What has just been said about an apparently "functionless" Messiah applies here as well. We must rid our minds of the presupposition that the Messiah simply cannot be mentioned and left functionless. He will obviously

---

64. For a discussion of kingship and the Hasmoneans, see M. Hengel, J. H. Charlesworth, D. Mendels, "The Polemical Character of 'On Kingship' in the Temple Scroll: An Attempt at Dating 11QTemple," *JJS* 37.1 (1986) 28–38.

65. I have tried to choose my words carefully. I have not insinuated that because no functions are described the Messiah is to be functionless. That exegesis is patently absurd. The Jew knew that God alone could explain the functions of the Messiah or of other mediators.

66. See E. Fruenwald's article on the concept of eschatology and messianology in Judaism, published in *The Messianic Idea in Jewish Thought* (Publications of the Israel Academy of Sciences and Humanities; Jerusalem, 1982) [in Hebrew].

67. See the excellent study by M. E. Stone: "The Concept of the Messiah in IV Ezra," in *Religions in Antiquity: Essays in Memory of Erwin Ramsdell Goodenough*, ed. J. Neusner (Studies in the History of Religions; Supplements to *Numen* 14; Leiden, 1970), pp. 295–312.

perform some function, but some Jews certainly refused to usurp God's prerogative and define those *ante eventum.*

Is the Messiah to assist in the resurrection of the dead? According to 1En 51:1, Sheol and Hell "will give back" all the dead; but there is no mention of acts performed by the Messiah. The tradition in 1 Enoch is complex and probably intentionally ambiguous; the one who chooses the righteous ones among the dead is "he," which is an example of the ambiguous relative pronoun in Semitics. "He" may refer back to "the Lord of the Spirits." But it is conceivable that some members of the Enoch community would have assumed that "he" may be the Messiah, since Enoch is told, "All these things which you have seen happen by the authority of his *Messiah* so he may give orders and be praised upon the earth" (1 En 52:4; italics mine). The Messiah is "his"—that is, he belongs to the Lord of the Spirits. Moreover, "all these things" may well refer back only to the events described in 1En 52:1–3, in which neither the Messiah nor resurrection is mentioned explicitly.

Both the Messiah and resurrection, however, may have been interpreted by members of the Enoch group to be included among "all these things." It is pertinent to remember that all the passages discussed above are from the same book of Enoch, which was probably composed before the turn of the era. It does contain explicit references to the Messiah, as we have seen.

According to 2 Baruch 30, the righteous alone will arise with the advent of the Messiah.[68] According to 4 Ezra 7:28–29, however, both the righteous and the unrighteous will be resurrected only after the Messiah dies, and the interlude of primeval silence begins and ends. These Baruch and Ezra traditions are very different, yet the Messiah is not the one who raises the dead.

Will the Messiah not establish a permanent and peaceful kingdom? This idea may have been once connected with early Jewish interpretations of Isaiah 7, 9, and 11, and Isaiah 42–45;[69] it seems to be found in PssSol 17:21–32. In contrast to this idea, the apocalypses present us with two mutually exclusive ideas. According to 2 Baruch 36–40 and 4 Ezra 7, the kingdom of the Messiah will be finite; his kingdom will be part of the limited messianic age that precedes the eschaton. According to 1 Enoch 38 and 48–52, and 2 Baruch 73 and 74, however, his kingdom will be eschatological and eternal.

Is the Messiah going to be a human? According to 2 Baruch, the Messiah seems to be a terrestrial king who shall embody all the dreams attributed to the kings of ancient Israel. According to 4 Ezra 12:31–34, the Messiah "will

---

68. In the following pages I will attempt to show that "advent" is meant here and not ascension.

69. Potentially misleading is the following comment by R. J. Werblowsky: "One may, perhaps, commit a technical anachronism and describe as "messianic' those scriptural passages that prophesy a future golden age, the ingathering of the exiles, the restoration of the Davidic dynasty, the rebuilding of Jerusalem and the Temple, the era of peace when the wolf will lie down with the lamb, and so on." See Werblowsky, "Messianism: Jewish Messianism" in *The Encyclopedia of Religion,* ed. M. Eliade (New York, 1987), vol. 9, p. 472.

arise from the posterity of David." But according to 4 Ezra 13:3–14:9, he is depicted as a man who ascends out of the sea: *hominem qui ascenderat de mari*.[70] Obviously we have seen contradictory traditions preserved by the authors of 4 Ezra and 2 Baruch; and this is only one reason to affirm that although these apocalypses were composed after the burning of the Temple in 70 C.E., they preserve traditions that antedate that catastrophic event.

What we observe is not chaotic thought. Instead, through literature we witness tangible indications of the creativity and liveliness of pre-70 Jewish thought, and the nonsystematic phenomenological expressions of real and enslaved people struggling with the impossibility of describing the future. One should not dismiss these passages as ideological; they are sociological deposits of a time of crisis. The apparent chaotic thought is actually the necessarily unsystematic expressions of Jews subjugated to the experienced evilness of a conquering nation.

It is necessary to stress emphatically that such texts should not be read as if we were in a proverbial ivory tower. They must be studied as if we were within the ambience of the Burnt House, the high priest's home burned by the Romans in 70 C.E., and now unearthed with the charred beams of wood virtually still smoldering.

According to the texts collected into the Pseudepigrapha, the earliest explicit use of the *terminus technicus*—"Messiah" or "Christ"—is the first century B.C.E. in the Psalms of Solomon and in the book of the Parables of Enoch. Prior to that time, the Jews had not experienced the horrifying corruption by Hasmonean "kings" and did not fear the Romans, with their massive, well-organized, and technically advanced armies under a seemingly invincible emperor or king. In the second century B.C.E. most Jews considered the Hasmoneans the agents of God and the Romans their allies and friends.[71] The successes of the early Hasmoneans or Maccabees left no vacuum in which to yearn for the coming of a Messiah.

THE DEAD SEA SCROLLS

The other body of early Jewish literature that contains explicit references to "Messiah" or "Christ" is the Dead Sea Scrolls. The discussions of this aspect in the Scrolls is so well published and known that some refer to a consensus:[72] At Qumran the belief in the Davidic Messiah was joined with, and

---

70. Why this "man" should be identified with the Messiah is because 4 Ezra was compiled or composed by one person, "man" corresponds with the perception of the "Messiah" in 4Ezra 11 and 12, and what is said about him links up with the other passages in which the noun "Messiah" appears. See Charlesworth, "The Messiah in the Pseudepigrapha," in *ANRW* II.19.1, p. 205. The Latin text of 4Ezra is from A. F. J. Klijn, ed., *Der Lateinische Text der Apokalypse des Esra* (Texte und Untersuchungen 131; Berlin, 1983).

71. See Charlesworth, "The Triumphant Majority as Seen by a Dwindled Minority: The Outsider According to the Insider of the Jewish Apocalypses, 70–130," in *To See Ourselves As Others See Us*, ed. J. Neusner, *et al.* (Chico, Calif., 1985), pp. 285–315.

made subordinate to, the belief in an Aaronic Messiah. The excesses and failures of the Hasmonean ruler (later called "king") in Jerusalem led the Qumranites to yearn for the coming of a priestly messiah. This thought seems a natural development, since the earliest Qumran Essenes were priests who had been expelled from the Temple and lived in exile in the Judean desert near the Dead Sea.[73]

At the present time I intend to modify this consensus in five significant ways. First, we now have well over 170 documents that probably were created, written, or redacted at Qumran. Most of them do not contain the noun "Messiah." Often this omission is startling, if the Qumran community was a messianic group. In addition to the Psalter's 150 Psalms of David, other Davidic psalms were found, and some of these were intentionally written as Davidic Pseudepigrapha. Not one of them is messianic. None of the Pesharim contains messianic exegesis.[74] The Isaiah Pesher 1 (4Q161) makes only a frustratingly brief reference to the Branch of David which shall arise at the end of days. The Temple Scroll, which may have been brought to Qumran from elsewhere and edited in a final form in the scriptorium, does not contain one reference to the "Messiah." The fact seems strange in a document that is characterized by a tendency to subordinate the king to the priest. Since a reference to the "Messiah" is found in the psalmbook attributed to Solomon, why is there no mention of "Messiah" in the Qumran Psalter, namely the Hodayoth or Hymns Scroll?[75]

Statistically we must admit that messianology was not a major concern of this community, at least not in its early history. The *terminus technicus* for the eschatological Messiah, מָשִׁיחַ, except for the obscure reference in the fragment of the Patriarchal Blessings (4QPBless), occurs in only three documents: 1QS, 1QSa,[76] and CD (which probably was brought to Qumran and redacted there). It seems that less than 3 percent of the Qumran documents contain the word מָשִׁיחַ.

72. See the paper presented in the Symposium by L. Schiffman. We both are critical of the so-called consensus, emphasize the diversity of thought at Qumran and the minimal role given to the Messiah in the few passages in which he is mentioned. These conclusions were obviously derived independently. We had access to each other's paper only after our own work was completed. Also, see the important earlier publication by A. S. van der Woude, *Die messianischen Vorstellungen der Gemeinde von Qumrân* (Assen, 1957). Good bibliographical data for Qumran messianology are found in G. Kittel's *TDNT* vol. 9 under *chriō* and in E.-M Laperrousaz, *L'attente du messie en Palestine à la veille et au début de l'ère chrétienne* (Collection Empreinte Dirigée par Henry Hierche; Paris, 1982).

73. See Charlesworth, "The Origin and Subsequent History of the Authors of the Dead Sea Scrolls: Four Transitional Phases Among the Qumran Essenes," *RQ* 38 (1980) 213–33.

74. See the similar comments by Schiffman in this volume.

75. D. Dimant correctly reports that the role of the messianic figures in the Dead Sea Scrolls "is not always clear, and some of the texts, like the *Hodayot*, lack reference to the Messiah altogether, even though they contain elaborate eschatological depictions." D. Dimant, "Qumran Sectarian Literature," in *Jewish Writings of the Second Temple Period*, ed. M. E. Stone (Compendia Rerum Iudaicarum ad Novum Testamentum 2.2; Assen, Philadelphia, 1984), p. 539.

76. 1QSb states that the Prince of the Congregation will disperse justice on behalf of the afflicted. The exegesis of this statement is far from clear.

Second, all work on the theology of the Dead Sea Scrolls is confused if it does not allow for diversity and development in the community.[77] We must acknowledge these two factors because of the increased variety in the community as attested by the successive archaeological expansions or alterations, and the discovery of a Pharisaic-type of phylactery in the caves, beginning with the first century B.C.E. Diversity and development is also reflected in the redactions and additions to texts, in the sheer length of time the Qumran Essenes lived at or near Qumran (from c. 150 B.C.E. to 68 C.E.), and by the variety of thought among the Scrolls.[78]

Third, at Qumran some fragments raise interesting questions. What is the original meaning of 4Q Florilegium? According to this fragment, the Qumran Essenes interpreted the prophecy of Nathan to David, so that the reference is transferred to David's descendant, and probably to the Messiah. Nathan told David that God had said, "I will be his father, he shall be my son" (see 2Sam 7:14). The interpretation of this fragment is not clear; but it may preserve the concept, well known from Psalm 2 and 4 Ezra, that the future king will be God's son. According to this fragment, the future "branch of David" shall interpret the Law, save Israel, and rule in Zion at the endtime. What is highly significant for us now is the recognition of a possibly messianic passage in which the king is not subordinated to the priest. According to 4Q Florilegium there are not two messiahs.

Likewise, in the Patriarchal Blessings (4QPBless) the "Messiah of Righteousness" will be of the branch of David. He apparently will renew the covenant through something like kingship.

Fourth, perhaps the most excitement for our discussion comes from the discovery of a fragmentary copy of what seems to be the earliest version of the Rule of the Community. The renowned Qumran expert J. T. Milik claims that he has identified the earliest copy of the Rule, and that it does not contain the famous passage in which the two messiahs are mentioned.[79] The earliest form of the Rule of the Community ostensibly does not contain a reference to one or two messiahs.[80]

This conclusion, however, is not possible. Larry Schiffman has found and

---

77. The nouns *mšyḥw* in CD 1.12 and *bmšyḥw* in CD 6.12 refer to "his anointed," and "by his anointed," but both of these comments denote *God's prophets*. In 1QSa 2.12 the context centers on the instructions for beginning a meal and the seating arrangements in the Council of the Community with the arrival of the Messiah of Israel—there is no clear reference to "the Messiah of Aaron."

78. An excellent monograph on the theology of Qumran, which does indeed incorporate diversity at Qumran, is H. Lichtenberger's *Studien zum Menschenbild in Texten der Qumrangemeinde* SUNT 15; Göttingen, 1980).

79. J. T. Milik, in his review of P. Wernberg-Møller's *The Manual of Discipline Translated and Annotated, with an Introduction*, in *RB* 67 (1960) 411. Also, see Charlesworth, *Judaisms and Their Messiahs*, pp. 232–33.

80. It is distressing that this fact was announced in a book review many years ago, but that the fragment is still not available to scholars. See the comments on this fragment by Schiffman.

examined the fragment that Milik claimed was the earliest copy of the rule and which did not contain the *locus classicus* for the "Messiah." The fragment is in fact two fragments of the Rule of the Community; and they were incorrectly stuck together in the fifties.

We should seriously contemplate the possibility that the earliest phases of the Qumran community were not messianic.[81] In fact, that is precisely what I wish to suggest. The Righteous Teacher, who led the priests from the Temple into the wilderness, may not have believed in a future Messiah. The recently published portions of 4QMMT disclose a letter dating from around 150 B.C.E. The letter may not necessarily have been composed by the Righteous Teacher, as J. Strugnell and E. Qimron have argued, but it certainly was written either by him or by one of his gifted cohorts.[82] What is important for us is the recognition that it was written to discuss halakoth, religious rules, and not messianology. Likewise, the Hodayoth probably contains psalms composed by the Righteous Teacher, but none of them is messianic.

This new perception is in line with my contention that the earliest explicit reference to "the Messiah," according to the documents collected into the Pseudepigrapha, was in the first century B.C.E. 1QS, the only full copy of the Rule of the Community, was copied in the early decades of the first century B.C.E. 1QSa and CD also date from the first century B.C.E. If we are seeking to discern the first use of "Messiah" to designate an eschatological figure in Jewish theology, these documents point us only to the first century B.C.E., and probably to the period 100–50.

In seeking to learn the *functions* of the Anointed One or Ones, Messiah or Messiahs, we shall unfortunately learn very little from 1QS or CD. Each only refers to "the Anointed Ones (or Messiahs) of Aaron and Israel" or "the Anointed (or Messiah) of Aaron and Israel." The reference is to the future appearance of one, or two, who is (are) the Anointed One(s). No descriptions or functions are presented to us. While some passages in CD do seem to associate future actions with the appearance of the Anointed One(s), no functions are portrayed as being performed by the Anointed One(s) or the Messiah. Only two passages seem significant. CD 14.19 states that when the Anointed of Aaron and Israel arises he will (probably) expiate the iniquity of the Covenanters (= Essenes). CD 19.10 (= B1) records the idea that those

---

81. Caquot astutely observes that the early Maccabean crisis did not cause Jews to look for the coming of the Messiah. I am in full agreement with Caquot that messianology developed in the Qumran community after John Hyrcanus. Note his keen insights: "À l'époque même de Jean Hyrcan, si l'on se fie à la datation maintenant proposée pour le plus ancien rouleau de la *Règle* (4QSe), le messianisme essenien est encore dans les limbes puisque la phrase du rouleau de la grotte I (1QS 9, 11) '. . . jusqu'à la venue du prophete et des messies d'Aaron et d'Israël' n'y figure pas." See his "Le messianisme qumrânien," in *Qumrân*, p. 237. Laperrousaz is critical of basing so much on paleographical dating of a fragment. See his *L'attente du messie en Palestin*, p. 82.
82. For bibliography and a photograph see Charlesworth, *Jesus Within Judaism*.

who do not belong to the members of the Covenant (= Essenes) will be put
to the sword when "the Anointed of Aaron and Israel comes." We can only
ask, does that mean that the Anointed One will use the sword?

According to 1QSa 2.12, there is a reference to the seating arrangements
in the Council of the Community and the instructions for beginning a meal
when the Messiah of Aaron and the Messiah of Israel are present. Again we
are left without answers to our questions. Is it possible that the ambiguity is
intentional? I think the answer is probably yes.

Fifth, in discussing the Qumran Scrolls we now should not refer to the
thoughts of one insignificant group of monks living in the desert. The consensus is that this community is related to a much larger group, the Essenes,
most of whom, if we can trust the reports of Josephus and Philo, lived somewhere besides Qumran. The archaeological work on the southwest corner
of present Old Jerusalem has unearthed ancient, probably first-century,
mikvaoth (small, carefully constructed cisterns for ritualistic purification)
and a first-century small gate. Many fine scholars have become convinced
that Essenes lived in the southwestern section of Jerusalem, and that the
tiny gate unearthed is the Essene gate mentioned in Josephus and in the
Temple Scroll.[83]

Evidence of Essenes living elswhere in Palestine, or at least similar
groups, is disclosed by the most recent work on the texts, especially the
biblical scrolls found at Qumran. These represent more than six text-types
and are divided into two major groups by Professor Emanuel Tov, one of the
leading experts on the Qumran biblical texts.[84] One category has scribal
characteristics identified with the scrolls known to be composed at Qumran.
The other category does not possess these scribal features, and the biblical
scrolls in it were probably composed elsewhere, but certainly not necessarily in "Essene" groups. All these observations prompt me to think about
Essenes living in various places in Palestine; after approximately 63 B.C.E.,
when the Romans entered Jerusalem, and some of them probably held some
type of messianology.

The complexity of messianic ideas, the lack of a coherent messianology
among the documents in the Pseudepigrapha and among the Dead Sea
Scrolls, and the frequently contradictory messianic predictions prohibit anything approximating coherency in early Jewish messianology.[85] If we were

83. See the chapter by R. Riesner in *Jesus and the Dead Sea Scrolls*, ed. Charlesworth, forthcoming.

84. E. Tov shared these insights in Jerusalem during a celebration of the fortieth anniversary
of the discovery of the Dead Sea Scrolls in July 1977.

85. Werblowsky contends that "Messiah" ultimately in Early Judaism "acquired the connotation of a savior or redeemer who would appear at the end of days and usher in the kingdom of
God, the restoration of Israel, or whatever dispensation was considered to be the ideal state of
the world." See his "Messianism: Jewish Messianism," in *The Encyclopedia of Religion*, vol. 9,
p. 472. The caution in referring to a description of the "ideal state of the world" in the future is

statisticians, we might conclude that we should ignore Jewish messianic references because they are so meager, and when present so vague or contradictory. There is no smooth transition from messianology to christology.

ADDED COMPLEXITY

To this insight let me add four suggestions. First, two passages in the Pseudepigrapha refer to the return of the Messiah. The distinguished pioneer in the study of the Pseudepigrapha, R. H. Charles, argued that 2Bar 30:1 referred to the return of the Messiah into heaven after the end of his responsibilities on earth. Here is his translation:

> And it shall come to pass after these things, when the time of the advent of the Messiah is fulfilled, that He shall return in glory.[86]

Charles added this footnote: "This seems to mean that after His reign the Messiah will return in glory to heaven." I am convinced that Charles has misunderstood this verse.

A better translation seems to be the following:

> And it will happen after these things when the time of the appearance of the Messiah has been fulfilled and he returns with glory. . . . [87]

2 Baruch 30:1 seems to refer to the preexistence of the Messiah, and it is not a Christian passage, as P. Volz contended.[88] As we have already seen, many early Jews thought that the Messiah, like Melchisedek according to the end of 2 Enoch, was preserved by God in a secret place (see esp. 1En 46:1–2, 48:2–3, 62:7; 4Ezra 7:28–29, 12:31–34, 13:26).[89] Notice the excellent translation of 4 Ezra 13:25–26 by Professor Bruce M. Metzger:

---

admirable, but it is not balanced by a similar circumspection in referring to the functions of the Messiah to "usher in the kingdom of God," and to "the end of days." The too systematic definition fails to note that in many texts no functions are attributed to the Messiah, and that his appearance is not always clearly eschatological.

86. R. H. Charles in *The Apocrypha and Pseudepigrapha of the Old Testament in English* (Oxford, 1913), vol. 2, p. 498.

87. For further discussion, see Charlesworth, *Judaisms and Their Messiahs*, pp. 246–47.

88. "Dass die Rückkehr des Messias in Herrlichkeit 30:1 wahrscheinlich ein christlicher Gedanke ist. . . ." P. Volz, *Die Eschatologie der jüdischen Gemeinde im neutestamentlichen Zeitalter* (Tübingen, 1934), p. 179; see also his comments on pp. 43 and 44.

89. If the (or that) Son of Man is identified with the Messiah, in some passages in 1En 37–71, then these references to the preexistence of the Son of Man need to be mentioned. In his paper in this collection, VanderKam rightly argues that the Son of Man is identified with the Messiah by the Enoch group, and that the statement that the Messiah is hidden does not necessarily mean that he is preexistent. Sometimes, however, the preexistence of the Son of Man, Messiah, seems clear in 1En 37–71: "At that hour, that Son of Man was given a name, in the presence of the Lord of the Spirits, the Before-Time, even before the creation of the sun and the moon, before the creation of the star, he was given a name in the presence of the Lord of the Spirits" (1En 48:2–3, trans. by Isaac in *OTP*).

As for your seeing a man come up from the heart of the sea, this is he whom
the Most High has been keeping for many ages. . . . [90]

This passage seems parallel to the Jewish idea that the Messiah was taken
from paradise, after the fall of Adam and Eve, and is protected by God until
the end of time. We have ample documentary evidence for this Jewish belief,[91] and it is similar to the preservation of other biblical heroes, most notably Melchisedek, Enoch, and Elijah. In 1 Enoch 48 we are told that the
Son of Man "was concealed" with the Lord of the Spirits before the creation
of the world (1En 48:6). If the Messiah had been in Paradise, here on the
earth, he can be said to return to the earth with glory, as in 2Bar 30:1.

This idea also seems to be found in the Greek text of the Psalms of Solomon:

May God cleanse Israel in the day of mercy and blessing,
In the day of election when he brings back his Messiah.   (PssSol 18:5)

The Greek verb (ἀνάξει) can mean "lift up," but here it probably means "to
bring back." The author was referring either to the return of an anointed one
like David or, as seems more probable, to the return of the Messiah, who is
like the wonderful King David.

If some Jews held a belief in the return of the Messiah, then we have an
important foundation for the Christian belief in the parousia of Jesus. At this
point messianology flows into christology.

My first suggestion is that we consider that some early Jews contemplated
the *return* of the Messiah. The second suggestion pertains to the transference of messianic functions from God to the Messiah and then back again to
God. In the theologies of ancient Israel much attention was given to God as
the actor or savior of Israel. During the late exilic period many of the activities reserved for God were transferred to his messengers and angels. By the
first century B.C.E. the Messiah was thought by some Jews to perform the
actions formerly attributed to God. He would save Israel. He would judge
the nations and Israel.

Now, I wish to suggest that in some segments of early Jewish theology
there seems to be a reaction against messianology. What some Jews had attributed to the Messiah was now retransferred by others back to God. This
retransference would be demanded under the force of a thoroughgoing
monotheism. We saw an example of this phenomenon in the Psalms of Solomon 17 and 18, with the final stress put upon the belief that God, not the
Messiah, is the king: "The Lord himself is our king forevermore." God is

90. B. M. Metzger in *OTP*, vol. 1, p. 552.

91. See L. Ginzberg, *The Legends of the Jews*, 7 vols. (Philadelphia, 1909–28; repr. more than
once). See vol. 1, p. 22; vol. 5, p. 33 ("On the whole, the Messiah plays an important part in this
description of the life of the pious in paradise.") vol. 6, p. 351 ("The 'Messiah, the son of David'
likewise entered paradise alive, and awaits there 'his time.'"). The textual evidence for this
concept is admittedly post-70 C.E.; but it is conceivable that the tradition is pre-70.

the Lord of the Messiah. The Messiah is God's; he belongs to God. He is the
Lord's Messiah (*christou autou*).

My third suggestion is that we no longer hold fervently to the contention
that messianic titles were not related to each other by some early Jews. We
professors have been taught and have taught that "the Son of Man" is a term
or title that is to be distinguished from the term or title Messiah. Now, with
the recognition that the Parables of Enoch are clearly Jewish, Palestinian,
and probably pre-70, we should rethink this assumption. Is it possible "that
Son of Man" (1En 48), who is concealed before the Lord of the Spirits (48:6),
is implicitly identified with the Lord of the Spirits' Messiah (48:10)? I am
now impressed with the similar functions attributed in the Parables of Enoch
to three eschatological figures, namely the "Messiah," "that Son of Man,"
"The Elect One," and "the Righteous One."[92]

My fourth and final suggestion is that we now contemplate the ways Jews
debated, even argued, with each other over messianology. Some believed in
the coming of the Messiah, others did not. Some felt the need to attribute
certain functions to the Messiah, others preferred to leave such guidelines
up to the sovereignty of God. There was probably a backlash against excessive messianology; perhaps some Jews believed the monotheism of Judaism
was undermined, or that the integrity and future of Judaism was threatened
by the excessive ideology of the militantly zealous messianic Jews (some of
whom were offensive in numerous ways to many Jews). Perhaps this factor
explains why there is no mention of the Messiah in Pseudo-Philo, as we
would expect in light of the celebration of David, and in the Testament of
Moses, in light of the conquest theme. Each of these pseudepigrapha were
composed in the first half of the first century C.E.

Earlier we asked if Jewish messianism could be isolated in or attributed
to known groups in Early Judaism. We have seen that messianology crossed
numerous social and economic boundaries.

CONCLUSION

We have seen why it is impossible to define, and difficult to describe the
messianology of the early Jews.[93] There is no discernible development in

---

92. It is important to note that this idea is not novel. Virtually the same conclusion was obtained by J. Theisohn, *Der auserwählte Richter: Untersuchungen zum traditionsgeschichtlichen
Ort des Menschensohngestalt der Bilderreder des Äthiopischen Henoch* (SUNT 12; Göttingen,
1975). Also, see Charlesworth, *Judaisms and Their Messiahs*, pp. 237–41; VanderKam's paper in
this collection; G. W. E. Nickelsburg's insightful comments in *Jewish Literature Between the
Bible and the Mishnah: A Historical and Literary Introduction* (Philadelphia, 1981) p. 223; and
A. Pinero, "Libro 1 de Henoc (*et y gr*)," in *Apocrifos del Antiquo Testamento*, ed. A. Diez
Macho, *et al.* (Madrid, 1984) vol. 4, p. 23.

93. There is no script that the Messiah is to act out. There is no clear, widely accepted Jewish
description of the Messiah. The references to him are often frustratingly vague and imprecise;
they are the opposite of the *post eventum* messianic pseudepigraphon composed by Nathan, the
"prophet" of the false Messiah Sabbati Ṣevi: "Behold a son will be born to Mordecai Ṣevi in the

messianic beliefs from the first century B.C.E. to the first century C.E. Some
Jewish writings in the first century C.E. before 70—namely Pseudo-Philo
and the Testament of Moses—show little interest in messianology and seem
even to be antimessianic. The traditions in 4 Ezra, 2 Baruch, and the New
Testament documents preserve a totally different picture. The simplest explanation of the reason for this significant difference is to appeal to Josephus'
antimessianism and to the effects of the Great War against Rome of 66–
73/74 placing the alleged antimessianic documents after it and the promes-
sianic documents before it. That solution is at once simplistic and unthink-
able. Fortunately the documents are collected in precisely the opposite way
from what historiography would expect, warning us against a too facile and
positivistic relation between documents and history.

These comments put into perspective some of the limitations of the present study. At the outset I admitted that virtually our only vehicle for learning
about the messianism of the early Jews is their own literature; but the documents do not lead us back to the mind of all early Jews, are only a portion of
the writings circulating at that time, and may not adequately represent the
swirling and living dimensions of oral traditions, not all of which were sacred
or *torah she-be'al peh*.

While, for example, we find virtually no literary evidence for the Jewish
belief in a *militant* Messiah in Philo[94] or other pre-70 authors, it is nevertheless conceivable that numerous and influential Jews, not necessarily scribes,
rabbis, and Temple authorities, believed that God would free his enslaved
elect ones by means of a warrior-Messiah.[95] Perhaps the possible polemic
against militant messianism in the Psalms of Solomon, mentioned earlier, is
a window through which to see some of these "popular" beliefs.

Similarly Schäfer does not find any numismatic or literary evidence that
Bar Kokhba desired or planned to rebuild the Temple and restore the cult;[96]
but some Jews probably expected the revolt to be successful and to culmi-
nate in the restoration of the Temple cult. It is conceivable that such ideas
are confronted in the Apocalypse of Abraham,[97] and that 2 Baruch, which is
contemporaneous with that apocalypse and was probably written a few decades prior to the revolt of 132–135 C.E., polemizes against such restoration

---

year 5386 [1626 C.E.] and he will be called Sabbatai Ṣevi. He will . . . be the true messiah." See
G. Scholem, *Sabbati Ṣevi: The Mystical Messiah 1626–1676*, trans. R. J. Zwi Werblowsky (Bol-
lingen Series 93; Princeton, 1973, 1975), p. 225.

94. See the learned and careful study in this collection by Borgen.

95. The War Scroll (1QM) comes to mind, but it is not a messianic document.

96. P. Schäfer, *Der Bar Kokhba-Aufstand*, p. 100.

97. See J. R. Mueller, "The Apocalypse of Abraham and the Destruction of the Second Jewish Temple," in *Society of Biblical Literature: 1982 Seminar Papers*, ed. K. H. Richards (Chico,
Calif., 1982) pp. 341–49; see esp. p. 347: The author of the ApAb, as "seen from the quotation of
25:4–6" puts "heavy emphasis" on the cult; "future redemption will bring about a renewal of
proper cultic practices (19:18)."

by stressing the centrality of Torah.[98] Both apocalypses in different ways, therefore, may provide evidence of Jewish expectations that the cult will be restored. Polemics may reveal a possible grass roots expectation of a restored Temple.

Messianology and One Dimension of New Testament Study

New Testament scholars have spent this century struggling with the problem of the so-called messianic secret in Mark.[99] Mark, and surely Matthew, believed that Jesus should be recognized as the Messiah.[100] The problem arises with the recognition that Jesus, according to Mark, does not proclaim that he is the Messiah, does not accept Peter's confession at Caesarea Philippi, and repeatedly orders those who comprehend who he is to keep this understanding secret.

The problem was caused, of course, by Mark's own social setting and theology; but certainly more must be said to comprehend the complexities involved. To a certain extent the problem appeared because Mark was working with some nonmessianic Jesus traditions. The problem, however, arose primarily because the Jesus traditions were swept forward by Jews who fervently claimed that he was the Messiah but had to struggle against a Jewish background that did not specify what such a declaration meant, and also—and more importantly—did not allow for a crucified "Messiah" and cautioned against any human declaration that a man was, or had been, the Messiah.

The polemical setting of the debate among Jews rejecting Jesus and Jews affirming Jesus is, moreover, an essential sociological perspective to be stressed. Maybe the claim that Jesus was the Messiah was offensive because of the fact that he had been crucified. Perhaps the proclamation that Jesus was the Messiah was not so offensive as the excessive, unsupported, and preposterous claim that one who had been crucified was still alive and resurrected. Maybe the offense came at the obsession Jesus' followers had with their very own teacher, whom they exalted as both Messiah and Lord, *and* their apparent rejection of, or shockingly peculiar interpretation of, scripture. Perhaps the offense came from the social strains caused by the missionary zeal of Jesus' aggressive followers.

These are complex issues; they help us grasp that messianology does not easily flow into christology. Paul knew this and referred to the stumbling

---

98. See the judicious suggestions by F. J. Murphy, *The Structure and Meaning of Second Baruch* (SBLDS 78; Atlanta, 1985), pp. 136–37.

99. See esp. W. Wrede, *The Messianic Secret*, trans. J. C. G. Greig (Greenwood, S.C., 1971); and C. Tuckett, ed., *The Messianic Secret* (Issues in Religion and Theology 1; Philadelphia, London, 1983).

100. As R. E. Brown states, Matthew concludes his genealogy so the reader will know that the end of the monarchy is connected "with the appearance of the final anointed king, the Messiah (Christ) Jesus" (p. 69). See Brown's *The Birth of the Messiah* (Garden City, N.Y., 1977).

block of faith. Why did Jesus' earliest followers hail him as "the Messiah"? No other title would have been so difficult to align with the life and thought of Jesus of Nazareth. What prompted them to articulate their unique faith in Jesus with this title?

These observations and questions lead us to William Wrede's *The Messianic Secret*. In light of our research it is seen to be full of numerous errors. First he assumed incorrectly that the Jews of Jesus' time held one idea concerning the coming of the Messiah. He wrote that Jesus had trouble with his disciples, because "the people and the disciples, it is said, did not have his idea of the Messiah but the Jewish, that is a political, one." [101] For Wrede the Jews held to the belief that the Messiah would be "political, patriotic and revolutionary" (p. 221).

Second, Wrede was amazingly ignorant of Jewish sources, referring to the concept of a hidden Messiah by citing only Justin Martyr and the Gospel of John, and bypassing the classic references to this idea in such works as 4 Ezra. Nowhere does he refer to the messianology found in the Psalms of Solomon, 1 Enoch, 4 Ezra, and 2 Baruch. It was unfortunately typical of his time for a New Testament scholar to study Greek thought and religion, and to ignore the detailed and fruitful research of such contemporaries as Kautzsch and Charles.

Third, he assumed that almost all Jews were looking for the coming of a Messiah. He claimed that the "expectation of a Messiah was in the air. Men's minds were everywhere full of it" (p. 30). We have seen the fallacy in that assumption.

Fourth, his sources for Jewish beliefs were the New Testament records. After writing the words just quoted, he stated the following: "This is certainly the impression created by the Gospels, and they are given credence for it in this matter" (p. 30). Likewise, much later, he claims, "Thus Luke attributes to the disciples as Jews an expectation of the Messiah which we may when all is said describe as national and political" (p. 171).

Fifth, his work is sadly anti-Semitic or better anti-Jewish. Note these words: ". . . Jesus is hinting at his passion in order to cleanse the disciples' messianic belief from Jewish sediment" (p. 15). We confront in these words the perennial attempt to remove Jesus and his followers from their Jewishness and from Judaism.

To turn to Wrede's work to illustrate some of the problems in New Testament research is not to pick on some scholar recognized as dated. Wrede's work is hailed as a classic and many New Testament theologians affirm that he wrote a masterpiece. For example, Professor Norman Perrin, in one of his last plenary addresses before the Society of Biblical Literature prophe-

---

101. Wrede, *The Messianic Secret* (the preface to the original German work is dated 1901). This is not a recent book, as some might assume from the English translation of 1971.

sied that the *Wredestrasse* had become the *Hauptstrasse* (the Wrede-street had become the main-highway).[102]

Summary. The major conclusions of this study may be summarized as follows: (1) Jewish messianology exploded into the history of ideas in the early first century B.C.E., and not earlier, because of the degeneration in the Hasmonean dynasty and the claim of the final ruling Hasmoneans, especially Alexander Jannaeus, to be "the king," and because of the loss of the land promised as Israel's inheritance to the gentile and idolatrous nation Rome. (2) Jews did not profess a coherent and normative messianology. (3) New Testament scholars must read and attempt to master all the early Jewish writings; there is much to admire about the genius of early Jewish theology. The Jewish social and ideological contexts of Christian origins are not the background for, but the foreground of, Jesus and his earliest followers. (4) One can no longer claim that most Jews were looking for the coming of the Messiah. (5) The gospels and Paul must not be read as if they are reliable sources for pre-70 Jewish beliefs in the Messiah.

We have seen that it is not easy to describe the messianology of pre-70 Jews. We have been left with numerous questions, most notably this one: Why did Jesus' followers claim above all that he was the Messiah?

---

102. N. Perrin, "The *Wredestrasse* Becomes the *Hauptstrasse:* Reflections on the Preprinting of the Dodd *Festschrift,*" *Journal of Religion* 46 (1966) 297–98. Also see C. R. Mercer, *Norman Perrin's Interpretation of the New Testament* (Studies in American Biblical Hermeneutics 2; Macon, Ga., 1986), see esp. pp. 23–24.

PART TWO

MESSIANIC IDEAS AND THE HEBREW SCRIPTURES

J. J. M. ROBERTS

THE OLD TESTAMENT'S CONTRIBUTION
TO MESSIANIC EXPECTATIONS

A discussion of the Old Testament's contribution to the development of the later messianic expectations can hardly be focused on the Hebrew word for messiah, מָשִׁיחַ. In the original context not one of the thirty-nine occurrences of מָשִׁיחַ in the Hebrew canon refers to an expected figure of the future whose coming will coincide with the inauguration of an era of salvation.

The word מָשִׁיחַ is an adjectival formation with passive significance from the verbal root מָשַׁח, "to anoint." It is used adjectivally in the expression הַכֹּהֵן הַמָּשִׁיחַ, "the anointed priest" (Lev 4:3, 5, 16; 6:15), to refer either to the Aaronid priests in general, all of whom were anointed (Ex 28:41; 30:30; 40:15; Num 3:3), or possibly to the high priest alone as the specific successor to Aaron, since the unction of high priest seems to be treated as something special (Num 35:25). The most common use of the term, however, is as a singular nominalized adjective in construct with a following divine name or with a pronominal suffix referring to the deity: מְשִׁיחַ יְהֹוָה "the anointed of Yahweh" (1Sam 24:7, 11; 26:9, 11, 16, 23; 2Sam 1:14, 16; 19:22; Lam 4:20); מְשִׁיחַ אֱלֹהֵי יַעֲקֹב, "the anointed of the God of Jacob" (2Sam 23:1); and מְשִׁיחוֹ, מְשִׁיחֶךָ, מְשִׁיחִי "his, my, your anointed one" (1Sam 2:10, 35; 12:3, 5; 16:6; 2Sam 22:51; Isa 45:1; Hab 3:13; Pss 2:2; 18:51; 20:7; 28:8; 84:10; 89:39, 52; 132:10, 17; 2Chr 6:42 [corrected from מְשִׁיחֶיךָ]). With one exception all these occurrences refer to the contemporary Israelite king, and the use of the term seems intended to underscore the very close relationship between Yahweh and the king whom he has chosen and installed.

The exception is Isa 45:1, where the Persian Cyrus is called Yahweh's anointed one: לְכוֹרֶשׁ כֹּה־אָמַר יְהוָה לִמְשִׁיחוֹ, "Thus says Yahweh to his anointed one, to Cyrus . . ." This usage, like Yahweh's earlier reference to Cyrus as רֹעִי, "my shepherd" (Isa 44:28), is analogous to passages in Jeremiah where Yahweh refers to Nebuchadnezzar as עַבְדִּי, "my servant" (Jer 25:9; 27:6; 43:10), an expression that is otherwise reserved in Jeremiah for David (Jer 33:21, 22, 26) or the collective Jacob (30:10; 46:27, 28). This unusual designation of a non-Israelite king with terms normally used to express the very special relationship that the Israelite king had to Yahweh is clearly intended by both Jeremiah and Second Isaiah to shock their Israelite audiences into looking at historical events in a new way. Yet the role assigned to Cyrus by Second Isaiah is quite different from that assigned to Nebuchadnezzar by Jeremiah.[1] Nebuchadnezzar was an agent of judgment against God's people, a role never assigned to a native Israelite king. Cyrus, however, is assigned a role as an agent of salvation for God's people. This is quite compatible with Israelite expectations for their own native kings, and Isaiah's oracle concerning Cyrus could be seen as modeled on Israelite coronation oracles. Nonetheless, one should not regard Second Isaiah's treatment of Cyrus as messianic in the later sense of the term. Despite the positive expectations associated with Cyrus, he, like Jeremiah's Nebuchadnezzar, was a contemporary ruler, not an expected figure of the future. At most one could say that Second Isaiah endowed him with the same royal expectations that were formerly bestowed on any new incumbent of the Davidic throne at his coronation.

The plural nominalized adjective occurs twice (excluding 2Chr 6:42, which should be corrected to a singular), both times with a first person singular suffix referring to Yahweh: אַל־תִּגְּעוּ בִמְשִׁיחָי וְלִנְבִיאַי אַל־תָּרֵעוּ, "Do not touch my anointed ones, and do not harm my prophets" (Ps 105:15; 1Chr 16:22). The context makes it clear that the anointed ones here are the Israelite patriarchs seen as prophets (cf. Gen 20:7). Whether Israelite prophets, like Israelite priests and kings, were normally anointed at their installation, as 1Kgs 19:16 might suggest, is disputed, but an early cultic practice of such anointing would help to explain the later metaphorical language that characterizes the prophet as anointed with the spirit of God (Isa 61:1; Joel 3:1).

One of the other three occurrences of מָשִׁיחַ is irrelevant for our discussion since it concerns the oiling of a shield (2Sam 1:21) and should probably be corrected to מָשׁוּחַ, but the final two are significant since they involve the nominal use of מָשִׁיחַ in the absolute state (Dan 9:25–26), and they occur in a late text only a century earlier than datable texts that use מָשִׁיחַ or its Greek translation χριστός to refer to expected eschatological figures of the future. The usage in Daniel is not messianic in this later sense, however. The expression צַד־מָשִׁיחַ נָגִיד, "until an anointed one, a prince [comes]" (Dan 9:25), apparently has a historical figure of the distant past in mind, perhaps the high priest Joshua or the governor Zerubbabel mentioned in Haggai and Zechariah (Hag 1:1–14; 2:21–23; Zech 4:6; 6:9–14; cf. 4:14, where the expression שְׁנֵי בְנֵי־הַיִּצְהָר, "the two sons of oil," presumably refers to these two anointed officials). On the other hand, the expression יִכָּרֵת מָשִׁיחַ וְאֵין לוֹ, "an anointed one will be cut off and will have nothing" (Dan 9:26), is nor-

---

1. I must thank Martin Hengel for reminding me of this during the discussion at the colloquium.

mally interpreted to refer to Onias III, the legitimate high priest who was deposed and eventually murdered during the reign of Antiochus IV. At the time of the writer of Daniel, both incidents were past events, so neither figure could be regarded as a messianic figure expected by him or his readers.

PASSAGES WHICH ACQUIRED A LATER MESSIANIC INTERPRETATION

Even if some of these passages where מָשִׁיחַ occurs were later understood as prophetic predictions of the Messiah, as happened for example with Ps 2:2, such passages provide an inadequate base from which to discuss the Old Testament contribution to the development of messianic expectations. By far the majority of biblical passages given a messianic interpretation by later Jewish and Christian sources do not contain the word מָשִׁיחַ. The passages selected as these messianic proof texts remain remarkably consistent for both Jewish and Christian interpreters, however, and this suggests that one might approach our task by analyzing the different types of material included in this fairly consistent body of messianic texts.[2]

Ex Eventu *Prophecies*

Some of these texts in their original settings appear to have been prophecies *ex eventu*. Balaam's oracle about the star that would step forth from Jacob and the staff that would arise from Israel (Num 24:17) probably dates from the early monarchy and celebrates the victories of a Saul or a David in the guise of prophecy. This seems to be literary prophecy in a triumphalist mode, not so much propaganda to further a political agenda as nationalistic literature celebrating an already achieved hegemony. Jacob's comment that the scepter or staff would never depart from Judah (Gen 49:10) would also appear to date to the early monarchy and to refer to the Davidic dynasty. Whether it is pure celebration, however, or whether it was intended to undergird the inviolability of the Davidic dynasty by rooting it in a prophetic word remains debatable. One might challenge the characterization of these texts as prophecies *ex eventu* if one accepted a pre-monarchical date for them on linguistic grounds, but, in any case, they found their fulfillment in the early monarchical period, and it is only by ignoring that original setting that they can continue to function as prophecies for the future.

---

2. The basic consistency in the choice of texts can be seen by a simple comparison of the work of the Jewish scholar J. Klausner, *The Messianic Idea in Israel* (New York, 1955), to any of the countless works by Christian scholars on the same subject. Nor is this consistency a modern phenomenon. Early Christians, rabbinic sources, and the sectarians at Qumran cite the same biblical texts in their portrayals of the royal messiah, as A. S. Van der Woude has pointed out (*Die messianischen Vorstellungen der Gemeinde von Qumrân* [Studia Semitica Neerlandica 3; Assen, 1957], pp. 243–44).

Enthronement Texts

Other texts appear to have their original settings in the enthronement ceremonies of particular Israelite or Judean kings. Psalms 2 and 110 and Isa 8:23b–9:6 have been plausibly interpreted in this fashion. The divine promises contained in these texts were made to particular kings or their subjects at particular points in the history of the monarchy. They were not prophecies holding out hope for a distant future but oracles that gave expression to political, social, and religious expectations for the reign of a contemporary king just being installed into office. As such, they served a political as well as a religious function; the propaganda value of such texts and of the larger ceremonial occasion in which they were originally embedded should by no means be overlooked.

Such enthronement texts, though composed for particular occasions, reflect the Israelite royal theology as it was developed and transmitted in the kingdom of Judah, and it will be helpful to highlight aspects of that royal theology before turning to the next category of "messianic" texts. The particular historical developments during the reigns of David and Solomon led to the widely accepted theological claims that Yahweh had chosen David to be his king and Jerusalem to be his royal city. The choice of David extended to David's descendants so that the Davidic dynasty was to retain David's throne in perpetuity and the choice of Jerusalem meant that Yahweh would make his abode there, first in David's tent where David had the ark transferred with great fanfare and then in the Temple that Solomon eventually built. This double choice, of dynasty and royal city, which has numerous parallels in the ancient Near East, was firmly linked in the royal Zion theology (Pss 2:6; 132:10–18), but the implications of each choice could be spelled out independently of the other.

The choice of Zion was elaborated by the glorification of the city, sometimes in strongly mythological terms, but I have treated that subject extensively elsewhere,[3] and while it would be central to any discussion of Israel's general eschatological expectations, it is not central to a discussion of "messianic texts" narrowly conceived. One should note, however, that the tradition of Zion as Yahweh's city presupposes the Temple, the cultus, and the priesthood in one fashion or another.

The choice of David was elaborated by the tradition of the eternal covenant God made with him and his dynasty. This tradition is already attested in the "last words of David" (2Sam 23:1–7), an old poem with close linguistic ties to the oracles of Balaam, and it is continued in such texts as Psalms 89

---

3. See my article, "Zion in the Theology of the Davidic-Solomonic Empire," *Studies in the Period of David and Solomon and Other Essays*, ed. T. Ishida (Tokyo, 1982), pp. 93–108, and the literature cited there.

and 132, and 2 Samuel 7, to mention only the most prominent. Israelite royal theology resembled that of its Near Eastern neighbors in stressing the king's responsibility to uphold justice, rule wisely, and ensure the general well-being and piety of his land, but David's imperial expansion gave the Israelite royal theology an added dimension. This royal ideology viewed David and his successors as regents of the divine suzerain; hence the surrounding nations should be their vassals, making pilgrimage to the imperial city to pay tribute to the Davidic overlord and his God and to submit their conflicts to the overlord's arbitration.

One other aspect of the enthronement texts should be noted—their strong mythological component. However the language was understood in the enthronement ceremony, Ps 2:7 speaks of God giving birth to the king; Ps 110:3, though textually difficult, also appears to refer to the divine birth of the king;[4] and Isa 9:5–6, after referring to the king's birth, assigns divine qualities to the king in the series of names that are given to him. These names in Isa 9:5–6 are best explained as royal names given to the new king in the coronation ceremony on the analogy of the five royal names given the new Pharaoh in the Egyptian enthronement ceremony,[5] and this suggests a strong Egyptian influence on the Judean coronation ritual. This influence may go back to the formative period of the Israelite state when Egyptian influence was quite strong. As is well known, Solomon married a daughter of the Pharaoh (1Kgs 3:1; 7:8; 9:16), and even earlier David appears to have adopted Egyptian models for many of the high offices in his empire.[6] In any case, the Egyptian influence on the Israelite royal ceremony brought with it the strongly mythological language of the Egyptian royal protocol. This language was probably not taken literally in the Israelite court—the language of divine sonship, for instance, was presumably understood in Israel as adoptive sonship—but once this mythological language had been deposited and preserved in texts whose original roots in particular court ceremonies were forgotten, the possibility for new, literalistic readings of this mythological language arose. Much of the mythological dimension in the later messianic expectations can be traced back to the remythologization of this borrowed mythological language of the royal protocol.

4. Note H.-J. Kraus' emendation of the text to בְּהַרְרֵי־קֹדֶשׁ מֵרֶחֶם שַׁחַר כְּטַל יְלִדְתִּיךָ, "On the holy mountains, out of the womb of Dawn, like dew have I given birth to you" (Psalmen 2 [Biblischer Kommentar 15.2; Neukirchen, 1961²], pp. 752–53, 758–60).

5. S. Morenz, "Ägyptische und davidische Königstitular," Zeitschrift für ägyptische Sprache 79 (1954) 73–74; H. Bonnet, "Krönung," Reallexikon der ägyptischen Religionsgeschichte (Berlin, 1952), pp. 395–400; A. Alt, "Jesaja 8,23–9,6. Befreiungsnacht und Krönungstag," Kleine Schriften zur Geschichte des Volkes Israel (Munich, 1953), vol. 2, pp. 206–25.

6. See the discussion and further bibliography in T. N. D. Mettinger, Solomonic State Officials: A Study of the Civil Government Officials of the Israelite Monarchy (Coniectanea Biblica, Old Testament Series 5; Lund, 1971).

Restoration and Dynastic Texts

The third category of messianic texts differs from the first two in that these texts do in fact envision a future ruler not yet on the scene. Because Israelite royal theology, at least as transmitted in Judah, regarded the Davidic dynasty as eternally guaranteed by God, in times of severe crisis the tradition of Yahweh's eternal covenant with David could serve as basis for the hope that God would soon restore the monarchy to its former glory by raising up a new scion of the Davidic line. Sometimes this figure is not described as a descendant from the Davidic line, but simply as David himself. Nonetheless, it is extremely doubtful that this usage should be pressed to imply that the long-dead king would return to life to assume the throne again. It is more likely that the usage simply implies a new embodiment of the Davidic ideal, a new David. As the founder of the dynasty, creator of the Israelite empire, and dominant influence in the creation of the national cultus in Jerusalem, David was the model of the ideal king, and a new embodiment of that ideal could be called David for short.

A number of these passages cluster in prophetic collections that come from the late eighth century, but the originality of that literary context is disputed for every one of the passages in question. Isa 11:10, 32:1–8; Hos 3:5; Amos 9:11–12; and Micah 5:1–5 are generally taken as later expansions of the genuine eighth-century material in these books. The judgment on Isa 11:1–9 is more divided, but a significant number of scholars would also date this material much later than the eighth century. I am not convinced that this general skepticism is warranted. There are other indications that the political disasters of the late eighth century, including the destruction of the northern kingdom and the deportation of a significant portion of the population of the southern kingdom, produced widespread longing for the unity, strength, and justice of the idealized united monarchy of the past. Isaiah reflects that longing in a number of oracles dating from the period of the Syro-Ephraimite war,[7] it is clearly expressed in Isa 1:21–26, and Hezekiah's attempt to extend his control into the north presupposes it. One should also note that the oracle in Zech 9:1–10, as difficult as it is to interpret, contains a number of elements that strongly suggest an original eighth-century context. The linking of Hadrach (Hatarikka in the Akkadian texts), Damascus, Israel, Hamath, and the Phoenician cities inevitably reminds the historically informed interpreter of Tiglath-pileser's victory over Kullani (biblical Calneh) in 738 B.C.E., when the south Syrian coalition apparently led by Judah under Azariah/Uzziah collapsed. All these states figure in that event according to

---

7. J. J. M. Roberts, "Isaiah 2 and the Prophet's Message to the North," *JQR* 75.3 (1985) 290–308; and "Isaiah and His Children," *Biblical and Related Studies Presented to Samuel Iwry*, ed. A. Kort and S. Morschauser (Winona Lake, Ind., 1985), pp. 193–203.

the Assyrian sources, and it is impossible to find a later event of which the same could be said.[8]

If such a longing for the golden days of the Davidic empire were prevalent in the late eighth century, one should reevaluate these texts. As von Rad argued years ago,[9] Amos can be interpreted as rooted in the Zion theology, and an eighth-century Judean prophet rooted in that theology could well author such an oracle as Amos 9:11–12, which envisions the restoration of the Davidic empire. One should note that both Amos (6:2) and Isaiah (10:9) specifically mention the fall of Kullani as an event with profound consequences for Israelite and Judean security.

Hillers has suggested a similar background for Micah 5:1–5.[10] The reference to the seven shepherds and eight princes is most easily explained against the background of the south Syrian league active in the late eighth century and in which Judah apparently played a leading role prior to the battle of Kullani. Isa 11:1–9 would also fit this period as a statement of Isaiah's hope in the context of the Syro-Ephraimitic war.

Micah's promise of a new ruler from Bethlehem and Isaiah's promise of a shoot from the root of Jesse both suggest a new David is needed and thus imply a serious criticism of the current occupant of the Davidic throne as less than an adequate heir to David. Such criticism fits the time of Isaiah and Micah quite well. With Azariah/Uzziah's demise there was ample room for dissatisfaction with the Davidic house. Jotham is hardly noted, but Isaiah's disappointment with Ahaz is well documented. It would seem that both prophets expected a new embodiment of the Davidic ideal, but both expected a refining judgment on the nation beforehand. That is certainly the case with Isaiah, who envisioned a humbling of the royal house and of the royal city before both would experience a new embodiment of the ancient ideal (Isa 1:21–26, 11:1–9, 32:1–8).[11] Nonetheless, it also seems certain that Isaiah expected this new David in the near future. His use of very similar language in his coronation oracle for Hezekiah probably suggests that, for a time at least, he expected Hezekiah to fulfill these expectations.

8. The best and most comprehensive treatment of this event remains that of H. Tadmor ("Azriyau of Yaudi," *Studies in the Bible,* ed. C. Rabin [Scripta Hierosolymitana 8; Jerusalem, 1961], pp. 232–71), but it should be supplemented or corrected by at least the following articles: M. Weippert, "Menahem von Israel und seine Zeitgenossen in einer Steleninschrift des assyrischen Königs Tiglathpileser III. aus dem Iran," *Zeitschrift des Deutschen Palästinavereins* 89 (1973) 26–53; N. Na'aman, "Sennacherib's 'Letter of God' on His Campaign to Judah," *BASOR* 214 (1974) 25–39; and K. Kessler, "Die Anzahl der assyrischen Provinzen des Jahres 738 v. Chr. in Nordsyrien," *Die Welt des Orients* 8 (1975–76) 49–63.

9. G. von Rad, *Old Testament Theology,* trans. D. M. G. Stalker (New York, 1960), vol. 2, pp. 130–38.

10. D. R. Hillers, *Micah* (Hermeneia; Philadelphia, 1984), pp. 65–69.

11. J. J. M. Roberts, "The Divine King and the Human Community in Isaiah's Vision of the Future," *The Quest for the Kingdom of God: Studies in Honor of George E. Mendenhall,* ed. H. B. Huffmon, F. A. Spina, and A. R. W. Green (Winona Lake, Ind., 1983), pp. 127–36.

Jeremiah, Ezekiel, and Related Texts

The next cluster of messianic texts envisioning a future king falls at the end of the Judean kingdom in the late seventh and early sixth century. These include Jer 23:5–8, 30:9, 33:14–26; Ezek 17:22–24, 34:23–24, 37:15–28. The originality of some of these passages in their present context or their attribution to the prophet in whose book they stand has been questioned, but there is little reason for redating any of the passages to a significantly later period. Jer 23:5–8 is normally attributed to Jeremiah, and the apparent play on Zedekiah's name in vs. 6 suggests that the oracle comes from the period of that king's rule. The oracle seems influenced by several Isaianic passages. The צֶמַח ("sprout") for David recalls Isa 11:1, 10; the expression וּמָלַךְ מֶלֶךְ וְהִשְׂכִּיל וְעָשָׂה מִשְׁפָּט וּצְדָקָה בָּאָרֶץ "the king will rule and act wisely, and he will do justice and righteousness in the land," resembles Isa 32:1a, הֵן לְצֶדֶק יִמְלָךְ־מֶלֶךְ, "Then the king will rule in righteousness"; and the themes of the reunification of Judah and Israel and of the new exodus remind one of Isa 11:10–16, all of which suggest that these passages antedated Jeremiah and influenced his outlook. Jeremiah envisions a new Davidic ruler who will embody the ancient ideals of just rule. In this ruler's days the unity of north and south will again be realized, and the exiles from both states will return to Israel to live in their own land. Jer 30:8–9 may be originally from an early period in the prophet's ministry, perhaps from the time of Josiah, when Jeremiah was appealing to the north. It shows close connections to Hos 3:5 and to some Isaianic passages (Isa 10:27, 14:25). If this early dating for the original setting of Jer 30:8–9 is accepted, it may suggest that Jeremiah at one point in his ministry saw Josiah as the new David. Exactly how Jer 30:18–21 fits into this picture is not clear, though it also seems to be an early oracle addressed to the north. What is meant by the ruler who would arise from the midst of Jacob? Could the prophet refer to a Davidic king in so obscure a fashion? Could Josiah, for instance, have claimed kinship with the northerners in an effort to persuade them to accept his rule in preference to that of the foreign nobility who had controlled Samaria since the fall of the north? Or does this passage envision a genuine northerner to rule over the north? The issue remains obscure. Jer 33:14–26 is also problematic. Since the passage requires extensive discussion and its attribution to Jeremiah is questionable, we will return to it later.

The messianic oracles in Ezekiel are roughly contemporaneous with those of Jeremiah and basically only elaborate the themes already found in Jeremiah. The long-standing division between north and south will be healed under the new David, and the exiles will return to their own land to serve God, where a Davidic prince will always rule over them. This emphasis on the eternal rule of the promised Davidic prince appears to be a response to a problem of faith created by the Babylonian termination of the Davidic dynasty in Jerusalem. Given the tradition of God's eternal covenant with David, how could the dynasty possibly come to an end? When it was seriously threatened, one could approach God with the accusation of a breach of covenant, as Psalm 89 very well illustrates, but when the dynasty no longer existed, what was left to say? Were the promises of God not reliable? Ezekiel suggests the reinstallment of the dynasty in such a way as to respond at least implicitly to this existential concern.

That such an existential concern was a serious problem in this general period is clear from Jer 33:14–26, which addresses it explicitly. This pericope is full of problems that make its attribution difficult. It is missing in the LXX of Jeremiah, which has been taken as an indication that the pericope is a very late secondary addition to the book. The pericope begins after an introductory statement in vs. 14 with a citation in vss. 15–16 of a slightly variant form of the genuine Jeremianic oracle of Jer 23:5–8. That in itself may also suggest secondary expansion of the Jeremianic corpus. The pericope, however, continues with a promise that God is not yet finished with the Davidic dynasty nor with the Levitical priesthood, and this promise is clearly formulated in response to a widespread opinion that was being expressed among the people. According to vs. 24 the people were saying that God had rejected the two families that he had chosen. He had annulled his covenant with David so that a member of the Davidic dynasty no longer ruled before him, he had annulled his covenant with Levi so that the Levites no longer served as priests before him, and he had spurned his people so that they were no longer a nation before him. Whatever one may think of the authorship of this pericope, such murmurings among the people can hardly be temporally situated anywhere but in the exile. They presuppose the end of the Davidic dynasty, the cessation of the regular Temple cultus, and the loss of Judah's independent existence as a nation. With the restoration of the Temple cultus after the return, it is unlikely that such a claim about the Levitical priests could have gained currency, and the nature of the prophet's response to the opinion of the people gives no grounds for thinking that the Temple cultus had yet been restored.

One should note that the three things which the people claim God has rejected are three central dogmas of the deuteronomic theology: Yahweh's choice of and covenant with David and his successors to be his king; Yahweh's choice of and covenant with Levi and his successors to be his priests; and Yahweh's choice of and covenant with Israel to be his special people. It should be clear then that the prophetic defender of these threatened dogmas is to be sought in those theological circles that were trying to preserve the deuteronomic legacy from its apparent failure in history. In the face of external reality, the prophet simply asserts that God has not abrogated his covenants with these parties any more than he has abrogated his covenant that upholds the order of creation. The implication is that he will once again install Davidic kings and Levitical priests in office for his people Israel. Moreover, it is very clear from the passage that the prophet envisions a series of Davidic rulers and Levitical priests. Given the decimation of these families caused by the disaster of the Babylonian conquest, the prophet is constrained to apply the old Abrahamic promise of national fertility to these specific families: "Just as the host of heaven cannot be counted and the sand of the seashore cannot be measured, so I will multiply the seed of David my servant and the Levites who minister to me" (Jer 33:22). This is probably an important exegetical comment on earlier prophecies of a new David since it provides a good indication that there had not yet developed any expectation for a last David who in his own person would rule forever.

The mention of the Levitical priests deserves further comment. At first blush their inclusion in such a prophecy concerning a restoration of the Davidic dynasty seems surprising, but further reflection shows that such a move was only to be expected. From the beginning the Zion Tradition had linked the choice of David to the choice of Jerusalem, and Jerusalem as the city of God was first and foremost Jerusalem the site of God's sanctuary, the national Temple built for Yahweh by Solomon. If the Davidic ruler was Yahweh's regent for maintaining just political rule, the priests were Yahweh's chosen servants for maintaining the cultus that allowed Yahweh to remain in the midst of his city among his people. One should recall that Psalm 132, which celebrates Yahweh's linked choice of David and of Zion, twice mentions the priests of Yahweh (vss. 9, 16).

Moreover, the tradition of Yahweh's election of a particular priestly family probably predates any tradition of his choice of a royal line, though the variety of such traditions and their possible contamination by later struggles over the priesthood make any attempt at clarifying the history of the priesthood highly speculative. Nevertheless, one should regard the tradition of Yahweh's selection of Levi for the priesthood, attested among other places in the early blessing of Moses (Deut 33:8–11), as pre-monarchic, and the same is probably true for the tradition of Yahweh's election of Eli's predecessors to the priesthood (1Sam 2:28–29), even though Eli's family was eventually rejected and replaced by Zadok (1Kgs 2:27). Num 25:13 also speaks of an eternal covenant of priesthood which Yahweh gave to Phineas and his descendants as a result of his actions on God's behalf at Baal Peor. One should note that each of these traditions is traced back to pre-settlement days and that two of them make the bestowal of the priesthood a reward for the priest's violent actions of killing on behalf of Yahweh. Their similarity in this regard raises the possibility that all these traditions may be variants of a single original.

In any case, some form of such a priestly tradition was undoubtedly cultivated by the priestly family or families that dominated the Jerusalem priesthood. As long as the normal functioning of the cultus was uninterrupted, the average Israelite was probably not much concerned which priestly family had the upper hand in the Temple. The threats to the Davidic house in the late eighth century find their reflex in texts from that period, but despite occasional prophetic attacks on the priests, there is no indication that there was any threat to the continuity of the Jerusalem cultus sufficient to call forth widespread and serious reflection on claims of priestly election. Josiah's radical cultic reform in the late seventh century probably altered this situation, since the closing of so many local shrines and the consequent unemployment of the local priests in favor of Jerusalem and its priesthood must have exacerbated rival priestly claims for the right to serve as priests in the Temple. If one may judge from the book of Deuteronomy, the deuteronomic reform certainly brought the claims of the Levites to public awareness. Then when the Babylonians brought an end to the Davidic dynasty, destroyed Jerusalem, burned the Temple, and killed or deported the priests, it was not just Yahweh's election of David that seemed abrogated; it was also Yahweh's choice of Jerusalem and, for a deuteronomist, of Yahweh's servants, the Levitical priests. It is no more surprising that an exilic deuteronomist should mention the Levitical priests alongside the Davidic king in his vision for the future than that an exilic Zadokite should mention the Zadokite priests alongside the Davidic prince in his vision of the restored community (Ezekiel 40–48).

Postexilic Texts

The attention devoted to Jer 33:14–26 may seem disproportionate to the intrinsic value of the text, but it is crucial to a correct evaluation of the next cluster of messianic prophecies, those of the early postexilic period. After the first return from exile following the edict of Cyrus in 539 B.C.E., the faith issues raised by the people in Jer 33:24 were still not resolved. There was no Davidic king, the Temple was still in ruins, and, given the state of the Temple, the priesthood was in no little disgrace. In 520 B.C.E. the prophets Haggai and First Zechariah began to address that situation, apparently initiating a campaign to rebuild the Temple. Haggai urged the Persian-appointed Davidic governor of Judah, Zerubbabel the son of Shealtiel, and the high priest, Joshua the son of Jehozadak, to finish the work, promising that God would soon intervene to make this disappointingly modest-looking building more glorious than the former Temple (Hag 2:1–9). Moreover, in a second oracle Haggai promised that on that day of divine intervention God would take Zerubbabel his servant and make him the signet ring on the divine finger, for God had chosen Zerubbabel (Hag 2:20–23). Given the context of God's promise to overturn other kingdoms, such an oracle clearly implied the elevation of Zerubbabel to the Davidic throne of his ancestors, a point that is even more explicit in the oracles of Haggai's contemporary Zechariah.

Zechariah addressed all of the issues raised by the complaint of the people in Jer 33:24. He proclaimed Yahweh's return to Zion and his reelection of Jerusalem as his place of abode among his people (Zech 2:5–17), and he promised that Zerubbabel who had begun the rebuilding of the Temple in Jerusalem would complete it (Zech 4:6–10). He proclaimed the rededication of the priesthood in a vision concerning Joshua, and he announced that God had renewed his covenant of priesthood with Joshua and his colleagues (Zech 3:1–10). Finally, picking up the older Jeremianic prophecies concerning the "sprout" (צֶמַח) of David, he announced that God was bringing his servant the צֶמַח (Zech 3:8), and in Zech 6:12 he identified the צֶמַח as the man who would build the Temple, that is, as Zerubbabel the Davidic governor. There can be little doubt that Zechariah identified Zerubbabel as the one who would restore the Davidic dynasty. Despite the secondary dislocations that the text of Zech 6:9–15 has suffered, the crown referred to there was originally intended for the head of Zerubbabel who would build the Temple and rule as king, while Joshua would be the priest who served by his throne and with whom the king would have amicable relations.

This linking of royal and priestly figures in Zechariah's prophetic expectations is not an innovation, since it simply continues that found in Jer 33:14–26, which may have influenced Zechariah, but Zechariah seems to be the first writer to call attention to the fact that both priest and king were anointed as God's chosen agents. That would seem to be the implication of his somewhat obscure reference, presumably to Zerubbabel and Joshua, as "the two sons of oil who stand before the lord of all the earth" (Zech 4:14). It is probably also the biblical source for the later dual expectations for "messiahs of Aaron and Israel." The secondary corrections to Zech 6:9–15 that resulted in the crown being placed on the head of the priest instead of the king may also have contributed to the superior position accorded the messiah of Aaron in priestly dominated circles like those of the Qumran community.

Sometime after Haggai and Zechariah, Malachi introduced a prophetic figure into Israel's expectations for God's future intervention with his announcement that God was sending Elijah the prophet before God's great day of judgment (Mal 3:23). This passage is dependent on his earlier oracle announcing God's sending of his messenger to prepare the way before him (Mal 3:1), though it is not clear in this earlier oracle that the מַלְאָךְ ("messenger") is even human, much less specifically a prophet. It is hard to determine the source for this new expectation of a particular prophetic figure. It does not seem dependent on the Mosaic prophet of Deut 18:15, though the introduction of Elijah as an eschatological figure may have influenced a new eschatological reading of this deuteronomic text. The more general announcements of the return of prophecy found elsewhere are less difficult to explain. Since the exile had raised doubts about the continuation of prophecy (Ps 74:9) just as it had about kingship and the priesthood, such prophecies as Joel 3:1–2 could be seen as a response to the longing for a reestablishment of the institutions of the idealized golden age. No particular family, however, had ever been promised an eternal prophetic line, so the hope for a prophetic future did not have the compelling tie to the progeny of a particular figure the way the expectations for a king or priest did, and as a result the later speculations about the prophet to come remain quite fluid.

SUMMARY

This paper has only touched on the high points of the Old Testament's prophecies of a new David, a new priest, and a new prophet. There are major dimensions of the Bible's eschatological hopes that I have not discussed or have discussed far too inadequately. The new Jerusalem is far more prominent in prophetic visions of the future than the Davidic king, but such eschatological hopes are not specifically messianic, so I have only mentioned this outgrowth of the Zion Tradition in passing. Many prophets left no oracles expressing the hope for a new David, and some may have been opposed to such views. Second Isaiah applied God's commitments to David to the nation as a whole (Isa 55:3), thereby implicitly renouncing the expectations for a new David, and at least one voice in the Third Isaiah collection appears to have also rejected the priestly claims. He seems to oppose the rebuilding of the earthly Temple (Isa 66:1), and he extends the priestly role to all Israelites (Isa 61:6).

Moreover, I have characterized a number of passages as not really envisioning a future king in their original contexts, and I have ignored other more peripheral passages for the same reason. That cannot be the last word on these passages. Once the expectation of a new Davidic king became an important hope in large circles of the Israelite people, these passages would be subject to eschatological reinterpretation, to new readings that were genuinely prophetic.

Nonetheless, within the self-imposed limits of this study, several conclusions stand out: (1) Nowhere in the Old Testament has the term מָשִׁיחַ acquired its later technical sense as an eschatological title. (2) Old Testament expectations of a new David are probably to be understood in terms of a continuing Davidic line. There is little indication that any of these prophets envisioned a final Davidic ruler who would actually rule for all time to come, thus obviating the need for the continuation of the dynastic line. The language of some of the prophecies is open to that interpretation, and such a reading was eventually given to them, but such passages as Jer 33:14–26 and Ezekiel 40–48 indicate that the dynastic understanding was the dominant interpretation of such promises as late as the exilic period, and the repeated references to the בֵּית דָּוִיד, "the house of David," in Third Zechariah (Zech 12:7–12; 13:1) suggest that this interpretation remained dominant well into the postexilic period. (3) The mythological language of the royal protocol, influenced as it was by Egyptian conceptions of the royal office, provided a textual base for the development of later, far more mythological conceptions of the awaited Messiah. (4) The later expectations of a priestly Messiah can be traced back to the promises of the restoration of the priesthood found in Jeremiah 33 and in Zechariah's oracles concerning the high priest Joshua. (5) Finally, Malachi provided the catalyst for further speculation about prophetic figures who would precede the great day of Yahweh's coming judgment.

ROYAL TRAITS AND MESSIANIC FIGURES:
A Thematic and Iconographical Approach

INTRODUCTION

The Field of Study

In the study of "royal messianism," it seems that every perspective for research has been taken up, but not pursued to the end. At any rate, that is the case for the attempt to gain a more concrete picture of messianic representations through the study of ancient Near Eastern (especially Mesopotamian and Syro-Palestinian) royal iconography. Situated at the intersection of a collective eschatology and a royal ideology, messianism depends upon both precisely at their point of contact, for the hope in a *Messiah* (מָשִׁיחַ) presupposes "a royal person whose coming is the sign of national salvation following a crisis that is insurmountable from a human point of view."[1]

Thus our field of investigation is well blocked out. The question is what we can learn from the Mesopotamian royal iconography in its relationship to the religious texts of the ancient Semitic domain, including the Old Testament. How and in what measure can the comparison of the textual and iconographic data clarify the difficult question of the origins of the messianic hope in ancient Israel, of its phraseology, and of its representations?

Even though I am appealing to the iconographic data of the ancient Near East, I will avoid an approach that is merely illustrative of the phraseology relative to messianism. On the contrary, my objective, from a more explanatory perspective, will be to isolate the constitutive elements of the best-characterized messianic representations. Let me state from the beginning, however, that I will not include a treatment of the theme of the "divine and royal triumph," a theme which has already been well studied in the past.[2]

---

1. The definition of A. Caquot, cited by J. Coppens, *Le messianisme royal: Ses origines, son développement, son accomplissement* (Lectio Divina 54; Paris, 1968), p. 228.
2. See O. Keel, *Wirkmächtige Siegeszeichen im Alten Testament* (Orbis Biblicus et Orientalis 5; Freiburg, Göttingen, 1974), p. 232 (illus. 78).

Method

Ideally this approach would presuppose a specific study of each monument decorated with figures in its historical and artistic context (synchronic), then a subsequent elaboration of a comprehensive dossier on the theme (and/or the motifs) represented (diachronic), with the view of reconstituting the total iconic syntax and coherence. Yet an undertaking of such magnitude would not be possible in the context of this symposium; it is why, in initiating this dialogue with specialists on messianism, I pose the question, first of all, of the methodological presuppositions of such an approach. I shall then attempt to disengage the two principle guidelines for research in this field.

Because of these limits and in order to clearly situate the approach proposed here, I will list below the methodological principles (according to their order of coherence and in the form of recall) on which I base my demonstration:

i. Word and Vision. The recognition of the literary genre of the "words of the seer(s)," of their original character (from the "prophetic" texts of Mari in the eighteenth century B.C.E. down to the classical prophets of the eighth century B.C.E. in Israel), and of their expressive coherence presses the exegete to take seriously the concrete and visual elements of a biblical text, especially if it is of religious and messianic character.[3] This applies especially to the *Sehersprüche* of the oracles of Balaam, in the poetic passages of Numbers 23–24, which constitute a first prelude of messianic representations in ancient Israel.[4]

ii. Figurative Language. From this same perspective, the exegete should take fully into account the concrete and plastic aspects of the figurative language of the Bible, from the prophetic oracles down to the Gospel parables. In effect, the philologist cannot isolate himself indefinitely in this "iconographic blindness" that allows him to study such topics as "the image of God" in the priestly tradition (p) without actually raising the question of the meaning of the "statue/image" (*ṣalmu/ṣelem*) in the ancient Near East.[5] By a systematic recourse to the continuously expanding data from Near Eastern and

---

3. See S. Amsler, "La parole visionnaire des prophètes," *VT* 31 (1981), 359–63; B. O. Long, "Reports of Visions Among the Prophets," *JBL* 95 (1976) 353–65; contrast C. Westermann, *Erträge der Forschung am Alten Testament: Gesammelte Studien* (Munich, 1984), vol. 3, p. 188: "Geschicht und Deutung treten auseinander."

4. D. Vetter, *Sehersprüche und Segensschilderung: Ausdrucksabsichten und sprachliche Verwirklichungen in den Bileam-Sprüchen von Numeri 23 und 24* (Calwer Theologische Monographien, Reihe A; Stuttgart, 1974), vol. 4, p. 151.

5. W. W. Hallo, "Cult Statue and Divine Image: A Preliminary Study," *Scripture: More Essays on the Comparative Method*, ed. W. W. Hallo, J. C. Moyer, L. G. Perdue (Winona Lake, Ind., 1983), pp. 1–17.

biblical archaeology, the biblical scholar—especially on the Protestant side—should be able to transcend this unconscious iconoclasm, undoubtedly based on a too absolute understanding of "the prohibition of any image" (Ex 20:4, Deut 5:8). To maintain this misunderstanding of the prohibition is to forget that the theme of the prohibited image should be taken up and reinterpreted, in the light of the all-embracing image, the *Imago Dei*. This is equally the center of gravity of the royal and messianic representations in the field of ancient semitic studies.

iii. The "Mimesis" - Imitation. In order to rediscover the "mimetic" dimension of biblical discourse, following the work of the literary critics (E. Auerbach, N. Frye, R. Girard, etc.), on the one hand, and the point of view of the art historians and iconographers, on the other, one should pay attention to the notions of a "model" (Heb. *tabnît*, Gk. *mimesis*). These notions persist for such a long time in the ancient documentation that they merit in this respect the rank of operational concepts. Thus the exegete has the task of extracting all the value of a reference to the original and to the unique in biblical discourse ("The Bible, the great code of art"—William Blake). He should certainly not resign himself to what appears to have become the fate of our present generation—the veritable loss of this original code![6]

iv. The Narrative and the Emblematic. In the framework of iconology, which ought to include the study of figured monuments as well as the descriptive textual data (in "figurative language"), the critic has the complementary task of maintaining a proper balance between two fundamental aspects of iconic representations, the "narrative" and the "emblematic." One of these aspects should not be allowed to prevail to the detriment of the other, but both should be expressed in complementary fashion, according to their full "sym-bolic" value. This is an open field of research, in which a synthesis should be achieved between the recent studies on the "narrative art" in ancient Mesopotamia, following H. Frankfort,[7] and the older studies of the *Symbol-Forschung*. Unfortunately, the methodological imprecisions of the latter have undermined its achievements. Nevertheless, it is evident that the biblical exegete cannot cut himself off from such sources of information without loss.

6. J. G. Heintz, "Ressemblance et représentation divines selon l'Ancien Testament et le monde sémitique ambiant," *L'imitation: aliénation ou source de liberté?* (Rencontres de l'École du Louvre, 3; Paris, 1985), pp. 89–106 (illus. 6).

7. H. Frankfort, *Kingship and the Gods: A Study of Ancient Near Eastern Religion as the Integration of Society and Nature* (Chicago, London, 1948, 1978); see also I. J. Winter, "After the Battle Is Over: The *Stele of the Vultures* and the Beginning of Historical Narrative in the Art of the Ancient Near East," *Pictorial Narrative in Antiquity and the Middle Ages*, eds. H. L. Kessler, M. S. Simpson (Studies in the History of Art 16; Washington, 1985), pp. 11–32 (illus. 17).

v. The Style of the Court ("Hofstil"). It is possible to easily isolate and characterize a group of texts and specific traditions that concern the person of the king, whether divine or human, namely the "style of the court." Situated in a precise context, that of the royal palace or the divine court, and expressing itself in the terms of praise, this language needs to be studied afresh. Rather than dismissing it as the "gratuitous flattery of the courtier"[8] or as oriental hyperbole, one should understand courtly language more as a genuine testimony to the royal ideology of this period. By its reference to the divine origin of the institution of the human monarchy it forms the substratum for the later messianic formulations of a "perfect king and savior."[9] Insofar as this is the case, this (too) human language of the court, whose literary and thematic connections with the prophetic oracles should be explored in still more depth,[10] reveals itself particularly apt in expressing the modalities of human hope in the coming of the Messiah, according to the plan of the living God.

On the basis of these introductory theses—cited here as methodological corollaries—I propose a first approach to the texts that possess a messianic character. This approach will be neither illustrative nor exhaustive, as I have already indicated, but it will attempt to close in upon the constitutive elements of the messianic hope. In spite of the works of remarkable pioneers, such as H. Gressmann, we are still at the beginnings of this methodological approach. This means that I am able to use the study of themes (and of the motifs that they include) only as *dicta probantia*, somewhat as the systematic theology at the end of the nineteenth century made reference to passages from the Bible. That is why I am devoting this communication to the study of some constitutive elements of the messianic hope. I will do this on two levels, and these levels will furnish at the same time the plan for my paper, the second level being illustrated by two examples. These two levels are the following: (1) *Messianic humanity,* the Messiah as a person, the origins of this representation, and its iconographic and religious (anthropological and theological) implications; (2) *Messianic authority,* the symbols of authority, the origins and significance of these symbols, and the extension and duration of this authority, illustrated by (a) the sword and the word, and (b) the son of the king.

Messianic Humanity

If the personal form of the messianic hope as a part of eschatology, based on the Hebrew word מָשִׁיחַ (Gk. χριστος), "the Anointed," might appear ob-

---

8. See P.-E. Dion, "Ressemblance (et image de Dieu)," *Dictionnaire de la Bible: Supplément* (Paris, 1981), vol. 10, cols. 365–403.

9. See H. Gressman, *Der Messias* (Göttingen, 1929), pp. 7ff.

10. For a partial approach to this subject, see my: "Langage prophétique et 'style de cour' selon *Archives Royales de Mari, X* et l'Ancien Testament," *Semitica* 22 (1972), pp. 5–12.

vious to us in terms of the biblical and Christian tradition, it by no means does so when one considers the long historical process which has given birth to these representations. Thus the Assyriologist Th. Jacobsen, who in his major work, *The Treasures of Darkness* (1976),[11] progressively unfolds the fundamental metaphors of Babylonian religion, places the emergence of individual divine figures in the third millennium B.C.E. On the other hand, the notion of a god who is near, a parent and mediator, appears only at the extreme end of the third millennium B.C.E. and asserts itself primarily at the beginning of the second millennium, during the time of the First Babylonian Dynasty (1894–1595 B.C.E.).[12] Two types of documents illustrate perfectly this emergence of the anthropomorphic form of the divine, but one particular monument, by its significant variation on a constant theme, will lead us into the heart of this *problématique personnaliste*.

At that period one of the fundamental aspects of the religion consisted in the desire of the pious individual to enter into a personal relationship with his deity. This desire is expressed abundantly by the scenes decorating the cylinder-seals, starting from the Neo-Sumerian period, at the time of the third dynasty of Ur (twenty-first century B.C.E.), in the form of the so-called "presentation scenes." *Figure 1* is a typical scene. These scenes require three personages, always in the same order: a superior deity, most often seated on a throne; a mediator deity, almost always feminine; and a worshipper, in a ritual posture.

Beginning from the Isin-Larsa period (twentieth to nineteenth century B.C.E.), this theme was significantly modified into that of "the adoration-intercession scene." In effect, according to the description given by A. Parrot:

> the personages are the same (principal deity, client, assistant deity), but they are no longer portrayed in the same order nor even in the same attitude; the pious is standing in front, hands joined or raised, while behind him the assistant deity intercedes.[13]

The classical form of these scenes of "presentation and intercession" extends into the Old Babylonian period, to which two major monuments bear witness. *Figure 2*, the relief on the upper part of the stele on which the Code of Hammurabi is inscribed, forms a genuine introduction to that text; it depicts the giving of the divine law by the sun-god Shamash as the omnipresent and

---

11. Th. Jacobsen, *The Treasures of Darkness: A History of Mesopotamian Religion* (New Haven, London, 1976), p. 273.

12. I follow the chronology established by J. A. Brinkman in his "Appendix: Mesopotamian Chronology of the Historical Period" in A. L. Oppenheim, *Ancient Mesopotamia: Portrait of a Dead Civilization* (Chicago; London, 1967, 1977), pp. 335–48.

13. See A. Parrot, *Abraham et son temps* (Cahiers d'Archéologie Biblique 14; Neuchâtel, Paris, 1962), pp. 27ff.

omniscient deity.[14] *Figure 3* shows the central part of the painting called "the investiture scene" from room 106 of Zimri-Lim's palace at Mari. Its archaeological and epigraphic context allows one to suppose a *hieros logos* in the form of a prophetic oracle of salvation (*Heilsorakel*).[15]

Finally, I must mention here a monument that, though from a later period, is of particular importance because of the changes it introduces in the classic theme of the "presentation"—changes sufficient to shift the interpretative axis. *Figure 4* is the cultic tablet from Sippar (British Museum, no. 91000). Its upper part (about a third of its total height) is occupied by this representation. In accordance with the schema of "the presentation to a divinity," there is depicted on the left a group of three personages advancing toward a divine figure who is seated on a throne to the right and portrayed in "heroic size." These personages represent, in this left-to-right order, the Babylonian king Nabû-apal-iddina (middle of ninth century B.C.E.), two inferior deities who, playing the role of intercessors, introduce and present him to the great deity, the great solar deity Shamash, the titular god of Sippar.

Though I cannot enter into the details of the interpretation of this monument, whose cosmic character is obvious,[16] it is only by recourse to the text of the cuneiform inscription that one is able to grasp its meaning. The king recalls how in times past the statue of the:

> god Shamash, who dwelt in the [temple] Ebabbara in Sippar, which the Suteans had destroyed, . . . and whose images they had destroyed . . . , the stele of the god and his insignia had gone out of usage, and no one was any longer able to picture them. The king of Babylon, Simbar-Shipak, consulted the deity concerning his form, but the deity did not reveal to him his face. Without having rediscovered his statue (*ṣalmu*) and his insignia, he nevertheless envisaged the emblem (*niphu*) of the god Shamash, and he reestablished the regular offerings. . . . But then [*i.e.*, under the reign of the present king] one rediscovered on the left bank of the Euphrates a relief on an oven-baked clay tablet, on which the deity was portrayed with his form and his insignia. The priest of Sippar [who found it] . . . showed it to the king . . . upon whom the responsibility thus fell, by divine command, to remake this image.

This takes us beyond the mythological and platonic interpretations which could be proposed for this monument back to the central point of its purpose and function. It is a simple scene of transfer. The representation seizes this moment of the removal of the solar disk, the substitute emblem (*niphu*) of

---

14. See A. Parrot, *Le Musée du Louvre et la Bible* (Cahiers d'Archéologie Biblique 9; Neuchâtel, Paris, 1957), pp. 102–7 (illus. 51).

15. See A. Parrot, *Le Musée du Louvre et la Bible*, pp. 10–13 (illus. 2). For an explanation of this interpretation see my article in SVT 17 (1969), pp. 112–38, (125–29).

16. See my "Ressemblance et représentation divines," pp. 89–106 (cf. n. 6).

Fig. 1   Presentation Scene from a Cylinder Seal,
Ur III period. (A. Parrot, *LE MUSÉE DU*
LOUVRE ET LA BIBLE [Neuchatel ett Paris: De-
lachaux & Niestlé S.A., 1957], p. 24)

Fig. 2   Code of Hammurabi, now in the
Louvre Museum. (Parrot, p. 105)

Fig. 3   The "investiture scene"; from court no 106 of the Palace of Zimri-
Lim at Mari. (Parrot, p. 11)

Fig. 4   Cult tablet from Sippar, now in the British Museum (B.M. 91000)

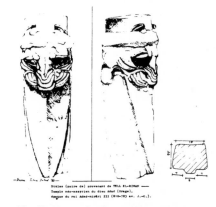

Fig. 5   Two steles from Tell Rimah in northern Iraq. The upper part represents a roaring lion and the lower part is an un-sheathed sword ("image et signification," Reconstres de l'Ecole du Louvre © Documentation Française Paris, 1983)

Fig. 6   Image of a roaring lion, Seal of "Shemaʾ, servant of Jeroboam," Meggido (A. Parrot, *SAMARIE*, 1955).

the deity, and its replacement by the deity's statue in human shape (*ṣalmu*) sitting enthroned in majesty. But this scene of ritual displacement really functions to render graphically the total supremacy accorded to the divine statue in human form in contrast to the emblematic substitute for the deity.

This theme of the divine absence (of the statue) or, more precisely, of his incomplete presence in a substitute manner is also found clearly expressed in the tradition of some recently discovered cuneiform texts conventionally called "Akkadian Prophecies" (abbreviated *Pr.A.*), although it would be more accurate to speak of "Akkadian Apocalypses."[17] In a textual tradition that is particularly fragmentary, five separate units can actually be discerned. It is the fifth fragment (= *Pr.A.*, no. 5), a document recently discovered at Uruk and dating from the neo-Babylonian period (first half of the sixth century B.C.E.),[18] that completes this file. As for the four others (*Pr.A.* 1, 2, 3/A–B, and 4), they are *vaticinia ex eventu* developed in a long sequence of historic apodoses (declaratory sentences). In regular succession these paragraphs mention the coming of future anonymous kings whose reigns will be successively beneficial and ill-fated. Here is how the reign of one of these latter is characterized:

> [After] him a king will come, but he will not enact the law in the country; he will not pronounce a [just] sentence on the land. He will lead the *protective-goddess* of Uruk away from Uruk and make her reside in Babylon. -A [*non*]*protective goddess* of Uruk he will establish in her sanctuary; he will bring to her as an offering some men who do not belong to her.

The opposite, hence beneficial rule could thus be described by a simple thematic inversion:

> He will lead the *protective goddess* of Uruk away from Babylon, and he will establish her in Uruk, in her sanctuary.

Here, as in a vast dossier that we are only beginning to master, it is necessary to recognize the theme of the "presence/absence of the divine statue in human form," the *conditio sine qua non* for the existence of a human in a stable cosmic order. This recurrent historiographical theme is present in the critical moments of the "Erra Epic," whose whole plot is marked by "the anger and distance of the god, the catastrophes which result, the divine statue deserted, lost, and soiled, before it is found, purified, and once again

17. According to the terminology of W. H. Hallo, "Akkadian Apocalypses," *IEJ* 16 (1966) 231–42; followed by my study: "Note sur les origines de l'apocalyptique judaïque, à la lumiére des 'Prophéties akkadiennes,'" *L'apocalyptique* (Paris, 1977), pp. 71–87.

18. It was discovered in 1969; see Warka inventory no. 22307/7 in H. Hunger, *Spätbabylonische Texte aus Uruk* (Ausgrabungen der Deutschen Forschungsgemeinschaft in Uruk-Warka 9; Berlin, 1976), part 1, pp. 21–23 and plate 3.

'living' and glorified."[19] It is also present in the sequence of events recounted in the historical preamble of the "cultic tablet of Sippar," as well as in the alternation between the beneficent and ill-fated reigns of the "Akkadian Prophecies." The theme expresses the placing into question of the national and religious cohesion of a whole people. Israel itself did not escape this law, as one can see from the traditions relative to the "Ark of the Covenant" (1 Samuel 2, 4, and 7) and from Ezekiel's treatment of the exile in Babylon.[20]

Conclusions

On the basis of this initial inquiry, it is important to state to what extent the mimetic search for the "human figure of the deity," far from being an original and obvious given, is the outcome of a long historical process. Thanks to the evidence provided by iconographic documents, I have also been able to note some of the significant stages of this process. After the emergence of individual divine figures there follows the intervention of divinities near to man, mediators, from whom come the gifts of the law and the promises of salvation. These functions can be transposed to the person of the king, who is at the same time the "re-presentative" of the divinity and mediator between the divine world and humanity. Parallel to this, on the religious and cultic level, man seeks and values the human form of the divine statue as the only true representation of the deity, and hence its absence, *a contrario*, is inevitably marked by a national and cosmic catastrophe. Over against this cultic vision, which can only lead to an apocalyptic perspective of the divine disappearance (of the statue) and of the cosmic catastrophe, the prophetic perspective offers the personal approach of a sovereign and free God, "who holds himself [momentarily and voluntarily] hidden" (Isa 45:15).[21] Does this not lead to an eschatological hope that is embodied in a person, that of God's "anointed," his present and living manifestation in the history of humanity?

The Messianic Authority

In the area of the fundamental metaphor, defined as the messianic humanity based on the divine representation, there is room for research on

---

19. See R. Labat, *Les Religions du Proche-Orient* (Paris, 1970), p. 116.
20. See P. D. Miller and J. J. M. Roberts, *The Hand of the Lord: A Reassessment of the "Ark Narrative" of 1 Samuel* (The Johns Hopkins Near Eastern Studies; Baltimore, London, 1977), note esp. pp. 77–87; see also D. Bodi, *The Book of Ezekiel and the Poem of Erra* Orbis Biblicus et Orientalis 104 (Freiburg: Göttingen, 1991), pp. 183–218.
21. See my "De l'absence de la statue divine au 'Dieu qui se cache' (Esaïi, 45/15): aux origines d'un thème biblique," *Revue d'histoire et de philosophie religieuses* 59 (1979) [= Hommages à E. Jacob], pp. 427–37 (illus. 1).

concrete details, sometimes transcribed by the iconography of the period. Thus one can attempt to recover the original sense of the "living metaphor" (P. Ricoeur) that forms the center of the prophetic oracle.

The transition point is provided by an Assyrian text, which a new interpretation allows to situate in this perspective. It is a proverb (Heb. *māšāl*, "comparison") that is transcribed in a letter that a high official addresses to his sovereign, Asarhaddon or Assurbanipal, during the neo-Assyrian period (between 680 and 627 B.C.E.), but which undoubtedly goes back to a much more ancient tradition. Here is an attempt at translation (= *LAS*, no. 145)[22]:

> As it is said, "The [human] king is the shadow of the god, and man [the human being] is the shadow of the [human] king." Thus the king himself is the perfect resemblance of the god!

This important text, though difficult to interpret, presents the interesting citation of an archaic proverb very relevant to the theme that qualifies the king as "the image of the god."[23] But here the learned commentator, making use of assonance, improperly called "play on words," points to the fundamental meaning of the text. Thus behind the word translated as "shadow" (the Sumerian logogram GIŠ.MI), the Semite would almost automatically hear the term *ṣalmu*, "the dark, the obscure," which is very close to the substantive that is habitually used in this context, *ṣalmu*, (Hebrew *ṣelem*), "the image, the statue." This equation is confirmed by the final line, which establishes the "resemblance" (*muššulu*) between the king and the god.

This theme is of fundamental importance for the *theologoumenon* of the "image of God" in the Old Testament, but it also forms the basis of the whole "royal ideology" of ancient Mesopotamia. This "royal ideology" appears to provide us a possible substratum for the messianic representations of ancient Israel, but it expresses itself through a phraseology, a figurative language, to which I will now turn our attention, at least with regard to two specific motifs: the sword and the word, and the son of the king.

1. THE SWORD AND THE WORD

Figure 5 is a drawing of the two orthostatic steles which were discovered *in situ* on each side of the entrance to the cella of a temple of the god Adad, which was built by King Adad-Nirari III (810–783 B.C.E.) at Tell Rimah, in

---

22. See Frankfort, *Kingship and the Gods* 3rd ed., (Chicago, 1958), p. 406, n. 35; W. G. Lambert, *Babylonian Wisdom* (Oxford, 1960), pp. 281–82; see S. Parpola, *Letters from Assyrian Scholars to the Kings Esarhaddon and Asshurbanipal* (AOAT 5.1–2; Neukirchen, 1970, 1983), vol. 1, pp. 112–13; vol. 2, pp. 131–32.

23. See my: "Ressemblance et représentation divines," pp. 89–106 (illus. 6), see esp. pp. 94ff.

northern Iraq. This monument, which would merit a detailed study,[24] presents an interesting iconography for the storm god, characterized by its significant biomorphism: (a) the upper part shows a roaring lion, symbolizing thunder; and (b) the lower part shows an unsheathed sword, symbolizing lightning.

Although very instructive, this interpretation does not exhaust the heuristic value of this figured monument. In effect, by integrating the unrepresented "symbolic node" with the "tongue"—the natural place for the blade of the sword according to a type of weapon well known in that period—one moves into a complementary theme, that of the "word."

Moreover, the Hebrew tradition has exploited precisely this imagery and its symbolic implications. It is not only the thunder of the storm god (*rigim d.Adad*) that corresponds to the "roaring lion"; the judging and sovereign word of Yahweh corresponds to it as well. Thus one reads in the "psalm of David":

The LORD thundered from heaven,
and the Most High uttered his voice.
(2Sam 22:14 = Ps 18:14, RSV; cf. Psalm 29).

In the same way it is not only the natural element of lightning, the visible manifestation of the storm, that corresponds to the "unsheathed sword"; the "devouring fire," which is a major expression for the divine power in the most ancient Semitic traditions (see Amos 1:3–4ff.), also corresponds to it. This theme is already well integrated in the book of Amos as the double parallelism of the programmatic, if not inaugural, prophetic oracle attests:

The lion has roared; who will not fear?
The Lord God has spoken; who can but prophesy? (Amos 3:8, RSV).

The simple iconography of a storm god is here taken up and assimilated by the Yahwistic theology—and by the popular religion, if one may judge by the Palestinian seals of the eighth to seventh centuries B.C.E. (see *Figure 6*)—in order to serve as a metaphor for the judging and sovereign word of Yahweh, the unique and living God of Israel. This rich symbolism does not stop in this period, however. It reemerges in the vision of the "glorified Christ" in the Apocalypse of John:

In his right hand he held seven stars, from his mouth issued a sharp two-edged sword, and his face was like the sun shining in full strength.
(Rev. 1:16, RSV; cf. 2:12b, 19:15a, 21).

24. See my study: "Langage métaphorique et représentation symbolique dans le prophétisme biblique et son milieu ambiant," *Image et signification* (Rencontres de l'École du Louvre 2; Paris, 1983), pp. 55–72 (illus. 7), see esp. pp. 57–68.

The discovery of the ancient figured steles from Tell Rimah has taught us two complementary lessons: (a) It has permitted the rediscovery of the precise symbolism that the figurative language of the texts had partly obscured. That the figurative language of the texts allowed only an approximate understanding of the symbolism can be seen in the contrast between the representation on this ancient monument and the illustrations of the Apocalypse of John by later artists such as A. Dürer and L. Cranach the Elder, during the sixteenth century C.E. (see *Figure 7*). (b) More important for our subject, it has shown that a constitutive theme of the divine theophany of Yahweh has been transferred to the person of the Son of Man in the visions of John on Patmos.

2. THE SON OF THE KING

We return here to the text of the "Akkadian Prophecies" (= *Pr.A.*, no. 5), which dates to the period of the coregency of Nebuchadnezzar II (604–562 B.C.E.) and his son Amel-Marduk (562–560 B.C.E.), but which refers to events that took place about two centuries earlier (in the middle of the eighth century B.C.E.).[25] In a thematic context that recalls the ancient religious and iconographic tradition of the city of Uruk, such as has been already illustrated by the ornate alabaster vase coming from this same site (fourth to third millennium B.C.E.),[26] this text (*Pr.A.* no. 5:15–18), in the lines immediately following the early citation of the same text, describes the reestablishment of the beneficent royal authority:

> He will renovate Uruk. The gates of the city of Uruk he will build with lapis-lazuli. The canals and the irrigated fields he will refill with plentitude and abundance.
> (The son of the just king):
> After him his son will come as king in Uruk, and he will reign over the four regions of the earth. He will exercise sovereignty and royalty over Uruk. His dynasty will last forever.
> *The kings of Uruk will exercise the sovereignty like the gods.*
> [*šarrū (LUGAL).MEŠ šá Uruk\<ki\> ki-ma ilī (DINGIR.MEŠ) ip-pu-šú be-lu-ú-tu.*[27]

In addition to the themes that characterize this text, from the reestablishment of the legitimate authority and of the social order (cf. the *mīšarum* edicts) to the restoration of the city and the fertility of the country, one should pay attention to its twofold final perspective. In the first place, follow-

---

25. See P. Höffken, "Heilszeitherrscherwartung im babylonischen Raum (Überlegungen im Anschluss an W 22 307.7)," *Die Welt des Orients* 9 (1977), pp. 57–71.

26. See A. Parrot, *Sumer* (L'univers des formes; Paris, 1960), pp. 70–73 (illus. 87–90).

27. Transcription and translation by Hunger, *Spätbabylonische Texte aus Uruk*, (Berlin, 1976) p. 21/b and plate 3.

ing the binary structure, positive and negative, which characterizes the whole of this small corpus, this brief and surprising epilogue mentions (this is a unique case) the "son of the just king" in terms specific to the oracle of royal salvation and messianic hope (i.e., universal sovereignty, legitimate royalty, and eternal duration). Then, secondly, the final line of the text furnishes the religious confirmation because "the kings of Uruk will exercise the sovereignty *like the gods.*" Could one find a better religious legitimation than this epilogue, which establishes and sums up all the re-presentative function of the royalty among humanity? By this personification of the hope in a legitimate royal dynasty, as well as by its projection into an ideal future, this text anticipates the "apocalyptic replacement of royal messianism," one of the themes underlined by recent biblical research,[28] and one that should remain an open and fruitful field for research.

Conclusions

Three fundamental themes are initiated in this neo-Babylonian text, following a problematic development that will never be completely foreign to the biblical traditions. First, according to the principle of the interpenetration between the divine and human spheres, which marks the Mesopotamian royal ideology, the sovereignty of the gods is proposed as a "model" for the legitimate dynasty. In Israel, however, this relation is limited to the king's function as the "re-presentative" of God. It remains a question whether this implies only a relation of simple vassaldom,[29] or whether there exists, in traces, the notion of a distant iconographic projection of the divine in the human king: "You have made him almost like a god!" (Ps 8:5).

Second, in both cases, the sovereign who brings salvation acquires a juridical and ethical significance. In Mesopotamia this justice is the hypostatic reflection of the divine world, but in ancient Israel it is referred both to the continuity of the ordinances of Yahweh and to the historic event of the Mosaic law. From this continuity, the Davidic king draws his legitimacy and his function as the agent of "law and justice" (cf. Isa 9:6, 11:3–5; Jer 23:5, 33:15; Ezek 37:24; Zech 9:9–10).

Third, this theme is expressed in both cultures by the motif of "the son of the king." In the neo-Babylonian text quoted above, this figure is an element in the continuity and discontinuity of the royal cycles. In Israel, on the other hand, this figure appears in the prophetic oracles as the bearer of the hope of the whole people of Israel, the ideal and divine personification of this aspiration of all humanity. The announcement of the birth of the Messiah, as

---

28. See J. Coppens, *La relève apocalyptique du messianisme royal* (BETL 50; Louvain, 1979), 1:325.

29. See R. de Vaux, "Le roi d'Israël: vassal de Yahvé," *Mélanges Eugène Tisserant* (Studi e Testi 231; Rome, 1964), vol. 1, pp. 119–33; reprinted in de Vaux's *Bible et Orient* (Paris, 1967), pp. 287–301.

it is expressed in the great prophetic texts (Isa 7:14, 9:1–6, 11:1–8; Micah 5:1–3),[30] combines this motif with the two discussed above. Rev 22:16, which combines Num 24:17 with Isa 11:1, shows that the theme was both fundamental and permanent: "I, Jesus, . . . I am the root and the offspring of David, the bright morning star."

Fig. 7 John's vision of the Son of Man in Revelation 1:12–16, by Lucas Cranach the Elder, sixteenth century (THE SEPTEMBER BIBLE [Baltimore: John Hopkins University Press, 1955])

30. See Th. Lescow, "Das Geburtsmotiv in den messianischen Weissagungen bei Jesaja und Micha," *ZAW* 79 (1967) 172–207; see also E. Lövestam, *Son and Savior: A Study of Acts 13, 32–37* (Coniectanea Neotestamentica 18; Lund, Copenhagen, 1961), p. 134, and G. Gerleman, *Der Menschensohn* (Studia Biblica 1; Leiden, 1983), pp. ix, 79.

P. D. HANSON 4

MESSIAHS AND MESSIANIC FIGURES IN PROTO-APOCALYPTICISM

TERMINOLOGY

The period extending from the Exile to the time of Ezra and Nehemiah was one of transition within the religious and political structures of the Jewish people. This was certainly true of programs and visions of cultic and national restoration, for the clash between traditional forms and contemporary realities placed a great strain upon attempts to formulate plans for the future.

At the center of the discussion was the question of the role to be played by God's anointed one(s). As demonstrated by J. J. M. Roberts in his article in this volume, "anointed one" (*māšîaḥ*) in scriptural usage does not normally refer to an eschatological figure whose coming would inaugurate a new era of salvation, rather to contemporary kings and priests.[1] By the first century B.C.E, however *māšîaḥ* and its Greek equivalent *christos* carried connotations that were distinctly eschatological in nature, connotations that continued to influence both Judaism and Christianity in succeeding centuries. An early stage in the development of eschatological understandings of the nature and role of the "anointed one" can be reconstructed on the basis of texts commonly designated as "proto-apocalyptic." These texts, arising within the period of transition from late prophecy to early apocalyptic, reflect the struggles of a community seeking to reestablish its social, economic, and cultic structures after years of disruption caused by national calamity and exile. From this period, three categories of materials will be relevant to our study: (1) Texts in which the noun *māšîaḥ* is used; (2) texts in which individuals are described as being objects of a divine action expressed with a verbal form of the root *mšḥ*, and (3) texts lacking any form of the root *mšḥ* but nevertheless relevant to our subject due to the presence of other terms undergoing transformation in the direction of eschatological connotations in a manner parallel

---

1. See the second essay by J. J. M. Roberts, "The Old Testament Contribution to Messianic Expectations."

to *māšîaḥ*. While the third category is difficult to define and delimit, it cannot be excluded from the discussion without leaving a serious gap in the relevant evidence.[2]

HISTORICAL BACKGROUND

Though we shall discern differences in the way various groups applied the notion of "anointed one(s)" to the new situation in which the Jewish community found itself, we first note two features that virtually all Jews shared in the wake of the Babylonian destruction of the Temple: (1) They all understood the essential nature of the Jewish people as a kingdom ruled by the divine King who had called it into existence; (2) they all struggled to understand how that rule was manifested under the conditions of Jewish subjugation to foreign rule.

As we move now to analyze the various reflections on the notion of God's "anointed one" in the relevant texts, we shall see that they fall into distinct traditions according to the way in which they attempt to resolve the tension between the Jewish community's understanding itself as a kingdom ruled by God and the existential experiences of Babylonian exile and subsequent integration into the Persian satrapy of Eber Nahara.

THE HISTORICAL-REALISTIC MESSIANISM
OF THE EARLY RESTORATION PERIOD

Within two decades after Cyrus' Edict of 538 B.C.E., a messianic interpretation arose that combined eschatological speculation with historical realism. God was about to accomplish the restoration of the Kingdom of Israel through the instrumentality of Zerubbabel, grandson of Jehoiachin and thus heir to the Davidic crown. The high level of expectation that could be engendered by this figure among Judahites longing for the restoration of their nation and cult is obvious. What is often overlooked, however, is the degree of historical realism that is also an essential part of the way in which Zerubbabel was interpreted by the main spokesperson of our first type of messianism, namely, Haggai. According to his oracles, God's answer to economic and political vicissitudes was restoration of cosmic order through the reestablishment of legitimate kingship and the rebuilding and reconsecration of the authorized Temple and cult. Chief among the mandated actions was the reinstitution of the official sacrificial system. This was not only a prerequisite for

---

2. In discussing the notions of "anointed one" (*māšîaḥ*) that develop within the texts discussed in this paper, it will be important to hold in suspension all those connotations that derive from later periods and from contemporary attitudes and beliefs. Helpful in this regard is the reminder that the root meaning of *māšîaḥ* has to do with the ritual anointing applied to the king and priest as part of an investiture ceremony.

reestablishing sanctity in the land and the assurance of divine blessing; on a very practical level it also involved the restoration of centralized control over distribution of the land's produce.[3] True to the theologoumenon of the Temple cult, Haggai could promise that once the Temple had been restored, God would secure all aspects of šālôm, from fertility of the land (Hag 2:18–19) to safety from enemy hostilities (Hag 2:20–22). Though the lavish nature of his promises indicates that Haggai drew freely upon themes of the preexilic Jerusalem cult that originated in a mythopoetic view of reality, the historical realism informing his announcement that a specific king was to reestablish a communal order in continuity with preexilic institutions and structures must not be overlooked. Though the vocable mšḥ is absent in Haggai, the divine favor, power, and authority associated with the sacral anointing of the king are invoked clearly by the terms 'abdî ("my servant"), ḥôtām ("signet ring"), and bǎḥar ("have chosen") in the divine decree concluding the book (Hag 2:23).

A restoration message similar in spirit to that of Haggai is found in a divine pronouncement that gives every appearance of having been interpolated into the original vision found in chapter four of Zechariah. Whereas the lampstand vision in that chapter presents a messianic program focusing on a priest-prince diarchy, verses 6aβ–10a lift up the royal messianic theme by naming Zerubbabel explicitly, and picturing him engaged in the royal activity par excellence, namely, rebuilding the Temple, an activity for which he is fully empowered by the divine rûaḥ ("spirit"). We can recognize behind this interpolation the same line of pro-Davidic propaganda that informs the message of Haggai, and which, more broadly still, can be recognized as the underlying intention of the original edition of the Chronicler's History.[4]

A MESSIANIC DIARCHY: ZADOKITE PRIEST AND DAVIDIC PRINCE

Zechariah developed a message that, while sharing Haggai's messianic thrust in a general way, manifests its own distinctive features. The message draws upon the tradition of Ezekiel, according to which restoration of the nation would come through God's designation of a diarchy consisting of a Zadokite priest and a Davidic prince (Ezek 37:24–28; 43:18–27). In the vi-

---

3. For the understanding of temple sacrifice that underlies the message of the prophet Haggai, see G. A. Anderson's study, *Sacrifices and Offerings in Ancient Israel: Studies in their Social and Political Importance* (Harvard Semitic Monographs 41; Atlanta, 1987), pp. 91–126.

4. On the relation of the Chronicler's History to the programmatic effort during the early postexilic period to restore the Temple cult and Davidic leadership, see P. D. Hanson, "Israelite Religion in the Early Postexilic Period," *Ancient Israelite Religion: Essays in Honor of Frank Moore Cross*, ed. P. D. Miller, Jr.; P. D. Hanson; and S. D. McBride (Philadelphia, 1987), pp. 498f.

sion of the lampstand in chapter four, the two olive trees flanking the lamp-stand are interpreted as representing "the two sons of oil (*běnê hayyiṣhār*) who attend to (*hā'ōmědîm*) the Lord of the whole earth" (Zech 4:14).

Though a form of the root *mšḥ* is not used, we have here a clear image pointing to those consecrated for sacred service by being anointed with oil. What is important in this vision for later developments is the presence of *two* anointed figures, one priestly and one royal. Moreover, the lampstand vision stands at the very center of the seven original visions in Zechariah 1–6, which taken as a whole proclaim that the anointing of these two figures marks a decisive turning point in the history of the Jewish people: The Lord of Hosts has taken the initiative to remove all that has reduced Israel to subser-vience and despair, including Israel's own faithlessness and sin as well as the hostility of the nations.[5] The sanctity of Israel would be reestablished, as the cult would again flourish under the Zadokite high priest, and the nation would be led by the anointed Davidic Prince. The visions of Zechariah thus depict a restoration in eschatological terms drawing on the tradition of a mes-sianic diarchy, a tradition that would reappear in writings of the late Second Temple period at Qumran and elsewhere.

THE ELEVATION OF THE PRIESTLY "MESSIAH"

It is difficult to determine whether Zechariah 3 belongs to the original words of the prophet. The form of the vision in chapter 3 does not conform to the distinctive form characterizing the seven other visions. What is more, this chapter features the High Priest Joshua virtually to the exclusion of his counterpart, the Davidic Prince. Here Joshua's investiture as high priest is depicted as a solemn rite occurring within the divine assembly. Upon him is conferred authority over God's house and charge of God's courts. He is even granted right of access to those attending on the Lord. Within this context, almost as an aside, mention is made of the "Branch" (*ṣemaḥ*), a term which in Hebrew, as in Phoenician, designates the "royal heir." The narrative then returns immediately to further description of the high priest and of the par-adisiacal conditions that his regime will introduce. We seem to be dealing with a tradition that sees the "messianic" age largely in terms of the authori-tative reign of the Zadokite high priest.[6]

Evidence for this tradition is also found in the received form of Zech 6:9–14. The original narrative apparently described a divine command that

5. For a description of the eschatological program depicted in the visions of Zechariah 1–6, see P. D. Hanson, "In Defiance of Death: Zechariah's Symbolic Universe," in *Love and Death in the Ancient Near East: Essays in Honor of Marvin H. Pope*, ed. J. H. Marks and R. M. Good (New Haven, 1987), pp. 173–79.

6. See F. M. Cross, "A Reconstruction of the Judean Restoration," *JBL* 94 (1975) 4–18 [repr. in *Int* 29 (1975) 187–203].

crowns be cast for the messianic pair, Davidic Prince and Zadokite High Priest. But as the narrative now stands, only one crown finds a head upon which to be placed, the head of Joshua the high priest. It appears that with the fall of the Davidide from power (for reasons that can only be conjectured), the Zadokites found it necessary (or availed themselves of the opportunity?) to move the nation toward a hierocratic form of local rule. This same development is reflected in secondary and tertiary strata within the Chronicler's history.

MESSIANIC THEMES WITHIN THE CONTEXT OF PROPHETIC CRITIQUE

Seminal in the development of messianic reflections from the perspective of prophetic critique is Isaiah 40–55. Rather than propounding a restoration program under a Davidic or a Zadokite Messiah, the author of this corpus makes pronouncements that point to an alternative, albeit one whose specifics are hard to determine due to the highly symbolic-poetic style of the author (commonly called Deutero-Isaiah or Second Isaiah). Most noteworthy in this alternative vision of restoration, however, is the fact that the *māšiaḥ* designated by God in Isa 44:24–45:7 is not a member of the family of David, nor even of the Jewish people. God's appointed Messiah is Cyrus, that is, the Persian king remembered for his enlightened policy of supporting the restoration of the customs and temples of his subject peoples. The themes developed in the so-called Cyrus Oracle in Isa 44:24–45:7 are precisely the ones expected in connection with pronouncements about the Messiah, namely, themes of the restoration of Jerusalem and Judah and the rebuilding of the Temple. Comparison with the messages of Haggai and Zechariah indicates how intimately promises of king, Temple, and royal city belong together. But precisely such comparison underscores the unique feature in Deutero-Isaiah. Whereas the Davidic prince Zerubbabel is celebrated in the books of Haggai and Zechariah as the chosen of God and the Temple builder,[7] in the present context the Lord designates Cyrus as "my shepherd" (*rōʿî*) and "my anointed" (*měšîḥô*) and announces that it is he who "shall fulfil all my purpose" (Isa 44:28 and 45:1). It can be no accident that standard royal ideology, which throughout the ancient Near East celebrated the ruler of the native dynasty as called by the patron deity of the nation, is here replaced by something quite different. The pattern followed is that of antiroyalist propaganda, such as also arose in Babylon at this time against the House of Nabonidus. But what was its intended function? There is no indication that Deutero-Isaiah shared the enthusiasm of the Babylonian Marduk priests for Cyrus' reign per se. Central to the message of this prophet is always the

---

7. See esp. Hag 2:20–23 and Zech 3:1–14.

reign of God; Cyrus is merely an instrument of God's sovereign purpose. The theme of God's anointing Cyrus as Messiah must therefore be interpreted as an instance of prophetic critique, that is, as a warning that God's restoration of the nation would not take the form of a reinstitution of the Davidic monarchy as it was known in the past.

This impression is corroborated by the rest of Deutero-Isaiah. In this work one finds other allusions to Cyrus as the chosen instrument of God (Isa 41:2–4; 41:25; 45:13; 48:14–15), where Yahweh otherwise exercises his kingship by direct, unmediated action, and where the divine blessings earlier associated with the Davidic covenant are extended to the people quite generally (55:3).

One other element finds its place in the vision of restoration developed in Isaiah 40–55: the description of another agent of divine purpose, the "servant" ('ebed) of YHWH. This agent also seems to function as an element in a critique of traditional royalist views of restoration, for the "servant" stands in starkest contrast to traditional descriptions of the anointed priest or king, at the same time as he is described as one who "shall *startle* many nations" and on account of whom "kings shall shut their mouths" (Isa 52:15). Though the exact meaning the author intended to convey with the figure of the "servant of the Lord" will perhaps ever remain a mystery, it does seem clear that this enigmatic figure takes its place as part of a picture of restoration offered as an alternative to the more traditional messianism of the most loyal supporters of the Davidic house.

We cannot begin to trace the long, complicated history of interpretation through which the alternative picture of Second Isaiah was developed in various directions, though some of them fall under the general category of messianic traditions. We must limit ourselves to the following observations.

Isa 61:1–3 is a passage which probably stems from the earliest wave of immigrants returning to the land. In it a first person voice, claiming to be empowered by God's "spirit" (*rûaḥ*) and anointed (*māšaḥ*) "to bring good tidings to the afflicted," apparently speaks for a group regarding itself as charged with carrying out divine purposes traditionally tied to the privileged status of royal and priestly houses.[8] If we can speak here of messianism, it is a democratized form of messianism, perhaps inspired by Second Isaiah's concept of a democratization of God's covenant with David (Isa 55:3), and paralleled by an apparent democratization of priestly prerogatives as well (Isa 61:6; cf. Zech 14:20–21).

There is another side of Second Isaiah's alternative vision of restoration that is developed within what can be loosely designated as a "School of Second Isaiah." Here restoration is increasingly portrayed in terms of God's direct intervention (Isa 59:15b–20, 64:1–3 and 66:15–16): "[God] saw that

---

8. See P. D Hanson, *The Dawn of Apocalyptic*, rev. ed. (Philadelphia, 1979), pp. 46–77.

there was no human . . . , then his own arm brought him victory" (59:16); "For YHWH will execute judgment with fire, and with his sword against all flesh, and those slain by YHWH will be many" (66:16). Within this general stream of tradition we can understand one of the verses that through extension became prominent in Christian messianic thought, Zech 9:9:

> Rejoice heartily, daughter of Zion!
> shout gladly, daughter of Jerusalem!
> Your king now comes to you,
> triumphant and victorious is he,
> humble and riding on an ass,
> on a colt, the foal of an ass.

The powerful intervention of YHWH as divine warrior to reestablish his rule is also depicted in Zechariah 12 and 14. In the latter, the divine warrior enters with his entourage of the *qĕdōšîm* ("holy ones," i.e., angels).

As indicated above, Deutero-Isaiah's alternative vision included the motif of the suffering of God's servant. Though some interpreters have tried to understand this motif against the background of so-called "ritual humiliation of the king" in the annual festival of enthronement, this line of interpretation lacks supporting evidence. The theme of suffering is better understood as arising out of the prophet's own understanding of the meaning of his nation's recent tragic history (and possibly out of his own personal history as well), leading to a delineation of God's purpose in nontriumphalistic ways capable of accounting for the humiliation suffered by Israel at the hands of foreign powers. In a later time when Jews who regarded themselves faithful followers of God experienced suffering at the hands of their own leaders, the tradition of the suffering servant was reapplied to an inner-community setting (Zech 12:10–14), though the social and historical circumstances of that setting and the referent intended by the enigmatic phrase "the one who was pierced" elude us.

MESSIANIC REFLECTION AMONG DISSIDENT PRIESTS

The Book of Malachi seems to stem from a priestly group (perhaps predominantly Levitical in composition though not necessarily excluding estranged Zadokites) unified in a harsh attack against the alleged negligence of the majority of the priests in two principle areas of sacerdotal responsibility: teaching of *tôrâ* and sacrifice. In a manner typical of protest groups, the critique of this group has two prongs, one looking back in time, the other to the future. The retrospective look invokes God's covenant with Levi (a covenant antedating the divine promises to which the Zadokites could appeal) as a model of priestly sanctity and responsibility (cf. Deut 33:8–11). The future look anticipates vindication and victory for the righteous minority in lofty eschatological images that would figure into later messianic speculation. Of

particular significance in that later speculation are the following three
themes: (1) To the tradition of God's direct intervention is added the theme
of the messenger who as a forerunner prepares the way (Mal 3:1); (2) The
remnant remaining faithful to YHWH is named *yir'ê yhwh*, "God-fearers,"
whose members are entered into a "book of remembrance." God describes
them as his "special possession" (*sĕgullâ*, cf. Exod 19:5), and promises that
they will be spared on the day in which separation will be made between the
righteous and the wicked, and in which those who fear YHWH will become
agents of divine retribution (3:16–21). (3) In an addition to the Book of Malachi, the messenger to be sent by YHWH as forerunner is designated as
Elijah (3:23).

As background to the messianic tradition found in the Book of Malachi,
one other text invites our attention, namely, Jer 33:14–26.[9] Its absence in
the LXX suggests a relatively late entry into the text of the Book of Jeremiah.
It can best be understood within the context of the tension and struggle
within the Jewish community in the two decades leading to the completion
of the Temple in 515 B.C.E.[10] To those despairing over the decline of the
Davidic House, it offers a divine word announcing YHWH's raising up a
Branch (*ṣemaḥ*) for David. That the Branch is not a specific, one-time eschatological redeemer, but the one who would continue the perpetual tradition
of the rulers of the royal Davidic House is indicated by the specific formulation of the divine promise. Much in the style of deuteronomistic tradition,
the assurance is given that there would never be lacking a Davidide to sit on
the Israelite throne. Parallel to this is the promise that the priesthood likewise would be maintained into perpetuity due to God's fidelity to his covenant with the Levitical priests. This parallelism, while recalling the diarchy
promised by Ezekiel and promoted by Zechariah, differs in one major point.
The priestly family represented here is Levitical in contrast to the Aaronide
and Zadokite emphasis of the Book of Ezekiel. This would seem to indicate
that Jer 33:14–26 originates within circles influenced by deuteronomistic
tradition and committed to the cause of reestablishing full priestly status for
the Levites, who since Josiah's reform had been forced to the periphery of
Israel's sacral structures.

If we are correct in dating this passage to the exilic or earliest postexilic
period, we can interpret it as an expression of the hopes of Levitical priestly
circles that God would soon restore the archaic conditions within which a
Davidide would reign along whose side Levites would serve as the divinely
appointed priesthood. The Book of Malachi in turn can be interpreted as a
composition stemming from the same Levitical circles several decades later.
A Davidide no longer presided over the people. And the Zadokites had taken

9. A discussion of this passage is also found in the article cited in n. 1 for this essay.
10. For evidence suggesting a postexilic dating of Jer 33:14–16, see W. Holladay, *Jeremiah 2*
(Hermeneia; Minneapolis: Fortress Press, 1989), *ad loc.*

the priesthood firmly in hand to the exclusion of the Levites. Their concerns found expression in a harshness and vindictiveness reflective of their imperiled situation. They attacked what they perceived to be the failures of the Zadokite priests as they combined words of divine imprecation with a defense of the abiding validity of God's covenant with Levi (Mal 2:4–7 and 3:3–4). The Book of Malachi indicates that this circle had also altered its view of the royal office, again in response to historical developments. In place of the picture of a Davidide enthroned over Israel, we read of God's direct intervention and establishment of dominion, a dominion no longer tied to the chosenness of the Davidic covenant, but drawing upon the faithfulness of those simply designated as "God-fearers" (*yir'ê yhwh*). The "democratizing" tendency discernible in Malachi is thus reminiscent of the restoration visions considered above.

CONCLUSION

We conclude that those traditions stemming from the Exile and the early Second Temple Period which later were drawn into various types of messianic speculation originally arose within a situation rife with tension and change. All of the groups involved sought to explain the contradiction between a corporate identity understood in terms of a people living under God's rule and the experience of living under the sovereignty of a pagan emperor. Given the co-existence of rival claims to leadership informed by different backgrounds and party affiliations, it is not surprising that the eschatological traditions arising from the period are characterized by wide diversity. Though the subsequent interpretation and reapplication of these traditions developed quite independently of their original meaning and setting, an awareness of origins is the proper starting point for the study of the history of interpretation of all traditions. The traditions developing the messianic themes discussed throughout this volume are no exception.

PART THREE

MESSIANOLOGY IN EARLY JUDAISM AND EARLY RABBINICS

S. TALMON

5

THE CONCEPTS OF *MĀŠÎAḤ* AND MESSIANISM IN EARLY JUDAISM

INTRODUCTORY REMARKS

A renewed examination of messianism in early Judaism can with some justification be likened to carrying coals to Newcastle or balm to Gilead. The issue has been intensively and extensively researched over centuries[1] so that bringing it under scrutiny once again does not seem to hold much promise for a discovery of previously uncharted approaches. However, there are at least two weighty, although quite different reasons which can be adduced in the defense of a reopening of the issue: (a) The meaning of messianism and its evaluation constitute a credal and intellectual challenge which confronts every generation of Jews and Christians, demanding a periodical reassessment, internally and separately, as well as a review of it in common. (b) In our days the discovery of new documents which reveal hitherto unknown or only dimly perceived configurations of the messianic idea which had been current at the turn of the era, require their comparison with conceptions of messianism which can be traced in the classical sources and their integration into the socioreligious contexts of Judaism and Christianity in the last centuries B.C.E. and the first centuries C.E. Pride of place must be accorded to the Qumran writings, discovered four decades ago in the Judean Desert near the shores of the Dead Sea, which may be dated confidently to the last three centuries of the Second Temple Period.[2] In these ancient writings surfaces a belief in Two Anointed Ones who carry the Hebrew title *māšîaḥ* and are

1. A useful selection of pertinent titles is provided by J. H. Charlesworth, "The Concept of the Messiah in the Pseudepigrapha," in *ANRW* 2.19.1, ed. H. Temporini and W. Haase (Berlin, New York, 1979), pp. 189–91, nn. 5–10. I would add: L. Dürr, *Ursprung und Ausbau der israelitisch-jüdischen Heilandserwartung* (Berlin, 1925); H. Ringgren, *The Messiah in the Old Testament* (SBT 18, London, 1956).

2. Publications pertaining to Qumran messianism are listed in S. Talmon, "Waiting for the Messiah: The Spiritual Universe of the Qumran Covenanters," in J. Neusner, *et al.*, eds., *Judaisms and their Messiahs at the Turn of the Christian Era* (Cambridge, New York, 1987), pp. 111–37; idem, *The World of Qumran From Within* (Jerusalem, 1989), pp. 273–300 (abbreviated as *Qumran*).

expected to arise contemporaneously at an imminently awaited turning point in history. The "Twin Messiahs" will ring in the fervently hoped-for future eon of immaculate bliss.

In the present discussion I can review only some pivotal aspects of the very complex phenomenon of early Jewish messianism, which at times contains quite dissimilar, even contradictory features.[3] Since selection is imperative, I shall attempt to highlight some facets in the overall picture which in my opinion do not always receive the attention they deserve in the discussion of early Jewish messianism.

There will be unavoidable overlaps of my ensuing analysis with comments offered in papers read by other participants in this symposium, and equally with previous publications which deal with the development of Jewish messianism. I shall nevertheless keep references to consenting and dissenting views to a minimum, so as not to overload my presentation of the matter with an unduly expanded bibliographical apparatus.

The title of my paper requires some clarification. I differentiate between the epithet מָשִׁיחַ, which is preponderantly used in the Hebrew Bible in reference to an actual ruling king or his immediate successor, and the concept messianism, which derives from that noun, but becomes increasingly invested as Jewish thought develops with a credal and visionary dimension that transcends the original terrestrial signification of the term māšîaḥ.

"Early Judaism" has been variously defined by modern scholars and schools of thought. These divergent interpretations cannot be explicated here in detail, since such an explication would lead us far afield. Let me therefore simply state that my remarks will be directed to the elucidation of some major characteristics which can be perceived in Jewish messianism in the prerabbinic age.

THESES

The phenomenon of early Jewish messianism, from the founding of the biblical monarchy around 1000 B.C.E. to the end of the Second Temple Period in 70 C.E., cannot be reviewed here in all its ramifications. Therefore I shall focus on two prominent configurations of the messianic idea: the one discernable in the seminal Hebrew biblical canon, and the other emerging in the already mentioned literature of the Qumran Covenanters. Further expressions of messianism which can be recovered from other sets of literature current in that age, will be mentioned only *en passant*. The two major configurations of the *māšîaḥ* idea appear to illustrate best and to corroborate

---

3. This characterization applies not only to messianism in the late Second Temple Period, as acutely discerned by E. Rivkin, "The Meaning of Messiah in Jewish Thought," *USQR* 26 (1970/71) 383–406, but also to earlier stages of its development.

the following theses which will serve as guidelines in my deliberations. They can be formulated as follows:

First Thesis. Initially the *māšîaḥ* idea is an intrinsically sociopolitical notion which must be assessed primarily in the historical setting and the conceptual context of the biblical institution of kingship.[4] Also in its later manifestations, it can be best evaluated in the framework of constituted groups that present to the viewer a specific socioreligious profile.[5]

Let me add the following observation, lest I be misunderstood. I know that the sphere of belief and ritual cannot be segregated from the sociopolitical domain when one comes to discuss the biblical society or, for that matter, any society in the ancient Near East. Biblical Israel must be appreciated as a unified polity that had not yet experienced the ideational and factual separation of *civis terrae* from *civis dei* which is to mark the contours of later conceptual systems and patterns of thought. However, in order to counterbalance a prevailing tendency to exceedingly "theologize" the notions of *māšîaḥ* and messianism in their biblical setting, I aim to bring into full light their down-to-earth political connotations. They must be appreciated within the existential context of the historical people that hammered them out and whose societal and credal development concurrently was to a large extent determined by these concepts. Israel wrote the books of the Bible as its corporate biography; ensuingly it became the People of the Book.

The above proposed thesis will be tested: (a) by an examination of some motifs, topoi, patterns, and literary imagery in the Hebrew Bible pertaining to the figure of an "anointed" *māšîaḥ* and (b) by a parallel analysis of the vision of the "Twin Anointed" which, as said previously, emerges in the New Covenanters' writings of Qumran.

As is well known, this particular late Second Temple modification of the basic biblical *māšîaḥ* concept came already under scrutiny in the early twenties, in the wake of the discovery of the *Zadokite Fragments* in the Cairo Genizah.[6] However, only since the albeit partial publication of the Qumran finds can we study and assess the phenomenon of "Twin Messianism" in the context of a structured socioreligious entity that flourished at the turn of the era, viz. the "Commune of the New Covenant" whose members conceived of themselves as the only true representatives of the biblical "People of Israel."

---

4. See S. Talmon, "Kingship and the Ideology of the State," in *King, Cult and Calendar in Ancient Israel* (Jerusalem, 1986), pp. 9–38 (abbreviated as *King*). Also, see J. J. M. Roberts' paper in the present volume.

5. See S. Talmon, "Types of Messianic Expectation at the Turn of the Era," *King*, pp. 202–24.

6. See esp. L. Ginzberg, *An Unknown Jewish Sect*, updated translation from the German by R. Marcus (New York, 1976).

The emphasis on the interpenetration of messianic thought and societal structure which makes Qumran messianology a ready topic for inclusion in our discussion, at the same time proves the messianic references in the Apocrypha and Pseudepigrapha to be most recalcitrant objects for this purpose. These vestiges of the messianic idea which were current in the Second Temple Period cannot be set within the parameters of a definable socioreligious entity. Therefore references to "the Messiah" in the Pseudepigrapha must be examined under different headings and are indeed being brought under scrutiny by other participants in our symposium.

For a different reason we can exclude from our discussion a consideration of what is sometimes presented as the Samaritan version of biblical messianism. The Samaritans were indeed constituted in the Second Temple Period as a clearly circumscribed socioreligious entity and have remained so to this day. But, as is well known, they accept only the Five Books of the Pentateuch as scripture and do not consider the other components of the Hebrew Bible, viz. the Prophets and the Writings, as being invested with authoritative sanctity. Now it is a fact that exactly these latter components of the Hebrew Canon reflect the Age of the Kingdoms, and it is in them that the concept of an "anointed" finds its most salient expression. The very figure of a *māšîaḥ* is indissolubly bound up with the historical experience of monarchy in which the Samaritans did not share. Therefore there is no cause for wonder that they also did not extrapolate the idea of a future ideal "anointed" from the famous verse in the Balaam pericope, "a star will arise from Jacob" (Num 24:17). Rabbinic exegesis construed that text to foreshadow the institution of kingship, embodied in the Davidic *māšîaḥ* in whom is captured the quintessence of the future blissful eon. Insofar as vestiges of a central figure can be discerned in Samaritan traditions concerning a future age, they appear to pertain to a *Moses redivivus*, designated *taheb*. This designation, best translated as "restorer," points up the dominant restorative character of the Samaritans' vision of that future era which lacks the utopian superstructure fashioned by the biblical prophets and which had a formative influence, although to varying degrees, on all configurations of messianic expectation in the late Second Temple Period.

Second Thesis. The unfolding of the messianic idea in early Judaism—from the earthly figure of an anointed king, the historical *māšîaḥ*, to the vision of an unique superterrestrial savior who will arise in an undeterminably distant future—may be seen, *grosso modo*, as a developmental process in three stages: it proceeds from the *historical realism* which prevailed in the age of the monarchies, to a *conceptualization* in the Second Temple Period, and it culminates in the *idealization* of the anointed after 70 C.E., i.e. in the Christian era, when "the Messiah" is center stage as the inaugurator of the final and unending era of universal salvation.

My ensuing remarks will be directed toward a discussion of the first two stages of this developmental scheme.[7] The intrinsically distinct characteristics by which these two stages are defined, can be subsumed under the next thesis.

Third Thesis. "Kingdom," *māšîaḥ*-dom, is determined by an orientation toward *space* and is acted out in the tangible parameters of a manifestly circumscribed geographical entity—the sovereign nation-state of biblical Israel in the Age of the Kingdoms. This space orientation enhances the marked quintessence of "topicality" which inheres in the very figure of an "anointed king."

In contradistinction, the frame of reference of messianism is *time,* with a concurrent recession from tangibility. *Time* cannot be enclosed in particular societal and geographical parameters, and thus messianism turns progressively away from the topicality of state and nation and tends to supplant it by the conceptuality of an all-embracing universalism.

We must, however, be reminded that the above transition will not unfold unilineally in a simple evolutionary pattern. Rather we can observe in most configurations of messianism an intertwining and interweaving of the characteristics which invest this phenomenon with traits that seem more germane to *māšîaḥ*-dom.

THE BIBLICAL BASIS OF MESSIANISM

I am fully aware of the fact that the diverse later configurations of the messianic idea cannot be directly and exclusively derived from the person of the biblical anointed king. Professor Roberts correctly shows that "In the original context not one of the thirty-nine occurrences of מָשִׁיחַ in the Hebrew canon refers to an expected figure of the future whose coming will coincide with the inauguration of an era of salvation."[8] But notwithstanding the palpable absence of Messiah-futurism in the Hebrew Scriptures, there is yet much truth in Martin Buber's assertion that messianism must be deemed "die zutiefst originelle Idee des Judentums," deeply rooted in the ancient Israelites' conceptual universe, and that it is the only source out of which the various postbiblical formulations of messianism could have sprung.[9] No equal to the messianic idea—its essence and its diversity—can be found outside the framework of the Judeo-Christian culture and belief systems. Even

---

7. The elucidation of the third stage is left to other participants in this symposium who are better equipped for carrying out the task.

8. See J. J. M. Roberts, "The Old Testament Contribution to Messianic Expectation," in this volume.

9. See M. Buber, *Drei Reden über das Judentum* (Frankfurt am Main, 1911), p. 91.

if one accepts without question the interpretation of some items of Mesopotamian iconography as representation of messianic figures,[10] the resulting
totality does not measure up to the weightiness of the concept of an
"anointed" in the Hebrew Bible—neither by volume nor by ideonic depth.
The Mesopotamian "pictorial account" of anointing never comes anywhere
near the conceptual and credal fullness captured in the biblical "verbal portrayal" of the *māšîaḥ* in a great variety of literary motifs and imagery. Likewise the expectation of a hero-figure that we encounter in the Cargo-Cults of
the Pacific, whose future coming is expected to inaugurate for the islanders
an era of well-being and an abundance of earthly goods, bears little resemblance to the hope for universal salvation and cosmic peace which permeates
Jewish and Christian messianism.[11]

It follows that the examination of any postbiblical expression of the messianic idea must take its departure from Hebrew Scriptures. The diversity
which we encounter in the later configurations of messianism can be explained, in part, as being inspired by different literary strata of the Hebrew
Canon that in turn served them all as a shared seminal source. Again, the
diversity resulted from the particular interpretation or reformulation of the
common heritage and from the distinctive emphasis which this or the other
group put on this or the other aspect of the biblical *māšîaḥ*-notion.[12] And
then one must yet take into account the variegated intellectual and spiritual
stimuli which external factors effected on these sundry groupings. The diver-
sification arose probably already in the Persian period under the impact of
the preceding dispersion of the Judeans after the debacle of 586 B.C.E. [13] The
process gained in force and was accelerated in the hellenistic and Roman era
when various groups of Jews were differently affected by the Greco-Roman
culture and by indigenous spiritual and religious phenomena, such as apocalypticism and gnosticism, to mention only the most conspicuous.

THE BIBLICAL *MĀŠÎAḤ* IDEA

The Hebrew Scriptures do not offer any systematic statement which could
serve as a clear guideline in an investigation of the conceptual content which
inheres in the *māšîaḥ*. As is the case with other phenomena in the realm of
speculative thought, biblical historiographers and narrators content them-

10. See J.-G. Heintz, "Royal Traits and Messianic Figures: A Thematic and Iconographical
Approach (Mesopotamian Elements)," in this volume.

11. See S. Talmon, "Der Gesalbte Jahwes—biblische und frühnachbiblische Messias- und
Heilserwartung," in *Jesus—Messias? Heilserwartungen bei Juden und Christen* (Regensburg,
1982), pp. 27ff., with references to pertinent literature.

12. See S. Talmon, "Types" (above n. 5).

13. See S. Talmon, "The Emergence of Jewish Sectarianism in the Early Second Temple
Period," in *Ancient Israelite Religion, Essays in Honor of Frank Moore Cross*, ed. P. D. Miller,
Jr., P. D. Hanson, S. D. McBride (Philadelphia, 1987), pp. 587–616 = *King*, pp. 165–201.

selves with factually recording instances of the anointing of kings without theorizing about the religious and political basis of this custom. Only in the Psalms and the Prophets does one find attempts at transcending factuality and at seemingly reaching out for an intrinsic understanding of the *māšiaḥ* phenomenon. Even then the cogitation remains topical, emanating out of the authors' historical experience, and it does not attain that level of abstraction and synthesis which characterizes classical writers and philosophers and is indicative of the modern scholars' approach to the Bible.

In view of these circumstances, the student of the Hebrew Bible can only attempt to achieve some measure of comprehensive appreciation of ancient Israelite messianism by collating and integrating partial descriptions and fragmentary formulations found in a great variety of texts stemming from widely separated periods, differing from and at times contradicting each other. There emerges, at best, a kaleidoscopic picture which lacks consistency. This state of affairs should cause no surprise. We are after all dealing with a corpus of writings which grew over an extended period and which necessarily reflects the heterogenous attitudes of authors who may have entertained diverging appreciations of the *māšiaḥ* concept and its actual crystallizations in history.

However, notwithstanding these severe limitations by which the quest for integration and systematization is beset, we may yet be able to trace some significant features which mark the contours of the biblical *māšiaḥ* idea.

From the very outset, the biblical conception of an "anointed," and also the Jewish messianism which grew out of it, exhibits a bewildering internal tension. It is stressed between a topical rationalism rooted in historical experience, and a mystical utopianism which transcends all reality.

The very title *māšiaḥ* and the custom of "anointing" originated in the world of the Israelite monarchy. The anointed king, scion of a dynastic house—as realized preeminently in the Davidic line—bears upon himself the imprint of two in essence contradictory principles:[14] inspired leadership which derives its authority from personal charisma and is by definition discontinuous, as it was known in the days of the Judges, coalesces with the automatically continuous monarchical regime which draws its strength from the office charisma of an acclaimed institution.[15] The principle of election, inherent in a leader on whom is the divine spirit, was grafted on the system of dynastic government which is intrinsically devoid of any religious or spiritual dimension. Due to the resulting amalgam, the anointed king and the monarchy were conceived as a basic tenet of the Israelites' body politic and

14. The resulting tension is captured *int. al.* in the motif of the "Barren Wife," as I suggested in "Literary Motifs and Speculative Thought in the Hebrew Bible," *Hebrew University Studies in Literature and the Arts* = HSLA 16 (1988) 150–68.

15. See Z. Weisman, "Anointing as a Motif in the Making of the Charismatic King," *Biblica* 57 (1976) 378–98.

world view. Nathan's prophecy (2Sam 7) which echoes in related traditions (1Kgs 8:22–26; 1Chr 28:4–7; 2Chr 6:16–17; 13:5 *et al.*) assured the House of David of everlasting divine support. Out of it grew the image of the ideal anointed king: blessed with infinite understanding and wisdom, inspired and righteous, a savior who would reunite Judah and Ephraim and regain for Israel its national splendor as in the days of the united monarchy under David and Solomon. Innumerable passages in the Hebrew Bible extol this vision of the perfect future age which Jeremiah portrays as follows:

> The days are now coming, says YHWH, when I will raise up from David['s line] a shoot [invested] with righteous might,[16] a king who shall rule wisely, maintaining law and justice in the land. In his days Judah shall be safe and Israel shall live securely. And this is the name by which he will be known: YHWH is our righteous might. (Jer 23:5–6; cf. 17:25, 22:4, further Isa 11:1–10, Hos 3:4–5, Amos 9:11–15, Micah 5:1–8, Hag 2:20–23 *et al.*)

In addition, the diverse configurations of *māšîaḥ*-messianism absorbed to varying degrees mythical elements which derive in part from ancient Near Eastern cultures and in part from later mystical and gnostic concepts. They mostly penetrated the ancient Israelites' world of ideas through the diffuse and undirected contact with neighboring peoples and their literatures. But it may be assumed that this interpenetration was at first also consciously fostered by the Israelite royal houses and their loyal followers. The ancient Near Eastern literatures proffered to the biblical kings and writers an ideological underpinning of the monarchy which they could not extrapolate from their own indigenous traditions. This assumption helps to explain the proliferation of mythopoeic royalist imagery in biblical writings which pertain to the age of the monarchies—foremost in the Book of Psalms where it is applied with special emphasis to the house of David.[17]

We further discern in the biblical portrayal of the future *māšîaḥ*, and of the new era that he will ring in, two discrete patterns which may be designated "utopian messianism" and "restorative messianism" respectively. Both can be set in either a particular-national or a universal-comprehensive framework. In most biblical oracles and visions of the future age these initially separate strands are already interwoven. However, by applying textual and literary analysis, they can yet be segregated to some extent and traced to presumably independent pristine traditions which spring from diverse socioreligious contexts.[18]

From these variously accentuated emphases on the utopian or the restorative outlooks which mark unequally distinct strata in the biblical literature

16. Biblical texts are quoted here according to the NEB, except where my understanding of the Hebrew original requires a departure from that translation.

17. See S. Talmon, "Kingship" (above n. 4)

18. See S. Talmon, "Biblical Visions of the Future Ideal Age," *King*, pp. 140–64.

appear to derive the differentiated manifestations of messianism in the post-biblical era. Messianic visions which bear upon them the imprint of utopianism will gravitate toward a reliance on "prooftexts" culled from the Psalms and the prophetic books. They will accordingly foreshadow an idyllic picture of the future, the likes of which humanity and Israel had never experienced. In contrast, types of messianism which are marked by a pronounced restorative thrust, will model the depiction of the "Age to Come" after a historical *Vorzeit* which is perceived as an idealized prototype. In these configurations of messianism, the conception of the "Age to Come" is intrinsically conceived as the memory of the past projected into the future. The identification of and the differentiation between these basic types of early Jewish messianism is of exceeding importance in the assessment of the Qumran Covenanters' twin *māšîaḥ* expectation which shall yet be brought under consideration.

THE SIGNIFICATION OF ANOINTMENT

The practice of anointing a secular-political leader with oil was an innovation which has no roots whatsoever in the socioreligious tradition of premonarchic Israel. This shows manifestly in the report about the first attempt to institute the monarchy in the days of Gideon, in which neither the verb *mšḥ* nor the title *māšîaḥ* are ever used (Judg 8:22–27). Equally these terms are altogether absent from the ensuing account concerning Gideon's son Abimelech whom the Shechemites actually made king over them (Judg 9:1–6, 16–20).

Prior to the monarchy, the Bible mentions anointing only in cultic contexts: (a) in reference to the installation rites of the High Priest (Ex 28:41; 29:7, 36; 40:13–15; Lev 8:10–12; Num 3:3; 35:25; 1Chr 29:22 *et al.*), who was accordingly known by the designation הַכֹּהֵן הַמָּשִׁיחַ (Lev 4:3, 5, 16; 6:15); (b) in reference to prophecy, when Elijah anointed Elisha as prophet (1Kgs 19:16), and possibly once in a paratactical apposition of *nābî'* with *māšîaḥ* (Ps 105:15); (c) pertaining to the sanctification of cultic implements (Gen 28:18; 31:13; Ex 30:25–26, 40:9–11; Num 7:10, 84, 88 *et al.*).

It must be emphasized that in practically all its occurrences, the noun *māšîaḥ* serves as a royal title, notwithstanding its apparent "adjectival formation with passive significance."[19] In this, as in many other instances, a contextual exegesis and functional analysis have the upper hand over grammatical and philological considerations. The noun *māšîaḥ* belongs in one category with a series of similarly construed terms which are designations of societal functionaries: (a) *pāqîd*, "office holder," both in the political arena (Gen 41:34; Judg 9:28; 2Kgs 25:19 = Jer 52:25; Esth 2:3) and in the cultic domain (Jer 29:26; Neh 11:9, 14, 22; 12:42; 2Chr 24:11; 31:13). Especially

---

19. See Roberts' contribution in this volume.

instructive is the combination of *pāqîd* with the royal epithet *nāgîd* in Jer 20:1. (b) *qāṣîn*, "nobleman" or "military commander" (Josh 10:24; Isa 1:10, 3:6–7, 22:3; Prov 6:7, 25:15), used interchangeably or in parallelism with *rōʾš* as designation of a tribal or national leader (Judg 11:6–8, 11; Micah 3:1, 9). (c) In the same category belong the very common titles *nāśîʾ* "tribal head," which can parallel *melek* and in fact replaces that term in Ezekiel; *nāsîk*, "prince"; and *nābîʾ*, "prophet"—to mention just a few.

Of special interest in the present context is the already mentioned title *nāgîd*, which in the seminal account of Samuel's being divinely instructed to anoint Saul as the first Israelite king is actually combined with the vocable *mšḥ*: וּמְשַׁחְתּוֹ לְנָגִיד עַל־עַמִּי יִשְׂרָאֵל (1Sam 9:16). The very same word combination is taken up in a description of Solomon's coronation ceremony (1Chr 29:22), where the technical connotation of the two terms is highlighted by the preceding verb *mlk*, which prevalently defines royal rule: וַיַּמְלִיכוּ שֵׁנִית לִשְׁלֹמֹה בֶן־דָּוִיד וַיִּמְשְׁחוּ לַיהוָה לְנָגִיד "They declared Solomon ben David king a second time and anointed him as YHWH's king."[20]

The application of the collocation *mšḥ lngyd* to Solomon, who built the City of Jerusalem and the Temple, gives rise to the supposition that his image served the author of Daniel as the prototype on which he modelled his portrayal of the *māšîaḥ nāgîd* who is said to arise after the completion of the divinely determined period of wrath which will last for seven times seventy years. Then the historical triad—Davidic king, prophet, and anointed high priest—will be reinstituted in the rebuilt holy city:

> Seventy weeks (of years) have been decreed (as the time of punishment) for your people and your holy city, to stop transgression, to expiate iniquity, and to bring in forever (the Davidic king of) righteousness, to mark (again with the seal of divine spirit) a prophet of vision, and to anoint a most holy (priest). Know then and understand: from the time that the word went forth that Jerusalem should be restored, seven (-year) weeks shall pass till an anointed king (*māšîaḥ nāgîd*)[21] will arise (Dan 9:24–25a).

Extrabiblical sources prove that the anointing of kings was also practiced in other ancient Near Eastern monarchies (see 1Kgs 19:15), including some Canaanite city-states. However, the royal title *māšîaḥ* is attested only in the Hebrew Bible. There it occurs exclusively in the construct form—מְשִׁיחַ יְהוָה (1Sam 24:7, 11; 26:9, 11, 16, 23 *et al.*) and מְשִׁיחַ אֱלֹהֵי יַעֲקֹב (2Sam 23:1), or with a poss. suff.—מְשִׁיחִי (1Sam 2:35, Ps 132:17), מְשִׁיחֶךָ (Hab 3:13; Ps 84:10, 132:10 *et al.*), מְשִׁיחוֹ (1Sam 2:10, 12:3, 5; Isa 45:1 *et al.*) and once in the plural מְשִׁיחָי (Ps 105:15).

The Bible mentions anointing explicitly only in reference to some kings: Saul (1Sam 10:1), David (1Sam 16:1, 12, 13; 2Sam 2:4, 5:3; Ps 89:21; 1Chr

---

20. This notation is missing in the parallel account in 1Kgs 1:38–40.
21. This word combination is taken up in the ensuing verse in a break-up pattern—9:26a:
יִשָּׁחִית עַם נָגִיר הַבָּא וְקִצּוֹ בַשֶּׁטֶף 9:26a: יִכָּרֵת מָשִׁיחַ

11:3), Solomon (1Kgs 1:39; 1Chr 29:22), Jehu (2Kgs 9:1ff.), Joash (2Kgs 11:12; 2Chr 23:11), and Jehoahaz (2Kgs 23:30). However, the recurring collocation *mšḥ lmlk* (Judg 9:8, 15; 1Sam 15:1; 2Sam 2:4; 1Kgs 19:15 *et al.*) and the often-used term *māšîaḥ YHWH* lead to the conclusion that all kings of Judah and most kings of Ephraim were actually anointed, even though our sources do not record the fact.

The ritual of unction was performed by the High Priest (1Kgs 1:39; 2Chr 23:11) with the holy oil kept at first in the Tabernacle and then in the Temple (Ex 25:6, 37:29; Lev 8:2; 1Kgs 1:39), or by a prophet (1Sam 10:1, 16:12–13; 2Kgs 9:6ff.; cf. 1Kgs 19:15–16 *et al.*) on divine command. The fact that representatives of both these offices are not mentioned in the Savior-traditions in the Book of Judges may have been a contributing factor to the author's abstention from using the root *mšḥ* in the Gideon and Abimelech stories in which kingship plays a prominent role (Judges 9–10).[22]

The Bible also mentions instances of kings being anointed by the people. According to 1Chr 29:22 the people acclaimed Solomon as king by anointing him at the customary coronation banquet which will serve as the model for the future "messianic banquet."[23] It is similarly said of Joash that "*they* [i.e. the people] made him king, anointed (or: by anointing) him, clapped their hands and shouted 'Long live the king' " (2Kgs 11:12). The text is even more explicit in the depiction of the enthronement of Jehoahaz: "The *ʿam hāʾāreṣ*[24] took Josiah's son Jehoahaz, anointed him[25] and made him king in place of his father" (2Kgs 23:30).

A synopsis of all these references prompts the conclusion that in biblical society, the ritual of unction was the formal expression of approval of the "anointed" by representatives of the religious-cultic echelons of the society—prophet or priest, and by "the people—in whatever composition, representing the body politic *in toto*.

This conclusion is buttressed by Jotham's Fable in which the above features are abstracted from historical-political realities and are raised to the status of principles encapsulated in literary imagery. Like "the Israelites" in Gideon's time (Judg 8:22) and later "the elders of Israel" in the days of Samuel (1Sam 8:4–5, 19–20), in their quest for a king "the trees" offer "anointing" to one after the other of the especially productive and estimated trees (Judg 9:8–15). Scholars are divided in the interpretation of the message transmitted by the fable.[26] But there can be no doubt that it signifies the decisive role played by the body politic in the appointment of kings: the

---

22. See my comments above, p. 87.

23. See J. Priest's "The Messianic Banquet Revisited," in this volume.

24. On the special connection of the *ʿam hāʾāreṣ* with the davidic dynasty, see S. Talmon, "The Judaean *ʿam haʾareṣ* in Historical Perspective," *King*, pp. 68–78.

25. The crucial phrase is missing in the parallel account in 2Chr 36:1.

26. It is debated whether the author of the fable intended it as a critique of monarchy as such or whether he only distanced himself from Abimelek, whom the Shechemites had made king over themselves.

trees, symbolizing the Shechemites or, for that matter, all Israel, initiate the introduction of the monarchy and propose to confer the royal office on the chosen individual by "anointing" him.

This conclusion leads to one other inference. Conceptually the rite of anointing with holy oil seemingly invested the *māšîaḥ* with the immunity which inheres in the act of sanctification by unction (1Sam 24:7, 11; 26:9, 11, 16, 23; 2Sam 1:13–16; Ps 105:15 = 1Chr 16:22 *et al.*; cf. also Ex 22:27). However, in reality the requirement that the king be anointed by the people reveals his dependency on his constituents and the control which the citizens of the realm retained over the *māšîaḥ*.

The effective circumscription of the *māšîaḥ*'s power and his sacred status shows in one other remarkable phenomenon which exclusively affected "anointed" rulers. Prior to the establishment of the monarchy, divine inspiration was never removed from a man who had been revealed as a savior, even if he transgressed and went wrong. Samson's marrying a Philistine woman indeed angered his parents (Judg 14:3; cf. Gen 26:34–35 and 27:46). But his action is ultimately justified—"for he looked for a pretext [to fight] against the Philistines" (Judg 14:4)—and the divine spirit did not depart from him (Judg 14:6). By erecting the Ephod in his city Ophrah, Gideon sinned and caused others to sin: "all Israel went astray after it . . . and it became a snare unto Gideon and his house" (Judg 8:27). Even so his mission was not terminated. He remained a judge until his death "at a ripe old age" (Judg 8:32).

How different was the fate of a *māšîaḥ* who failed. Notwithstanding his being anointed with holy oil, his mission could be voided altogether or he could suffer severe punishment. The very first *māšîaḥ* was also the first leader to be deposed. Samuel, who had anointed Saul, stripped him of his office (1Sam 10:1, 13:13–14, 15:26–28). The rule over most of Israel was divested from Solomon (1Kgs 11:11–13), whom Zadok the priest and Nathan the prophet had anointed (1Kgs 1:45), because he had sinned by marrying foreign women (1Kgs 11:1–4)—as Samson had done—and by introducing illegitimate cultic objects (1Kgs 11:5–10)—like Gideon. Ahab's transgressions caused his son to be deprived of the throne and in his stead Jehu was anointed king over Israel by an emissary of Elisha the prophet.

It follows that in historical reality the ritual of anointing was a ceremonial manifestation of the checks and balances which the agents of unction— priest, prophet, or people—imposed upon the *māšîaḥ*, rather than being a symbol of sacred immunity which they wished to bestow upon him.

THE PROGRESSIVE CONCEPTUALIZATION OF THE *MĀŠÎAḤ*

The gradual emergence of an increasingly critical attitude toward kings in actual history, voiced predominantly by the prophets, caused the title *mā-šîaḥ* to be transferred to the idealized figure of a "King to Come" who was expected to arise in an appreciably near future. As a result, the concept lost some of its initial concreteness and became invested with a measure of utopian nonreality. But in the last count, the designation retained its unmistakably tangible connotation. The vision of an "Anointed to Come" who would rectify the wrongs perpetrated by the ruling king and remedy the ills of the present situation, is set within the frame of actual history. In this as in other aspects of the conception of time, the biblical writers' historical horizon appears to span no more than seven to eight generations: three to four, viewed retrospectively, constitute "the past"; and three to four, seen prospectively, make up "the future."[27]

With the discontinuance of the royal line of David in the wake of the conquest of Jerusalem by the Babylonians in 586 B.C.E., there sets in a progressive "ideazation" of the no longer extant "anointed." The fervent hope that the *māšîaḥ absconditus* will be revealed again in another Davidic anointed indeed did not cease altogether. At first it was riveted to palpable pretenders to the title, like Zerubbabel the Davidide, hailed as the "anointed" by the prophets Haggai (Hag 2:20–23) and Zechariah (Zech 3:8, 4:1–14, 6:9–15), who were active in the period of the Return from the Exile.

The expected imminent realization of the hopes pinned on the incumbent anointed reverberates in the prophets' visions concerning Zerubbabel, the shoot grown from the stock of Jesse (Isa 11:1): "I will take you, Zerubbabel son of Shealtiel, my servant (says YHWH), and will wear you as a signet-ring, for you it is that I have chosen" (Hag 2:23). While the title *māšîaḥ* is not used in this passage, and even the Davidic patronymic is omitted, the employment of collocations with distinct Davidic overtones—such as *ᶜabdî*, "my servant"; *běkā bāḥartî*, "you I have chosen"; and *kaḥôtām*, "like a signet-ring"—fully evince the *māšîaḥ* character of this oracle.[28]

It would appear that for Haggai and some of his contemporaries the existential gap between their historical "now" and the messianic "then" had been closed. "This day," the twenty-fourth of the ninth month in the second year of Darius's reign, "the momentous day of Temple refoundation,"[29] is seen as "the day of YHWH" envisaged by earlier prophets. There is no mention in Haggai's or in Zechariah's message of an *'aḥărît hayyāmîm* which lies yet ahead. The promised "future age" has become "historical reality." The Return from the Babylonian Exile is the New Exodus. Now God will again "shake heaven and earth, overthrow the thrones of kings, break the power of heathen realms, overturn chariots and their riders" (Hag 2:22), as he had

27. I expect to discuss this phenomenon in a separate publication. For the present, see S. Talmon, *Eschatology and History in Biblical Judaism* (Ecumenical Institute, Jerusalem, Occasional Papers 2; Tantur-Jerusalem, 1986), pp. 15–16.

28. The messianic interpretation of this oracle is debated by C. and E. Meyers in their recent commentary on *Haggai-Zechariah 1–8* (AB 25B; New York, 1987), p. 82.

29. See Meyers, *Haggai-Zechariah 1–8*.

done in the past to the Egyptians at the crossing of the Red Sea (Ex 15:4–13, 19). And just as the Exodus from Egypt had constituted the historical prerequisite for the ensuing introduction of the monarchy and the anointing of Saul (1Sam, 16), so the Exodus from Babylon serves as the backdrop for the reemergence of a Davidic scion—Zerubbabel, whom Haggai's contemporary Zechariah likens to an olive tree "consecrated with oil" (Zech 4:1–14).

However, Zechariah appears to offer to his audience a correction of Haggai's overoptimistic interpretation of current events as evidencing the realization of the messianic age. Also, Zechariah uses collocations which evoke associations with Davidic *māšîaḥ* phraseology. He speaks of YHWH's "choosing again Jerusalem" as his dwelling place and of "Jerusalem and the cities of Judah," which, as Martin Noth has acutely discerned, "is a patently political designation for the realm of the Davidic ruler."[30] But in contradistinction from Haggai, Zechariah refrains from harnessing his vision of restoration to a definite timetable (Zech 1:12) such as had been proclaimed by prophets of the monarchic age. Then, (First) Isaiah could yet perceive in the unborn son of the reigning king Ahaz the new *māšîaḥ*, destined to ring in an eon of bliss:

> For a boy has been born to us, a son given to us to bear the symbol of dominion
> on his shoulders . . . to establish and sustain it with righteousness and just
> might from now and for evermore. (Isa 9:5–6, cf. 7:14–16)

The age of eternal joy and bliss of which the passage speaks (Isa 9:2) was deemed to lie but one generation ahead. And Jeremiah could foresee in his oracles of woe Judah's subjugation to Babylonian rule to last for seventy years (Jer 25:11–12, 29:10; Zech 7:5; Dan 9:2; 2Chr 36:21; cf. Isa 23:15, 17), a time span which is coterminous with the already mentioned realistic conception of the future as comprising three generations.

Zechariah's reticence to proclaim that this period of punishment had run its course, as Haggai unhesitatingly does, is tantamount with a refusal to consider his own times as the realization of the promised era of salvation. Zechariah's vision of the reconstitution of Jerusalem in an undetermined future—עוֹד—contains an implied criticism of Haggai's viewing Zerubbabel as the incumbent *māšîaḥ*, divinely appointed to assume dominion over Israel in this age in which for him the visionary future had become reality.

The controversy between two contemporaries over the interpretation of the *māšîaḥ* idea respective to their own days indicates that already in biblical times the development of this concept was not unilineal. Being rooted in the realities of a historical society, its formulations and reformulations reflect reactions to changing circumstances to which that society was subjected. To

---

30. M Noth, *The Laws in the Pentateuch and Other Studies* (London, 1984), p. 138.

some degree, this multiplicity persisted into a later age. In the Second Temple Period, the vision of the future *māšîaḥ* progressively lost its distinctness and ultimately could not be fitted anymore into a definite chronological schema. But at the end of this period—when, on the whole, *ideation* had replaced the earlier *historical realism* of the *māšîaḥ* concept—Qumran documents still reflect the notion of a messianic eon to be imminently realized. We can, *mutatis mutandis*, apply to this dichotomy in Jewish messianism Buber's pithy characterization of biblical eschatology:

> Eschatological [*lege:* messianic] hope—in Israel, the historical people par excellence (Tillich)—is first always historical hope; it becomes eschatologized only through growing historical disillusionment. In this process faith seizes upon the future as the unconditioned turning point of history, then as the unconditioned overcoming of history. From this point of vantage it can be explained that the eschatologization of those actual-historical ideas includes their mythicization . . . Myth is the spontaneous and legitimate language of expecting, as of remembering, faith. But it is not its substance . . . The genuine eschatological life of faith is—in the great labour-pains of historical experience—born from the genuine historical life of faith; every other attempt at derivation mistakes its character.[31]

MĀŠÎAḤ IMAGERY AND MOTIFS

The above proposed thesis that we can discern in the biblical *māšîaḥ* concept a development—indeed multilinear, even erratic—from historical reality to ideazation and then to idealization, can be verified by an analysis of literary patterns and motifs in which this development is encapsulated. The study of this aspect of the issue under review cannot be carried out in full in the present context. It must suffice to illustrate the matter by bringing under scrutiny only two salient characteristics of *māšîaḥ* imagery:

(a) Besides being conceived from the outset as a historical royal person, the *māšîaḥ* is unfailingly seen as a member of an ascriptive social unit: family, clan, or tribe. This ascription is fully in keeping with the manifestly familistic orientation of the Israelite society, abundantly documented in the biblical writings. The anointed is usually introduced as the son of a named father to whom he was born in the process of natural procreation by a wife, who is also sometimes named. The *māšîaḥ* is never a loner. Rather he is ostentatiously portrayed in his varying relations and interactions with parents, siblings, offspring and other kin and, being a political figure, with a wide spectrum of public personages: courtiers and military personnel, prophets, and cultic functionaries. Born like any other human being, he will die the death of

---

31. M. Buber, *Kingship of God*, trans. from the German by R. Scheimann (London, 1967), "Preface."

mortals: of old age in his own home—like *David*[32] (1Kgs 2:1–10 = 1Chr
28:28), *Solomon* (1Kgs 11:43 = 2Chr 9:31), Rehoboam (1Kgs 14:30 = 2Chr
12:16), Abijah (1Kgs 15:8 = 2Chr 13:23), *Jeroboam* (1Kgs 14:20), Baasha
(1Kgs 16:6), Omri (1Kgs 16:28), Jehoshaphat (1Kgs 22:51 = 2Chr 21:10) and
Jehu (2Kgs 10:35); or due to illness—like Asa (2Chr 16:12–14),[33] Ahab's son
Ahaziah (2Kgs 1:2, 6, 15–17), Jehoshaphat's son Jehoram (2Chr 21:18–19),[34]
and Azariah-Uzziah (2Kgs 15:5 = 2Chr 26:21). Some anointed were slain on
the battlefield—like *Saul* (1Sam 31:3–6 = 1Chr 10:3–6), Ahab (1Kgs
22:34–38 = 2Chr 18:33–34), and *Josiah* (2Kgs 23:29–30 = 2Chr 35:19–
24). Occasionally they fell victims to a court cabale—like Nadab (1Kgs
15:27–29), Elah (1Kgs 16:9–12), Jehoram (2Kgs 9:24), Ahaziah son of Joram
(2Kgs 9:27), *Jehoash* (2Kgs 12:21–22 = 2Chr 24:25–26), Amaziah (2Kgs
14:19; 2Chr 25:27), Zechariah (2Kgs 15:10), Shallum (2Kgs 15:14), and Pe-
kahiah (2Kgs 15:25).

(b) In this context it is certainly of interest to note that the Hebrew Bible
has not preserved any "miraculous birth" traditions concerning anointed
kings. Thus, for example, all tales about a "barren wife" who after divine
intervention[35] gives birth to a son destined to greatness, are set in the premonarchic era. The latest of these tales centers on Samuel (1Sam 1:1–28),
who opened the door for the introduction of the monarchy and was the first
to anoint a *māšiaḥ* (1 Samuel 8–12). I have discussed the conceptual implications of the "barren wife" motif in a separate publication.[36] Therefore it
suffices to point out here that not one of the "heroes" who were ultimately born
by these women—Isaac, Jacob, Joseph, Samson, and Samuel—was ever
anointed. Likewise, we have no *māšiaḥ* versions of the "endangered progeny" motif, which is best exemplified by the Moses tradition (Ex 1:15–
2:10),[37] although anointed kings indeed encountered dangers in their life-
times and, as said, in some instances died violent deaths. The abstinence of
biblical writers from embroidering their *māšiaḥ* accounts with miraculous
and mythopoeic elements appears to disclose a conscious insistence on the
preservation of the realistic propensity of these traditions.

However, concomitantly with the realistic portrayals of kings, all of whom
presumably were anointed, we note a progressive extrication of the *māšiaḥ*
from the network of natural family and societal-political relations. The detailed and plastic reports on the life of the first anointed kings, Saul, David,

<hr>

32. The names of kings whose unction is expressly mentioned are italicized.
33. The fact is only cursorily noted in the parallel account in 2Kgs 15:23–24.
34. The parallel in 2Kgs 8:24 does not record this circumstance.
35. See G. Wallis, "Die theologische Bedeutung der Wundergeburten im Alten und Neuen
Testament," in *De la Tôrah au Messie, Mélanges Henri Cazelles*, ed. J. Doré, P. Grelot, M.
Carrez (Paris, 1981), pp. 171–78.
36. "Literary Motifs," above, n. 13a.
37. See *int. al.* R. Polzin, "The Ancestress of Israel in Danger," *Semeia* 3 (1975) 81–
98; D. B. Bedford, "The Literary Motif of the Exposed Child," *Numen* 14 (1961) 209–28.

Solomon, and Jeroboam—their childhood and youthful exploits—are increasingly replaced by the much vaguer depictions of later royal figures, also of those whose unction is expressly mentioned, like Jehu and Jehoash. This diminution of details may point to a waning of the historiographers' interest in these "anointed," or it may have resulted from the nature of the sources which were at their disposal. But at the same time we observe in prophetic literature the concurrent development of a seemingly nonrealistic conception of the (anointed) king such as is not present in the prophetic tales spliced into the historiographies of Samuel and Kings. This "nonrealistic" trend is most prominent in oracles and visions pertaining to the anointed out of David's stock, in which a measure of possibly intended opaqueness is recognizable.

A case in point is (First) Isaiah's prophecy given to King Ahaz, whom he encounters in the outskirts of Jerusalem, where Ahaz had gone to prepare the defense of the city in the face of an imminent attack on it by an Aramean-Ephraimite coalition (Isaiah 7). Perceiving a pregnant young woman, who may have been in the king's entourage, Isaiah foresees a radical change for the better in Judah's political situation which will occur in the yet unborn son's infanthood. The thrust of the prophet's message to the king and his people is epitomized in the name "Immanuel" by which that son is to be called (Isa 7:14–16).[38]

The expectant mother is not named, and her husband's name is not revealed. She is referred to by the term ᶜalmāh, which has been variously explained, in some instances with far-reaching theological implications. The indistinct identity of the *dramatis personae* and the distinctly soteriological content of this passage have given rise to widely differing interpretations of the episode which cannot and need not be explicated here.[39] Viewing the pericope in the framework of the collection of predominantly pro-Davidic oracles in Isaiah 7–11, I unhesitatingly side with commentators who identify the ᶜalmāh as the king's pregnant wife and her unborn son as his heir and prospective successor to the throne. Understood thus, this tale assumes the character of a first royal version of the above-mentioned premonarchic "annunciation type-scene," with topical and linguistic adjustments to the prophetic literary genre.[40] The vignette-like depiction may be compared with a

---

38. The implied promise is underpinned in an ensuing pericope which speaks of a son born to the prophet by his unnamed wife, *hannebî 'āh*. That son's name, "Speedy-Spoiling–Prompt-Plundering"—*mahēr šālāl ḥāš bāz* (Isa 8:3–4) epitomizes the utter destruction of Aram and Samaria, the foes of Judah. It thus complements the propitious message encapsulated in the name "*Immanuel.*"

39. A convenient summary of the interpretation history of this text is provided by H. Wildberger, *Isaiah 1–12* (Continental Commentaries; Minneapolis, 1991); O. Kaiser, *Isaiah: One to Twelve. A Commentary, The Old Testament Library* (Philadelphia, 1983), translated from the German originals.

40. See Th. Lescow, "Das Geburtsmotif in den messianischen Weissagungen bei Jesaja und Micha," ZAW 79 (1967) 172–207.

similar type scene[41] in Judges—the annunciation of Samson's birth (Judges
13)—the prophet Isaiah takes the place which the annunciating angel (another type of divine emissary) occupies there; King Ahaz replaces Manoah
(of whom it is never explicitly said that he fathered the son to be born); the
unnamed ᶜalmāh comes in lieu of Manoah's unnamed wife; and the son to be
born is to be given by his mother (MT: wĕqārāʾt) the portentous name "Immanuel" (cf. Isa 8:10), just as it is the mother who in the other story bestows
upon her son (wattiqrā) the equally auspicious appellation "Samson" (Judg
13:24).

However, notwithstanding the soteriological setting of the Immanuel episode (and vision), the particulars pertaining to that son's birth reflect the
process of normal procreation. In contradistinction to the aforementioned
narratives concerning "barren" wives, we have here no mention whatsoever
of an unduly delayed pregnancy by which the child's mother had been afflicted, nor is the eventual birth of Immanuel in any way brought about by
supraterrestrial intervention. Even in the Immanuel tradition, charged with
incipient messianic soteriology, realism yet manifestly outweighs the miraculous.

This characterization can be underpinned by a comparison of the wording
of the birth annunciation formula in Isaiah 7 with parallel passages which
speak of the natural conception and imminent birth of an heir, especially in
reference to the Davidic line:

Isa 7:14   הִנֵּה הָעַלְמָה הָרָה וְיֹלֶדֶת בֵּן
Gen 16:11   הִנָּךְ הָרָה וְיֹלַדְתְּ בֵּן
Judg 13:5, 7   הִנָּךְ הָרָה וְיֹלַדְתְּ בֵּן
1Kgs 13:2   הִנֵּה־בֵן נוֹלָד לְבֵית־דָּוִד
1Chr 22:9   הִנֵּה־בֵן נוֹלָד לָךְ

Compare further:
Gen 18:10   וְהִנֵּה־בֵן לְשָׂרָה אִשְׁתֶּךָ
22:20   הִנֵּה יָלְדָה מִלְכָּה גַם־הִוא
25:24   וְהִנֵּה תוֹמִם בְּבִטְנָהּ

The theophoric name Immanuel must be taken as a royal epithet which belongs to the category of the Hoheitstitel affiliated with the Davidic
anointed.[42] It can be comfortably joined with the string of titles by which
"the son born for us" is designated in an ensuing Isaiah oracle as "Wonderful
adviser, godlike in battle (ʾēl gibbôr), everlasting (lit., Father for all time)

---

41. For this term in its application to biblical literature, see R. Alter, *The Art of Biblical
Narrative* (London, 1981), pp. 47–62.

42. See H. Wildberger, "Zu den Thronnamen des Messias Jes 9 5b," *TZ* 16 (1960) 314–22;
contrast Lescow's statement "Beispiele für solche Thronnamen finden sich im AT indessen
nicht," *ZAW* 79 (1967) 181.

Prince of Peace" (Isa 9:6), and with other theophoric appellations, such as
YHWH ṣidqēnû—"YHWH is our righteous might," which Jeremiah adds to
that roster (Jer 23:6) and which may be compared with the royal proper name
sidqiyyāhû (2Kgs 24:17 et al.) and yĕhôṣādāq (Hag 1:1 et al.). The annunciation episode recorded in Isaiah 7 appears to have altogether the character of
a prolepsis of the Davidic visions assembled in the ensuing chapters, sharing
with them a similar terminology and imagery and, above all, their soterio
logical outlook. There annunciation imagery, or the *Geburtsmotif*, is recurrently taken up in an ever expanding visionary scope: while in one oracle (Isa
9:5–6) "the son to be born for us" is yet conceived as a wise and just ruler in
an appreciably near future, "from *now* on and forever"(*mēʿattāh wĕʿad-
ʿôlām*, Isa 9:6), in the other "the shoot out of Jesse's stump" is seen in a futuristic perspective, unbounded by historical reality (Isa 11:1–10). It could be
said that the structurally not directly connected but nevertheless consecu-
tive three Isaiah oracles reflect in their juxtaposition the posited three stages
in the development of the biblical *māšîaḥ* theme: historicity (Isa 7:14–16);
ideation (Isa 9:5–6); idealization (Isa 11:1–10). That progressive dehistoriza-
tion of the *māšîaḥ* notion appears in the oracles of the postexilic prophets
Haggai and Zechariah concerning Zerubbabel, the last anointed of the Davidic line in the biblical era.

One notes a parallel obfuscation of the circumstances of Zerubbabel's life
and his person in the first six chapters of the historiographical Book of Ezra,
which relate the man's exploits. This text block constitutes in fact a self-
contained unit which was prefixed to Ezra's history. There is good reason for
entitling the clearly circumscribed section: The Book of Zerubbabel.[43] It is
remarkable that this fairly extensive corpus of texts which pertain to Zerubbabel's days, altogether some sixteen chapters,[44] contains practically no information on the man Zerubbabel. Not a word on his background, the events
which preceded his return to the Land of Israel, his kin and his descendants.
Even his father's name remains in doubt. While in the above-mentioned prophetic and historiographical sources he is referred to (*passim*) as Zerubbabel
ben Shealtiel, in the genealogical roster of the Davidic line (1Chr 3:1–24) he
is listed as the son of Pedaiah (1Chr 3:19). In addition, that very roster records several generations of Zerubbabel's descendants, none of whom is ever
mentioned in the books of Haggai, Zechariah, and Ezra.[45]

43. See S. Talmon, "Ezra and Nehemiah," in *Literary Guide to the Bible*, ed. R. Alter and F.
Kermode (Cambridge, Mass., 1987), pp. 358–59.

44. Haggai 1–2; Zechariah 1–8; Ezra 1–6.

45. Not even Zerubbabel's daughter Shelomith (1Chr 3:19) is named, although she appears
to have been a person of some importance in her time. N. Avigad has published a seal which
belonged to her and which identifies her as the wife of the governor Elnatan, who may have
succeeded Zerubbabel as head of the province of Jahud. See N. Avigad, *A New Discovery of an
Archive of Bullae from the Period of Ezra and Nehemiah*, Qedem IV: Monographs of the Institute of Archaeology of the Hebrew University of Jerusalem (Jerusalem, 1975); S. Talmon, "Ezra
and Nehemiah (Books and Men)," *IDBS* (1976) 325ff.

Likewise these sources are totally silent on the causes and circumstances of Zerubbabel's sudden and unexplained disappearance from the historical scene. Their silence has caused scholars to engage in wholly undocumented and unprovable hypotheses in their various attempts to recapture the events which led to his fading from the horizon.[46] The total absence of any biographical information about the man whom the contemporary prophets certainly extolled as a *māšîaḥ*, and his beclouded exit from the scene, contrasts palpably with the detailed knowledge of the fates of the individual anointed in the First Temple Period which the biblical sources preserve, even though to varying degrees.

We may observe here the very same waning of historical realism which is at the roots of the annunciation stories and the "barren wife" motif. The "annunciation type scene" has extrabiblical parallels and is prone to absorb mythical and mystical overtones, especially when the *māšîaḥ* figure is invested with godlike faculties, or is altogether presented in a *Geburtsmotif* setting as the "son of God" (Ps 2:7).[47] In the context of the Hebrew Bible this phraseology must be understood as adoption language, as correctly stressed by Lescow.[48] The total abstraction of the *māšîaḥ* from all reality and topicality should be judged a sign of literary license. The father-son imagery, applied to God and king, did not attain in ancient Judaism and its literature the status of more than a marginal theme.[49]

THE EXPANDING HIATUS BETWEEN "NOW" AND "THEN"

A corresponding development comes into view in the overall chronological framework in which the anointed is shown to operate. In this context attention must be given to the introduction of an ever deepening disjunction between the historical present and the messianic future. I have already remarked on that progressively widening gap in the discussion of the series of Davidic *māšîaḥ* oracles in Isaiah (Isaiah 7–11). The phenomenon is put into an even sharper focus when one compares actual figures given for the expected expanse of the intervening period in various biblical texts. While these texts cannot be securely arranged in a definite chronological succes-

46. S. Talmon, *IDBS*, 319–20.

47. G. Cook, "The Israelite King as the Son of God," *ZAW* 73 (1961) 202–5; H. Bronstein, "Yahweh as Father in the Hebrew Scriptures," *Criterion* 8 (1968/69) 8–11. This image plays an important role in the later "Son of Man" concept. This matter is discussed in several essays in this volume. The virtual identity of king and nation finds an expression in the transposition of this motif to the God-People level. See D. J. McCarthy, "Notes on the Love of God in Deuteronomy and the Father-Son Relationship Between Yahweh and Israel," *CBQ* 27 (1965) 144–47.

48. Lescow, *ZAW* 79 (1967) 181: "Die Phraseologie von der Zeugung muss im Bereich des Jahweglaubens adoptianisch interpretiert werden."

49. For a different appreciation see M. Hengel, *The Son of God* trans. J. Bowden (London, 1976), pp. 21–56.

sion, it would seem that such a developmental progress can nevertheless be ascertained in the relation of the various premessianic time schemes.

I argued above that the premonarchic annunciation traditions and the *māšîaḥ* visions of the monarchic period perceive the onset of the messianic "Age to Come" as lying within the orbit of historical reality; that is, they are seen to be one to three generations ahead of the respective present time. The hoped-for new *māšîaḥ* is conceived as the reigning king's son, his grandson, or his great-grandson. (First) Isaiah's son-imagery and vocabulary must be taken at face value. Less accurately circumscribed but yet located within that historical-genealogical framework is Jeremiah's vision of a reconstitution of the Davidic *māšîaḥ*-dom at the end of a period of doom lasting seventy years (Jer 25:11–12; 29:10—cf. Isa 23:15, 17 in reference to Tyre), which is taken up by the postexilic authors of the books of Zechariah (Zech 1:12, 7:5), Daniel (Dan 9:2), and Chronicles (2Chr 36:21; cf. Ezra 1:1). The restitution was obviously expected to materialize within the lifetime of one generation, since biblical tradition considers seventy years to be a man's normal life expectancy: "Seventy years is the span of our life" (Ps 90:10). In that period of time, one hopes to see children and grandchildren. It follows that Jeremiah anticipates the change for the better in Judah's history to occur in the fourth generation hence.

This anticipation is more fully explicated in another pronouncement in which he exhorts the deportees of 597 B.C.E. to "normalize" their lives in exile for the duration so that there will be a fourth generation to experience that great event:[50]

> Marry wives, beget sons and daughters; take wives for your sons and give your daughters to husbands, so that they may bear sons and daughters. (Jer 29:5–6; cf. 2:9)

Then,

> when seventy years will be completed for Babylon, I will take up your cause [says YHWH] and fulfill the promise of good things I made you . . . (Jer 29:10)

This promise entails the ingathering of the exiles and their return to the Land (Jer 29:10–14). But it foresees also the restoration of the Davidic anointed, if the above passage is read, as it should be read, in the overall context of Jeremiah's consolatory prophetic message:

> The days are coming, says YHWH, when I will make a righteous branch spring from David's line, a king who shall rule wisely, maintaining law and justice in

---

50. It is likely that we have here an allusion to the prospective Pentateuchal tradition which speaks of a fourth generation that will experience the Exodus from Egypt (Gen 15:14–16). See S. Talmon, " '400 Jahre' oder 'vier Generationen' (Gen 15.13–15): Geschichtliche Zeitangaben oder literarische Motive," *Die Hebräische Bibel und ihre zweifache Nachgeschichte. Festschrift R. Rendtorff*, ed. E. Blum, C. Macholz and E. W. Stegemann (Neukirchen, 1990), pp. 13–25.

the land. In his days Judah shall be kept safe, and Israel shall live undisturbed. This is the name to be given to him: YHWH is our Righteous Might. (Jer 23:5–6; cf. 33:15 and also Zech 3:8, 6:12)

Again:

> then kings shall come through the gates of this city who shall sit on David's throne; they shall come riding in chariots or on horseback . . . and this city shall be established for ever. (Jer 17:25, cf. 22:4)

The interval between the "now" and the "then" takes on a new dimension when we come to consider Ezekiel's oracle in which he foresees a period of punishment for Israel and Judah which is to last 390 + 40 years (Ezek 4:4–6). The sum total of 430, which is most probably patterned after the tradition that gives the same number of years to the enslavement in Egypt (Ex 12:40), transcends by far the biblical conception of historical reality. Accordingly, the restitution which is to follow at the end of this period (Ezek 28:25–26; 38:8–16, 39:25–29 et al.) is foreseen to occur at a no longer tangible turn of the times. But it is yet situated within history.[51] At that preordained terminus, God will restore Israel in its land and will restore for Israel the Davidic anointed whom Ezekiel also depicts in traditional royal imagery:

> Then I will set over them one shepherd to take care of them, my servant David . . . I, YHWH, will (again) be their God and my servant (ʿabdî) David shall be ruler over them (nāśîʾ bĕtôkām) . . . I will make a covenant of peace with them . . . and they shall live in safety and no one shall threaten them. (Ezek 34:23–28; cf. Hos 2:20–25; Amos 9:13–15; Micah 4:4–5 et al.)[52]

A further expansion of that time gap is effected in the apocalyptic visions contained in Daniel. The increase of the intervening period of war and strife to the schematic total of 7 × 70 years evinces the intensified abstraction of the hoped-for "then" when the māšîaḥ nāgîd will arise, from the existentially experienced "now" (Dan 9:25). This dehistoricized notion leads conceptually to the total abstinence from any "millenarian" speculations. This is ex-emplified by Zechariah's refusal to take at face value Jeremiah's prophecy of Israel's predetermined rejuvenation after a seventy-year period of doom.[53] Zechariah's indefinite בְּ which characterizes his restitution prophecy— וְנִחַם יְהוָה עוֹד אֶת־צִיּוֹן וּבָחַר עוֹד בִּירוּשָׁלָ͏ִם, "YHWH will yet comfort Zion, and will again make Jerusalem the city of his choice" (Zech 1:17, cf. 2:16)[54]—is recurrently echoed in the Daniel visions "for those days to come." Also there, the added ʿôd divests the terms qēṣ, ʿēt, môʿēd (Dan 11:27, 35) and

---

51. See the discussion on the following pages.
52. The motif of "Israel Dwelling in Safety" permeates int. al. the Gog of Magog oracles in Ezekiel 38–39.
53. A parallel development can be observed in Qumran millenarianism (see below).
54. I tend to see in this wording an intended allusion to Zerubbabel, the Davidic "chosen" of whom Haggai says "kî-bĕkā bāḥartî" (Hag 2:23).

yāmîm (Dan 10:14) of their inherent connotation: predestined (and therefore ascertainable) time or date.

The evolving disengagement from the topical, and the concomitant accentuation of a proclivity toward a time beyond history, reaches its climax in the closing passage of Daniel. The revolution in Israel's fate is expected to completely transcend history. In a double entendre, "appointed time"—*qēṣ*—is deferred to the end of a period of 1,335 years and is conceived as being coterminous with "the end of all time"—*qēṣ hayyāmîn*. Significantly, no "anointed" is any longer perceived on that distant horizon (Dan 12:8–13).

QUMRAN MILLENARIANISM

We can now turn our attention to an examination of the peculiar formulation in which the biblical *māšîaḥ* notion surfaces in the Qumran Covenanters' writings.

The surprising peculiarity of the Qumran "Twin Messianism" highlights the diversity in which the *māšîaḥ* idea expressed itself in Second Temple Judaism by supplying a novel, hitherto unknown, configuration of this concept. At that time Judaism was altogether "a richly varied phenomenon."[55] In that diversity no one mainstream can be identified due to the lack of pertinent contemporary source material. This circumstance has led scholars to realize that George Foot Moore's concept of a "normative Judaism" which he employed, *nota bene*, in a discussion of Judaism in the much better documented Tannaitic Period, the first and second centuries C.E., is not applicable at all to the much earlier age in which the Covenanters' Community, the *Yaḥad*, arose.[56]

The Qumran scrolls reflect the credal concepts of a group of Jewish extremists who propounded a millenarian messianism. They had constituted themselves as the "New Covenant"—or the *Yaḥad běnê Ṣādôk*—roughly at the beginning of the second century B.C.E., seceding from what may be called proto-Pharisaic Judaism. The community persisted into the first or possibly the early second century C.E. An appraisement of the Covenanters' socioreligious outlook and their history can therefore throw new, albeit indirect, light on the messianic conceptions of Rabbinic Judaism and nascent Christianity. Such enlightenment can be gained by pointing out features which Qumran messianism shared with this or the other or with both, or else by putting in relief specific traits which contrast with characteristics of one or the other, or both.

55. J. H. Charlesworth, "The Concept of the Messiah" (above n. 1), p. 191.

56. The dictum pertains to many aspects of Jewish thought and societal life in those times, as is most consistently and insistently argued by J. Neusner. The remarkable variety of configurations in which messianism is then encountered is given a pointed expression in the title of a book edited by J. Neusner *et al.*: *Judaisms and Their Messiahs at the Turn of the Christian Era* (Cambridge; New York, 1987).

In thus proceeding we must bear in mind that not all the documents which are being brought under review in such a study are necessarily of Qumran origin or exhibit exclusively Qumranian contours. While some or possibly a great part of the manuscripts were indeed penned at Qumran and many are copies of works authored by members of the community, others may have been in the possession of novices who added them to the already existing collection of books when joining the *Yaḥad*. Therefore, such scrolls—which cannot though be identified with certainty—preserve facets of the cultural heritage which was shared by diverse factions of Jewry in the outgoing Second Temple Period.[57]

As said, the founding fathers of the *Yaḥad* were possessed of an ardent messianic vision. By extrapolating a prophetic key text and subjecting it to millenarian arithmetic, they believed to have worked out the exact date of the onset of the "Age to Come" and held themselves in readiness to welcome its harbingers, the "Twin Anointed." They had established that date by applying a literal interpretation to a visionary act performed by the prophet Ezekiel under divine instruction in face of the besieged city of Jerusalem:

> Lie on your left side and (I will) lay Israel's iniquity on it (or: you); you shall bear their iniquity for the number of days that you lie on it (that side). I count for you the years of their iniquity as a number of days, three hundred and ninety days . . . When you have completed these, lie down a second time on your right side, and bear Judah's iniquity for forty days; I count for you one day as one year. (Ezek 4:4–6)

Irrespective of the intrinsic meaning of this passage, which at times was taken to have a "retrospective"[58] rather than a "prospective" thrust, the Qumranians read Ezekiel's symbolic act of woe in a pesherlike fashion as an oracle of weal, deftly balancing the implicit threat of exile with an implied message of hope and applying it to their own history. In an account of the genesis of the *Yaḥad* we read (CD 1.3–8):

> For when they were unfaithful and forsook him, he [God] hid his face from Israel and his sanctuary and delivered them up to the sword. But remembering the covenant of the forefathers, he left a remnant for Israel and did not deliver it up to [utter] destruction. (cf. Jer 5:18, 30:11, 46:28; Neh 9:31)

> And in the age of wrath (i.e. their own days), three hundred ninety years after he had given them into the hand of King Nebuchadnezzar of Babylon, he remembered them (cf. CD 6.2–5) and caused the root he had planted to sprout

---

57. See L. Schiffman's "Messianic Figures and Ideas in the Qumran Scrolls" in this volume. S. Talmon, "Waiting for the Messiah," above, n. 2.

58. See the remarks of the medieval commentator Shelomo Yitzhaki (Rashi) on 2Chr 36:22; W. Zimmerli, *Ezechiel* (*Biblischer Kommentar*, 13.1; Neukirchen-Vluyn, 1969), pp. 118–22.

from Israel and Aaron[59] to take (again) possession of his land and enjoy the fruits of its soil. (cf. Hag 2:18–19; Zech 3:10, 8:12)

Exegetes have found it difficult to make heads or tails of the figure 390 in Ezekiel's oracle and often follow the Greek translation, which has 190. However, conjoined with the figure of forty days, which signifies the schematic span of life of one generation and is rooted in the "wilderness-trek" tradition,[60] we arrive at a total of 430 years, which in Exodus 12:40–41 is given for the duration of the Egyptian bondage.[61] Moreover, the extrapolation of the passage in the (Cairo) Damascus Document gives irrefutable witness to the originality of the Massoretic Text. Ezekiel's oracle of 430 years of woe took on for the Covenanters the same meaning which Jeremiah's prophecy of a period of tribulation lasting 70 years had for the Judeans who were exiled to Babylon in 597 and 586 B.C.E. as for those who after 538 returned to their homeland.

WAITING FOR THE MESSIAH

When the great event extrapolated from Ezekiel's vision failed to materialize, the Covenanters did not any longer venture to establish once again the exact date of the onset of the ideal future eon by millenarian computations.[62] The vista of that messianic age was indeed not lost from sight. However, their ignorance of the expected occurrence of the (next) appointed day caused a profound modification in the Covenanters' messianic perspective.

It appears that in their waiting for the Messiah they had initially adopted a quietist stance. Since the onset of the messianic age had been divinely ordained, history was expected to unfold in a smooth progression. Man was not called upon to assist in any way in bringing that day about. But the non-fulfillment of Ezekiel's vision engendered a revolution in their attitude. The failure was seen to have been partly caused by their own sinfulness (CD 1.8–9) and partly by hostile agents—the Wicked Priest and his followers—who obstructed the unfolding of the historical-millenarian drama. Together with repentance to atone for their transgressions, the inimical forces would have to be overcome by concerted action so that the New Jerusalem could be achieved and the way be paved for the arrival of the "Twin Messiahs." An

---

59. I suggest that the dichotomy "Israel and Aaron" alludes to the diarchy of anointed which typifies Qumran messianism (see my following comments).

60. See S. Talmon, "מִדְבָּר *midbār*, עֲרָבָה ʿarābāh," *TWAT* 4 (1984) 660–95.

61. This correspondence alone would be reason enough for giving the MT the edge over the LXX. See W. Zimmerli, *Ezechiel* (above n. 53); J. Kreuzer, "430 Jahre, 400 Jahre oder 4 Generationen—Zu den Zeitangaben über den Ägyptenaufenthalt der 'Israeliten,'" *ZAW* 98 (1986) 208–9.

62. Cf. the previous remarks concerning the visionary dates given in Daniel.

apocalyptic battle in which they would vanquish the evil adversaries with divine help became a categorical *conditio sine qua non* for the aspired transition from the dismal present time to the illumined future era.[63] They conceived of that fearful battle in the image of Ezekiel's Gog of Magog oracle (Ezekiel 38–39) and the visionary engagements of which Daniel speaks (Daniel 7–12).

A TWIN MESSIANISM

The victorious termination of that last war will open the door for the advent of the "Twin Anointed": a *māšîah* of Israel and a *māšîah* of Aaron, one representing the royal line of David, the other the high-priestly house. This doctrine surfaces with sufficient clarity foremost in the (Cairo) Damascus Document (CD), known *in extenso* only from medieval manuscripts which were salvaged from the Cairo Genizah. However, fragments found at Qumran, only some of which have been published to date, attest to the antiquity of the work and to its currency in the Covenanters' Community. In addition, references to the Twin Messiahs are found in the Community Rule (1QS) and the Rule of the Congregation (1QSa) connected with it.

The relevant passages are concerned with two different situations: (a) there are texts which deal with matters relating to the *Yaḥad* in its historical actuality but at the same time involve the perspective of the "Age to Come"; (b) other texts pertain directly to that realized ideal eon, offering prescriptions which are then to be followed by the Covenanters.

The two discrete sets of texts exhibit a persuasive internal similarity in matters of community structure and ritual customs. Thus they buttress the contention that also at Qumran the messianic "Age to Come" was conceived as an infinitely improved reenactment of history experienced, or else that history was seen to foreshadow the brilliance of the future immaculate eon. More important: as will yet be demonstrated, both conceptions are modelled upon a historical past—the period of the Return from the Babylonian Exile—which is perceived as the prototypical *Vorzeit*. Thus the past, the present, and the future are bound up together in a three-tiered structure, all three being founded on the very same sociopolitical principles and cultic-religious tenets.

This overall congruence will now be illustrated (a) by an interpretation of passages which speak of the two anointed and (b) by having reference to texts which mirror the community structure.

---

63. The presumed evolution of the Covenanters' millenarian messianism leads to the assumption that the War Scroll (1QM) was composed at a later stage in the *Yaḥad* history. This assumption, though, cannot be substantiated by paleographic or any other evidence.

1QS 9.10–11   They shall be judged by the first statutes (or: the statutes laid down by the first -founders) by which the *yaḥad* members were ruled at first, until there shall arise (*bô'*) the prophet and the Anointed (*ûmĕšîḥê*) of Aaron and Israel.

CD 12.22–23   This is the rule of the assembly of the camps who walk in it in the age of wickedness (*bĕqēṣ hāriš°āh*) until there shall arise the Anointed (*°ad °ămûd mēṣ ûaḥ*)[64] of Aaron and Israel.

CD 13.20–22   This is (the rule for) the assembly of the camps during all (the age of wickedness; *wĕkōl qēṣ hāriš°āh*) and whosoever will not abide by these (statutes) shall not be (considered) worthy to live in the land when there shall come the Anointed of Aaron and Israel (*bĕ'aḥărît hayāmîm*). (cf. 6.8–11)

CD 19.34–20.1   None of the backsliders . . . shall be counted among the Council of the People and in its records they shall not be entered, from the day of the demise of the Teacher of the *Yaḥad* (*môrēh hayyāḥîd*) until there shall arise the Anointed of Aaron and Israel.

CD14.18–19   This is the exact (or: detailed) account of the statutes in which [they shall walk in the appointed period of evil until there shall arise the Anoin]ted of Aaron and Israel who will atone for their iniquity.

CD 19.9–11   Those who watch for him (or: observe his commands) are
[7.20–21]   the humble of the flock; they shall be saved in the age of the visitation (*bĕqēṣ happĕqûddāh*), whereas the backsliders shall be delivered up to the sword when there shall come the Anointed of Aaron and Israel. (Cf. 4Q 174, 2.5: [The Anointed of Is]rael and Aaron.)

The duality of the Anointed appears also to be mirrored in the already mentioned opening passage of the Damascus Documents.

CD 1.5–7   And in the age of (his) wrath (*bĕqēṣ ḥărôn*) . . . he remembered them and caused the root he had planted to sprout (again) from Israel and Aaron.

---

64. As in the ensuing texts, the distributive singular here signifies the plural.

A BIBLICAL DIARCHY

The duality of a Davidic lay *māšiaḥ* and an Aaronide priestly anointed reflects dependence on a biblical pattern that evolved in the postexilic period. At the same time it underscores the sociohistorical character of the messianic idea in Hebrew Scriptures and in Qumran literature, revealing a striking spiritual consanguinity. The Qumran authors' predilection for depicting their own community—its structure, history, and future hopes—by having recourse to idioms, technical terms, and motifs that are manifestly drawn from biblical writings, discloses the *Yaḥad's* self-identification with biblical Israel and its conceptual universe.[65] From this source, the *Yaḥad* drew also the religiopolitical concept of "Twin Anointed" who in the "New Age" would together govern their community, and ultimately the reconstituted polity of the People of Israel.

The roots of this scheme can be traced to the world of ideas of the returnees from the Babylonian Exile. At that time, Zechariah had presented to the repatriates a *blueprint* for the organization of the Province of Jahud— *yh(w)d mdnt'*—as a state *in nuce* within the framework of the Persian Empire. The prophet proposed a societal structure that differed quite distinctly from the organization of the Judean body politic in the First Temple Period. Then the king, in charge of the mundane affairs of the realm, had also wielded controlling power over the sacred institutions. The priesthood was dependent on him so much that the high priests were considered royal officials (2Sam 8:17 = 1Chr 18:16; 2Sam 20:25–26; 1Kgs 4:2, 4–5) whom the king could appoint and depose at will (1Kgs 2:26–27, 35; see also 2Chr 24:20–22).

In the early Persian Period the situation changed radically. The loss of political sovereignty in the wake of the fall of Jerusalem in 586 B.C.E. had undermined the status of royalty. It was probably further weakened by the Persian authorities' granting the returnees only a measure of administrative autonomy, in fact restricted to the domain of ritual and sacred institutions (Ezra 5:3–5; cf. 1:1–4 and see 4:8–23). The combination of these factors enhanced the standing of the priesthood,[66] whose position was further strengthened by collaboration and marriage alliances with the upper classes in the Palestinian population that had not been exiled (Hag 2:10; Ezra 9–10; Neh 6:18, 13:4–9). As a result, the prestige of Joshua the high priest, Zerubbabel's contemporary, rose to an unprecedented height, so much so that he appears to have contested Zerubbabel's supremacy in matters of the body politic.

Zechariah's intervention must be evaluated against this background. Realizing the changed circumstances, he proposed a plan of "shared responsi-

---

65. See S. Talmon, *Qumran* (above, n. 2), pp. 32–52.
66. See E. Meyer, *Geschichte des Altertums* IV (repr. Darmstadt, 1980), pp. 88–89.

bilities": the Davidic Anointed and the Aaronide Anointed were to be assigned separate spheres of competence (Zechariah 3). Monarchy and priesthood are to complement each other, their mutual relations guided by "a counsel of peace" (Zech 6:13), a sign and an example for the entire community (Zech 8:9–17) and, beyond that, for the family of nations (Zech 8:20–23; cf. Isa 2:2–4 = Micah 4:1–5 et al.). As distinguished from the "monocephalic" structure of the Judean realm in the First Temple Period,[67] the New Commonwealth of Israel was to be diarchic.[68] In his vision, the prophet perceives two Anointed (šěnê běnê yiṣhār), symbolized by "two olives [olive trees or branches] pouring oil through two golden pipes" (Zech 4:2–3, 11–12), "standing before the Lord of the whole world" (Zech 4:14; cf. CD 20.1; 12.22; 14.19 restored).

This duality is given a more realistic expression in a divine word which accords a crown and a throne to both Joshua the high priest and to (Zerubbabel) the shoot (out of David's stock) as insignia of their complementary functions of government in the res publica (Zech 6:9–14 restored; cf. CD 1.5–7; 4Q 174, I, 1–2:10–13; 4Q 161, 8–10:11).

HISTORY AND "THE WORLD TO COME"

It cannot be ascertained whether that prophetic scenario was indeed realized in the returnees' community. The unexplained disappearance of Zerubbabel, the last Davidic scion, upset the intended balance, turning the scales in favor of the priestly anointed. However, it appears that the Qumran Covenanters embraced Zechariah's balanced scheme and modelled upon it their vision of the future. Identifying with an idealized period of Return from the Exile, they conceived in its image the ideal "Age to Come." Then the Yaḥad is to be established as the axis of a world freed from all tension. The "New Age" will be a shining creation, healed from all religious blemishes and societal evils which had marred the historical Israel also in the days of Zerubbabel, Ezra, and Nehemiah.

The character of the "Age to Come" remains largely restorative. It will unfold in the geographical frame of the Land of Israel to which the Yaḥad returns victorious. The Covenanters expected to experience a new Landnahme, culminating in the rebuilding of the Temple in Jerusalem, portrayed as an infinitely improved but nevertheless realistic, not spiritualized, replica

---

67. The evident predominance of the king in the monarchic period militates against the tracing of the later balanced standing of king and priest to those early times, as suggested by K. Baltzer, "Das Ende des Staates Judah und die Messiasfrage," in Studien zur Theologie der alttestamentlichen Überlieferungen, G. von Rad zum 60. Geburtstag, ed. R. Rendtorff and K. Koch (Neukirchen-Vluyn, 1961), pp. 38–41, n. 50.

68. The emerging picture differs considerably from the prevalent portrayal of Judah in the Restoration Period as an exclusively religious community whose sole representative was the high priest of the Jerusalem Temple.

of the historical city. The messianic era will be lived out by the Covenanters as a structured ethnic-national entity—the renewed People of Israel—not as a congregation of inspired individuals. This notion once again reflects the conceptual universe of biblical Israel. However, into the ascriptive designation "People of Israel" the idea of elective association was infused. The Covenanters are the chosen remnant of biblical Israel (cf. Mal 3:13–21; Ezra 9:2 with Isa 6:11–13). To the Covenanters alone out of all his people God granted a new lease on life and the right to reconstitute Israel's sovereignty, epitomized in the "Twin Anointed" of Israel and Aaron.

We should be reminded that Israel had once before experienced an almost-realized messianism.[69] The returnees from the Babylonian Exile, led by Zerubbabel, Ezra, and Nehemiah, conceived of their return and the restoration of a religiopolitical Judean entity, however restricted, as the realization of Jeremiah's prophecy. The postexilic biblical books bear witness to the fact that the returning exiles took Jeremiah's prophecy at face value. They appear to be uncertain whether the appointed time indeed had run its course, and whether the stage was set for the rebuilding of the Temple, God's time-honored abode, which would signify his residing again in the midst of his redeemed people (Hag 1:2). But the prophets Haggai (Hag 1:3ff.) and Zechariah (Zech 6:9–15; 8:1–23) have no doubts. However, in the final reckoning the returnees' flighty expectations did not come to fruition. The world that had been seen to be in upheaval (Hag 2:20–22) came to rest (Zech 1:11). Mundane, real history took over once more. With the fading of Zerubbabel from the scene, the hopes that had fastened upon the "Anointed" came to naught. The actual "Restoration" did not measure up to the anticipated profound reshaping of the historical world.

The founding members of the Yaḥad may have thus judged the return from the Babylonian Exile. The references to that period in their literature are so scanty that one is inclined to assume that they intended to obliterate it entirely from their perception of Israel's history, and to claim for themselves the distinction of being the first returnees after the destruction of the Temple. In their view, the divine promise had not yet been fulfilled. It remained open-ended. Now it fell to them to close the circle and to assume the preordained task of the Restoration Generation.

HISTORICAL MESSIANISM

The Covenanters invested their conception of the messianic age with the same real-historical character which biblical thinkers had given to their visions of the future. They saw themselves standing on the threshold of a new

---

69. See B. Vawter, "Realized Messianism," in *Festschrift H. Cazelles* (above n. 33), pp. 175–79.

epoch, infinitely sublime, but in essence not different from preceding stages in actually experienced history. The *ʾaḥărît hayyāmîm* is the preordained age when the Twin Anointed will ring in the New Eon—*qēṣ neḥĕrāṣāh waʿăsôt ḥădāšāh* (1QS 4.25). The Anointed will come, not at the *end of time*, but rather at a *turn of times*, at a profound crisis in history marked by tribulations of cosmic dimensions (cf. Hag 2:20–22). After that upheaval, the world shall settle down to "a time of salvation for the people of God" which is *eo ipso* "an age of (world) dominion for all members of his fellowship"—that is to say for the *Yaḥad* (1QM 1.5; contrast Zech 1:10ff.).

The congruence of historical past, present actuality, and visionary future shows not alone in the messianic diarchy, but also in the structure of the community led by the "Twin Anointed." A case in point is the depiction of the "Messianic Banquet," which becomes visible when the curtain is raised for the millenarian era, the *ʾaḥărît hayyāmîm*. In that visionary "Banquet of the Two Anointed," there are reflected distinct features of the *Yaḥad*'s societal structure and communal-cultic customs which also pertain to the returnees' community as manifested in Ezra-Nehemiah. In some respects, this banquet seems to be construed as a theologically refurbished reflection of the ceremonial coronation banquet—*mištēh hammelek* (1Sam 25:36)—which was known in the period of the monarchies (see 1Sam 9:22–24; 1Kgs 1:5–10, 19, 25, 41, 49; 3:15). But the correspondence becomes especially apparent in the three-tiered comparison between the returnees' *res publica*, the historical *Yaḥad*, and the messianic community. The juxtaposition of relevant texts discloses in all three instances characteristics of a tightly knit socioreligious entity with a restricted and spatially compressed membership.

The Rule of the Congregation prescribes the future standing order of members in the assembly:[70]

1QSa 1.1–3   *bĕʾaḥărît hayyāmîm* when they will gather [in the *yaḥad* and con]duct themselves in accord with the ordinances of the *bĕnê Ṣādôk* the priests and the men of their Covenant. who re[frained from walking in the] way of the people. They are the men of his council who kept his Covenant in the time (*qēṣ*) of iniquity, expia[ting for the lan]d (or: world).

This arrangement is foreshadowed in passages that detail the rules by which the Covenanters' life was regulated in actuality (e.g. 1QS 5.1ff.; CD

---

70. D. Barthélemy correctly points out the difference in size between the Community to which the Manual (1QS) is addressed and the Congregation of which the fragment 1QSa speaks (DJD I [1955] 108). But this differential in numbers does not obfuscate the absolute compactness of both these units, compared with the larger Community of the Essenes and the Congregation of the Hasidim (Barthélemy, *ibid*).

12.22–23). At the same time, it also mirrors the recurring biblical references to postexilic assemblies in which rules were laid down and statutory acts proclaimed (e.g. Ezra 9:1ff., 10:7ff.; Neh 5:1ff., 8:1ff., 9:1; cf. also Haggai and Zechariah).

Especially striking is the linguistic similarity between the passage in the Rule of the Congregation that speaks of the future public reading of the statutes in front of the entire community, and the report on the Reading of the Torah in Nehemiah 8:

1QSa 1.4–5	they (the priests) shall covene (*yaqhîlû*) all those who come, (including) infants and women, and they shall read in th[eir hearing] al[l] precepts of the Covenant, and shall explain to them (*ûlĕhābînām*) all their sta[tut]es lest they stray in [their] er[ror]s.
Neh 8:1–8	all the people gathered as one man on the square in front of the Water Gate . . . Ezra the priest brought the Torah before the assembly -*qāhāl*- (consisting of) men, women and all (children) who were capable of understanding . . . He read from it . . . in the presence of the men, the women and those (children) who could understand . . . and the Levites expounded (*mĕbînîm*) the Torah to the people . . . and gave instruction in what was read.

Into this *Yaḥad-bĕʾaḥărît-hayyāmîm*-assembly the Anointed are inducted:

1QSa 2.11–17	[This shall be the se]ssion of the men of renown [called to the] (appointed) meeting of the *Yaḥad* Council, when [God] shall lead to them[71] the (Davidic?) Anointed. With them shall come the [Priest at] the head of all the Congregation of Israel and all f[ather (house)s of the] Aaronide priests, the men of renown [called] to the [appointed] assembly. And they shall sit be[fore him each] according to his dignity. And then shall [come the Anoin]ted of Israel and before him shall sit the head[s of] the [thousands of Israel ea]ch according to his dignity, according to his st[anding] in their camps and marching [formation]s. And all the heads of [clans of the Congrega]tion together with the Wis[e of the holy Congregation] shall sit before them each according to his dignity.

71. Instead of Barthélemy's reading יוליד, I read with Milik יוליך. See Qumran Cave I, ed. D. Barthélemy and J. T. Milik, *DJD* I (Oxford, 1955), p. 117. Hengel follows Barthélemy and paraphrases the Qumran text: "The birth of the Messiah will be God's work" (*The Son of God*; above, n. 45a, p. 44). However, even this understanding of the passage does not yet make the Qumran Messiah the Son of God.

The division into priestly and lay leaders that shall obtain in the "Age to Come" mirrors the Covenanters' community structure and formal seating arrangements, as the following excerpts indicate. At the same time, both reflect the identical partition of the returnees' community (Ezra 1:5; 2:2–39 = Neh 7:7–42 *et al.*):

1QS 6.8–9   This is the rule for an assembly of the many, each in his (assigned) place: the priests shall sit first and the elders second, and the rest of the people each in his (assigned) place.

These factions are similarly represented on the *Yaḥad* tribunal of judges:

CD 10.4–6   This is the rule concerning the judges (or: court) of the Congregation: (A number of) ten men selected from the Congregation for a (definite) time (or: for the occasion), four from the tribe of Levi and Aaron, and of Israel six, knowledgeable (*měbônenîm*) in the Book *hehāgû/î* and in the tenets of the Covenant . . .

In the biblical rosters in Ezra and Nehemiah the lay leaders always precede the priests. As against this, the inverted order obtains in the Qumran texts: the priests precede the lay leaders, both in reference to the actual structure of the *Yaḥad* and in the *'aḥărît hayyāmîm* assembly.

In keeping with this arrangement, and because of the cultic character of that solemn event, the (anointed?) Priest takes precedence over the Anointed of Israel in the opening ceremony of the messianic banquet:[72]

1QSa 2.17–22   And [when they] shall assemble for the *yaḥad* [ta]ble (to eat) [and to drink the w]ine, and when (*ha yaḥad*) table shall be set and [the] wine [poured] for drinking, [no] man [shall extend] his hand to the first (loaf of) bread and the (first cup of) [wine] before the (anointed) Priest; for [he shall b]less the first bread and the win[e and extend] his hand first over the bread. Thereaft[er shall ex]tend the Anointed of Israel his hands over the bread;[73] [and then] the entire Yaḥad Congregation [shall make a bles]sing (over the food), ea[ch man according to] his

---

72. See J. Priest's "The Messianic Banquet Revisited" in this volume.
73. Cf. Ezek 44:3. It seems that a similar notion is expressed in 1Sam 2:29, where we should probably read לְהַבְרִיאָם instead of MT לְהַבְרִיאֲכֶם. The reading appears to underlie the Targum that censures Samuel for according his sons undue preference in the distribution of sacrifices: וַיְקַלֵּה יַת בְּנֵי קֳדָמְתָא לְאוֹכְלוּתְהוֹן מֵרֵישׁ כָּל קֻרְבָּן יִשְׂרָאֵל.

dignity. In accord with this statute they shall proceed at
every m[eal at which] ten me[n are ga]thered.

Again, the rules foreseen to be operative in the messianic future are effective also in the actual *Yaḥad* community, when no "Anointed" are as yet involved:

1QS 6.3–5   Wherever there are ten men of the *Yaḥad* Council to-
                     gether, a priest shall be present, and they shall sit before
                     him according to their rank, and thus they shall be asked
                     for their counsel in all matters. And when they lay the
                     table to eat or to drink, the priest shall first stretch out
                     his hand to make a blessing over the first bread and
                     wine.

It has been argued that these texts give the priests and the Anointed of
Aaron pride of rank over the lay leader(s) of the community and the future
Anointed of Israel respectively. But this interpretation remains open to
doubt. Rather it would appear that the precedence accorded to the Aaron-
ides is meant to achieve a balance in the standing of the Two Anointed in the
community, in contrast to the societal setup of monarchical Israel, which patently favored the (anointed) king over the (anointed) priest. Such symmetry
is probably intended also in the already mentioned Zechariah passages:
when the text speaks of the crown with which each of the *běnê-hayyiṣhār*
(Zech 4:14, cf. 4:3, 11–12)—the Two Anointed—is to be endowed, the High
Priest Joshua precedes the Davidic scion Zerubbabel (Zech 6:12—restored),
whereas in respect to the thrones which they are assigned, the Davidic
"sprout" precedes the priest (Zech 6:13).

The above survey points up a striking characteristic of the millenarian-
messianic idea at Qumran: the expected "New Eon" will unfold as an age in
which terrestrial-historical experience coalesces with celestial-spiritual uto-
pia. Salvation is viewed as transcendent and imminent at the same time. The
New Order to be established by the anointed is not otherworldly but rather
the realization of a divine plan on earth, the consummation of history in history. Qumran messianism reflects the political ideas of the postexilic returnees' community. It is the *politeia* of the New Commonwealth of Israel and
of the New Universe. Viewed from the angle of typology, the *Yaḥad* must be
assessed the most decidedly millenarian or chiliastic movement that arose in
Judaism at the turn of the era and possibly altogether in antiquity, Christianity included. However, unlike the followers of Jesus, the Covenanters did
not live to see their hopes materialize and remained suspended in limbo
between their topical reality and their vision of the impending onset of the
future immaculate era. Like the men in Beckett's play who were waiting for
Godot, who never came, the Covenanters stood in watch for the Twin Mes-

siahs who ultimately failed to appear on their horizon. *Yaḥad* messianism is a prime example of stumped millenarianism.

CONCLUDING REMARKS

In conclusion, I wish to highlight some of the focal characteristics of early Jewish messianism that became manifest in the foregoing reflections and may be seen to constitute the matrix of the ensuing configurations of this idea in post-70 Judaism.

We should first keep in mind Charlesworth's statement, echoed by other speakers in this symposium, that "most Jewish texts from the turn of the era do not reveal an expectation of a Messiah."[74] This holds true also for rabbinic literature of the first centuries C.E. Wherever references to a Messiah surface, he is seen, *pace* W. D. Davies, as "a purely human figure."[75] The Mishnah maintains a nonmessianic stance. In this authoritative compilation of Jewish laws that determine the individual's and the community's way of life, the Messiah as a supernatural or eschatological figure does not make an appearance.[76] The figure of *māšîaḥ* remains rooted in sociopolitical realities— viz. in the realities of post-70 Judaism.[77] There is hardly a trace of a utopian superstructure. Viewed against the backdrop of later configurations of the messianic idea in Judaism, and the more so in Christianity, we may indeed define that phenomenon with W. D. Davies' "a paradoxical messianism."[78]

It may be surmised that this inherent realism caused those Jewish sources not to offer a particularized description of the messianic age. Due to its predominant restorative thrust the future eon is in essence conceived as a vastly improved replica of a status experienced in the past which is imprinted in the collective memory. Therefore it does not stand in need of being spelled out in detail. The messianic era is not characterized by a total revamping of man's nature and societal structures, nor of the constitution of the universe. Rather it is seen as a sublime reenactment of the favorable conditions which obtained in the idealized period of the united monarchy under David and Solomon. Then Israel had been saved by David's exploits from any immediate danger of wars and vassaldom to other nations, and had achieved in the days of his son an unmatched state of peace and well-being:

> The people of Judah and Israel were countless as the sands of the sea(shores);
> they ate and they drank and enjoyed life. Solomon ruled over all the kingdoms

---

74. See J. H. Charlesworth's "From Messianology to Christology: Problems and Prospects" in the present volume.

75. See W. D. Davies' "The Gospel of Matthew and the Origins of Its Messianology," in the present volume.

76. J. Neusner, *Messiah in Context* (Philadelphia, 1984); see esp. pp. 18–19.

77. See W. D. Davies' remarks in this volume.

78. *Ibid.*

from the river Euphrates to Philistia as far as the frontier of Egypt; they paid tribute and were subject to him all his life . . . For he was paramount over all the land west of the Euphrates from Tiphsah to Gaza, ruling all the kings west of the river; and he enjoyed peace on all sides. All through his reign Judah and Israel lived securely, every man under his vine and his fig-tree, from Dan to Beersheba (1Kgs 4:20–5:1; 5:4–5; cf. Gen 15:18–21).

The memory of those days inspired later biblical writers, and upon it they modelled their vision of the future. In doing so they drew explicitly on past experience:

Was it not this that YHWH proclaimed through the prophets of old, while Jerusalem was populous and peaceful, as were the cities around her, and the Negeb and the Shephelah? . . . These are the words of YHWH Ṣebaoth: See, I will rescue my people from the countries of the east and the west, and bring them back to live in Jerusalem . . . [unlike] before that time . . . [when] no one could go about his affairs in peace because of enemies . . . but now . . . there shall be sowing in peace, the vine shall yield its fruit and the soil its produce . . . with all these things I will endow the survivors of this people. You, house of Judah and house of Israel, . . . I will save you, and you shall become the symbol of a blessing. Courage! Do not be afraid. (Zech 7:7–8:13, cf. Gen 12:2–3)

These words of the postexilic prophet Zechariah evince an expectation that the sublime vision will be realized in an attainable future which will carry upon itself the stamp of the Solomonic era: "On that day, says YHWH Ṣebaoth, you shall invite one another to come and sit (each) under (his) vine and (his) fig tree" (Zech 3:10). It should be noticed that this vision is unintermittently followed by an oracle which conspicuously displays "anointing" imagery and pertains to the Davidide Zerubbabel and the high priest Joshua (Zech. 4:1–3, 11–14).[79]

In other prophetic oracles which cannot be securely dated, the hoped-for realization is transported into an uncharted future, and the range of the vision is expanded to embrace all peoples on the inhabited earth who will be blessed with eternal peace. Thus in Isaiah:

They shall beat their swords into ploughshares and their spears into pruning knives; nation shall not lift sword against nation, nor will they ever train again for war. (Isa 2:4)

In the book of the contemporaneous prophet Micah, that same oracle is adduced with a text expansion which appears to attenuate the utopistic-romantic overtones of the Isaiah version:

---

79. This topical cohesion militates against the sometimes proposed transfer of Zech 3:1–10 after 4:14. See NEB.

> Each man shall live under his vine and his fig tree and no one shall make them afraid. (Micah 4:4)

In these passages no "anointed" is explicitly mentioned. But their dependence on the wording and the imagery of the 1 Kings pericope which depicts the rule of Solomon—the third biblical *māšîaḥ*—leaves little doubt that the prophetic oracles speak of a "messianic" future.

The quest for a peaceful national existence under a *māšîaḥ*, an anointed king, to which the above texts give expression is echoed in rabbinic literature. A saying of the Sages, recorded in the Babylonian Talmud, states that, in contrast to the situation which obtains in their historical world, the distinguishing mark of the "Age to Come" will be "the delivery of Israel from the yoke of other nations" (b. Berakhot 34b *et al.*). While this saying and others like it cannot be construed to reveal the Sages' one and only view concerning the future world, it certainly reveals widespread sentiments which found acceptance in Rabbinic Judaism.

The fundamental realism of biblical *māšîaḥ*-dom never ceased to inspire Jewish messianism also in the post-70 era.[80] One hoped for and foresaw a restoration of the splendor of old, realized in the ingathering of the dispersed in the Land of Israel so as to reconstitute the monocentricity of the monarchic age, and the restoration of national sovereignty under a Davidic Anointed. The spiritual dimension of Jewish messianism continued to manifest itself in historical realism and societal factuality.

---

80. See P. Schäfer, "Die messianischen Hoffnungen des rabbinischen Judentums zwischen Naherwartung und religiösem Pragmatismus," in *Zukunft in der Gegenwart,* ed. C. Thoma (Bern–Frankfurt am Main, 1976), pp. 96–125 = idem, *Studien zur Geschichte und Theologie des rabbinischen Judentums* (Leiden, 1978), pp. 214–43.

MESSIANIC FIGURES AND IDEAS IN THE QUMRAN SCROLLS

The opportunity to survey the "messianic" or "eschatological" materials in the corpus of scrolls found at Qumran, usually known as the Dead Sea Scrolls, is a source of both satisfaction and trepidation. The satisfaction stems from the central role which these still recent finds (we are now in the fortieth year since the discovery of the scrolls) must play in the reconstruction of the history of the messianic idea in Judaism and Christianity. The trepidation results from two concerns. First, there is little need for another in the long series of syntheses which attempt to present "the" messianism of the scrolls. Second, serious methodological problems—better, pitfalls—await anyone who seeks to investigate this area of Qumran studies.

Chief among these problems is the definition of the corpus to be studied. The Dead Sea Scrolls include a variety of materials. Central to our study will be the texts authored by the Qumran sect. Other materials, composed by earlier or related circles, including various apocryphal and pseudepigraphic works, some previously known and others not, constitute background for our work. Finally, biblical materials are important as they shed light on the state of the scriptural sources which underlie the messianic ideas of the Qumran sect. (A detailed study of the eschatology of those materials not authored by the sect itself would also contribute greatly to our understanding of the background of the messianism of Judaism and Christianity, but unfortunately space does not permit it here.) We must also be mindful that fully 25 percent of the Qumran material, some 50 percent of the titles in the corpus, remains unpublished. Except for a few hints from those entrusted with publication, we shall have to limit our study to the published texts. Our conclusions, then, must at best be regarded as tentative.

This corpus, even as we have defined it, will provide us with a variety of messianic or eschatological approaches. This pluralism of ideas is susceptible to two possible explanations. It may result from the coexistence of different approaches within the group. Such is the case, for example, in regard to eschatological matters in the rabbinic tradition.[1] It may also be indicative of historical development within the group. Certain ideas may be earlier; others later.

More difficult to reckon with, and probably the case at Qumran, is the confluence of both these factors. The traditions of pre-Hasmonean Judaism, new ideas evolving both within the sect and in the general community outside, and the momentous historical forces at work in this period all join together to produce a set of related but differing concepts distributed over both time and text, echoing certain common elements, yet testifying to diversity and pluralism, even within the Dead Sea sect.

These considerations make it virtually impossible to separate instances of historical development from those of the coterminous variety, except in certain particular cases. For this reason, it will be advisable to analyze the major texts of the Qumran corpus individually, to determine the messianic and eschatological teachings of each. In this respect we will follow a method similar to that of J. Neusner's *Messianism in Context*[2] which deals with rabbinic literature. Like Neusner, we shall also be mindful of the absence of messianism in specific texts, and, further, of the absence of certain motifs and ideas which we have come to identify with the end of days. We shall also attempt to pay careful attention to the terminology used in the various texts. Yet at the outset it must be admitted that there is little likelihood that we shall be able to sort out the complex history and variety of messianic figures and ideas in the Qumran scrolls in a definitive manner.

THE ZADOKITE FRAGMENTS *(DAMASCUS DOCUMENT)*

The Zadokite Fragments is certainly a composite work, consisting of an Admonition which serves as the preface to a number of short legal collections. Even within the Admonition, different documents may be discerned. Yet the final product presents a consistent approach to eschatology.[3] In CD 2.12, the phrase *mĕšîḥ[ê] rûaḥ qŏdšhô*, "those anointed with his holy spirit (of prophecy)," appears, parallel to the probable emendation *ḥôzê 'ĕmet*, "true prophets." CD 6.1 also uses *mêšîḥê ha-qôdeš* (emended from *bmšyḥw*), "holy anointed ones," to refer to the prophets. Clearly, the term *māšîaḥ* has not yet acquired its later, virtually unequivocal meaning of "Messiah."

1. See L. H. Schiffman, "The Concept of the Messiah in Second Temple and Rabbinic Literature," *Review and Expositor* 84 (1987) 235–46.

2. J. Neusner, *Messianism in Context*, 2nd ed. (Philadelphia, 1984). See also my review "Neusner's *Messiah in Context*," *JQR* 77(1987) 240–3.

3. See L. H. Schiffman, *Sectarian Law in the Dead Sea Scrolls, Courts, Testimony, and the Penal Code* (Chico, Calif., 1983), pp. 7–9.

In 4.4 the author refers to the period of the life of the sect as *'aḥărît ha-yāmîm*, "the end of days." This usage betrays the text's concept of the periodization of history. The author sees the present age as being an intermediate step from the present into the future age. With the rise of the sect this intermediate stage began. It will end when the final age is ushered in. These stages are designated with the term *qēṣ*, meaning "period" in the terminology of Qumran. This term appears in CD 4.9–10, 5.20, and elsewhere. The present *qēṣ* (*qēṣ hā-reša*ʿ, "the period [or age] of evil," CD 6.10, 14) requires that the sect separate itself from the house of Judah because of various violations of Jewish law (CD 6.11–7.4). Indeed, to the author of the *Damascus Document*, the primary difference between this period and that of the future age is the correct observance of the Law, both the revealed (*nigleh*) and hidden (*nistar*).[4] Indeed, the *qēṣ hā-resha*ʿ will come to an end when "there shall arise the one who teaches righteousness (*yôreh ha-ṣedeq*) in the end of days (*'aḥărît ha-yāmîm*)" (6.10–11). It is not yet clear, however, if this refers to the teacher of the sect himself, the sect's own period being the end of days, or if these terms refer to an eschatological teacher who is yet to arise. Unfortunately, the syntax of this passage is exceedingly difficult.

Further evidence for the notion that the author saw the eschaton as having already partially dawned comes from 7.18–21. Here Num 24:17, a passage taken in later tradition as eschatological, is understood to refer to the sect and its leaders. "The Star is the searcher of the Law (*dôrēš ha-tôrâh*). . . . The Sceptre is the prince of all the congregation (*nĕśî' kol hā-ʿēdāh*)."[5] It has been suggested that the imagery of exile to Damascus used in 7.15–18 (immediately preceding) should also be taken as messianic. Evidence has been cited from various Jewish and Christian sources to confirm the widespread use of the Damascus motif.[6]

The clause *bĕ-bôʾ mĕšîaḥ* or *mĕšîḥ[e] 'aḥărôn we-yiśrā'ēl* "with the coming of the Messiah" or "Messiahs" "of Aaron and of Israel" in 19.10–11 is certainly a reference to an eschatological era which is yet to arrive. Some seek to claim that this text expects one messianic figure, representative of the priesthood and the people of Israel. Others emend so that the text describes two Messiahs, the Aaronide, high-priestly Messiah, and the lay, temporal Messiah. A further possibility is to eschew the emendation, yet to understand *mĕšîaḥ* (construct) as distributive over both modifiers, i.e., referring to two Messiahs.

The problem is more acute in regard to 20.1 where the text has *ʿad ʿamôd māšîaḥ mē-'āhărôn û-mi-yiśrā'ēl*, "until the rise of a Messiah from Aaron and from Israel." Here there are only two possibilities. We can conclude that the text envisions only one Messiah, or we can understand the word *māšîaḥ* as

---

4. See L. H. Schiffman, *Halakhah at Qumran* (Leiden, 1975), pp. 23–60.
5. Trans. C. Rabin, *The Zadokite Documents* (Oxford, 1954).
6. N. Wieder, *The Judaean Scrolls and Karaism* (London, 1962), pp. 1–51.

being modified by both prepositional phrases, yielding a two-Messiah scheme. In 4QD^b, the still unpublished Qumran manuscript corresponding to CD 14.19, the editor informs us that the text has ʿad ʿămôd měšîaḥ ʾahărôn wě-yiśrāʾēl, which he takes as showing that it is one Messiah who was expected.[7] Whatever interpretation we follow, it is clear from the context of this passage that the present age is that between the death of the Righteous Teacher and the coming of the messianic era. According to 20.15, this period, like that of the desert wandering, is supposed to span forty years.

Attention must be called to the appearance of David in 5.5. Yet David is in no way linked to the end of days or to a messianic role. The Messiah of Israel, even if he is distinct from the Aaronide Messiah in the Damascus Document, is not singled out to be Davidic.

THE MEGILLAT HA-SERAKHÎM (RULE SCROLL)

The Rule is clearly a composite document. At the very least it is comprised of three distinct compositions: the Rule of the Community (Manual of Discipline), Rule of the Congregation, and the Rule of Benedictions. These three components were joined by a redactor, or at least by a scribe. We shall have to treat each component separately and then inquire about the unified scroll.

Rule of the Community

The Blessing and Curse ritual, 1QS 2.19 tells us, will continue only through the period of the reign of Belial. This certainly is evidence of a notion that a new age will dawn at some time. The appointed period (or end) of this rule is termed qēṣ in 3.23. The same notion appears in 4.16–17 where reference is made to qēṣ ʾahărôn, "the final period (age)." Indeed a final destruction of all evil (pěqudâh, "visitation [for destruction])" is expected to take place after which the world will be perfected (4.18–20, 25–26). Here the text is speaking of a sort of Day of the Lord, although the term does not appear.

The most significant passage for our purposes is 9.11–12. Here it is stated that the prohibition on mingling property with those outside the sect is to remain in effect ʿad bôʾ nābî û-měšîḥê ʾahărôn wě-yiśrāʾēl, "until the coming of a prophet and the Messiahs [or anointed ones] of Aaron and Israel." In this text, as opposed to the Damascus Document, there can be no question that we are speaking of two Messiahs, as is the case in the Rule of the Congregation. This passage, however, is the conclusion of the section of 8.15b–9.11

---

7. J. T. Milik, *Ten Years of Discovery in the Wilderness of Judaea,* trans. J. Strugnell (London, 1959), pp. 125f. This text is now published in B. Z. Wacholder, M. G. Abegg (eds.), *A Preliminary Edition of the Unpublished Dead Sea Scrolls: The Hebrew and the Aramaic Texts from Cave Four* (Washington, DC, 1991) frag 18, col III, 1.12 (p. 20).

which is reported to be missing in MS. E, identified as the earliest copy of the Rule of the Community.[8] On the basis of this omission, it has been assumed by some that the original sources of the Rule of the Community made no mention of these messianic figures and that they were introduced either by the redactor of the Rule of the Congregation or even by the compiler of the entire *Megillat Ha-Serekhîm*.

It is difficult to accept such conclusions as long as the manuscript evidence is unavailable for inspection. Further, the priestly role was strongest in the earliest stages in the history of the sect and gradually weakened as lay power increased. We would therefore expect to encounter the notion of priestly preeminence in the end of days early in the notion of priestly preeminence in the end of days early in the history of the sect, not later on. Second, the two-Messiah concept is known from various other Second Temple sources,[9] and it could have entered the sect's thinking at any time.

Most important is the omission again of David from this scheme. The Messiah of Israel is nowhere said to be Davidic. On the other hand, an eschatological prophet appears here alongside the Messiahs. This prophet is to join the Messiahs in deciding outstanding controversies in Jewish law.[10] This role was understood to belong to Elijah in later rabbinic traditions.

The communal meals of the sect are described in 1QS 6.2–5. At these repasts, the priest presided and received the first portions. Elsewhere we have shown that these meals were a reflection of the sect's eschatological banquets as described in the Rule of the Congregation. These eschatological banquets were to be presided over by the high priest and the Messiah of Israel. The meals in the present age were led only by the priest, however.[11] The description in this same passage (6.6–7) of the *ʾîš dôrēš ha-tôrāh*, "the man who interprets the Torah," as "alternating, each with his fellow," shows that at least in the context of 6.6–7 this is not an official and certainly not a messianic figure.

What emerges here is that there may or may not have been a two-Messiah concept in the original text of the Rule of the Community. There was a notion of periods of history and the eventual destruction of the wicked on a day of visitation. Neither David nor Davidic descent plays any role whatsoever.

Rule of the Congregation

This text, also known as *Serekh Hā-ʿĒdāh* (1QSa), is an appendix to the Rule of the Community, at least in the present manuscript.[12] Nonetheless, it

8. Milik, *Ten Years*, p. 123.
9. See the sources cited in Schiffman, *Halakhah at Qumran*, p. 51, n. 202, and Schiffman, *Sectarian Law*, p. 208, n. 94.
10. See 1Mac 14:41, 4:46.
11. Schiffman, *Sectarian Law*, pp. 191–210.
12. See my detailed study of this text, *The Eschatological Community of the Dead Sea Scrolls: A Study of the Serekh Hā-ʿĒdāh*, the SBL Monograph Series 38 (Atlanta: Scholars Press, 1989).

may have originally been a separate composition. It begins by referring explicitly to itself as a *serekh*, a list of sectarian legal prescriptions for the life of the sect in the end of days (*ʾaḥărît ha-yāmîm*). Foremost among these regulations is the series of stages of life which are described in detail, as well as the scroll's requirement of the absolute purity and purification of the members of the community, who are expected to fulfill the laws required for fitness for priestly service found in the Pentateuch.[13]

This text does not refer to the notion of historical ages since it concerns only the period after the dawn of the eschaton. The list of the stages of life does refer to subduing the nations (1.21) and to various military officers (1.24–25, 28–29). In these matters, the text stands roughly in agreement with the War Scroll (to which we will turn below). The Rule of the Congregation emphasizes the role of the Zadokite priests as leaders of the eschatological council (2.3).

This scroll also describes the eschatological assembly, as well as the banquet presided over by the high priest and the Messiah of Israel. We will not discuss the restoration of 2.11 except to note the possibility that it refers to the birth of the Messiah. Line 12 refers to the Messiah (*ha-māšîaḥ*) in the singular alongside the priest, *ha-kôhēn* (restored). In 1QSa 2.15 there is another reference to the Messiah of Israel, and in 19–21 the priest and the Messiah of Israel are again mentioned together. The priest is given prominence both in seating and in the recitation of the benediction over the bread and the wine. This dinner is an eschatological reflection of the almost identical pattern we observed in the Rule of the Community for the pre-messianic era. Indeed, the communal meals of the sect constituted an attempt to live in the present age in a way similar to that of the end of days. In the life of utmost purity and perfection, that goal was ultimately to be achieved.[14]

It is important to emphasize a distinction between what appears here and what is the case in the Rule of the Community and, according to most readings, in the Damascus Document. Whereas in 1QS two Messiahs, both termed *māšîaḥ*, are expected, in the Rule of the Congregation there is a priest and a *māšîaḥ* of Israel. The term *māšîaḥ* only refers to the lay Messiah.

Again, David is not mentioned, only Israel. There are no details regarding the onset of the eschatological era or of the notion of periods in the history of the world. This is, indeed, a text describing the fulfillment of Jewish law and sanctity in the end of days.

---

13. Those physically deformed are therefore to be excluded from the eschatological community. See Schiffman, "Purity and Perfection: Exclusion from the Council of the Community in the *Serekh Hā-ʿĒdāh*," *Biblical Archaeology Today*, ed. J. Amitai (Jerusalem, 1985), pp. 373–89.

14. See above, n. 12.

Rule of Benedictions

The last item in this trilogy is the Rule of Benedictions, also called the *Serekh Ha-Bĕrakhôt*. Opinions differ on the exact reconstruction of this fragmentary series of blessings for various figures. It appears that 1QSb 4.22–28 is a fragment of a benediction for the high priest. It follows a benediction for the Zadokite priests (1QSb 3.22–28). Neither of these is in any way eschatological in character. Yet, after the blessing of the high priest, in another fragmentary passage (4.18), there is mention of the *qiṣê ʿad*, "periods of eternity."

According to Licht's restoration, 5.20, the beginning of a benediction for the *nĕśîʾ hā-ʿēdāh*, "the prince of the congregation," refers to an eschatological leader.[15] This restoration is supported by the fact that the benediction for the prince which follows is based on Isa 11:2–5, a passage referring to the Davidic Messiah. If so, we have here another designation for the Messiah of Israel, clearly based on the Ezekiel tradition (Ezek 34:24, 37:25). Ezekiel saw the eschatological community as led by a *nāśîʾ* (chaps. 44–48, passim). No idea of how the messianic era will come about is provided here.

The Rule of Benedictions, then, to the extent that it can be reconstructed, assumes a Davidic Messiah to arise in the end of days. As we have seen, this is not the case with most of the Qumran sectarian writings. The author apparently has a notion of the periods of history. No explicit mention of a priestly Messiah appears, but it is possible that the full text did make a reference to such a figure.

War Scroll

The Scroll of the War of the Sons of Light Against the Sons of Darkness is generally understood to describe the war which will usher in the end of days in the teaching of the Dead Sea sect. This scroll uses the key word *qēṣ*, "period, age" (cf. 1.8), and talks about the complete destruction of the wicked (1.5–7) which is predestined (1.10). This battle is to be fought not only on this earth but by the heavenly beings above (1.15). The statement of 1QM 6.6 regarding victory, "And the kingdom will belong to the God of Israel . . . ," must refer to the eschaton. This notion is so central to the scroll that it is repeated in 12.15 (partially restored) and 19.8

Israel and Aaron appear on the banner of the entire congregation along with the names of the twelve tribes (1QM 3.12). According to 5.1–2, on the shield of the *nāśîʾ* of the entire congregation is written his name, Israel, Levi, and Aaron, as well as those of the twelve tribes. Again we see the same duality of Aaron and Israel which we have encountered elsewhere, but no mention is made here of two Messiahs. But it is important to note that the term *māšîaḥ* in 11.7–8 refers to prophets in the phrase *mĕšîḥêkā hôzê*

---

15. J. Licht, *Megillat Ha-Serakhim* (Jerusalem, 1965), p. 288.

tĕ⁽ûdôt, "your anointed ones, the seers of things ordained."[16] We cannot simply assume that *māšiaḥ* must refer to a messiah. Although 11.1–3 mentions David's defeat of Goliath, the passage has absolutely no messianic overtones. Num 24:17–19 is interpreted noneschatologically in 11.6–7,[17] in contrast to the interpretation of this passage in the Damascus Document.

The War Scroll, despite its clear description of an eschatological battle, does not mention the messianic figures, although the idea of stages of history lies behind it. At the same time, the omission of messianic figures can be explained as the result of the text's describing only the events leading up to the messianic era, not that era itself. If, on the other hand, the prince of the congregation is identical with the lay Messiah, we would look in vain in this text for a two-Messiah concept.

The Thanksgiving Scroll

The Thanksgiving Scroll (*Hôdayôt*) contains a poem in 3.5–18 which seems to describe the birth of the Messiah. He is designated by reference to the "wondrous counselor" of Isa 9:5. The poem as a whole recounts the initial spread of evil, followed by the rise of the Messiah, and then the destruction of all evil. In this sense it is apocalyptic in character. There is no mention of the word Messiah, however, nor of David nor Aaron. 1QH 3.35–6 seems to foretell the destruction of the wicked as does 15.19. It has been suggested by some that the *nēṣer* of 6.15, 7.19, and 8.6 is to be taken as a messianic figure, based on the prophetic background of this word (Isa 11:1).[18] However, there is little in the context of the Qumran hymn itself to support such a conclusion. It is more likely that this term is based on Isa 60:21 and refers to a plant.[19]

All in all, there is no real messianism to speak of in the Thanksgiving Hymns. There is no Messiah, Davidic or otherwise, and only the echoes exist of the eventual dawning of an age in which the destruction of the wicked will take place.

PESHARIM

The biblical commentaries from Qumran provide a form of contemporizing biblical exegesis which sees the words of the scriptures as being fulfilled

---

16. Trans. in Y. Yadin, *The Scroll of the War of the Sons of Light Against the Sons of Darkness,* trans. B. and C. Rabin (Oxford, 1962), p. 310.

17. Ibid.

18. See J. Carmignac ("Les Hymnes," in *Les Textes de Qumran,* ed. J. Carmignac, P. Guilbert [Paris, 1961], vol. 1, pp. 222f.), who also rejects this view.

19. J. A. Fitzmyer, "The Aramaic 'Elect of God' Text from Qumran Cave 4," in *Essays on the Semitic Background of the New Testament* (Missoula, Mont., 1974), p. 132.

in the age of the author. These texts and related materials contain a significant amount of eschatological material.

Pesharim *on Isaiah*

4Q161 (*Pesher Isa^a*) refers to ʾaḥărît ha-yāmîm, "the end of days," in interpreting Isa 10:28–32 (frags. 5–6). The Qumran passage speaks of the něśîʾ hā-ʿēdāh, "the prince of the congregation," who will participate in an eschatological battle. The same text, in frags. 8–10, lines 11–24, interprets Isa 11:1–5 as referring to a Davidic Messiah who will arise in the end of days and rule over the nations ([pišrô ʿal ṣemaḥ] dāwîd hā-ʿômēd bě-ʾaḥă[rît ha-yāmîm][20]). The fragmentary material suggests that he will judge his people according to the rulings which the priests will teach him.

4Q162 (*Pesher Isa^b*) speaks of the end of days in which there will be pě-quddat hā-ʾāreṣ, "a visitation [of punishment] on the earth" (2.1–2), but the context is insufficient to determine what is being discussed. The passage may even refer to events of the author's own time period. In 4Q 163 (*Pesher Isa^c*), frags. 4–7, 2.10–14, Isa 10:24 is taken to refer to the end of days in which, it appears, the evildoers will be taken into captivity.[21] Yet frag. 23, 2.10, shows how for the author the present Greco-Roman period can also be called the end of days. In this period there will arise the "seekers of smooth things" (dôrěšê halāqôt), probably a pun meant to designate the Pharisees. 4Q 164 (*Pesher Isa^d*) frag. 1.7 refers to the heads of the twelve tribes in the end of days. This fragmentary passage appears to be messianic.

The author or authors of the *Pěšarîm* on Isaiah clearly expected the sect to be led in the end of days by the prince of the congregation and/or the Davidic Messiah. These texts expect a final destruction yet do not speak of the periodization of history. No mention of a priestly eschatological figure appears in the preserved portions of the text.

Pesher Habakkuk

Pesher Habakkuk 7.7 and 12 allude to the qēṣ hā-ʾaḥărôn, "the final age," but it is not clear if in these passages the author speaks of the messianic future or of his own day. It is most likely that he sees his own times as the beginning of the future age, soon to lead to the eschatological fulfillment. This period, according to the author, is to be longer than the prophets had expected. The end of days mentioned in 9.6 must refer to the years preceding the dawn of the eschaton when the evildoers will be punished.

This text, then, seems to mention the periodization of history, believing the author's own day to be the very verge of the end of days. Yet no mention of any specific messianic figures occurs here.

---

20. Restoring with J. M. Allegro, *Qumrân Cave 4, I (4Q 158–4Q 186)* (DJD V; Oxford, 1968), p. 14.
21. See frags. 13 and 14, which also mention the end of days.

Pesher Hosea *and* Pesher Nahum

4Q166 (*Pesher Hos^a*) 1.9–10 refers to *qēṣ*, "period," and *dôr ha-pĕqudâh*, "the generation of the visitation [for punishment]," and line 12 mentions the *qiṣê ḥārôn*, "periods of wrath." According to 4Q169 (*Pesher Nahum*) 3.3, in the final period (*bĕ-ʾaḥărît ha-qēṣ*), the evil deeds of the *dôrĕšê ḥalāqôt* ("seekers after smooth things"), a term for the Pharisees, will be revealed to all Israel. In 4.3 the author tells us that in the final age (*lĕ-qēṣ haʾ-aḥărôn*), Menasseh (probably a hellenistic or Sadducean group) will cease to rule over Israel.

While these texts have a sense that there will be a better future in the end of days, they exhibit nothing like the developed messianism of other texts. This is especially surprising in the case of *Pesher Nahum* which is so extensively preserved.

Other Pesharim

1Q14 (*Pesher Micah*) frags. 17–19.5 speaks of *ha-dôr hā-ʾaḥărô[n]*, "the final generation," but the fragmentary context does not allow any conclusions. 4Q171 (*Pesher Pss^a*) 2.6–8 mentions a forty-year period after which all evil will be destroyed. This seems identical to the forty years of the eschatological war of the War Scroll. A fragmentary comment in 4Q173 (*Pesher Pss.^b*) 1.5 on Ps 127:2–3 talks about [*kô*]*hēn lĕ-ʾaḥărît ha-qē*[*ṣ*], "a priest for the final age." Needless to say, these brief references do not allow any conclusions about the messianic views of the authors of the respective texts.

4Q FLORILEGIUM

The 4Q Florileqium (4Q174) refers to an eschatological temple, *ha-bayit ʾăšer . . .* [*bĕ-*]*ʾaḥărît ha-yāmîm* ("the house which . . . [in] the end of days"). This temple will be of the highest purity and, accordingly, Ammonites, Moabites, the *mamzēr*, foreigners, and converts will be excluded from it (frags. 1–2, 2.3–5). In addition, in the end of days there is to arise the shoot of David (*ṣemaḥ dāvîd*), clearly a Davidic Messiah, to save Israel. Along with the shoot of David, there will arise the *dôrĕš ha-tôrāh*, "the expounder of the Law" (frags. 1–2, 2.10–13) whom some have seen as a priestly, messianic figure. The text interprets Ps 1:1 as foretelling the rise of the sect, which is constituted of those who have turned aside from the ways of the wicked (lines 14–19). We have here the explicit notion that the rise of the sect constitutes the onset of the end of days (*ʾaḥărît ha-yāmîm*).[22]

Here again we encounter explicit reference to a Davidic Messiah, as well as the notion that the rise of the sect signals the onset of the eschaton. The notion of an eschatological temple of perfect purity appears as well, but there

22. See also frag. 14, which mentions the end of days.

is really no mention of the priestly Messiah, unless we assume that the expounder of the law is to be so identified. Elsewhere, however, the function of the eschatological priest is envisioned as cultic, not educational or exegetical.

11Q MELCHIZEDEK

11Q Melchizedek is a text similar in literary character to 4Q Florilegium.[23] The text explicitly alludes to the end of days, interpreting the commandment of the Sabbatical year (Lev 25:13; Deut 15:2) to refer to this period. At that time, Melchizedek will proclaim release for the captives (?). He and his lot (nahălâh) will also be granted a special Sabbatical of atonement. He will then take vengeance on Belial and his lot with the help of the angels. The eschatological Isa 52:7 is then quoted, apparently to identify Melchizedek with the herald of the future age. There is a mention of the qiṣê ḥā[rôn], "the periods of wrath." But Melchizedek here is not himself a messianic figure. It seems best to see him as taking the very same role Michael takes in the War Scroll, leading the forces of good in the cosmic battle with Belial and his lot of evil. It is after this battle that the eschaton will be inaugurated.

This text mentions no Messiah or Messiahs and says nothing of a Davidic rule (even though David is mentioned explicitly before a quotation from Psalms). The notion of stages of history, however, does appear.

OTHER TEXTS

In this section we will survey a few texts which, because of size or state of preservation, yield material too scant to allow useful conclusions, yet at the same time are worthy of notice. 4Q177 (Catena (A)) at the beginning mentions the end of days and qîṣîm, "periods" (frags. 1–4.10), but nothing can be gleaned from the context. The term qeṣ occurs as well (line 11). The mention of a second book of the Torah (line 14) has been taken by some to refer to an eschatological, new Torah, or even to the Temple Scroll,[24] but the fragmentary nature of the context allows absolutely no interpretation to be supported. Frag. 9.4 mentions the "seekers after smooth things" (partially restored) in an eschatological context (line 2, bĕ-ʾaḥărî[t hā-yamîm], line 9, bĕdôr hā-ʾa[ḥărôn]). Again, context is insufficiently preserved for any analysis. The same is the case with frags. 12–13, 1.2 (cf. 2.3) and 4Q178 frags. 2 and 3. 4Q182 (Catena (B)) frags. 1 and 2 also contain eschatological references, but they are too fragmentary for consideration.

23. See J. A. Fitzmyer, "Further Light on Melchizedek from Qumran Cave 11," Essays, pp. 245–67.

24. Y. Yadin, The Temple Scroll (Jerusalem, 1983), vol. 1, pp. 396f.

4Q *Divrê Ha-Mĕʾôrôt* 3.13–14 refers to *ʾaḥărît ha-yāmîm*,"the end of days," but the passage is simply a reflex of Deut 31:29 and has no eschatological significance. In 4.6–8 the text refers to God's covenant with David as permanent king over Israel. 4Q Prayers for Feasts (509) II 7.5 mentions the end of days, but the context is not understandable. The notion of periodization of history appears in 4Q Wisdom Canticles (511), frag. 35. 1Q Book of the Mysteries speaks of the disappearance of evil. The David Apocryphon (2Q22) supplies nothing messianic. The so-called New Jerusalem texts (1Q32, 2Q24, 5Q15, 11QJN) may describe a vision of the messianic Jerusalem, but they seem to be based on Ezekiel and make no reference to messianism or the end of days. 4Q Testimonies (4Q175) cites verses which may have had eschatological significance but provides no interpretation.

These minor references suffice to show that eschatological ideas were originally found in many other texts of the Qumran corpus but that these are not sufficiently preserved. We can expect additional manuscripts to be published in the future which may shed further light on the messianic consciousness of the sect.

Two texts are notable for their nonmessianic character. The so-called Psalms Scroll from cave 11 is in actuality a liturgical compilation of Psalms, some in our biblical canon and some not. The section entitled "David's Compositions" (11Q Pssᵃ 27.2–11) makes absolutely no reference to messianism. The same is the case in the supernumerary Psalm 151 A (11Q Psᵃ 28.3–14) dealing with David's musical ability and his anointment.

Another text which should not be taken as eschatological is the Temple Scroll. This text describes a temple to be in use until the dawn of the eschaton. This is explicitly stated in col. 29. At that time, God will create his own eschatological sanctuary.

It has been maintained by some that the Elect of God Text (4Q Mess ar) speaks of the birth of the Messiah. In actuality, this text mentions the *bĕḥîr ʾĕlāhā*, "the elect of God," and never uses the word *māšîaḥ*. There is no evidence from within the text that *bĕḥîr ʾĕlāhā* is a messianic designation. Further, the evidence of one manuscript reading in the Gospel of John 1:34 (*ho eklektos tou theou*) as the sole basis on which to take the text as messianic is not justified. Even if this manuscript represented the correct text, we would have to assume that this designation in John was indeed a title, and this does not seem to be the case.[25] Instead the Elect of God Text seems to belong to one of the previously unknown pseudepigraphal compositions now attested at Qumran. Finally, the Aramaic literature from Qumran on the whole was not composed by the sect but was imported. It is usually dated earlier than the sectarian compositions.

25. Fitzmyer, *Essays*, pp. 157–60.

CONCLUSION

If anything is clear from the foregoing survey, it is that a variety of motifs and beliefs are distributed in almost random fashion throughout the texts. Thus, either we are dealing with an example of the historical development of ideas, or of parallel approaches, or, most likely, of a combination of these factors.

J. Starcky[26] sought to construct a history of the messianology at Qumran which went hand in hand with the stages in the archaeologically attested occupation of the site. In the Maccabean period the teacher authored the Thanksgiving Scroll and the Rule of the Community. Messianic expectations do not appear in the hymns, and the earliest manuscript of the Rule of the Community does not contain the messianic allusion. Hence, Starcky concludes that messianic speculation was absent in this period. In the Hasmonean period, Pharisaic influence leads to the presence of messianism in the Rule (1QS), as well as in its appendices. Here we find the notion of two Messiahs. Starcky identifies the Pompeian period references in the Damascus Document where the two Messiahs have become one priestly figure: the teacher was the eschatological prophet, the interpreter of the Law. In the last period, the Herodian, the anti-Roman feeling exemplified in the War Scroll developed.

It seems to us, however, that there are numerous problems with this theory.[27] Chief among them is the presumption that the Damascus Document should be dated much later than the Rule of the Community and that the omission of material found in 1QS from the still unpublished MS. E of the Rule can be taken as evidence for the history of the text. Furthermore, the claim that the messianic idea only entered through Pharisaic influence is a gross oversimplification. Finally, the theory in no way accounts for Davidic versus non-Davidic lay Messiahs.

We can augment the quest for a historical explanation by recognizing the various messianic trends which existed in Second Temple Judaism. Guided by the programmatic essay of G. Scholem,[28] we will explore the dominant trends in Jewish messianism and the tension between them. He noted the poles of restorative vs. utopian messianism. The restorative seeks to bring back the ancient glories whereas the utopian constructs a view of an even better future, one which surpasses all that came before. The restorative can be described as a much more rational messianism, expecting only the improvement and perfection of the present world. The utopian is much more apocalyptic in character, looking forward to vast catastrophic changes in the

---

26. J. Starcky, "Les quatres étapes du messianisme à Qumran," *RB* 70 (1963) 481–505.

27. See Fitzmyer, *Essays*, pp. 136–40.

28. "Toward an Understanding of the Messianic Idea in Judaism," *The Messianic Idea in Judaism* (New York, 1971), pp. 1–36; see S. Talmon, "Types of Messianic Expectation at the Turn of the Era," *King, Cult, and Calendar in Ancient Israel* (Jerusalem, 1987), pp. 202–24.

world with the coming of the messianic age. It is not that either of these approaches can exist independent of the other; rather, both are found in the messianic aspirations of the various Jewish groups. However, the balance of creative tension between these tendencies is what determines the character of the messianism in question.

Elsewhere we have traced the roots of this distinction through biblical and early Second Temple literature.[29] What is important for our purposes is that these two approaches, the restorative and the utopian, ultimately are based on different biblical traditions. Restorative messianism looks forward to the reestablishment of the Davidic Empire, a process which can come about through natural developments. Utopian messianism expects a world that never was, perfect and ideal. Such a world can only be built upon the ruins of this world, after the annihilation of its widespread evil and transgression. Whereas the prophecies of the reestablishment of Israel's power and prosperity inform the restorative trend, notions such as the Day of the Lord serve as the basis for the utopian approach.

With this background, we can return to the Qumran corpus. Those texts which espouse the Davidic Messiah tend toward the restorative. They therefore emphasize much more the prophecies of peace and prosperity, and do not expect the cataclysmic destruction of all evil. The more catastrophic, utopian, or even apocalyptic tendencies usually do not envision a Davidic Messiah. They seek instead to invest authority in a dominant priestly religious leader and a temporal prince who is to be subservient to the priestly figure. In this case, there is no Davidic allegiance, and the prominent role of the priesthood in the life of the sect is transposed onto the end of days. Some of the utopians sought to limit the leadership to one messianic figure. Sometimes we may encounter both trends side by side in the same text, influencing its author equally. This is testimony to the fact that these two trends were at this very time beginning the long process of being fused into what later became the messianic ideal of Rabbinic Judaism.

We will never be able to construct an exact historical sequence of the messianic ideas and texts found at Qumran. Yet a matrix of history on the one axis and the restorative-utopian dichotomy on the other is the only framework within which to explain the rich and variegated eschatological ideas and approaches which are represented in the literature of the Dead Sea sect. This study should again caution us against seeing the materials found in the Qumran caves as a monolithic corpus, the elements of which may be harmonized with one another at will.

29. See n. 1 of this essay.

FURTHER REFLECTIONS ON
"THE SON OF MAN:"
The Origins and Development of the Title

"'Embarrassing' might be the kindest word for it," is how I described the status of the Son of Man problem in 1967.[1] Unfortunately, despite all that has been written on the subject during the past twenty years, not much has changed in this regard. The term, so central to the Gospels' presentations of Jesus, is yet elusive with respect to its background, its possible use by Jesus, and its role in the mission and Christology of the early churches. After reviewing studies by S. Kim and B. Lindars, P. J. Achtemeier concluded, "Despite the careful work of both scholars, the mutually exclusive nature of their respective conclusions shows that there is as yet no scholarly consensus even on the way to approach the problem of Jesus as the 'Son of Man.'"[2]

Certainly, however, there are camps of scholarly opinion, and at several points during this period it did appear that a broader consensus was beginning to emerge. Following Rudolf Bultmann and the work of H. E. Tödt, a number of scholars in the middle 1960s, including Ferdinand Hahn, Reginald Fuller, Günther Bornkamm, and A. J. B. Higgins, believed that a reasonably clear picture could be delineated.[3] There were permutations in their

1. F. H. Borsch, *The Son of Man in Myth and History* (Philadelphia, 1967), p. 15 [hereafter *SMMH*].

2. P. J. Achtemeier, *JBL* 105 (1986) 335. In his reviews (pp. 332–35) of S. Kim, *"The Son of Man" as the Son of God* (Grand Rapids, 1985) and B. Lindars, *Jesus Son of Man: A Fresh Examination of the Son of Man Sayings in the Gospels in the Light of Recent Research* (Grand Rapids, 1984).

3. R. Bultmann, *History of the Synoptic Tradition*, 2nd ed. (New York, 1968), pp. 120–30; H. E. Tödt, *The Son of Man in the Synoptic Tradition* (Philadelphia, 1965); F. Hahn, *The Titles of Jesus in Christology: Their History in Early Christianity* (London, 1969); R. H. Fuller, *The Foundations of New Testament Christology* (New York, 1965), pp. 119–25; Günther Bornkamm, *Jesus of Nazareth* (New York, 1960), pp. 175–78, 228–31; A. J. B. Higgins, *Jesus and the Son of Man* (London, 1964). Similarly also C. Colpe, ὁ υἱὸς τοῦ ἀνθρώπου in *TDNT*, vol. 8 (1972), pp. 400–77, and "Der Begriff 'Menschensohn' und die Methode der Erforschung messianischer Prototypen," *Kairos*, N.F. 11 (1969) 241–63; 12 (1970) 81–112; 14 (1972) 241–57. (See Higgins, *The Son of Man in the Teaching of Jesus* [SNTS MS 39; Cambridge, 1980], who also uses the theory of the circumlocution idiom to explain the origin of some of the earthy Son of Man sayings). See my review of this and other positions in 1967 in *SMMH*, 15–54.

theories, and differences over the degree to which Jesus may or may not have linked himself and his mission with the figure, but it was agreed that the references to the Son of Man as a figure on earth and as one who was to suffer were compositions of the early communities (or possibly in a few cases they resulted from a misunderstanding of "son of man" used as a first person circumlocution). The earliest of the Son of Man sayings spoke of a heavenly figure who would appear as judge and vindicator. While Jesus may have looked for his own vindication and that of his followers in association with this Son of Man, sayings which may be attributed to him are characterized by his speaking of the Son of Man as another.[4] These relatively few sayings are traceable to the community responsible for the putative Q source. Their eschatological expectation and faith in Jesus formed the crucible in which the more developed Christian Son of Man teachings began to take shape.

The vision of Dan 7:13–14 was the source for the conception of the Son of Man figure, though Daniel's "one like a son of man" (כבר אנש) was descriptive rather than titular in character. The so-called Similitudes of Enoch (1 Enoch 37–71) and 4 Ezra 13, and perhaps certain rabbinic references, were parallel developments within Judaism and constituted evidence for a generalized expectation regarding a Son of Man figure at the time of Jesus.

Two factors were critical in the questioning of this consensus. In the first place, a number of scholars became far less certain that there was any general Son of Man conception in Judaism at the time of Jesus. The lack of 1 Enoch 37–71 at Qumran, and a possible later date for it with its Son of Man references, along with a different way of reading the Gospel sayings and other materials, led to the suspicion that this Jewish Son of Man conception was "created, not by the thinkers of New Testament times, but by modern critical scholarship."[5] It was still possible, however, to preserve a form of the consensus by arguing that Jesus or later disciples had first fashioned the Son of Man conception on the basis of Dan 7:13–14. In the more sophisticated form of this theory, it was held that the font of the Son of Man tradition was a pesher which brought an earlier statement about vindication and exaltation ("sit at my right hand") drawn from Ps 110:1 together with Dan 7:13 and perhaps with other scriptural references as well.[6] This basic saying (now

---

4. Higgins in *Son of Man* (1980) maintains that Jesus thought of himself as the destined Son of Man.

5. Lindars, *Jesus Son of Man*, p. 8. Among others see R. Leivestad, "Exit the Apocalyptic Son of Man," *NTS* 18 (1971–72) 243–67.

6. Perrin developed and refined this position in a series of essays, "Mark xiv.62: The End Product of a Christian Pesher Tradition?" *NTS* 12 (1965–66) 150–55; "The Son of Man in Ancient Judaism and Primitive Christianity: A Suggestion," *BR* 11 (1966) 17–28; "The Creative Use of the Son of Man Traditions by Mark," *USQR* 23 (1967–68) 357–65; "The Son of Man in the Synoptic Tradition," *BR* 13 (1968) 3–25. They are now collected in his *A Modern Pilgrimage in New Testament Chronology* (Philadelphia, 1974). Zech 12:10 was also seen to have played a part and W. O. Walker, Jr., added Ps 8, esp. vss. 5–8, a suggestion accepted by Perrin, *Pilgrimage*, pp. 19, 21–22. See Walker's survey, "The Son of Man: Some Recent Developments," *CBQ* 45 (1983)

found in Mk 14:62 and parallels), which Tödt and others had seen as a later development,[7] was now viewed as the basis for the entire Son of Man tradition.

Far more damaging to the consensus has been the contention that the earliest of the Gospels' Son of Man sayings derive from utterances which made use of the Aramaic phrase בר (א)נש(א) as a way of referring to the speaker. Sayings such as "the son of man has nowhere to lay his head" in Mt 8:20, (Lk 9:58), and "whoever says a word against the son of man" in Mt 12:32, (Lk 12:10), are based on this way of speaking and could go back to Jesus in reference to his earthly ministry. Originally, however, these logia did not use בר (א)נש(א) as a title, much less with reference to a heavenly, exalted figure. That phase came relatively later when the idiom was linked with Dan 7:13–14 and Jesus was seen as the heavenly one referred to in scripture. This identification then interacted with the whole of the developing tradition.

A version of this way of solving the Son of Man problem was first proposed in its modern dress in a paper delivered by Geza Vermes in 1965, and it has been refined, with significant variations, by Vermes and developed by Maurice Casey, Barnabas Lindars, Günther Schwarz and others.[8] Schwarz is in-

---

584–607, and, for more detail, "The Origin of the Son of Man Concept as Applied to Jesus," *JBL* 91 (1972) 482–90. In the same discussion Perrin also made use of Hendrikus Boers' suggestion that Psalms 16 and 18 were critical in the formation of resurrection faith which came to include an identification of Jesus with the Son of Man. See Boers, "Psalm 16 and the Historical Origin of the Christian Faith," *ZNW* 60 (1969) 107–10 and "Where Christology Is Real: A Survey of Recent Research on New Testament Christology," *Int* 26 (1972) 300–27.

7. Tödt, *Son of Man*, pp. 36–40.

8. Vermes' 1965 paper was published as "The Use of בר נש/בר נשא in Jewish Aramaic" in the 3rd ed. of M. Black's *An Aramaic Approach to the Gospels and Acts* (Oxford, 1967), pp. 310–28, and also in his *Post-Biblical Jewish Studies* (Leiden, 1975), pp. 147–65. Then see his "'The Son of Man' Debate," *JSNT* 1 (1978) 19–32 and "The Present State of the 'Son of Man' Debate," *JJS* 29 (1978) 123–34, also in his *Jesus and the World of Judaism* (Philadelphia, 1984), pp. 89–99; M. Casey, *Son of Man: The Interpretation and Influence of Daniel 7* (London, 1979); B. Lindars, *Jesus Son of Man: A Fresh Examination*: G. Schwarz, *Jesus "der Menschensohn": Aramaistische Untersuchungen zu den synoptischen Menschensohnworten Jesu* (BWANT 119; Stuttgart, 1986). See also M. Müller, *Der Ausdruck "Menschensohn" in den Evangelien: Voraussetzungen und Bedeutung* (Acta Theologica Danica 17; Leiden, 1984) and "The Expression 'the Son of Man' as Used by Jesus," *ST* 38 (1984) 47–64. The earlier stages of the debate were carried on by H. Lietzmann, J. Wellhausen, A. Meyer, N. Schmidt, N. Messel, R. H. Charles, G. Dalman, and P. Fiebig over a fifteen-year period around the beginning of this century. For a bibliography and a review of that discussion, see E. Sjöberg, *Der Menschensohn im äthiopischen Henochbuch* (Lund, 1946), pp. 40–60 and his "בן אדם and בר אנש im Hebräischen und Aramäischen," *Acta Orientalia* 21 (1950) 57–65, 91–107.

In subsequent discussion Casey has continued to argue for a more generic use of the idiom inclusive of all men, including the speaker. See his "The Jackals and the Son of Man (Mt 8.20, par. Luke 9.58)," *JSNT* 23 (1985) 3–22. Lindars has resisted Richard Bauckham's suggestion ("The Son of Man: 'A Man in My Position' or 'Someone'?" *JSNT* 23 [1985] 23–33) that the idiom was more likely used indefinitely to refer to "someone" with whom the speaker could more appropriately identify himself and which usage would better fit a number of Jesus' sayings. The phrase, Lindars argues, was used emphatically with the generic article in such a way as to allow

sistent that by recognizing and trying to recreate the Aramaic origins of many Gospel sayings, we can often find their earlier meaning.[9] Lindars has nuanced the understanding of the use of the idiom with the "generic article" by maintaining that it was not a means of making a general statement in which the speaker included himself, nor an exclusive self-reference, but a form making "idiomatic use of reference to a class of persons with whom he identified himself"[10]—"a man in my position" or "a man such as I." It was a way of making a self-reference, often obliquely and sometimes as a way of defending oneself. At times there is a certain irony intended in its use and a measure of deference.

It is a strength of this thesis that it seeks to explain the remarkable fact that the Son of Man phrase/reference is used only by Jesus and never confessionally by the churches. Because it was remembered as a distinctive form of Jesus' speech, the developing tradition continued to put it only on the lips of Jesus. The turning point came with the translation of the tradition into Greek, thus losing any sense of the idiom and giving the phrase a peculiar status in Greek. ". . . [T]he translation of the sayings in Greek had a catalytic effect on the development of Christology."[11] The phrase became an exclusive self-reference and later became linked with Dan 7:13–14 in the process of viewing Jesus as an exalted, heavenly figure.

Lindars goes on to seek a setting-in-life for many of the Son of Man logia. A number of the sayings which refer to the Son of Man on earth and even some of the logia about suffering likely go back to Jesus' use of the idiom. Other sayings are interpreted as part of the developing tradition.

Although Lindars, Casey, and Schwarz also do not see the need to posit a Son of Man conception which existed in Judaism prior to the Gospels, they, of course, diverge widely from those who view Dan 7:13 and a Christian pesher usage as the source of the Son of Man teaching. The two camps almost wholly invert the order in which they see the sayings being formed.

Those who favor an origin of the Son of Man tradition in sayings about exaltation and eschatology are joined by others who have raised various criticisms of the idiomatic periphrasis thesis. Even granted the coinage of the idiom at the time of Jesus in Palestine, they ask whether some of the very Son of Man sayings on which Lindars and others most rest their case make good sense as having reference to a class of human beings of whom Jesus would have been one. Is there not a sense of distinctive status to "the son of man has authority on earth to forgive sins" (Mk 2:10, par. Mt 9:6, Lk 5:24)

reference to the speaker as one of a class of persons. See Lindars, "Response to Richard Bauckham: The Idiomatic Use of Bar Enasha," *JSNT* 23 (1985) 35–41.

9. See his *Und Jesus Sprach* (BWANT 118; Stuttgart, 1985).

10. Lindars, *Son of Man*, pp. 23–24

11. Ibid., p. 26.

and "For John came neither eating nor drinking, and they say, 'He has a demon'; the son of man came eating and drinking, and they say, 'Behold, a glutton and a drunkard, a friend of tax collectors and sinners!'" (Mt 11:16–19, par. Lk 7:33–34)? Indeed, in the latter case what would be the point of contrast between the man John and a class of men among whom Jesus includes himself? Even in what appears to be the most obvious case for human lowliness ("the son of man has nowhere to lay his head" in Mt 8:20, par. Lk 9:58), it may well seem that some distinctive situation is being referred to. In the critical saying of Lk 12:8–9 (however it is reconstructed and seen in relation to Mt 10:32–33 and Mk 8:38 with Lk 9:26),[12] it is not easy to view the one who will acknowledge before the angels of God those who acknowledge him as but a member of a class of human beings.[13]

Nor does everyone grant the widespread character of the idiom at the time of Jesus. In a series of articles[14] J. A. Fitzmyer has been the leading critic in this regard, holding that Vermes has been able to produce only one unambiguously circumlocutional usage of the idiom and that "it remains to be shown that this represents a first-century Palestinian usage."[15] Fitzmyer questions whether Vermes' major examples come from the Aramaic of Jesus' time. He points particularly to the lack of the initial aleph in these examples as a sign of lateness.

One must also ask questions about the role of the final aleph. We, of course, cannot be sure that בר (א)נשא was used emphatically in any underlying Aramaic sayings, but the almost invariable definite Greek usage in the Gospels could well suggest that it was, even if (which is not certain) the emphatic and nonemphatic forms could be used interchangeably in the Aramaic of Jesus' time. It has reasonably been suggested that this consistent use of the noun with a definite article may indicate a special emphasis; i.e., not just any son of man but *the* Son of Man whom hearers are expected to regard in a significant manner.[16]

---

12. See Lindars, *Son of Man*, pp. 48–58 and below pp. 143–44.

13. See also the critique of the interpretation of Lk 12:8–9 as using the בר (א)נש(א) idiom by M. Black, "Aramaic Barnāshā and the Son of Man," *ExpT* 95 (1984) 200–6 and the response by M. Casey to this and Black's other criticisms in "Aramaic Idiom and Son of Man Sayings," *ExpT* 96 (1985) 233–37.

14. J. A. Fitzmyer, "The Contribution of Qumran Aramaic to the Study of the New Testament," *NTS* 20 (1973–74) 382–407; "Methodology in the Study of the Aramaic Substratum of Jesus' Sayings in the New Testament," in *Jésus aux origines de la christologie*, ed. J. Dupont (BETL 40; Gembloux, 1975), pp. 73–102. Both these essays (the latter revised as "The Aramaic Background of the New Testament") are in his *A Wandering Aramean: Collected Aramaic Essays* (SBLMS 25; Missoula, 1979), pp. 85–113 and 1–27 respectively, as is "The New Testament Background Philologically Considered," pp. 143–60. Also "Another View of the Son of Man Debate," *JSNT* 4 (1979) 56–68.

15. Fitzmyer, *Wandering Aramean*, p. 153.

16. C. F. D. Moule suggests that the insistent use of the Greek articles indicates a demonstrative force ("that Son of Man" referring to Dan 7:13) and that the underlying Aramaic used some demonstrative form as do the Syriac translations of the Gospels and the Similitudes of Enoch.

It would be somewhat foolish, however, to argue that some form of (א)שׁנ(א) בר could not have been used as a means of circumlocution on occasion. "Man" or "a man" can be employed as a periphrasis for the speaker in a number of languages. In my 1967 response to Vermes' thesis, I suggested an example in English: "A man can't work miracles. What do you expect of me?"[17] The argument, therefore, should not be over whether such a form of periphrasis can occur in Aramaic, but whether it seems to have been current and widespread, and also makes the best sense of the Gospel sayings. In the first respect the evidence seems at least to be scanty, and the case for best sense is highly debatable.

It is an aspect of our "embarrassment" regarding the Son of Man materials that the evidence seems so open to different understandings by the best trained scholars. People who find good measures of consensus on a number of other New Testament issues can differ widely about the Son of Man. What for one group is early and Aramaic is for another late and formed in a Greek-speaking milieu, and vice versa. For some it is eschatology and then reflection on the resurrection and exaltation of Jesus which gave birth to the Son of Man tradition. For others this stage came relatively late in the development.

In these circumstances it is understandable that scholarship might want to minimize or even partially overlook the problem. In some discussions of Jesus and the Gospels it could be hard for an outsider to recognize the importance that the Son of Man phrase has in the Gospels.[18] One way of dealing with the problem as far as the historical Jesus is concerned is, of course, to locate the formation of all Son of Man sayings in the churches, and one must wonder if there is not today a bias in that direction in order to help deal with the "embarrassment." Scholarship is still obligated, however, to find convincing life-settings for the origin and development of the Son of Man tradition in early Christianity (remembering that the evangelists' redactional use of materials does not always also explain their origin), and clearly no consensus has emerged in this regard.[19]

"Neglected Features in the Problem of 'the Son of Man' in *Neues Testament und Kirche*, ed J. Gnilka (Freiburg, 1974), pp. 413–28 and *The Origin of Christology* (Cambridge, 1977), pp. 11–16.

17. Borsch, *SMMH*, p. 23, n. 4.

18. In a recent popular article on Jesus, researched through conversation with and the reading of a number of contemporary New Testament scholars and theologians, Cullen Murphy speaks only once of the some seventy occasions in which Jesus refers to himself as "'the Son of Man,' a designation that appears to be somehow mystical and significant." *The Atlantic Monthly* (December 1986) 37–58.

19. Walker offers the suggestion that "the Son of Man Christology originated, flourished, and, for the most part, died within what can be called the 'Q Community'," *CBQ* (1983) 607. This has the virtue of some specificity but places the origin and development in a hypothetical community about which little is really known despite all the research on the subject. It also seems

One can appreciate, therefore, why some scholars would want to stand back and look at the totality of the tradition again. While it is not hard to find reasons for relegating various sayings and particular parts of the tradition to later church creativity, might it not be that where there is so much smoke there once was a fire—that there is something deeper in the tradition that has caused this rather widespread phenomenon? It at least continues to be remarkable that the phrase is, for all intents and purposes, confined to use by Jesus. It remains surprising that what has touched, if not profoundly colored, many strands of Gospel tradition has had no clearly evident effect on other New Testament writers. By the two toughest standards of "authenticity" with respect to the traditions (dissimilarity and multiple attestation), the Son of Man usage has much better than a prima facie case for being taken seriously. Those who hold that a Son of Man conception was not current in Judaism recognize its dissimilarity from Jewish thinking. Although one can make a circular argument that the Gospels themselves are evidence for its currency among early Christians, there continues to be virtually no evidence outside the Gospels that this was so.

With respect to the criterion of multiple attestation, the phrase is found in Mark, in so-called Q as well as special Lucan and special Matthean material, and in John. It is in miracle and pronouncement stories, in strands of parabolic tradition, and in the passion narratives. In a number of different settings in the Gospels it is found in various kinds of sayings, wisdom logia, prophecies, and judgment pronouncements.

Joachim Jeremias argued that, where there were parallel sayings in which one version had a form of the first person pronoun and another the Son of Man, the latter were secondary.[20] This was an indication that use of the designation was in the process of development. I have countered that the evidence points the other way round.[21] Others, assessing our arguments, have judged that the evidence is too mixed to draw a directional line.[22] Nonetheless, there is at least some cause in this regard, and also with respect to the criteria for authenticity, for holding that the Gospels are witness to a way of speaking that had been dying out rather than being formulated. Although research into this possibility runs counter to most contemporary critical approaches to the Gospels, it certainly is historically credible in principle. If one does not in every instance hold to the theory of Markan priority, the evidence might be seen as even stronger in this regard.

Chrys Caragounis and Seyoon Kim are among recent scholars who have

---

somewhat in conflict with his apparent acceptance of the suggestion (p. 603) "that the Son of Man christology appeared relatively late in the exegetical tradition of the early church."

20. J. Jeremias, "Die älteste Schichte der Menschensohn-Logien," ZNW 58 (1967) 159–72.

21. Borsch, *The Christian and Gnostic Son of Man* (SBT 2nd series 14; London, 1970), pp. 1–28.

argued for the authenticity of a large number of the Son of Man sayings.[23] They obviously believe that others have been too quick to dismiss the understanding that there was a known conception of a Son of Man in Judaism at the time of Jesus. The Similitudes of Enoch, 4 Ezra 13, other later Jewish materials,[24] and the various strands in the Gospels themselves[25] (perhaps along with Rev 1:13, 14:14) are sufficient evidence, they argue, not necessarily for a definitive titular figure, but for a powerful symbolic image.[26] This likely derives from, or is at least closely allied to Dan 7:13–14, and has affected several Jewish groups of the time in somewhat different ways.

Some twenty years ago I was similarly impressed by indications that some form of Son of Man ideology had strongly influenced the most formative stages of the Gospel traditions. I did not find, however, that the sufficient cause of this flowed from the Danielic symbolic figure. That seemed only a part of the traditions. If the variegated conception that is found in the Gospels is not largely a later creation by the churches, then one might surmise that the initial impetus was itself more complex. Moreover, there were other materials in the Gospels which had never seemed to me to be satisfactorily explained as creations by the later churches in their entirety. I looked particularly at the baptism, temptation, and transfiguration narratives which seemed to bear elements not fully understood by their church users.[27]

Looking for a fresh approach, I suggested that the setting-in-life for several of these strands of tradition was a baptizing sectarianism in the Palestine of Jesus' time. I was particularly intrigued by signs that somewhat later forms of this sectarianism spoke of the Son of Man, along with the possibility that aspects of this sectarian belief (but not practice) were preserved in gnostic traditions. While use of the Son of Man designation practically disappears among other Christians, it is found in use by over a dozen gnostic and Christian gnostic-influenced groups.[28] A common concern in important strands of the baptizing sectarianism and of later gnostic materials was an interest in Adamic lore—associated with a more general conception with a long and varied history, of the first man as a royal figure.[29]

22. Higgins, *Son of Man in the Teaching of Jesus*, p. 116.

23. C. C. Caragounis, *The Son of Man: Vision and Interpretation* (WUNT 38; Tübingen, 1986) and Kim, "Son of Man as the Son of God."

24. For a review and analysis of these materials with bibliographies, see Caragounis, *Son of Man*, pp. 35–144.

25. Colpe, *TWNT*, vol. 8, pp. 429–61 deals with the synoptic sayings as a fourth source for the Son of Man conception.

26. It is interesting that Perrin became willing to speak of the Son of Man figure as "an ancestral symbol" capable of exerting evocative power, *Modern Pilgrimage*, pp. 36–40.

27. See *SMMH*, esp. pp. 365–89.

28. See Borsch, *Christian and Gnostic Son of Man*, pp. 58–129.

29. A number of scholars would agree with R. Kearns that the Son of Man conception in Daniel 7 goes back to Canaanite lore, but without necessarily accepting his derivation of בר נשא

It was and is novel to consider the possibility that Jesus may have been allied with a cultic practice—of which most of the clear indications would have died out by the time the Gospel traditions were given shape. Such an idea is probably not at first congenial to many Christians and does not fit easily with the dominant picture of the historical Jesus that critical scholarship has delineated nor with its theories of development. Worse for the case is the fact that our knowledge of the baptizing sectarian movements is sketchy and usually secondary. But that, of course, is also the case with much of our first-century evidence, and it was within this sectarian setting that I attempted to understand many aspects of the Son of Man traditions and what I held to be allied materials. I was particularly interested in showing how the apparently disjunctive conception of an earthly but heavenly Son of Man—one who suffered and was vindicated—could have a life-setting in relation to ritual practice.

By analogy with the hard sciences, one might wish that there were new experiments that could be devised—perhaps even new evidence that could be uncovered—which would lead to some more certain and agreed solutions to the Son of Man problem and overcome this embarrassment for New Testament scholarship. It is not inconceivable, however, that the problem will remain, with the evidence continuing to yield only several possible if conflicting scenarios. Recent studies have asked whether the problem is insoluble,[30] and other reviews of the issue have been silent or very tentative about suggesting ways forward.[31]

Yet clearly there are avenues which need to be given further study. Here are but a few of them which should be followed.

1. Sociological investigations are certainly worth pursuing. This, of course, begs the question as to which sociological context is to be used as a setting for particular Son of Man sayings—early or late, pre-resurrection or post-resurrection, in Palestine or the diaspora, country or city, along with other possibilities and combinations of them. But there is no reason that several hypotheses cannot be tried, recognizing, too, that the problem may

---

from an ancient, honorific title for Baal or Hadad. See his three-volume *Vorfragen zur Christologie: I. Morphologische und Semasiologische Studie zur Vorgeschichte eines christologischen Hoheitstitels* (1978); II. *Überlieferungsgeschichtliche und Receptionsgeschichtliche Studie zur Vorgeschichte eines christologischen Hoheitstitels* (1980); III. *Religionsgeschichtliche und Traditionsgeschichtliche Studie zur Vorgeschichte eines christologishen Hoheitstitels* (1982) (Tübingen); and his study of the later use, *Das Traditionsgefüge um den Menschensohn: Ursprünglicher Gehalt und älteste Veränderung im Urchristentum* (Tübingen, 1986).

30. So A. J. B. Higgins, "Is the Son of Man Problem Insoluble?" in *Neotestamentica et Semitica: Studies in Honor of Matthew Black*, ed. E. E. Ellis and M. Wilcox (Edinburgh, 1969), pp. 70–87; M. Hooker, "Is the Son of Man Problem Really Insoluble?" in *Text and Interpretation: Studies in the New Testament Presented to Matthew Black*, ed. E. Best and R. McL. Wilson (Cambridge, 1979), pp. 155–68.

31. J. R. Donahue offers several suggestions in "Recent Studies on the Origin of 'Son of Man' in the Gospels," *CBQ* 48 (1986) 484–98.

be compounded by the use of some of the sayings in several settings before they were finally incorporated into Gospels.

Do Son of Man sayings and related materials come from the poor or the relatively well-off, or some group escaping poverty or one being forced into it? Are the communities franchised or disenfranchised? Settled or wandering? Dominant or persecuted? Gerd Theissen has made a useful beginning in this regard. He finds that "many sayings about the attitude of members of the Jesus movement display an unmistakable parallelism to sayings about the Son of Man."[32] There is "a structural homologue between the wandering charismatics and the local communities on the one hand and that of the Son of Man on the other."[33] Both are said to have the experience of being outsiders—because of being persecuted but also, in a more positive sense, by transcending the norms of their environment. Theissen concludes that "all these parallels between sayings about the Son of Man and early Christian wandering charismatics (and community members) cannot be coincidence. Evidently the images of the Son of Man Christology had a significant social function."[34]

2. It would be helpful better to understand the baptizing sectarianism of Palestine at the time of Jesus in sociological and other terms. It is conceivable that later tradition tied Jesus more closely to John the Baptist than was actually the case, but there is good evidence in the narratives and sayings, as well as in geographical and sociological terms, indicating that the Jesus movement was born in relationship to baptizing sectarianism. Are references to the Son of Man in some of the surviving sectarian traditions only the result of Christian influence, or do they betray some parallel ideology?[35] Do references to humiliation and exaltation in cultic baptismal life have any relationship to the scenario about the Son of Man? What connections may there be with an interest in Adam among the sectarians and among later gnostics— Adam as the first man, as a kind of representative humanity, as the one who stood closest to the creation and the secrets of God?[36] What is the significance in this regard of the importance of Seth (son of Adam, son of the first man) to much gnostic thought?[37] Is the second article in the Greek phrase ὁ υἱός τοῦ ἀνθρώπου quite as innocent of significance as is usually assumed?

---

32. G. Theissen, *Sociology of Early Palestinian Christianity* (Philadelphia, 1978), p. 25.
33. Theissen, *Sociology*, p. 26.
34. Ibid., p. 27.
35. See Borsch, *SMMH*, pp. 174–231.
36. See Borsch, *The Christian and Gnostic Son of Man*, pp. 58–121, with reference to the important Apocalypse of Adam and other works. The background of the "Odes of Solomon" also needs much further investigation in this regard. See Borsch, *SMMH*, pp. 188–99, and J. H. Charlesworth, *The Odes of Solomon* (Oxford, 1973) and in *OTP*, vol. 2, pp. 725–71.
37. See *The Rediscovery of Gnosticism: Proceedings of the International Conference on Gnosticism at Yale, New Haven, Connecticut, March 28–31, 1978*; vol. 2 *Sethian Gnosticism*, ed. B. Layton (Sup. *Numen* 41.2; Leiden, 1981); and A. F. J. Klijn, *Seth in Jewish, Christian and Gnostic Literature* (Sup. *NovT* 46; Leiden, 1977).

3. Whether reference to the Son of Man in Christian circles was dying out or being formulated in the roughly two decades between Jesus' death and Paul's correspondence, and whether its usage was confined to certain Palestinian areas or not, it would have been remarkable if Paul knew nothing of it. Is it because it is solely a self-reference of Jesus in the tradition that he makes no mention of it? Does he not employ it because he is aware that it is barbaric in Greek and loses much of its nuance in translation? Does he then, as some have suggested, translate or transpose it into other language? One thinks especially of the "one man" Adam and "one man" Christ contrast in Rom 5:12–21 and the "first man Adam" and "the last Adam," "the second man," and the "man of dust" with "man of heaven" contrast of 1Cor 15:45–49. Adam is viewed as "a type of the one who was to come" (Rom 5:14).[38] The idea of a man below in some relation to a man above seems to have had a foothold in both baptizing sectarianism in Palestine and later gnostic thought. Is it only the result of Pauline or other Christian influence?

Probably of most importance in this regard is the *hymn* in Phil 2:6–11 — usually held to be based on themes that were not originally Christian. The Christ story here, in other words, has been at least partly influenced by a previously extant pattern. On the basis of little or no evidence which can be linked with the dates and locations of early Christian writings, this pattern has been held to be the myth of a descending and then ascending savior figure.[39] There is, however, some evidence for a contemporary Adamic typology and speculation. I and others have argued that the language of Phil 2:6–11 best suits one who is born into circumstances like those of Adam—in "the form (μορφή)[40] of God" and "the likeness of men." But unlike the first Adam, this one does "not count equality with God a thing to be grasped," but rather "empties himself"—is humble and a servant. After humbling comes vindication and exaltation.[41]

Is this pattern of humbling and exaltation in any way related to the humbling and vindication/exaltation of the Son of Man found in several forms in the Gospels' traditions? Can one detect an earlier Aramaic hymn behind

---

38. On these passages and the conception more generally, see R. Scroggs, *The Last Adam: A Study in Pauline Anthropology* (Philadelphia, 1966); also Colpe, *TWNT*, vol. 8, pp. 470–72, U. Wilckens, "Christus, der 'letzte Adam,' und der Menschensohn. Theologische überlegungen zum überlieferungsgeschichtlichen Problem der paulinischen Adam-Christus-Antithese," in *Jesus und der Menschensohn: für Anton Vögtle*, ed. R. Pesch and R. Schnackenburg (Freiburg, 1975), pp. 387–403, and R. P. Martin, *Carmen Christi: Philippians 2:5–11 in Recent Interpretation and in the Setting of Early Christian Worship*, rev. ed. (Grand Rapids, 1983).

39. E.g., F. W. Beare, *A Commentary on the Epistle to the Philippians* (New York, 1959), p. 75. ". . . probably of Iranian origin."

40. It is argued that there is no reference to the creation story (Gen 1:26–27) here, since μορφή is used instead of εἰκών, but see Borsch, *SMMH*, p. 251, n. 3.

41. Borsch, *SMMH*, pp. 250–56. For a critique of the Adamic interpretation, see C. A. Wanamaker, "Philippians 2:6–11: Son of God or Adamic Christology?" *NTS* 33 (1987) 179–93.

Paul's words?[42] Does the "as [a] man" (ὡς ἄνθρωπος) of vs. 8 have any connection with the "as a son of man" background?

If none of these references has any genuine association with Son of Man themes in the Gospels, the issue remains even more remarkable. Why does Paul make no reference to a designation/description which must have then been playing a significant role in the developing traditions behind the Gospels?

4. There is a growing consensus among those who work most closely with 1 Enoch that the Similitudes are fully Jewish and were probably written before 100 or quite possibly before 70 C.E.[43] But even if this material was composed after the Gospel traditions had been shaped, it is probably evidence for non-Christian reflection on the figure from Dan 7:13–14 that goes back to the time of Jesus. Attempts to minimize its significance on the grounds that "that Son of Man" is not titular in 1 Enoch but is a way of referring to Daniel's hero are not very telling because the designation may well have been used in a more descriptive and nontitular way in earlier Christian settings as well.[44] It is in this sense that whatever the Ethiopic demonstrative is translating and the definite use of the phrase in the Gospels may bear some relation to each other; i.e., they may be making reference to the/that Son of Man-like one.

We may now ask about the sociological background of the Similitudes and how the writing relates to various Christian settings. Is the strong association of the Son of Man with messianic attributes and titles in 1 Enoch 37–71 a formulation of this work or a sign of a more widespread phenomenon?[45] To which strands of New Testament Son of Man sayings (e.g., the Matthean) is the language and imagery of 1 Enoch 37–71 more closely related and what does this tell us about provenance and sources? Some time ago, for example, I pointed out that the three key phrases in Mk 14:62 (which Perrin saw as a result of Christian pesher activity using Dan 7:13; Ps 110:1 and Zech 12:10)[46] are found in the same order (they see—Son of Man—sitting) in 1En 62:5.[47] Is this but a coincidence, the result of the Similitudes or Mark influencing

42. As did E. Lohmeyer, *Kyrios Jesus: Eine Untersuchung zu Phil. 2:5–11* (Heidelberg, 1928).

43. In the course of this symposium, J. H. Charlesworth further reinforced this agreement on the thoroughly Jewish character of 1En 37–71 and its dating in first century C.E. Charlesworth pointed to the discussions of the several SNTS Pseudepigrapha Seminars on the subject. See Charlesworth, *The Old Testament Pseudepigrapha and the New Testament: Prolegomena for the Study of Christian Origins* (SNTS MS54; Cambridge, 1985), pp. 102–10. For more on the contemporary discussion see J. R. Donahue, *CBQ* 48 (1986) 486, n. 8.

44. M. Hooker refers to the designation as a role rather than a title, "Is the Son of Man Problem Really Insoluble?" p. 167.

45. Fitzmyer (*Wandering Aramean*, p. 153) holds that the Son of Man designation has been regarded as messianic only because of its association in 1 Enoch 37–71.

46. See n. 6 above.

47. F. H. Borsch, "Mark xiv.62 and I Enoch lxii.5," *NTS* 14 (1967–68) 565–67.

the other, or is it due to some other factor? Ps 110:1 may be as important to this strand of the Enoch tradition as it is in the New Testament.[48] See also below (p. 144) on the themes of shame, angels, and the role of the Son of Man in the Gospel sayings and in 1 Enoch 37–71. A better understanding of such issues may also help us to determine how Daniel 7 was interpreted in this period and how widespread was its influence.[49]

5. A critical question for Son of Man research pertains to the relationship of synoptic and Johannine traditions.[50] What is, on any explanation, so remarkable about these sets of traditions is that they say many of the same things about the Son of Man in quite distinctive language. In both we hear of a Son of Man who is an earthly and a heavenly figure. In both he is pictured as a judge (so Jn 5:27). Most remarkable in both traditions is the manner in which the passion and vindication predictions are made of the Son of Man—John accomplishing this in terms of his *double entendre* about the "lifting up" (on the cross and in exaltation) of the Son of Man (Jn 3:14; 8:28; 12:34) and the Son of Man's being "glorified" (Jn 12:23–25; 13:31) through passion to exaltation.

In both the synoptic and Johannine Gospels this is what must ($\delta \epsilon \hat{\iota}$) happen—probably implying a sense of scriptural warrant and perhaps eschatological *mustness*. There is no question but that the Fourth Evangelist and his community have put all the traditions he inherited through the wringer of their worldview and Christology. This accounts for much of the distinctive character of his Son of Man logia. But how does one account for these striking parallels?[51]

If on other grounds one holds that John knew one or more of the synoptics by reading or hearing them, or that he was acquainted with earlier aspects of synoptic traditions about the Son of Man when they were fairly well formed, this parallelism is remarkable but explicable and not necessarily important in accounting for earlier ideas about the Son of Man. If, however, one holds that the synoptic and Johannine strands separated at a fairly early stage, then it would seem that there were factors in the early tradition which caused

48. On Ps 110:1 in 1 Enoch 37–41 see Johannes Theisohn, *Der auserwählte Richter Untersuchungen zum traditionsgeschichtlichen Ort der Bilderreden des äthiopischen Henoch* (SUNT 12; Göttingen, 1975), pp. 94–98. In the NT see D. M. Hay, *Glory at the Right Hand: Psalm 110 in Early Christianity* (Nashville, 1973).

49. On the various theories of how Daniel intended the Son of Man to be perceived, see Caragounis, *Son of Man*, pp. 35–81.

50. See F. J. Moloney, *The Johannine Son of Man* (Rome, 1976) and for further bibliography, both favoring and questioning a Johannine dependency on the synoptics in this regard, see R. Maddox, "The Function of the Son of Man in the Gospel of John" in *Reconciliation and Hope: New Testament Essays on Atonement and Eschatology Presented to L. L. Morris on His Sixtieth Birthday*, ed. R. Banks (Grand Rapids, 1974), pp. 186–204.

51. M. Black asks whether the Johannine "the Son of Man must be lifted up" may not be the more primitive and even authentic form parallel to the synoptic passion and resurrection sayings. "The Son of Man Problem in Recent Research and Debate," *BJRL* 45 (1962–63) 305–18. See p. 317.

both strands to tell of a Son of Man judge, somehow both earthly and heavenly, of whom (not of the Son of God, Lord, or Christ!) passion and vindication with exaltation are predicated.[52]

6. On a somewhat broader scale one might describe a persecution-vindication or rejection-exaltation pattern with respect to the Son of Man in the several traditions. This is presented in terms of the Johannine "lifting up" sayings and at several points in the synoptic tradition in addition to the passion predictions. As we have seen, Theissen draws the parallel between the experience of the Son of Man and that of the disciples. The more important passages in this regard are Mt 12:32, par. Lk 12:10; Mt 19:28, 25:31–46; Lk 6:22; 21:36. Are there any links between this scheme and that of the persecution-vindication pattern in Daniel 7 with reference to "one like a Son of Man" (perhaps to be viewed as a representative or corporal figure) and "the saints of the most high"?[53]

7. In a number of studies dealing with the Son of Man, Lk 12:8–9 is a pivotal passage even while it is handled very differently.[54] Tödt viewed it as coming from Jesus and argued for its importance for an understanding of the basis of the Son of Man tradition. The passage, he held, is soteriological rather than christological in character and views the heavenly Son of Man, who is other than Jesus, as a guarantor (more than a judge) of the vindication of the followers of Jesus. The Son of Man becomes "I" in Mt 12:32 (and perhaps in Rev 3:5b as well; "he" in 2Tim 2:12b) because the churches found it difficult to speak of the Son of Man as though another than Jesus.[55]

Lindars, on the other hand, finds the logion of special interest because, together with Mt 12:32–33 and Mk 8:38, par. Lk 9:26, it represents a tradi-

---

52. Further on the Son of Man in the Fourth Gospel, see Borsch, *SMMH*, pp. 257–313. S. Schulz held that the Son of Man sayings and related materials in John's Gospel derived from a special stratum in the tradition having to do with the eschatological Son of Man. *Untersuchungen zur Menschensohn-Christologie im Johannesevangelium; zugleich ein Beitrag zur Methodengeschichte der Auslegung des 4. Evangeliums* (Göttingen, 1957).

53. See Cargounis, *Son of Man*, who argues throughout his book for a close and detailed relationship between the Gospels' Son of Man and the Book of Daniel. He believes that Jesus' view of the Son of Man and kingdom of God are both Danielic in origin.

54. In his seminal essay arguing that Jesus never used the Son of Man designation, P. Vielhauer held that the argument for some degree of authenticity regarding Jesus' use of the phrase hung or fell on Lk 12:8–9. Maintaining that the apparent distinction between Jesus and the Son of Man was the result of the legal function of the church's use of the logion, Vielhauer held that this and all of the Son of Man sayings were church creations. See his "Gottesreich und Menschensohn in der Verkündigung Jesu," in *Festschrift für Gunther Dehn*, ed. W. Schneemelcher (Neukirchen, 1957), pp. 51–79, and "Jesus und der Menschensohn: zur Diskussion mit Heinz Eduard Tödt und Eduard Schweizer," *ZTK* 60 (1963) 133–37. Both essays collected in *Aufsätze zum Neuen Testament* (Munich, 1965), pp. 55–91, 92–140. Lk 12:8–9, in other words, is not distinguishing between Jesus and another, but between the status of Jesus in this age and the Age to Come. See Von Gösta Lindeskog, "Das Rätsel des Menschensohnes," *ST* 22 (1968) 149–75.

55. Tödt, *Son of Man*, pp. 55–60, and, in debate with Vielhauer regarding the saying's authenticity, pp. 339–47.

tion which bifurcated at an early stage. The variation between Son of Man and I, and between sayings with Son of Man (Mk 8:38; Lk 9:26) and without (Lk 12:9), are signs of the בר (א)נש(א) idiom being differently understood and used in translation.[56] The basic logion underlying the several versions is authentic, but Jesus was referring discretely to himself by use of the idiom.

Thus both scholars see the saying as early and formative. Both of them argue for a more primitive form of Lk 12:8–9 which included "Son of Man" in some form in both halves. Otherwise they vary in just about every important understanding.

From differing perspectives agreement might be reached on an early saying which read something like this:

> Everyone who acknowledges me before men (sons of men?) בר (א)נש(א) will also acknowledge before the angels of God; everyone who is ashamed of me before men (sons of men?) בר (א)נש(א) will be ashamed of before the angels of God.

I frankly find it difficult to hear a speaker referring to himself by different means in the same sentence. (Why not use בר (א)נש(א) all around? It could even be substituted for "everyone.") And if one substitutes "a man like me" or "a man in my position" for בר (א)נש(א), the saying does not seem to make good sense. The matter is complicated by Luke's linking of 12:10, another saying in which בר (א)נש(א) may well have been used, but which Marcan tradition seems to have interpreted as "sons of men."

One may notice, too, that the motifs of "shame" and angels at the judgment, along with the picture of the Son of Man as a vindicator of followers, have important roles in 1 Enoch (particularly 61:10; 62:9–12; 63:11: "their faces will be filled with shame before that Son of Man"). Do these parallels not also suggest that the בר (א)נש(א) here is more than an ordinary mortal?

Lk 12:8–9 is a critical passage for anyone trying to understand the Gospels' Son of Man, but there are many others and, evidently, more questions than answers all around. It is clear that there is no consensus solution to the Son of Man problem on the immediate horizon, though one recognizes why it would be convenient to embrace a solution or to try to minimize the issue. But still it stands—a very large rock in the stream of New Testament research—troubling but also making the flow more interesting.

---

56. Lindars, *Jesus Son of Man*, pp. 48–58.

THE MESSIANISM OF THE PARABLES OF ENOCH
Their Date and Contribution to Christological Origins

Since R. H. Charles' two editions of 1 Enoch were published (Oxford, 1893 and 1912), it has been Charles' views of Enochic messianism, in particular the messianism of the Parables, which have dominated discussion of the subject until very recent years. According to Charles, there was only one Messiah in 1 Enoch outside the Parables, the "white bull" at 1En 90:37.[1] The Parables, however, presented, in a series of pre-Christian Jewish visions or apocalypses, a quasi-human transcendental figure, known as the "Son of Man," alias "Elect One," "Righteous One," as well as the "Anointed One" or "Messiah," who was to act as the Vicegerent of God at the Last Judgment.

While not all of Charles' contemporaries agreed with him without question or qualification (few, if any, approved of his adventurous handling of the text at ch. 71, where Enoch is identified with the Son of Man), it was not till the late thirties and early forties that two longer monographs appeared— H. L. Jansen's *Die Henoch Gestalt. Eine vergleichende religionsgeschichtliche Untersuchung* (Oslo, 1939) and Erik Sjöberg's *Der Menschensohn im äthiopischen Henochbuch* (Lund, 1946). Following Jansen, Sjöberg, while in no way challenging the main features of Charles' Son of Man Messiah, sought also, in the fashion of the time, to place the Enoch figure in its religio-historical context by relating the Son of Man to a pre-Danielic *Urmensch* or "heavenly Man" (Bousset, Reitzenstein, Creed, Kraeling). While relating the Son of Man to a possible pre-Danielic tradition, Sjöberg firmly rejected the theory (e.g., of Paul Billerbeck) that there was any connection with Isaiah 53 (ch. 6, "Der leidende Menschensohn?"), at the same time drawing prominent attention to traits in the Enoch Son of Man borrowed or adapted from the traditional Davidide or King Messiah tradition (ch. 7, "Menschensohn und Messias"), "The possibility of a connection between the Son of Man and national hopes is, therefore, to be affirmed without qualification" (p. 145),

---

1. See Black, *1 Enoch*, p. 279f. See p. 146, n. 3.

though these, he argues, have not influenced "the actual picture of the Son of Man" in the Parables.

The subject received a fresh impetus with the discovery of the Dead Sea Scrolls, and from Milik's intimation, in the late fifties, of the absence, in the extant fragments of 1 Enoch from Qumran Cave IV, of any trace of the Parables, followed up by his conclusion that the latter "are probably to be considered the work of a Jew or a Jewish Christian of the first or second century A.D. . . ."[2] In the last three decades there have not only been five new editions of 1 Enoch,[3] which necessarily deal with the Parables and their messianism, but a veritable spate of monographs and articles.[4]

We are confronted, therefore, with an *embarras de choix*, which I have endeavored to solve by dividing this paper into two parts: (1) theological, the messianism of the Parables and its contribution to New Testament Christology, and (2) the dating of the Parables, in which I shall also try to say something about the evidence of the putative influence of the Parables on the Gospel Son of Man traditions. The division is, for those who know the subject, a patently artificial one, made only for convenience of presentation.

THE MESSIANISM OF THE PARABLES

That the Son of Man figure in the Parables has been inspired by Dan 7:13 has never been in doubt:

I saw in the night visions, and behold, with the clouds of heaven
there came one like a son of man,
and he came to the Ancient of Days
and was presented before him.   [RSV]

1En 46:1:

And there I saw One who had a head of days,
And his head was white like wool,
And with him was another whose countenance had the appearance of a man,
And his face was full of graciousness, like one of the angels.

---

2. *Ten Years of Discovery in the Wilderness of Judaea*, trans. J. Strugnell (London, 1959), p. 33.

3. J. Milik, *The Books of Enoch: Aramaic Fragments of Qumran Cave 4*, (Oxford, 1976); M. Knibb, *The Ethiopic Book of Enoch:* A New Edition in the Light of the Aramaic Dead Sea Fragments, 2 vols. (Oxford, 1978); also Knibb in *The Apocryphal Old Testament*, ed. H. F. D. Sparks (Oxford, 1984); E. Isaac in *The Old Testament Pseudepigrapha*, ed. J. H. Charlesworth, vol. 1; S. Uhlig, *Das äthiopische Henochbuch*, *JSHRZ* 5.6 (Gütersloh, 1984); M. Black, *The Book of Enoch or 1 Enoch*, New English Edition, with Commentary and Textual Notes by M. Black in consultation with J. C. VanderKam, with an Appendix on the astronomical Chapters (78–82) by O. Neugebauer (Leiden, 1985).

4. A full bibliography by J. Theisohn (see p. 147), covering the century to 1975, runs to 31 pages, with 17–21 items per page.

There is also a wide consensus of scholarly opinion that, for the author of Daniel, the "one like a son of man" is a symbol or cipher for "the people of the saints of the Most High" of Dan 7:27. But it is at this point that scholars are divided: obviously, in this composite expression, "Israel" in some sense is meant, but in what sense? A comparatively recent interpretation is one proposed by the late Joseph Coppens in his posthumously published *Le Fils d'Homme vétéro- et intertestamentaire* (Leuven, 1982), a study which includes an exhaustive analysis of the term "saints" in the Old Testament and the Dead Sea Scrolls (pp. 69–100). Overwhelmingly, in Hebrew usage in the Old Testament and elsewhere, it refers to "angelic beings," but can also refer to members of the priesthood or to "faithful Israelites." Coppens is not satisfied with the last (or the last two) meanings for Dan 7:27 and comes up with the novel idea that the symbol of the "son of man" is interpreted by Daniel with reference to both the coming reign of angelic beings and of a Jewish people reborn through persecution. Their reign is not in opposition; they are complementary (p. 112).

As I have stated in a review,[5] this idea of a celestial diarchy, however complementary, will satisfy few exegetes; nevertheless, the valuable insight that the "saints of the Most High" may contain a suprahuman dimension need not be lost, once it is recognized, as I have argued,[6] that the faithful Israelites of the regenerated Israel of the Last Days are being envisaged by Daniel, not only as "like a human/humane being" (a meaning stressed by Coppens), but also as those who have undergone a transformation akin to apotheosis; they have become "like the angels." We can rule out altogether any reference to angel-archons; the Kingdom is to be given to the angel-archons of Israel. We have thus, in Daniel itself, before we come to 1 Enoch, both a quasi-human and suprahuman dimension in the one "like a son of man."

In a detailed study of the two main designations of the Messiah in the Parables, the "Elect One" and the "Son of Man," the work of Coppens has been revised by J. Lust, from previous studies of Coppens and by the use of the important monograph of Johannes Theisohn, *Der auserwählte Richter* (SEUNT Göttingen, 1975) to which Coppens had frequently referred. The results are as follows (*Le Fils d'Homme*, p. 133f.):

---

5. *Theologische Revue* 81.2 (1985), 104f.

6. See the Festschrift for Vögtle in *Jesus und der Menschensohn* (Freiburg, 1975), pp. 92–99. This view is not novel. See, e.g., J. Barr on Dan 7:18 and 27 in Peake's *Commentary on the Bible*, ed. M. Black and H. H. Rowley (Edinburgh, 1962) and, more fully, R. H. Charles on Rev 14:14 (*Revelation*): ". . . 'like a man' = 'like an angel,' i.e., a being who is of a supernatural character but not an angel. Thus in Daniel we are to infer that the faithful remnant in Israel are to be transformed into supernatural beings as in 1En 90:38: . . . That this is the meaning of the text is proved by the adjoining clause 'There came with the clouds of heaven.' This clause implies beyond question supernatural authority." See F. Lang (*TDNT*, vol. 6, p. 946): ". . . the appearance of the Son of Man (at Rev. 1:9) is described with attributes from Daniel 7 and 10, whereby attributes of deity are transferred to Jesus."

(1) The entire Book of the Parables is dominated by the vision of the Great Judgment as well as with the deliverance of the elect.

(2) With the Great Judgment in view, the Parables know of two personages called to carry out the role of judge at the side of God, the Lord of Spirits, namely the Elect One and the Son of Man. The Elect One is, without question *le personnage fondamental*, and, consequently, the sections he dominates are no less fundamental and primitive.

(3) The Elect One is essentially a judgment figure, which does not derive from the Book of Daniel, but from a literary tradition completely different. The Son of Man, on the other hand, does depend on Daniel 7:13–14 and does not postulate any pre-Danielic source or *Vorlage*. New features it receives, foreign to the figure in Daniel, proceed principally from the unification[7] of this figure with that of the Elect One.

(4) Three hypotheses have been advanced to account for the presence in the Parables and the alignment (*rapprochement*) of texts relating to the Son of Man and the Elect One: (1) that of the influence of two sources, allowing for two distinct strata of tradition; (2) that of "interpolations," sometimes judged to be Christian; (3) that which Theisohn calls "*assoziative Komposition*," which Coppens takes to mean that "the author of the Parables has, on his own, in the composition of his work, 'coalesced' the two judgment figures," the "Elect-Son of Man" then being called to the role of eschatological judge. The end result is that "one will only have to do in the Parables with a single eschatological figure."[8]

(5) Coppens goes on to develop his own theory of three successive "rereadings" ("relectures") of the Son of Man/Elect One traditions in the Parables. (1) The Elect One tradition, original and fundamental, has been revised, amplified, interpolated to create a first "relecture" (Coppens, perhaps influenced by Theisohn, seems to avoid the words "sources" or "recensions"), identifying the Elect One with the Danielic Son of Man. (2) A second recension, much less ample, identifies the Elect Son of Man with the Anointed One, the Messiah. (3) The third and final recension identifies the Elect Son of Man with Enoch, but this last novel reinterpretation has taken place "outside the Book of the Parables."

That there has been editing and perhaps reediting in the production of the Parables, and distinct and disparate sources, traditions or recensions, is generally acknowledged. And whoever first brought together into the Parables the Elect One and the Son of Man pericopes, as these now appear in

---

7. P. 133, "Les traits nouveaux, étrangers au personnage daniélique, proviennent en ordre principal de la fusion de cette figure avec celle de l'Elu."

8. See Theisohn, *Richter,* p. 203. See also M. D. Hooker, *The Son of Man in Mark* (London, 1967), pp. 43f.

the *mixtum compositum* of this section of 1 Enoch, meant the twin titles (and their related texts) to refer to the one and the same Elect Son of Man. Moreover, the Elect One pericopes may well have provided the original basic document, though this is certainly not "incontestable" (Coppens, p. 134); and the redactional unification of these, in some respects, disparate traditions, probably did take place prior to the final redaction or compilation of the Parables. It is certainly also widely held that chs. 70–71 represent a separate Enoch "ascension" tradition-piece, though on what grounds it can be held to be "outside the Book of the Parables" is by no means apparent.

But do we have to posit an additional "recension" to account for the two applications of the epithet "Anointed One" to the Elect Son of Man (48:10, 52:4)? It clearly comes from the "royal" messianic tradition, which, as Sjöberg emphasized, is also woven, as it were, into the variegated canvas of the Elect Son of Man portrait in the Parables.[9] We have, however, almost certainly to do with a two-tier development of Elect–Son of Man traditions before the Parables assumed their final redactional shape. The further problem of chapters 70–71 is discussed below, p. 165f.

In this revision of his earlier study, it is difficult at times to distinguish what is Coppens' own original contribution from the views of Theisohn. What is common to both is that the Enoch/Son of Man figure is inspired by Daniel 7 (Theisohn also rejects any idea of pre-Danielic "sources"; the Book of Daniel known to the "author" of the Parables is the Book of Daniel in its classic form). Theisohn stresses, particularly, that the Parables reinterpret the Danielic "one like a son of man" by the Elect One tradition, and he shares with Coppens (and other earlier scholars, back through Jansen, Sjöberg, Jeremias, etc., to Charles) in the idea of the "redactional fusion" of the Elect One with the Son of Man.

Since he goes on to elaborate other features of this composite *Menschensohn-auserwählte Richter* Elect Son of Man—the Ebed Jahweh influence,[10] the Wisdom aspect, the royal-messianic strand—Theisohn's Elect Judge (*auserwählte Richter*) title is much too narrow a designation for the composite figure. While it does emphasize a central function of the Elect Son of Man, his judicial role, it tends to overshadow these other, equally important, attributes of the figure, especially the Ebed Jahweh dimension and the influence of the royal-messianic tradition, which relates the transcendental Son of Man to the mainstream royal messianism of Israel. The only full designation would be "the Elect Son of Man Servant Messiah," if it is concluded that, for the final author-editor of the Parables, all these traditional traits related to one and the same person.

Before considering these several (related) aspects of this Elect Son of Man, clarification of the origin and significance of the composite title, in par-

---

9. Above, p. 146 and below, p. 161.
10. See Coppens, *Le Fils d'Homme*, p. 133, n. 22; 1En 48:4 calls for special explication.

ticular for the author or final redactor of the Parables (and for his prospective readers), is an essential introduction.

The origin of the Son of Man title in Daniel need not detain us, nor its original use in the Old Testament as a poetic synonym for "man." As I have argued, it has been used in Daniel as a symbol or cipher for a quasi-angelic Israel ("the people of the saints of the Most High") while at the same time signifying a human kingdom in stark contrast to the bestiality of the brutal regimes it will supersede.[11] "The Elect One" is a noun formation from the Hebrew/Aramaic *ba/eḥir*, "elect/chosen one," used most frequently in the plural, always in combination with "Jahweh," "the elect ones of Jahweh," and applied either to ethnic Israel or to the pious in Israel, and sometimes coupled with the designation of Israel as Jahweh's servant.[12] In addition to the naming of an individual, Jacob at Isa 45:4 (but as head and inclusive representative of Israel, Jacob = Israel), there are three other named individuals in the Old Testament so designated—Moses (Ps 106:23), Saul (2Sam 21:6), and David (Ps 89:3), all of whom, like Jacob, can be regarded in their different ways as representative heads of Israel.

The Elect One and the "elect ones" in the Parables are clearly modeled on the Old Testament use of this (comparatively) rare compound expression to describe Israel and its founder-rulers and kings (Jacob, Moses, Saul, David). It is not only used, however, to describe ethnic Israel, but also as Jahweh's chosen servant at Isa 42:1 it is expressly applied to the Ebed Jahweh, who stands also for Israel, the Israel of the Remnant. The Elect One and the "elect ones" in the Parables are also Israel, the remanent Israel of the post-Danielic age; and what cements the partnership of the Son of Man and the Elect One is, quite clearly, that they are two different ciphers for Israel, the "redeemed Israel," the Remnant.[13]

The Elect Son of Man as Judge, Vindicator/Deliverer

His Enthronement and (Royal) "Sessions" as Transcendental Judge. In a contribution to the W. D. Davies *Festschrift*,[14] I traced the *Traditionsgeschichte* of the throne-vision apocalypses at 1 Enoch 14 and 71 to the Old Testament theophanies at 1Kgs 22:19f. (the vision of Micaiah), Isaiah 6, Ezekiel 1, and Daniel 7. These have been described as *Berufungszenen*, since their main purpose is to provide a theophanic stage, as it were, for the

---

11. Cf. *Le Fils d'Homme*, pp. 108, 111.

12. E.g., 1Chr 16:13; Ps 105:6, 43 and 106:5; Isa 42:1, 43:20, 45:4 ("Jacob my servant," par. "Israel my elect"), and 65:9, 15, 22.

13. In *Studies in the Gospels and Epistles* (Manchester, 1962), p. 140, T. W. Manson draws attention to the remarkable parallelism between "the Elect One" and "the elect ones." The Elect One, like Jacob (Gen 34:30), is a "corporate personality," Head, and inclusive representative of the elect/chosen "Israel." See also J. Coppens, *L'Elu et les Elus dans les Ecritures Saintes et les Ecrits de Qumran*, ETL 57 (1981) 120–24.

14. Black, *1 Enoch*, p. 188.

call and divine commission of the prophets, and in Daniel 7 and 1 Enoch of the "one like a son of man." They all have in common the vision of a celestial Throne, on which, in the Old Testament, Jahweh/the Ancient of Days is seated: at 1 Enoch 14, the "glory of the Great One"; at 1 Enoch 71, the Chief of Days. The pattern is strikingly similar in all of them—a vision of God on his celestial throne, followed by a commissioning of the prophets (Micaiah, Isaiah, Ezekiel, or of Enoch as the Son of Man in the Parables and 1En 71:14) or the transfer to authority to the "one like a son of man" in Dan 7:22.

1 Enoch 14, with its Throne-vision (vs. 18f.) is a classic example where Enoch is transported to the Presence of God, then given his commission to condemn the Watchers.[15] Especially important for the messianism of the Parables is the Throne-vision apocalypse at 1 Enoch 71, which, as I have claimed for Daniel 7,[16] shows the same close literary dependence on 1 Enoch 14–15. "It seems undeniable, as many have noted, that there, as in the earlier vision at ch. 46, the author of the Parables is drawing on Dan 7:9–13, but no less certain is the fact that the author is *modeling this climactic vision on the Throne-vision of chs. 14–15.*"[17]

"And he translated my spirit into the heaven of heavens, and I saw there as it were a structure built of crystals, and between these crystals tongues of living fire . . ." (71:5, trans. Charles). The source is 1En 14:18–22; as Charles comments, "This passage (vv. 18–22) is used by the author of 71:5–8."[18]

What we have is, in fact, another developed Throne-vision apocalypse, but in this case the commissioning of the Prophet Enoch is his designation as "the Man who is born for righteousness":

> And the angel [Michael] came to me and greeted me . . . and said:
> You are the Son of Man who is born for righteousness,
> And righteousness abides upon you . . .
> And all shall walk in your ways . . .

This vision is certainly post-Daniel and could antedate our Gospels. It is a purely Jewish apocalypse with an image of a Son of Man figure which has survived, as Hugo Odeberg pointed out, in the Enoch-Metatron speculations where Enoch is translated to a throne next to the Throne of God him-

---

15. Jude 6 and 2Pet 2:4 (from Jude) are familiar with this Watcher legend, describing the punishment of the Watchers "in eternal chains in the nether gloom until the judgment of the great day." This is a clear reference to 1En 14:5 (the Watchers are to be bound "in bonds in the earth for all the days of eternity"). A detailed comparison of this chapter in Jude and in 2 Peter 2 shows how familiar the whole Watcher legend was to the authors of these epistles—not surprisingly in Jude's case, for he can cite 1En 1:9 virtually as scripture (Jude 14). See my note on 14:5 in *1 Enoch*, pp. 145f., and on Jude and 2 Peter in the *Bible Review* 3 (1987) 23f.

16. *1 Enoch*, pp. 151f.

17. *1 Enoch*, p. 188.

18. *The Book of Enoch*, p. 34.

self (one derivation of *metatron* is *metathronios*, the one seated on the Throne after God), and where he can also be described as "the lesser Yahweh" (יהוה הקטון).[19]

This last Enoch Throne-vision is a typical example of the use made by the author of the "Second Vision" of the "First Vision."[20] Moreover, it may well dispose of the theory, in current circulation, that 1 Enoch 70–71 is a separate piece from outside the Book of Enoch; it seems part and parcel of 1 Enoch. The question of its date is discussed later.[21]

In his thesis, *Der auserwählte Richter,* Johannes Theisohn has traced the tradition history of "the motif of the 'session' of the Elect One on the/his Throne of glory" (p. 68f.) also back to 1Kgs 22:19f., Isaiah 6, Ezekiel 1, and Daniel 7 (p. 83f.). He is not concerned with the Throne-vision of 1 Enoch 14–15 and treats 1 Enoch 70–71 as an extraneous appendix to the Parables outside the terms of reference of his thesis (p. 211, n. 17). The passages in question—45:3; 51:3; 55:4; 61:8; 62:2, 3, 5; 69:27, 29—in fact belong within the same tradition history as the Throne-vision at 1 Enoch 14–15 and 1 Enoch 70–71, falling between 1 Enoch 14–15 in the older book, where it is God who sits on the Throne as Judge and 1 Enoch 70–71, the commissioning of the Patriarch Enoch as Son of Man. The link between the older Enoch eschatology with God as Judge and the Son of Man as "seated on the Throne of glory" as Judge occurs at 1En 47:3, 60:2 in the Parables, where it is the Lord of spirits/Chief of Days who sits upon the Judgment-Throne. In the remaining Throne-visions, it is the Elect Son of Man who now sits on the Throne of Judgment, to be finally identified with the Patriarch Enoch.

As noted, the older eschatology of God as Judge is found in two places only in the Parables—1En 47:3 and 60:2—where, just as in the Old Testament Throne-visions and elsewhere in the Old Testament, especially in his advent for final judgment,[22] and in the older Enoch Book, it is God/the Lord of spirits who occupies His Throne of glory and exercises His judicial role. In the other Throne-vision passages in the Parables, where it is the Elect Son of Man who now sits on the Judgment-Throne, 1En 61:8[23] is of special

---

19. *1 Enoch*, p. 189. Cf. *3 Enoch or the Hebrew Book of Enoch* (Cambridge, 1928), Introduction, p. 63f.

20. For these titles for the Parables and the older Book of Enoch, see Black, *1 Enoch*, p. 193f.

21. See below, p. 165.

22. Pss 50:6, 75:7, 96:13 (1Chr 16:33), Joel 3:12.

23. Theisohn (*Richter*, p. 87) takes 62:2, not 61:8, as his first example of the enthronement of the Elect Son of Man by the Lord of spirits. His text for 62:2, however, is based on a conjecture of Dillman (adopted by Charles), who emended the Ethiopic "received text," which reads, ". . . the Lord of spirits sat on the throne of his glory" (an impossible reading in this context) to "the Lord of spirits seated him (i.e., the Elect One) on the throne of his glory." In my edition (*1 Enoch*, pp. 59, 235), I have replaced this conjecture by a variant reading preserved in the *Liber Nativitatis* 41:59, which I regard as the correct reading, ". . . the Elect One sat on the throne of glory" (Wendt, *Lib. Nat.* 42:52 mistranslates *nabara* as if it read *anbaro*); and this leaves only one passage, 61:8 cited above, where the Elect One is enthroned by the Lord of spirits.

significance, for it is in this apocalypse that a truly remarkable development in the "divine judgment" traditions of Judaism is placed on record: *the Lord of spirits enthrones the Elect Son of Man on the Judgment-Throne.*

> 61.8 And the Lord of spirits placed the Elect One on the Throne of glory,
> And he shall judge all the works of the holy ones in heaven above,
> And in the balance shall their deeds be weighed.

Theisohn (p. 94f.) seeks to trace this unique theologoumenon (to become a christologoumenon in the New Testament) of the Elect Son of Man as eschatological Judge, enthroned as such by the Lord of spirits Himself, to Ps 110:1, or rather to the enthronement imagery which, following a popular exegesis of the Psalm, Theisohn is convinced lies behind this verse in the Parables. (He also finds the Old Testament background of 62:3, the judgment of the kings, at vv. 5–6 of the same Psalm, as well as at Isa 11:4 [p. 98, n. 100; cf. p. 63].)

> The Lord says to my Lord:
> "Sit on my right hand, till I make your enemies your footstool."
> (Psalm 110:1, RSV)

Behind this opening verse in this "royal Psalm," it is suggested, lies the image of the (Davidic) king, taking his place on Jahweh's Throne "on his right hand" and exercising judgment. (The Psalm has been frequently explained as an enthronement psalm for the accession of a king.) The hypothesis is supported by oriental parallels and by 2Chr 9:8 where it is said that Jahweh placed Solomon on his (Jahweh's) throne. (cf. 1Chr 28:5)

This single Old Testament verse from Psalm 110, Theisohn suggests, has provided the conceptual model (*Denkmodell*) for the transference of the formula "sitting on the glorious Throne" applied in the Old Testament to Jahweh, to the Elect Son of Man (p. 98). He goes on to argue that in all the passages where the Elect Son of Man sits in judgment on the glorious throne, the reference is invariably to God's Judgment-Throne; the Elect Son of Man is co-occupant with the Lord of spirits of His glorious Throne.

On his exegesis of Ps 110:1, Theisohn concedes that "it cannot yet be concluded that the passage was only understood in this way" (p. 96), i.e. of the king on Jahweh's right hand on Jahweh's Throne. Nevertheless the hypothesis is an attractive one, and many will find it convincing, associating, as it does, the Elect Son of Man with royal messianic traditions. The next stage in the tradition history of this theologoumenon would then be represented by 1En 62:8 translated above, where God, the Lord of spirits, is presented as installing the Elect Son of Man as eschatological Judge on the "Throne of glory." Perhaps these Elect Son of Man Throne-visions of judgment may be best accounted for as stemming from a midrash on Ps 110:1f., where the Psalmist's "Lord," addressed by "the Lord," i.e. Jahweh, has been identified with "the one like a son of man" of Dan 7:13, reinterpreted (as Theisohn maintains) in the light of the Elect One tradition as Elect Judge.[24] The same figure of speech as at Ps 110:1, of one "at the right hand of God," but without any expressed or implied Throne imagery, is applied at Ps 80:17, most probably to the "king" as Jahweh's "righthand man," a parallel which suggests that the Elect Son of Man as Judge, seated at God's right hand, was envisaged by the apocalyptist as Vicegerent or Plenipotentiary of God in judgment, his authority a delegated authority (Theisohn, p. 236, n. 100).

There is a problem with Theisohn's further claim that in all these Throne-vision passages it is on the Throne of the Lord of spirits the Elect Son of Man is installed and seated. The difficulty is that a number of these passages appear to refer to the Elect Son of Man as seated on his own Throne—e.g. 62:2, 5; 69:27, 29. In these cases Theisohn argues that the third-person-singular suffix in the Ethiopic text simply represents the definite article in the Greek *Vorlage*, so that the reference is in all cases to "*the* (well-known) glorious Throne," the Judgment Throne of God. 1En 51:3, where the best text reads: ". . . the Elect One shall sit on My Throne," i.e. the Lord of the spirits' Throne, might seem conclusive.[25]

The possibility of so construing the third-person-singular suffix in the Ethiopic texts as the definite article in Greek appears first to have been mooted by Sjöberg, only to be rejected as improbable, especially in view of Mt 19:28, 25:31 where the Son of Man is seated 'ἐπὶ θρόνου δόξης αὐτοῦ.[26] In a review of Theisohn,[27] Michael Knibb, while tending to follow Sjöberg, recognizes that the cases where *manbara / sebhatihu* = "the/his throne of glory" referring to the throne of the Son of Man, does pose problems, but thinks an explanation in terms of possession still seems to be a possibility, especially "in view of the New Testament evidence to which Sjöberg refers." Certainly the ambivalence of the Ethiopic third-person suffix remains in all these cases; and if we accept the reading "My Throne" at 51:3 (as Knibb seems to do), the possibility that these suffixes reproduce the Greek definite article remains, translating a Greek text ἐπὶ τοῦ θρόνου τῆς δόξης.

Sjöberg and Theisohn both considered the problem on the assumption that the Ethiopic translated a Greek text such as ἐπὶ τοῦ θρόνου τῆς δόξης, with or without αὐτοῦ. But we have also to ask what the Greek translator may have had before him in a (putatively) Hebrew or Aramaic original, also now a more than defensible assumption, especially for these short Son of

24. For the use of Ps 110:1 in the Gospels, see below, p. 164, n. 57.

25. The "vulgate" text has "his throne." See 55:4 where, in addition to "My Throne" and "the Throne," one manuscript reads "on the right of My glorious Throne." See Black, *1 Enoch*, p. 353.

26. *Der Menschensohn*, p. 64f., n. 14 and p. 65f.

27. *JSS* 21 (1976), 198f.

Man apocalyptic passages. At 51:3 a Hebrew original could be understood either as "my throne" or "his throne," given the orthography of the Hebrew or Aramaic square script at this time, since *waw* or *yodh* are frequently indistinguishable, rendering "his" or "my" respectively.[28] In view, however, of the "conceptual model" behind these Elect Son of Man predictions, Ps 110:1, "The Lord said to my Lord, 'Sit at my right hand . . .,'" it is inherently improbable that the original text was ever construed (except perhaps by a Greek translator) in any other way than as "My glorious Throne" or "*the* glorious throne," denoting the Lord's own glorious Throne.

So far as the Ethiopic textual evidence is concerned, the Theisohn alternative is certainly the more convincing; and the New Testament parallels may well have arisen from a desire to magnify the person of the Christian Son of Man by seating him on his own glorious Throne. This latter possibility would have important implications for the relationship of the Parables to the New Testament in its Elect Son of Man messianism; it would represent a Jewish alternative to the Gospel tradition.

More important than the textual problem, whether a single or a double Throne is involved, is the theological implication of either alternative, that such an elevation of the Elect Son of Man implies an apotheosis. In the Parables he is a transcendental figure, envisioned as seated on a Judgment Throne of God, probably at God's right hand. As a symbol or cipher for Israel, his position is identical with that of the "one like a son of man" in Daniel, the apotheosized "people of the saints of the Most High," i.e. he is a quasi-human transcendental Judge or, more probably, as seated on God's right hand, as the Vicegerent or Plenipotentiary of God at the Great Judgment.

The "Royal" and "Wisdom" Traditions and the Son of Man. At 49:3 and 62:2 the Elect Son of Man is equipped for his role as eschatological Judge with wisdom, insight, understanding, might (49:4, cf. 62:3f.). The motif, and indeed the actual phraseology, are drawn from the prophetic "messianic oracle" at Isa 11:2f., originally and traditionally applied to the scion of the house of David, the Davidide. Chapter 49:3 follows closely on 48:10, where, as we have seen,[29] the designation "Anointed One" (once again only at 52:4) is applied to the Elect Son of Man ("Son of Man" at 48:2, "Elect One" at 52:4). The role of the Elect Son of Man as vindicator is especially emphasized at 62:2 (= Isa 11:4), and of deliverer at 62:8. The use of the same Isaianic oracle at 1QSb 5:20–28, in a passage with remarkably similar phraseology to 62:9 (cf. 46:5f., 62:6), even suggesting a shared tradition, shows that it was

---

28. See Black, *1 Enoch*, p. 214. In Aramaic there is not such ambiguity.
29. Above, pp. 148, 149.

the Royal Anointed One, to whom the Judaism of Qumran applied Isa
11:2f.[30]

> ". . . the mighty kings . . . who rule the earth
> Shall fall down . . . and worship . . . that Son of Man,"

So too at 1QSb 5:27f. ". . . and God has raised thee (the Nasi) up as a sceptre
of rulers, they shall come before thee [and worship thee and all] nations shall
serve thee . . ." Even if the expression "worship" here means no more than
"do obeisance to," it is still to a "royal" personage, seated on a royal throne
the "rulers" do homage. Moreover, the royal role of the Elect Son of Man is
clearly also a development of the Danielic tradition, for its was "to him (the
'one like a son of man') was given dominion and glory and kingdom, that all
peoples, nations, and languages should serve him . . ." (Dan 7:14, RSV).

Much has been made by A. Feuillet[31] of the influence of the Wisdom literature on the portrayal of the Danielic and Enochic Son of Man, but the
assured results of this research, certainly with regard to the Enochic Son of
Man, have been disappointing. In this connection the views of Coppens have
been decisive, certainly as far as Daniel is concerned.[32] Particularly striking
is the parallel of 1En 49:3, 62:2/Isa 11:2f. and Prov 8:12/Isa 11:2f.[33] But while
noting that the Parables do attribute to the Son of Man the *charismata* of the
Spirit described at Isa 11:2 exactly in the same way as Prov 8:12 applies them
to the hypostatized Wisdom,[34] Coppens does not pursue the parallel further,
since he appears, in general, to regard passages such as WisSol 9:4 (". . . give
me wisdom who sits beside thy throne . . .") as purely metaphorical.[35]

Theisohn allows for the possibility of some less limited influence than
Coppens, e.g. the motif of the Son of Man's preexistence may well be traceable to Prov 8:23.[36] More than one tradition stream has certainly contributed
to the composite picture of the Elect Son of Man; and Wisdom tradition,
though less influential than others, has also contributed.

The Elect Son of Man and the Ebed-Jahweh

Before and since the work of Sjöberg,[37] the connection between the Elect
Son of Man and the Ebed-Jahweh has been debated in numerous studies,

---

30. See my *The Scrolls and Christian Origins, Studies in the Jewish Background of the New
Testament* (Edinburgh and New York, 1961); rep. in Brown Judaic Studies 48 (Chico, Calif.,
1984) 151.

31. "Le Fils d'Homme de Daniel et la tradition biblique" in *RB* 60 (1953) 170–202, 321–46.

32. "Le messianism sapiential et les origines littéraires du Fils de l'homme daniélique" in the
H. H. Rowley Festschrift, *Wisdom in Israel and the Ancient Near East* (VT Supp. 3; Leiden,
1955), pp. 33–41.

33. Feuillet, pp. 322, 327; Theisohn, *Richter*, pp. 57f., 137f.

34. Coppens, op. cit., p. 39, n. 4; Theisohn, *Richter*, p. 247, n. 36.

35. Op. cit., p. 36.

36. *Richter*, pp. 131, 141.

37. Above, p. 145.

most notably in a controversial essay of Paul Billerbeck[38] and later in the work of Joachim Jeremias,[39] followed up in recent decades by that of Coppens[40] and Theisohn.[41] To the best of my knowledge, since the latter was published in 1975, no other substantial monograph or study has appeared on the subject.

All of these scholars inevitably call attention to the prominent allusion to the Isaianic Servant at 1En 48:4 as *lux gentium* (Isa 42:6, 49:4), with a possible further allusion in this verse to Isa 61:1 (even if not strictly in the "Servant Songs"),[42] and to a possible background to the title the "Elect One" itself at Isa 42:1 ("Behold my servant . . . mine elect" [*beḥiri*]). The description "the righteous one" (1En 38:2, 3) has also been traced to Isa 53:11.

Theisohn's work offers a critical assessment of that of his predecessors. The influence of the Ebed-Jahweh tradition, e.g. he regards as having been considerably overestimated by Billerbeck; a more realistic assessment is that of Jeremias, who refers to the Ebed-Jahweh tradition as one only among other traditions, which have shaped the eschatological figure of the Parables (Theisohn, p. 118). Theisohn agrees, however, with Sjöberg against Jeremias, in rejecting the idea of a suffering Son of Man (or one "capable of suffering," *leidensfähig*) in the Parables (p. 117).

A detailed comparison by Theisohn of 1En 48:2f—Isa 49:1f., 1En 62:1f.—Isa 49:1f. fully corroborates the fact of the influence of the Isaianic Servant on the figure in the Parables, if not of its extent. While such influence should not be underrated, it is only at Isa 49:1f. that Theisohn considers the evidence to be conclusive (p. 123). Thus (in Theisohn's view) Isa 49:2 "in the shadow of his hand he hid me" is the source of 1 Enoch 48:6 ". . . he (the Son of Man) has been chosen and hidden from everlasting." The motif of his "preexistence" is traced, as we have seen, to Wisdom tradition influence. The relationship of the Elect One to the mighty kings (1En 62:1, Isa 49:7) and to "the elect ones" (1En 48:4f., 62 passim) stems also from the Ebed-Jahweh tradition (p. 124). Finally, the Ebed-Jahweh tradition could have contributed something to the motif of "election" itself, but one cannot derive the designation Elect One exclusively from Isa 49:1f., since the whole idea of "election" is basic in Hebrew thought (p. 124).

Theisohn goes on to seek to define more specifically the "fusion" or

---

38. "Hat die alte Synagoge einen präexistenten Messias gekannt?" in *Nathaniel* 19 (1903) 97–105; 21 (1905) 89–150. See also Strack-Billerbeck, *Kommentar zum Neuen Testament aus Talmud und Midrasch*, vol. 2, p. 282, n. 1.

39. E.g. in *TDNT* 5 (1954) 617–717.

40. *Le Fils d'Homme*, p. 136f. in his second *relecture messianique*, Isa 42:6, 48:4, 49:6, and 61:1.

41. *Richter*, pp. 114–24.

42. See 1QH18.10–15 where Isa 61:1f. becomes a "Servant Song" for the Qumran psalmist (who refers to himself repeatedly as the "servant" of Jahweh and has been identified by several scholars with "the rightful Teacher"). See Lk 4:16f.

"blending" (*Verschmelzung*) of the Elect Judge tradition (*Richtertradition*) with the Ebed-Jahweh tradition, with the following conclusions (p. 124):

(1) The motif of the "concealment" of the Son of Man is unique to the Ebed-Jahweh tradition [Isa 49:2], but now converges with the"Elect Judge" tradition stream.

(2) In the description of the relation of the Elect One to the elect ones, the influence of the Ebed-Jahweh tradition requires nothing more by way of evidence than the specific formulation "Light of the peoples" (*Licht der Völker*). (The relationship is described in the Parables else-where in ways which cannot come from Isaiah 49; here there is an overlapping of the traditions which offered the possibility of "fusion.")

(3) Even more evident is the overlap in the relationship of abasement and obeisance between the "kings and mighty" and the Elect One, a "mo-tif" anchored in the "royal-messianic tradition," though not without variations.

(4) Finally, the idea of "election" itself offers a possibility of "fusion" of Ebed-Jahweh and Elect Son of Man but is too general an idea to pro-vide an adequate basis for specific research.

On (1) it is unlikely that all students of the Parables will agree, but *faute de mieux*, it is a possible, if not probable, explanation of the motif of the Son of Man's "concealment."

On (2) no one has ever questioned the significance of the expression "Light of the Gentiles," in the only verse, 1En 48:4, where it occurs in the Parables (raising the inevitable suspicion that it is a Christian "interpola-tion"):

(a) He shall be a staff to the righteous whereon to stay themselves and not fall,

(b) And he shall be the light of the Gentiles,

(c) And the hope of those who are troubled in their hearts.

The expression "light of the Gentiles" is found at both Isa 42:6 and 49:6, but it is on the latter that it is based (as a kind of midrash), with possibly at line (c), as Coppens suggested, an idea from Isa 61:1.[43] Isa 49:6 reads:

It is not enough for you to be my servant, to restore the tribes of Jacob and bring back the survivors of Israel;
I will make you the light of the nations so that my salvation may reach to the ends of the earth.   (JB)

43. See p. 157, n. 40.

Second Isaiah is concerned to emphasize the Servant's wider role, his terrestrial mission to the nations; his "interpreter" in the Parables is concerned only with what the Son of Man can do for "the righteous," no doubt equated by him with the "elect," in their own way and time "the survivors of Israel." The midrash is faithful to its Isaiah text, but the Son of Man as "the light of the Gentiles" theme is not further developed.[44] The verses that follow at 1En 48:8–10 do develop the theme of Isa 49:7, the abasement and obeisance of the "kings of the earth," but the emphasis again is on the "portion of the righteous" which the Son of Man will preserve, not on Jahweh's "salvation to the ends of the earth," but on the fearful retribution, at the hands of the elect, which awaits "the kings of the earth" (vss. 8–10). At the same time the wider role of the Son of Man as Ebed-Jahweh is there, plainly stated and not only by implication: 48:5, "All who dwell on the earth shall fall down and worship before him . . ."

Thus while 1En 48:4, like 48:7, does certainly define the relation of the Elect One to the "elect" or "righteous," and is also "a verse attributing to the Son of Man a terrestrial mission which no other Son of Man or Elect One passage (in the Parables) attests" (Coppens, p. 137), one must ask how important a role, if any, does the Elect Son of Man play as Ebed Jahweh, *lux gentium*, in the Parables? Is it no more than one among other "motifs" which have shaped the figure in the Parables, but, basically, a subordinate one? Certainly, in Theisohn's view, the Elect Son of Man is Elect Judge and appears to have no other role or function to perform, other than that of eschatological Judge on his Judgment-Throne at the right hand of God. I shall return to this point after considering Theisohn's final conclusion (4).

(3) Theisohn concluded that the "pairing" of the kings with the Son of Man is anchored in the "royal messianic" tradition (Psalm 110).[45] This also must include Isa 11:2f. and perhaps also Psalm 2.[46] The tradition-historical development is from Isa 11:2f., etc., to Isaiah 49 and then to 1En 62:1f. These passages along with Psalm 110, however, may not be the only background and origin of the motif of the triumph and vindication of the Elect Son of Man: Isa 52:13, 53:12 in the Servant Songs also portray the exaltation and triumph of the lowly Servant, simply repeating the central theme of Isa 49:7, the triumph of the Ebed Jahweh over his enemies.[47]

44. Lines (a) and (c) at 1En 48:4 are in synonymous parallelism, but (b) breaks the thought. A more logical order would be (a), (c), (b). While faithful to his Isaianic tradition, one has the impression that the author is not anxious to stress this universal role of his Elect Son of Man as *lux gentium*.

45. Above, p. 156.

46. Theisohn, *Richter*, pp. 58f., 125; cf. M.-A. Chevallier, *L'Esprit et la Messie dans le Bas-Judaisme et le Nouveau Testament* (Paris, 1958), p. 17f.

47. A possibility mooted by Billerbeck and Jeremias, and rejected by Sjöberg (p. 125). See, however, Jeremias in *TDNT*, vol. 5, p. 688 and in *TLZ* 74 (1949) 406.

(4) The rejection of the concept of "election" as too "general" to contribute to the "fusing" of the Ebed Jahweh and Elect Judge traditions is only less surprising than Theisohn's evident reluctance to explore the Old Testament for this basic theme in Hebrew tradition. As I have pointed out,[48] the whole idea of the "elect" of Jahweh, whether applied to an outstanding individual (Moses, David, etc.) or to the elect/chosen people, is the scriptural foundation of the Elect One and the "elect ones" of the Parables. The tradition-historical progression from the purely ethnic ideal ("the chosen people") to the Elect One and elect ones of the Parables begins with the Remnant (1 Isaiah), reappears at the next stage as the Ebed Jahweh, the humiliated but one-day-triumphant "Israel" (2 Isaiah), and finally finds expression in the Danielic "son of Man," "the saints of the Most High."[49]

The last stage in the tradition history of the Elect Son of Man, who is also the Ebed Jahweh, is his role in the Parables, along with the elect/righteous ones he represents.

The fusion of the tradition of the Elect Judge and Ebed Jahweh through the idea of election raises no insurmountable difficulties. Even if the title "Elect One" was not necessarily derived from Isa 42:1 and Isa 49:7 does not expressly mention the judgment of the kings, the idea of judgment is central at Isa 11:3f., another of the fused traditions.

The main problem is to find an answer from the Parables to the question of whether the Ebed Jahweh motif in the composite Figure implies the full Isaianic concept of the rejection, suffering, and death of the Son of Man before his final vindication and exaltation as God's Vicegerent in judgment.

Most exegetes have been content to accept Sjöberg's conclusion that there is no evidence for the idea of a "suffering Son of Man" in the Parables. Certainly there is nothing in any of the Elect One or Son of Man pericopes which explicitly or even implicitly connects the Elect Son of Man with Isaiah 53. But the situation is more complex than this simplistic and clear-cut solution offers; and I have revived the view that at 1 Enoch 47 there is at least an implicit reference to the role of the Isaianic Servant at Isaiah 53.[50] As we have seen, the Elect One as a symbolic figure and elect/righteous ones in the Parables are interchangeable expressions for the redeemed Israel, the familiar oscillation between the One and the Many, in the Hebrew concept of "Israel." (Even though the Elect Son of Man is individualized in the Parables, as the transcendental Head of the elect and their inclusive representative, he still remains a symbol of the eschatological people of God.) What

48. Above, p. 150.
49. Cf. T. W. Manson, *The Teaching of Jesus* (Cambridge, 1951), p. 227.
50. Black, *1 Enoch*, p. 209. The idea goes back several generations, originally to Weisse (who used it in support of his theory of a Christian origin of the Parables), then to Billerbeck and Jeremias. See Sjöberg, p. 129; Colpe, *TDNT*, vol. 8, p. 426, notes the possibility of an *explicit* reference to Isa 53 at 1 Enoch 47:1, 4, but considers "the blood of the righteous ones" a collective singular for the sufferings of the martyrs and not predicating suffering of the Son of Man.

happens to "the righteous" and the "righteous one" is shared by their representative Head; 47:1 and 4 allude, if not directly then certainly obliquely, to
the destiny and fate of the Elect Son of Man, as Head, representative, and
symbol of the redeemed Israel.

And at that time the prayers of the righteous shall ascend,
And the blood of the righteous one from the earth before the Lord of spirits.

(1En 47:1)

In this connection, it must be admitted, the Elect Son of Man in the Parables, while exhibiting Ebed Jahweh features, nevertheless is given a low
profile; but for readers familiar with the Ebed Jahweh tradition, such a profile would be recognized as present, if only by implication, whenever his role
is explicitly mentioned. Was it for this reason that he was the "Son of Man"
absconditus, revealed only to "the elect" (1En 48:6–7)?

The most significant theological result, however, of the discussion of this
composite Elect Son of Man Messiah in the Parables is the recognition of the
implications of his elevation to a place next to the Lord of spirits, to be seated
as eschatological Judge on a judgment throne. Such an exaltation amounts,
in effect, to *apotheosis*, similar to what I have sought to maintain for "the one
like a son of man" = "the saints of the Most High" in Daniel, except that in
Daniel the "one like a son of man" is a symbol only, a cipher for Israel or the
"redeemed Israel," the Remnant, whereas, the Son of Man in the Parables is
both transcendental Messiah, as well as symbol of the new Israel, the Elect
One as Head of the elect, but also as a cipher for the elect Israel.

He is a composite Figure also in the sense that his portrayal as eschatological Judge in the Parables draws on "royal messianic," "Wisdom," and Ebed
Jahweh traditions, and it is probably from this last tradition that the idea of
his "concealment" by God derives (his "pre-existence" seems best traced to
the Wisdom tradition). He is the *lux gentium* and so, at least by implication,
the instrument of God's salvation to the end of the earth (Isa 49:6).

THE DATING OF THE PARABLES AND THEIR
CONTRIBUTION TO CHRISTOLOGICAL ORIGINS

The most recent critical surveys of the problem of the dating of the Parables are those of Uhlig[51] and Coppens.[52] The dating by Milik,[53] who ascribed
different parts to a Christian authorship in the second and third centuries
C.E., with a final redaction c. 270 C.E., has been generally rejected.[54] Scholars have differed on whether the Parables were a Jewish and pre-Christian

51. S. Uhlig, *Das äthiopische Henochbuch*, p. 574f. See also M. Black, "A Bibliography of 1
Enoch in the Eighties." *JSP* 5 (1989) 6–9.
52. *Le Fils d'Homme*, pp. 148–55.
53. *HTR* 64 (1971) 333–78, *The Books of Enoch*, pp. 4, 58, 91–96. Also see above, p. 146.
54. See Uhlig and Coppens, loc. cit.

or a Jewish/Jewish Christian, but post-Christian composition, uninfluenced or influenced by the New Testament. While one can hardly speak of an *opinio communis* or perhaps even the likelihood of one, views have certainly been hardening in favor of a basically Jewish work, composed around the turn of the millennium, c. first century B.C.E.–first century C.E.

The view to which I have finally committed myself is that "the Parables contain pre-Christian Jewish traditions, Hebrew and/or Aramaic, including some, at any rate, of the Son of Man visions. . . ."[55] As I have noted, however, in commenting on 1En 70:1, one cannot rule out altogether a Christian "editing" of some of these traditions. It is hardly possible, within the limits of this paper, to rehearse the arguments (already, in any case, in print) for and against this position; the problem has been discussed, by myself and many others, and, failing the dramatic discovery of fresh data, will no doubt continue to be hotly debated. There is, however, a case for a reassessment of the evidence for the influence of the Parables, in particular their messianism, on the New Testament, and especially for this colloquy, on the Gospel Son of Man traditions, since it is almost certainly there that we are to look for christological origins.

Such a reassessment is, in my judgment, now imperative in view of the enormous influence, especially on younger scholars, of the radical position taken on this question by C. Colpe, author of the erudite article in the *TDNT*, vol. 8, pp. 400–77, on ὁ υἱὸς τοῦ ἀνθρώπου. If, in the earlier decades of the century, there may well have been a too enthusiastic reception of the messianism of the Parables as the Jewish key to the Son of Man christology of the Gospels, in recent works (e.g. that of Johannes Theisohn), some not uninfluenced by *TDNT* "fundamentalism," there has been a marked tendency in the opposite direction, to "play down" and minimize the relevance and contribution of the Parables to New Testament christology. Certainly, in so far as Colpe's article is concerned, the influence of the Parables on the Gospel Son of Man traditions has been grossly underestimated.

After a characteristic expression of critical opinion that the allusions to Dan 7:13 on the lips of Jesus (e.g. Mk 13:26, 14:62) will prove to be "secondary additions by the primitive community," Colpe writes, "The Son of Man messianism of the Ethiopic Enoch is, in its details, so markedly rarely reflected in the Synoptics, and seems clearly to belong only to a special group, that it yields nothing directly pointing to it as a source of New Testament Son of Man christology" (*TDNT*, vol. 8, p. 429). Where "details" are given later, where an Enochic Son of Man messianism is reflected in the Synoptics, Mt 25:31, with its imagery of "the Son of Man" who will "sit on his glorious Throne," is noted (p. 448), and 1En 45:3, 61:8, 62:2, 69:27, 108:12 compared (p. 448, n. 342). Theisohn adds Mt 19:28 (p. 153), describing such "reflec-

---

55. See *ExpT* 95 (1984) 201 and *The Book of Enoch*, p. 187f.

tions" as "a type of partial influence" in contrast to "a type of full influence," the latter starting from a complete picture of a Jewish Son of Man concept (op. cit., p. 150f.). For Colpe, Mt 25:31 has been "stylized" according to apocalyptic imagery; Theisohn, more precisely, limits the "partial influence" of the Parables' imagery to a stage or stratum in the Matthean redaction at both Mt 19:28 and 25:31 (p. 182).

We may take these two passages as test cases for the nature and extent of the influence of the Parables on the Synoptic Son of Man sayings (Theisohn, p. 152f.). The main question is the source of the expression about the "session" of the Son of Man on his glorious throne. Theisohn considers the possibility that it is traceable to the Son of Man saying at Mk 14:62 or to New Testament passages other than Son of Man sayings where the expression occurs (e.g. Lk 1:32, Acts 2:30) and decides that they do not support the hypothesis of an inner–New Testament development; the question of an influence other than a Christian one is justified (p. 158). After a scrutiny of the formula in the Old Testament and later Jewish sources, Theisohn concludes that it is peculiar and individual to the Parables (p. 160 bottom). But one cannot count on literary dependence: the expression is a short one and could have come into Matthew from an oral tradition (p. 161 top). We have to do with "a partial influence."

This is, in itself, a positive and important result, and certainly a step beyond Colpe's "apocalyptic stylization." But how are we to evaluate such a "partial influence" when it has to do with a central "conceptual model" so unique and theologically radical as the idea of "one like a man" seated on a glorious judgment throne, especially if we accept Theisohn's view that it is always God's Judgment Throne on which the Son of Man is seated? Had the expression been, as at 1En 47:3, about the Chief of Days seated on His glorious Throne, there would have been nothing innovative about it; the expression would at once have been traced to the biblical imagery of Jahweh "seated on His Throne" (1Kgs 22:19, Isa 6:1, etc.). But it is the Elect Son of Man in the Parables who sits on God's Judgment Throne, which is said to be "reflected" or "partially influencing" the Matthean passages. So far from being a "reflected detail" or a "partial influence" we have to do with the sum and substance of a whole Jewish Son of Man messianism, based on the "one like a man" at Dan 7:13, individualized and interpreted in the Parables as an eschatological judge. It is an idea found nowhere else in the Old Testament or Jewish traditions examined by Theisohn until we come to the New Testament. And if Theisohn is right in maintaining that the Parables' imagery is of the session of the Elect Son of Man on the Lord's "glorious Throne," then we have a significant development at Mt 19:28, 25:31, where the Son of Man sits on his own "glorious Throne."

Theisohn seeks to confine this so-called "partial influence" of the Parables to these two passages in St. Matthew's Gospel, coming from a stage in Matthean redaction. And it is true that Mt 19:28 and 25:31 are the only Son of

Man sayings in the Gospels which employ the imagery of the "session" of the
Son of Man on his glorious throne. The more frequent image is of the "coming" of the Son of Man (Mk 8:38, Mt 16:27; cf. 1En 51:5, 69:29). But the
imagery of the "session" of the Son of Man, "seated at God's right hand," does
occur in another saying, parallel, in this respect, to Mt 19:28, 25:31—
namely at Mk 14:62, where the imagery also comes from Ps 110:1.

As we have seen, Ps 110:1f. are key verses in the development of the
messianism of the Parables. As Theisohn has shown, it provided the "conceptual model" (Jahweh's "enthronization" of the Israelite monarch) for the
transference in the Parables of the formula "sitting on his Throne" (of judgment) by Jahweh to the "session" of the Elect Son of Man on this Throne (p.
98). Theisohn draws attention to Mk 14:62, where Ps 110:1 is also a constitutive messianic element, but he is mainly concerned to show that it did not
contribute anything to the use of imagery at Mt 19:38, 25:31. What has, however, surprisingly gone unnoted by Theisohn is that, while the expression
"seated on his glorious Throne" at Mt 19:38, 25:31 and "seated at the right
hand of the Power" at Mk 14:62 are formally different, *the imagery is conceptually identical:* both verses are referring to the exaltation or elevation to
(royal) status—an eschatological Judge *beside* the Lord of spirits—of the Son
of Man. Should Mk 14:62 not then also be a case of "partial influence?"

The Son of Man as eschatological Judge is a basic element, a fundamental
tenet, of the messianism of the Parables: it is no less basic in the christology
shared by Mark and Matthew's special source tradition. Mk 14:62 probably
represents the oldest stratum of such a tradition[56] (or is there a Son of Man
christology implicit at Mk 12:35f.?[57]); Mt 19:28, 25:31 probably exemplifies
the youngest. Within this tradition history we need to fit passages such as
Mk 13:26, Lk 18:8 and 21:36, etc.,[58] which speak of the coming of the Son of
Man to judge the world.

When these Gospel Son of Man sayings are set down side by side with
their parallels in the Parables, there are two possible alternative explanations only: either, as has been argued, the Parables have been directly influenced by the Gospel Son of Man sayings, or, that the latter derive their Son
of Man messianism from the sayings in the Parables. It is true that there are
no direct verbal quotations from the Parables in the Gospels; and if the criterion is adopted which requires a "Son of Man saying specific to the Par-

56. In the use of "the Power" as a surrogate for God, Mk 14:62 shows traces of Palestinian
Aramaic origin. Cf. *ExpT* 95 (1984) 204f. and n. 23.

57. Cf. above, p. 154, n. 24. Was there a messianic midrash on Ps 110:1 in circulation at the
time of Jesus (and known to him), identifying the psalmist's "Lord" with the apocalyptic Son of
Man, and to which Jesus is cryptically referring in this Markan episode? Theisohn has one reference to Mk 12:36 as alluding to Ps 110:1 but no discussion of it.

58. Among passages judged by Jeremias (*ZNW* 58 [1967] 171f.) as representing an early stage
in the Son of Man sayings traditions.

ables" to prove literary dependence (Theisohn, p. 153 and n. 4 on p. 251), then "partial influence" may be a possible explanation, provided it is recognized that a whole New Testament christology—the session of the Son of Man at the right hand of God, etc.—is based on the Elect Son of Man messianism of the Parables. On the whole it seems to me more likely that there was a literary deposit, a core of Elect Son of Man sayings, originally in Hebrew, on which the Gospels are drawing than that we have to do only with an oral tradition.

Colpe attributes the most distinctive Jewish feature of the Parables, their closing identification of their Elect Son of Man with the immortalized Patriarch Enoch himself as stemming from the theology of a special Jewish sectarian group.[59] I have already noted that it is widely held that chapters 70–71 represent a separate Enoch "ascension" tradition piece, an extraneous appendix to the Parables or a late Jewish "recension." The dependence of 1En 70–71 on 1En 14–15, as we have noted, tends, however, to support the view of the integrity of the Parables and of chapters 70–71 as the climactic revelation of the Book, a view which has been most recently stated in an article by M. Jaz.[60] The clear link with the cabbalistic speculations about the Metatron-Enoch, suggests, however, a late post-Christian date, though Jaz dates the Parables to the first half of the first century C.E.[61] I myself drew attention to this evidence and have committed myself to the view that these chapters have been "pieced together from the relics of an old tradition of glorification of the immortalized Enoch . . . open to the suspicion that Enoch as Son of Man was an invention of late esoteric cabbalistic Judaism, as a Jewish rival to the Gospel figure."[62]

Since the stimulus of this colloquy has led me to look again at this problem, I feel that the case for regarding these chapters as containing an early Hebrew Enoch–Son of Man tradition has never been fully presented, in particular, the "addition" or "appendix" theory never convincingly refuted. In spite of my late dating in my recent article (and my suspicion about the motivation of this Enoch–Son of Man figure), I still adhere to my view of the integrity of the Parables. The author or final redactor of the Parables may have been a member of a cabbalistic group, of the first or second Christian century, but he may also be reproducing an earlier pre-Christian Enoch–Son of Man tradition.

This may well be speculation, but the fact of Enoch's "elevation" as Son of

---

59. *TDNT*, vol. 8, p. 427. See earlier Sjöberg, *Der Menschensohn*, p. 167, especially n. 50.

60. "Hénoch et le Fils d'homme" in *La revue réformée* 30 (1979) 105–19. See J. Coppens, *Le Fils d'Homme*, p. 152f. For M. Jaz, chapters 70–71 were a late post-Christian Jewish polemic to counter the Christian belief in Jesus as the Son of Man.

61. "Hénoch," p. 119.

62. *ExpT* 95 (1984) 201; cf. *The Book of Enoch*, p. 189.

Man is not: the surprising thing is that no Christian scribe (until R. H. Charles) tampered with the text to remove the *skandalon* of identifying Enoch with the Son of Man.

In modern theological discussion of the problem, that of Colpe has probably exercised the widest influence. While regarding chapters 70–71 as an "appendage" (*TDNT*, vol. 8, p. 426) (Theisohn [p. 234, n. 80 and p. 211, n. 17] excludes consideration of the "addition" altogether from his book), Colpe seeks to do full justice to these chapters as evidence for the theology of a distinctive group, for whom the immortal Patriarch was both hero and founder as well as expected World Judge (*TDNT*, vol. 8, p. 427). The latter expectation certainly constitutes an analogy to the role of Jesus as Son of Man in the early Church, and he refers to the statement of C. K. Barrett: "If there were, in the first century A.D., Jews who believed that it was possible for a man to be exalted to heaven so as to be identified with a supernatural being who was called Son of Man and was to come in glory as judge and saviour, their existence and their belief can hardly fail to be relevant to the study of the Gospels."[63] The relevance, or rather irrelevance, of this "theology"—it is, properly speaking, a distinctive type of transcendental messianism—is, however, dismissed by Colpe in the concluding sentences of a summary of his views on the Son of Man christology. "In what concerns the relationship of Jesus' own person to the figure of the Son of Man, Jesus was neither rabbi nor member of a group reflecting on the founder of his own organisation. A messianic-dogmatic equation of himself with the Son of Man lay just as much beyond his mental horizon as the equation of the Day of the Son of Man with the Reign of God"(*TDNT*, vol. 8, p. 440).

The last sentence quoted makes it perfectly clear that for Colpe, Jesus' own self-designation as υἱὸς τοῦ ἀνθρώπου (*brnš*), when applied to the coming World Judge, also named υἱὸς τοῦ ἀνθρώπου, referred to someone other than Jesus himself—a view which for the generation of Bultmann, Bornkamm, and others has been accepted as New Testament theological dogma. There has, however, been another school of thought, led by Jeremias and others on the European continent, and consistently represented in Anglo-Saxon scholarship, which is prepared to consider that such an equation of his own person with the coming Son of Man World Judge, did not lie beyond the mental horizon of Jesus of Nazareth; and that the equation of the Day of the Son of Man with the consummation of the Reign of God has as much in common as the Danielic symbolic son of man with the Kingdom of God.

Colpe's previous sentence, however, is far from clear. The statement that Jesus was no rabbi is strange coming from a representative of a German exegetical school: Bultmann has a section in his *Jesus/Jesus and the Word* which

63. *The New Testament Background* (SPCK, 1956), p. 255.

is headed "Jesus as Rabbi."[64] The statement was perhaps intended to prepare the way for the last sentence, which questions whether such "rabbinical" speculations, equating himself with the Son of Man, lay beyond Jesus' mental horizon.

Even more enigmatic is the second half of this sentence, but it does appear to be an allusion to the Jewish sectarian group referred to in *TDNT*, vol. 8, p. 427, with Enoch as its hero and founder and expected Son of Man–World Judge. If I have not misunderstood Colpe's intention, he is declaring that Jesus was not a member of such a Jewish sectarian group, allowing himself reflections on the founder Son of Man, Enoch.

If we take seriously the possibility, however, mooted above, that the Son of Man-Enoch, as eschatological Judge, was a known—if, like its later Metatron parallel, esoteric, possibly Essene or North Palestinian—form of early pre-Christian Jewish messianism, then it may well have been known or in circulation among apocalyptic circles of the time of Jesus. As we know from the Synoptics there was a lively expectation in the time of Jesus of a "return" of Elijah, or Jeremiah, or one of the other prophets (Mk 8:28f.), or of one of the "ancients" (Lk 9:8, 19, a word usually applied to the patriarchs). At Lk 9:8 Luke is thinking of the appearing of a "prophet redivivus," whereas Mk 6:15 speaks of "a prophet, like one of the prophets." Jesus himself was prepared to think of the Baptist, not necessarily as *Elijah redivivus*, but as an Elijah-like prophet (Mk 9:9–13). It is by no means inconceivable that the tradition of Enoch as the Son of Man, preserved in the Parables, was also known to Jesus of Nazareth, and similarly interpreted and applied by him to his own role in his mission as a prophet of the coming Kingdom—not in terms of an *Enoch redivivus* Son of Man–Messiah, but as an Enoch-like apocalyptic teacher and prophet, adopting and adapting the classic Enoch tradition to the Son of Man's futuristic role as eschatological Judge, but first to his earthly ministry as the Servant of the Lord.

A not dissimilar line of thought appeared in an essay by the Jewish scholar and theologian Martin Buber, republished in his *Two Types of Faith* (London, 1951). In chapter 10, Buber, while fully aware of the minefield he is entering, allows himself some intriguing remarks on the "self-consciousness" of Jesus and his personal connection with the Jewish faith. Buber is prepared to include in the Judaism of the period belief in an Ebed Jahweh "hidden Messiah" (Isaiah 53, 1En 62:7) which came to be modified by apocalyptic notions and finally to be incorporated into the Danielic and Enochian Son of Man (p. 112). While rejecting the view of Otto that Jesus "lived among the ideas of the Enoch tradition" (p. 113), he accepts as relevant evidence for Jewish messianism the development in the Book of Enoch of the "Messianic

---

64. Cf. *TDNT*, vol. 8, p. 440, n. 194, for a parallel with Enoch, who is both "scribe" and apocalyptic prophet (1En 15:1; cf. 12:3, 91:1).

man": "the 'from the outset hidden' (1 Enoch 62:7) heavenly 'Son of Man' is he who, having come down, will be 'the light of the world' (48:4)."

In an original exegesis of the rare verb at Mk 2:20 par., in the Parable of the Bridegroom, "The day will come when the bridegroom is taken away [ἀπαρθῇ] from them," Buber suggests that "in the Aramaic original the verb which appeared in the Old Testament texts about the removal (of Enoch, Gen 5:24, Elijah, 2Kgs 2:9, and the Ebed Jahweh, Isa 53:8) was obviously used here at Mark 2:20." [65] In an imaginative surmise, Buber suggests further that, in the mind of Jesus, there may have been the thought of his own demise, perhaps like that of Enoch and Elijah, [66] but, as events shaped his destiny, to be "taken away" like the Ebed Jahweh. Buber asks, "Will he be 'taken' like Enoch and Eliah, whom God removed to a special office and bestowed the power for it, the one to a heavenly office as the 'Prince of the Presence' . . . the other to an earthly office as the 'Angel of the Covenant,' the helper in need and herald of the kingship, who had just appeared as John the Baptist and had performed his office? Or must it happen otherwise? It was written of yet another, of the servant of JHVH (Isaiah 53), that he was 'taken' and 'cut off from the land of the living . . .' This too is a removal, a removal also to a particular, especially elevated office: he shall become a light to the nations (42:6, 49:6) . . . ; through his mediation the salvation of God shall rule unto the borders of the earth (49:6)" (Buber, p. 104f.).

Jeremias has perceptively summarized Buber's position: "If we see the connection correctly, Jesus under the influence of the Isaianic concept [of the Servant] has understood himself to be the transmitter (*Träger*) of a hidden messianism" (Buber, p. 107); "The figure of the Servant modified by apocalyptic [through the combination with the Son of Man] has entered 'into the actual life-history' of Jesus" (Buber, p. 113, *TDNT*, vol. 5, p. 717, n. 486).

I find a masterly summary of the vocation of Jesus as Son of Man (as does also Professor C. F. D. Moule of Cambridge) in some words of the late Professor George Caird of Oxford:

> It [the phrase] enabled [Jesus], without actually claiming to be Messiah, to indicate his essential unity with mankind, and above all with the weak and humble, and also his special function as predestined representative of the new Israel and bearer of God's judgment and kingdom. Even when he used it as a title, its strongly corporate overtones made it not merely a title, but an invitation to others to join him in the destiny he had accepted. And when he spoke of the glory of the Son of man he was predicting not so much his own personal victory as the triumph of the cause he served. [67]

---

65. *Two Types of Faith*, p. 104, n. 1. The verb is Πος "to take away (by death)" or "to take up (to heaven)." See P. Grelot in *La Legende d'Hénoch* in *RSR* 46 (1958) 11. Was the verb used in Judaean Aramaic?

66. The only other instance of the verb in the New Testament is at Acts 1:9 (D).

67. Cited by Moule in *The Origin of Christology* (Cambridge, 1977), p. 20.

RIGHTEOUS ONE, MESSIAH, CHOSEN ONE, AND SON OF MAN IN 1 ENOCH 37–71

The Similitudes of Enoch have been the subject of so many studies that it seems unlikely anything new could be said about them and about the messianic designations which appear in them. These chapters have proved to be of special interest to scholars of the NT because in them one meets a "son of man" whose traits resemble, at least in some respects, those which some Gospel texts attribute to the Christian Son of Man. The conclusions which scholars of the Gospels have reached about the son of man in the Similitudes have diverged widely, with some claiming to find in him a crucial precedent for Jesus' use of the term while others have dismissed the Similitudes as either too late or too absurd to have influenced Jesus.[1] In this paper the possible relevance of the Similitudes for NT Christology will be left aside, as will the traditional question whether "son of man" in 1 Enoch is a title. The emphasis here will be on the four messianic terms which play so prominent a role in 1 Enoch 37–71. The paper is divided into three parts: I. The Occurrences of the Four Designations; II. Literary Issues (which affect the interpretation of the terms); and III. The Interrelations and Meanings of the Four Designations.

I. THE OCCURRENCES OF THE FOUR DESIGNATIONS

In the various pictures of the end times in the Similitudes, four terms are used for a leader or leaders: righteous one, anointed one, chosen one, and son of man. The relations which obtain between these epithets will be treated later (part III below), but here the basic facts about their occurrences should be presented. Two of these designations—righteous one (*ṣādeq*) and anointed one (*mas/šiḥ/h*)—the writer uses very infrequently; the other two—chosen one (*x/ḥeruy*) and son of man (*walda sab'*, *'walda be'si*, or

---

1. For brief references to these positions, see M. D. Hooker, *The Son of Man in Mark* (Montreal, 1967), p. 33.

walda 'egʷāla 'emma-ḥeyāw)—dominate the passages which deal with an eschatological figure.[2]

A. The Infrequent Epithets

1. *Righteous One (ṣādeq)*. The adjective, in the singular form and without a modified noun, can be found in at least four passages; but of these one is text-critically dubious and two are probably meant in a collective sense. At 1En 38:2 several MSS read *ṣādeq* in the phrase *wa-soba yāstarē'i ṣādeq ba-gaṣṣomu la-ṣādeqān* (literally: when the righteous one appears before the face of the righteous ones), and this reading is reflected in most translations of the passage. Charles, however, correctly saw in his critical edition that the abstract noun *ṣedq* (righteousness) has superior support among the MSS and is thus the preferred reading from a text-critical standpoint—despite the curious line that results (when righteousness appears before the face of the righteous ones).[3] The two forms of the root *ṣdq* could, of course, easily have been confused by copyists, but the strangeness of the resulting line in the best MSS may have been what led later scribes to emend the noun *ṣedq* to the adjective *ṣādeq*.

The two cases in which *ṣādeq* is undoubtedly the correct reading (there are variants in both passages) and is apparently used in a collective sense are in 1En 47:1,4. The proper interpretation of these verses is particularly important because the word *dama* (blood of) precedes *ṣādeq* both times. If the adjective is being used absolutely as a title, then the righteous one suffers.[4] The context in 1En 47:1, 4 strongly suggests, nevertheless, that these singular adjectives are employed with a collective meaning. In vs. 1 poetically parallel clauses demonstrate the point: *wa-ba-we'etu mawā'el 'argat ṣalota ṣādeqān / wa-dama ṣādeq 'emenna medr qedma 'egzi'a manfasāt* (in those days there ascended the prayer of the righteous ones / and the blood of the righteous [singular] from the earth before the Lord of spirits). Here *ṣādeqān*

---

2. All citations from the Eth. text of 1 Enoch are taken from R. H. Charles, *The Ethiopic Version of the Book of Enoch* (Anecdota oxoniensia; Oxford, 1906). Convenient English translations may be found in Charles, *The Book of Enoch or 1 Enoch* (Oxford, 1912; repr. Jerusalem, 1973); M. A. Knibb, *The Ethiopic Book of Enoch*, vol. 2: *Introduction, Translation and Commentary* (Oxford, 1978); E. Isaac, "1 (Ethiopic Apocalypse of) Enoch" *OTP*, vol. 1; M. Black, *The Book of Enoch or 1 Enoch* (SVTP 7; Leiden, 1985). See also S. Uhlig, *Das äthiopische Henochbuch* (*JSHRZ* 5.6; Gütersloh, 1984). When an English translation is cited in the text, the name of the translator whose rendering is quoted is given between parentheses, unless the present author has given his own translation. All biblical quotations are from the RSV.

3. Charles, *The Ethiopic Version*, p. 77, n. 19. He gives "Righteous One" at this point in his translation and offers only the following in explanation of his changed view: "Though less well attested the former [*ṣādeq*] is preferable." Black (*The Book of Enoch*, pp. 43, 195) thinks that one should read "Righteous One" in both 38:2 and 3; while Uhlig (*Das äthiopische Henochbuch*) reads the abstract noun.

4. For a discussion of this point, see E. Sjöberg, *Der Menschensohn im äthiopischen Henochbuch* (Skrifter Utgivna av kungl. Humanistiska Vetenskapssamfundet i Lund 41; Lund, 1946), pp. 128–30.

and ṣādeq parallel one another and seem to refer to the same group. It should be noted that vs. 2 contains the phrase ba'enta dama ṣādeqān (regarding the blood of the righteous ones) which further supports the collective sense in vs. 1 (see also ṣalotomu la-ṣādeqān [the prayer of the righteous ones] in vs. 2). The same kind of argument holds in vs. 4 where the parallel lines wa-ṣalotomu la-ṣādeqān tasamʿa/wa-damu la-ṣādeq ba-qedma 'egiz'a manfasāt tafaqda (the prayer of the righteous ones was heard / and the blood of the righteous [singular] was required before the Lord of spirits) also indicate that ṣādeq does not refer to an individual.[5]

The single case in which ṣādeq is used absolutely as an epithet of the eschatological leader is in 1En 53:6: wa-'em-dexra-ze yāstare''i sādeq wa-xeruy bēta mešteguba'a zi'ahu. There is some dispute about the meaning of yāstare''i in this passage,[6] but, following G. Beer[7] and Charles, most translators render the verb in a causative sense: "And after this the Righteous and Chosen One will cause the house of his congregation to appear" (Knibb). It is noteworthy that, though this is the only certain occurrence of "righteous one" as a title, it is here used as another designation for the chosen one. Consequently, "righteous one" in the Similitudes never alone refers to the eschatological leader. It is employed for him just once as another way of describing the chosen one. As will be seen below, however, the chosen one/son of man is regularly associated with the attribute of righteousness.

2. *Anointed One (mas/šiḥ/h)*. This familiar title is used only twice in the Similitudes (1En 48:10; 52:4). In the former passage one reads that the kings and the mighty will fall prostrate before the son of man but no one will help them rise because "they have denied the Lord of spirits and his Anointed one" (Black; keḥdewwo la-'egzi'a manfasāt wa-la-mašiḥu). As the commentators have noted, the author here echoes the words of Ps 2:2 where kings and rulers "take counsel together, against the Lord and his anointed." That is, a biblical allusion conditions the use of "anointed one" in this context. In 1 Enoch 52 there is reference to the secrets of heaven and earth, which include several different kinds of mountains. Enoch, upon asking the angel who accompanied him for an explanation of these secret phenomena, learns that they are to serve the authority or dominion (selṭāna; see the Aramaic cognate šolṭān in Dan 7:14, 27) of his anointed (vs. 4). As these are the only two uses of the title in the Similitudes, it is clear that it plays a modest role in the author's thinking and that little can be gleaned about the meaning

---

5. See J. Theisohn, *Der auserwählte Richter* (SUNT 12; Göttingen, 1975), pp. 33–35. Black (*The Book of Enoch*, p. 209), however, believes that there is an "oscillation" between a singular and a group referent in the terms. "In that case we cannot exclude at the same time a deliberate allusion to 'the Righteous One' par excellence of 38.2, 53.6."

6. See Black, *The Book of Enoch*, p. 218.

7. "Das Buch Henoch," *APAT*, vol. 2.

which he attached to it. Some scholars have questioned whether these references are original to the text, but there are no adequate grounds for excising them.[8]

B. The Frequent Designations

1. *Chosen One* (x/ḥeruy). There are fifteen and perhaps sixteen instances in which *xeruy*, an adjectival form, is used as a substantive to designate an eschatological hero. There is also one passage (1En 48:6; 49:4 is possibly a second) in which it is used adjectivally to describe a character who is called by another name. The evidence is presented here with brief indications of the context in which "chosen one" figures.

39:6. Enoch sees in a certain place *xeruya la-ṣedq wa-za-ḥāymānot* (the Chosen One of righteousness and faith).

40:5. Enoch views hosts of angels standing before the Lord and four different figures on the four sides of him. He hears the second of these four "blessing the Chosen One and the chosen who depend on the Lord of Spirits" (Knibb; *ʾenza yebāreko la-xeruy wa-la-xeruyān ʾella sequlān ba-ʾegziʾa manfasāt*).

45:3. After referring to the "day of affliction and distress" (Knibb) in vs. 2, the writer says that "on that day my chosen one will sit on the throne of glory" (*wa-ba-yeʾeti ʿelat yenabber diba manbara sebḥat xeruyeya*). At the end of the same verse some MSS read a second instance of the singular adjective: "and their spirits within them will grow strong when they see my Chosen One and those who appeal to my holy and glorious name" (Knibb). It seems better on text-critical grounds, however, to accept the reading *la-xeruyāna* (plural), rather than either *la-xeruya* or *la-xeruya lita* (the source of Knibb's rendering).[9]

45:4. On the same day as the one mentioned in the preceding verse, the Lord of Spirits "will cause my Chosen One to dwell among them (*ʾanabbero māʾkalomu la-xeruya* [plural in several MSS][10] *ziʾaya*), and I will transform heaven and make it an eternal blessing and light" (Knibb).

48:6. In this verse *xeruy* is quite clearly employed as an adjective to describe the son of man.

49:2. Chapter 49 deals with the wisdom of the chosen one: "for the Cho-

8. Cf. Sjöberg, *Der Menschensohn*, pp. 140–41; Theisohn, *Der auserwählte Richter*, pp. 55–56.

9. See Charles, *The Ethiopic Version*, p. 85, n. 28.

10. Ibid., n. 34.

sen One stands [*'esma xeruy qoma*] before the Lord of Spirits, and his glory (is) for ever and ever" (vs. 2; Knibb).

49:4. It may be that *xeruy* in the statement *'esma xeruy we'etu ba-qedma 'egzi'a manfasāt* (either: for he is chosen before the Lord of spirits; or: for the Chosen One is before the Lord of Spirits) is used as a title, but it is also possible that it is used adjectivally here rather than as a substantive.

51:3. In a context which speaks of the earth and sheol giving up what they had received and of the salvation of the righteous and holy ones, one reads "in those days the Chosen One will sit on his [or: my][11] throne, and all the secrets of wisdom will flow out of the counsel of his mouth" (Knibb).

51:5. It is obvious that the same time as in vs. 3 is meant (note *ba-'emāntu mawā'el* [in those days]), but the writer resorts to a perfect-tense verb with "Chosen One": *xeruy tanše'a* ("the Chosen One will have arisen" [Knibb]).

52:6. In yet another eschatological context it is said that sundry mountains "before the Chosen One will be like wax before the fire" (Knibb; *qedmēhu la-xeruy yekawwenu kama ma'āra gerā ba-qedma 'essāt*).

52:9. Just three verses later, Enoch learns that different metals will be destroyed "when the Chosen One appears before the Lord of Spirits" (Knibb; *soba yāstare'i heruy ba-qedma gaṣṣu la-'egzi'a manāfest*).

53:6. In a passage that was treated under I.A.1 above, the eschatological figure is called both the "righteous one" and the "chosen one."

55:4. The previous verse refers to "the day of distress and pain," while vs. 4 mentions that the mighty kings "will be obliged to watch my Chosen One sit down on the throne of my [or: omit my][12] glory, and judge" (Knibb; *ter'ayewwo hallawakemu la-xeruya zi'aya kama yenabber westa manbara sebhateya* [or *sebhat*] *wa-yek^wēneno*) Azazel and his cohorts.

61:5. The phrase used here is *ba-'elata xeruy* (on the day of the chosen one).

61:8. In preparation for the judgment "the Lord of Spirits set the Chosen One on the throne of his (or: omit his)[13] glory" (Knibb; *wa-'egzi'a manfasāt diba manbara sebhatihu* (or: *sebhat*) *'anbaro la-xeruy*).

61:10. In a list of angelic powers, the author includes the Chosen One.

---

11. Ibid., p. 94, n. 8. Charles read the first-person-singular suffix.
12. Ibid., p. 100, n. 5. Charles preferred the form without a suffix.
13. Ibid., p. 110, n. 18. Charles opted for the suffix-less form.

62:1. The kings and the powerful are ordered to look "if you are able to acknowledge (or: recognize) the Chosen One" (Knibb; *'emma tekelu 'a'meroto la-ḥeruy*).

As the above references show, the epithet "chosen one" appears in all three parables (parable 1 is in chs. 38–44, parable 2 in 45–57, and parable 3 in 58–69), but after 62:1 the author no longer resorts to it. In fact, of the four designations the only one that is found after 62:1 is "son of man."

2. *Son of Man.* This designation, which occurs about as frequently (sixteen times) as "Chosen One," has certainly attracted the largest amount of scholarly attention. Though the reason for the changes is not always clear, the author uses three different expressions for "son of man."[14]

a. *walda sab'*. This phrase surfaces in parable 2 alone and only in a small part of it (1En 46:2, 3, 4; 48:2). The strong influence of the vision in Daniel 7 on these chapters is evident from the fact that the term "head of days"—the near equivalent in the Similitudes for the ancient of days in Dan 7:9, 13, 22—can be found in the immediate context of each use of *walda sab'*. It is worth noting that *walda sab'* is not the rendering in the Eth. version of Dan 7:13 for the "one like a son of man" (see section c. below).

b. *walda be'si*. This expression, too, is met four times (1En 62:5; 69:29 [twice]; and 71:14). The occurrences are in the third parable and in the concluding chapter. In 1En 62:5 the (or: that) son of man is sitting on his glorious throne (*la-zeku walda be'si*[15] *'enza yenabber diba manbara sebḥatihu*). The sight of him there terrifies the kings and the powerful who are punished. 1En 69:29, which uses the phrase twice, is part of a description of the situation which will result after the judgment:

> And from henceforth there shall be nothing corruptible,
> For that Son of Man has appeared (*'esma we'etu walda be'si tare'ya*),
> And has seated himself on the throne of his glory,
> And all evil shall pass away before his face,
> And the word of that Son of Man (*la-we'etu walda be'si*) shall go forth
> And be strong before the Lord of Spirits (Charles).

The final appearance of *walda be'si* is the most controversial: in 1En 71:14, Enoch, as he appears before God himself in the heaven of heavens, is iden-

---

14. The list that follows does not include *walda sab'* in 60:10 where Noah is addressed as "son of man" in a manner reminiscent of the frequent *ben 'ādām* in Ezekiel. See Charles, *The Book of Enoch*, p. 116. For a discussion of the three Ethiopic expressions, see Isaac, "Enoch," 43, n. j; and Black, *The Book of Enoch*, pp. 206–7.

15. A number of MSS read *walda be'sit* (= son of a woman; Charles, *The Ethiopic Version*, p. 112, n. 35). It is possible that this reading was mistakenly introduced under the influence of vs. 4, which speaks of a woman in the pangs of childbirth.

tified with the Son of Man: *'anta we'etu walda be'si za-tawaladka le-ṣedq* (you are the Son of Man, [you] who were born for righteousness).

c. *walda 'egʷāla 'emma-ḥeyāw.* This more elaborate phrase, which is the usual translation of "son of man" in the Eth. Bible—both OT and NT,[16] is the preferred one in the Similitudes because it occurs twice as often as either of the other two phrases for "son of man." The eight occurrences are in 1En 62:7, 9, 14; 63:11; 69:26, 27; 70:1; 71:17. Like the phrase *walda be'si*, it appears in the third parable and in the final section (chs. 70–71). The text of 62:7, which will be discussed in more detail below, speaks of the hiddenness of the son of man and the revelation of him to the chosen. It is set in a context of the final judgment, as is vs. 9 where the term also appears (the kings and mighty fall before him and ask his mercy). 62:14 indicates that after the wicked are judged, the righteous and chosen will live with the son of man forever. 63:11 also brings him into contact with the kings and powerful who feel shame in his judgmental presence. At 69:26–27 those to whom the son of man was revealed rejoice, while the sinners are destroyed by his judicial decree. The final two passages—70:1 and 71:17—are summary statements about the ultimate removal of Enoch (70:1) and about the length of days which the son of man, now identified as Enoch, will enjoy. They form a kind of *inclusio* around the final chapters of the Similitudes which fall outside the three-parable structure of the body of the book.

Hooker and Theisohn have observed that the epithets "chosen one" and "son of man" (in its various formulations) appear in groups or in blocks of text.[17] That is, they are almost never used together. As Hooker presents the pattern it appears thus:

A. 38–45 The Elect One (= Chosen One)
B. 46–48 The Son of Man
C. 49–62:1 The Elect One
D. 62:2–71 The Son of Man

It should be underscored that one must wait until parable 2 to meet the phrase "son of man." The first designation to be used and the only one that figures in all three parables is "chosen one."

It is useful to have these data assembled, but it will be more valuable to study how the author of the Similitudes employs each one, where he found them, and how he transformed older sources in his composition. These issues will be discussed below. Before turning to them, however, it will be necessary to face some literary problems because not all scholars are con-

---

16. See T. W. Manson, "The Son of Man in Daniel, Enoch and the Gospels," *BJRL* 32 (1949–50) 177; C. Colpe, "*ho huios tou anthrōpou*," *TDNT*, vol. 8, p. 424, n. 186.
17. Hooker, *The Son of Man in Mark*, pp. 34–37; Theisohn, *Der auserwählte Richter*, pp. 47–49.

vinced that each of the passages in which the four designations occur belongs to the original form of the Similitudes.

II. LITERARY ISSUES

A. *Introduction*

The text of the Similitudes has not survived in the form in which one would like to have it. Like the other parts of 1 Enoch, it was probably composed in a Semitic language and subsequently translated into Greek. Unlike the other parts of the book, no fragments of either the Semitic original or the Greek translation(s) have survived. Hence one is reduced to working with the Ethiopic rendering which is a granddaughter version of the Similitudes. This fact means that one should make only rather humble claims about details in the text; one simply cannot be sure in many cases what the original may have read.

Nevertheless, the state of the text has not deterred scholars from asking their predictable questions about source divisions, glosses, etc. The Similitudes have, at one time or another, been considered a Christian document (though 71:14 has always been somewhat of an embarrassment for this view), a Jewish text with Christian interpolations (such as the son of man passages), or a Jewish work with Jewish additions (e.g., chs. 70–71).[18] A variation on this last-named position—one associated with the distinguished names of Beer and Charles—was that two principal sources underlie the composition: a "chosen one" source and a "son of man" source.[19] Although contemporary scholars generally find such views inadequate, there remains widespread agreement that at least a few significant sections were added to the Similitudes during their textual history. In the most thorough and in some respects still the most impressive study ever written about 1 Enoch 37–71, Sjöberg listed the following passages as the ones that have often been regarded as secondary:[20]

1. the noachic sections: 39:1–2a; 54:7–55:2; 60; 65–69:25
2. the cosmological sections: 41:3–8; 43–44; 59
3. the wisdom chapter: 42
4. the national messianic sections: 50; 56:5–8; 57
5. the conclusion: chs. 70–71

---

18. For a survey of these older views, see Sjöberg, *Der Menschensohn*, pp. 1–24.

19. Beer, "Das Buch Henoch," 227; Charles, *The Book of Enoch*, pp. 64–65. Sjöberg (*Der Menschensohn*, pp. 24–33) has refuted their source divisions.

20. *Der Menschensohn*, pp. 33–35.

Sjöberg himself argued that several of these were original to the text (41:3–8; 43–44; 50; 56:5–8; 57),[21] but since, with one major exception (no. 5), none of these involves the epithets which are the subject of this paper (on *walda sab'* in 60:10 see above, n. 14) their role in the text will not be examined here. The status of chs. 70–71 is, however, absolutely crucial to one's understanding of the phrase "son of man" and eventually of all the other epithets. For that reason, these two chapters must be treated in more detail.

B. Arguments About the Textual Status of Chs. 70–71

Many scholars today believe that 1 Enoch 70–71 did not form part of the original text of the Similitudes.[22] It is obvious, of course, that they do not fit in the three-parable structure of the book; but then neither does the introductory ch. 37. It would hardly be surprising if an author chose to write an introduction and a conclusion to a composition that otherwise consisted of three major parts. Two specific arguments that one meets in various places are the following: (1) Chs. 70 and 71 are repetitious in themselves; and (2) It is difficult to reconcile the preexistence of the son of man in the Similitudes with the claim of 71:14 that Enoch is the son of man; moreover, in the remainder of the Similitudes (even including ch. 70), Enoch is distinguished from the son of man while in ch. 71 he is identified with him. If Enoch were to be regarded as the son of man throughout the book, he would be seeing himself in visionary form and not recognizing the familiar face.[23]

In response to these arguments, chs. 70–71 should first be analyzed. After this, the difficult problem of preexistence will be examined, and finally it will be asked whether one can harmonize the author's teachings with the idea that Enoch is the son of man throughout the book, though the reader learns of the identification only at the end.

1. An analysis of 1 Enoch 70–71. The charge that these chapters form a double or even a triple epilogue to the Similitudes is based on a failure to understand their structure and their relation to the remainder of the work. A close examination of the text such as the one that Sjöberg devoted to it shows that it is carefully crafted and tightly unified. There are three clearly

---

21. Ibid., 33–34, 140–46.

22. See the related views discussed in ibid., 147–67; and Uhlig, *Das äthiopische Henochbuch*, p. 573 (the chapters appear to him to be a secondary supplement). Black ("The Eschatology of the Similitudes of Enoch," *JTS* 3 [1952] 8; see *The Book of Enoch*, p. 250) reverses the standard proposal by suggesting that chs. 70–71 form the older text from which 37–69 have developed. For his more recent view about this issue, see his paper in the present volume.

23. For arguments of these sorts, see Sjöberg, *Der Menschensohn*, pp. 159–67; U. B. Müller, *Messias und Menschensohn in jüdischen Apokalypsen und in der Offenbarung des Johannes* (StNT 6; Gütersloh, 1972), pp. 54–60; and J. J. Collins, "The Heavenly Representative: The 'Son of Man' in the Similitudes of Enoch," in *Ideal Figures in Ancient Judaism*, ed. G. W. E. Nickelsburg and J. J. Collins (SCS 12; Chico, Calif., 1980), pp. 122–24.

identifiable sections: 70:1–4; 71:1–4; 71:5–16 (17). About them Sjöberg
wrote:

> both stages of the exaltation in ch. 71 connect well with what is pictured in ch.
> 70. There one was told how Enoch was removed to paradise; then in ch. 71 one
> is told how he was exalted to the heavenly world and finally stands before God
> in the highest heaven and is greeted by him as the son of man. Only through
> this does the exaltation appear to have reached the goal mentioned in 70:1:
> Enoch was exalted "to that son of man and to the Lord of the spirits". The
> removal to paradise would not suffice in the same way for this expression. The
> structure of the whole, then, can be understood well: after the introductory,
> summarizing notice, in which Enoch is spoken of in the third person, there
> follows Enoch's own report about the three stages of the exaltation. (my trans-
> lation)[24]

Thus Enoch first enters paradise (70:2–4), then the lower heavens (71:1–4),
and finally the heaven of heavens (71:5–16). 1 En 71:17 is a concluding statement by the author and not a direct continuation of vs. 16. The three major
units are not parallel accounts about the same event but are rather a series of
reports regarding the stages in Enoch's ultimate ascent.

A few points should be added to Sjöberg's perceptive analysis. First, in
70:2 (as in vs. 1) the verb for Enoch's elevation is *tala'āla*. A form of the same
verb appears in Isa 52:13 for the exaltation of the servant[25]—a fact that will
be noted again in part III below. As Sjöberg has seen, the verbs used in 71:1,
5 for the two subsequent phases of Enoch's ascent are forms of *kabata*—the
verb that the Ethiopic Bible employs in Gen 5:24 for God's taking of Enoch
after his 365 years were completed.[26] So, the verbs which describe the experience show a twofold progression in which the second part is broken
down into two stages.

Second, a biographical point about Enoch should be made because it
demonstrates the intimate connection between chs. 37–69 and 70–71. The
author of the Similitudes has furnished several notices which indicate that
he has the entire biblical career of Enoch in mind as he presents the visions
that constitute the book. In the first verse of the Similitudes, 37:1, he provides a reversed genealogy of Enoch which is drawn from Gen 5:1–24. It is
intriguing that two of the names in the genealogy offer a suggestive idea.
Since *walda* is used before each name, one twice reads expressions which in
the original language meant literally "son of man": Enoch is *walda hēnos* (son
of Enosh = son of man) and *walda 'adām* (son of Adam = son of man). It is

---

24. *Der Menschensohn*, p. 164.
25. A. Dillmann, *Lexicon Linguae Aethiopicae* (Leipzig, 1865; repr. New York, 1955, and
Osnabrück, 1970), p. 55. The description in vs. 2 is related to the account of Elijah's ascent in
2Kgs 2:11 (Beer, "Das Buch Henoch," p. 277, n. a; Charles, *The Book of Enoch*, p. 141).
26. Sjöberg, *Der Menschensohn*, p. 161. Dillmann (*Lexicon*, p. 848) listed 1En 12:1; Isa 45:3;
and Heb 11:5 as other verses in which the word is utilized.

not impossible that the writer is indulging in a sort of wordplay which prepares the reader, however obliquely, for Enoch's identification of son of man
in 71:14. After ch. 38, which introduces the first parable and states its theme,
ch. 39 prepares for the vision report itself and describes the circumstances
in Enoch's life when the experience came to him. 1En 39:1–2 state that at
the time of the descent of the watchers from heaven (here called the chosen,
holy children) and their union with human beings, Enoch took "books of zeal
and wrath, and books of disquiet and expulsion" (Charles). In vs. 3 one learns
that in those days "a whirlwind carried me off [mašaṭani] from the earth,
/ And set me down at the end of the heavens" (Charles). Here it is essential
to see that it is not Enoch's final translation to celestial realms with which the
writer is dealing; on the contrary, he is talking about an event within Enoch's
365 years. In fact, all of chs. 37–69 are set in the time before Enoch's ultimate removal from earth—the time when he still has opportunity, following
his visions, to recount his experiences for his contemporaries (see 37:2).

The ancient exegetes of Gen 5:21–24, the Enoch pericope, observed that
there were two places in which the scriptural writer used the words way-
yithallēk ḥănôk 'et hā'ĕlōhîm (vss. 22, 24). They interpreted this to mean that
both during his 365 years (vs. 22) and after them (vs. 24) he sojourned with
the angels (hā'ĕlōhîm was understood to mean "the angels" and the anarthrous 'ĕlōhîm in vs. 24 to refer to God).[27] If one applies this pattern of two
sojourns to the Similitudes, 39:2–3 introduce the occasion during his 365
years when he saw the visions that are related in the three parables (cf. 39:8–
10 in which he sees the place of the righteous—a place where he will be in
the future; 52:1). But this removal of the patriarch would not bring him to
the end of his career. Chs. 70–71 provide the concluding elements: the accounts of Enoch's final, post-365-year translation from the company of mankind. As noted above, the verbs used in 71:1, 5 are forms of the one employed in Gen 5:24 for the deity's taking of Enoch from the earth. These
chapters, therefore, provide the natural conclusion to the description in the
Similitudes of Enoch's entire biblical life.

2. The preexistence of the son of man. Scholars have argued that in the
parables sections of the Similitudes, the son of man is said to be preexistent,
that is, he existed before other creatures, and that this constitutes a fundamental objection to identifying the son of man with the man Enoch as 71:14
does. If the notions of the son of man's preexistence and of Enoch's identity
as the son of man in the Similitudes are irreconcilable, it is highly unlikely
that 71:14 and thus the whole chapter belong to the Similitudes. If the son of
man existed before creation, he is clearly not the same being as Enoch, the

---

27. See D. Dimant, "The Biography of Enoch and the Books of Enoch," *VT* 33 (1983) 14–29;
and J. VanderKam, *Enoch and the Growth of an Apocalyptic Tradition* (CBQ MS 16; Washington, 1984), pp. 30–31. Jub 4:17–25 draws the distinction clearly.

seventh from Adam. So the argument runs.[28] The principal passages that are adduced in this connection are 1En 48:3, 6; 62:7 (cf. also 39:6–7; 40:5; 46:3; and 70:1).

The texts which according to some experts document the son of man's preexistence may be saying much less than is claimed for them. In fact, they may assert no more than that he existed before the revelation of his true identity to others. 1En 48:3 can be dismissed quickly because in itself it does not support the idea that the son of man existed before creation.[29] It says: "And before the sun and the 'signs' were created / Before the stars of the heavens were made, / His name was named before the Lord of spirits" (Black). That is, only the *name* of the son of man was called in the presence of the Lord of spirits prior to creation of the celestial bodies (see Isa 49:1). As T. W. Manson wrote: "The naming of the name of a group or an individual can mean simply the designation of that group or individual to some high destiny. And this seems to me to be the most likely meaning in this passage in Enoch."[30] It appears that somewhat stronger support for the doctrine of preexistence comes from 48:6: "And because of this he was chosen and hidden before him before the world was created, and forever" (Knibb). Here the verb "hidden" may appear to imply more than naming or choosing, and Sjöberg himself has concluded from it that the verse teaches the preexistence of the son of man.[31] This motif of hiddenness is probably related to Isa 49:2 where the servant of the Lord is hidden in the divine hand and concealed in his quiver—that is, he is protected by the Lord.[32] It is difficult to discern precisely what is meant by this concealment, but it is important to notice that in 1En 48:6–7 it is contrasted with the Lord's subsequent act of revealing him to the holy and righteous ones. Perhaps, then, the choosing and hiding refer to no more than premundane election and concealment of his identity.

The sturdiest backing for the teaching of the son of man's preexistence comes from 1En 62:7:

---

28. For treatments of the evidence and arguments, see Sjöberg, *Der Menschensohn*, pp. 83–101; Müller, *Messias und Menschensohn*, pp. 47–51. See also Theisohn, *Der auserwählte Richter*, pp. 128–39, who thinks that there is heavy influence at this point from the wisdom tradition of Proverbs 8. Each of these scholars concludes that 1En 37–71 teaches the preexistence of the son of man.

29. Sjöberg, *Der Menschensohn*, p. 93.

30. "The Son of Man," p. 182. Both Manson (pp. 181–82) and Sjöberg (*Der Menschensohn*, pp. 88–90) point to Mesopotamian statements to the effect that a god or the gods had named monarchs already in the remote past. These claims do not entail that the rulers had existed when the naming occurred. Cf. Jer 1:5.

31. *Der Menschensohn*, pp. 88–90. He maintains that vss. 3, 6, and 7 speak not about a vision of future phenomena but of the present nature of the son of man.

32. See Theisohn, *Der auserwählte Richter*, p. 124.

For from the beginning the Son of Man was hidden,
And the Most High preserved him in the presence of His might,
And revealed him to the elect (Charles).

Here, although it seems that the words "hidden" (*xebu'*) and "preserved [him]" (*'aqabo*) are parallel in meaning and are contrasted with the revelation of him to the elect (as in 48:6–7), it can be argued that "preserved" entails more than "hidden." There must be something existing if it can be preserved. This may indeed be the proper way to read the passage, and it may, then, imply some sort of existence for the son of man before he was revealed to the elect. A problem arises, however, in trying to specify when that time of preexistence was. The phrase which Charles and most others have translated as "from the beginning" (*'em-qedmu* seems to be the best reading)[33] may apply only to the hiddenness of the son of man—the veiling of his actual identity, not to his preservation which is mentioned only in the next poetic line. If it is correctly rendered, then the first line says only what 48:6b has already said: the son of man was hidden from the beginning. The Lord of spirits then preserved him in his power and revealed him to the elect (apparently in the last, critical days). In that case, one might have in 62:7 a terse summary of the son of man's career until the last days: hidden with God from the beginning, preserved by him throughout history, and finally revealed to the elect during the eschaton.

The English word "beginning" may, however, convey more than the author intended. The phrase *'em-qedmu*, which may derive from Micah 5:1 (ET 5:2; cf. also 7:20; Isa 45:21; 46:10), can also mean *tempus praeteritum, prius*,[34] and the setting does suggest that this is its significance here, as Beer, who translated with "vorher," recognized. The context deals with the astonishment of the kings and the powerful when they see the son of man sitting on the throne of glory (vss. 1–6). Then vs. 7 adds as an explanation that before this time he had been revealed only to the elect, not to the ones who are, at the final judgment, amazed at seeing him. 1En 62:7 may not be talking about ultimate origins but only about the time before the kings and mighty see the enthroned son of man (cf. Isa 52:13–15). It seems unlikely, therefore, after a close reading of the verse, that it teaches the precreation existence of the son of man.[35] In this sense one can agree with Manson's declaration about the passages which supposedly teach his preexistence: ". . . they clearly support a doctrine of pre-mundane election both of the Son

---

33. Charles, *The Ethiopic Version*, p. 113, n. 7.

34. Dillmann, *Lexicon*, p. 462. Uhlig (*Das äthiopische Henochbuch*) renders the phrase with "zuvor."

35. Influence from Prov 8 is less noticeable for this verse than for 48:3, 6, despite the material in Theisohn, *Der auserwählte Richter*, pp. 121–23.

of Man and of all the righteous and elect ones. . . . But pre-mundane election does not necessarily involve pre-mundane existence except as a project in the mind of God." [36]

3. *Enoch as the Son of Man.* Is Enoch's identification as the son of man in 71:14 consistent with the teachings of the remainder of the Similitudes? That is, do the Similitudes actually draw a distinction between Enoch and the son of man? There appear to be no other convincing grounds for separating chs. 70–71 from the remainder of the document. Is this question the decisive one? First, it should be recalled that the author may already be hinting at the identification in the genealogy at 37:1. Also, the biography of Enoch would be completed, as noted above, if his climactic ascent were told in chs. 70–71. Moreover, the notion that Enoch was the son of man was an inference that a member of the Enoch circle(s) might have drawn by juxtaposing 1 Enoch 14 (the earlier text) with Daniel 7 (a later document). Both of these chapters were written before the Similitudes, and in 1 Enoch 14 the patriarch appears in a role very much like that of the "one like a son of man" in Daniel 7 (regarding the close connections between the son of man in the Similitudes and ch. 7 of Daniel, see part III below). That is, Enochic tradition in association with Daniel 7 may have suggested the identification to the author of the Similitudes.

It may indeed be the case, as Collins has written, that there are no other examples in apocalyptic literature of a seer having an "auto-vision" but failing to recognize himself.[37] But it hardly follows from this circumstance that therefore ch. 71 did not originally belong with the preceding chapters. The dramatic way in which the identity of the son of man is disclosed in the Similitudes is a literary device which begins with Enoch's overt questions about the "man's" identity in 46:2 and concludes with the stunning but perhaps not entirely surprising revelation of 71:14. It should not be forgotten that it is the earthly Enoch who sees what his future role will be, and it is overwhelmingly clear that at the eschaton he will be exalted far above his human form and will become the judge of all. In addition, if the seer's inability to recognize himself in a vision is unique to the present form of the Similitudes, it joins a series of other unusual phenomena in the text—such as the text's multifaceted picture of the eschatological judge.

In this connection it may be useful to adduce an idea which is attested in several ancient Jewish texts that could shed some light on the problem at hand. In them one reads that a creature of flesh and blood could have a

---

36. "The Son of Man," pp. 183–84; see also p. 185.

37. "The Heavenly Representative," p. 122. A. Caquot ("Remarques sur les chap. 70 et 71 du livre éthiopien d'Hénoch," in *Apocalypses et théologie de l'espérance* [Lectio Divina 95; Paris, 1977], pp. 121–22) has cited TLevi 8 as another example of such a vision, but Collins has properly noted that it is not analogous.

heavenly double or counterpart. GenR 68:12 seems to intend this when it says of Jacob that his "features are engraved on high; they [the angels of Gen 28:12] ascended on high and saw his features and they descended below and found him sleeping."[38] That is, Jacob's features exist in some form in heaven while he exists on earth. The Prayer of Joseph may provide a more helpful example, again one involving Jacob. "I, Jacob, who is speaking to you, am also Israel, an angel of God and a ruling spirit. *Abraham* and Isaac *were created before any work.* But, I, Jacob, who[m] men call Jacob but whose name is Israel am he who[m] *God called Israel* which means, a man seeing God, because I am the *firstborn of every living thing to whom God* gives life" (A, 1–3).[39] In the sequel, there is reference to his incarnation, and he is called an archangel, "*chief captain* among the sons of God," and "*first minister before the face of God*" (A, 7–8). In this text, Jacob not only has a heavenly, angelic counterpart, but he also existed before other creatures.[40]

These texts offer a model by which one could interpret the references in the Similitudes to the visionary son of man who is identified as Enoch in 71:14. Enoch would be viewing his supernatural double who had existed before being embodied in the person of Enoch. 1En 61:10 even includes the chosen one (= son of man) among the angelic powers; his status throughout the Similitudes is surely no less than angelic. This model could also explain the verses that have often been interpreted as teaching the preexistence of the son of man. They would be referring to Enoch's celestial counterpart. As shown above, however, those verses are open to a different reading.

1En 70:1 should be discussed in this context. In this verse one reads: "And it came to pass that after this his name during his lifetime was raised aloft to that Son of Man and to the Lord of Spirits from amongst those who dwell on the earth" (Charles). Scholars naturally have concluded that if Enoch could be raised to that son of man, then the writer is distinguishing two beings. Some students of the text have tried to avoid this conclusion by adopting the reading of MS *u* which could be translated: ". . . the name *of a son of man* [i.e., Enoch] *was raised up to the Lord of spirits.* . ." (Black).[41] That is, if one follows the reading of this MS, the distinction between Enoch and the son of man disappears. Since, however, it has the support of just this one MS, it

---

38. Translation of H. Freedman, *The Midrash Rabbah,* vol. 1: *Genesis* (London, Jerusalem, New York, 1977), p. 626.

39. Translation of J. Z. Smith, "Prayer of Joseph" *OTP,* vol. 2, p. 713 (the following phrases are also from Smith's rendering).

40. See the discussion in Smith, "Prayer of Joseph," pp. 700–5; and J. H. Charlesworth, "The Portrayal of the Righteous as an Angel," in *Ideal Figures in Ancient Judaism,* pp. 135–51. The author is indebted to Professors A. Yarbro Collins and M. Hengel for directing his attention to the passages discussed in this paragraph.

41. M. Casey, "The Use of the Term 'Son of Man' in the Similitudes of Enoch," *JSJ* 7 (1976) 25–26; *Son of Man* (London, 1979), p. 105; Caquot, "Remarques," p. 113; Black, *The Book of Enoch,* p. 250.

should be rejected as most unlikely to be the original reading. It would be more logical to understand it as a scribal correction made to sidestep the separation that the text seems to make between Enoch and the son of man—a separation that is denied in 71:14. It should be added that it is also possible to translate MS *u* at this point as "his name was raised to that son of man."

Yet, despite appearances, it seems in the final analysis unlikely that 70:1 draws a separating line between Enoch and the son of man. The verse functions as an introduction to all of chs. 70–71, as Sjöberg noted[42] and summarizes what happens from 70:2 to 71:16. It would be remarkable if, at the beginning of this artistically structured unit, there was a statement that contradicted what the unit itself forthrightly declared. What the author appears to have intended in 70:1 was that Enoch's name was elevated to the place where those characters whom he had seen in his visions were to be found, namely in the throne room of the celestial palace. That is, he does not see the son of man here but begins his ascent to the place where he himself will perform that eschatological role—perhaps at this time becoming one with his heavenly double, now that his earthly sojourn has ended. If the text said that Enoch joined an already existing heavenly duo, thus forming a kind of trinity with the Lord of spirits and the son of man, one might have expected some reference to this result in the remaining verses of these chapters. But of this there is not the slightest hint.

If the explanations which have been offered above are correct—and, given the fact that we do not have the original form of the text, some reserve is in order—then the passages which are usually adduced to prove the preexistence of the son of man in the Similitudes may not in fact do so; or, if they do, the preexistence taught may not be inconsistent with the identification of Enoch and the son of man. Even if one rejects the heavenly double theory as foreign to the Similitudes, it may still be said that no passage requires that one think of a separate being called the son of man existing in heaven while Enoch lives elsewhere. Enoch sees the son of man in visions of the future, not in disclosures of the present. He is seeing only what he will become.

A few comments about one other passage—1En 39:6—should be appended to this section. It, too, has been claimed as a proof-text for the preexistence of the eschatological leader, though here he is called the chosen one.[43] Since, however, the chosen one and the son of man are identified in the Similitudes (see part III below), by implication what is said here also applies to the son of man. In 39:4–5 Enoch sees the places where the righteous and holy ones live with the angels. These saints are presumably the righteous who have died. They now supplicate on behalf of mankind. Then

42. *Der Menschensohn*, p. 164.
43. Ibid., pp. 91–92.

vs. 6 adds that Enoch saw the chosen one in the same place. Since the deceased saints are praying on behalf of mankind (unless it is the angels who are doing this), there must be people on the earth for whom they can intercede. This suggests that what Enoch sees exists now; it is not merely a vision of the future. It should be objected, nevertheless, that this is an eschatological vision and that the prayers of the righteous dead are offered at that future time. Furthermore, the only verb that is used in connection with the chosen one is in the imperfect tense (*yekawwen*), as are the verbs in vs. 7. Consequently, it again seems unlikely that the passage deals with a chosen one now existing in heaven or in the abode of the righteous while Enoch is living out his 365 years in other places. The chosen one and Enoch are not necessarily two separate beings. The notion of a celestial double could also explain 39:6.

In conclusion, it may be said that nothing in the Similitudes separates Enoch and the son of man/chosen one in the sense that they are two distinct beings. This entails that the identification of Enoch as the son of man in 71:14 is not inconsistent with the remainder of the composition. There is every reason to believe that chs. 70–71, therefore, formed the original and organic conclusion to the Similitudes and that they should be included in a study of what the book teaches about the son of man.[44]

III. THE INTERRELATIONS AND MEANINGS OF THE FOUR DESIGNATIONS

The passages that are presented in part I above reveal that in the Similitudes one reads, in eschatological contexts, about a righteous one, an anointed one, a chosen one, and a son of man (to whom three different expressions refer). How are these titles related to one another and what do they signify in this text?

A. The Four Epithets Refer to the Same Individual

The four terms, in the present text of 1 Enoch 37–71, very clearly refer to the same being.[45] This thesis can be supported by three kinds of evidence.

1. Equivalence of terms. In some passages the terms are interchanged or identified with one another. 1En 48:6 (cf. 46:3) mentions that the son of man

44. This is also the conclusion of Hooker, *The Son of Man in Mark*, pp. 37–42; Casey, "The Use of the Term 'Son of Man,'" pp. 18–19; *Son of Man*, p. 102; and Caquot, "Remarques," pp. 111–22.

45. See J. Coppens and L. Dequeker, *Le Fils de l'homme et les Saints du Trés-Haut en Daniel, VII, dans les Apocryphes, et dans le Nouveau Testament* (2d ed.; ALBO, series 3, 23; Bruges, Paris, 1961), p. 78; Theisohn, *Der auserwählte Richter,* pp. 31–49. See also Colpe, "*ho huios,*" pp. 423–25.

(*walda sab'* in vs. 2) was chosen (*xeruy*), while ch. 62 uses these designations together: in vs. 1 the chosen one is seen by the kings and the mighty on his glorious throne (cf. vss. 3, 5), but the one who occupies this throne in vs. 5 is the Son of Man (*walda be'si*). Then in vs. 7 he is called "son of man" (*walda 'eg*ʷ*āla 'emma-ḥeyāw*), as he is in vss. 9 and 14. These passages, incidentally, also show that the expressions for "son of man" have the same referent. Once it is established that the son of man and the chosen one are the same individual, one can show that the other epithets, too, are designations for him. 1En 52:4 is one of the two passages which mention the anointed one, but vs. 6, part of the same context, calls him the chosen one (cf. also vs. 9). And, conveniently, the only certain reference to the righteous one names him the chosen one as well (53:6). So, the chosen one is both the righteous one and the anointed one, and he is also identified with the son of man.

2. *Similarity of descriptions.* The functions and descriptions of the chosen one and the son of man, the two frequent epithets, are the same. In part I it was observed that these designations occur in blocks, but, as Theisohn has remarked: "Entirely in contradiction to the formal distinction of the terms stands the observation that the expressions are found almost completely with both designations" (my translation).[46] Since he has devoted a thorough study to this issue, there is no point in reproducing his evidence. He has found that they have in common their function, attributes, role in the plan of salvation, and special relationship with God.[47] Here it will suffice to note that both are epithets for the judge at the final assize (chosen one: 45:3; 49:4; 51:2, 3; 55:4; 61:5, 8, 9; 62:1–3; son of man: 69:27, 29); in that court the one who sits on the glorious throne is called by both designations (chosen one: 45:3; 51:3; 55:4; 61:8; 62:2–3; son of man: 62:5; 69:26–29). The counterparts to both are regularly the kings and powerful (chosen one: 53:5–6; 55:4; 62:1; son of man: 46:4–6; 63:1–11). When one of these terms appears, words such as "righteous" and "righteousness" are almost certain to accompany it (e.g., 39:4–7 for the chosen one, and 48:1, 4, 7 for the son of man).

3. *Reversal of descriptions.* Some phrases that one would expect to be associated with the chosen one are used with the son of man and vice versa. As will be seen below, "chosen one" is a title derived from some of the servant songs in 2 Isaiah and "son of man" comes from Daniel 7, but in 1En 48:4 the son of man is said to be "the light of the nations" (Isa 42:6; 49:6), while the chosen one shares a scene with the "head of days"—a divine title taken from Dan 7:9—in 55:1–4.

---

46. Theisohn, *Der auserwählte Richter,* p. 48.
47. Ibid., pp. 35–44. The remaining sentences in this paragraph are largely dependent on these pages.

B. Influence of the Contexts

The designation used is at times conditioned by the context.[48]

1. "Righteous one": The designation occurs so infrequently that little can be said about it. The eschatological leader is, however, characterized by righteousness so that it is not surprising to find him so labeled. In ch. 53, the only passage where the epithet figures (vs. 6), both the righteous and righteousness are mentioned (vs. 7). If 38:2 were accepted as another instance of the title, the same could be said about its context (vss. 1, 2, 3, 4, 5).

2. "Anointed one": This title is also employed very infrequently, but in the first instance (48:10) it is part of a near citation from Ps 2:2 where kings and rulers likewise oppose the Lord and his anointed (in 1En 48:10 they deny them). The only other reference to the anointed one (52:4) also uses a political word in connection with him (dominion/authority), and in this context, too, one meets the verb "deny" (vs. 9).

3. "Chosen one": The name surfaces often in connection with the chosen ones: 39:6 (see vss. 1 [though the elect here are angels], 6, 7); 40:5 (vs. 5); 45:3, 4 (vss. 3, 5); 49:2, 4 (see 50:1); 51:3, 5 (vs. 5); 53:6 (cf. vs. 6); 61:5, 8, 10 (vss. 4, 12, 13); and 62:1 (vss. 7, 8, 11, 12, 13, 15). The terms "righteous" or "righteousness" are also very common in the passages where "chosen one" appears (e.g., 39:4, 5, 6, 7).

4. "Son of man": The familiar epithet comes from Daniel 7, and in the Similitudes it is used in connection with other features of that chapter. It will be recalled that three Ethiopic phrases underlie this one English designation. It is possible that there is some relationship between context and which of these three is used. This is true in particular about *walda sab'* which occurs only in 1En 46:2–4; 48:2. These verses belong to a section which is heavily indebted to Daniel 7 (note the head of days in 46:1, 2; 47:3, 48:2). Verse 46:1 introduces the deity's special companion by saying that his "countenance had the appearance of a man" (Charles). In this expression the word "man" renders Ethiopic *sab'* which then becomes a fixed part of "son of man" in this setting. The other two Ethiopic phrases for son of man are confined to the third parable and the two concluding chapters. The title "head of days" is not used in connection with them except in 71:10, 12, 14. What other considerations may have motivated the author's choice of these two terms are unknown.

C. The Sources of the Designations

Obvious questions at this point are: From what sources did the writer derive his remarkably varied pictures of the eschatological judge, and what motivated him to combine sources as he did?

---

48. See Müller, *Messias und Menschensohn*, p. 45 (for the chosen one/chosen ones and the righteous one/righteous ones).

1. The principal sources. As many scholars have noted, the author has drawn his portrait of the eschatological hero primarily from Daniel 7 and from some of the servant songs in 2 Isaiah. He has supplemented these sources from a variety of biblical and extrabiblical traditions such as Isaiah 11, Psalm 2, Proverbs 8, Psalm 110,[49] 1 Enoch 14, etc.—that is, passages which are especially susceptible to messianic interpretation.

a. Daniel 7.[50] The most obvious borrowing from this chapter is the term "son of man," but the Similitudes are indebted to it for several other motifs, including the divine title "head of days" and the judgment scene which is so prominent in it. Something of the extent of the writer's dependence on Daniel 7 can be seen by comparing it with 1 Enoch 46 (Daniel 7 continues to supply elements elsewhere [e.g., 47:3 is related to Dan 7:9–10]).

(1) In 1 Enoch 46 God is called the "head of days" (vss. 1, 2) whose head is white like wool (vs. 1); in Daniel 7 he is the "ancient of days" (vss. 9, 13, 22) whose head is white like wool (vs. 9).

(2) The one who looked like a man (46:1), the son of man (vss. 2–4) is the counterpart to Daniel's "one like a son of man" (7:13).

(3) Kings oppress the righteous (1En 46:2–8) as in Daniel they afflict the saints of the Most High (7:24–25). For their teeth (1En 46:4), compare Dan 7:5, 7, 19.

The writer who is responsible for the present form of Daniel 7 identifies the "one like a son of man" as "the saints of the Most High" (vss. 18, 22) or "the people of the saints of the Most High" (vs. 27). In the Similitudes, however, the son of man is an individual. In addition, Daniel 7 does not claim that the one in human likeness does any of the judging (the ancient of days performs this function in vss. 10, 22), although the plural "thrones" in vs. 9 has been taken to imply that he did.[51] In 1 Enoch 37–71, the son of man is definitely the judge in the eschatological courtroom. One may, therefore, agree with Charles when he wrote: "The title 'Son of Man' in Enoch was undoubtedly derived from Dan. 7, but a whole world of thought lies between the suggestive words in Daniel and the definite rounded conception as it appears in Enoch."[52] The writer of the Similitudes did not just borrow; he transformed.

---

49. Regarding the contributions of these passages, see Theisohn, *Der auserwählte Richter*, pp. 53–99, 130–43.

50. For studies of the author's use of Daniel 7, see L. Hartman, *Prophecy Interpreted* (Coniectanea Biblica, New Testament series 1; Lund, 1966), pp. 118–26 (for 1En 46:1–8 alone); Casey, *Son of Man*, pp. 107–12; and Theisohn, *Der auserwählte Richter*, pp. 14–47. As Black (*The Book of Enoch*, p. 206), commenting on the phrase "appearance of a man" in 46:1, has noted, not only Daniel 7 but also Ezek 1:26 (and he adds, in a private communication, Dan 10:18) provide the wording of 1 Enoch 46.

51. An example is S. Mowinckel, *He That Cometh* (New York, Nashville, 1956), p. 352.

52. *The Book of Enoch*, p. 307.

b. *Some of the servant songs in 2 Isaiah.*[53] That these poems are another principal biblical base cannot seriously be disputed, but, as a number of writers have insisted, it is not valid to extrapolate from the fact that some of the servant's traits are applied to the eschatological figure in 1 Enoch to the assertion that he inherits all of the servant's characteristics.[54] The following are some of the elements that the author took from 2 Isaiah.

(1) The epithet "righteous one" may well derive from Isaiah 53:11 where the servant of the Lord is called "the righteous one, my servant." Elsewhere in this part of Isaiah terms from the root *ṣdq*, which figure so prominently in the Similitudes, are not uncommon (Isa 42:6, 21; 45:8, 13, 21, 23, 24; 48:18; 51:7; 53:11; 54:14).

(2) "Chosen one" is another description of the servant (Isa 41:8, 9; 42:1; 43:10, 20; 44:1, 2; 45:4; 49:7). In the Similitudes the word *xeruy* has the first-person, singular pronominal suffix added to it in several cases (= my chosen one: 45:3 [possibly twice], 4; 55:4; 61:5). In Isaiah the servant is also called "my chosen one" (42:1; 43:20 [= my people]; 45:4).

(3) The passages which some experts have interpreted as references to the preexistence of the eschatological ruler (see the discussion above in part II) seem to be related to verses in 2 Isaiah which speak of the Lord's choice or call of the servant before his birth. 1En 48:3, 6 place the naming, choice, and concealment of the son of man before creation (cf. 62:7). This is considerably more than Deutero-Isaiah claims, but he at least does have the servant say: "The Lord called me from the womb, / from the body of my mother he named my name" (49:1; see also vs. 5 and 42:6; 44:2, 21, 24; 48:1). Yet it should also be noted that in 2 Isaiah the creator's foreknowledge of what was to take place is stressed (e.g., 44:6–8 and 46:10: "declaring the end from the beginning"). Thus, one might infer, he could have designated the servant in the beginning. The related idea in the Similitudes that the Lord has hidden the son of man (48:6; 62:7) reminds one of verses such as Isa 49:2 and 51:16.

(4) The kings and the mighty, who appear frequently in 1 Enoch 37–71 as ones who oppress the righteous (62:11 is an example) but who will be judged, are also mentioned in Isaiah (40:23; 41:2, 25; 45:1; 49:7; 52:15) where they, too, treat God's people harshly (49:7; 51:17–23) and will pay the price (e.g., 51:23).

---

53. For surveys of the elements shared by 2 Isaiah and the Similitudes, see Sjöberg, *Der Menschensohn,* pp. 118–34 (especially regarding whether the Son of Man suffers); J. Jeremias, "pais theou," *TDNT,* vol. 5, pp. 687–88; and Theisohn, *Der auserwählte Richter,* pp. 114–26 (he finds Isa 49:1–7 to be the real textual base). Cf. also G. W. E. Nickelsburg, *Resurrection, Immortality, and Eternal Life in Intertestamental Judaism* (HTS 26; Cambridge, Mass., 1972), pp. 70–78, 85–86. That the borrowing was directly from 2 Isaiah is a more satisfactory explanation than that of F. Borsch (*The Son of Man in Myth and History* [New Testament Library; Philadelphia, 1967], p. 154) who thinks the two texts share a common background.

54. E.g., Sjöberg, *Der Menschensohn,* pp. 118–19.

(5) The familiar phrase "a light to the nations" (48:4) is from Isa 42:6; 49:6; cf. 51:4.

(6) The verb *tala'āla* in 1En 70:1, 2 is also found in the Ethiopic version of Isa 52:13 for the exaltation of the once lowly servant.

(7) There is no reason for thinking that the writer borrowed the epithets "anointed one" and "son of man" from Isaiah, but perhaps it is worth mentioning that both occur there, though in different senses. In Isa 45:1 Cyrus is called the Lord's anointed, one whom he has called by name (vs. 3) for the sake of Israel his chosen (vs. 4). Later, one reads about the "son of man" (Isa 51:12; *ben 'ādām*) but here the term is merely a poetic parallel to the word *'ĕnôš* (cf. also 52:14).

The dependence of the Similitudes on 2 Isaiah is undoubted, but, as with Daniel 7, the author has reinterpreted his biblical base. In 2 Isaiah the servant is, of course, explicitly identified as Israel (41:8; 44:1; 49:3, etc.), but in 1 Enoch the titles of the servant are applied to an individual. 1 Enoch 37–71 is perhaps the most ancient but hardly the only witness to the messianic interpretation of the servant. Moreover, the theme of a *suffering* servant in Isaiah does not form part of the writer's appropriation of motifs from his biblical source.[55] In the Similitudes, the chosen one/son of man does not suffer. Rather, the focus there is upon his exaltation and his extraordinary status at the end of time. In these two respects—messianic understanding of the servant and separation of suffering from him—the Similitudes offer a precedent for the treatment of the servant found in Targum Jonathan.[56]

c. Conclusions about Daniel 7 and 2 Isaiah. These indications of borrowings from Daniel 7 and 2 Isaiah (and the two lists are not exhaustive) justify Theisohn's *Arbeitshypothese:*

> The demonstrable connections with the book of Daniel and the manner of the borrowing and revision of the Danielic material show that in the transition from Daniel to the son of man concept of the Similitudes one is dealing with a process of interpretation, with an interpretation of the Danielic figure of the son of man. The relation of the designations "chosen" and "son of man" in the Similitudes and of the almost completely identical expressions connected with them lends a particular character to the process of interpretation: The interpretation of the one like a man of Daniel 7 takes place through his identification with the chosen—an eschatological figure—the eschatological judge of a group or class, from which the Similitudes come. So the Similitudes fill the son of man title with a completely new concept (new interpretation) and thereby constitute their own completely new son of man tradition.[57] (my translation)

---

55. A number of scholars have noted this; see, for example, Sjöberg, *Der Menschensohn*, pp. 128–32; Colpe, *"ho huios,"* p. 426.

56. C. R. North, *The Suffering Servant in Deutero-Isaiah*, 2d ed. (Oxford, 1956), pp. 11–12; cf. also p. 8; D. S. Russell, *The Method and Message of Jewish Apocalyptic* (Old Testament Library; Philadelphia, 1964), pp. 334–36, 339–40.

57. *Der auserwählte Richter,* p. 51.

D. Reasons for the Combination

In sections a. and b. above, some of the motifs which the writer borrows from Daniel 7 and 2 Isaiah are listed. It is evident that several of them, which are fundamental in the Similitudes, appear in both biblical books: an exalted individual who is closely associated with God, with future judgment for oppressing nations and rulers, and with the vindication of the suffering saints. The description of Enoch in 1 Enoch 14 would have suggested a connection with the one like a son of man in Daniel 7, and the traits shared by the servant of the Lord and this one in human likeness could easily have induced the writer to combine them. It would not have been a giant step next to attach both traditions to Enoch, the scribe of righteousness (1En 12:4) who also had been hidden (12:1), had pronounced judgment on angels (12:4–6), had blessed the elect righteous (1:1–3; cf. vs. 8), and had been taken by God to himself (Gen 5:24). The writer than added to the resulting figure attributes which he drew from other messianic passages in the scriptures.

THE CHRIST AND JEWISH WISDOM

INTRODUCTION: A DASH OF WISDOM WOULDN'T HURT

The current scholarly approach to the origins of Christology has been guided by the apocalyptic hypothesis. The apocalyptic hypothesis is that Jesus proclaimed the imminence of the kingdom of God, a reign or domain ultimately imaginable only in apocalyptic terms. Early Christians somehow associated Jesus himself with the kingdom of God he announced (thinking of him as the king of the kingdom) and thus proclaimed him to be the Messiah. If Jesus was an apocalyptic prophet, as the logic seems to have run, it was only natural for early Christians to conclude that he must have been the expected Messiah and that it was therefore right to call him the Christ.[1]

With this hypothesis in place, the field of christological "background" studies has naturally been limited to the search for "messianic" figures in Jewish apocalyptic literature.[2] Seldom have the anthropological poetries of

---

1. The apocalyptic hypothesis was first proposed by J. Weiss, *Die Predigt Jesu vom Reiche Gottes* (Göttingen, 1892; ET *Jesus' Proclamation of the Kingdom of God* [Philadelphia, 1971]) and continues in force as shown by the recent study of E. P. Sanders, *Jesus and Judaism* (London, 1985). The hypothesis is based upon a judgment about the content of Jesus' message, but it includes an assumption of his effectiveness as a charismatic reformer and even accommodates early Christian myths of Jesus' death and resurrection. These early Christian views are usually fit into the apocalyptic scenario of Christian origins as "eschatological events." The term "Christology," then, is normally reserved for the subsequent mythic identifications used by early Christians to claim for Jesus a special authority and role in the larger scheme of things. Thus these mythic identifications are thought to be elaborations upon the primary recognition of Jesus as the expected Messiah. That Jesus was thought of as the Messiah is inferred mainly from the title Christ ("anointed") in combination with the apocalyptic hypothesis. For a critique of the apocalyptic hypothesis with regard to the language of the kingdom of God, see B. Mack, "The Kingdom Sayings in Mark," *Foundations and Facets Forum* 3.1 (1987) 3–47.

2. A theological pattern has guided a full scholarly quest for evidence of the Jewish "expectation" of "the Messiah" that Jesus "fulfilled." Because of the apocalyptic hypothesis, privilege has been granted to Jewish apocalyptic literature as the natural context for expressing messianic expectations. The pattern of "promise and fulfillment" allows for discrepancies among "messianic" profiles without calling into question the notion of a fundamental correspondence. Only

contemporary Jewish wisdom writings been taken as seriously as apocalyptic texts when asking about the "earliest Christology" and its Jewish derivations. Jewish wisdom has entered the picture, of course, but mainly to account for what has been considered second-level developments. Wisdom thought and imagery were important for early Christians, according to this view, but only as an aid in the elaboration of the primary (apocalyptic) christological identification of Jesus as the Christ. Connections have been drawn, for instance, between various expressions of wisdom thought and the following aspects of a "high Christology": (1) the notion of preexistence;[3] (2) the humiliation-exaltation pattern in kerygmatic and hymnic formulations;[4] (3) the logos proem in John;[5] (4) the "Sophia-Christology" in Q and Matthew;[6] and (5) the esoteric content of Christian gnosis.[7] Few studies have engaged the question

---

recently has the failure to establish a commonly held expectation of "the" Messiah led to a questioning of the apocalyptic hypothesis. See J. Neusner, ed., *Judaisms and Their Messiahs* (Cambridge, New York, 1987). The papers in this present volume also reveal a restlessness with regard to the adequacy of a generic designation (Messiah) for the ideal figures depicted in early Jewish and Christian literature, though most of these papers are still devoted to the exploration of apocalyptic texts. The paper by James Charlesworth sets the issue clearly in perspective and provides the proper context for discriminating judgments in the reading of the papers as a set. The present essay is meant to offer an alternative approach to the origins of Christology in light of the serious questions Charlesworth has identified with respect to the prevailing messianic model.

3. On the wisdom background of the notion of preexistence, see E. Schweizer, "Zur Herkunft der Präexistenzvorstellung bei Paulus," *EvT* 19 (1959) 65–70 (Repr. *Neotestamentica*, Zürich, 1963); and R. Hamerton-Kelly, *Pre-Existence, Wisdom, and the Son of Man: A Study of the Idea of Pre-Existence in the New Testament* (SBLMS 21; New York, 1973).

4. For the wisdom background to the Christ-hymns, see R. Deichgräber, *Gotteshymnus und Christushymnus in der frühen Christenheit* (SUNT 5; Göttingen, 1967); J. T. Sanders, *The New Testament Christological Hymns: Their Historical Religious Background* (SNTS MS 15; New York, 1971); and E. S. Fiorenza, "Wisdom Mythology and the Christological Hymns of the New Testament," in *Aspects of Wisdom in Judaism and Early Christianity*, ed. R. Wilken (Notre Dame, 1975), pp. 17–41.

5. On the wisdom background to the prologue (and Christology) of the Gospel of John, see R. Bultmann, "Der religionsgeschichtliche Hintergrund des Prologs zum Johannesevangelium," *Eucharisterion II: Festschrift H. Gunkel* (FRLANT 36.2; Göttingen, 1923), pp. 1–26; ibid., *The Gospel of John: A Commentary*, trans. G. R. Beasley-Murray, *et al.* (Philadelphia, 1971), pp. 22–23; B. Mack, *Logos und Sophia: Untersuchungen zur Weisheitstheologie im hellenistischen Judentum* (SUNT 10; Göttingen, 1973); and E. J. Epp, "Wisdom, Torah, Word: The Johannine Prologue and the Purpose of the Fourth Gospel," *Current Issues in Biblical and Patristic Interpretation*, ed. G. F. Hawthorne (Grand Rapids, Mich., 1975).

6. On a "Sophia-Christology" in the Q (synoptic) tradition, see F. Christ, *Jesus Sophia: Die Sophia-Christologie bei den Synoptikern* (ATANT 57; Zürich, 1970); M. J. Suggs, *Wisdom, Christology and Law in Matthew's Gospel* (Cambridge, Mass., 1970); J. M. Robinson, "Jesus as Sophos and Sophia: Wisdom Tradition and the Gospels," *Aspects of Wisdom in Judaism and Early Christianity*, ed. R. Wilken (Notre Dame, 1975), pp. 1–16; J. S. Kloppenborg, "Wisdom Christology in Q," *Laval Théologique et Philosophique* 33/34 (1977–78), pp. 129–47; and A. D. Jacobson, "Wisdom Christology in Q" (Ph.D. dissertation, 1978).

7. Early Christian claims to a special wisdom "revealed" through Jesus have been studied in their relation to various christologies. On Paul's statement that "God made Christ Jesus our wisdom" (1Cor 1:30) in the context of 1 Corinthians 1–2, see U. Wilckens, *Weisheit und Torheit: Eine exegetisch-religionsgeschichtliche Untersuchung zu 1. Kor. 1 und 2* (Beiträge zur historischen Theologie 26; Tübingen, 1959). On the wisdom backgrounds to 1 Corinthians 15, see

of wisdom thought and Christology in broad perspective, and none has succeeded in displacing the scholarly consensus on "messianic" backgrounds.[8]

Even when acknowledged, however, these traces of Jewish wisdom in early Christian thought have not invited thorough investigation. That is because the logic of wisdom discourse has not seemed as fundamental to early Christian thinking as the assumed apocalyptic mentality. There are several reasons nonetheless for keeping wisdom in view: (1) A reassessment of the apocalyptic hypothesis with regard to the historical Jesus is now underway. The alternative appears to be an aphoristic Jesus whose social critique was more like that of a Cynic than that of an apocalyptic prophet.[9] (2) The notion of a single, first Christology can in any case no longer be held. The alternative is a recognition of plural christologies produced in different early Jesus movements at distinct junctures of their social histories. These christologies appear to address specific issues of group identity arising at different times in relation to particular configurations of Judaism.[10] (3) Recent studies in Q, the pre-Pauline kerygma, the passion narrative, and Mark, to name only the more obviously critical textual loci, have traced assumptions fundamental to these texts, and the modes of reasoning basic to their logics, to patterns of wisdom imagery and thought.[11] These findings suggest that wisdom as an intellectual tradition may have contributed far more to early Christian thinking than has normally been considered.

The position taken in the present paper is that wisdom as a mode of thinking was pervasive throughout early Judaism and Christianity. The connections between Jewish wisdom mythology and early Christian Christology are

---

K.-G. Sandelin, *Die Auseinandersetzung mit der Weisheit in 1. Cor. 15* (Abo, 1976). On wisdom in the GThom, see S. L. Davies, *The Gospel of Thomas and Christian Wisdom* (New York, 1983).

8. Way stations in the history of investigating wisdom and Christology include: H. Windisch, "Die göttliche Weisheit der Juden und die paulinische Christologie," *Neutestamentliche Studien für Georg Heinrici* (Leipzig, 1914), pp. 220–34; B. Botte, "La sagesse et les origines de la christologie," *Revue de sciences philosophiques et théologique* (1932) 54–67; E. Schweizer, "Aufnahme und Korrektur jüdischer Sophiatheologie im Neuen Testaments," *Neotestamentica*, (Zürich, 1963), pp. 110–21; H. Gese, "Die Weisheit, der Menschensohn, und die Ursprünge der Christologie als konsequente Entfaltung der biblischen Theologie," *SEÅ* 44 (1979) 77–114; and G. Schimanowski, *Weisheit und Messias* (WUNT 2/17; Tübingen, 1985).

9. Way stations in the investigation of a sapiential Jesus include: J. M. Robinson, "'Logoi Sophōn': On the *Gattung* of Q," *Trajectories Through Early Christianity*, ed. J. M. Robinson and H. Koester (Philadelphia, 1971), pp. 71–113; J. D. Crossan, *In Fragments: The Aphorisms of Jesus* (San Francisco, 1983); L. Vaage, "The Community of Q: The Ethics of an Itinerant Intelligence" (Ph.D. dissertation, 1986); J. S. Kloppenborg, *The Formation of Q: Trajectories in Ancient Wisdom Collections* (Studies in Antiquity and Christianity; Philadelphia, 1987); and M. J. Borg, "A Temperate Case for a Non-Eschatological Jesus," *Foundations and Facets Forum* 2.3 (1986) 81–102.

10. On plural Jesus movements and their different christologies, see B. Mack, *A Myth of Innocence: Mark and Christian Origins* (Philadelphia, 1988).

11. For recent studies on Q, see the references in n. 9. For wisdom influence in the formation of the kerygma and the passion narrative, see G. W. E. Nickelsburg, "The Genre and Function of the Markan Passion Narrative," *HTR* 73 (1980) 153–84; and B. Mack, *A Myth of Innocence*.

not therefore direct. There may be no straight-line developments or "identifications" of Jesus with a particular image or myth of Jewish wisdom or of "wisdom's child." The texts at our disposal cannot adequately be explained at the level of the history of ideas in any case. They document something far more interesting than the explication of some idea or concept "borrowed" and "developed" from an intellectual tradition. What we have in hand are the products of intellectual labor engaged in making sense of social circumstances. This labor was expended in the imaginative mode as a means of reflection upon social histories in the interest of group identity and legitimation. Creative rearrangements of traditional images, symbols, categories, models, and narrative patterns served to explain and interpret current events. Social critique and/or experimentation requires by definition the manipulation of traditional symbols. To determine typical patterns of thought in early Jewish literature, therefore, and then discover these same patterns of thought at work in the constructions of early Christian mythologies, would be to learn something about Jewish reflection upon contemporary social history, as well as about the accommodation of Jewish traditions by Christian movements for their own purposes. We might actually discover what was at stake in the social experimentations, both Jewish and Christian, characteristic of the times.

It should be emphasized that fantastic depictions of the special man are not limited to apocalyptic writings during our period. The so-called messianic figures of apocalyptic writings and early Christian imaginations of the Christ are only two types of many ideal figures that occur across the wide range of literatures produced. Moreover, the connections between those figures usually designated messianic and the several profiles of the Christ are not direct and do not describe equational correspondence. It will be argued, therefore, that the manipulation of imagery is more important to understand than its imitation, and that several of the imageries of major importance for early Christian mythmaking can and should be traced to the provenance of Jewish wisdom thought in general, rather than to Jewish apocalyptic in particular.

"Wisdom" is a tricky term, of course, and can come to mean everything and therefore nothing. The tendency for the term to be used in broad and multiple connotation is, however, a partial clue to the phenomenon under investigation. Wisdom in broad connotation was the Jewish analogue to Greek *paideia* and philosophy. The term "wisdom" referred to all forms of human intelligence and skill, as well as to the distillation of typical behavior and its consequences won by patient observation, the poetic facility to formulate observations in precise and memorable sayings, the ability to discern the match or misfit of a situation with a proverb. Wisdom included the formulation of a culture's insights into codes of etiquette and rules for making judgments, the control of behavior in keeping with a culture's codes, the accumulation of a culture's knowledge about life and ethics, the capacity of some to master the accumulation and pass it on through teaching, the sagacity of some to use the accumulated knowledge to analyze a social-historical juncture and assess alternative responses. Wisdom also referred to the systematic arrangement of imageries to acknowledge a culture's ideals, study a circumstantial loss, and project a culture's desire for order in the situation of its absence, as well as the learning required to read and the intellectual effort involved in writing, the sensibility involved in persuasive rhetorical choices, the genius of a penetrating mind, and the intelligence involved in constructive proposals. In short, wisdom included the full range of intellectual activities of which humans are capable. It is this broad and multilayered connotation that makes the use of the term tricky as the designation of an alternative to the apocalyptic derivation of particular figures. If wisdom finally refers to Jewish intelligence, which it does, even apocalyptic will have to be included.

Nevertheless, it is also the case that wisdom can be used in a slightly narrower sense to designate an activity and a literature of reflection that focused upon the phenomenon of wisdom itself. It is in this sense that certain patterns of thought and recurring images, including those of personified wisdom and a set of anthropological figures, may be specifically designated as reflections of and upon wisdom and its social incarnations. A delineation of this intellectual tradition will be necessary in order to identify three anthropological figures that appear to have been common coin. Only then will it be possible to suggest the extent to which wisdom thinking might be discerned in the formation of early christologies. The broad sweep is necessary in order to get to the heart of the matter. The reader is therefore asked to regard the paper as a programmatic suggestion rather than a fully presented demonstration.

The paper will unfold in two major parts. In the first part, the emphasis will fall upon the intelligence and intellectual activity of Jewish authors in the tradition of wisdom, and upon the social horizons of their interests and concerns. It is necessary to do this as a counter to modern perceptions of poetic activity that are based upon romantic and individualistic psychologies. It will be argued that wisdom poetry should be read in relation to its social circumstance, and that its speculative and idealistic features functioned as large, imaginative frames of reference by which perspective could be won upon the times. These imaginative frames, moreover, bear striking comparison with the revisionary projections that occur in paradigm shifts where antepenultimate models (in this case of society) are idealized, then used to criticize the recent past and status quo, and to call for adjustments in line with the selected ideal.[12] Those who cultivated the traditions of wisdom be-

---

12. For this assessment of patterns of thought embedded in a culture and their relation to social constructs, I have been helped by the following studies in the theory of cognition and the sociology of knowledge: T. Kuhn, *The Structure of Scientific Revolutions* (Chicago, 1970);

longed to the scribal class, shared elitist and conservative interests, and drew upon the imagery of the ordered society when casting up ideals. But in the late Second Temple Period, many paradigms from the Hebrew epic were called upon as well. It is the function of these paradigms, frequently compressed in the delineation of ideal figures, that deserves our attention.

In the second major part of the paper, several early "christologies" will be discussed in relation to their use of wisdom idiom. It will be argued that different christologies can be related to specific junctures in the various histories of new social movements, that the formation of these christologies can be understood as mythmaking on the model of the intellectual activity of the wisdom scribes (authors), and that the function of these myths of origin was similar to that of the ideal figures produced by wisdom thinkers—creating paradigms for social critique, charter, and legitimation.

I. THE ANTHROPOLOGY OF JEWISH WISDOM

Collective wisdom was articulated and transmitted by means of proverbs, riddles, maxims, instructions, prohibitions, codes, biographical snippits, fables, and stories. Studies of these genres show that their wisdom was won by astute observation of life situations, human responses to these situations, and the usual consequences of each kind of response. The wisdom gained could then be gathered up and taught, and teachers for their part could reflect upon the whole in relation to a society's well-being and a culture's claim on its values.[13]

A logic has been discovered underlying the wisdom discourse of the ancient Near East. Based upon proverbial insight into recurring situations, wisdom thinking worked with the notion of the typical case. The typical case was a generalization, but it was not the statement of a universal principle, nor was it treated as a universal principle. Hebrew sages did not locate the truth of a proverbial insight in an order of reality from which predictions, explanations, and philosophical knowledge could be derived. The typical case was a generalized description based upon a telling discernment. This was brought to bear upon actual situations, then, as a guide for probing judgments and as an invitation to further reflection upon them.[14]

Older scholarship saw this as the failure of ancient Near Eastern wisdom to conceptualize ideal systems, to grasp the significance of order, precise definition, discrete classification, and the logics of inductive and deductive

---

H. Margolis, *Patterns, Thinking, and Cognition: A Theory of Judgment* (Chicago, 1987); and J. Z. Smith, *To Take Place: Toward Theory in Ritual* (Chicago, 1987).

13. For an introduction to the wisdom tradition of Israel and the scholarship devoted to it, see J. L. Crenshaw, *Old Testament Wisdom: An Introduction* (Atlanta, 1981).

14. On the logic of proverbial wisdom, see H. H. Schmid, *Wesen und Geschichte der Weisheit* (Berlin, 1966); and G. von Rad, *Wisdom in Israel* (Nashville, 1978).

reasoning. This view overlooks both the practical and the theoretical advantages of adequate description appropriate to human intercourse, as well as the sharp refinements in situational assessments of which wisdom thinking was capable. Wisdom thinkers were not ignorant about the orders of things, nor unaware that, in order to make sense of human endeavors, some alignment with both the "natural" (created) and the social (covenantal) orders was required. But they knew that these orders were not to be taken for granted, that they were constructions, not ontological entities, and that, in the case of the human social orders, those constructs were fragile and precious. The strength of ancient Near Eastern wisdom was its frank acknowledgment of human frailty, the contingency of human situations, the limits of human perception and knowledge, and the fact that civilization was marvelous just because, as a human achievement, its stability could not be taken for granted. That is why there was always need for discernment, vigilance, reflection, instruction, encouragement, and constant care of the system of social relationships. It was wisdom that produced the environment for human well-being.[15]

Wisdom thought was fully capable of reasoned reflection upon the most complex phenomena. Devastatingly sophisticated analyses of social crises are recorded, as well as profound studies of the subtleties of theodicy from an individual's perspective. Intellectuals were not hindered from explorations into the reasons for social failures, nor from the invention of models for the construction of social systems. The sages were there at every critical juncture of Israel's social history, offering meditations on the reasons for failure, and calling for the return of sane social circumstances. They did it, however, with pictures, comparisons, configurations, and ethical injunctions, not by means of philosophical argumentation. They did it by casting up depictions of the imaginable juxtaposed to the actual state of affairs. They played the gaps between the ideal and the real, and asked their readers to think with them about their social situation, its need of rectification, and how one might live in the meantime.[16]

A very serious exploration took place during the Hellenistic age. The experience of the exiles had raised the question of whether wisdom was still to be imagined anywhere in the world. Wisdom scholars such as Ben Sira had

---

15. On the question of order, historical crisis, and theodicy in the wisdom tradition, see W. Zimmerli, "The Place and Limit of Wisdom in the Framework of Old Testament Theology," *SJT* 17 (1964) 146–58 (repr. *Ancient Israelite Wisdom*, ed. J. L. Crenshaw [New York, 1976], pp. 314–26); G. von Rad, *Old Testament Theology* (New York, 1962), vol. 1, pp. 441–59; and J. L. Crenshaw, "Popular Questioning of the Justice of God in Ancient Israel," *ZAW* 82 (1970) 380–95 (repr. in *Studies in Ancient Israelite Wisdom*, ed. J. L. Crenshaw [New York, 1976], pp. 289–304).

16. For an exploration of one creative reflection in the mode of wisdom upon a critical juncture of social history, see B. Mack, *Wisdom and the Hebrew Epic: Ben Sira's Hymn in Praise of the Fathers* (Chicago, 1985).

found it possible to answer in the affirmative once the Second Temple state was firmly in place. But merely to affirm wisdom's relocation in Second Temple society was not enough. A thorough analysis of the newly configured social institutions and roles was called for in order to be more specific about where among them wisdom was again to be found and what it now required. It was in this period of reimagining the sane society that attention had to be given to new anthropological imagery.

To speak merely of the wise and the foolish was no longer sufficient. And so one finds a range of types and social roles under study. Piety, godliness, and righteousness, for instance, came to be emphasized as manifestations of wisdom, as were the labors of the teacher and the scribe. But particular focus fell upon the high leadership roles that belonged to the structure of the Temple state and its epic precursors. Priests, kings, prophets, warriors, scribes, and counselors all came under critical review. They were reviewed, moreover, in keeping with wisdom idiom, by studied depiction in scenes of social consequence. Special attention was paid to the models given with Israel's epic history, including Adam, the antediluvian figures, and especially Moses. Each office and each hero figure was taken up for investigation. The questions had to do with the kind of wisdom each possessed or should possess, and what the particular contribution of each was supposed to be toward the general well-being of the people. Thus the quest was on for a social anthropology, and the many fine and fantastic poetries in the depiction of anthropological figures created during this time can easily be understood as constructive efforts toward this end. Note that the human, generically defined, was not comprehended with a concept but a figure. And as with Adam, a storied figure of the Hebrew epic that served as well to represent generic humankind, so with the other figures repeatedly reimagined. Ideal figures served to concentrate reflection upon comprehensive social constructs. Thus, depiction was a mode of thinking.[17]

Three images created by wisdom thinkers played significant roles in the process of studied reflection upon the nature and destiny of Israel. They were (1) the figure of wisdom personified, (2) the king who rules by wisdom, and (3) the righteous one rescued from trouble by wisdom. Each deserves a brief description.

A. A Typology of Anthropological Figures

1. Personified Wisdom. The figure of wisdom described in Proverbs 1–9, Job 28, Sirach 1, 24, and elsewhere, is best understood as an objectification of social sanity in the experience of its lack. The common motifs are the absence of wisdom from the social order, the consternation that caused, and

---

17. For a study of three anthropological poetries in the mode of wisdom reflection, including the "messianic" figure in Psalms of Solomon 17–18, see B. Mack, "Wisdom Makes a Difference," *Judaisms and Their Messiahs*, ed. J. Neusner (Cambridge, New York, 1987), pp. 15–48.

various quests to have her returned to the world of human endeavor. The particular features of wisdom's personification betray a little help from the mythologies of Maat and Isis, but the fact of personification is the more important datum. It demonstrates the capacity of Jewish thinkers for abstraction in the mode of imagery, and it illustrates the social dimension of their intellectual labor. Imagining wisdom personified was not a result of armchair theological speculation. It was the result of an astute reflection by cultural critics fully engaged in their social histories. They were greatly concerned about the loss of the kingdoms, about the exiles, and about the consequence of both for human intercourse in a world in need of repair.[18]

The imaginative linkage of personified wisdom to God, a constant mythologoumenon in this imagery, did not mean that the wisdom thus objectified was not in fact a personification of the (human, social) wisdom once known to have prevailed in Israel. If the loss was to be acknowledged as devastating, if, that is, social sense was not to be made of any arrangement unless and until that wisdom "returned," some location had to be imagined for the figure of wisdom while away. To locate wisdom with God was a happy solution, serving several conceptual needs at once. It garnered the order of things in creation as an argument for the continued manifestation of wisdom, though one step removed from the social-historical arena, even while allowing the thought that, under different circumstances, the wisdom God intended for the world could again be replicated in the social order. This narrative logic can be viewed as the Jewish analogue to the Greek philosophical notions of ideality and eternity. Wisdom became "divine" in the process of wanting to affirm its continued existence even while having to acknowledge that, under the present circumstances, it could not be found anywhere in the world. The affirmation of wisdom in the experience of its lack was a remarkable display of tenacious optimism in a constructive mode.

Wisdom thinkers were fully aware of the inadequacy of such an affirmation for any serious investigation of the grounds for ethical judgments, as the books of Job and Qoheleth show. The location of wisdom beyond or in the created order of things did not cancel out an admission of social distress. Using categories conceptualized by the Greeks for the purpose of illustration, the middle term of a mimetic triad was simply missing. Without wisdom at work in the *polis,* the schema of *cosmos, polis, anthrōpos* could devolve into a cynic, apocalyptic, or gnostic gameboard for sectarian or individualistic survival. Thus the notion of divine wisdom-in-creation was not enough to carry out the necessary theological and ethical program. The no-

---

18. On the relation of wisdom mythologoumena to the Egyptian mythologies of Maat and Isis, see H. Conzelmann, "Die Mutter der Weisheit," *Zeit und Geschichte: Festschrift R. Bultmann* (Tübingen, 1964), pp. 225–34; C. Kayatz, *Studien zu Proverbien 1–9* (WMANT 22; Neukirchen-Vluyn, 1966); J. Reese, *Hellenistic Influences on the Book of Wisdom and Its Consequences* (Rome, 1970); B. Mack, *Logos und Sophia;* and J. S. Kloppenborg, "Wisdom Christology in Q."

tion of wisdom-in-creation was, however, one important way to cultivate the affirmation and, during the Hellenistic period, wisdom thinkers found ways to enhance the persuasion by correlating the image of wisdom-in-creation with Greek philosophical concepts. Thus the concepts of *pneuma, logos, physis, nomos, nous,* and *sophia* were all explored as ways to press Greek thought into the service of maintaining a wisdom affirmation in the face of contrary social histories.

The problem with the imagination of wisdom as divine was that another step was required in order to relocate wisdom in the world of human affairs and get on with the business of living. Relocating wisdom might be imagined in any number of ways, but, once declared present in this or that perception, behavior, or social institution, real tests could be applied. Only three of the many attempts to bring wisdom "back down" can be judged successful from this point of view. They were Ben Sira's relocation of divine wisdom in the Second Temple system, Philo's use of wisdom mythology to comprehend the Diaspora synagogue, and the later rabbinic mythologization of Torah as the locus of Israel's wisdom. In each case the mythology worked because the social construct it supported was successful.

Job's audition of the thunderous affirmation of God's supreme wisdom and power brought to climax an intense investigation of the recondite subject of individualistic theodicy. It could not be used to grant a social formation charter. Qoheleth also resigned in the face of social history and made the attempt instead to salvage some wisdom for the individual willing to live pensively. The author of the Wisdom of Solomon, on the other hand, dared still to address the plight of the people of righteousness in yet another time when righteousness was not on the throne. But in order to imagine the readiness of wisdom to intervene, the figure of wisdom had to be hymned in greatly exaggerated stanzas. The author claimed to see it working in the rhythmic patterns of the cosmic order and thus "at all times" prepared to rescue the righteous from despair. The poetry is strong, and his social vision is conscience clear, but his myth of wisdom works only at a distance from the social circumstances that called it forth. It was only the articulation of a desire that things be other than they were.

The Wisdom of Solomon shows how difficult it was during the early Roman period to continue to affirm that the world was ordered in wisdom. That is because wisdom thought imagined the world to be modeled after the ancient Near Eastern Temple state. With the Second Temple experiment now approaching its demise, there was a scramble for envisioning new arrangements. The wisdom mythologies in apocalyptic and gnostic literatures corroborate this finding. Both were born of the judgment that the world was not worthy of the wisdom imagined with God, though each succumbed to a deeply nostalgic despair and found distinctly different ways to rearrange the mythic sequences.

Given the mythic personification, and given the desire to find the world worthy of wisdom once again, wisdom discourse soon gave prominence to two narrative mythologoumena. One was that of the quest for wisdom, frequently reduced to the simple injunction to "seek" her out; the other was that of wisdom's own quest for a place to dwell in the world. The sages who thought to claim this or that social institution as a manifestation of wisdom frequently expressed the connection narratively by means of some metaphor of "descent." Those who denied the world wisdom's presence frequently made the connection by imagining some form of human "ascent." (Apocalyptic imagination often used both narrative mechanisms, reserving the descent of wisdom upon the world until some future transformation of the present evil conditions.)

2. *Wisdom's Royal Anthropology.* Nurtured in the citadels of the ancient Near Eastern civilizations, wisdom thought put palaces and temples in the middle of the picture and imagined kings and priests in charge. Kings were singled out for special consideration because of their privilege, power, and symbolism. How to make sure of their wisdom was the ever recurring question, and the answers came in myths, rituals, counselors, the social construction of the courts, and the social roles of prophets. The ideal king was wise, and the wise king was exalted. But real kings needed lots of help to keep from forgetting what wisdom required.

This close connection between social structure, cultural values, and intellectual functions determined that the king became a common topic in wisdom discourse ("Wisdom exalts her sons") and royal qualities common traits in anthropological depiction. Tracing through the imagery used to describe the epic heros in the literature of the hellenistic period, for instance, attributes befitting a king are frequently found for Adam, the patriarchs, Moses, and Aaron, as well as for the favorites acknowledged really to have been the kings of Israel. Mythologically, the king was wisdom's son. Ideally, the king was the anthropological image par excellence.

During the hellenistic period, kingship was a burning issue both for Near Eastern cultures under the hegemony of hellenism and for Greeks caught between the rhetoric of colonial democracy and the reality of tyrannical rule. The ideal king was imagined and discussed as a topic in ethical and political theory. "King" encapsulated *anthrōpos* at the acme of endowment and achievement. "Ruling" was the favorite metaphor for the achievement of virtue, and as the Stoics and Cynics said, "only the wise are truly kings." Thus the image of the king was democratized even while it centered theoretical efforts to rethink entire political systems.

A funny thing happened among the Jews. In the eyes of many intellectuals, the Hasmonean experiment with kingship had not gone well. Pictures of the golden age of David and Solomon could still be used to set the present in perspective and offer critique. But even then, sharp profiles of royal power increasingly suffered erosion. This was already true for Ben Sira who

assigned the royal functions of his anthropological typology to the high priest
as the highest convenantal office. The author of the Wisdom of Solomon emphasized the king's piety, righteousness, and wisdom as the only credentials
he had for ruling. Philo portrayed Moses as king, but also as prophet and
priest. Moses' principal act of royal decree was the "legislation" of the "law"!
And in the poem about the "son of David," "the Lord's anointed" in the
Psalms of Solomon 17–18, one of the classical "messianic" texts, the desired
king is cast as one who will rule, not by means of the customary instruments
of power, but by his wisdom and the word of his mouth. No ordinary ruler,
this king, for he will be among the people and the nations as their teacher!

Thus kings were put in their place by the exigencies of social history and
the requirements of wisdom's social anthropology. For Jews working out the
implications of both sets of data, the issue finally focused on the relationship
between wisdom and power. The imagination of ideal royal figures endowed
with wisdom offered an arena of serious reflection that could move beyond
the insufficient affirmation of divine wisdom in creation and take up the task
of reimagining social institutions. The purpose of such poetry could range
from social critique, through political program, to the construction of charters for novel social experiments.

3. *Wisdom and the Righteous One.* George Nickelsburg has studied the
story of rescue from the Joseph cycle through such tales as Ahikar, Esther,
and Daniel, and into the Maccabean literature and the Wisdom of Solomon.[19] He is no doubt right about the fact of a narrative pattern common to
all of these performances. A pious Jew is falsely accused and brought to trial.
Wisdom saves the day, however, for his innocence is revealed and his piety
vindicated. Thus the situation is inverted and his last state better than the
first.

Nickelsburg is also probably right to call this narrative pattern a "wisdom
tale." The pattern is pervasive throughout early Jewish literature and occurs
with frequency as idiom in wisdom contexts. The idiom can be recognized in
the humiliation/exaltation pattern, the two-stage schema (first trial, then reward), the cry-of-distress/praise-for-rescue sequence in the Psalms of the
suffering righteous, Philo's levels of progress on the king's way, and the martyrological topos of persecution/vindication. Thus it appears that the wisdom
tale of rescue and vindication was a popular Jewish narrative genre.

That such a plot belonged to the popular Jewish imagination may at first
not seem surprising. The sequence from trial to rescue is natural enough and
corresponds nicely with the general pattern found as well in Greek novels
and comedy. But when it is seen that the point of the story turned on the

---

19. On the wisdom tale, see G. W. E. Nickelsburg, *Resurrection, Immortality, and Eternal
Life in Intertestamental Judaism* (HTS 26; Cambridge, Mass., 1972).

question of justice, and that the story was popular, not in spite of that, but because of it, a bit of amazement would not be inappropriate. Note that the plot, though focused on an individual in distress, follows the pattern of the Exodus epic. Note also that the righteousness in question is never solely a matter of personal virtue gained or lost, but of identification as an observant and loyal member of the Jewish nation. The Jewish popular tale was about the wisdom of righteousness in a world that threatened to snuff it out.

Two points need to be made about the pressures put upon this storyline during the early Roman period. One is that endings appropriate to the times were very difficult to come by. The other is that, in all honesty, the more traditional trial scenes were far too romantic and novelistic for application to the realities of the social histories experienced. Part of the solution to these problems was to admit into the story the fact that rescue did not always happen in this life, that persecution frequently ran its course unto death. Both the Wisdom of Solomon and the Maccabean literature dared to entertain this admission. The wisdom tale was not subverted, however, for in each case the story still ended in vindication. The difference was that vindication now had to be imagined as a sequel to the death, a vindication that involved a post-mortem destiny.

B. A Sociology of Creative Combinations

Authors may be credited with creativity even within the perspective of a sociology of literature and collective imagination. Creativity will be discerned, however, in terms of fresh combinations and rearrangements of familiar material, rather than in *de novo* formulations. Motivation and intention will also be distributed by situating a literature in relation to cultural currents and social histories. Thus situated, the implicit rhetoric of even highly imaginative literature can be regarded as the result of a thoughtful account of contemporary social circumstances. Three examples of the creative use of wisdom imagery will be given.

1. The Wisdom of Solomon. A situation of political distress for the people is evident, although the author's involvement seems not to have been first-hand. The meditation is a reflection on the situation, interpreted in light of a conflict of worldviews. The ungodly think that might is right while the pious know that righteousness must ultimately win. Thus the author attempts to justify an optimism about Jewish destiny in spite of the fact that ungodly kings have succeeded in their plan to squelch the righteous. What the ungodly kings have done cannot be accepted as the way the world is made to work. The way creation is ordered, together with the lessons from Israel's history, teach instead the story of reversal when wisdom intervenes.

This alternative view was created by means of a combination of the myth of personified wisdom, a reflection on kingship under wisdom's tutelage, and the wisdom tale of rescue. The resulting imagery of reversal was then closely connected to the Exodus story in order to establish the epic paradigm.

The presence of personified wisdom, both with God and in the hidden structures of the world, is greatly amplified. The author admits, however, that since wisdom is hidden from view, moments of manifestation are required. Most of these moments follow the common pattern of wisdom's "descent."

The motif of wisdom's descent is cleverly used to link the myth of wisdom with the imagery of the king in need of wisdom and with the story of the rescue of wisdom's righteous child. Solomon's prayer for wisdom is used as the moment when all three mythologoumena can be imagined in combination (1Kgs 3:7–9). Solomon's prayer corresponds formally both to the prayer of the righteous for deliverance and to the quest of the king for wisdom. Recast by the author, the prayer is that God will "send her forth from the throne of thy glory, that she may be with me and toil" (WisSol 9:10). In chapter 10 a series of rescues is recounted for seven figures of the primeval era (from Adam to Moses). These rescues draw their power from the wisdom tale but emphasize the imagery of "fall" in the trial scene and the imagery of "ascent" in the rescue. An intentional overlap with the wisdom myth of descent is evident throughout, especially in the statement that "She descended with him [one of the seven "righteous ones," i.e., Joseph] into the dungeon, and when he was in prison she did not leave him, until she brought him the scepter of a kingdom, and authority over his masters. Those who accused him she showed to be false, and she gave him everlasting honor" (WisSol 10:13–14). Note that each wisdom motif makes its contribution to the power of the interlocking imagery even while it draws support in return from its correlations with other motifs.

The astounding thing about this poetry is that the author knew that the wisdom myth and story of rescue were in trouble. He understood that it was all but impossible to imagine either any longer. The alternative, however, was to agree with the ungodly that "might makes right" (WisSol 2:11), a proposition the author was unwilling to consider. So even if the righteous have been "condemned to a shameful death," the logic of the wisdom story must prevail. That is because there really was no other story to tell. That is because, according to the author, the story of Israel *was* the story of wisdom. That is why the meditation comes to climax in a midrash on the Exodus. The lesson to be drawn from the paradigmatic event was precisely that of vindication and rescue: "For in everything, O Lord, thou hast exalted and glorified thy people; and thou hast not neglected to help them at all times and in all places" (WisSol 19:22).

2. 4 Maccabees. This book picks up on the legends of the martyrs in 2 Maccabees and turns them into mimetic examples of obedience to the Torah.

It has been difficult to situate 4 Maccabees, although one helpful hypothesis puts it in Antioch during the first half of the first century C.E. and interprets it as a speech on the occasion of a memorial for the martyrs. The author is well-versed in popular Greek philosophy and in fact claims that the loyalty of the Jewish martyrs to Torah is proof that "religious reason is sovereign over the emotions." Thus, even though it honors Judean heroes, the memorial's protreptic fits best in a Diaspora synagogue.[20]

Two narrative patterns were used to elaborate the legendary deaths: (1) the depiction of the noble death, a concept deeply embedded in Greek traditions, and (2) the trial/vindication plot from the Jewish wisdom tale. Because of this creative combination, an important differentiation was made in respect to the narrative motif of vindication: the martyr's post-mortem glory was treated as a personal vindication of his righteousness; and the effectiveness of his death in "defeating" the tyrant and thus "cleansing" the land of foreign dominion was treated as a vindication of the "cause" for which the martyr died. Thus the motif of vindication from the wisdom tale was doubled as a result of its combination with the Greek tradition of the noble death. Since the importance of this development for early Christian views of Jesus' death can hardly be exaggerated, it will be helpful to illustrate the pattern by citing a clear instance of its articulation:

> The tyrant himself and his whole council admired their endurance, whereby they now do both stand beside the throne of God and live the blessed age. For Moses says, "All also who have sanctified themselves are under thy hands." And these men, therefore, having sanctified themselves for God's sake, not only have received this honour, but also the honour that through them the enemy had no more power over our people, and the tyrant suffered punishment, and our country was purified, they having as it were become a ransom for our nation's sin (4 Mac 17:17–22).

That the notion of the vicarious effectiveness of the noble death is Greek, not Jewish, should be clear. Demonstration is given in studies by Sam Williams and David Seeley.[21] That the vindication motif stems from the popular Jewish wisdom tale has been documented by George Nickelsburg. It is extremely important to see that the sequel to the death of the martyr is understood as a vindication, not an apotheosis. It is the wisdom rationale in the stories of the martyrs that describes the limits of Jewish accommodation of the Greek notion of the noble death. However, 4 Maccabees does show just

20. On the date and occasion of 4 Maccabees, see G. W. E. Nickelsburg, *Jewish Literature Between the Bible and the Mishnah* (Philadelphia, 1981), pp. 226–27.

21. On the noble death tradition and its reflections in 4 Maccabees and the Pauline corpus, see S. K. Williams, *Jesus' Death as Saving Event: The Background and Origin of a Concept* (Harvard Dissertations in Religion 2; Missoula, Mont., 1975); and D. Seeley, "The Concept of the Noble Death in Paul" (Ph.D. dissertation, 1986).

how far the wisdom patterns could be stretched in order to address difficult social histories.

Even though these stories are set in the land and are impelled by the exigence of foreign occupation, they were not written in defense of the Second Temple system. They were written in defense of Torah obedience and general codes of Jewish piety and identity. Thus a piety appropriate to the Diaspora comes into view, rationalized by a peculiar twisting of a wisdom pattern of thought. The particular twist in 4 Maccabees is aberrational when judged historically, for the notion of the effective death of the wisdom martyr did not commend itself to subsequent generations of Jewish thinkers. But, should a more acceptable combination of wisdom myth be found in support of the Diaspora synagogue, a post 70 C.E. continuation of the institution of Israel might be thinkable.

3. Philo of Alexandria. It has not been customary among scholars to regard Philo as a wisdom theologian nor to classify his commentaries as Jewish wisdom literature. The reason for this, no doubt, is that the figure of wisdom is not as prominent as one might expect of a sage in the tradition of wisdom thought. Nevertheless, stock wisdom metaphors abound, and the narrative patterns of wisdom mythologies are pervasive. Philo thought in the genres of wisdom but developed a discourse focused upon other figures.

What happened to the figure of wisdom can be explained. The term "wisdom" was reserved primarily for two particular functions in Philo's project. One was to symbolize the beginning and ending of a complex process that involved both the rhythms of creation and the purposes of history. The other was to allegorize biblical figures as encoded allusions to the role of hidden wisdom in the complex cosmic process. Philo wanted to distinguish between human and divine wisdom, and he wanted to imagine stable absolutes at either end of the cosmic processes. Thus he no longer pictured personified wisdom in the world at all, whether as a continuously generative power in creation or as a figure that entered social history in quest of human habitation. Instead, divine wisdom was pictured only in the presence of God. She was there to set the world in motion at the beginning, and she would always be there to bless her children at the end of their journey. She represents rest, nourishment without labor, home without conflict, and the bright, clear, unfading vision of God. She is the goal toward which all creation and history is directed.[22]

In the meantime, however, the processes of enlightenment, learning, and progress for humans on the way through the world were surely cared for. Wisdom metaphors, tropes, and narrative patterns abound in the description of these processes, but they are used without reference to the figure of wis-

---

22. On Philo in the tradition of Jewish wisdom, see B. Mack, *Logos und Sophia*.

dom. Instead, a variety of concepts and figures appears to have taken wisdom's place, each with a more or less specific function in the large system of dynamic relations Philo had in mind. Thus the following concepts are regularly described in language clearly reminiscent of wisdom mythology: *physis, pneuma, dynamis, logos, nous,* and *psychē.* By means of wisdom imagery these concepts were turned into figures similar to that of personified wisdom. In Philo, therefore, the dense concentration of the wisdom symbol, traditionally interesting and workable because of its layered nuances and purposive ambiguity of reference, was distributed to other figures across a vast screen of vision in which the dynamic forces of creation and history were imagined to be working in Israel's behalf. Wisdom was parceled out, as it were, for more detailed analysis.

Of the many figures substituting for wisdom in Philo's system, the most important is that of the *logos.* That is because *logos* is the preferred figure for elaborating the largest number of traditional wisdom functions. By means of clever description and imagery, the maleable figure of the *logos* was used (1) to depict the cosmos as created order; (2) to imagine the descent into the world of God's instruction; (3) to symbolize Israel as God's son; (4) to specify the stages on the king's highway that Israel traverses; (5) to claim paradigmatic significance for the leaders of Israel storied in the epic, especially Adam, Abraham, Isaac, Jacob, Moses, and the High Priest; (6) to identify the order of truth contained in the five Books of Moses if allegorized; and (7) to visualize the ascent of the obedient disciple finally into the house of wisdom and the presence of God.

All of the classic wisdom anthropologies occur in multiple combinations as Philo makes his exegesis of the epic and constructs his fantasy of the world. But some shifts in emphasis are noteworthy as well as the major change introduced by the substitution of the *logos.* Wisdom's royal anthropology is still discernable, for instance, especially in the attribution of royal traits to the epic incarnations of the *logos,* but it is overshadowed by the strong tendency to depict the patriarchs as students, Moses as teacher, and the *logos* as priest. In Philo's picture of Israel in the cosmos, the only true king was God, and the only human approximation was the sage. Real kings did not really count.

The sequence of trial/reward from the wisdom story of rescue is fundamental to the entire Philonic system with its notion of the way through the world as trial and the ascent-vision as reward. But in the application of the story to the experience of "the soul," the motif of persecution was dropped, and there was no need for introducing a meditation on the death of the righteous, much less a martyrology of the sage.

Thus the mythic functions from the traditions of wisdom were transferred to other figures, psychologized, and then applied to the experience of Jewish life in Alexandria. The structure of the cosmos was still imagined on the model of the Temple, and the cosmic rhythms of generative blessings from above, followed by the ascents of human spirits from below, inscribed the pattern of the Temple's liturgies. But the great cosmic temple of God now encompassed more than Judea. And the path to the sanctuary could be traversed by following the markers of the Exodus epic and reliving Moses' grand allegory of the soul. Thus the five books were basic to the project. The Books of Moses were the chart and charter for the congregation of Israel. Moses was the leader on the King's highway, and all Israel was, by definition, in the "school of Moses." One learned how to "follow" the path that Moses laid out for the children of Israel in the synagogue school with its lessons and teachers. No wonder wisdom mythology was rearranged. No wonder the *logos* was imagined entering the world to guide it on the way to wisdom. Philo's fantastic view of the world was a scholar's mythology of the hellenistic synagogue, a grand vision in the wisdom mode to justify a social institution other than the Temple state as a legitimate form for Israel taking place in the larger scheme of things.

II. THE CHRISTOLOGY OF EARLY CHRISTIANITY

Early Christian imagination was not more fantastic than that of Jewish authors writing during the same period, except for one thing. Christian fantasies were used to claim significance for new social formations by mythologizing a founder of very recent memory. This conjunction of myth and history creates the riddle of Christian origins. If Christology is the mythology of a new Jesus movement, how can one know how the movement began, and how can one know why the mythmaking settled on just the figures it did?

There are some clues toward the solution of this riddle. The first is the plurality of early Christian movements and their views of Jesus. The second is that, though these several views of Jesus do not match, they all have in common the concern to emphasize the novelty he introduced into the world. The third clue is that interest in the historical person is way down in every case, whereas interest in his authorization of community practices and beliefs is high. And a fourth is that, though the movements stemming from Jesus emphasized their novelty, they all found ways to lay claim to the heritage of Israel, a most intriguing case of having one's cake and eating it too. Since these claims had to be made by manipulating the myths, rituals, and symbols of Judaism already in place, a fifth clue can now be added. Where it is possible to demonstrate the domestication of Jewish wisdom, the rationalization of some social experiment may be suspected.

The thesis of this essay is that early Christians recognized the novelty of their various social experiments and, accustomed to thinking in the genres of wisdom, mythologized Jesus as founding figure in keeping with those genres. This would mean that the various images of Jesus as the special man functioned as an imaginative locus for working out new social arrangements and positioning new social formations within the larger world. Christology would be a rationalization of social formation. Social formation then would be the missing factor in the equation that must be solved in order to get from the historical Jesus to the Christ of mythic imagination.

Three early histories can be used to explore the wisdom component in early Christian thinking about Jesus. They are the view of Jesus as sage in the early Jesus traditions, the view of Jesus as martyr and Christ-king in the hellenistic communities, and the combination of the two in the formation of the Gospels.

A. The Jesus Traditions

1. *Jesus as Sophos.* In the movements that transmitted his sayings, Jesus was remembered as an enigmatic sage. This memory has some historical value and may come close to telling the truth about the historical Jesus. Of greater importance, however, is clarity about the fact itself and its function for those who cultivated it. Four considerations establish the probability that the tradents of Q, and those who created the pronouncement stories, imagined Jesus' role as sapiential.

a. The genres used to collect and replicate Jesus' sayings are most appropriate to the memory of a person known for his wisdom. Q has been established as an example of the genre *Logoi sophōn;* and the pronouncement stories are formally comparable to *chreiai,* hellenistic anecdotes that featured the sageness of leading philosophers and teachers. The genres implicate the characterization of Jesus his early followers had in mind.[23]

b. The style of discourse is aphoristic throughout. The smaller forms of speech feature highly crafted figural compositions that make their point by clever turns of phrase and fresh perspectives. The attribution of an aphoristic discourse to Jesus indicates that he was most likely thought of as a popular sage.[24]

c. It now appears that the earliest layer of the Q tradition is to be characterized as "sapiential," and that the prophetic and apocalyptic sayings entered the tradition later at some point of disillusionment with the Q program. Certainly it is the case that the sayings of Jesus in the pronouncement story tradition display wisdom, not apocalyptic persuasion. Thus the content of Jesus' sayings puts them largely within the tradition of wisdom.[25]

It does need to be said that the content of Jesus' wisdom is very difficult to determine. That, however, may be a clue to the kind of wisdom he employed. The sayings are not philosophical maxims, nor reasoned ethical in-

---

23. On the genre of Q as *Logoi Sophōn,* see J. M. Robinson, *"Logoi Sophōn,"* and J. S. Kloppenborg, *The Formation of Q.* On the pronouncement stories in the synoptic gospels as *chreiai,* see B. Mack and V. Robbins, *Patterns of Persuasion in the Gospels* (Sonoma, Calif., 1989).
24. On the aphoristic quality of the teachings of Jesus, see J. D. Crossan, *In Fragments.*
25. On the earliest layer/stage of the Q tradition as sapiential, see J. S. Kloppenborg, *The Formation of Q.*

junctions. They do not use proverbs to elucidate the wisdom of conventional codes and behavior. Jesus' wisdom is more like the *mētis* of the Cynics—disruptive wisdom aimed at the soft spots of social conventions. Much of his wisdom is occasional and daring. Some is risky or even quite offensive. One has to imagine a sageness fit for social critique, though without a definite institutional target in view to receive the barbs, and without a grand design for an alternative social formation. The movements stemming from Jesus show that social formation *did* take place in the context and cultivation of such discourse. It is also clear that the new groups soon took themselves very seriously. Thus the essential attraction of early Christianity may very well reside in the experience of community construction. But the variety of these movements also shows that Jesus did not propose any plans for such an eventuality.[26]

d. When those who cultivated the sayings of Jesus did venture characterizations befitting his importance to them as founder of their movements, the profiles created for him all fell within the category of the (uncommon) sage. The most important designation was "teacher," although traits definitely associated with scribes, Pharisees, and the mythologies of wisdom and her intimates were not uncommon. The lines can be drawn from Q to the Gospels of Thomas, Matthew, and Luke on the one hand, and from the pronouncement stories in Mark to Matthew and Luke on the other.[27]

Two characterizations do not seem to fit. Both clearly belong to the Jesus traditions, rather than to the hellenistic congregations of the Christ reflected in the Pauline literature, and thus must be accounted for as a development among those who cultivated Jesus' sayings. They are the figures of the prophet and the Son of Man. Both figures occur in oblique reference to Jesus in Q and then are used specifically to characterize the activity of Jesus in Mark's narrative. Since both figures enter the tradition at the secondary layer of Q, they can be explained as rationalizations on the part of the tradents at that point when disillusionment due to failure had turned to threats of judgment upon their gainsayers, the inclusive "evil generation."[28]

2. Jesus as Prophet. It is important to note that in Q the term "prophet" is not used expressly in relation to Jesus. It occurs as a reference to the motif

---

26. For an introduction to the logic of *mētis*, a Greek cultivation of the wisdom required of threatening circumstances, in contrast to the *sophia* of the philosophers, see M. Detienne and J.-P. Vernant, *Cunning Intelligence in Greek Culture and Society*, trans. J. Lloyd (Atlantic Highlands, N.J., 1978). For a study of the Cynic-like traits of Jesus' wisdom, see B. Mack, *Anecdotes and Arguments: The Chreia in Antiquity and Early Christianity* (Occasional Papers 10; Claremont, Calif., 1987).

27. On the wisdom of Jesus in the Gospel of Thomas, see S. L. Davies, *The Gospel of Thomas and Christian Wisdom*. On Jesus as a teacher in Mark, see V. K. Robbins, *Jesus the Teacher: A Socio-Rhetorical Interpretation of Mark* (Philadelphia, 1984).

28. For a reconstruction of the second layer of Q, see J. S. Kloppenborg, *The Formation of Q*.

of the killing of the prophets as a class (Lk 11:49–51; 13:34–35), and in application to the tradents of Q themselves: "Blessed are you when men hate you . . . for so their fathers did to the prophets" (Lk 6:22–23). Odil Steck has traced this motif to a homiletic topos in deuteronomistic preachments of the Second Temple Period. Its purpose in Q was to explain the rejection of the Q people and their message by their own generation. It is obvious, however, that Q tradents had come to think of Jesus' activity also on the model of the prophets, as the comparison with John the Baptist shows (Lk 7:19–35; a second level development), and that they probably had thought of Jesus' death on the model of the slain prophets as well, as the sayings about "the blood of all the prophets" (Lk 11:49–51) and the lament over Jerusalem (Lk 13:34–35) lead one to believe.[29]

To think of Jesus' death on that model would have been an important moment in the history of this movement, for it would have been one way to enhance the historical significance of Jesus and thus of their own work. It would also have meant that Jesus' message was right, just as the messages of the prophets were understood to have been right. But the deaths of the prophets were not understood to have been redemptive, vicarious events. And the prophets were not said to have been resurrected or rewarded by some postmortem transformation. So the claim that Jesus should be counted among the prophets implies nothing more than a validation of his message according to Q.

It is, however, significant that both John and Jesus are called "wisdom's children" (Lk 7:35), and that the topos of the prophets killed occurs in a wisdom saying: "Therefore also the wisdom of God said, 'I will send them prophets . . .'" (Lk 11:49). Jack Suggs has called attention to the Wisdom of Solomon where wisdom "makes . . . friends of God and prophets . . . in every generation" (WisSol 7:27), and he has discussed the possibility that the Hebrew prophets had come to be thought of as the "envoys" of wisdom. Such a wisdom reading of the epic history of Israel could serve as a bridge to the accommodation of the homiletic topos of the killing of the prophets, as does in fact occur in the Q saying where the epic scope is comprehended in the sweep from Abel to Zechariah (Lk 11:51). This means that the shift in characterization from Jesus as sage (early layer Q) to Jesus as prophet (later layer Q) can be understood as an exercise in wisdom mythology. The new characterization was called for by the experience of rejection suffered by the Q tradents and their own response to rejection by taking up prophetic and apocalyptic language to pronounce judgment upon the "evil generation."[30]

29. On the motif of the killing of the prophets, see O. H. Steck, *Israel und das gewaltsame Geschick der Propheten: Untersuchungen zur Überlieferung des deuteronomistischen Geschichtsbildes im Alten Testament, Spätjudentum und Urchristentum* (WMANT 23; Neukirchen-Vluyn, 1967).

30. On the question of wisdom's "envoys," see M. J. Suggs, *Wisdom, Christology and Law in Matthew's Gospel.*

3. *Jesus as Son of Man.* It is the same with the apocalyptic figure of the Son of Man. It was not used in Q to characterize Jesus directly but to add argument to the threat of judgment against those who did not receive the Q message. The equation is clever: The one who acknowledges Jesus before men will be acknowledged by the Son of Man before the angels of God; the one who denies Jesus before men will be denied before the angels of God (Lk 12:8–9). The apocalyptic consideration enters the Jesus tradition just in order to make this threat of judgment stick.

The use of the term "Son of Man" in Q should therefore not be referred to as a "christological title"; it is neither titular nor a surrogate designation for Messiah. Of the nine clearly attested occurrences in Q, only one appears in the earliest layer of tradition, the saying about the Son of Man having nowhere to rest (Lk 9:58). This saying is easily understood as a poignant observation about (generic) humankind (in keeping with the normal Aramaic idiom that must lie behind the curious Greek formulation). The tenor of the saying fits the Cynic hypothesis, moreover, and the saying's traits correlate nicely with wisdom forms, motifs, and logic.[31]

In the second layer of Q there are eight occurrences of the term "Son of Man," and with them a number of problems do arise with respect to the sources for the figure, and especially with regard to its intended reference in relation to Jesus.[32] Nevertheless, six of the occurrences are apocalyptic projections, four of which use some form of the "prophetic correlative" illustrated above (Lk 12:8–9), and one of which supports the correlative in Luke 12:8–9 (Lk 12:10; the other references are Lk 12:40; 17:24, 26, 28). Thus it is clear that the curious figure of the Son of Man functions mainly in support of the threat of judgment that characterizes this stage of Q discourse. The logic of this correlation between the response given to Jesus and the judgment to be received from the Son of Man is, however, thoroughly compatible with wisdom thought, as Klaus Berger has shown.[33]

This manner of apocalyptic projection cannot be called a mythologization of Jesus, although the basis upon which one will be judged does shift away from response to the message of Jesus and toward an acknowledgment of his importance as the messenger. This corresponds to the way in which Jesus' importance as wisdom's child was being enhanced by alignment with the prophets. In the two remaining occurrences, then, it should create no great surprise to find the term "Son of Man" used in reference to Jesus himself in the context of comparison with prophets. He (as the Son of Man) is compared

31. On Cynic wisdom in Lk 9:58, see J. Butts, "Jesus the Fox," unpublished paper presented to the New Testament Seminar, Claremont Graduate School, April 19, 1983.

32. On the unresolved issues in regard to the Son of Man sayings, see the survey by F. Borsch in the present volume, "Further Reflections on the 'Son of Man': The Origins and Development of the Title."

33. On the wisdom logic of sayings that correlate present behavior with eschatological consequence, see K. Berger, "Zu den sogenannten Sätzen heiligen Rechts," *NTS* 17 (1970–71) 10–40.

firstly with John the Baptist (Lk 7:19–35; cf. "For John the Baptist has come eating no bread and drinking no wine; and you say, 'He has a demon.' The Son of Man has come eating and drinking; and you say, 'Behold a glutton and a drunkard'" [Lk 7:33–34]) and then with Jonah the preacher (Lk 11:29–32; cf. "For as Jonah became a sign to the men of Nineveh, so will the Son of Man be to this generation" [Lk 11:30]). Note that the point in each case is just that Jesus' appearance is to be taken as of supreme importance, even though his curious wisdom makes identification all but impossible in terms of standard roles.

The use of the term "Son of Man" is intentionally enigmatic, as the contexts show. When thinking of Jesus, that is, it is as if one might well find some helpful comparisons with the prophets, or with John the Baptist (who, however, was himself "more than a prophet," Lk 7:26), or with Jonah the preacher (a funny "prophet" whose generation did repent), or even with the notion of the Son of Man (bearing, no doubt, its own strange ambiguities of reference, location, and function). But do not forget the differences! Do not take offense (Lk 7:23). Eating and drinking, indeed. "Behold, something greater than Jonah is here; something greater than Solomon is here" (Lk 11:31–32). The conclusion must surely be that these attempts at characterization in the later Q tradition, though they trade in prophetic and apocalyptic idiom for the purpose of calling down judgment upon those who have rejected the Q messengers, and though they play daringly with potentially mythic attribution, have not yet resulted in a clear designation of Jesus' role, much less in an apocalyptic "Son of Man Christology."

It was Mark who introduced "high christological" characterization into the Jesus traditions, and it is extremely important to note that. In the materials that reflect pre-Markan traditions, such as Q, some pronouncement stories, the miracle story chains, some parables, and so forth, Jesus is not referred to as "Christ" (or Messiah), much less as the Son of God familiar from the writings of Paul. It should also be emphasized that these materials are not to be read in the light of any "post-Easter" enthusiasm, for they neither mention nor presuppose any mythology of the saving significance of Jesus' death and/ or Resurrection. This means that the traditional scholarly consensus of a Resurrection datum for all early Jesus traditions, a datum that allows for the construction of a "Son of Man Christology," has no textual basis and in fact should not be assumed.

At the beginning, the Jesus movements apparently did not require a king for a founder, think of themselves as substitutes for particular institutional forms of Judaism, or feel the need of explaining Jesus' innocence, righteousness, or undeserved death by recource to the wisdom tale of rescue. There is no evidence of interest in a royal anthropology for Jesus anywhere before the time of Mark, nor are associations with the wisdom tale of rescue drawn in the obviously pre-Markan material. This does not mean that, in the process of repeated appeals to Jesus' precedence in order to justify group practice, Jesus did not become an imperious authority for those who cultivated his counterculture wisdom. When the time came to notice that authority as constitutive for the Jesus movements, however, the natural move was to enhance the notion of Jesus' superior wisdom as a sage. This happened in the pronouncement story tradition where Jesus' wisdom became self-referential and his pronouncements simply beyond adjudication, in the Gospel of Thomas where Jesus' words hold the secret of immortality, in Q where Jesus eventually is imagined speaking oracles appropriate only to the divine, personified wisdom, and in Matthew and Luke where it is Jesus' incomparable message that marks the turn of the ages. There is even the possibility that Matthew made some direct connection between the divine wisdom and Jesus.[34] But of course, by Matthew's time, the high christologies of the Christ cult and the low "christologies" of the Jesus traditions had long since been intertwined in the story Mark wrote. So by then, almost any imagination was possible. We shall return to Mark's accomplishment below.

B. The Christ Cult

1. *Jesus as Martyr.* The Pauline correspondence with Christian groups in Asia Minor provides a window into an altogether different social terrain. It was here that the image of the Christ was created to serve as the symbol for a fully independent and self-conscious religious society.[35] There is no evidence of interest in cultivating the memory of Jesus the sage, even though Jesus traditions must be assumed at the beginning. Some form of the Jesus movements must have reached northern Syria at a very early period and experienced great change in the transition. The changes are reflected in the marks of the Christ cult: a full-blown myth (kerygma), rituals (entrance baptism, symbolic supper, signs of recognition), liturgical productions (doxologies, prayers, hymns, etc.), codes, leadership roles, ideologies, and conflict over authority. Some would-be leaders apparently thought that something worth fighting for was in the mix.

The jump from Jesus to Paul has always been too great for the scholarly imagination. That is because several missing links in the process of social formation and its mythologization were buried by Paul's intense theological argumentations. Paul's intellectual exercise in the dialectic of judgment and grace (apocalyptic and wisdom) appears to have been the product of his own anxiety about the excesses of freedom, rather than the kind of message upon which a new religious enthusiasm could have emerged. If one isolates the evidence for the thought and practice of the Christian movement indepen-

---

34. On Matthew's "Sophia Christology," see M. J. Suggs, *Wisdom, Christology and Law in Matthew's Gospel.*

35. For a tally of the occurrences of the term Christ in the New Testament and the overwhelming evidence of its provenance in the hellenistic Christ cult, see the essay in this volume by D. Aune.

dent of Paul, some of the missing links are recoverable, and these missing
links do begin to make some social sense. It is here that Jewish wisdom made
a significant contribution.

The clues are available in the logic of the myth and rituals. The first steps
have been taken by Sam Williams, David Seeley, and others, who trace the
language of the kerygma to the martyrological literature of hellenistic Judaism, especially 4 Maccabees. The language includes the symbols of death
(body, blood, crucified, etc.) as well as allusions to the motivation and vicarious effectiveness of the martyrdom (obedience, faithfulness, and the cause
"for which" the martyr "gave" his life). In the case of the early Christian
employment, the "cause" for which Jesus was imagined to have died was the
Jesus movement itself. Why this movement needed that kind of justification
is the next question.[36]

The clues to the "why" question are given with the language of application. The vexing problem was precisely the "justification" of "sinners" (a social category) within a group that wanted to lay claim to the legacy of "Israel."
Thus the question was a Jewish question. And the answer was also found
(admittedly by a great stretching of normal thinking) from within the Jewish
bag of intellectual categories. It was the notion of vindication (*dikaiosunē*
means both "justification" and "vindication") from the wisdom tale. The notion of vindication put all of the pieces together, for it could vindicate Jesus
and his fate, implicate a theological perspective on the event (absolutely necessary for the myth to work), and justify the cause "for which" he died, including those among the group who did not stand a chance of being considered "righteous" (another social category) without some such foundation
myth.

Note that the kerygma is structured on the model of the wisdom tale
(cross/Resurrection as trial/vindication), but that the kerygma cannot be narrated or historicized without hopelessly complicating its logic. That is because, if the opponents are named, the focus must shift to include a conflict
of cultures as the context for deciding what the basis for the definition of
righteousness will be.

2. *Jesus as the Christ-king.* With a wisdom-martyrology as founding
myth, second-level elaborations and poetic embellishments could easily
make use of all varieties of wisdom mythology. In the wisdom-martyrology
the narrative form of expression for vindication was a postmortem status. It
could be portrayed as a Resurrection or an Ascension (the terms can be translated either way), and this became the preferred formulation in early Christian circles. The pre-Pauline tradition cited in Rom 4:25 shows that not only

---

36. References to the works of S. Williams on Rom 3:24–26, and on its martyrological background, and to D. Seeley on the noble death tradition in Paul are given in n. 21.

the death, but also the resurrection of Jesus (his own personal vindication as martyr) had been interpreted vicariously by using the same language of motivation or effect ("for . . ."): "raised for our justification." The interesting thing about this formulation is that the logic of martyrology was expanded upon by including a reflection on the significance of the vindication motif. Note that the vindication of the martyr Jesus (raised) and the vindication of the society "for which" he died ("our justification") have been connected by noticing the similarity of function (result) and aligned by means of the similarity of logic (cause).

In the cluster of wisdom images created by the combinations of wisdom genres characteristic for this period, the notions of rescue, ascension, inversion of status, and lordship were merged. The image of the king belonged to the model of ancient Near Eastern society from which these narrative themes derived. Though many forms of early Judaism modified their royal imageries in the direction of priestly and scribal functions, early Christians emphasized their king's sovereignty and power. If Jesus' death inaugurated a "kingdom" in which the mix of Jew and Gentile (righteous and sinners) was justified, what about his Resurrection? Narrative logic implied his status now as lord, Lord of the world and King of the kingdom for which he died.

The evidence for the attractiveness of this imagery among early Christians is very strong. As startling as it may seem, the notion very quickly passed from social rationale to cultural fetish. A cult developed, replete with all of the accoutrements, focused on the cultivation of the spiritual presence of the Christ-king. The evidence includes the Christ-hymns, the doxologies, the liturgical formulations of the kerygmatic credo, the rationalizations for the entrance rites, the symbolism for the ritual meal, the eager pursuit of scriptural allegorization, the Christian accommodation of the Psalms of enthronement, the cultivation of ecstatic (transcendental) experiences, the Christian accommodation of the hellenistic clichés about freedom and knowledge as the signs of a "king," or, on the other hand, Paul's emphasis on an ethic of obedience to complement the proper lordship of Christ. The Pauline dictum sums things up quite nicely: "We preach Christ crucified . . . to those who are called, both Jews and Greeks, Christ the power of God and the wisdom of God. . . . He is the source of your life in Christ Jesus, whom God made our wisdom, our righteousness. . . ." (1Cor 1:23–24, 30).

The reason why it has been so hard to trace the lineaments of wisdom thinking into early Christianity is not that they were not fundamental to the mythologization of the new social experiments. It is because the logic of wisdom discourse had to be violated in order to rationalize (justify) the new social experiment. Paul was quite right to note that the ensuing wisdom was only "ours," and that to both Greeks and Jews outside of the community it could make no sense ("folly," "stumbling block," 1Cor 2:23). The answer must be that, at least in this case, logos did not precede praxis. The essential attraction of early Christian movements must have resided in the space they created for experimenting with new social relationships and experiences, not in the power of the new logos itself as Paul would have it.

C. The Gospel Tradition

Mark is the one who picked up on the possibility of fitting Jesus into an apocalyptic reading of the history that brought the Second Temple Period to its end. He cast Jesus as one who announced the reign of God, predicted the destruction of the Temple, and was killed as the rightful king of the kingdom of God in the first encounter between the two opposing forces. Mark suggested that the people understand enough to think he was a prophet. They were only partially right, however, according to Mark, for Jesus' true identity could only be indicated by a complex merger of imageries otherwise associated with the Son of Man, the Son of God, and the Christ. Mark's composition was a special case of mythmaking, performed at a particular juncture of early Christian tradition to rationalize a specific problem of social identity. It cannot be used to argue for the pervasive influence of apocalyptic mentality either in the early or in the subsequent chapters of the Jesus traditions. Note that both Matthew and Luke go to great lengths to tone down Mark's apocalyptic frame and retrieve the sayings tradition for a more sapiential interpretation.

Mark's composition of the Gospel is an excellent example of recasting the image of Jesus in order to provide a rationale for a particular group at a specific juncture of its social history.[37] Mark's group was one of the Jesus movements, most probably the group responsible for the pronouncement stories, a group that had thought of itself essentially as Jewish by virtue of participation in some synagogue until just before Mark's time. Because Mark's group, along with other Jesus movements, had already learned to appeal to the figure of Jesus for authority, the new rationalization had to stand in continuity with the tradition of Jesus as sage. Thus Mark availed himself mainly of Jesus materials in order to create the new characterization.

But the Jesus traditions alone were inadequate for the charter now necessary. That is because a completely independent social formation required a full complement of social codes, markers, myths, and rituals, and Mark's group had apparently "borrowed" most of its identity from the synagogue, either by claim to share in its heritage or by contrastive symbiosis. Suddenly now, however, a complete set of substitutes had to be crafted, and Mark turned to the Christ cults for a little help.

That Mark knew about the Christ cult is documented textually: (1) Mark's account of the Last Supper is best understood as a narrative historicization of the kind of etiological legend for the Lord's meal cited in 1Cor 11:23–26; (2) the three predictions of the passion are best understood as narrativized

---

37. This section on Mark's Gospel is a tight summary of B. Mack, *A Myth of Innocence*.

versions of the kerygmatic formulations characteristic for the Christ cult; (3) Mark's use of the term "Christ" as well as his use of the term "Son of God" are best understood as resignifications of mythological terminology embedded in the Christ cult; and (4) the cautious but conscious and ironic employment of the language of salvation in Mk 10:45, the supper text, and the taunt at the cross ("He saved others; he cannot save himself" [Mk 15:32]), is best understood as an accommodation of the language of the Christ cult.

That Mark combined Jesus traditions with Christ-cult traditions is a common scholarly understanding. The problem has always been, however, that the story Mark told of Jesus' death does not reflect the form of religious experience known to have been characteristic for the Christ cult. Mark's account does not present Jesus' death as a vicarious and effective event, nor does it provide the basis for a cult of presence, personal transformation, mimetic participation in self-sacrificial rituals, or grounding for the justification of sinners. One has therefore to be suspicious, for these characteristics of the Christ cult are definitional. They are the very aspects that distinguish the religious society of Christ from the Jesus movements, and they are the features missing from Mark's picture.

A solution to this conundrum is not difficult to find. Mark only took from the Christ traditions what he wanted, and that was the martyr myth, a sufficiently powerful logic to justify a Jesus movement desperately in need of a myth of origins. That he did so can be demonstrated in the way in which Mark toned down each of the Christ-cult traditions mentioned above by reducing them to their common core—the pattern of trial and vindication. That pattern could be combined with the image of Jesus as sage and provide a Jesus movement with an effective founding event. But how to write it up?

The clue to Mark's achievement is hidden in the passion narrative. Recent studies have called attention to Mark's firm hand in the composition of the passion narrative, and George Nickelsburg has shown that the basic plot follows the outline of the wisdom tale of the persecution and vindication of the righteous one. The conclusion must be that Mark saw the wisdom tale as the common link between the Jesus traditions (Jesus as sage) and the Christ cult (Jesus Christ as vindicated martyr), and used it as the pattern for his plot, interweaving both sets of material in order to lead from Jesus' activity as a sage to his martyrdom as a figure of destiny.[38]

Not interested in a cult of the presence of the cosmic Christ, however, Mark imagined Jesus' destiny in apocalyptic terms. He thus preferred to think of Jesus as the Son of Man whose (first) appearance inaugurated the beginning of the endtime, and whose final appearance would be the same as

---

38. On the passion narrative in Mark as a Markan composition, see W. Kelber, ed., *The Passion in Mark: Studies on Mark* (Philadelphia, 1976), pp. 14–16. On the passion narrative as a wisdom tale, see G. W. E. Nickelsburg, "The Genre and Function of the Markan Passion Narrative."

the manifestation of the kingdom of God in power and glory. In the meantime the followers of Jesus were to continue in the hope that the kingdom
they represented would eventually make some difference in the real world
as it should, but also now recognize the evil of the times, and thus be prepared to watch and wait for that full manifestation of divine power and glory
without which their story would have no satisfactory ending. The large-scale
frame for Mark's Gospel was certainly an apocalyptic reading of his violent
times. But the core of its logic was provided by the vindication motif of the
wisdom tale. Jesus *must* be vindicated (i.e., manifested in power), if, that is,
he was martyred as wisdom's child.

CONCLUSION: UNCOMMON WISDOM TELLS THE TALE

In the Jesus traditions the various memories that were cultivated and created for him softly focused around the image of an uncommon sage. This was
true for Q, for the pronouncement stories, for the parables, and for the Gospel of Thomas. Since Jesus' wisdom was of the unconventional variety, and
since the movements stemming from him were novel social experiments,
they all created different profiles of their founder when called upon to authorize their unprecedented behavior. In Q and Mark, Jesus the sage took on
the features of a prophet-but-not-quite; in the pronouncement story tradition Jesus was cast more in the mold of the scribe who made the exegesis of
his own text; and in those traditions that eventually surface in the Gospels of
Thomas and John, Jesus' wisdom was reified to become the self-knowledge
of the divine man or even the incarnation of wisdom itself, but a wisdom not
to be found in the world at large.

In the Christ cult, narrative patterns and characterizations underlying the
very logic of the kerygma and the symbolism of the ritual meal were taken
from hellenistic applications of traditional Jewish wisdom thought. Wisdom
imagery was also the model for the subsequent mythologies of cosmic lordship and destiny that were crafted in the hellenistic communities. And in
Mark, the passion narrative and the plan for the Gospel as a whole followed
the wisdom tale of vindication, though the message to which Jesus was true
and the kingdom for which he died were dialectically contrastive with the
Jewish wisdom that the story once assumed. So apparently early Christians
were much at home in the imagery and thought characteristic of the Jewish
tradition of wisdom, even though they violated that tradition when putting
its logic to their own use.

The story of early Christian domestication of Jewish wisdom could easily
be continued through the formative period of the late first through third
centuries. The use of wisdom idiom is obvious, for instance, in the post-
Pauline letters, the Johannine tradition, Matthew's Gospel, Christian gnosticism, and many of the fathers, both apostolic and beyond.

Nevertheless, there are no direct lines to be drawn from the figure of divine wisdom and her mythology to the figure of the Christ. There is no such thing as a Sophia-Christ or Christology until, perhaps, the gnostics created one by fusing two fully mature mythologies of cosmic destiny. Thus the scholarship has been right not to trace the origins of Christology to a direct identification of Jesus with the divine wisdom. What then?

The thesis proposed here is that wisdom thought was capable of mythologizing social systems and histories and in fact included in its repertoire a variety of anthropological figures and functions laden with Jewish sociologies. These were put to use by early Christians in much the same way as early Jewish intellectuals used them—to rearrange symbol systems in the interest of reassessing ideals in the light of contemporary circumstances and vice versa. Thus the missing links between Jewish wisdom and early Christology are the social formations of the Jesus and Christ movements that required rationales, and the creative borrowing from Jewish wisdom of its anthropological imageries in order to work out those rationalizations. Evidence for reconstructing both of these links is available to the historian. The novelty Christianity claimed to introduce into the world may therefore best be tested by having a closer look at the way in which Jewish wisdom was domesticated for Christian purposes.

It should be acknowledged that the relation of wisdom idiom to apocalyptic language has been left unexplored in this essay. The justification for that was the desire to offer an alternative to the apocalyptic hypothesis at the point of the "earliest christologies" and their fundamental logics. It is obvious, however, that early Christians entertained apocalyptic persuasions in various applications from an early time, second-layer Q, Paul, and Mark being the prime loci. It is also obvious that a form of apocalyptic mythology became normative for the patristic period where the decisive moment for or against eternal salvation was reserved for the day of judgment. In this literature, the function of apocalyptic language in almost all cases appears to be a theodicy with respect to the just deserts of an intransigent world, on the one hand, and a threat intended to control the behavior of the faithful, on the other. But the question of the persuasive power of apocalyptic rhetoric needs to be asked, especially in relation to fundamental claims to truth that are grounded in the genres of wisdom, and more especially in relation to the fascination with power that marked early Christianity almost from the beginning. Why was it, so the question must be phrased, that Christians were attracted to images of royal authority, in contrast to Jews who turned rather away from kings, and cultivated the offices of priests, scribes, and teachers? Can a study of Christian wisdom and apocalyptic tell the tale? Or must the social histories of diverse groupings and their bids for a place in the scheme of things provide the clues for the rationale?

A NOTE ON THE MESSIANIC BANQUET

One element included in Jewish and Christian speculation about the end time was a great feast for the faithful in the age to come. If the Messiah is host at the meal, it is properly called the Messianic Banquet; if no mention of the Messiah is made, the term eschatological banquet is more appropriate. For purposes of convenience the former appellation will be used in this note unless specific attention is called to the significance of the absence of a messianic figure.

D. S. Russell's comment that the "idea of an eschatological banquet is, of course, a familiar one in the apocalyptic tradition"[1] is representative of statements in standard treatments of apocalyptic literature. The central purpose of this note is to examine the textual evidence for this assumption. What follows is a considerably abbreviated version of a more inclusive paper which I hope to make available later. Two criteria are operative in limiting the scope of this presentation. First, only texts which speak more or less directly about a meal set in an eschatological context will be discussed. Other texts which allude to some element of such a meal, e.g., the bread of paradise, the restoration of the manna, fellowship with the heroes of old, Behemoth and Leviathan, etc., will, for the most part, be omitted. Their inclusion will be mandatory for a broader examination of tradition history of the topic, but that is a separate project.

The second criterion relates to chronology. The chronological limits proposed for the Symposium were 250 B.C.E.–200 C.E. Application of this criterion raises a methodological difficulty since scholars differ considerably in dating some of the texts. I have chosen to err on the conservative side, that is, to include only texts which can almost certainly be dated within the proposed limits. A discussion of texts which are earlier than 250 B.C.E. or later than 200 C.E. will be relevant for a fuller treatment of the topic.

---

1. *The Method and Message of Jewish Apocalyptic* (Philadelphia, 1964), p. 322.

I

Given the common assumption of the pervasiveness of the theme of a messianic/eschatological banquet in Jewish apocalyptic thought, it may be somewhat surprising that so few overt references are to be found. The parade examples, cited over and over, are 1En 62:12–16 and 2Bar 29:1–8. (Unless otherwise noted I shall use the numeration and the translations in *OTP* vol. 1, ed. Charlesworth.) The former, following a vivid description of the judgment, reads:

> It shall become quite a scene for my righteous and elect ones. They shall rejoice over (the kings, the governors, the high officials, and the landlords) because the wrath of the Lord of the Spirits shall rest upon them and his sword (shall obtain) from them a sacrifice.[2] The righteous and elect ones shall be saved on that day; and from henceforth they shall never see the faces of the sinners and oppressors. The Lord of the Spirits will abide over them; they shall eat and rest and rise with that Son of Man forever and ever. The righteous and elect ones shall rise from the earth and shall cease being of downcast face. They shall wear the garments of glory. Those garments of yours shall become the garments of life from the Lord of the Spirits. Neither shall your garments wear out, nor your glory come to an end before the Lord of the Spirits.

Three points in this passage should be noted for future reference: (1) mention of the sword and the sacrifice; (2) emphasis on a specific (that) day; but (3) also a continuation of being with and eating with that Son of Man in perpetuity.

The second passage, 2Bar 29:1–8, contains many more details.

> That which will happen at that time bears upon the whole earth. Therefore, all who live will notice it. For at that time I shall protect only those found in this land at that time. And it will happen that when all that which should come to pass in these parts has been accomplished, the Anointed One will begin to be revealed. And Behemoth will reveal itself from its place, and Leviathan will come from the sea, the two great monsters which I created on the fifth day of creation and which I shall have kept until that time. And they will be nourishment for all who are left. The earth will also yield fruits of ten thousand fold. And on one vine will be a thousand branches, and one branch will produce a thousand clusters, and one cluster will produce a thousand grapes, and one grape will produce a cor of wine. And those who are hungry will enjoy themselves and they will, moreover, see marvels every day. For winds will go out in front of me every morning to bring the fragrance of aromatic fruits and clouds

---

2. This is the trans. of E. Isaac in *OTP,* vol. 1, p. 44. He notes that "sacrifice" is literally "memorial feast." M. Knibb in *Apocryphal Old Testament,* ed. H. F. D. Sparks (Oxford, 1984), p. 245, gives the following translation: "And the sword of the Lord of Spirits will be drunk with them." Charles, *APOT,* vol. 2, p. 228, translates the passage as "Because the wrath of the Lord of Spirits resteth upon them, and His sword is drunk with their blood" (p. 228). The textual problem does not affect the general sense of the passage.

at the end of the day to distill the dew of health. And it will happen at that time that the treasury of manna will come down again from on high, and they will eat of it in those years because these are they who will have arrived at the consummation of time.

The following points in this account should be noted: (1) though there is no specific reference to an "inaugural" messianic meal, such may be inferred from the comments that all this will take place when the Messiah will begin to be revealed and that the monsters will provide nourishment for all who are left; and (2) eating in the messianic age takes place not on a single occasion but "every day." Both Enoch and Baruch agree that the messianic banquet not only marks the beginning of the eschatological age but is a feature of it in perpetuity.

Baruch does, however, introduce a new element. Among the foods mentioned as constituting the meal, in addition to the return of the heavenly manna and fruit, the food of Adam in Paradise, is the flesh of the primeval monsters Behemoth and Leviathan. This last viand warrants comment. 1En 60:7–10 describes the creation and preservation of these two monsters and 60:24 states "And the angel of peace who was with me said to me, 'These two monsters are prepared for the great day of the Lord (when) they shall turn into food.'" The role and function of Leviathan and Behemoth in the mythic sources which underlie the development of the theme of a messianic banquet in Jewish apocalyptic will be discussed in the summary section of this note, but mention of a passage in 4 Ezra is germane:

> Then you kept in existence two living creatures; the name of one you called Behemoth and the name of the other Leviathan. And you separated one from the other, for the seventh part where the water had been gathered together could not hold them both. And you gave Behemoth one of the parts which had been dried up on the third day, to live in it, where there are a thousand mountains; but to Leviathan you gave the seventh part, the watery part; and you have kept them to be eaten by whom you wish, and when you wish.

The passage is set in the context of creation, not consummation, and thus in its present form does not allude to the messianic meal. Nevertheless, the concluding sentence "and you have kept them to be eaten by whom you wish, and when you wish" almost certainly is a modified utilization of the theme.

The passage in 5 Ezra (= 2Esdras) 2:33–41 is presented with reservation. Although most scholars date this section no later than the end of the second century C.E., some suggest that it is not earlier than the middle of the next century.[3] Consequently it may not meet our dating criterion operative in this note and will not be discussed in detail. Ezra, in a vision of the end time, is

3. B. Metzger, *An Introduction to the Apocrypha* (New York, 1957), p. 22.

shown "at the feast of the Lord the number of those who have been sealed. Those who have departed from the shadow of this age have received glorious garments from the Lord" (38-39). No details of the feast are given, and one might almost assume that the motif was so much a common part of apocalyptic stock in trade that no explanation was considered necessary. To this we shall return. (A potentially interesting item in this passage which cannot be pursued here is the mention of the Lord's supplying "glorious garments." In Matthew's version of the parable of the marriage feast [22:1–14], surely an allusion to the messianic feast, one without a proper wedding garment is consigned to outer darkness. Has the author of 5 Ezra attempted to deal with the enigmatic Matthean passage?[4])

Finally, with even more reservation than with the preceding passage, I would call attention to material in the Testaments of Abraham, Isaac, and Jacob. They are cited not as primary witnesses to a full-blown description of the messianic meal in the period under consideration but as examples of the use made of the theme near the very end of that period or at the beginning of the subsequent era. The relationship among these three Testaments and their dates and provenance remain matters of dispute, but I believe that their substratum at least warrants inclusion.[5]

The Testament of Abraham does not mention a meal, but it does introduce a theme which is later conflated with the banquet: "Take, then, my friend Abraham into Paradise, where there are the tents of my righteous ones, and (where) the mansions of my holy ones, Isaac and Jacob, are in his bosom, where there is no toil, no grief, no moaning, but peace and exultation and endless life" (20:14).

Two passages in the Testament of Isaac (as translated in *OTP* 1) mention the banquet. Here, again, the choice of the text used for translation is significant. Stinespring in *OTP* 1 uses the Arabic version (with some help from the Coptic and Ethiopic), while Kuhn in AOT uses the Sahidic version.[6] The latter does not include mention of the banquet. The inclusion of the Arabic version here should not be construed as a text-critical judgment on my part, and if the Arabic is later and dependent on the Sahidic, the passages may more properly belong to later developments of the tradition. I shall cite only the crucial lines dealing specifically with the banquet. The context of both

4. It is probable that this passage is from a Christian editor. However 1 Enoch, certainly pre-Christian, also mentions "garments of glory" and "garments of life" (62:15–16).

5. An explanatory note justifying the inclusion of these three testaments is in order as the passage in TAb does not directly allude to a meal (one of the criteria for inclusion), and there is question as to whether the other two fall into our chronological criterion. (For the dating see *OTP*, vol. 1, pp. 903, 913; *AOT*, pp. 424–25, 441.) Because of the intimate relationship among the three, the presence of the meal in TIsaac and TJac warrants, in my judgment, the inclusion of TAb, and conversely the admittedly early date for TAb, again in my judgment, justifies inclusion of the other two.

6. *AOT*, p. 425; "The Sahidic Version of the Testament of Isaac" *NTS* 8 (1957) 225–39; idem, *NTS* 18 (1967) 325–36.

passages deals with the rewards in store for those who have performed acts of mercy in the name of Isaac. The first passage is 6:22:

> There shall not be any trouble in their departure (from this world), I will grant them a lifetime in my kingdom, and they shall be present from the first moment of the millenial banquet.

The second is 8:5–7:

> behold, I will give him [the righteous] to you [Abraham] in the kingdom of heaven and he shall be present with them at the first moment of the millenial banquet to celebrate with them in the everlasting light in the kingdom of our Master and our God and our King and our Savior, Jesus the Messiah.

Two points about the passages in the Testament of Isaac, one of which appears in the context of the second citation, are worthy of mention. First is the mention of "first moment" and reference to the millennium. The translations cited above allow of ambiguity. Is the reference to a single banquet which will inaugurate the millennium or to a banquet which will last throughout the millennium? M. R. James' translation of the Arabic version clearly implies the latter: "and he [the righteous] shall be present with you at the first hour of the banquet of the thousand years."[7] Both themes, an inaugural banquet and a continuing banquet, appear in other traditions of the messianic/eschatological banquet.

The second potentially significant allusion is in 8:5. "[F]or each of them [the righteous] shall have a dwelling in the kingdom of heaven, because our Lord has made with them his true covenant forever." (I note that mention of the covenant also appears in the Sahidic version.) We shall see that both in the Old Testament backgrounds and in at least one passage in the New Testament covenant and meal are brought into conjunction.

TJac 7:21–28 is quite similar to the two passages cited from TIsaac. (There is considerable repetition among all three Testaments, and some scholars have concluded that the Testament of Isaac consciously builds upon the Testament of Abraham and the Testament of Jacob upon both. The righteous are to be rewarded for the good deeds performed in life. The most relevant section of the passage is 7:23–24:

> O my sons, do for the poor what will increase compassion for them here and now, so that God will give you the bread of life forever in the Kingdom of God. For to the one who has given a person bread in this world God will give a portion from the tree of life.

Although no specific banquet is mentioned, allusion to eating in the kingdom of God is patent. We may infer, therefore, that this passage, as it relates

---

7. *Texts and Studies* 2 (Cambridge, U.K., 1892), 149–51.

to our topic, can point in two directions. It can be understood as an example of how a theme (messianic/eschatological banquet) can be broken and only partially utilized in another connection, or it can be understood as an example of how bits and pieces of diverse material may be brought together in a larger complex. I believe that in this case the former is operative, but both possibilities should be kept in mind in evaluating the total configuration of the messianic/eschatological banquet in both Jewish and Christian traditions.

In the version of this note prepared for oral presentation, I included three other texts, 2En 42:5; 3En 48:10; and scattered passages from the Hebrew Apocalypse of Elijah. Participants at the symposium persuaded me that there are no reasonable grounds to include the last given the chronological framework adopted in this note. I remain ambivalent about the passage in 2 Enoch. I have omitted it on two counts: (1) the textual evidence is highly uncertain; and (2) the allusion to the meal is quite vague.[8] It would, of course, be included in a broader study dealing with broken elements of the meal.

It is altogether possible that some relevant pseudepigraphical texts have escaped my attention or that I have arbitrarily omitted some that should be included. On the basis of the above study, however, the following preliminary summary may be useful.

Two overall themes are present. On the one hand, and this is the more dominant, the meal is an occasion of joy for the redeemed, while on the other, judgment and destruction of God's enemies is stressed. In some passages both themes are present, either explicitly or implicitly. The meal reflects both judgment and joy.

Attention may also be called to specific elements present in the picture of the banquet. Some of these are found in several passages, others in a few, and still others in a single instance. I include all of them for future reference after evidence from the rest of our texts has been presented. (1) A "messiah" may or may not be mentioned. Thus, in some instances we may speak of a messianic banquet proper, while in others the more general reference to an eschatological banquet is more appropriate. (2) There is fluidity between emphasis on a particular meal which may imply the inauguration of the future era and on the perpetual festal bliss of the redeemed. (3) Heroes of the past, Adam and the Patriarchs are participants. (4) The eschatological era is characterized by a lush renewal of nature. (5) The mythical monsters Behemoth and Leviathan are fed upon.

---

8. The text translated by F. I. Andersen in *OTP*, vol. 1, p. 168, does refer to a heavenly meal, but the text used by Hugo Odeberg, *3 Enoch* (Cambridge, 1928) does not. Furthermore, Pennington in *AOT* and Forbes-Charles in *APOT* 2 omit the passage altogether.

II

A text from Qumran contains an important but unfortunately ambiguous contribution to study of the Messianic meal. The conclusion of 1QSa, commonly called the Rule of the Congregation and attached as an annex to 1QS, the Rule of the Community,[9] sets forth the protocol to be observed at a communal meal or communal meals. A closely parallel passage in 1QS 6.4–6 is clearly descriptive of the appropriate protocol for the recurring communal meals of the community, and some have interpreted the passage in 1QSa simply as a variant description of the regular common meal. The 1QSa passage, however, contains one significant element lacking in the 1QS parallel, mention of the presence of the Messiah (1QSa 2.12, 14, 20). This could be construed as prima facie evidence that we have a clear reference to the messianic meal. But do we?

Lacunae and blurred readings in the manuscript have led to a wide diversity of scholarly reconstructions, and the nature of those reconstructions is crucial for determining whether the text does in fact contain an unequivocal reference to the messianic meal. The heading of the section, 2.11–12 is badly broken, and a suspension of final judgment is in order. I propose the following reconstruction, with the most debatable points underlined: "And this is the order of the session of the men of renown, called to the session of the council of the community when *God begets* the Messiah. With them shall come *the priest* at the head of the whole congregation of Israel." The word translated *begets* is very blurred and has been variously emended. Emendations such as "sends" or "causes to be present" do not affect the messianic nature of the passage. On such readings the meal described in 2.18–21 would be a messianic meal. Other emendations, however, remove any reference to the Messiah or assume that it is an honorific title for one of the leaders of the community. The inference drawn is that the meal in 2.18–21 is simply a variant description of the regular common meal known from 1QS 6.4–6, and that no messianic significance should be attached to it. This contention is apparently supported by the rubric which concludes the protocol for the meal "And they shall act according to this decree at every me[al when] at least ten men are gathered."[10]

At one time I maintained that the meal described in 1QSa was purely eschatological and that its repetition referred to repetition in the messianic age. I now believe that this was a mistaken view. It seems more probable that the Qumran community understood their regular communal meals as anticipations of *the* great meal which would be celebrated when the Messiah

9. *DJD* 1, ed. D. Barthelemy and J. T. Milik (Oxford, 1955), pp. 107–18.

10. For a detailed examination of the textual problems and proposed reconstructions, see my *The Two Messiahs at Qumran* (Ann Arbor, 1960) and a summary in *JBL* 82 (1963) 95–100. Two useful recent treatments with considerably different conclusions are by J. J. Collins, *The Apocalyptic Imagination* (New York, 1984), pp. 122–26, and L. Schiffman, "Communal Meals at Qumran" *RQ* 10 (1979) 45–56.

appeared among them. This perception, as shall be noted below, recurs in some of the New Testament materials.

1QSa 2.11–21 is, in my judgment, of paramount importance for understanding the Two Messiahs at Qumran, the influence of Qumran messianism on the organizational structure of the community, and the possibility of tracing changing messianic beliefs and structural organization of the life of the community.[11] Discussion of these matters, however, is not appropriate to an examination of the messianic meal as such. With respect to that, the following conclusions seem most appropriate. The Qumran community's scenario of the end time, at least as reflected in 1QSa, included a festal meal at which the Messiah was present. His role, however, was subordinate to that of the (eschatological?) priest. In the interim period before the consummation, the communal meals of the community were considered to be a proleptic anticipation of the feast of the age to come. Finally, this conjunction of present and future had a profound effect on the liturgical life of the community.

There is another Qumran text where it is surprising that mention of the messianic/eschatological banquet is absent. 1QM, the War Scroll, which clearly draws upon and eschatologizes holy war ideology (Deuteronomy 20), depicts graphically in a number of passages the mighty triumph over God's enemies.[12] Elsewhere, for example in a number of Old Testament texts, the book of Revelation and 1 Enoch 62, there is an intimate connection between the battle and the banquet.[13] In 1QM the meal is never mentioned. I do not presume to offer an explanation of its absence in 1QM, but mention it to sound a note of caution about assuming that there is a "pattern" into which the theme of the messianic banquet may be placed. Generalized conclusions regarding apocalyptic materials, including the theme of the messianic banquet, should always be checked by specific textual evidence. In this instance inclusion of a messianic meal was not considered to be an integral element.

III

The New Testament is a most valuable source of data concerning the messianic/eschatological banquet. For the purpose of this note I shall omit critical discussion of the passages presented except in those cases which relate directly to the meal itself. Reference to, or at least allusions to, the meal may be divided into six categories.[14]

1. At least two passages clearly refer to Jesus as the host at the messianic

---

11. See "Mebaqqer, Paqid, and the Messiah," *JBL* 81 (1962) 55–63.

12. For a comprehensive treatment, see Y. Yadin, *The Scroll of the War of the Sons of Light Against the Sons of Darkness* (Oxford, 1962).

13. See esp. J. D. M. Derret, *Law in the New Testament* (London, 1970), pp. 126–55.

14. I need to emphasize that in this provisional study I have largely ignored textual, form critical, and redactional issues in the New Testament texts examined. Our present concern is with their utilization of the theme of the meal. A fuller study would, of course, include a more detailed analysis of these issues.

meal. Rev 19:9 simply states "Blessed are those who are invited to the marriage supper of the Lamb." The title Lamb is, of course, a code name for Jesus. Further, the passage includes the "marriage" motif (cf. Mt 22:1–14; 25:1–13) into the messianic meal, a motif which appears also in later Jewish writings.

The second passage, Lk 22:28–30 requires more extensive comment.

> You are those who have continued with me in my trials; and I assign (*diatithemai*) to you, as my father assigned (*dietheto*) to me, a kingdom, that you may eat and drink at my table in my kingdom, and sit on thrones judging the twelve tribes of Israel.

Reference to *my* table in *my* kingdom can hardly be interpreted in any way other than an allusion to the messianic meal. Both the Matthean and the Markan parallels omit the Lukan passage, although as we shall see below, both may have in this context a more veiled allusion to the messianic meal. Matthew in another context (19:28) does speak of the disciples who will "sit on twelve thrones judging the twelve tribes of Israel," but does not include any mention of eating and drinking with the Son of Man. Thus, while Luke surely relates the messianic meal to Jesus, no central significance is given to it by Mark and Matthew.

A final comment on the Lukan passage is presented with some diffidence. The verb translated "assign/assigned" in the RSV is rendered in a wide variety of ways in current English translations. It may evoke a covenantal frame of reference and imply that the messianic meal will be the seal of the new covenant. A connection between meal and covenant is made in TIsaac 8:5 and in some OT passages (see below). I do not place too much stress on this allusion, but do consider it to be worthy of continued reflection.

2. The second category consists of texts which seem to bring the Last Supper into relationship with the future meal. The relevant passages are Mt 26:26–29; Mk 14:22–25; and Lk 22:15–18. The crucial sentence, in its Markan version, is "Truly, I say to you, I shall not drink again of the fruit of the vine until that day when I drink it new in the kingdom of God" (vs. 25). Matthew adds "with you," while Luke does not speak of drinking again in the kingdom, stating rather that Jesus said he would not drink again until the kingdom of God comes. We noted earlier that Luke does subsequently make overt reference to the messianic meal and its intimate connection with Jesus, and it is probable that both Matthew and Mark are implicitly making use of the messianic meal theme. That they do not make that theme explicit indicates, however, that it was a peripheral rather than a central motif for them.

One other section of the pericope of the institution of the Lord's Supper is found only in Luke. He prefaces his version with "And he said to them, 'I have earnestly desired to eat this passover with you before I suffer; for I tell you I shall not eat it until it is fulfilled in the kingdom of God'" (22:15–16). We shall not address the textual problem—some MSS add "again," which is important for identifying the last supper as a passover meal—but simply call attention to the fact that Luke may be attaching an eschatological significance to the Passover. Some later Jewish writings do make this connection. Last Supper, Lord's Supper, messianic meal, present Passover, eschatological Passover intertwine.

3. The third category is closely related to the second. Some early Christian writings depict the Lord's Supper in the church both as a commemoration of the death of Jesus (Last Supper) and as an anticipation of the coming messianic meal. In the New Testament this understanding is most clearly found in 1Cor 11:23–26.

4. There are some passages which advert to the messianic/eschatological meal simply as an illustrative motif, apparently well known to Jesus' hearers, which could be used without further explanation, and which made no overt connection between Jesus and the coming meal. Mt 8:11–12 (= Lk 13:28– 30) affirms that the faithful, even the faithful Gentiles, will sit at table with Abraham, Isaac, and Jacob. The presence of the heroes of ancient Israel at the feast, as was noted above, was a fairly common feature of Jewish depictions of the banquet. Jesus could assume that his hearers were familiar with an application of that motif to this particular situation.

The parable of the Great Supper (Mt 22:1–10 = Lk 14:15–24) raises a special problem.[15] On the one hand, I think it appropriate to include it in this category. On the other hand, it contains some elements which may make it more appropriate to include it in category one, passages which refer directly to the messianic meal with Jesus as host. The Lukan introduction to the parable, "Blessed is he who shall eat bread in the kingdom of God" (14:15b) and the Matthean introduction which refers to king/son could certainly alert the hearer/reader to a nuance of the messianic/eschatological meal. Above all, Lk 15:24, "For I tell you, none of those men who were invited shall taste of *my* banquet" (lacking in the Mt par.), may be a specific reference to the messianic meal. At best, however, we have an elusive allusion which serves an illustrative purpose and is not a central thematic motif.

5. It is often asserted that the accounts of the miraculous feedings (Mt 14:13–21; Mk 6:30–44; Lk 9:10–17; Mt 15:32–39; Mk 8:1–10; Jn 6:5–14) reflect a retrojection of the Eucharist and/or the messianic meal into the life of the historical Jesus. If this be true, and it seems probable, we have additional evidence that the motif of the messianic meal is operative even where it is not set forth in an overt manner. Even less direct allusions, for example, the post-Resurrection meal accounts in Lk 24:28–43 and Jn 21:9–14, the Lukan beatitude, "Blessed are you that hunger *now,* for you shall be satis-

---

15. In addition to the standard commentaries, special attention is called to the section in Derrett, mentioned in n. 13, and to the treatment by J. Sanders in *Essays in Old Testament Ethics,* ed. J. L. Crenshaw and J. T. Willis (New York, 1974), pp. 245–71.

fied" (6:21a), and the story of the Rich Man and Lazarus (Lk 16:19–31) may well draw on the imagery of the meal. Caution should be exercised in seeing allusions to the meal wherever a faint reminiscence is present, and in the concluding section of this note, attention will be called to the necessity of distinguishing between ideology and imagery.

6. The final passage to be considered is Rev 19:17–21:

> Then I saw an angel standing in the sun, and with a loud voice he called to all the birds that fly in midheaven, "Come, gather for the great supper of God, to eat the flesh of kings, the flesh of captains, the flesh of mighty men, the flesh of horses and their riders, and the flesh of all men, both free and slave, both small and great." And I saw the beast and the kings of the earth with their armies gathered to make war against him who sits upon the horse and against his army. And the beast was captured, and with it the false prophet who in its presence had worked the signs by which he deceived those who had received the mark of the beast and those who worshiped its image. These two were thrown alive into the lake of fire that burns with brimstone. And the rest were slain by the sword of him who sits upon the horse, the sword that issues from his mouth; and all the birds were gorged with their flesh.

The background of this passage is surely the widespread combat myth.[16] Many Old Testament passages (see below) reflect this myth, particularly in its Ugaritic version. The emphasis is on the destruction of God's enemies, not on the festal rejoicing of the redeemed. Taken in conjunction with Rev 19:9, this passage indicates clearly that the author of Revelation understood the messianic meal to depict both joy and judgment.

The theme of judgment and the meal is perhaps also alluded to in Mt 8:11–12 = Lk 13:28–29, and in the parable of the marriage feast (Mt 22:1–14 = Lk 14:16–24), particularly in the Matthean conclusions (vss. 11–14), but with nothing like the vividness of the language of Revelation.

IV

A curious and tantalizing lacuna in our evidence pertaining to the messianic meal exists in the preserved literature of tannaitic Judaism. Two noted scholars of that period asserted with confidence that there is no mention of it at all in that literature.[17] That it does reappear(?) in later rabbinic materials

16. For a superb treatment of the use of this myth in Revelation and a detailed examination of its backgrounds, see A. Yarbro Collins, *The Combat Myth in the Book of Revelation* (Missoula, Mont., 1976).

17. L. Ginzberg, *Legends of the Jews* (Philadelphia, 1928), vol. 5, pp. 42–48; G. F. Moore, *Judaism* (Cambridge, Mass., 1927), vol. 2, p. 364. Moore, in his notes in vs. 3, does allow that Pirke Aboth 3:20 may refer to the banquet. Other scholars, e.g., J. Bloch, *On the Apocalyptic in Judaism* (Philadelphia, 1952), attempt to maintain a continuity of apocalyptic in the tannaitic period. I am convinced that this issue is one of the most pressing ones for the study of the development of early Judaism and early Christianity. Ginzberg, to whom all of us are indebted

is obvious, and I think that a thorough examination of the possible continuity of the tradition in the tannaitic period is of utmost importance. I do not presume, however, to venture into the turbulent waters of dating the rabbinic sources. I would hope that others competent in that area may undertake such an investigation. Two passages in Pirke Aboth, surely to be dated prior to 200 C.E., warrant comment.

Pirke Aboth 3:20, attributed to Akiba, teaches that actions in this world have consequences not only for this world but also for the world to come. It concludes with the cryptic comment that "everything is prepared for the banquet." The second, 4:21, attributed to a certain Rabbi Jacob and usually dated in the latter half of the second century C.E., reads "This world is like a porch before the world to come. Make thyself ready in the porch, that thou mayest enter into the banquet-hall." (The translations are those of R. T. Herford, *APOT* 2.702 and 706.)

Obviously, neither of these passages delineates any details about the messianic/eschatological banquet, but what is important for our consideration is the fact that they can refer to it in such an offhand manner as to imply that it would be common knowledge to their hearers or readers. I consider this important for a final evaluation of our topic.

If these passages imply that the messianic meal theme was so well known that it could be cited for illustrative purposes, without explanation, one might infer that apocalyptic ideas had much more influence on the Judaism(s) of the tannaitic period than has been generally assumed. Pursuit of that question lies outside the scope of this note. Re-examination of the influence of apocalyptic, in general, on Judaism and Christianity in the first two centuries of the common era is, in my judgment, of primary importance. A detailed re-examination of the theme of the messianic meal may make a contribution to that enterprise.

The following brief summary of the Qumran, New Testament, and Pirke Aboth evidence is in order. First, both at Qumran and in some passages in the New Testament, the meal is clearly messianic and not simply eschatological, though there are some passages in the New Testament (e.g., Mt 8:11 = Lk 13:28–30) which seem to maintain the more general image. Second, it is probable that both at Qumran and in the early church, the theme of the messianic meal affected communal liturgical practices. Third, some passages in the New Testament and both allusions in Pirke Aboth imply that the theme was so well known that it could be used without any explanation in a variety of illustrative ways. (The saying in the Gospel of Thomas 64

---

for his massive learning, once wrote: "Of apocalyptic Pseudepigrapha it may well be said that the new therein is not Jewish and the Jewish is not new," *Students, Scholars, and Saints* (New York, 1953), p. 91. This is from a lecture originally given in the summer of 1920. It is altogether probable that the enormous research which has been done on apocalyptic since that time might have changed the opinion of this venerable scholar.

points in the same direction.) Fourth, the meal was not a universal or indispensable element in the eschatological scenario. Finally, the judgment/combat theme, especially in Rev 19:17–21, replicates a motif found in some texts examined in section I above.

V

I perceive two lacunae in the foregoing presentation. (Readers may well call attention to others.) The first has to do with the body of material from which the evidence has been drawn. No evidence has been adduced from noncanonical Christian writings of the period. Neither consultation of major secondary sources nor a preliminary reading of a considerable portion of the so-called New Testament Apocrypha, the Nag Hammadi Library, sub-apostolic, and early apologetic literature has uncovered any direct references except insofar as the Eucharist is interpreted as having a proleptic eschatological dimension. I do not claim, however, to have made an exhaustive study of this vast body of material, and a detailed examination of this material by specialists in these areas is a desideratum. Further, the so-called rabbinic literature has not been discussed (except for the Pirke Aboth passages). The problem here is not lack of evidence—such is abundant—but the dating of that evidence. Particularly important in this connection is the question of how the messianic/eschatological banquet in particular and apocalyptic motifs in general reappear in post-tannaitic literature, while they are largely absent in the tannaitic period. (Or, perhaps, are they all that absent?) Detailed studies of this particular instance of tradition history may well provide valuable evidence of the role comparative midrash may play in enhancing our fuller understanding of early Judaism and early Christianity. In an extended version of this note I shall attempt to deal with this issue, but in the long run I must defer to rabbinic specialists.

The second lacuna also has a chronological origin. A comprehensive study of the messianic banquet would require not only a detailed examination of the afterlife (i.e., post 200 C.E.) of the theme, but also of its antecedents in the Old Testament and, indeed, of non-Israelite and pre-Israelite material which affected the formulation of those Old Testament texts. Although the following violates the chronological strictures mentioned at the beginning of this note, a very brief summary of the Old Testament and non-Israelite non-materials may be appropriate and will indicate the general contours of a more comprehensive study.

There are in the Old Testament texts three themes which, in my judgment, are pertinent.[18] The first refers to eating and drinking before YHWH,

---

18. I repeat with respect to the Old Testament texts here mentioned the same strictures applied to relevant New Testament texts in n. 14 above. In a fuller discussion, detailed textual and exegetical comments would be mandatory. Especially important for delineating the devel-

and stresses joy and communion (e.g., Deut 12:7–18; 2Sam 6:18–19; 1Chr 29:22, etc.). Often the meal is set in a covenantal context. The parade example is Ex 24:1–11 where the Sinaitic covenant is sealed with sacrifices and culminates with the statement that they (the covenant participants) beheld God, and ate and drank. The renewal of the covenant in the postexilic period was also accompanied by a meal (Nehemiah 8–10, esp. 8:9–12). A meal could also be involved in human covenants, binding together the covenanting parties (e.g., Isaac's covenant with Abimelech, Gen 26:26–32; and Adonijah's conspiracy, 1Kgs 1:22–26). The first theme, then, may be summarized as joyous covenantal communion.

Both of the other themes are, to a certain extent, "eschatological" in nature. The first, and more predominant, emphasizes the sacrificial slaughter of God's enemies "on that day." Many of the usually adduced texts do not explicitly mention a meal, e.g., Isa 27:1; 34:5–7; Jer 25:15–34; (unless mention of "the cup of wrath" be an extremely vague allusion); Jer 46:10. The emphasis is on vengeful triumph.

Three passages in Ezekiel 29:3–5; 32:2–8; and 39:17–20) do refer to sacrificial slaughter and a subsequent meal. The eaters are not the redeemed, however, but the beasts and the birds of the air (cf. Rev 19:17–18). The first two passages clearly adapt this "eschatological" theme to a historical situation. The slain enemy is Pharaoh and by extension Egypt as a whole. (This is also the case with the two passages from Jeremiah which were cited above.) A historical application of the theme is found also in Zeph 1:7–9 and probably in the somewhat enigmatic verse in Obad 16. I shall return to this "historization" in the conclusion of the note. The third passage from Ezekiel (39:17–20) is more clearly "eschatological" in nature, but as was noted above, its emphasis is on God's slaughter, not communion with his people. They are spectators, not participants in the meal.

The first two passages in Ezekiel contain an element which requires attention (29:3–5, 32:2–8). In them the food of the sacrificial feast is the flesh of the dragon (tannin). Ps 74:13–14 reflects this motif: The dragons (tanninim = Leviathan), crushed by YHWH, are the food which will be eaten by the creatures in the wilderness. There are, of course, many allusions in the Old Testament to the myth of the triumph of YHWH over the primeval dragon.[19] Many of them have been "naturalized" or "historicized," though the mythic-eschatological dimension, a somewhat strange combination,

---

opment of the history of the tradition would be dating the passages in Jeremiah and Ezekiel. If they are "authentic," then the mythic-historic-eschatological complex belongs to an early, exilic, period in the biblical literature.

19. A list of the most relevant Old Testament texts, with brief commentary, may be found in T. H. Gaster, Thespis, 2nd rev. ed. (Garden City, N.Y., 1961), pp. 42–48. The most comprehensive study, with full citation and discussion of Old Testament and cognate texts, is that of J. Day, God's Conflict with the Dragon and the Sea (Cambridge, Mass., 1985).

should not be overlooked. In some passages, above all Isa 51:9–11, the mythic, the historical, and the eschatological are fused in a dramatic fashion. A full-scale investigation of this theme would constitute a significant section of a larger study, but for our immediate purposes I shall simply note that no Old Testament passage directly relates the slaying of the "dragon" to a meal shared by the faithful.

The third theme depicts the joyous participation of the redeemed in the eschatological meal. (No Messiah, of course, is directly mentioned. The passage in Zech 9:9–17 *may* be an exception. See below.) Evidence of this theme, to say the least, is scanty. The clearest example is Isa 25:6–8:

> On this mountain the Lord of hosts will make for all peoples a feast of fat things, a feast of wine on the lees, of fat things full of marrow, of wine on the lees well refined. And he will destroy on this mountain the covering that is cast over all peoples, the veil that is spread over all nations. He will swallow up death forever, and the Lord God will wipe away tears from all faces, and the reproach of his people he will take away from all the earth; for the Lord has spoken.[20]

Most commentators also cite Isaiah 55, and this is, in all probability, correct. The author, however, has reshaped the theme in a remarkable manner. Even more attenuated are the passages in Isa 49:9–12; 65:13–16; and Zeph 3:8–13. Peaceful feeding in the future *may* reflect a nuance of the motif, but if so, the allusion is highly indirect.

Zech 9:9–17 requires special comment. If this passage does refer to an eschatological meal,[21] then vs. 15 may be a direct witness to the combination of themes of judgment of enemies, their slaughter, and the feasting of the redeemed.[22] The interpretation of the passage is, however, too problematical to be used unequivocally as direct testimony. I am inclined so to understand it, but caution is warranted.

The Old Testament evidence can be summarized briefly. First, joyous communion with YHWH, often in a covenantal context, could be projected to a feast in the eschatological era. Second, drawing upon mythic themes depicting the mighty triumph of God over his enemies, judgment is emphasized. These two themes, joy and judgment, can operate separately or can coalesce.

A final topic—which would require detailed examination in a fuller treatment of the messianic meal, its post 200 C.E. development, and its antecedents—is the pre-Israelite combat myth (Divine Warrior) which, as we have

20. A detailed study of the material in Isaiah 24–27 may be found in W. R. Millar, *Isaiah 24–27 and the Origin of Apocalyptic* (Missoula, Mont., 1976).

21. So, for example, P. Hanson, *The Dawn of Apocalyptic*, rev. ed. (Philadelphia, 1979), pp. 292–324, esp. p. 316; *JBL* 92 (1973) 37–59.

22. S. B. Frost, in *Old Testament Apocalyptic* (Epworth, 1952), remarks that this is the only passage in the Old Testament where Yahweh's people share in the feast after the destruction of their enemies (p. 128).

seen, has been incorporated into a number of Old Testament texts. Here we can only mention it and refer to some of the more important representative discussions.[23] Since Gunkel, it has been a commonplace to refer to apocalyptic as the eschatologizing of myth, though there is a lack of clarity on a precise definition of each of the three terms. Gunkel, of course, could utilize only the Mesopotamian materials, but since the Ras Shamra discoveries a more immediate influence is patent. In both its Mesopotamian and Ugaritic forms, the myth includes a banquet as a consistent component.

Though scholars differ slightly in their reconstruction of the details of the myth, the following is a representative consensus: threat, war, victory, banquet. (Temple building also often appears.) Investigation of the utilization of pre-Israelite mythic themes in the Old Testament and their appearance in a radically transmuted form in apocalyptic literature is an important enterprise. Extreme caution must be exercised, however, in distinguishing between the persistence of imagery and the persistence of ideology. (One might mention Milton in this connection.) Is there some reasonable ideological connection between the banquet in its mythic (cultic) setting and its eschatological setting in apocalyptic? That is a question more easily asked than answered, but it has an important bearing on traditio-historical studies. Consideration of this issue must be deferred to a later occasion.

VI

The following observations may sharpen certain central conclusions and point to the directions desirable for further research and expansion.

1. The theme of a messianic/eschatological banquet was well known in Jewish and Christian apocalyptic thought. Although it is found in its developed form in only a surprisingly few texts, its pervasiveness is attested by allusions to it which can be given without explanation or comment.

2. The immediate background of the theme is to be derived from a number of Old Testament texts which depict the slaughter of God's enemies on the day of his triumph and/or which speak of the festal meal of the redeemed on that day. The former theme is dominant, but occasionally the two are brought into conjunction. Both judgment and joy are ingredients of the motif.

---

23. F. Cross has been a pioneer in this area. Good introductions to his program may be found in "New Directions in the Study of Apocalyptic," *JThC* 6 (1969) 157–65; "The Divine Warrior" and "The Song of the Sea and Canaanite Myth," in *Canaanite Myth and Hebrew Epic* (Cambridge, Mass., 1973), pp. 91–111 and 112–44 respectively. In addition to the works of Millar and Hanson mentioned in nn. 20 and 21 above, the treatment by P. D. Miller, *The Divine Warrior in Early Israel* (Cambridge, Mass., 1973), is relevant.

3. The New Testament, as would be expected, associates the meal with Jesus, both in his earthly career and in his future coming. In the New Testament and in early Christian writings the motif is incorporated into the celebration of the Eucharist as a proleptic participation. (This would seem to be the case also at Qumran.)

4. More detailed examination of fragments of the motif in Jewish and Christian literature of the period (200 B.C.E.–200 C.E.) should be pursued.

5. Careful attention should be given to the use and development of the motif in post 200 C.E. Jewish and Christian literature.

6. The pre-Israelite and non-Israelite backgrounds of the motif should be examined, especially in the context of the problem of the continuity of imagery and the continuity of ideology. Mowinckel's warning that we should not confuse exegesis with the history of motifs is cogent.[24]

7. The messianic/eschatological banquet is by no means a central and indispensable element in Jewish and Christian apocalyptic. More intensive study of it, however, may enhance our understanding of the diverse ways Jewish and Christian apocalyptic writers utilized their traditions to meet the needs of their own times. This is no small contribution.

---

24. *He That Cometh*, trans. G. W. Anderson (Oxford, 1956), p. 218.

B. M. BOKSER   12

MESSIANISM, THE EXODUS PATTERN, AND EARLY RABBINIC JUDAISM

Two issues are raised by the now generally accepted observation that early rabbinic documents, in particular the Mishnah and Tosefta, do not take active messianic stances, that is, do not orient themselves or structure their teachings around the end of time or a victory over history, and do not expect divine intervention in the near future to rectify worldly problems: First, how may we properly assess the implications of these findings regarding the common need to look to the future? As Charles Dickens suggests in *Hard Times*, unless an individual is caught up in his or her own illusionary perfect world or intends to oppress people and prevent them from aspiring to self-improvement, that person needs to be receptive to hopes and dreams. Hence, how do the early rabbinic sources treat idealized visions of the future and integrate them into their notions of religious life? Second, keeping in mind that messianism took diverse concrete forms, do the early rabbinic references, although admittedly not part of a utopian, radical cataclysmic system, belong to a restorative, less radical type of hope that aims at recreating a past condition felt as an ideal?[1]

Let me explain the basis for these questions. We are able to address the question of interpretation, asking how to evaluate the adaptation of messianic themes in early rabbinic Judaism, because scholars have completed the basic descriptive research. In two stages, they have mapped out the broad contours of rabbinic views of the messianic kingdom. In the first stage, writers such as Joseph Klausner and George F. Moore, despite an uncritical use of early and late documents, found that amoraic teachings treat messianic

---

1. See G. Scholem, "Towards an Understanding of the Messianic Idea in Judaism," in idem, *The Messianic Idea in Judaism* (New York, 1972), pp. 1–36. Cf. R. Werblowsky, "Messianism in Jewish History," in *Jewish Society Through the Ages*, ed. H. Ben-Sasson and S. Ettinger (New York, 1971), pp. 30–45; S. Talmon, *King, Cult, and Calendar in Ancient Israel* (Jerusalem, 1986), pp. 202–24.

themes more extensively than tannaitic traditions.[2] In the second, more recent, stage, scholars became more attentive to differentiate between sources; some even analyzed the structural role of the messianic motifs and how they are employed in the diverse rabbinic documents.[3] Since they— like the students of other Jewish writings such as the Dead Sea Scrolls, Philo, the New Testament, 4 Ezra, and 2 Baruch—recognized that we cannot impose a single messianic view on the varieties of ancient Judaism, they have investigated how diverse writers adapted the earlier heritage and their diverse visions of the future.[4] Recent scholars have thus demonstrated that in tannaitic traditions in particular, messianic themes are present but not determinative; they are references but not organizing principles; they refer to the past or future but neither to an imminent present nor to a future whose realization is desperately sought.

In 1977, Anthony Saldarini notably found that:

> The rabbinic texts [the Mishnah and Tosefta] . . . do not reflect a live apocalyptic impulse. Many elements of apocalyptic (as well as of eschatology in general) are present, but mostly in a muted and fragmentary form. The references to the world to come do not occur in a visionary context or with the help of a heavenly mediator. There are no elaborate scenes of battle or judgment. Rather the heavenly realities which are the stuff of apocalyptic are presented as adjuncts to other discussions or in the course of exegeses. Neither the pressure of persecution nor the ecstasy of vision seem to have motivated the authors of rabbinic literature, but rather a concern to live the law in ordinary life, a task which is given more depth and dimension by attention to the future which is the completion of and integral to the present. To this complex belief system with its subordinate category of eschatology, apocalyptic thought has made a small contribution.[5]

2. J. Klausner, *The Messianic Idea in Israel* (New York, 1955); see esp. pp. 32, 389–407, 420, 437, 458–59, 465, 469; G. F. Moore, *Judaism in the First Centuries of the Christian Era*, 2 vols. (New York, 1971), see esp. vol. 2, p. 346.

3. See B. Bokser, "Recent Developments in the Study of Judaism. 70–200 C.E.," *The Second Century* 3 (1983) 26–27, for references (esp. to L. Landman, *Messianism in the Talmudic Era* [New York, 1979], an introduction [n.b. pp. xxiii–xxiv, xxxii], anthology, and bibliography; and A. Saldarini, "Apocalyptic and Rabbinic Literature," *CBQ* 37 [1975] 348–58)—to which add: M. Smith, "What Is Implied by the Variety of Messianic Figures," *JBL* 78 (1959) 66–72; S. Lieberman, "Mishnat Shir ha-Shirim," in G. Scholem, *Jewish Gnosticism, Merkabah Mysticism, and Talmudic Tradition* (New York, 1965), pp. 118–26, and I. Gottlieb, "Sea and Sinai, Tent and Temple: From Allegory to Idea," the last two of which compare tannaitic with amoraic comments on the Song of Songs; E. Urbach, *The Sages* (Jerusalem, 1979), pp. 649–92; D. Roskies, *Against the Apocalypse* (Cambridge, 1984), pp. 23–25.

4. See P. Hanson, "Apocalyptic Literature," in *The Hebrew Bible and Its Modern Interpreters*, ed. D. Knight and G. Tucker (Chico, Calif., 1985), pp. 465–88; J. Collins, "Apocalyptic Literature," in *Early Judaism and Its Modern Interpreters*, ed. R. Kraft and G. Nickelsburg (Atlanta; Philadelphia, 1986), pp. 345–70, esp. pp. 359–60; G. W. Sayler, *Have the Promises Failed? A Literary Analysis of 2 Baruch* (SBLDS 72; Chico, Calif., 1984); F. J. Murphy, *The Structure and Meaning of Second Baruch* (SBLDS 78; Atlanta, 1985); esp. J. Neusner et al., eds., *Judaisms and Their Messiahs* (Cambridge, 1987).

5. A. Saldarini, "The Uses of Apocalyptic in the Mishna and Tosefta," *CBQ* 39 (1977) 396–409.

This approach was more broadly adapted by Jacob Neusner, who comprehensively reviewed the rabbinic canon, document by document. He laid out, first, how various works draw on the repertoire of messianic terms and themes, adapting them for ulterior purposes, and second, how they treat history and historical information, elements usually considered central in messianic thinking.[6] My own research on notions of redemption associated with Passover in the Mishnah and in the Palestinian Talmud,[7] coincides with Neusner's overall observations. On the one hand, the Mishnah refers to the world to come in general terms, treating the ultimate future situation of the individual and not the group; it focuses not on salvation but on sanctification; it may mention the messiah but in doing so refers to a factual matter or point of reference or an unidentified person who does not figure prominently and who does not resolve any of the major religious issues of the day; and it does not project the belief in the coming of this person or time as the foundation for structuring current existence. On the other hand, postmishnaic sources—and this is important—openly confronting the reality of an unredeemed world, turn to the future and reintroduce messianic hopes but yoke them to the Mishnah's foundation so that what counts and what provides meaning is salvation in the present and not a hoped-for, fundamentally new future; hence the means to obtain those messianic hopes entails, for example, changing the current human condition.

This paper will enable us to appreciate the significance of this overall distinction and to illuminate how in the process of emphasizing personal sanctification and in creating an ahistorical vision of the current world, even the tannaitic sources had to channel messianic hopes in a concrete fashion. In addition, we will see that the early rabbinic position cannot be simply identified with the "restorative" type of messianism, for it does not make dominant the restoration of the past glories of the Davidic dynasty nor otherwise actively look for a victory over history, even of a future growing out of history.[8]

The two mishnaic references to the "messiah" demonstrate that the issue is not whether or not the Mishnah mentions the messiah but what a source does with the reference. The first reference, m. Soṭ 9:9–15 (actually part of a probable postmishnaic addition closing the Mishnah tractate), need not de-

6. J. Neusner, *Messiah in Context* (Philadelphia, 1984). See, e.g., how L. Schiffman—"The Concept of the Messiah in Second Temple and Rabbinic Literature," *Review and Expositor* 84 (1987) 235–46—builds on Neusner.

7. B. Bokser, *The Origins of the Seder* (Berkeley, 1984) and "Changing Views of Passover and the Meaning of Redemption According to the Palestinian Talmud," *AJS Review* 10 (1985) 1–18.

8. Cf. P. Schäfer, *Studien zur Geschichte und Theologie das Rabbinischen Judentums* (Leiden, 1978), pp. 37–43; Urbach, *Sages*, pp. 649–52; E. Schürer, *The History of the Jewish People in the Age of Jesus Christ. A New English Version*, vol. 2, rev. and ed. G. Vermes, F. Millar, and M. Black (Edinburgh, 1979), p. 495.

tain us since its transformation of the messianic orientation on the future by making worldly virtues primary is readily recognizable, as Neusner proves.[9] Hence we turn to m. Ber 1:5, the other reference and the one which connects the notion to the paradigm of the Exodus from Egypt:

A. They mention the Exodus from Egypt at night.

B. Said R. Eleazar ben Azariah, I am like a seventy year old and was not worthy (of understanding) that the Exodus from Egypt be said at night, until ben Zoma expounded it.

C. As it is said, "So that you remember the day on which you left the land of Egypt *all the days of your life*" (Deut 16:3).

D. "The days of your life"—(refers to) the days. "*all* the days of your life"—(includes) the nights.

E. And sages say, "The days of your life"—(refers to) this world. "*all* the days of your life"—includes the days of the messiah.[10]

Since line A indicates the passage's redactional perspective to validate the mention of the Exodus at night, which is spelled out in Eleazar ben Azariah's and ben Zoma's view, their opinion in B through D is primary, and the opposing opinion of sages in E is secondary. Paradoxically, the latter position, reminding us of the usual connection between the Exodus from Egypt and the days of the messiah, may provide a key to understand the Mishnah by underscoring that a shift has taken place. The significance of that new association of the Exodus event is revealed by noting the Mishnah's use of the term "Exodus from Egypt," *yĕṣî'at miṣrayim,* a phraseology that the Bible never employs. As David Daube observes, the development of this expression may represent a "decisive step from thinking about that event in concrete terms towards a historical-theological concept."[11] This development would build on the Bible which had made the event into a primary model of redemption and a legal and religious concept centering on the notion that God saves Israel in dire situations. To depict the great deliverance of Israel which made them a people, gave them the Torah, and led them into the promised land where they were to build a sanctuary, Scripture uses diverse formulary concepts of law and customs, thereby anchoring the story in solid legal relations, ethics, and justice, which gives it eternal validity, confidence, and stability. As Daube observes:

9. Neusner, *Messiah,* pp. 26–30, 37–38. The tractate closes with an addition whose first part may draw on toseftan materials; cf. S. Zeitlin, in Landman, pp. 110, 512; J. Epstein, *Introduction to the Text of the Mishnah* (Jerusalem, 1964), pp. 684–85, 956, 976–77.

10. The Leiden MS's variant, cited by Klausner, *Messianic Idea,* pp. 410–14, 419, is otherwise only attested in the K MS's margin; N. Sachs, ed., *Mishnah Zeraim with Variants* (Yad haRav Herzog—Makhon haTalmud haYisraeli haShalem; Jerusalem, 1971), p. 13, n. 89.

11. D. Daube, *The Exodus Pattern in the Bible* (London, 1963), p. 34; see pp. 31–34.

The consequence was to lift the Exodus out of the sphere of the accidental, the arbitrary, the mythological and, instead, to link it to norms of—in the eyes of the authors and their successors—eternal validity. It is from that moment that Biblical salvation acquired that connection with ethics and justice, social and international, which marks it off throughout the centuries from otherwise comparable Oriental and Hellenistic notions. God was seen as intervening, not like a despot, but in the faithful exercise of a recognized privilege—which would, in turn, impose lasting obligations on those on whose behalf he intervened. . . . What we are at the moment concerned with is the confidence and stability which resulted from this anchoring in firm legal relations. As God had vindicated those relations in the Exodus, one could be certain that he would vindicate them again, and again, unto the last. The kind of salvation portrayed in the Exodus was not, by its nature, an isolated occurrence, giving rise to nebulous hopes for similar good luck in the future: it had its root in, and set the seal on, a permanent institution—hence it was something on which absolute reliance might be placed. . . . By being fashioned on the Exodus, later deliverances became manifestations of this eternal, certainty-giving relationship between God and his people. . . . [E]ven events prior to the Exodus were made to approximate the latter, so as to gain still earlier proof of this role of God. (Pp. 13–14)

The prophets in particular played up the notion of "a change of master" so as to convince the Israelites that they remained under divine rule and could be assured of future deliverance. Samuel E. Loewenstamm[12] documents how this pattern is reflected in historiographic and prophetic biblical texts that depict the Exodus as a source of inspiration or a paradigm of a divine saving act, which provided the basis for other acts of benevolence in the past and in the future and which made up the core of a present promise (2Sam 7:23–29; Micah 7:15; Isaiah 11; Jer 23:7–9; Num 24:5–9; Josh 9:9–13). In the eyes of biblical writers, since even Gentile nations knew of the Exodus's significance, they were wary of offending Israel (1Sam 4:8; cf. Ps 136), something credible considering Weinfeld's research, which points to the ancient Near Eastern background of these legal and customary patterns.[13] Loewenstamm expands on the point that the Exodus created both a requirement to follow divine laws and a basis of the promise for Israel's future redemption (esp. Judg 6:13; Ps 80).

We can now appreciate the Mishnah. When one mentions the Exodus one refers not merely to a past historical event but to a concept rich with impli-

---

12. S. Loewenstamm, *The Tradition of the Exodus in Its Development*, 2nd ed. (Jerusalem, 1972), pp. 15–24; Daube, *Exodus*, pp. 42–46. For the pattern's NT use, see W. D. Davies, *The Setting of the Sermon on the Mount* (Cambridge, 1964), pp. 25–93, 113–24.

13. M. Weinfeld, *Justice and Righteousness in Israel and the Nations* (Jerusalem, 1985), pp. 133–41.

cations for the present and future.[14] But despite the fact that the Mishnah's prooftext of Deut 16:3 comes from an account of the Passover festival, which provides a natural setting for mentioning the Exodus, the Mishnah surprisingly associates the Exodus with the Shema prayer. This contrasts with the Mekilta *Bo* 16 and SifDeut 130 parallels to this passage which speak of remembering the Exodus without specifically mentioning the Shema, and also contrasts with the Passover haggadah, which appropriately includes the mention of the Exodus as part of the seder night liturgy, to wit, the annual holiday of Passover provides an opportunity to remember and to be open to the message and experience of redemption.[15]

What the Mishnah has done is to *extend the ritualized act of remembering the Exodus to a daily recitation of the Shema*, either in the third paragraph of the Shema (Num 15:37–41), which directly mentions the Exodus, or else in the blessing following the Shema.[16] In such daily recitation an individual affirms that the Exodus finds relevance in daily life—at "all hours"—and is not something projected to the future.[17] Likewise, the individual in prayer experiences a divine nearness which the concept of *yĕṣî'at miṣrayim* had spoken of in terms of God dwelling amidst the people at Zion. Accordingly, since the Mishnah makes the spiritualized adaptation of *yĕṣî'at miṣrayim* primary and the view of the sages, which projects the relevance of the Exodus to the future, secondary, it casts the standard association of *yeṣiat miṣrayim* with a future redemption—as a "tag-along" opinion.[18]

The use of this concept in m. Ber 1:5 fits in with the tractate's overall efforts at mandating and standardizing a system of blessings and prayers projected not merely as the pious acts of individuals but as the community *'ăbodah* or service of God. In doing so, it confronts a central theological problem. In the words of Joseph Heinemann:

> How can we further hope that our prayers will be heard and answered after the destruction of the Temple, which entailed the removal of the Divine Presence

14. On rabbinic recognition of the Exodus's relevance for future redemptions see: Klausner, p. 17; L. Ginzberg, *An Unknown Jewish Sect* (New York, 1976), pp. 233–38; M. Kadushin, *The Rabbinic Mind* (New York, 1952), pp. 73–74, 358–61; Daube, *Exodus*, pp. 45–46; D. Berger, "Three Typological Themes in Early Jewish Messianism," *AJS Review* 10 (1985) 141–43.

15. T. Zahavy, *Eleazar ben Azariah* (Chico, Calif., 1977), p. 14. N.b. Josephus *Ant* 4.8.13 #212, cited by L. Ginzberg, *A Commentary on the Palestinian Talmud*, 4 vols. (New York, 1941–61), vol. 1, pp. 206–7; R. Kimelman, "The Shema and Its Blessings," in *The Synagogue in Late Antiquity*, ed. L. Levine (Philadelphia, 1987), pp. 74–76.

16. Although the former identification seems self-evident, the latter accords with the previous Mishnah's treatment of the blessings encasing the Shema, and with m. Ber 2:2, which suggests that the third paragraph need not be said at night. See Ginzberg, *Commentary*, vol. 1, pp. 207–8; S. Lieberman, *Tosefta Kifshuṭah*, 10 vols. (New York, 1955–88), vol. 1, p. 12; H. Albeck, *Shisha Sidre Mishnah*, 6 vols. (Jerusalem, 1958), vol. 1, p. 327.

17. See the usage at SifDeut 161 (ed. Finkelstein, p. 212); cf. Schäfer, p. 38.

18. On the derivation from "*all (kol) the days of your life*," see GenR 91.10 (ed. Theodor and Albeck, p. 1134) and n. to 1.6.

and the break in the nearness between Israel and their Father-in-Heaven? The Temple's destruction not only brought the end of the sacrificial worship but also prevented the possibility of prayer, of worship of the heart.[19]

Mishnah Berakot responds by rejecting this logic and its conclusion. It conveys that response not by openly discussing the issue but by speaking as if it were not a problem. Indeed the discussion is predicated on the notion that prayer is possible, that through prayer a person can relate to the divine and experience God's presence and that, in turn, the divine is accessible. Likewise, it builds on the idea that everyday experiences become opportunities to be reminded of the divine and to relate to the divine's manifestation in the world.[20] For example, m. Berakot chapter 9 provides rules for the proper behavior facing Jerusalem and the Temple mount—subtly assuming or suggesting that despite the recent traumatic events, the original holiness of the Temple mount remains in effect.[21] Similarly, m. Ber 4:5–6, reflecting the notion that God's Potent Presence, the Shekinah, is still most effectively addressed through the Temple mount, requires people to orient their prayers to Jerusalem. The Mishnah, in accord with its general tendency, does not justify these assumptions nor tell us that they form a message especially relevant to post-*hurban* and post-Bar Kokhba Jewry who were bereft of the Temple and denied access to Jerusalem.

While we can now understand the role of m. Ber 1:5 within the tractate, the question becomes, Why include the sages' view? I submit that the presence of the sages' opinion impresses on us that *Eleazar ben Azariah and ben Zoma provide an alternative to the standard perception*, insisting that a person remembers the Exodus day and night—and not in the future, and *highlights the shift from the plain meaning of Deut 16:3*. Accordingly, through its place in a liturgical ritual, the mention of the Exodus reminds people of God's role in helping Israel and in living in a world as recipients of the divine act. This works on two levels. First, people's daily lives elicit the memory of the Exodus because they are able to enjoy life as a result of that liberation. The words of prayers, in this case the Shema, therefore suggest that the relationship with God remains intact, that God's gift of the Torah is the loving symbol of that relationship, and the human response is acted out by performing the commandments.[22] Second, in these moments of prayer, particularly

19. J. Heinemann, *Prayer in the Period of the Tanna'im and the Amora'im* (Jerusalem, 1964), p. 21.

20. See Heinemann, *Prayer*, pp. 17–28; M. Kadushin, *Worship and Ethics* (New York, 1963); and esp. B. Bokser, "The Wall Separating God and Israel," *JQR* 73 (1983) 349–74.

21. See B. Bokser, "Approaching Sacred Space," *HTR* 78 (1985) 279–99.

22. Cf. Kadushin, *Worship*, pp. 78–96; E. Schweid, *Mysticism and Judaism According to Gershom G. Scholem* (Jerusalem Studies in Jewish Thought Sup 2; Jerusalem, 1983), pp. 47–49; J. Heinemann, *Studies in Jewish Liturgy* (Jerusalem, 1981), pp. 12–21; Kimelman in *The Synagogue*, pp. 73–86.

in reciting the Shema, when people turn and open themselves to God, they can experience an intimacy with the divine that was traditionally associated with the Exodus and with hopes for future redemption. Because, therefore, in the ritual moment of prayer, a person can overcome the dissonance caused by comparing the ideal of redemption with current reality, religious life is not dependent on an apocalyptic intervention into history. The Mishnah thus spiritualizes or depoliticizes the notion of *yĕṣî'at miṣrayim*. Whatever the future will bring, one central aspect of the messianic heritage has already found fulfillment in current religious life.

This interpretation of the Mishnah is not a modern homily, for it is not only in accord with spiritualization of the messianic belief in m. Soṭ 9:9–15, as noted above, and implied in t. Ber 1:10–15, as we shall see, but already attested and expanded on in Mekilta *Bo* 16 (ed. Lauterbach 1:135–39; ed. Horowitz-Rabin, pp. 60–61). Let us pause to examine this midrashic text.

The Mekilta passage, commenting on the mention in Ex 13:3 of "remembering this day on which you went out from Egypt . . . ," cites an exposition of the similarly phrased verse "that you may remember the day when you went out from Egypt all the days of your life" (Deut 16:3). Structuring the discussion to respond to an opening inquiry as to the scriptural origin of mentioning at night the Exodus from Egypt, the Mekilta draws on the m. Ber 1:5 material. It then presents a supplementary debate setting out the reasons for the two positions, a debate which with some variations also appears in the Tosefta, and goes on to speak of the recital of the blessings after and before food and over the Torah. [23]

On examination, we find that the Mekilta's treatment of these blessings echoes the transformation in m. Ber 1:5 of the Exodus from Egypt pattern. [24] The grace after meals consists of four blessings. The first blessing speaks of God's ongoing act of salvation in sustaining people with food from the earth. The second, further developing the latter point, refers to God providing the Israelites with: (a) good and ample land, after having redeemed them from Egypt and having given them a covenant of the Torah with its laws; (b) life; and (c) the ongoing gift of food. By including the last item, it may suggest that the previous acts are continued in the everyday gift of food. The third blessing, providing the acknowledgment of current reality, appeals for the rebuilding of Jerusalem and (in the earliest version) implies, if not mentions, divine compassion for the Temple. [25] Significantly, including these hopes in a

---

23. See Ginzberg, *Commentary*, vol. 1, p. 219; S. Abramson, "Four Matters in Midreshe Halakhah," *Sinai* 74 (1974) 1–7.

24. See Lieberman, *TK*, vol. 1, pp. 101, 102; Heinemann, *Studies*, pp. 3–6, 12–18.

25. The use of Deut 3:25 in the Mekilta and the t. Ber 6:1 parallels decisively supports the identification of the referent with the Temple; see G. Vermes, *Scripture and Tradition in Judaism*, 2nd ed. (Leiden, 1973), pp. 26–39. The prayer's later versions specify Israel, Jerusalem, and Zion.

context which actually states that God has not abandoned but has continued to redeem Israel in effect channels the aspirations in a manner that downplays any dissonance. Hence, it is as if this blessing (in particular, if, in its original form, it was brief and uncomplex) simply states that the rebuilding of Jerusalem and the Temple also need attention. The fourth blessing brings home this point, as well, by acknowledging that God does all good for Israel.

In its references to the set of blessings over the Torah, the Mekilta likewise channels eternal hopes into a ritual act and an acknowledgment that the ultimate good—the Torah—resides with Israel. The Mekilta thus not only calls the Torah ḥayê ʿolām, "life eternal" or the "good," par excellence, but also cites a tradition that requires mentioning the Torah in the grace after meals.[26] The overall notion is somewhat differently conveyed by the next pericope, which for an unspecified context, possibly over the Torah or in the invitation to grace after meals, prescribes blessings that evoke or suggest that God is being encountered, blessed, and exalted, thereby underscoring the point that the object in question, be it the Torah or the food, provides the very gift of redemption, that is, the experience of the divine.[27]

The Mekilta, confirming our reading of the deeper structure of m. Ber 1:5, expresses the thought that God sustains life and gives food in the here and now as well as in giving the Torah which the people read and over which they recite blessings, encounter the divine, and gain life eternal. A person, therefore, does not have to wait for the Messiah. These passages strikingly illustrate my observations from 1983: "rabbis applied eschatological motifs to nonmessianic activities such as study of Torah and channeled messianic hopes into prayer and rites such as the Passover evening celebration or preserved them as a future goal."[28]

Mishnah Ber 1:5 hence associates ben Zoma with a theological position stressing the potentiality of current religious life and attributes to the sages a view holding that the experience of the Exodus also applies in the future. In Scholem's terms, we might see in the *latter* opinion a restorative messianic notion, which through replaying the past engenders and encourages hope for the future. Although we must put off further discussion of the nuances of these positions until after analyzing the Tosefta, it is clear, at this point, that if ben Zoma or Eleazar ben Azariah's opinion was formulated to respond to sages, the latter opinion must have circulated in their day, in the first century, and perhaps should be understood in light of messianic trends

26. Lieberman, TK, vol. 1, p. 102.

27. Cf. ibid.; Horowitz-Rabin, p. 61, n. to line 11; t. Ber 6:1; SifDeut 306 (ed. Finkelstein, pp. 342–43).

28. "Recent Developments," p. 26. My analysis is supported by individual studies of the Mekilta such as N. Zohar, "The Living and the Dead in the March of Redemption—Editing and Meaning in *Mekhilta de-Rabi Yishmael*—An Interpretation of the First *Parshah* of Massekhet Beshalaḥ," *Jerusalem Studies in Jewish Thought* 4.3–4 (1984–85) 223–36.

that came to the forefront in the two rebellions against Rome.[29] But however
we assess and interpret that opinion, the Mishnah and Mekilta—and, we
shall see, the Tosefta—choose to deemphasize that approach.

T. Ber 1:10–15 (ed. Lieberman, pp. 4–6) extensively supplements Mishnah Berakot chapter 1. In bringing out the assumption of the Mishnah, it not
only supports my reading of m. Ber 1:5 but also adds a second nuance to the
depoliticizing of the messianic heritage. Dividing the Tosefta, for the sake of
discussion, into five units, we find that it: (I) opens by quoting the dispute in
m. Ber 1:5 between ben Zoma and sages; (II) appends a debate in which the
two parties argue the matter; (III–IV), supplementing the interchange in (II)
regarding the possibility that the future redemption will overshadow the Exodus, presents other instances in which a new experience might change the
character of the old; and (V), closing with a final application of this pattern,
focuses on the Temple mount and the presence of God. The Tosefta reads:

I = t. Ber 1:10 *(ll. 41–46).*

A. *They mention the Exodus from Egypt at night.*
B. *Said R. Eleazar ben Azariah, I am like a seventy year old and was not
   worthy of hearing*[30] *that the Exodus from Egypt be said at night, until
   ben Zoma expounded it.*
C. *As it is said, "So that you remember the day on which you left the land
   of Egypt all the days of your life" (Deut. 16:3).*
D. *"The days of your life"—(refers to) the days. "all the days of your
   life"—(includes) the nights.*
E. *And sages say, "The days of your life"—(refers to) this world. "all the
   days of your life"—includes the days of the messiah.*

Except for one slight variation, I. A–E follow the Mishnah rather closely.
II, providing rationales in the form of a debate, adapts a Jeremian approach
to affirm the divine covenant relation with Israel. It reads:

II = t. Ber 1:10 *(ll. 46–54).*

F. Said to them ben Zoma, And will they mention the Exodus from Egypt
   in the days of the messiah? And is it not already said, "Assuredly, a time
   is coming—declares the LORD—when it shall no more be said, 'As
   the LORD lives, who brought the Israelites out of the land of Egypt,'
   but rather, 'as the LORD lives, who brought the Israelites out and led

---

29. Cf. esp. Schäfer, *Studien*, pp. 37–39.
30. See Lieberman, *TK*, vol. 1, pp. 12–13.

the offspring of the House of Israel from the northland (and from all the lands to which I have banished them)'" (Jer 23:7–8).[31]

G. They said to him, Not that the Exodus from Egypt be uprooted from its place (in memory); rather the Exodus from Egypt will be an addition to the kingdoms[32]: the (consummation of the four world) kingdoms will be the main thing and the Exodus from Egypt will be secondary.

H. Similarly, "Your name shall no longer be called Jacob but rather Israel," etc. (Gen 35:10): not that the name of Jacob should be uprooted from him but rather that Jacob should be added onto Israel, Israel the primary (name) and Jacob (the) secondary (name).

Note, first, how F's claim that the new future redemption will be different asserts that the hopes associated with the Exodus are distinct from those connected to the ultimate future. By therefore projecting redemption as a future liberation from Israel's current oppressor, it divorces the hope for divine intervention from the Exodus concept and makes yĕṣi'at miṣrayim stand for something else. Sages in G, on the other hand, assert that the traditional aspiration associated with the Exodus remain relevant for the future.

To appreciate the role of these thoughts in the Tosefta's wider thinking we should, secondly, note two literary features of the text. First, G employs the verb la'aqor, "uproot," which is used to state that the Exodus experience will not be uprooted, a word that reappears in the chapter's last tradition, S, which speaks of Jerusalem being uprooted (paradoxically to suggest that while Jerusalem is being uprooted, the Exodus experience is not uprooted); and, second, F and G (and subsequent traditions) use a similar pattern, the former in citing Jeremiah's reference to a change in God's name, and the latter in a diverse set of related teachings. As we shall see below, these two

---

31. Witnesses to the Tosefta and parallels vary in citing the similarly worded Jer 16:14–15 or 23:7–8. While the Tosefta's p.e. cites only their common beginning, the Erfurt and Vienna MSS (with some verbal forms fitting the Jeremiah 16 alternative) cite Jeremiah 23. Lieberman, TK, vol. 1, p. 13, however, prefers Jer 16:14–15, which is found in Mekilta Bo 16, possibly attested by remnants in the Erfurt and Vienna MSS, and appropriate for the abbreviated p.e. It reads: "Assuredly, a time is coming—declares the LORD—when it shall no more be said, 'As the LORD lives, who brought the Israelites out of the land of Egypt,' but rather, 'As the LORD lives, who brought the Israelites out of the northland (and from all the lands to which He banished them).'"

32. Although one could read mlkwt, "sovereignty [of God]," in accord with t.Ber 2:1 (which contains a dispute over adding, in the blessing after the Shema, the mention of mlkwt, "sovereignty of God," in addition to the Exodus from Egypt; see Kimelman, p. 78), it is preferable to read mlkywt, "kingdoms," following the MSS and p.e., for: (a) 1.56 attests this usage; (b) the verse in question contrasts the Exodus redemption with that of the future (the one "from the North"); (c) the notion of the "sovereignty of God" may be inappropriate here (despite later being interpolated into diverse prayers, as Kimelman notes) because the Jeremiah verse treats the restoration of Israel.

repeated features bring attention to the Tosefta's adaptation of a central Jeremian response to the Temple's destruction. The prophet transformed the covenant relationship between God and Israel to redefine the soteric tradition by arguing that the destruction indicated that the covenant was in effect; since God had to punish as a response to sin, the fulfillment of the punishment proved that the sin was now forgiven.[33]

Unit III, to underscore the proceeding point, supplements ben Zoma's association of Jer 23:7–8 with Isa 43:18, which states that the future will bring something new:

III = t.Ber 1:11 (ll. 54–62).

I. Likewise, "Do not recall what happened of old, or ponder what happened of yore" (Isa 43:18). "Do not recall what happened of old"—these (are God's acts) of (redemption from) the kingdoms, "or ponder what happened of yore"—these (are God's acts) of (redemption from) Egypt. "I am about to do something new. Even now it shall come to pass (, suddenly you shall perceive it: I will make a road through the wilderness and rivers in the desert)" (Isa 43:19)—this (refers to) the war of Gog and Magog.

J. They drew a parable to what does the matter resemble? To one who was walking on the road and a wolf attacked him but he was saved from it and he would continually tell of the incident of the wolf. (Later) a lion attacked him but he was saved from it; he forgot the incident of the wolf and would tell of the incident of the lion. Afterwards he was attacked by a snake but he was saved from it; he forgot the other two incidents and would continually tell of the incident of the snake.

K. So too are Israel, the later travails make them forget the earlier ones.

III.I reinforces the support for ben Zoma, though J and K, through a parable, refine that position by redefining how the messianic experience will provide a new type of deliverance. Despite some ambiguity, it speaks of one encounter causing the previous experience to be forgotten and thus sees the relation of the events not just as a matter of what is primary but of the lack of an ongoing relevance.[34] The messianic days will, therefore, provide a new

---

33. H supports the sages, though one could employ its citation of Gen 35:10 in the manner of Mekilta *Bo* 16 (ed. Horowitz-Rabin, p. 59) to support Eleazar ben Azariah (to wit, only regarding Jacob does Scripture, e.g., at Gen 46:2, indicate that the initial name may also be used). See Ginzberg, *Commentary*, vol. 1, p. 220; Lieberman *TK*, vol. 1, p. 13. Although clause I apparently lends weight to Eleazar ben Azariah and ben Zoma, it opens in I with the term "similarly," the word with which H begins. This anomaly may have been caused by the use of a stereotypic structure in which the traditions are cast or may indicate that we have a remnant of a different understanding or use of these traditions, which has been reworked in the Tosefta.

34. Cf. Ginzberg, *Commentary*, vol. 1, pp. 221–22.

type of deliverance. The next unit, IV, provides a transition to the Tosefta's main point that a change does not always entail a change in reality:

IV = t.Ber 1:12–14 *(ll. 62–72)*.

L. Similarly (the change in name denotes a change in function or character), "No longer shall your name be Abram, but your name shall be Abraham" (Gen 17:5). At first, lo, you are the father of Aram. Now, lo, you are the father to the entire world, as it is said, "For I have made you the father of a multitude of nations" (ibid.).

M. Similarly, "As for Sarai your wife, you shall not call her name Sarai, but Sarah shall be her name" (Gen 17:15). At first, lo, she was the ruler of her people. Now, lo, she is the ruler over all the world, as it is said, "But Sarah shall be her name" (*srh* = ruler).

N. (Yet the change of a name does not change one's true identity:) Even though (Scripture) went and called Abraham Abram (Neh 9:7), it was not (done) pejoratively but rather in praise; and Joshua (who Moses, at Num 13:16, had named, was subsequently called after his initial name) Hosea (Num 13:18 and Deut 32:44), it was not (done) pejoratively but rather in praise. It was the same Abram before (God) spoke with him as after (God) spoke with him; it was the same Hosea before he entered greatness (as the people's leader) as after he entered greatness. (In these cases the new name or office did not go to Moses' or Joshua's head; rather each remained modest.)

O. (The second half of another tradition makes the same point:) (The doubling of the name) Moses Moses (Ex 3:4), Abraham Abraham (Gen 22:11), Jacob Jacob (Gen 46:2), Samuel Samuel (1Sam 3:10) all of these (repetitions) are expressions of endearment, expressions of encouragement.
    [Alternatively,[35]] They are the same before (God) spoke with them as after (God) spoke with them; they are the same before they entered greatness as after they entered greatness.

Note how N and O modify L and M's additional support for Eleazar ben Azariah and ben Zoma by asserting that despite Abraham and Sarah's change in name, which marked a change in their place or role in history, their personality did not change; they remained the same modest people, a point spelled out in the partial parallel in SifDeut 334 (ed. Finkelstein, p. 384). By implication, the change in the name of future redemptions, no longer characterized by the Exodus and its experiences, does not mean that the future redemption involves a changed reality or a total departure, for it will not

---

35. This term is found in the Sifra Vayiqra 1:12 (ed. Finkelstein, p. 13) parallel.

change the nature of things. The final section, unit V, spelling out the nuance of this thought, suggests that similarly God's presence, the Shekhinah, is not in exile awaiting a messianic return but maintains its customary nature. Hence, while God's relationship to Israel may appear to change depending on its adherence to the covenant, God remains the same as does the divine manifestation in Zion.

V = t.Ber 1:15 *(ll. 72–82)*.

P. Similarly, "*Salem* has become his abode; Zion, his dwelling place" (Ps 76:3). Why does Scripture reapply its (Jerusalem's) former name? Because it says, "This city has aroused my anger and my wrath" (Jer 32:3). Perhaps (erroneously one might think that) even now lo it is (is regarded) with anger and wrath? Therefore the teaching says (to the contrary), "toward that *mountain* which God desired for his dwelling" (Ps 68:17). Lo, it is (regarded) with desire and craving. (This) teaches that its destruction effected atonement for it.

Q. And from where (do we learn) that the Divine Presence (*haššĕkînāh*) does not return to its (Zion's) midst until it becomes (again) a mountain? As it is said, "*salem* has become his abode" (it will be God's dwelling place when it is Salem). We find that when it (the Temple mount) was Salem (it) was called a "mountain." (Hence what is crucial is its quality as a mountain:) Lo, the Divine Presence does not return to its midst until it becomes (again) a (desolate) "mountain." (God's presence will thus be on the mountain just as it had been before the Temple had been built, when it was still Salem.)

R. And (another verse, which attests that Abraham had called the place a "mountain") says, "And Abraham called the name of that place 'The Lord will provide' (or "will be seen") as it will be said today, 'On the *mountain* God will be seen'" (Gen 22:14).

S. And (Ps 137:7) says, "Remember, O Lord, against the Edomites the day of Jerusalem." When? When its (the Temple's) foundations will be uprooted from it. "How they cried, 'Strip her, strip her to her very foundations!'" (That day became a day to remember because then the Divine Presence could return to the mountain).

This section caps the redactor's orchestration of a long series of traditions which build on and refine antecedent comments to create a subtle essay on the fate of the Shekinah and the relation of messianic beliefs to current religious life. Since it, in contrast to units II through IV (and the Mishnah in I), is lacking in the tannaitic analogues to Eleazar ben Azariah's exposition and, therefore, may not have circulated as part of the larger composition, it may in particular reflect the editor's hand in manipulating earlier teachings and thus reveal the section's overall design.[36] Just as with the change of names of individuals, so with the Temple mount's return to its pre-Temple name, after the Temple's destruction, the state of the Divine Presence dwelling in Zion does not change. In fact, restoring the mount to its initial stage as a mountain provided for atonement.[37]

Roots for this idea are found in Jeremiah, Deutero-Isaiah, and Ezekiel's transformation and radicalization of the earlier soteric tradition which tied together destruction and deliverance, as T. Ludwig notes.[38] These prophets made the notion that God saves Israel by destroying their enemies subservient to Israel's responsibility to live up to the demands of the covenant relationship. They emphasized that YHWH's activity in saving the people could include judging and destroying them when they did not live up to their responsibilities. Yet, since they also thereby opened the way for renewal, they pressed the people to return to the covenant with God.

The parallel between the situation of Jewry after the first and second destructions is striking as is the role of the prophets and rabbis in working out a viable response. At such times of "disjunction," there is an "overriding need for religious meaning and security" and people "question the continuing efficacy of YHWH's saving power . . . [and] the continuing existence of the covenant community which could be faithful to YHWH," experiences which the prophets reflected.[39] Jeremiah in particular may offer a precedent for the Tosefta's idea that the very act of destruction provided atonement and may illuminate how the Tosefta's seemingly contrasting uses of the verb "uproot" ties together the whole text and how the uprooting of the Temple and Jerusalem becomes a sign of the emerging new redemption which did not fully "uproot" the Exodus experience. Accordingly, if previous Israelite or Jewish sins had caused the Shekhinah to depart the city (as portrayed in prophetic oracles), the Divine Presence could now return, in accord with those very same prophetic models.

> [The prophets] extended the sacred history to include the present historical process; the motif of passing through YHWH's judgment to reach new life became the scheme for an understanding of a new and greater act of salvation taking place in their present experience. [P]recisely in the present crisis they were confronting the power of the God of the covenant.

---

36. Cf. Lieberman, *TK*, vol. 1, p. 14.

37. Cf. A. Goldberg, *Untersuchungen über die Vorstellung von der Schekhinah in der frühen Rabbinischen Literatur* (Berlin, 1969), pp. 321–22, 523–24. See Bokser, "Wall"; R. Ḥayyim Yosef David Azulai, *Rosh David, Vayeṣe* (p. 25c), cited by Lieberman, *TK*, vol. 1, p. 14.

38. T. Ludwig, "'Remember Not the Former Things,'" in *Transition and Transformation in the History of Religions: Essays in Honor of J. M. Kitagawa*, ed. F. Reynolds and T. Ludwig (Leiden, 1980), pp. 22–55.

39. Ibid., pp. 26, 30, 34.

Ludwig's observation regarding the Exodus paradigm in Deutero-Isaiah is most relevant to our analysis:

> [F]or all the disjunction in the sacred history, the soteric traditum from the past shapes the vision of the new saving event. Of primary eschatological significance to Deutero-Isaiah was the *Heilsgeschichte* centering on the Exodus from Egypt, the journey through the wilderness, and the entry into the promised land; these old saving events provided the pattern for this description of the crucial events of the new age just now breaking forth. [40]

Since works like Jeremiah are known to have inspired ancient Jewish thinkers in time of crisis, [41] we may properly employ a nuanced reading of the prophets to illuminate the Tosefta. On the one hand, according to ben Zoma, who (in t.Ber 1:10F) avers that the new redemption or messianic days will usher in a new type of experience, the hopes associated with the Exodus differ from those of the ultimate future. Hence, if this *future* redemption brings liberation from Israel's *current* oppressor, the promises of the Exodus experience do not support a belief in a divine intervention in the present. [42] In the face of the Temple and Bar Kokhba catastrophes, one should, therefore, not simply fall back on "traditional" answers that God will intervene. Sages in G, on the other hand, asserting that those traditional aspirations will be relevant in the future, must hold that experiences previously attested in human history will recur in the future. But note, since the Tosefta's formulation in G–H makes the sages focus on what comprises the major or essential quality of the redemption, they would recognize that the future is not a simple retelling of the past redemption. Likewise, the apparent support for ben Zoma, in I–K, finding three referents in the Isaiah verse, envisions, as over against the Exodus, one form or stage of redemption other than the ultimate unprecedented one (of Gog and Magog). That is, even if the Exodus is not a paradigm for the messianic days, the intermediate stage of redemption, here associated with the "kingdoms," may involve some type of familiar experience. Moreover, the parable, in J–K, in speaking of "remembering" and "forgetting" previous saving acts, focuses more on human experience and memory than on the objective quality of what takes place. Significantly, as the Mekilta *Bo* 16 parallel speaks neither of primary or secondary matters nor of three stages, but only two, "now" and the "future," [43] the Tosefta may

---

40. Ibid., pp. 44, 46, 50.
41. See S. Cohen, *From the Maccabees to the Mishnah* (Philadelphia, 1987), pp. 28–29.
42. See M. Herr, "Realistic Political Messianism and Cosmic Eschatological Messianism in the Teaching of the Sages," *Tarbiz* 54 (1985) 344–45.
43. The Mekilta's casting of the parable, except in the Munich MS, and its preceding parable of a parent with a female and then a male child, even in the Munich MS, likewise make this simple contrast. Moreover, it is the Munich MS's addition to the animal parable alone which has the person "forget" instead of "leave aside" the encounter with the previous animal. See Ginzberg, *Commentary*, vol. 1, pp. 221–22. Different conceptualizations of the future undoubtedly

be slightly aligning the sages' opinion with ben Zoma's, thereby shifting the issues in accord with the coming modification in N–O. Making the same point, H refers to Jacob's name in a manner that likewise anticipates the focus, though with a different slant, on the change of names in L–O (= IV = t.Ber 1:12–14).

In suggesting that the uprooting of the city insured that the Exodus would not be uprooted, the Tosefta may build on the biblical strand such as in Exodus 15 that held that the Exodus experience culminated in the divine dwelling in the sanctuary or holy mountain. Since the model of redemption built on this pattern promised a religious encounter with the divine or the divine dwelling within God's special place, usually identified as Zion,[44] it is not surprising that the Tosefta runs counter to many messianic accounts which stress a rebuilding of the Temple at the end of days or messianic period.[45] The key point is that while the Tosefta may assume that the rebuilding is to take place, religious life is not dependent on it.

Accordingly, the destruction was an act of atonement restoring Zion to its natural state as the divine dwelling place. This notion of Zion is seen in Ps 76:3, which calls the spot by its original name *šalem*, reminding us that the later role of Jerusalem was foreshadowed even before the Temple was built on it.[46] Similarly Ps 68:17 speaks of the place as a *har*, mountain where God desires to dwell, a point further attested by the Tosefta's reading of Gen 22:14 that God was seen on the mountain—when it was a mountain—and will in the future also be so experienced. This understanding of Genesis 22 both contrasts with other readings which see verse 14 as a prophetic statement that the site will be rebuilt and exemplifies how the Tosefta goes beyond its sources, reworking and expanding diverse traditions and combining them so as to make a new point.[47]

---

help account for the diverse uses of the terms "future," "World/Age to Come," and "messianic age"; cf. Klausner, *Messianic Idea*, pp. 410–17, and S. Talmon, "Waiting for the Messiah," in *Judaism and Their Messiahs*, pp. 115–28.

44. Weinfeld, *Justice*, pp. 136–38; cf. D. Freedman, "Temple Without Hands," in *Temples and High Places in Biblical Times*, ed. A. Biran (Jerusalem, 1981), pp. 21–30. See also, e.g., Ben Sira 36:11–117; Schürer, vol. 2, pp. 498–500, 529–30, 531–37.

45. See, e.g., D. Juel, *Messiah and Temple* (SBLDS 31; Missoula, Mont., 1977), pp. 150–51, 169–209; and the references to P. Schäfer, R. J. McKelvey, and L. Gaston, in Bokser, "Wall," p. 368, n. 52.

46. See M. Weinfeld, "Zion and Jerusalem as Religious and Political Capital," in *The Poet and the Historian*, ed. R. Friedman (Chico, Calif., 1983), p. 103, who notes that Genesis 14 foreshadowingly depicts Abram appearing at Salem after defeating the northern kings, earning the blessing of Melchizedeq, and donating a tithe of the spoil to the LORD.

47. As attested in SifDeut 28 (ed. Finkelstein, pp. 44–45), R thus supplies Q's referent; Lieberman, *TK*, vol. 1, p. 14. An alternative and later rendering of Gen 22:14 (found first in SifDeut 352 [ed. Finkelstein, p. 410], to which GenR 56.10 [ed. Theodor-Albeck, p. 608] adds prooftexts), construing the verse as a prophetic precedent (in Abraham's mouth) that the site will go through three stages (built, destroyed, and rebuilt), uses the word *har* ("mountain") as the second referent. While SifDeut primarily treats the third—future—stage, seeking to give Israel

The Tosefta may indicate that its final comment represents its main point by closing with a citation of an exegesis of Psalm 137 that employs the verb "uproot," which echoes the use of this verb above in G and which suggests that the "day of Jerusalem," when the city's foundations were *uprooted*, is not a sad day but actually a momentous one.

Let me summarize our analysis. I have demonstrated that the Tosefta provides an early understanding of the Mishnah and brings out its basic assumption. With a two-pronged approach deftly responding to the theological problem posed by the Temple's destruction, the Tosefta rejects the assumption that one must await the messianic period to experience a full religious life and a restored Judaism. First, it suggests that the return of the Divine Presence is not predicated on a new and ultimate redemption, for the earlier changes overcoming the Temple mount, in both name and physical reality, did not prevent it from remaining a place of theophany and dwelling for the Shekhinah. Second, by having people mention the Exodus in the liturgy, it impresses on them the importance of the pious acts of prayer and has them learn to appreciate the fulfillment of the *yĕṣī'at miṣrayim* in this life.

Tosefta's approach in effect makes the destruction an act of divine dispensation, a position expanded on in postmishnaic circles. But in contrast to many amoraic traditions (in their confrontation with current reality and reincorporation of messianic themes though linked to mishnaic principles), the Tosefta, like the Mishnah as a whole, does not project hopes for a better life to the future. As a result, while the Tosefta's wording does not reveal the intent of those who expressed these thoughts, they would appear to downplay the need to find compensation in the face of the Temple's destruction. These circles would probably, therefore, have held that although it would have been preferable if the Temple did not deserve destruction, considering, however, that it did, the destruction was purposeful.

I can now interpret my close reading and analysis of these texts. Four points stand out.

First, Jews in the first two centuries held diverse views regarding the traditional hopes for the future. Rabbinic circles, although apparently not preoccupied with the problem, did discuss the relationship of past redemptions to the future one(s), and masters differed over the place of the prophetically envisioned later days or messianic period within the scheme of the future. Certain early authorities, in effect, see in messianism the hopes for a political improvement and utopian transformation—projected to a distant future. The Mishnah's editor (perhaps responsible for including the sages' opinion in m. Ber 1:5 to highlight the subtle shift taking place) drew on these traditions to emphasize that prayer and the encounter with the divine was still possible in the present—and hence an individual in this life can be satisfied in yearning for divine nearness. The Tosefta's editor both articulated the assumption behind this spiritualization of messianic ideas and suggested that the Potent Presence remained on the mountain; he thus squarely confronted the religious problem posed by the Temple's destruction and the traditional notions regarding the messianic restoration of the Divine Presence at the end of days. In doing so, he apparently modified both ben Zoma's tradition and the opposing opinion, bringing the two positions closer together. Mekilta *Bo* 16, in an expanded analogue to the Tosefta, likewise personalizes and channels the messianic notions into experiences and religious acts in the present world. Downplaying the notion of compensation, these sources thus validate alternatives to a central cult, though—perhaps paradoxically—still maintain the belief in the special quality of the Temple mount. The fact that the Tosefta adopts both approaches may mean that they could be perceived to be complementary. We might be able to understand this in light of Urbach's suggestion that the notion of the Presence in the Temple was believed to ensure that the Presence was also available in the world at large.[48]

Second, studying the editorial work reflected in the rabbinic sources proves more fruitful than the necessary but difficult task of probing the preredactional stages of the documents, which would illuminate the first- to mid-second-century developments. Analysis of other materials may shed additional light, in particular on the common suggestion that rabbis from 70 C.E. until after the Bar Kokhba revolt were not as antithetical to messianic aspirations as were later masters.[49] Our analysis, however, indicates that unless the sources totally misrepresent first-century masters, some of those rabbis already sought to transmute messianic hopes into personal experiences. This picture, moreover, accords with recent research on other first-century works such as Josephus and Pseudo-Philo.[50]

Third, in seeing how these early rabbinic circles differentiated between aspects of traditional messianic beliefs, we can appreciate how they responded in a positive and creative fashion to the inherited views of the future. Like Jeremiah and his colleagues, who radicalized traditional soteric notions, these rabbis transformed, while continuing, messianic ideas and the Exodus pattern. The choices therefore lay not just between accepting or rejecting messianic beliefs.

---

encouragement that it is forthcoming, the Tosefta assumes that the "mountain" is not desolate from God.

48. Urbach, *Sages*, pp. 52–53; on the two approaches coexisting, see R. Goldenberg, "The Broken Axis: Rabbinic Judaism and the Fall of Jerusalem," *JAAR Supplement* 45 (1977), 869–82; Bokser, "Sacred Space." Cf. Philo's dehistoricizing which appears to internalize virtues linked to the soul and to neutralize popular messianism; R. Hecht, "Philo and Messiah," in *Judaisms and Their Messiahs*, see esp. pp. 155–58.

49. See, e.g., Saldarini, "Apocalyptic," pp. 357–58.

50. L. Feldman, "Messianism and Josephus"; D. Mendels (chap. 13, below); Neusner, *Judaisms and Their Messiahs*.

Fourth, early rabbinic circles hence sought to restore order and hold back the chaos that Jews would have felt at the destructions of 66–70 C.E. and 135 C.E. While early rabbinic sources admittedly do not describe that chaos, they point to a comprehensive response to such a crisis. They speak of spiritualizing in everyday rituals messianic notions of nearness to God and also assert that the destruction, in effecting atonement, enabled the Potent Presence to remain on Zion. Consequently, because the editors of these documents and the authorities that they highlight depict (and assumably participate in) a world for which the rebuilding of the Temple might be desirable but is not urgently needed for living a full religious life, they understandably do not reveal what Scholem has called the restorative messianic notion, for the restorative approach is based on openly acknowledging the need to restore. Moreover, in focusing on the *individual's* experience of the divine nearness, they lack messianism's interest in the plight and restoration of the *community*. Similarly, they do not suggest that life should be lived in "deferment," to use another famous Scholem term.[51] Rather, while keeping alive hopes for the future, they suggest that a fulfilling religious life is currently possible.

51. Cf. Scholem, *Messianic Idea*, pp. 19–21, 35, 49–57.

PART FOUR

"MESSIANISM" IN SOCIAL CONTEXTS AND IN PHILO

PSEUDO-PHILO'S *BIBLICAL ANTIQUITIES*, THE "FOURTH PHILOSOPHY," AND THE POLITICAL MESSIANISM OF THE FIRST CENTURY C.E.

In memory of Arnaldo Momigliano

Two major trends can be discerned in the scholarship of the last fifty years concerning so-called messianic groups in Palestine in the first century C.E. up to 70. One view, represented by M. Hengel, suggests that most groups fighting the Romans acted together in one way or another, and that they had a common messianic vision. According to Hengel, these groups were the Zealots and Sicarii.[1] The other view, put forward by L. I. Levine, D. M. Rhoads, and others, is that all the groups terrorizing the Romans acted separately and that few, if any, had a messianic ideology.[2] Within this second group of scholars we can find different attitudes, as for instance in the works of D. M. Rhoads and R. A. Horsley. Horsley, in agreement with M. Stern, claims that there were local messianic groups which were organized around the various pretenders who rose up after Herod the Great's death in 4 B.C.E. and during the Great War (Athronges, Simeon, Menachem).[3]

It is important to stress that Josephus tends to avoid messianism when he relates the history of the first century C.E.; hence we hear little about messianism from the main historical source for this period.[4] Also, the problem of

---

1. M. Hengel, *The Zealots* (Edinburgh, 1989), claims that the Sicarii and Zealots are one and the same movement.

2. L. I. Levine, "Megamoth Meshihiot Besof Yemei Habait Hasheni," in Z. Baras, ed., *Messianism and Eschatology* (Jerusalem, 1983), pp. 135–52 [Hebrew]; D. M. Rhoads, *Israel in Revolution 6–74 C.E.* (Philadelphia, 1976), see esp. pp. 54–93; R. A. Horsley ("Ancient Jewish Banditry and the Revolt Against Rome, A.D. 66–70," *CBQ* 43 [1981] 409–32), in line with M. Smith and S. Zeitlin, argues against Hengel that the Sicarii and Zealots are different groups.

3. M. Stern, "Hamanhiguth Bikvutzoth lohamei Haheruth Besof Yemei Bait Sheni," in *The Great Man and His Age* (Jerusalem, 1963), pp. 70–78 [Hebrew]; Horsley, "Popular Messianic Movements Around the Time of Jesus," *CBQ* 46 (1984) 471–95.

4. See G. Vermes, *Jesus the Jew* (New York, 1973), pp. 129–59 (see esp. n. 20). Rhoads (*Israel*, p. 82) contends that "in general, Josephus suppressed the religious motivations of the revolutionaries by ascribing to them evil and dishonorable intentions." R. A. Horsley and J. S. Hanson (*Bandits, Prophets, and Messiahs* [Minneapolis, Chicago, New York, 1985], p. 114)

the identity of the Zealots and Sicarii, the two groups most strongly identified with messianism, and the precise time of their formation, in the first
century C.E. or earlier, is debated *ad nauseam*.[5] This problem cannot really
be solved until more evidence is found to support one view or the other, and
it is not central to the theme we are now discussing.[6]

---

reach the following conclusion: "Although he is apparently quite familiar with the distinctively
Jewish 'messianic' language, Josephus studiously avoids terms such as 'branch' or 'son of David'
and 'messiah' (*Ant* 10.210; *War* 6.312–13)." Yet he does not hesitate to use the language of 'kingship' (This contention is against Horsley's arguments: Josephus probably used kingship terminology in a regular hellenistic manner rather than a "messianic" one). In fact, scholars pointing
to Josephus' "silence" draw this conclusion *e silentio*. In general, see V. Nikiprowetzky, "La mort
d'Eleazar fils de Jaïre et les courants apologétiques dans le de Bello Judaico de Flavius Josèphe,"
in *Hommages à André Dupont-Sommer* (Paris, 1971), pp. 486–90. For a study of eschatology in
Josephus, see U. Fischer, *Eschatologie und Jenseitserwartung im hellenistischen Diasporajudentum* (Berlin, New York, 1978), pp. 144–83.

   5. As far as one can judge from the available sources, before 65 C.E. a wide consensus existed
which expressed the zealous attitudes of the Jews. There was no clear differentiation between
"Zealots" and "others" (*War* 2.228–31 and Josephus' opinion about the matter in *Ant* 20.257).
For a discussion of the related activity of "robbers," "rebels," and the common people, see *War*
2.234–35 (against the Samaritans; for Pseudo-Philo's anti-Samaritan polemics, see A. Spiro, "Samaritans, Tobiads, and Judahites in Pseudo-Philo," *Proceedings of the American Academy for
Jewish Research* 20 [1951] 279–355; not all of Spiro's arguments can be accepted). Scholars have
not sufficiently examined this upheaval in light of revolutionary movements in the Greek world.
See in particular the following: G. E. M. de Ste. Croix, *The Class Struggle in the Ancient Greek
World* (London, 1981); D. Mendels, "Polybius and the Socio-Economic Revolution in Greece
(227–146 B.C.)," *L'Antiquité Classique* 51 (1982), pp. 86–110; A. Fuks, *Social Conflict in Ancient
Greece* (Jerusalem, Leiden, 1984). From *War* 2 it seems that Josephus does not make a precise
distinction between the various groups that caused unrest, but uses the familiar "topoi" of hellenistic historiography to describe revolutions. Thus Josephus himself does not always know,
even *post-factum*, who is who (even in modern armies it is difficult to recognize who is who
during a war). In his history of the war Josephus frequently makes inexact observations. However, in the later books of the *War* (5.1–22), when he depicts the situation in Jerusalem, he
attempts an exact definition of the various groups; here it becomes clear that *lēstai* is a pejorative
term. Also, his generally exaggerated and emotional statements are at times misleading.

   Ant 17.285 contains a remark that is typical of hellenistic historiography (cf., for instance,
Polybius' "observations" in his description of the *Bellum Achaicum*, 38.9–14). Josephus, apropos
of the pretenders of 4 B.C.E., states: "And so Judaea was filled with brigandage. Anyone might
make himself king as the head of a band of rebels with whom he fell in; then he would press on
to the destruction of the community, causing trouble to few Romans and then only to a small
degree, but bringing the greatest slaughter upon their own people." This is a retrospective generalization which is true only of the year 4 B.C.E. The same is true of his description of 6 C.E.
(*Ant* 18.4–10 and see also *Ant* 20.124, 252).

   6. According to *War* 2.254–57, the Sicarii emerged at the time of Felix (52–60), after the
lēstai of Eleasar Ben Dinai were eliminated. Josephus emphasizes that the *lēstai* were active for
twenty years (*War* 2.253). From Josephus himself it becomes clear that only during the fifties
did matters in Palestine deteriorate regarding banditry (*War* 2.250–308; *Ant* 20.124, 160–82).
Throughout Book 2 of the *War*, Josephus differentiates between the "rebels" (*stasiastai*), "Jews"
(*Ioudaioi*), "multitude" (*dēmos*), and the "robbers" (*lēstai*) (513–56). He himself was later among
the "rebels," but from *War* 2.577–82 it becomes clear that his army contained many *lēstai*. Many
of them were also *neoi* (*War* 2.576). When Josephus speaks of his enemies, as in the case of John
of Gischala, he speaks of *lēstai* (*War* 2.585–89). See also his commentary on Simeon Bar Giorah
(*War* 2.652–54). The "rebels," however, he praises (*War* 3.11). In *War* 3.450 he mentions the
"rebels" of Tiberias but calls Joshuah Ben Shafat "the ringleader of this band of brigands." He
makes a similar comment about Bar Giorah (*War* 4.84–86). The *Vita* (33) also shows that the
situation should not be schematically systematized.

Some years ago M. Stern referred to this question again, highlighting the problem of the identity of Zealots and Sicarii with reference to their messianic fervor. He argues—correctly in my view—that the groups constituted two different wings of the so-called "Fourth Philosophy."[7] It should be emphasized that Josephus claims in his famous description of the four "sects" in Israel that the "Fourth Philosophy" was in fact similar to the Pharisaic group but differed in one respect—namely, its adherence to God alone as its sole master (*Ant* 18.23: "This school agrees in all other respects with the opinions of the Pharisees, except that they have a passion for liberty that is almost unconquerable, since they are convinced that God alone is their leader and master."[8] No messianism is mentioned by Josephus when he refers to either group. Judging from the Essene writings and the Pseudepigrapha, which antedate 70 C.E., messianism is not of major importance.[9] In many well-known instances, even in the Gospels with their messianic allusions, messianism is toned down.[10] Moreover, we can deduce from Josephus and from other sources of the period that messianism was understood in accordance with biblical notions concerning this phenomenon. The leaders of the "Fourth Philosophy" movement were, after all, but "commentators" on the Torah. These leaders were "wise" people, as Josephus emphasizes many times (viz. *War* 2.118, 433).[11]

As we examine the literature of the first century C.E. (and the centuries before it), we discover two trends of messianic thought. One is full of messianic tension, referring in particular to the biblical concept of Messiah Ben David. A classical passage is found in Psalm 51 of Ben Sira (preserved only in Hebrew; it mentions "Keren le-David"); another is in the Psalms of Solomon 17.[12] Other examples are found in many passages of the Gospels where people identify Jesus as the king of the Davidic dynasty (viz. Mt 9:27, 12:23, 20:30).[13]

The other trend is an "anti-present messiah" concept which can be discerned in some of the Gospels. This concept may be the reason for Jesus' dissociation from Ben David (Mt 22:41–46 and par.).[14] People who were

7. M. Stern, "The Suicide of Eleazar Ben Yair and His Men at Masada, and the Fourth Philosophy," *Zion* 47 (1982) 367–97 [Hebrew].

8. See I. Gafni, in Sh. Safrai, ed., *The Literature of the Sages* (Assen, Maastricht, Philadelphia, 1987), pp. 12–13.

9. See in general E. E. Urbach, *The Sages* (Jerusalem, 1978), pp. 591–600 [Hebrew]. Concerning Qumran we find references in 1QS and 1QSa; cf. J. Licht, *The Rule Scroll* (Jerusalem, 1965), pp. 190, 269–70 [Hebrew], and J. A. Fitzmyer, *Essays on the Semitic Background of the New Testament* (Missoula, Mont., 1974), pp. 120–21. (Also see L. H. Schiffman in the present volume, ch. 6). The view that Judah and Levi are messianic figures is problematic: D. Mendels, *The Land of Israel As a Political Concept in Hasmonean Literature* (Tübingen, 1987), pp. 105–7.

10. Consult, for instance, Mt 16:13–20; Mk 8:27–30, 9:2–13, 10:47–52.

11. Interestingly, Ps-Philo 20:2–3 emphasizes the *sapientia* which Joshua inherited from Moses.

12. Urbach, *The Sages*, pp. 592–94 [Hebrew].

13. J. Liver, *The House of David* (Jerusalem, 1959), pp. 143–44 [Hebrew].

14. For the various interpretations see Fitzmyer, *Essays*, pp. 113–26.

against a messianic figure for their own time were not against the idea of messianism in general, as we can learn from Mk 13:21–22 and parallels (see Jn 9:22). Thus we can possibly say that all groups within Judaism expected messianism in its biblical form; but they differed in their attitudes toward an actual messiah.

Two questions are now posed: (1) Can these attitudes be related to particular classes in Jewish society? (2) What was the spiritual origin of messianism for people who had messianic expectations? The first question is complex and cannot be answered thoroughly within this short paper. It is now clear that many of Jesus' followers came from among the poor, but the wealthy and "middle" class also showed an interest in, and joined, Jesus' movement (Mt 19:16–30, 27:57–60; Lk 19:1–10). This particular movement—like that of the Essenes—may have been exceptional. It is very difficult to get a clear picture from Josephus of exactly which classes fought the Romans and were therefore (as many scholars would say) imbued with messianic fervor. E. J. Hobsbawm's generalizations of banditry in modern times cannot be automatically applied to the historical context under discussion.[15] Josephus, it should be emphasized, writes in line with hellenistic historiography and thus when he mentions such groups as *lēstai, hoi polloi, neoi, Joudaioi, ponēroi, kinetikoi, stasiastai, Galilaioi, gerontes, ochlos, dynatoi* he does not refer to clear sociological groups.[16] In fact, many of these terms are used loosely and pejoratively[17] to denote the "rebels." Since this issue is complex, it suffices now to state only that messianism in its biblical connotation no doubt permeated all classes, groups, and sects. It was found among the *hoi polloi, prōtoi,* Pharisees, Zealots, Sicarii, and other Jews who adhered to the Torah. From Josephus we learn at least one thing with certainty: the God-fearing Jews came from all strata of society, hence it is not surprising that he refers to "Jews" in many revolutionary contexts. This brings us to the second question.

What was the spiritual origin for Jews who held messianic expectations?

---

15. E. J. Hobsbawm, *Bandits* (London, 1969). B. D. Shaw, who did some more comprehensive work on banditry in the Roman Empire from a sociological viewpoint, does not elaborate on the question of *lēstai* in Palestine. See his "Bandits in the Roman Empire," *Past and Present* 105 (1984) 3–52. However, see his "Tyrants, Dynasts and Kings." On *lēsteia* in Judaea, consult B. Isaac, "Bandits in Judaea and Arabia," *HSCPh* 88 (1984) 171–203.

16. For this problem in general, see T. Rajak, *Josephus* (London, 1983), pp. 84–94. From a different angle, see S. J. D. Cohen, *Josephus in Galilee and Rome* (Leiden, 1979), pp. 181–88. Cohen (p. 183) rightly claims that "Josephus too often oversimplifies and writes as if there were a clean dichotomy . . ." (A good demonstration for our case is Acts 17:5 when all the enemies of Paul in Thessalonica are depicted in a pejorative manner: *andras tinas ponērous kai ochlopoiēsantes ethoruboun*).

17. Another example: Eusebius (*Church History* 4.6.2) refers to Bar Kokhba as follows: "The Jews were at the time led by a certain Bar Chochebas, which means 'star,' a man who was murderous and a bandit (*phonikos kai lēstrikos tis anēr*), but relied on his name, as if dealing with slaves, and claimed to be a luminary who had come down to them from heaven and was magically enlightening those who were in misery."

It is evident that they looked back to their past which was in many aspects so frustrating. I cannot enter here into the problem of the character of biblical messianism; this subject is elaborated upon elsewhere in this volume.[18] However, on this particular point I can state, in agreement with Hengel, that it is almost axiomatic to assume that people who followed the Torah and were fighting the Romans and other gentiles had in one way or another messianic expectations (although I cannot wholeheartedly agree with Hengel's claim regarding a major political movement starting at the beginning of the century).[19] But what were the *contents* of this messianic thought? We know that among other messianic concepts, people played with the idea of a figure who would hail from the House of David. This is significant, because, as in analogous instances, an expectation of a messianic character turns the minds of people to their past.[20] The reference to the House of David conjures up associations with the history connected to the ascendance of this house (it is not necessarily an expectation of the coming of a "branch" of the House of David [Jer 23:5]; we also find the idea of a *David redivivus* [Ezek 37:21–28]). Thus, despite the fact that messianism is concerned with the future, namely with eschatological concepts, it is basically imbued with past history. This is particularly true of the Jews, who so vehemently lived in relation to their past. Hence we can easily assume that David and the circumstances of his ascendance to the throne played a significant role among the so-called messianic Zealot groups. The Pharisees, who were spiritually similar to the Zealots (and/or Sicarii), were against contemporary messianic figures, but they certainly did not deny the hope of a future arrival of a descendant of David. In their view such a descendant would have nothing in common with any of the figures who pretended to be messiahs. Unfortunately we have no Jewish document which gives details of any of the so-called messianic groups and we find only occasional references in our sources to messianism.

However, we do possess a long work which goes into the nature of the historical associations concerning messianism and the king of the House of David. This document, the *Biblical Antiquities* of Pseudo-Philo, can be dated to c. 70 C.E. and may refer to the historical origins of messianism at that time. It is, I believe, an ideological book directed against the very ex-

---

18. Consult J. Liver, "Messiah," in *EncBibl* 5 (1968) 507–26 and S. Talmon, P. Hanson, J. J. M. Roberts, and others in the present volume. Cf. also recently Ursula Struppe, ed., *Studien zum Messiasbild im Altem Testament* (Stuttgart, 1989).

19. Hengel, *Zealots*, passim; W. R. Farmer, *Maccabees, Zealots and Josephus* (New York, 1956) insightfully shows that the Torah was highly honored among the Zealots (pp. 47–83 and passim). Many of Farmer's parallels to the Maccabean period are, however, unacceptable to me.

20. In other cultures a "messiah" figure is in fact a "culture hero," a divine man who taught his people their culture, disappeared, and is expected to come back and be a reformer of all things that went wrong. The Aztecs waited for their culture hero, the God-Snake, who promised to return as a human being. The Germans in the Middle Ages expected the return of Carl the Great; later they waited for the hiding Friedrich Barbarossa to come back. The Bretons awaited King Arthur, and the Bohemians, King Venzel.

treme Zealots and Sicarii of the first century C.E. It uses Israel's history to prove its particular standpoint, and may have originated either in pre-70 Pharisaic circles or among moderate Zealots.[21] In fact, we hear of the Zealots as an organized group only at the beginning of the war in 66; before that time we hear only of a single zealot in Mt 10:4.[22] The *Biblical Antiquities* of Pseudo-Philo presents a unique opportunity to understand what people who were in contact with messianic ideas thought of their history, how they reinterpreted their past in accordance with changing circumstances. Even more importantly for our case, Pseudo-Philo enables us to understand what people who were opposed to a present kingship thought of kings who were not recognized as descendants of the House of David. In the following discussion we will also try to reconstruct some aspects of the ideology behind the so-called "Fourth Philosophy," ironically through a document written by its opponents.

Before going into a more detailed examination of this document, I would like to note that the author of the *Biblical Antiquities*, which was written originally in Hebrew, seems to have been reliving the history leading to the ascendancy of David. Pseudo-Philo, it seems, attempts to experience once again the historical dynamics which led to the foundation of the House of David; but he concludes the story with Saul's death.[23] It is no accident then

---

21. I follow here the text of D. J. Harrington and J. Cazeaux, *Pseudo-Philon Les Antiquités Bibliques* I (Paris, 1976); C. Perrot, P. M. Bogaert, and D. J. Harrington, *Pseudo-Philon Les Antiquités Bibliques* II (Paris, 1976). Most scholars tend to date the document at some point in the first century C.E. Consult, for instance, L. Cohn, "An Apocryphal Work Ascribed to Philo of Alexandria," *JQR* O.S. 10 (1898) 326–28; M. R. James, *The Biblical Antiquities of Philo* (with a prolegomenon by L. H. Feldman; New York, 1971), pp. xxviii–xxxi; C. Dietzfelbinger, in *JSHRZ* II.2 (1975) 95–96; G. Kisch, *Pseudo-Philo's Liber Antiquitatum Biblicarum* (Notre Dame, Ind., 1949), pp. 17–18; D. J. Harrington, "The Biblical Text of Pseudo-Philo's *Liber Antiquitatum Biblicarum*," *CBQ* 33 (1971) 1–17, and in J. H. Charlesworth *OTP*, vol. 2, pp. 297–303. See also J. H. Charlesworth, *The Pseudepigrapha and Modern Research* (Missoula, 1981), pp. 170–73 and 298–99. The crucial passage is 19:7: "I will show you the place where they will serve me for 740 years. And after this it will be turned over into the hands of their enemies, and they will destroy it, and foreigners will encircle it. And it will be on that day as it was on the day I smashed the tablets of the covenant that I drew up for you on Horeb; and when they sinned, what was written on them flew away. Now that day was the seventeenth day of the fourth month." Cohn's argument concerning this passage is indecisive—see A. Zeron, "The System of Pseudo-Philo" (unpublished thesis, Tel-Aviv University, 1973), esp. pp. 45–51 [Hebrew]. Also see Bogaert, *Pseudo-Philon* vol. 2, pp. 66–74. It is likely that *LAB* was composed at some point between 44 C.E. (or rather 52 C.E.) and 66 C.E. I plan to discuss the problem of dating in a future article. An exact date for *LAB* is not necessary for the argument presented now.

22. *War* 2.408–10, but even here Josephus does not use yet either "Sicarii" or "Zealots"; he simply mentions "rebels" (*neōterizontes*). In *War* 2.425 he mentions the "Sicarii" for the first time in the context of the war (before that in 2.254). In *War* 2.444 Josephus mentions the "Zealots" as an organized group (Menachem's murder). Consult the following: O. Cullmann, *The State in the New Testament* (London, 1957), pp. 8–23; S. G. F. Brandon, *Jesus and the Zealots* (Manchester, 1967), pp. 42–43, and Rhoads, *Israel*, pp. 84–87. In Acts 21:20 "Zelotai" denotes individuals who possess a spiritual trait. Cf. E. Haenchen, *The Acts of the Apostles* (Philadelphia, 1979), *ad loc.*

23. Zeron, "The System," esp. pp. 107–16. I cannot enter here into the question of the similarities between Josephus' account of this period and Pseudo-Philo. Consult L. H. Feldman, "Epilegomenon to Pseudo-Philo's *Liber Antiquitatum Biblicarum*," *JJS* 25 (1974) 305–12, and

that our author highlights the period of the Judges, feeling it most analogous to his own lifetime.[24]

The Judges were not popular in Hasmonean literature of the second century B.C.E. They only became fashionable in the first century C.E.[25] The author of the *Biblical Antiquities* shows no particular interest in Israel's history prior to the period of the Judges; he does not bother with Israel's history after Saul's death.[26] Throughout the book the author is concerned about the lack of leadership in Israel at the time of the Judges, but he omits from the traditions in Judges the refrain that anarchy results from the absence of kingship (Ps-Philo 33:4–6). The author compares the first century (probably ante-70 C.E.) to the time of the Judges, which in turn was reinterpreted according to the new conditions. The first century (up to 66) was a time of disintegration; there was no Jewish sovereignty over the Land. A superpower was ruling the country, which was heavily torn by conflicts between Jews and pagans in the cities. Many figures claimed local leadership, and prophets, pseudo-kings, and "magicians" rose up throughout the land. Thus it is not surprising that the author of the *Biblical Antiquities* should have turned to the period of the Judges to find a historical precedent for his own time. By so doing, he transferred his own fears and thoughts to this general historical period. Through his rewriting of history we can discover his own anti-messianic feelings as well as the thoughts of his opponents. In other words, through our author's views, which he transplants into his own interpretation of history, we can discern not only what issues were at stake at the time, but also how the dynamics of history were seen by people who believed that the Messiah Ben David was due. Let us now present some examples:

(A) Pseudo-Philo highlights the Judges as local leaders and launches a strong attack against kingship.

In some recently published papers, R. A. Horsley argues that the pseudo-kings who emerged after Herod's death (as well as the later ones) were eventually looked upon as messianic figures. These charlatans may have been associated with the revival of ideas connected with popular kingship found in the Bible[27]; however, we have too little evidence to ascertain whether the

---

Feldman's *Josephus and Modern Scholarship (1937–1980)* (Berlin, New York, 1984), pp. 418–19.

24. This matter is alluded to briefly by G. W. E. Nickelsburg, "Good and Bad Leaders in Pseudo-Philo's *Liber Antiquitatum Biblicarum*," in J. J. Collins and G. W. E. Nickelsburg, eds., *Ideal Figures in Ancient Judaism* (Chico, Calif., 1980), p. 63; and in M. E. Stone, ed., *Jewish Writings of the Second Temple Period* (Philadelphia, 1984), p. 109.

25. Mendels, *The Land*, passim.

26. L. Cohn, "An Apocryphal Book," *JQR* o.s. 10 (1898) 277–332; G. Kisch, *Pseudo-Philo*, pp. 5–15.

27. In *CBQ* 46 (1984) 471–95, and n. 3, above. This point is elaborated by Horsley and Hanson, *Bandits*, ch. 3. Also, see W. R. Farmer, "Judas, Simon and Anthronges," *NTS* 4 (1957/58) 147–55.

obscure pretenders of c. 4 B.C.E. had any messianic visions. They may simply have been pretenders to kingship, so commonly found in the hellenistic world (like Pseudo-Philip, Eunus, and others[28]). Athronges and Simeon seemed to be eager to imitate Herod the Great, who had no messianic ambitions.[29] Moreover, there is no evidence in the surviving sources of a revival of any popular ideology of kingship. Even if the adherents of the pretenders did refer back to the Bible, Horsley has not proved any of the links that may have existed between the pretenders he mentions and this particular ideology. Also, the terminology denoting kingship which many scholars detect in Josephus relating to the pretenders (including Menachem, Simeon Bar Giora, and John of Gischala) is also common in cases where no messianism is involved (Pseudo-Alexander, Archelaus, and others; viz. *War* 2.26–27; *Ant* 17.202, 232, 269–84, 324–38).[30] However, it is true that certain circles among the Jews wished to revive a kingship deriving from the House of David, but others were vehemently opposed to it. Many instances in the Gospels serve as evidence of this complex situation; for example, Jesus' followers apparently wished to crown him as a king of the Davidic House. The Pharisees were fiercely against this action (Lk 19:36–40 and Jn 6:14–15). The latter concept can also be seen in Pseudo-Philo.

As I have already mentioned, the author of the *Biblical Antiquities* highlights the period of the Judges. Here, when the people of Israel, as in the biblical story, wish to have a king, our author, in contrast to the Bible, says the following (56:2–3):

> And when Samuel heard talk of a kingdom, he was very sad in his heart and said, "Behold, now I see that it is not yet the time for us to have an everlasting kingdom and to build the house of the Lord our God, for these people are seeking a king before the proper time. But even if the Lord so wished it, it seems to me that a king could not be appointed." And the Lord said to him by

---

28. Josephus does not use descriptions which would associate these pretenders with messianic figures. But even if he would have, this does not mean that they were messianic figures. We can illustrate that easily from Polybius' description of Pseudo-Philip (36.10.1–2: "As for the false Philip, at first the story seemed utterly inadmissible. Here is a Philip fallen from the skies who appears in Macedonia, making light not only of the Macedonians but of the Romans too. . . ."), and from Diodorus Siculus, when he referred to Eunus (34/5.2.5–16: "There was a certain Syrian slave, belonging to Antigenes of Enna; he was an Apamean by birth and had an aptitude for magic and the working of wonders. He claimed to foretell the future, by divine command, through dreams, . . . he not only gave oracles by means of dreams, but even made a pretence of having waking visions of the gods. . . . Prior to his revolt he used to say that the Syrian goddess appeared to him, saying that he should be king. . . . Thereupon Eunus was chosen king. . . ."). If the latter passages would have appeared in Josephus, we would no doubt have attributed messianic traits to figures who were not messiahs.

29. The Jews did not understand messianism in this way (*pace* A. Shalit, *King Herod* [Jerusalem, 1964], pp. 270–73 [Hebrew]).

30. The case of the Egyptian false prophet (*War* 2.261–63) may be exceptional; here we see a combination of religious motifs and signs of kingship (although Josephus uses here *tyrannein;* in this line we can also explain Menachem's behavior).

night, "Do not be sad. For I will send them a king who will destroy them, and he himself will be destroyed afterward. (See also 58:4, 59:1–5.)

This is a more negative view of kingship than we find in 1 Samuel 8, even predicting that the *melech beṭerem ʿet* will be killed. This antikingship spirit also emerges from the abbreviated story about Abimelech in Pseudo-Philo 37. The author does not mention that the affair occurred at Shechem. Thus he transfers the antimonarchic atmosphere from the local to the national scene. Later in the book, when Jonathan takes leave of David, he says (62:9):

> Come to me, my brother David, and I will tell you of your righteousness. My soul will pine away in sadness over you, because we are now separated from each other. And our sins have caused this, that we should be separated from each other; but let us be mindful of one another night and day while we live. Even if death separates us, I know that our souls will know each other. For yours is a kingdom in this world, and from you is the beginning of a kingdom which will come in its own time . . . (see also 51:6, 62:2).

Although our author emphasizes the future ascendancy of the House of David, he ends the book with the death of Saul, thus fulfilling Samuel's prophecy recorded in ch. 56. In other words, the author of the *Biblical Antiquities*, who re-creates his past history, puts forward the idea that the time has not yet come for the ascendancy of a king of the House of David. Is he following the same line as those who killed Menachem because he was a "king before the proper time" (*War* 2, 441–48; *Vit* 21), or those who for the same reason wanted to establish a democracy (*War* 4.319–20, and 4.358[31])?

(B) Our author's attitude to Phinehas is significant. In Pseudo-Philo, Phinehas emerges as a figure who is reminiscent of Elijah (Pseudo-Philo 48). According to our author, Phinehas has an eschatological role to fulfill; perhaps he, like Elijah, constitutes an anticipation of the messiah, but this is not stated explicitly (48:1). Although Phinehas may have been a central figure in

---

31. Persons like Hanan and Gurion. John of Gischala's ambitions of becoming "tyrannos" and heading toward "monarchy" (*War* 4.389–97) should not be viewed within this same line. Also, Simeon Bar Giorah's ambitions do not seem to be messianic (*War* 4.510). Concerning the latter point, see G. Fuks, "Simon Bar Giora Gerasenos," *Zion* 52.2 (1987) 141–52 [Hebrew]. Neither Simeon nor Bar Giorah were Zealots in the narrow sense. Menachem was, and hence may have had "real" motivations to become a "messianic" king. See R. A. Horsley, "Menachem in Jerusalem: A Brief Messianic Episode Among the Sicarii—Not 'Zealot Messianism,'" *NovT* 27 (1985) 334–48; but this position is not certain.
  It is impossible to accept the notion that Menachem as well as Ezekias regarded themselves as heirs of the Hasmonean throne. For this notion, see M. Black, "Judas of Galilee and Josephus' 'Fourth Philosophy,'" in M. Hengel *et al.*, eds., *Studien zu Josephus* (Festschrift O. Michel, Göttingen, 1974), pp. 45–54. See also F. Loftus, "The Anti-Roman Revolts of the Jews and the Galileans," *JQR* 68 (1977–78) 78–98. At any rate, it should be emphasized that the Hasmoneans did not view themselves as being messianic figures, and there exists no evidence in the sources that a continuation of the Hasmonean dynasty was on the horizon in Galilee of the first century C.E.

the ideology of the Zealots (as Farmer, Hengel, and Brandon attempted to demonstrate[32]), it can be assumed that he was also not unpopular among wider Jewish circles at the time, especially among those who adhered to the Torah and were not necessarily Zealots or Sicarii. Perhaps he was even used as a figure antithetical to Elijah who was so frequently mentioned by the first Christians.[33] However, more relevant to our case is the fact that the book emphasizes the legitimacy of priesthood bestowed on the House of Phinehas (48:2). In 17:3–4 the author includes the following:

> Now that which happened then was like what Israel did while he was in Meso-
> potamia with Laban the Syrian when he took almond rods and put them at the
> cisterns of water; and the flocks came and drank and were divided among the
> peeled rods, and they brought forth white and speckled and many-colored
> kids. So the assembly of the people was like the flock of sheep. And as the
> flocks brought forth according to the almond rods, so the priesthood was estab-
> lished through almond rods.

This passage, I contend, should be read against the background of the Zealot attempts to reform the method of the nomination of high priests (*War* 4.151–54). It is as if our author was saying that a new method is acceptable, but not elections by lot from a new priestly house. History was interpreted by our author to accord with the new conditions of his day.

(C) The Zealots and Sicarii strongly believed that they should resist the foreigners occupying their land; they adhered to God as their sole master. Thus they fought their Roman oppressor, and in cases where no other choice remained they committed suicide to avoid falling into the enemy's hands.[34] Part of their messianic fervor was their belief in life after death. However, this does not mean that they did not often fight heroically (*War* 3.186–89; 229–33). At this point one should differentiate between a war waged against a foreign oppressor and a conflict with the people living alongside the Jews in Palestine. These conflicts were a matter of course during the forties, fifties, and sixties of the first century C.E.

Pseudo-Philo incorporates these conflicts and transplants them into the past. There is only one "foreign" oppressor mentioned throughout our book. He is Pharaoh, the king of Egypt. In one case a foreign enemy (i.e. one coming from outside the Land) appearing in the Bible is eliminated by our author (Kushan Rishataim; Josephus, referring to Judg 3:8, connects him

---

32. W. R. Farmer, "The Patriarch Phineas," *ATR* 34 (1952) 26–30; Hengel, *Zealots*, pp. 147–79; Brandon, *Jesus*, pp. 43–45.

33. Consult Mt 11:14, 16:14; Mk 6:15, 8:28–29; 9:4–13, 15:36–37; Lk 1:17, 4:24–28, 9:28–36; Jn 1:18–28. In fact, Phinehas was identified with Elijah (Brandon, *Jesus*, p. 5). In general, see R. Hayward, "Phinehas—the Same As Elijah: The Origins of a Rabbinic Tradition," *JJS* 29 (1978) 22–34.

34. In the forties of the first century C.E. we still see how a very wide circle of Jews was prepared to die without being "members" of one group or another. They were zealous in the broad sense of the term, but probably did not belong to an organized group (*War* 2.195–98).

with Assyria). Concerning the Exodus, our author provides a highly interesting elaboration which is unbiblical. He writes (10:3–5):

> Then in considering the fearful situation for the moment, the sons of Israel were split in their opinions according to three strategies. For the tribe of Reuben, and the tribe of Issachar, and the tribe of Zebulun, and the tribe of Simeon said, "Come let us cast ourselves into the sea. For it is better for us to die in the water than to be killed by our enemies." But the tribe of Gad, and the tribe of Asher, and the tribe of Dan, and that of Naphtali said, "No, but let us go back to them; and if they are willing to spare our lives, we will serve them." But the tribe of Levi, and the tribe of Judah, and that of Joseph, and the tribe of Benjamin said, "Not so, but let us take our weapons and fight with them, and God will be with us." And Moses cried out to the Lord and said, "Lord God of our fathers, did you not say to me, 'Go and tell the sons of Israel, "God has sent me to you"'? And now behold you have brought your people to the edge of the sea, and the enemy has pursued them; but you, Lord, remember your name." And God said, "Why have you cried out to me? Lift up your rod and strike the sea, and it will be dried up."

Here we have a midrashic embellishment on the theme of how to react in the face of a threatening enemy. There are three views: (1) Let us commit suicide; (2) let us give ourselves up and be servants of the Egyptians; and (3) the view put forward by the "best" tribes—Levi, Judah, Joseph, and Benjamin—let us struggle against the Egyptians with the help of God.[35] None of these views prevailed. A fourth one materialized: God rescued his people and they did not have to take any of the first three measures. Through this episode our author expresses his practical message for the present time: do not fight the oppressor; God will, provided you believe in him. We know from Josephus and the New Testament that Passover was always a time of trouble for the relations of the Jews with the Roman oppressor (viz. *War* 2.10–11; *Ant* 17.213–16[36]). It was a time of mass gathering in Jerusalem. The association with an abrupt change from servitude to liberty linked to this event caused much commotion among the Jews. Against this background one should read Pseudo-Philo, especially ch. 10.[37] The Zealots and Sicarii used violence to fight the oppressor; others surrendered to the Romans, but some did commit suicide (apparently members associated with the Sicarii movement[38]). It is against all those currents that our author launches his new

---

35. S. E. Loewenstam (*The Tradition of the Exodus in Its Development* [Jerusalem, 1965], pp. 99–100, 123) brings parallels from the Midrash; but he does not refer to any actuality which eventually emerges from our text.

36. And *Ant* 18.29–31, 20.105–12, and Josephus' comment in *War* 4.399–404 and 5.98–105.

37. The story of Theudas (*Ant* 20.97–99) is reminiscent of the Exodus in face of the Roman oppressor; consult also Acts 5:36 and Rhoads, *Israel*, p. 83.

38. See S. J. D. Cohen, "Masada: Literary Tradition, Archaeological Remains, and the Credibility of Josephus," *JJS* 33 (1982) 385–405; and Stern, "The Suicide of Eleazar Ben Yair," *Zion* 47 (182) 367–97 [Hebrew].

interpretation of the biblical story. Unfortunately his opinion did not prevent the great war from breaking out.

The other case concerned the fight which the Jews initiated or were forced to wage against the gentiles living in the Land (for instance, see *War* 2.457–80[39]). Here our author uses the period of the Judges to express his opinion about the struggle with the actual people of the Land. Many significant alterations, additions, and eliminations are made by our author; all of them are unbiblical. One example alone must now suffice to illustrate these alterations. Cenaz, a judge invented by our author, fights the gentiles, but succeeds only when he receives God's approval. The warriors may participate in the fight against their enemies only after they are purified and prove their belief in God. All those from among the "mob" who are nonbelievers are eliminated by the leader. They are not allowed to fight for God.

The motto which emerges from Pseudo-Philo concerning the fight against the gentiles living in the Land is clearly revealed in 27:14: "Now we know that the Lord has decided to save his people; he does not need a great number but only holiness." Our author's perspective is singularly significant; this problem did *not* preoccupy any of the Pseudepigrapha written during the Hasmonean period, which dealt with ancient wars. The last verse seems directed against those—probably Zealots—who relied on the "vast mob" when initiating the war (*War* 2.410). Josephus seems to agree with our author's view on the matter (*War* 2.577–82[40]). Moreover, the success in local wars always depended upon God's will (for instance, Ps-Philo 27:12). It seems that no territorial acquisition was made as a result of these wars.

Our book emphasizes a strong opposition to paganism and foreign temples in Palestine.[41] The Land seems to be amorphous, and in many instances our author transfers events from their biblical loci to other sites.[42]

---

39. For the impact of those relations on the war of 66–74, see, in general, U. Rappaport, "The Relations Between Jews and Non-Jews and the Great War Against Rome," *Tarbiz* 47 (1977–78) 1–14 [Hebrew]. Except for some sporadic incidents with the Samaritans, up to the sixties of the first century C.E. the relations between Jews and foreigners in the Land of Israel seem to be good (Josephus emphasizes the exceptional cases: *War* 2.266–70, 284–92; *Ant* 19.299–312; and see D. R. Schwartz, *Agrippa I* [Jerusalem, 1987], pp. 22–26 [Hebrew]); *Ant* 20.2–5; 173–78. According to *War* 2.457–86 and *Life* 24–27 the clashes between Jews and pagans in the mixed cities commenced only in 66 C.E.—see Cohen, *Josephus*, p. 195.

40. Josephus expresses similar views through his departures from the original text of 1 Macc. See I. Gafni, "On the Use of 1 Maccabees by Josephus Flavius," *Zion* 45 (1980) 81–95 [Hebrew]. Cf. in general for the role of God in Pseudo-Philo F. J. Murphy, "Divine Plan, Human Plan: A Structuring Theme in Pseudo-Philo," *JQR* 77 (1986) 5–14; idem, "God in Pseudo-Philo," *JSJ* 19 (1988) 1–18.

41. Ps-Philo 36:4; 38 includes an invented story about the judge Yair and the temple of Ba'al. Gilead is not mentioned as a scene, which means that Pseudo-Philo wants us to believe that we are on a "national" level. See also Pseudo-Philo 44, which is an embellishment on the story of Michah. In Ps-Philo 45:6 we read: *non sunt tunc zelati*; see also Ps-Philo 47:12.

42. This is significant, as Harrington has shown in his "Biblical Geography in Pseudo-Philo's *Liber Antiquitatum Biblicarum*," *BASOR* 220 (1975) 67–71.

Our author mentions the divine promise, but shows little interest in the acquisition of the Land for the Jews. This becomes evident from his description of the various wars of the Judges, as well as from his lack of interest in the conquest of the Land by Joshua. Such an opinion concerning the Land is opposed to the practices of the Zealots and Sicarii. They fought to drive the Romans out of Palestine in order to bring it under Jewish sway. The Land must be pure (namely free from any oppressor) when the messianic figure from the House of David comes. From Josephus we hear about raids performed by Sicarii. They demolished temples in the region of En Gedi and elsewhere (War 4.408) and were totally opposed to idols.[43]

(D) Our author exhibits a clear opposition to everything which is connected with an escape to the wilderness (= deserted places; mountains, and cliffs; see for instance Ps-Philo 6:11, 7:3, 15:6, 20:3). This opposition is not accidental; both the Zealots and the Jesus group (as well as the Essenes) held some wilderness ideal (War 2.258–63, 6.351).[44] The very important period of "the Children of Israel" in the wilderness is hurriedly passed over by our author. He seems to have no special interest in that particular period and in the code of laws linked to it.[45] He reveals a negative approach to the wilderness, but highlights the Temple (ch. 22) and emphasizes the continuity between the successive temples of ancient Israel (Ps-Philo 11:15, 13:1, 15:6, 19:10, 21:10, 22:8–9, 26:12, 32:18). In 56:2 our author connects kingship with the founding of the Temple. There is no doubt that there existed a consensus between the Pharisees and the Zealots concerning the centrality of the Temple. D. R. Schwartz has shown that the Zealots thought that the Temple in Jerusalem should be recognized as a political center as well as a spiritual and religious institution. The Pharisees and the early Christians opposed such a view.[46] This spirit also emerges from Pseudo-Philo. The Temple is only a spiritual and religious center; so it was in history, and so it should remain in the present. Our author's opposition to the wilderness is, I contend, unique when examined against the background of the "Fourth Philosophy" movement.

(E) The author of the Biblical Antiquities shows a persistent opposition to suicidal acts. The latter were common among the adherents of the so-called "Fourth Philosophy."[47] Our author demonstrates this through the story of

---

43. The noun "temples" denotes here pagan sanctuaries rather than synagogues. Also, see Ps-Philo 22:6; 38; 44.

44. Farmer, Maccabees, pp. 116–22; Hengel, Zealots, pp. 249–56, and D. R. Schwartz, "Midbar uMikdash," in Kehunah uMelucha (Jerusalem, 1987) 61–78 [Hebrew].

45. Ps-Philo 10:7–19 (at one point [11:8] the author writes: et universam orbem et inhabitabilem heremum).

46. D. R. Schwartz, "Midbar uMikdash" (art. cit. [n. 44]), pp. 61–78. Cohn's argument that Pseudo-Philo is not interested in the Temple and its cult should be restricted to the actual Temple cult. Pseudo-Philo does show interest in the historical concept of the Temple.

47. Cf. Hengel, Zealots, pp. 256–71.

Abraham and the furnace (ch. 6), as well as by bringing the story of Jeph-thah's daughter up to date by emphasizing her martyrdom (chs. 39–40). He praises a heroic death like that of Samson (43:5–8), but is wholeheartedly against suicidal acts in the face of the enemy (ch. 10). This is exactly in line with Josephus' ideas when he was still a "rebel." He encouraged people to die heroically during the war with the Roman troops (*War* 3.186–89; 222–61), but he was against suicidal acts (*War* 3.350–82).

(F) Our author is opposed to anything connected with witchcraft and ma-gicians (see ch. 34: Aod the magician). Josephus frequently links the Zealots with magicians (in *War* 2.261, 264, 565 Eleazar ben Simeon is connected in a pejorative way to magic; and so also is John of Gischala in *War* 4.85; see also *Vit* 149).[48]

Other examples could easily be given to show how our author reinterprets biblical history predating the ascendancy of the Davidic dynasty. The above examples should serve to substantiate that although our author has messianic hopes (like most of the Jews at the time), he seems to be against a messiah in the present. His position is similar to that of the Pharisees, according to Lk 19:38–39. Through this interpretation of the *Biblical Antiquities*, we arrive at an understanding of what went on in some Jewish minds concerning mes-sianism. It is thus possible to reconstruct from the above the associations of the Zealots and Sicarii regarding the period preceding the coming of the messiah. These accord either with what we know about their deeds, or with what we learn about their ideas.[49]

To conclude: In our discussion about the motives which inspired the mes-sianic groups, we referred to the past, because Jewish messianism is imbued with a historical dimension. Messianic groups thought in terms of patterns of events which may recur in the future. J. Liver has shown that from Hasmo-nean times onward Jews were reminded of the Davidic dynasty.[50] Hence I suggested that their associations were probably linked to the historical events which led to the founding of the House of David. This is why both messianic groups and their opponents showed a tremendous interest in past

48. Cf. Acts 8:9–24, according to which Simeon the magician is depicted in a negative way. Also, note Acts 19:13–20, in which witchcraft is seen negatively.

49. For instance, the Zealots thought that one must fight the oppressor with all his might in any circumstances, even if he has at his disposal an "impure mob." This notion emerges from their actions during the first century C.E. as described by Josephus. The historian may have at least partially been right in calling the Zealots and Sicarii *lēstai*. Also, we know that the Sicarii in particular adhered to the belief that suicide is an ideal way of escaping servitude to an enemy. Moreover they were of the opinion that although the Temple is central, the Wilderness consti-tutes the right solution when the Temple is no longer a religious or a political center. The Zealots were of the opinion that a radical reform in the method of electing a new priestly house should be followed. They were certain that the time had come for a king (of the House of David) to arise. This may have been true of other militant groups as well; see *War* 4.510—but as I already mentioned, we should be cautious about drawing hasty conclusions from the various pretenders. For the ideology of the Zealots and of related groups, see Brandon, *Jesus*, pp. 26–64, 146–220.

50. Liver, *The House of David*, pp. 117–47.

events seen to be charged with messianism. They referred to memories so that they could put themselves within the linear historical process. This approach obviously proved dangerous, as the phenomenon of the Sicarii shows. The latter, as well as the Zealots, apparently thought that the time had come, and so acted accordingly within the political circumstances.[51] However, their interpretation of messianism proved wrong, as Josephus emphasized (*War* 6.312–15). History proved very soon that the author of the *Biblical Antiquities* was right, and that messianism in its political mode brought a terrible disaster upon the Jews.

I am grateful to Prof. James H. Charlesworth and Dr. D. R. Schwartz for their comments.

51. Jesus of Nazareth wished to dissociate himself from this political trend. He wanted to stay out of politics at a time when political messianism was in the air. See the discussion by Cullmann, *The State*, pp. 24–49, and a very useful survey of modern attitudes about the matter by E. Bammel, "The Revolution Theory from Reimarus to Brandon," in E. Bammel, C. F. D. Moule, eds., *Jesus and the Politics of His Day* (Cambridge, 1984), pp. 11–68. It seems to me that Jesus was ahistorical in the sense mentioned above. In the four Gospels, we find no reference to a linear historical epitome concerning Israel's history. Such epitomes were very popular in Judaism at the time (recall for instance TMos, Ps-Philo 23 and 32, and Josephus' *War*, passim). Only after Jesus' resurrection, especially in the communities of Peter and Paul, do we find a comprehensive linear approach to Jewish history. In both cases this linear description reaches up to the ascendancy of the Davidic dynasty (Acts 7:1–53; 13:17–23, 33–39). This description is interesting because epitomes of this kind usually turn to history to show a continuity from the distant past to the event which is meaningful in the author's eyes at the time of writing. Why is this so? I would suggest that the Gospels still preserve the traditions concerning Jesus' reaction against his identification with Ben David (see, for example, Mk 12:35–37; Mt 22:41–46; also Mt 16:15–20, where the mention of Ben David is clearly avoided; see also R. Bultmann, *The History of the Synoptic Tradition* [Oxford, 1963], pp. 136–37, and the earlier literature). This identification was made only by Jesus' followers (at a certain point when they wished to make him king, he withdrew to the mountain, Jn 6:15). The instances are well known and reveal Jesus' antipolitical messianism. Paul and Stephen, according to the author of Acts, reflect a different atmosphere. They become "historically" oriented and do not hesitate to emphasize Jesus' historical associations with the House of David. By doing so, they reflect Christian thought after Jesus' resurrection. They continue the trend of many of Jesus' followers as well as of the evangelists themselves, who went on to fabricate the "Davidic" genealogy (in Mt 1:1–14; cf. Mt 2:1–14 and Lk 1:26–35; 2:4–5). The secondary nature of these genealogies is obvious. See Vermes, *Jesus*, p. 156; also Acts 2:29–36 and E. Haenchen, *The Acts of the Apostles, ad loc.*

For the influence of messianic ideas on Josephus' portrayal of David, see L. H. Feldman, "Josephus' Portrait of David," *HUCA* 60 (1989) 123–74. Feldman claims that "in his portrayal of David in his paraphrase of the Bible in the *Antiquities*, Josephus was confronted with a dilemma. On the one hand, as the beneficiary of so many gifts from the Romans, he could hardly praise David, who was the ancestor of the Messiah, and who *ipso facto* would lead a revolt against Rome and establish an independent state. On the other hand, David was a great folk hero. . . . Josephus' solution was to adopt a compromise: Thus he gives David a distinguished ancestry without stressing it unduly."

14

"MESSIANIC" FIGURES AND MOVEMENTS IN FIRST-CENTURY PALESTINE

PRELIMINARY CONSIDERATIONS: CRITICAL SHIFTS IN ASSUMPTIONS

The highly diverse Hebrew biblical and other Jewish literature prior to the time of Jesus exhibits a number of notions about future leaders. Early Christians used some of these notions more prominently than others in their attempt to understand and elaborate the great significance they found in the "person and work" of Jesus Christ. Because many of those notions or images of salvific figures became parts of the composite symbol "Christ" through the subsequent centuries of "christological" reading and reflection, they also tended to be carried over, in highly synthetic fashion, into the concepts of "Messiah" and "messianic" in modern biblical studies. Recent generations of biblical scholars, moreover, came to believe that many of these notions and expectations, somewhat literalistically understood, pertained to final, "eschatological" events at the "end time" (sometimes more cosmically conceived as the "end of the world"). Although they are used variously in modern scholarship, the term "Messiah" usually refers to a vaguely and generally conceived agent of final salvation while the term "messianic" is used almost indiscriminately with reference to an inspired agent and/or movement of eschatological salvation, an idea or expectation of such an agent or salvation, or anything apparently eschatological.

If this is what the terms "Messiah" and "messianic" usually mean, however, then there were no messianic figures in first-century Palestine. That is, judging from a critical assessment of the fragmentary evidence available, none of the historically attested leaders or movements were concerned with eschatological salvation, and none of the figures (including Jesus of Nazareth) match the synthetically conceived "job-description" so heavily influenced by Christian theology. Indeed, if "Messiah" and "messianic" are understood in such broad composite fashion, there were not even any messianic ideas or expectations in first-century Palestine other than what was forming in nascent Christian christologies.

To carry out any sort of serious historical analysis, therefore, we must cut through (if not simply abandon) the inherited composite concepts of "Messiah" and "messianic." At least until we attain a more precise sense of what was happening historically, we should conduct our research and reflection in very conservative fashion as "strict constructionists."

The most obvious term to be abandoned is "messianic." Neither in Hebrew Bible texts nor in Jewish texts of the second and first centuries B.C.E. is "Messiah" used of a figure or a configuration that could be labeled "eschatological."[1] Moreover, once we abandon the old-fashioned literalistic misunderstanding of prophetic and apocalyptic literature, there is little or no solid evidence that the more general expectations expressed therein were "eschatological" in the sense of the end of the world or the "final" events of history. Rather, such literature uses often fantastic imagery in reference to historical crises and their future resolution. There is thus no reason to continue to use "messianic" in the sense of eschatological. Since "Messiah" was only one among many images of agents of salvation, there is no reason (other than the composite concept that evolved centered around Jesus Christ) to use "Messiah/messianic" as the generic term. Such usage simply sets up confusion as to whether the general or the specific is meant in certain contexts. The principal reason for not using "messianic" as the general term is the misunderstanding that has resulted from the composite Christian theological concept, a misunderstanding that continued use would perpetuate.

The term "Messiah," however, should also be abandoned at least in the composite sense that has been standard in Christian biblical studies. "Christ," the Greek-derived term used in most of the early Christian literature, will do quite well for composite references. The terms "Messiah" and "messianic" can thus be used sparingly, if at all, with reference to historical and literary phenomena only where the Hebrew term "Messiah" or its equivalent is used, where another term that can be clearly established as closely associated is used, and perhaps where a particular social-historical form is evident that has previously been associated with the term. In none of these cases would the meaning of "Messiah" be evident except from the literary and/or historical context. It should also be kept in mind that the occurrence of the term does not necessarily entail the presence of the concept, and the presence of the concept does not necessarily imply the existence of a movement. Terms and concepts must be assessed in literary and, insofar as possible, historical context.

A related aspect in the recent shifts in our historical understanding of biblical literature and history is that we can no longer assume that the sub-

---

1. See the chapter by J. J. M. Roberts in this volume; F. Hesse, *"chrio," TDNT*, vol. 9, p. 504; J. J. Collins, *The Apocalyptic Imagination* (New York, 1984), p. 123; S. Talmon, "Waiting for the Messiah: The Spiritual Universe of the Qumran Covenanters," *Judaisms and Their Messiahs at the Turn of the Christian Era*, ed. J. Neusner, W. S. Green, and E. S. Frerichs (Cambridge and New York, 1988), pp. 115, 131.

ject matter of biblical and related studies is only or primarily "religious." In most traditional societies the religious dimension is inseparable from the other dimensions of life. For example, just as the rule of Rome and the Roman emperor were political-economic realities with an inseparable religious dimension, so the Jewish Temple and high priesthood in Jerusalem were political-economic realities with an inseparable religious dimension. Whatever particular term or symbol was used, God was a "political" as well as "religious" concept. With regard to biblical prophets and kings or messiahs, if any dimension was primary it was the political.

Of crucial import for exploration of "messianic" ideas or figures, we can no longer blithely assume that "the Jews" generally in late Second Temple times thought in a certain way. Our evidence for what the ancient Jews were thinking about anything is almost exclusively literary. But nearly all literature from the past was produced by literate people, and most people who were literate in antiquity worked for and were supported by the rulers or other wealthy patrons, and as we now recognize, literature reflects the interests of those who produced it. Of course some of the Palestinian Jewish literature of the late Second Temple Period was different. Literature such as the Dead Sea Scrolls or the Psalms of Solomon was produced by people discontent with or in reaction to the policies and practices of the ruling elite. But those who were literate and who produced literature were still a tiny fraction of the society. Is there any reason to believe that the extant literature, which was produced by a tiny fraction of the population who occupied a social position very different from the vast majority, reflected the attitudes and ideas of the whole society?[2] As we work toward more precise understanding of ancient Palestinian Jewish history, we must distinguish more carefully the social origins and interests that particular literature expresses. We must also then inquire what the dynamics of the historical situation were so that the ideas and interests expressed in particular literature from people in a particular social location is understood in terms of its concrete historical context.

THE RELATIVE UNIMPORTANCE OF A "MESSIAH" OR "MESSIANIC" IDEAS IN LATE SECOND TEMPLE JEWISH LITERATURE

There are precious few occurrences of the term "Messiah" in Palestinian Jewish literature in late Second Temple times.[3] That is, we have little or no

---

2. For a provisional attempt to discern whether apocalyptic literature can be used as evidence for what Palestinian Jews more generally may have been thinking in the late Second Temple Period, see R. A. Horsley, *Jesus and the Spiral of Violence* (San Francisco, 1987), pp. 129–31.

3. M. de Jonge, "The Use of the Word 'Anointed' in the Time of Jesus," *NovT* 8 (1966), 132–48; and *"chrio,"* etc., *TDNT*, vol. 9, pp. 509–27.

literary evidence *that*, let alone *how*, Palestinian Jews at the time of Jesus were thinking with regard to some sort of "anointed" figure. The relative paucity of the term "Messiah" in Palestinian Jewish literature suggests that expectations of a Messiah were relatively unimportant among literate groups in particular. Even where the term "Messiah" occurs, its usage must be disappointing to those looking for an agent of redemption. In the book of Daniel and the Enoch literature, the term is barely present, and not important; the agents of salvation are primarily God and certain angels. By comparison with its almost complete absence in other literature of the period, the handful of occurrences of "anointed" in the Dead Sea Scrolls and the reference to the anointed Davidic king in Psalms of Solomon 17 stand out prominently. Even then, considering the extensive literature produced by the Qumran community, the term "anointed" occurs relatively infrequently. Many of the key occurrences, moreover, are in phrases (such as "until there shall arise the anointed of Aaron and Israel") that refer to the time of fulfillment, not to some sort of agent of redemption (e.g., 1QS 9.10–11; CD 12.22–23; 13.20–22; 19.9–11; 20.1). The Aaronide priest and the "anointed of Israel" will preside at the banquet of fulfillment as *primi inter pares* (1QSa 2.11–22), but they are not portrayed as exercising any particular function as agents of salvation. The Qumran community understood itself predominantly as a new exodus and a new covenant, and its leadership was primarily priestly and scribal. Apparently it imagined virtually no significant function for an anointed royal figure. Almost alone in all of the Jewish literature prior to the destruction of Jerusalem in 70 C.E., the Psalms of Solomon assign an "anointed" king a significant role. Contrary to the old composite construction of "standard Jewish messianic expectations," however, this future Davidic king is not a military leader but has strong scribal and sapiential functions.[4]

In the literature of late Second Temple times there appears to be little interest in a "Messiah" or in a future Davidic king. Why? For several centuries Judea had been a Temple-state headed by a high priesthood that was assisted in governing by scribes and sages trained in the Torah, which provided the "constitution" and laws of the society. The scribes and sages were, in effect, the only literate people, hence the only ones to leave literary remains (on which modern biblical and historical study is so dependent). Their special concerns motivated their production of this literature in the first place, and the literature reflects their own experience, interests, and roles in society. An anointed and/or Davidic king was simply not important, or even present, in their recent historical experience, in the Torah, or in their concerns for and visions of the ideal Israel. The dominant roles and functions of the powerful and/or literate were priestly and scribal-sapiential.

---

4. See B. Mack, "Wisdom Makes a Difference: Alternatives to 'Messianic' Configurations," in *Judaisms and Their Messiahs*, pp. 38–41.

It is, of course, conceivable that ideas and expectations of a "Messiah" were kept alive in late Second Temple times through use of psalm and prophetic texts. Indeed, this must have been the implicit assumption behind the old synthetic concept of the Jewish Messiah, for some of the principal biblical texts cited as expressing expectations of "the Messiah" are certain royal psalms (e.g., Psalms 2, 110) and prophetic oracles concerning kings (e.g., Isa 9:1–6). Many of the psalms and prophecies that have traditionally figured in the older composite construct of the Messiah, of course, were originally parts of the ceremonial propaganda of the official royal theology that provided legitimation for the Davidic monarchy.[5] Some of the mythological and imperial imagery of such psalms and prophecies has even been the likely source of the "eschatological" misunderstanding of modern messianology. There is no evidence, however, that the imperial Davidic ideology was perpetuated or revived in late Second Temple times, although this may be due partly to limited literary remains from this period generally. Without such evidence we cannot use these earlier psalms and prophecies as evidence for later times. Hence the unavoidable conclusion remains that ideas or expectations of a "Messiah" of any sort were not only rare but unimportant among the literate groups in late Second Temple Jewish Palestine.

Concrete Figures and Movements

The lack of literary evidence for Jewish "messianic" expectations makes all the more significant the occurrence of several concrete figures and movements among the common people. First-century Jewish Palestine, although fairly simple in its social structure, featured a wide variety of groups and movements.[6] There is little or no evidence that any of these were eschatologically oriented. And most of them had no leadership that could be legitimately labeled as "messiahs." The ad hoc popular protests that occurred from time to time were neither eschatologically oriented nor apocalyptically inspired, judging from available evidence and comparative material. Josephus, our principal source, mentions no distinctive leadership at all. There is no indication that the Fourth Philosophy in 6 C.E., or the Sicarii, the terrorist group active in the 50s C.E. were eschatologically oriented or apocalyptically inspired. The leadership of both groups was scribal-scholarly, as Josephus says explicitly, and neither prophetic nor royal nor priestly. The brief "messianic incident" among the Sicarii in the summer of 66 C.E. will be discussed further below.

The Jewish Revolt of 66–70 C.E. involved a variety of groups, most of

---

5. See F. M. Cross, *Canaanite Myth and Hebrew Epic* (Cambridge, Mass., 1973), pp. 241–65; and the chapter by J. J. M. Roberts in this volume.

6. R. A. Horsley with J. S. Hanson, *Bandits, Prophets, and Messiahs: Popular Movements at the Time of Jesus* (San Francisco, 1988); Horsley, *Jesus and the Spiral of Violence,* ch. 4.

them regional in origin and popular in composition. Josephus suggests that during the Roman siege of Jerusalem some apocalyptic inspiration may have been involved, but there is no evidence of eschatological orientation among any of the regionally rooted groups. The initial insurrection involved some priestly leadership in Jerusalem itself (the Temple captain Eleazar) and brigand leadership in the Judean and Galilean countryside. From the winter of 67–68 C.E., the popular regional groups that originated largely or partly from the devastating reconquest by the Roman armies took up their positions in Jerusalem and, when not quarreling among themselves, resisted the prolonged Roman siege. The Zealots proper, a coalition of brigand bands formed in reaction to the Roman reconquest in northwestern Judea, conducted an election (by lot) of priestly leadership.[7] Josephus mentions no distinctive type of leadership among the Idumeans. He does say at one point that John of Gischala, among the Galileans who fled to Jerusalem, was aiming at sole leadership of the struggle, but gives no suggestion of "messianic" pretensions. By contrast, the popular movement originating in southeastern Judea was distinctively "royal" in its leader, Simon bar Giora (on whom see below).

POPULAR PROPHETS AND PROPHETIC MOVEMENTS

During the middle of the first century, a number of prophetic figures appeared in Jewish Palestine.[8] These figures mentioned by Josephus and/or the NT Gospels and Acts were all from among the people rather than associated with one or another of the literate groups such as the Pharisees or Qumranites. Reports about these figures in Josephus and the Gospels, when placed against the background of earlier (biblical) Israelite prophetic phenomena, indicate that these prophets were of two distinctive types, each reminiscent of or in continuity with a biblical tradition. Jesus son of Hananiah and probably John the Baptist as well are primarily individual spokespersons for God delivering oracles of judgment to their respective historical situations. Jesus is particularly reminiscent of Jeremiah in his lament over the doomed city of Jerusalem. During the Jewish Revolt other prophets (none of them named by Josephus) delivered oracles of deliverance. Judging from Josephus' reports, some of these may have been more apocalyptic in their inspiration and style, but the visionary imagery suggests that these prophecies concerned historical deliverance, not any "end of the world." These prophets, whether

---

7. R. A. Horsley, "The Zealots: Their Origin, Relationships, and Importance in the Jewish Revolt," *NovT* 28 (1986) 159–92.

8. For more elaborate analysis, see R. A. Horsley, "'Like One of the Prophets of Old': Two Types of Popular Prophets at the Time of Jesus," *CBQ* 47 (1985), 435–63; and "Popular Prophetic Movements at the Time of Jesus: Their Principal Features and Social Origins," *JSNT* 26 (1986) 3–27.

their oracles were of judgment or of liberation, were individual messengers, and none of them (including John the Baptist) appear to have organized or led a mass movement.

The other prophets, such as Theudas and the "Egyptian," inspired, organized, and led mass movements that were suppressed by Roman troops. These have been labeled "messianic" prophets or "prophetic pretenders to messiahship."[9] But that label blurs both their distinctive character and their distinctive difference from the movements led by popular kings who might more properly be designated "messianic." Contrary to suggestions by some and the misleading label "messianic," there is no overlap or confusion between these two types of movements and their leaders. Our principal source Josephus writes explicitly that Theudas and the "Egyptian" appeared as *prophets*, not that they assumed some royal posture. Josephus himself shared the (proto-) rabbinic view that the succession of truly inspired prophets ceased after Haggai, Zechariah, and Malachi, and he apparently avoids the term *prophetes* in reference to his own and other prophetic activity of which he approves. Thus it is all the more significant that he uses the term in his hostile accounts of the movements led by figures he denigrates as "deceivers" or "charlatans."

On the basis of Josephus' general descriptions of several such movements along with his accounts of Theudas, the "Egyptian," and a Samaritan prophet, we are justified in discerning here a distinctive type of prophet and prophetic movement. That is, these prophets, while also messengers of God, do not simply announce the will of God but (a) lead actions of deliverance (b) involving "revolutionary changes" (c) in accord with God's "design" and (d) corresponding to one of the great historical formative acts of deliverance led by Moses or Joshua.

Actions: According to Josephus' summary statements, there must have been several prophetic figures who at some point or another led their followers out into the wilderness in anticipation of new deliverance (*War* 2.259; *Ant* 20.168, 188). The most important, judging from their memory in NT literature as well, were those led by Theudas and the "Egyptian."

> During the period when Fadus was procurator of Judaea, a certain impostor named Theudas persuaded the majority of the masses to take up their possessions and to follow him to the Jordan River. He stated that he was a prophet and that at his command the river would be parted and would provide them an easy passage (*Ant* 20.97).

9. R. Meyer, *"Prophetes," TDNT*, vol. 6, pp. 826–27; M. Hengel, *Die Zeloten* (Leiden, 1961), p. 237; D. Hill, "Jesus and Josephus' 'messianic prophets,'" in *Text and Interpretation: Studies in the New Testament Presented to M. Black*, ed. E. Best and R. McL. Wilson (Cambridge, 1979), pp. 143–49.

There came to Jerusalem from Egypt a man who declared that he was a prophet and advised the masses of the common people to go out with him to the Mount of Olives, which lies opposite the city at a distance of five furlongs. For he asserted he wished to demonstrate from there that at his command Jerusalem's walls would fall down, through which he promised to provide them an entrance into the city (*Ant* 20.169–70; cf. *War* 2.261–62).

The placement of Theudas prior to Judas of Galilee (6 C.E.) in Acts 5:36 is merely either a chronological confusion or a lack of solid information by Luke. In Acts 21:38 Luke has simply confused the "Egyptian's" movement with the terrorism by the Sicarii during the same period under the governor Felix (52–60 C.E.). The fundamental reality of all of these movements appears to be that the prophets were leading their followers out to participate in some great anticipated liberating action by God. Josephus surely exaggerates a bit with "the majority of the masses" and "thirty-thousand dupes" (*Ant* 20.197; *War* 2.261), but these movements were clearly sizeable actions, with at least hundreds and perhaps thousands of participants.

"Revolutionary changes" (*War* 2.259): From Josephus' explicit reference to "the masses" and "the common people" it is clear that the social base of these movements was the Judean peasantry.[10] The participants in these movements were hardly from the comfortable strata. Their quest for "rest from troubles" and "freedom" or "liberation" implies an indictment of the established order and its supercession by a just social order. In some cases the movements appear simply to be withdrawing from an intolerable situation. The prophet from Egypt is more explicitly confrontational: He apparently led his followers out to participate in God's overthrow of the Roman-dominated established order in Jerusalem. There is no real evidence in our texts that any of these movements were in any way violent, let alone armed, as has sometimes been suggested. But they were apparently understood as a threat to the dominant order. Modern interpreters might dismiss their anticipations of divine actions as mere apocalyptic fantasies. To Josephus and others of the ancient Jewish ruling groups, however, these movements appeared as a genuine threat. Indeed, the ruling groups' brutal suppression of these movements by overwhelming military force indicates just how anxious they were about the "revolutionary changes" that these prophets and their followers apparently anticipated. At the very least, of course, if the participants in such movements abandoned their fields in anticipation of divine deliverance, the prophets and their followers posed a genuine threat to the continuing productive base that the ruling groups depended upon in their peasantry.

10. See further Horsley, "Popular Prophetic Movements," pp. 12–13.

"In harmony with God's design" (*Ant* 20.168): This and other phrases used by Josephus in these reports should surely be read against the background of Jewish apocalyptic literature. "God's design" appears to be a reference to the "mystery" of God that figures so prominently in Daniel and the Qumran texts. Josephus also writes that the prophets he considers charlatans operated "under the pretence of divine inspiration . . . persuading the masses to act like madmen" (*War* 2.259). In more positive traditional Palestinian Jewish terms, these prophets were charismatic leaders filled with the Spirit of God, by means of which their followers as well were inspired with the conviction that God was about to act and they were called to participate as the people to be liberated. Josephus thus does not conceal the apocalyptic features of these prophetic figures and their movements. One might still question whether "eschatological" (abandoning the use of "messianic" in that sense) is an appropriate interpretative term to apply in these cases. More precisely we can say that the anticipated act of deliverance was conceived in somewhat fantastic (apocalyptic) terms.

A new action corresponding to one of the great historical acts of deliverance: The historical analogies according to which the new acts of salvation were imagined are clear at least in general if not in particulars. The prophet from Egypt and his followers were clearly informed by the great battle of Jericho. Apparently now God would dramatically liberate Jerusalem from Roman domination. The "charlatan" who promised his followers "deliverance and rest from troubles if they chose to follow him into the wilderness" (*Ant* 20.188) was surely attempting to realize a new exodus from bondage out into the wilderness, in imitation of Moses of old. The precise analogy in Theudas' case is less clear. Perhaps it should be seen as a new exodus and/or entry into the land: As Moses parted the waters for the deliverance from Egypt and/or as Joshua had parted the waters of the Jordan for the entry into the promised land, so Theudas was acting as God's agent in the new deliverance from Roman oppression and/or in reentry into the land of promise. Israelite traditions had long since juxtaposed the exodus from Egypt and entry into the land. And prophetic traditions such as Isa 51:9–11 had long since conceived of new redemption in terms of the original formative acts of redemption.

There is virtually no literary evidence for the currency of an expectation of an eschatological prophet like Moses in the first century.[11] But in the cases of Theudas, the "Egyptian," and the "charlatan" there occurred concrete movements led by prophets in actions of liberation that correspond typologically to the great constitutive historical actions led by the prototypical prophet(s) Moses (and Joshua). Even though Josephus is careful to say only

---

11. Horsley, "'Like One of the Prophets of Old,'" pp. 441–43.

that Theudas and the "Egyptian" claimed to be prophets and that these leaders were really "deceivers and impostors" or "charlatans," he nevertheless used the same distinctive language that he used in his accounts of Moses and his "signs and miracles" of deliverance (e.g., *Ant* 2.286, 327; cf. 20.168, 188; *War* 2.259). Close analysis of Josephus' reports gives us the distinct impression that there must have been a particular and distinctive social form of *prophetic movements* in first-century Palestinian Jewish society.

MOVEMENTS LED BY FIGURES POPULARLY RECOGNIZED AS "KINGS"

Very different while equally distinctive in concrete social form are a number of other movements in which the participants recognized their leader as a "king." These movements occurred significantly at two important points of historical crisis: after the death of the tyrant Herod in 4 B.C.E. and in the middle of the struggle against the Romans in the late 60s. To these popular movements we can also compare the brief messianic episode among the Sicarii focused on Menahem. [12]

These movements headed by popularly acclaimed kings might more legitimately be described as "messianic" movements because they apparently stand in or hark back to an ancient Israelite tradition in which the people "anointed" a leader as "king/chieftain." In his reports of these movements, Josephus uses terminology familiar from other hellenistic historiography, such as that the leaders "donned the diadem." [13] It is thus at least conceivable that these leaders appear as "kings" only because of Josephus' use of standard hellenistic historiographical terms. It is also conceivable that these movements had certain similarities to popular movements elsewhere in the Roman empire that Josephus recognized and described accordingly. Most likely, however, is that the social form of these movements was somehow informed by the Israelite tradition of popularly acclaimed kingship, one that left several historical paradigms in the historical narratives of the Bible. Compared with the official Davidic royal ideology, this tradition of popular kingship has received little attention from modern scholars. Cross recognized that the covenantally and prophetically "limited monarchy" of Saul and the northern kingdom of Israel was quite different from "the imperial rule of Solomon" and "the Davidic royal theology." [14] When one looks more closely

---

12. On these movements, see further R. A. Horsley, "Popular Messianic Movements Around the Time of Jesus," *CBQ* 46 (1984) 471–95; and "Menahem in Jerusalem: A Brief Messianic Episode Among the Sicarii—Not 'Zealot Messianism,'" *NovT* 27 (1985) 334–48.

13. See, e.g., Diodorus Siculus 34/5.2.14–41.

14. Cross, *Canaanite Myth and Hebrew Epic*, pp. 219–64. See also Z. Weisman, "Anointing as a Motif in the Making of the Charismatic King," *Bib* 57 (1976) 378–83; and H. Tadmor, "The People and the Kingship in Ancient Israel: The Role of Political Institutions in the Biblical Period," *Cahiers d'histoire mondiale* 11 (1968) 46–68.

at such "limited monarchy," however, it is clear that it originated in popular movements in which the people acclaimed the leader as "chieftain" or "king" (e.g., 1Sam 11:15; 1Kgs 12:20). The term used in some of these cases, particularly David, was that the people or elders of Israel "anointed" the leader as king (2Sam 2:4; 5:3; 15:10–12 and 19:10). The popularly acclaimed king, moreover, was also thought to be "anointed" by Yahweh, through the action of a prophet (such as Samuel, Ahijah, or Elisha) and was thereafter known as "the anointed of Yahweh" (e.g., 1Sam 24:7, 11; 26:9, 11, 16, 23; etc.; cf. 2Sam 23:1). There is no way to prove that this Israelite tradition of popular kingship continued to or revived in Herodian times, although its embodiment prominently in biblical narratives means that it was definitely remembered. For the hypothesis that it was this tradition that informed the movements led by popularly acclaimed kings in 4 B.C.E. and 68–70 C.E., we are assuming that what anthropologists call "the little tradition" as well as the (written) "great tradition" was operative in Palestinian Jewish society in somewhat the same way as it operates in other peasant societies. Thus, if we are to utilize the term "messianic" at all, insofar as the late Second Temple movements led by "kings" were informed by the biblical tradition of popularly "anointed" kings, they might legitimately be called popular "messianic" movements.

The popularly acclaimed "kings" who led revolts after the death of Herod were all men of the people. There is simply no evidence of any survival of Hasmonean leaders, and it is highly unlikely that popular movements would have looked to government officials or gentry for leadership since they would have been involved in collaboration with the Herodian regime. Athronges, the "king" in Judea, was a "mere shepherd," as was David, according to tradition (*War* 2.57, 60; *Ant* 17.273, 278). Simon, the leader in Perea, had been a "royal servant," conceivably a lower-level Herodian official but more likely a tenant-farmer on the royal estates east of the Jordan. Judas, who led the revolt in Galilee, was the son of the famous brigand-chief Hezekiah, who had been pursued and killed by the young Herod nearly forty years earlier. Several scholars, seizing upon every conceivable shred of evidence that might support the modern (mis)conception of "the Zealots," have mistakenly identified Judas son of Hezekiah with "Judas of Galilee," leader of the "Fourth Philosophy" in Judea ten years later. Far from suggesting any identification between the two Judases, Josephus states explicitly that Judas of Galilee was a teacher-scholar (*sophistēs, War* 2.118), the same term he used with reference to the distinguished teachers whose students cut down the Roman eagle from over the Temple gate (*War* 1.648–55; *Ant* 17.149–68). Judas the popular king was most likely from the peasantry. Because of the fame of his father as a brigand-chief murdered by the arrogant young Herod, of course, he may already have been recognized as a popular leader.

The sizeable movements led by Judas, Athronges, and Simon were based in the countryside, and the followers were almost certainly from among the peasantry. Judging from Josephus' reports, these movements were quite separate from the active resistance in Jerusalem itself as well as from the separate revolt by a group of the veteran royal troops. It is difficult to discern whether "the brigands he collected" among Simon's followers were peasants who had been driven into banditry by the difficult circumstances under Herodian rule or simply Josephus' denigrating description of the rebels (*War* 2.57). Similarly the "desperate men" following Judas may reflect the social-economic circumstances at the end of the Herod's long exploitative and repressive reign, or it may simply be Josephus' pejorative term for the rebellious riffraff he so despised (*Ant* 17.271). At least the movement led by Athronges appears to have been organized into some sort of subdivisions or "companies," probably for military purposes, with the leader's brothers as the lieutenants. Josephus states explicitly that Athronges held councils to deliberate on courses of action (*Ant* 17.280–81). A special spirit or inspiration probably motivated these movements, as indicated in Josephus' comments that the Pereans had proclaimed Simon king in their "madness" and that they fought with "more recklessness than science."

The regional "kings" and their followers attacked both royalists and Romans. The principal objects of their attack mentioned by Josephus, the royal palaces at Sepphoris and at Jericho, were surely both symbols of Herod's tyranny and sources of weapons for the rebels. But Josephus also mentions explicitly that the rebels were also attempting to retrieve the property that had been seized by Herodian officers and stored in those places (*Ant* 17.274; *War* 2.57; cf. Solomon's royal fortresses that served also as tax-collection and storage depots). The aims of the movements would thus appear to be not only liberation from Herodian (Roman) domination, but a restoration of egalitarian social-economic relations. We can reasonably speculate, on the basis of cross-cultural materials, that the Jewish peasantry's long pent-up resentment at Herodian exploitation and repression was now releasing itself into an anarchism typical of peasant uprisings.

By far the most important "messianic" movement of the first century was that focused on Simon bar Giora, who eventually became the principal political-military commander in Jerusalem during the Jewish Revolt and whom the Romans ceremonially executed as, in effect, the king of the Jews. Josephus provides far more information concerning Simon and his career than he does for those who were acclaimed kings following the death of Herod, so there is far less speculation involved in analysis of Simon. Josephus also portrays Simon as an active instigator and organizer of the movement he headed. For Simon we can rely on two previous brief but complementary scholarly treatments.[15]

Like the popular kings seventy years earlier, Simon came not from a no-

15. C. Roth, "Simon bar Giora: Ancient Jewish Hero," *Commentary* 29 (1960) 52–58; O. Michel, "Studien zu Josephus," *NTS* 14 (1967–68) 403–8.

table family, but from humble origins, as indicated by his name bar Giora, "son of a proselyte." As the revolt erupted in the summer of 66, he must have become the leader of a substantial fighting force. He emerged as one of the heroes of the bold Jewish victory over the Roman forces advancing on Jerusalem that October (*War* 2.521). The aristocratic junta that set themselves up as a provisional government, however, could hardly have wanted to leave a popular hero in command of a nascent peasant militia, hence they passed over Simon when making appointment of district commanders. With his "physical strength and courage," however, Simon continued to catalyze popular insurrectionary activity in the toparchy of Acrabetene (*War* 4.503–4; 2.652–53). When the provisional government in Jerusalem attempted to suppress his activities in Acrabetene, he simply moved elsewhere. He even spent some time with the Sicarii who had fled to Masada after their rejection in Jerusalem in the summer of 66.

However, after the death of the High Priest Ananus, one of the principal leaders of the Jerusalem junta, Simon, began building a movement, apparently deliberately and systematically. According to Josephus, our sole source for Simon, his career is remarkably parallel to that of David, the great popular messianic prototype. It is unlikely that this is the literary artifice of Josephus himself, who displays a special hostility to Simon, probably because this "despot" had imprisoned his parents in Jerusalem during the Roman siege. Like David, Simon began as the leader of a localized guerrilla band, one that posed a threat to the existing government, and rose to become one followed as king by thousands of people, as well as by a large army. In both cases, the initial followers were the "worthless" and discontented (*War* 4.507–13). But with the people searching for effective leadership against impending foreign conquest in both cases, David and Simon came to be recognized as kings by masses of people, including some of the notables. Moreover, when Simon moved first to consolidate control of much of southern Judea and Idumea, including the town of Hebron, before moving on to Jerusalem, he may have had more than military strategy in mind. That is, following the great Davidic prototype, he may have been liberating and establishing "righteous" rule in Judah. Hebron may have been especially symbolic in this strategy, since it was surely remembered as the place where David was first anointed prince of Judah, and from which, once he was recognized as head of all Israel, he went on to take Jerusalem and to liberate the whole country. Josephus' attempt to divert the reader's attention just at this point in his narrative to the great antiquity of Hebron and its association with Abraham lends credibility to our somewhat speculative reconstruction of the "Davidic" features of Simon bar Giora's career (*War* 4.529–34).

The social revolutionary program of Simon bar Giora's movement is far more explicit in Josephus' reports than that of the popular kings at the death of Herod. After decades of economic hardship under the exploitative rule of Herod and the double taxation of tribute to Rome and dues to priests and

Temple, Simon and his movement were apparently attempting to restore social and economic justice. Unless it can simply be dismissed as some secret sympathy of Josephus, Simon's proclamation of "liberty for slaves and rewards for the free" has both an apocalyptic overtone and a ring reminiscent of prophetic promises. Equity for the meek and justice for the poor were to be features of the program of the future anointed king, the righteous branch of David, according to the prophecies such as Isaiah 11 and Jer 23:5 (cf. Jer 34:8–9).

Simon's movement, however, was by no means a "thieving and murderous horde of peasants" (as in Luther's fearful fantasies), wildly plundering the mansions of the wealthy or storming the barricades of Jerusalem. Judging from their War Scroll, the Qumranites were apparently at times caught up in fantasies of God's holy war against the oppressive enemy, and it is conceivable that Simon's followers may have been inspired by some far less ritualized and fantastic sense of God's imminent deliverance. If we can rely on Josephus' report, however, Simon and his movement are especially impressive for their military organization and discipline. With striking long-range forethought, they even made provision for the support system necessary for a prolonged war of liberation. Simon would also appear to have maintained a rigorous social discipline once he became the principal ruler in Jerusalem, a discipline that corresponded to the strategy and planning that brought him there. It would be uncritical to follow the bias of the wealthy deserter Josephus to interpret Simon's conduct of affairs in the besieged city as a "reign of terror." Behind Josephus' bitter condemnation of Simon's execution of deserters is simply the social-political discipline necessary to maintain order among the people under prolonged siege.[16] Simon's discipline could be understood as a fulfillment of how the Psalm of Solomon 17 anticipated the anointed king would govern: In the great "war" against the oppressive alien rulers, the king would "thrust out sinners from [the] inheritance" and "not suffer unrighteousness to lodge anymore in their midst, thus purging Jerusalem, making it holy as of old" (PsSol 17:26, 29, 33, 36).

Two final highly symbolic ceremonial events indicate unmistakably how Simon bar Giora had assumed the role of the king of the Jews. After the destruction of Jerusalem and the Temple, according to Josephus, Simon surrendered to the Romans in a dramatic and ceremonious act. Michel's analysis concludes that Josephus' account here rests on solid historical tradition. "Simon . . . dressed himself in white tunics and buckling over them a purple mantle arose out of the ground at the very spot whereon the Temple formerly stood" (War 7.29). The apparel is that of a king, symbolism that would have been clear to both Jews and Gentiles. Agrippa I as well as Jesus had been mocked as kings dressed in such garments (Philo, Flacc 36–39; Mk 15:16–

---

16. Michel, NTS 14 (1967–68) 406.

20). And such was the attire of the king on formal state occasions, such as the funeral of Herod the Great (War 1.671; Ant 17.197). While Simon's appearance in this apparel clearly indicates his kingly role, the purpose of his action as a whole is not obvious. Was his dramatic appearance intended as some apocalyptic sign of imminent divine intervention? Or, in inviting the Romans to take him as the unmistakable king was he hoping, by this self-sacrifice of the leader to the enemy, to mitigate the severe punishment that would otherwise fall on his people?

Whatever Simon's purpose in his dramatic surrender, the Romans did indeed execute him as the enemy general or head of state, as part of the triumphal procession and celebration of the great Roman victory over the rebellious Jewish nation (War 7.153–55, with a due sense of "pomp and circumstance"). The Roman treatment of Simon's rival for leadership during the prolonged siege of Jerusalem forms a striking contrast: John of Gischala was simply imprisoned. Simon, however, was ceremonially paraded (appropriately robed, judging from War 7.138),[17] scourged, and executed as the leader (perhaps explicitly as "king") of the Jews as one of principal events in the triumphal celebration in Rome. It is clear that Pontius Pilate was neither the last nor the first Roman imperial official to deal with a popular Palestinian Jewish leader recognized as a king of the Jews.

Prior to the emergence of Simon bar Giora as a popularly acclaimed king, there had been another "messianic figure" in connection with the Jewish revolt. The appearance of Menahem as a royal pretender was relatively insignificant historically, a mere episode among the group called Sicarii by Josephus. This incident, however, has been blown up out of all proportion, primarily by North Atlantic Christian scholars who use Menahem as evidence for a violently revolutionary "Zealot Messianism" which serves as a foil for their image of Jesus of Nazareth as a sober prophet of spiritualized salvation and individualized nonresistance.[18] It has even been claimed that Menahem stood in a dynasty of (messianic) leaders stemming from Judas of Galilee, founder of the Fourth Philosophy, which is identified with the Zealots, understood as a longstanding movement of armed resistance to Roman rule. Menahem is thus understood as the original leader of the Jewish revolt which was doomed nearly from the start because the Zealot movement splintered when he was struck down by the resentful priestly faction led by the temple captain Eleazar.

It is now finally being more widely recognized that the Zealots proper did not emerge until the middle of the Jewish revolt, in the winter of 67–68 C.E., by which time the Sicarii, who have often been mistakenly identified with

---

17. Ibid., p. 407.
18. E.g., M. Hengel, Was Jesus a Revolutionist? (Philadelphia, 1971); Victory Over Violence (Philadelphia, 1973); and Die Zeloten (Leiden, 1961), pp. 299, 369, 372–73; cf. O. Cullmann, Jesus and the Revolutionaries (New York, 1970).

the Zealots, had long since withdrawn to Masada, where they sat out the duration of the revolt. Moreover, there is no evidence of "messianism" or any messianic figure among the Zealots proper. The latter, a coalition of brigand groups created by the devastating Roman advance through northwestern Judea, operated in strikingly "democratic" and egalitarian fashion, electing by lot new priestly leadership from among legitimate Zadokite families who had long since been located in peasant villages. The Zealots were social-revolutionary like the popular messianic movements, but the social form taken by the Zealot movement was not popularly acclaimed kingship, but popularly recognized legitimate priestly leadership. Clearly, Menahem could not have been a "Zealot Messiah."[19]

Nor was Menahem part of some sort of messianic dynasty. This claim is based on scholarly confusion of fragments of evidence in Josephus, some of which pertain neither to the Fourth Philosophy nor to the Sicarii, particularly the false identification of the two Judases. But the scholar (*sophistēs*) Judas of Galilee, founder of the Fourth Philosophy in 6 C.E. and the "father" (or more likely grandfather) of Menahem, was clearly a different person from Judas son of Hezekiah, the popularly acclaimed king of Galilee in 4 B.C.E. There was apparently some continuity of leadership in resistance to Roman rule from Judas of Galilee through two of his sons who were executed by Tiberias Alexander, governor of Judea 46–48, to his (grand)son Menahem in 66 and his relative Eleazar son of Jairus, a leader of the Sicarii who sat out the revolt atop Masada. But Josephus gives no indication of any sort that Judas of Galilee or any other figure among either Fourth Philosophy or the Sicarii posed or was viewed as a king. There is absolutely no basis for projecting Menahem's "messianic" posturing back into his ancestors' activities. Menahem's royal pretensions are apparently unprecedented not only among the Sicarii, but among any of the known literate or scholar-led groups, i.e., the Pharisees, the Qumranites, and the Fourth Philosophy.

Menahem's "messiahship" was in fact merely a brief episode, although perhaps a turning point, in the activities of the group called the Sicarii. Far from being the head of a large organized movement that (supposedly) finally succeeded in catalyzing a large-scale revolt against Roman rule, Menahem was simply one of the leaders of a group that joined the revolt only after others had inaugurated the hostilities. The Sicarii of course had been active in terrorist activities since the 50s, primarily directed against high priestly collaborators with Roman rule. But Josephus does not even mention them in his reports of the early stages of the revolt in the summer of 66. Only after the Jerusalem populace was utterly outraged by the Roman governor Florus' mindless provocations, after a different group of militants had stormed and taken the fortress on Masada, after the temple captain Eleazar and other

---

19. Hengel's subheading, *Die Zeloten*, p. 299.

priests had boldly cut off the sacrifices for the emperor, and after the insurgent Jerusalem populace had pressed their attacks against the royal troops and the aristocracy in the upper city, only then did some of the Sicarii force their way into the action (*War* 2.408–25). Thus, Josephus does not even mention Menahem until the revolt was well underway.

Josephus finally reports three incidents involving Menahem, in rapid succession. First, he and his followers obtained arms from Herod's arsenal at Masada, whereupon Menahem "returned like a king to Jerusalem and, becoming a leader of the revolt, directed the siege of the royal palace" (*War* 2.433–34). Although there is no indication in Josephus that he became *the* leader of the insurrection, he clearly became a prominent leader at this point, for the garrison besieged in the royal palace negotiated "with Menahem and the leaders of the insurrection" (*War* 2.437). The "infatuated" Menahem, having become an "insufferable tyrant" (*War* 2.441–42), however, was plotted against by the followers of the temple captain Eleazar.

> So they laid their plans to attack him in the Temple, where he had gone up in state to pay his devotions, arrayed in royal robes and attended by his suite of armed fanatics. Eleazar and his companions rushed upon him, and the rest of the citizens [of Jerusalem], to gratify their rage, took up stones and began pelting the arrogant doctor . . . (*War* 2.443–45).

A few of the Sicarii escaped to Masada where they sat out the rest of the revolt. Menahem himself, having escaped temporarily, was soon caught, tortured, and killed (*War* 447–48).

Besides being unprecedented among the literate or scholar-led groups, the "messianic figure" Menahem is highly unusual in some other respects. All of the other figures who behaved like kings were from the common people and were popularly acclaimed. Menahem was known as a "teacher" (*sophistēs*, *War* 2.445) and a leader of an urban-based terrorist group apparently without any previous popular base. On the other hand, Menahem and his group appear to have been oriented toward popular interests. While they apparently posed a threat to and were attacked by the followers of the Temple captain, Eleazar, they seem to have fought for the interests of the common people. Specifically, they joined in the burning of the public archives "to destroy the money-lenders' bonds and to prevent the recovery of debts . . . in order to cause a rising of the poor against the rich" (*War* 2.427).

In the case of the popularly acclaimed kings, those in 4 B.C.E. and Simon bar Giora, Josephus mentions activities of a social-economic, political, and military sort. In the case of Menahem, he includes also a dramatic religious feature: The Sicarii gave ceremonial expression to Menahem's kingly position precisely in the Temple.

How can we explain this unprecedented appearance of a messianic figure from one of the scholarly groups? The Qumran community had at least a somewhat indefinite expectation of (an) "anointed one(s) of Aaron and Israel" who would have primarily ceremonial functions. The scholars who produced the Psalms of Solomon apparently expected an anointed son of David with certain pedagogical features (Psalm of Solomon 17). Thus the ideological ground may have been prepared for Menahem's more active pretentions. The Sicarii, of course, had for years been engaged in direct agitation against Roman rule and Jewish high priestly collaboration.[20] Suddenly, in the course of a few weeks, Jerusalem had been liberated from Roman rule by a spontaneous popular uprising. The recent events must have appeared as a vindication of their own judgment about the situation and a fulfillment of their own hopes for liberation. They may have been eager to assume control of the revolt in Jerusalem itself. Thus the unprecedented action of Menahem's appearance as "king" was likely due at least partly to the excitement that must have pervaded Jerusalem during the summer of 66. Of course, it did not fit the expectations expressed in the Psalm of Solomon 17 that Menahem began the rebuke of alien rulers and the removal of sinners by the might of his sword rather than "by the might of his word."

Menahem's kingship, finally, had only a very narrow base, apparently only among the Sicarii, and it was cut short before it could become a broader movement. Its principal significance appears to have been that after the followers of the Temple captain Eleazar attacked Menahem and company, the surviving Sicarii fled to Masada in rejection or disillusionment.

USE AND ABUSE OF HISTORY

Christian biblical scholars have often used stereotypes of ancient Jewish phenomena as foils for their own preferred Christian nova. For generations the stereotype of Pharisaic or rabbinic "works-righteousness" and self-justification has been used as a foil for the Pauline (= Lutheran) doctrine of "justification by faith." The supposedly widespread and fanatical "Zealot" movement or "Jewish nationalism" has been used as a foil of violent rebellion over against which Jesus was then portrayed as a sober prophet of nonviolence or even nonresistance. Or the supposedly crudely "political" Jewish messianic expectation has been used as a counterpoise for Jesus as the truly "spiritual" Messiah. These stereotypes and nonhistorical Christian interpretations of Jesus are also persistent. It would be utterly inappropriate for historical investigations—which are attempting, among other things, to challenge and replace nonhistorical stereotypes such as "the Zealot movement" and Palestinian Jewish society as a hotbed of violent resistance—to be used in support of the same old stereotype in slightly different form. In particular,

20. R. Horsley, "The Sicarii: Ancient Jewish 'Terrorists,'" *Journal of Religion* 59 (1979) 435–41.

it would simply perpetuate one of these Christian stereotypes if the popular "messianic movements" were simply to be substituted for "the Zealots" as the foil of violence to highlight Jesus as the eirenic advocate of nonviolence. Perhaps it would be well to place the popular messianic and prophetic figures and movements in some biblical perspective.

In the Hebrew Bible / Old Testament there are two traditions of messianic figures. Besides the popularly "anointed" kings such as Saul, David, Jeroboam, Jehu, in which (revived) tradition the popularly acclaimed kings of 4 B.C.E. and 68–70 C.E. stood, there was the official Davidic monarchy's tradition of imperial kingship. As noted above, it was rooted in and borrowed heavily from the widespread ancient Near Eastern mythic tradition of imperial kingship. Psalms 2 and 110, along with other "royal psalms," are vivid ceremonial expressions of the sacral legitimation and mystification of the royal power. The people, including conquered subjects, are not only to be absolutely obedient to him, but their welfare is utterly dependent upon his divinely ordained power. Much of the historical narrative and much of the classical prophetic corpus in the Bible is sharply critical of such imperial kingship. More specifically, the popularly anointed kings led movements in opposition to the imperial "messiahs." Ironically kings who started as popularly acclaimed often set themselves or their sons up as imperial monarchs. "Popular kingship" was by definition charismatic and unstable. One of Freire's generalizations is highly pertinent to ancient biblical history in such cases: the only model that the oppressed have of humanity (or government) is taken from their oppressors.[21]

The messianic and prophetic movements of late Second Temple times constituted widespread, organized popular resistance to Roman imperial rule and its client regimes in Palestine. Just as Ahijah and the Israelites who acclaimed Jeroboam as king rebelled against the forced labor of Solomon's imperial rule, and Elijah, Elisha, and the Israelites headed by Jehu overthrew the oppressive rule of the Omrides, so the popular messianic and prophetic figures and their followers in the first century sought liberation from the tyranny of Herod or the depredations of the priestly aristocracy under the overall domination of the imperial "Savior" and his *pax Romana*. Subjected to the imperial kingship against their will and against the ideals expressed in their own biblical traditions, the participants in the popular messianic and prophetic movements sought liberation from oppression, some sense of self-determination, and a more just social order.

Christian scholars who want to criticize these popular Jewish movements for not being sufficiently eirenic or nonresistant may want to train their critical eye on New Testament Christology and its use by Christian missions and theology in subsequent generations as well. Certain followers of Jesus,

21. P. Freire, *Pedagogy of the Oppressed* (New York, 1971), p. 30.

whose writings were to become highly influential in subsequent centuries, chose imperial images for their "Lord" and "Savior." One need think only of the prominence of Psalms 2 and 110 in literature that found its way into the New Testament canon. And Paul, after emphasizing the absolute humility and humiliation of Jesus Christ, then insisted that he had become the universal lord, savior and master. It was one thing for tiny groups of insignificant, poor, and alienated people in hellenistic cities to proclaim that the hero of their faith had become the universal lord and regent for the divine King. The resurrected and exalted Christ served as inspiration for their own resistance to the "principalities and powers." But when that imagery carried over into the establishment of Christianity as the official religion, the resultant imperial Christ came to legitimize domination rather than resistance to it.

The Hebrew Bible offered two traditions of anointed kingship. Even though some of his followers borrowed passages from the royal psalms to articulate what they saw as his world-historical significance, it seems clear that Jesus and his movement did not stand in the tradition of the established Davidic royal ideology. It is ironic and inappropriate, therefore, for Christian interpreters to denigrate other movements that stood in the more popular tradition of kingship in the name of, or ostensibly in defense of, a Messiah elevated into an imperial position.

It is becoming increasingly evident that there was little interest in a Messiah, Davidic or otherwise, let alone a standard messianic expectation, in the diverse Palestinian Jewish literature of late Second Temple times. It could be that, until we attain a far more precise historical sense of groups and expectations in the Jewish Palestine from which "Christianity" and "Judaism" emerged, we should simply drop the concept "Messiah/messianic" altogether. Meanwhile it seems possible, on the basis of Josephus' reports, to discern distinctive types of concrete social movements and their leaders. Figures such as Theudas and "the Egyptian" would appear to have been "prophets" who, like Moses and/or Joshua in paradigmatic biblical history, were leading their followers to join in what they anticipated as new acts of liberation. The movements led by Judas, Simon, and Athronges in 4 B.C.E. and that led by Simon bar Giora in 68 would all appear to share the same social form, in which the people recognized the leader as "king," somewhat as the ancient Israelites had acclaimed Saul or David as king. These figures and movements were directed toward asserting the independence of the people from Roman and Herodian or high-priestly rule and a more egalitarian social-economic order in Jewish society.

15

CONVERSION AND MESSIANISM
Outline for a New Approach

1. SOME PROVISIONAL DEFINITIONS

Longing for a better future may be a worldwide aspiration, but it is especially characteristic of biblical literature. Furthermore, messianic hopes are quintessentially Jewish, because only YHWH so typically appointed his agents by anointing them. The messianic tradition contained a future orientation because of the words of the prophet Nathan to David. In 2 Samuel 7, God promised through Nathan that a Davidic king would always rule. This prophecy was remembered carefully by the Judean kingship. Especially after the disappearance of last legitimate Davidic king, the prophecy infused Judean religious history with a hope for a restoration of the Davidic monarchy. Along with the restored kingship came a vision of future justice and fairness, under the rule of a Davidic descendant.

Jewish life, as evidenced by the literature of Second Temple times, continued with little mention of a future Messiah. So we are speaking of a small minority who were involved actively in messianic speculation. Of course, "messiah" could refer to the reigning king, so he could come before the end of time (4 Ezra), and the end of time could come without an explicitly messianic figure (Daniel). And messiahs patterned on priestly officials (Qumran) or non-Judean kingships (Bar Kokhba) were also expected. But it is safe to say that messianic language was one particularly Jewish way of discussing future redemption. Thus it had a religious context.

These messianic hopes received a special boost during Roman occupation. Josephus mentions about a dozen rebels in the century before the Great Revolt of 66–74 C.E.[1] Perhaps this was because the Roman regime was

---

1. Ezekias and Judas *War* 1.204–5 (see also Acts 5:37); James and Simon, sons of Judas, *Ant* 20.102; the Sicarii, *War* 2.254–57, 4.400–5; Eleazar, son of the high priest Ananias, *War* 2.409; Menahem, son of Judas of Galilee, *War* 2.433–48; Eleazar, son of Jairus, *War* 7.253; "the zealots," *War* 4.160f.; John of Gischala, *War* 4.84ff.; Simon bar Giora, *War* 4.503; "Galileans," *War* 4.558–63; Eleazar, son of Simon, *War* 4.5ff. See R. A. Horsley and J. H. Hanson, *Bandits, Prophets, and Messiahs: Popular Movements at the Time of Jesus* (Minneapolis, 1985).

crueler and more exploitative than previous occupations. But the result of Roman occupation was not only the production of more dramatic messianic language. It also brought two centuries of courageous, hopeless, and tragic political rebellion against Rome.

Some of these movements may have been entirely political, carrying no messianic imagery. Josephus gives us an almost completely political description of the rebels, which is apparently designed to protect Jewish religious sentiments from Roman censure. Like most movements in traditional societies, the majority, it is safe to say, were partly political and partly religious. Besides seeking the establishment of a messianic king, some envisioned a world disciplined, corrected, and perfected by God, where the good alone survived and the evil persecutors were destroyed. Because of this, it is possible to associate some messianic movements in the first centuries with apocalypticism and millenarianism.[2] It is clear from a survey of the various groups of the first few centuries that the terms "messianic," "apocalyptic," and "millenarian" are closely associated.

That is not to say that the expectation for an end of time and messianic expectations always went together in the same way. Each group discovered its own formula for combination. But in the first century C.E. of Jewish history, the bonds between the two ideas were almost palpable. Christianity was the result of one such messianic movement. The Bar Kokhba revolt, a much more explicitly political movement, certainly had messianic overtones. It is safe to say that the other revolts were viewed as messianic signs by many others in Judea.

Millenarian movements, those movements for political or religious freedom, hoping to inaugurate a new moral order, are certainly not uniquely Jewish. Many cultures facing exploitation by colonizing powers produce millenarian movements.[3] These movements have captured the attention of so-

2. Of course, messianic movements do not have to be millenarian or vice versa. Indeed there is a big difference between the widespread use of messianic language and the establishment of a community or sect actively preparing for the end of time.

3. The literature about these movements is endless, but here is a fair representation. See my book *Rebecca's Children: Judaism and Christianity in the Roman Empire* (Cambridge, Mass., 1986), pp. 69–80, for more detail. See also Y. Talmon, "Pursuit of the Millennium: The Relationship Between Religions and Social Change," in W. Lessa and E. Vogt, eds., *Reader in Comparative Religion: An Anthropological Approach*, 2nd ed. (New York, 1965), pp. 522–37; Bernard Barber, "Acculturation and Messianic Movements," in Lessa and Vogt, eds., *Reader in Comparative Religion: An Anthropological Approach*, 3rd ed. (New York, 1972), pp. 512–16; R. Linton, A. F. C. Wallace, W. W. Hill, J. S. Slotkin, C. S. Welshaw, D. Aberle and C. Geertz, "Dynamics in Religion," in Lessa and Vogt, eds., *Reader*, 3rd. ed., pp. 496–543. R. Bellah, E. J. Hobsbawm, *Primitive Rebels: Studies in Archaic Forms of Social Movement in the 19th and 20th Centuries* (Manchester, 1971); S. Sharot, *Messianism, Mysticism, and Magic: A Sociological Analysis of Jewish Religious Movements* (Chapel Hill, 1982); P. Worsley, *The Trumpet Shall Sound: A Study of "Cargo" Cults in Melanesia* (London, 1957), pp. 225–27; V. Lanternari, *The Religions of the Oppressed: A Study of Modern Messianic Cults*, trans. L. Sergio (New York, 1965); A. F. C. Wallace, "Revitalization Movements," *American Anthropologist* 58 (1956) 264–81; J. Gager, *Kingdom and Community: The Social World of Early Christianity* (Englewood

ciologists and anthropologists for decades. I want to focus on but one aspect of these movements: they are filled with people who have been converted from a less activist form of religion to a more activist form, which exists in special highly committed cells or communities. As we know from modern examples and historical records, belonging to a millenarian movement is not often the result of casual affiliation or dillitantish curiosity. It is a serious and life-changing commitment.[4] In other words, although messianic language may be widespread in the first century, a few specifically millenarian movements were organized for the purpose of preparing for the Messiah's arrival or even bringing about the messianic age. This goal of bringing about God's kingdom might be seen in political or religious terms or both. In this paper, I want to reflect on issues of conversion as they affect our understanding of social groupings in the first century.

2. THE STUDY OF CONVERSION

The great Harvard classicist Arthur Darby Nock set the groundwork for the study of conversion in the ancient world by showing that conversion was a distinctly specialized and rare religious experience.[5] Most religious rites of the time helped maintain the political order because they were civic ceremonies. Participation involved "adherence," a low level of involvement, as an act of civic piety. But prophetic religions such as Judaism and Christianity stimulated conversion, raising commitment far above simple adherence. Conversion necessarily involved a radical change of lifestyle, often to a socially stigmatized group. Professor Nock showed that the strong personal commitment of conversion was characteristic of Judaism, of some of the philosophical sects and mystery religions, and preeminently of Christianity. He maintained that conversion uniquely suited Christianity to gain in popularity while conquering opposition. Furthermore, highly personal piety, an effect of the conversion experience, was characteristic of Christianity and a small number of other cohesive religions in the Roman Empire. Thus, conversion provided the dynamo for a true religious revolution in the late Roman Empire and a startling innovation in religious patterns. According to Nock, the phenomenon of conversion was also remarkably important for understanding the popularity and attractiveness of Christianity even before Paul. Christian

---

Cliffs, N.J., 1975); S. Isenberg, "Millenarianism in Greco-Roman Palestine," *Religion* 4 (1974) 32. Also see the proceedings of the interesting colloquium on apocalypticism in Uppsala, August 12–17, 1979, D. Hellholm, ed., *Apocalypticism in the Mediterranean World and the Near East* (Tübingen, 1983).

4. See my *Rebecca's Children*, pp. 22–28, 58–60.

5. A. D. Nock, *Conversion: The Old and the New in Religion from Alexander the Great to Augustine of Hippo* (Oxford, 1933).

communities organized all their resources for the dissemination of the Gospel, quickly spreading throughout the Roman world.

Nock recognized and emphasized an extremely important dynamic in the spread of early Christianity, a perception which has largely lain fallow. To be sure, Nock may have overstressed internal factors, disallowing the importance of Constantine and the Christian emperors for the success of Christianity.[6] His understanding of conversion was stereotypic, for Nock followed William James in limiting the experience of conversion to a radical emotional experience or a quick turning to a new way of life, a complete reorientation in attitude, thought, and practice. He left out the perhaps more common religious experience of deciding rationally for a religious change—training for it and undergoing a ritual symbolizing the change.[7] In short, Nock's understanding of conversion was stereotypically and traditionally Christian (hence strongly influenced by Luke's description of Paul). Furthermore, Nock probably underestimated the level of commitment which adherence to a civic form could generate among the local pagan aristocrats, who vied with each other for social prominence through public benefaction. It turns out that the easiest definition of conversion has not to do with interior states, as Nock thought, but in the decision to change religious communities.

In violation of the usual scholarly methods, I would like to use Christian documents to explore larger issues within the Jewish community. After all, rabbinic Judaism has left us documents of uncertain origins in oral tradition from the third century and later, while the New Testament, while also having oral roots, was in written form by the beginning of the second century. The New Testament is hence much better evidence for the history of Judaism than is rabbinic Judaism for the origins of Christianity. This is precisely the converse of standard methodology. Instead of producing scholarly documents like Strack-Billerbeck's *Commentar zum neuen Testament* we should be writing a commentary to the Mishnah which includes Christian and other first-century sectarian evidence. Thus, the relationship between conversion, high personal commitment, and group cohesion is crucial for understanding the success of early Christianity and, at the same time, may give us important evidence about Judaism in the first century.[8]

6. See R. MacMullen, *Christianizing the Roman Empire A.D. 100–400* (New Haven, 1984); also his *Paganism in the Roman Empire* (New Haven, 1981), pp. 94–137, for issues of conversion in paganism, dynamic religions, and the death of paganism. See also R. L. Fox, *Pagans and Christians* (New York, 1986).

7. Modern research now sees a close relationship between the two different styles of conversion in terms of the behavior change, as we shall see.

8. A great many questions were left unanswered by Nock's intuition which we cannot go into now: Why did conversion become important in Judaism and Christianity? How did conversion continue to play an important role in Christianity in the second and succeeding generations of family membership? Nock saw conversion as a continuous engine, typical of the way in which all Christians entered their movement, but this cannot be entirely true. Only in the first generation

More recent studies in the social sciences have pointed out that Nock's intuition can be confirmed by contemporary behavior, but with certain reservations and only under certain circumstances. The highest degree of commitment is only evident when sudden conversions are followed and supplemented by reinforcement from other members, through education to the values of the group. Thus, even radical converts must be trained to understand the decision which they made so emotionally. Since all communities establish what Peter Berger has called a "plausibility structure," a state in which beliefs seem self-evident and need no proof, a more exact analysis of the relationship of conversion to commitment is necessary.[9] Viewed from the perspective of social commitment, conversion resembles a new and conscious choice to socialize to a particular group—a resocialization, if you will.[10] The convert builds up a new structure of reality, corresponding to the structure of the group he joins. The values of the new group become the convert's new reality.

The degree of resocialization depends on the distance the convert must go between the old and new communities and the strength of the new commitment. Thus, conversion can take place into a single religion, where less resocialization needs to take place. This is important, for instance, in judging the differences between the kind of conversion that Paul underwent and that of his mostly Gentile followers, who had a somewhat different experience from a social perspective. Paul went from a highly committed Pharisee to a highly committed member of an apocalyptic form of Judaism. His converts went from paganism to a new religion whose relationship to Judaism shortly became a vexing issue. Both Paul and his Gentile converts underwent conversion, but the experience was very different in each case. Thus, the experience of conversion within a group may be very different for closely associated members, even when the exact same language is used by the members to describe it.

---

of Christianity in a family did all enter by conversion. Thereafter the progeny of the converts was socialized into Christianity. The child needs no conversion for social mores, values, and institutions present themselves as self-evidently true in a family which provides instruction into its religious rites. Primary socialization of the child, the process by which self-evidently true assertions about the world become internalized and recognized as objective reality, may therefore be an important analogy to the way in which conversion works in developing commitment. Thus we must also factor in the most ascetic and monastic varieties of Christianity, Christian communities which eschewed family life, who continued to have a strong influence on the progress of the movement. See D. Macdonald, *The Legend of the Apostle*, and E. Fiorenza, *In Memory of Her: A Feminist Theological Reconstruction of Christian Origins* (New York, 1983). In radically ascetic Christianity, conversion would continue to be the primary experience of "entrance" into the religion.

    9. P. Berger and T. Luckmann, *The Social Construction of Reality: A Treatise in the Sociology of Knowledge* (Garden City, N.Y., 1967), p. 15; R. N. Bellah, *Beyond Belief: Essays on Religion in a Post-Traditional World* (New York, 1970).

    10. See H. Remus, "Sociology of Knowledge and the Study of Early Christianity," *Studies in Religion* 11:1 (1982), 47f.

3. CONVERSION AND THE STRENGTH OF RELIGIOUS COMMITMENT

In the religious life of most communities, the commitment of converts is legendary.[11] Many studies have noted and explored the relationship between conversion and strong religious commitment. Perhaps best known of these is *Commitment and Community*. In it, Rosabeth Kanter records her interest in the psychology of commitment while investigating the factors influencing the survival of apocalyptic communities.[12] After studying nine successful communities and many unsuccessful ones, she defined commitment as a group of necessary internal controls which support the group. Personal commitment and those conversion experiences in which a new social world is learned become two aspects of the same dynamic of socialization in sects and in apocalyptic or utopian communities. Whenever a group is made up almost entirely of converts, its cohesiveness will tend to be much greater than that of a group whose membership is filled by casual affiliation, with no decisive action rejecting other choices. But the phenomenon of commitment includes more aspects than merely conversion.

Kanter observed that the highest degree of cohesiveness is signaled in groups that present new moral communities, such as where members come to share property or other resources and form a single household. Since this is a common feature of Jewish and Christian messianic sects, the relevance to first-century sectarian life should have been noted before. As expected, one characteristic of sects that are highly dependent on conversion for membership is that they also tend to be highly aware of the special nature of their group, stressing the differences between themselves and the outside world as part of their cohesiveness. The Qumran community is an obvious example of this phenomenon, because they sharply distinguished between themselves and anyone else, Jew or Gentile.

In analyzing the history of these groups, Kanter observed three principal types of commitment and the processes which enhance them. Although hers is not the only possible scheme and possibly not the most satisfactory one from the point of view of general theory, it is especially relevant to the study of early Christianity and other apocalyptic forms of Judaism, since her observations were made on the basis of modern examples. She divided commitment into three aspects: affective commitment, instrumental commitment,

---

11. There is no need to document this in detail. But it happens that a recent survey by the American Jewish Committee in New York has demonstrated it again. Egon Mayer and Amy Avgar interviewed partners of 309 intermarried couples. About a third of the couples identified contained a partner who had converted to Judaism. The overwhelming majority of partners converted to Judaism were women. They reported that the children of these couples are raised as Jews and the spouses were highly identified with the synagogue and the Jewish community, *New York Times* (June 22, 1987), section B, p. 9.

12. *Commitment and Community* (Cambridge, Mass., 1972), p. 64.

and moral commitment.[13] Kanter characterized instrumental commitment as a commitment to the *organization and its rules,* affective commitment as commitment to its *members* and moral commitment as commitment to the *ideas of the group, as spelled out by its leaders.* This results in three major aspects of commitment in a particular group: retention of members, group cohesiveness, and social control. Though Kanter does not discuss the issue, her typology allows for a neat distinction between the two types of conversions which were isolated by psychologists: Sudden conversions would necessarily begin with a sudden high degree of affective commitment, while gradual conversions work explicitly to develop high dimensions of moral and instrumental commitment as well. Since these are observations based upon evaluations and interpretations of her narrative data, it is hard to maintain the distinctions strongly, as hard and fast definitions of every society's mechanism of commitment, but they are important descriptive tools in helping to analyze why conversion helps galvanize community and ensure success.

Although radical conversions relate to the affective side of group commitment, they may also have ramifications on the other two scales as well. Gradual conversions typically address all three aspects of group commitment as part of the training process. This explains why successful groups tend to encourage gradual conversions. Indeed without successful socialization to the values of the group, the radical convert is bound to disaffiliate. *Radical conversions are less stable than gradual ones.* But some radical conversions may be important for the development of commitment, where emotions are understood to be a mark of religious experience. Radical conversions can dramatize the workings of spirit, the ecstasy, or the bliss sought within the movement, and give urgency to the claims of the group. But, for the stability of the membership, it is important to balance the emotional contribution of radical converts with the more even enthusiasm of gradual converts, who appropriate the rules and roles of the group more thoroughly and so add stability.

More recently, several psychologists have investigated the relationship between conversion and commitment by examining the language of converts. Snow and Machalek[14] proposed that the surest way to identify the phenomenon of conversion would be to look for changes in the subject's "universe of discourse." Studying the Nichiren Shoshu Buddhist movement, they suggested that converts may be identified by four "rhetorical indicators": (1) adopting a master attribution scheme; (2) biographical reconstruction; (3) suspending analogical reason; and (4) embracing a master role. Subsequent research has shown that all these four rhetorical indicators are

---

13. Ibid., pp. 61–74.

14. D. Snow and R. Machalek, "The Convert as a Social Type," *Sociological Theory,* ed. R. Collins (San Francisco, 1983), pp. 259–89, and "The Psychology of Conversion," *Annual Review of Sociology* 10 (1984) 167–90.

important for locating religious commitment. Yet, in modern "born-again" Christianity at least, only one of them—biographical reconstruction, where the subject actively reinterprets past experiences or self-conceptions from the vantage point of the present in such a way as to change the meaning of the past for the subject—is a clear indicator of religious conversion.[15] Staples and Mauss were explicitly asking whether the criteria deduced by Snow and Machalek from studying an Eastern sect would hold true for a sect of born-again Christians. The answer was positive, but only one of the criteria was specific to conversion: the desire to revalue one's life. This criterion surprisingly places Paul squarely within the category of convert. It is surprising because Paul does not clearly use conversion language to describe himself, though he constantly talks about how his life changed on account of his fame. Nevertheless, as we shall see, with Staples' and Mauss' help, *convert* becomes a very sensible term to use about Paul, and it teaches us a lot about the character of early Christianity. In turn, that gives us interesting information about the messianic dynamics in first-century Judaism. But before we can enter this thorny issue, we must glean what we can from the explicit discussions of conversion in first-century Judaism.

4. CONVERSION AND COMMUNITY IN HELLENISTIC JUDAISM

The perception that strong personal decisions lead to highly cohesive groups can be profitably applied to sectarian life in Judaism. And one clear rule can be advanced at the beginning: Gradual conversion was the typical and expected pattern for virtually every sectarian group in Judaism, though sudden and emotional conversion may have occurred occasionally. Admittedly we know very little about the many messianic movements which left no documents behind, and even the community which John the Baptist led cannot be defined very clearly. But Greco-Roman Judea valued learning of special meanings of difficult texts. In fact, in providing special instruction in the truths of the sect, each of the sects set up the closest thing to educational institutions in Jewish society. The systems of catechesis developed in each sect for the purposes of conversion and education made possible Josephus' claim to be a religious quester, spending most of four years investigating the religious alternatives of first-century Judea before he decided for the Pharisees. A Jew's conversion to one of the Jewish sectarian positions—let us say either Essenism or Pharisaism—might have involved a radical change of some aspects of his existence. But at the same time, it was not a radical change in every respect. After all, Josephus was already a Jew before he

---

15. C. L. Staples and A. L. Mauss, "Conversion or Commitment? A Reassessment of the Snow and Machalek Approach to the Study of Conversion," *JSSR* 26 (1987) 133–47.

became a Pharisee (if he really did become a Pharisee). He claims that he searched and only chose Pharisaism in the end, after having tried several varieties of Judaism, because Pharisaism was a virtual necessity for anyone seeking a public career. For Josephus the decision to explore the Jewish sects was in some ways equivalent to a decision to seek higher Jewish education.[16] Although Josephus was guided by the Pharisees in the end, he appears to have been more intrigued by the Essenes, given the tone of his lengthy description of them. Had Josephus actually joined the Essenes as well as lauding them, he would have become a convert, although conversion to this group was normally envisioned as a gradual process of internalizing group norms. Essene membership came only by conversion. Even an orphan would have had to go through the same lengthy initiation as any other convert. Virtually no member of this group could be called merely an adherent because all members adopted a radically different lifestyle.[17]

The single most obvious characteristic of the Dead Sea Scroll sectarians was their dualism. Strongly apocalyptic, the community divided the world into a battle between the children of darkness and the children of light. But this is not to be confused with a philosophical impetus toward dualism—they believed in a single deity. The distinction, rather, has as much to do with sociology as theology. Their dualism was parallel to their division of the world into sons of light and sons of darkness, which served to separate members of the group from everyone else. This theology of radical dualism functioned as a social barrier. It kept the new member away from any contradictory information. They virtually identified themselves with the community of the saved at the end of time. There was thus a perfect symmetry between their personal decision states in joining their community and their views of the ultimate purpose of history.[18]

Even though ecstatic prayer, heavenly journeys, and other paranormal experience appear to have been part of their lives, the Qumran group did not describe conversion in ecstatic or emotional terms, stressing the rigors of the life of purity instead. They prescribed ritual immersion for purity as did the Pharisees and Christians. But among them baptism had a mark that

16. By the time Josephus wrote, Pharisaism, by his own report, was the most popular and politically powerful Jewish sect, a position which it may not have attained at the beginning of the first century. Josephus' decision, far from being a conversion, may only have been an act of expediency. In fact, the motif of spiritual quest was a literary convention for establishing one's credentials as a religious commentator. See Justin, *Dial* (beginning), Dio Chrysostom, and St. Augustine. See N. Heydahl, *Philosophie und Christentum: Eine Interpretation der Einleitung zum Dialog Justins* (Copenhagen, 1966).

17. See L. Schiffman, *Sectarian Law in the Dead Sea Scrolls: Courts, Testimony, and the Penal Code* (Chico, Calif., 1983), pp. 155–74.

18. In this respect they are quite close to the flying saucer group which L. Festinger, H. W. Riecken, and S. Schacter studied in *When Prophecy Fails: A Social and Psychological Study of a Modern Group That Predicted the Destruction of the World* (New York, 1956) or many of the new religions today, which set up monastic or ascetic or retreat communities based on the notion that they alone will survive.

was unequivocally Essene. Ritual immersion made the Dead Sea Scroll community pure enough to fight in the same army as with the angels at the end of time. Hence, the member could be saved at the final battle. The practice helps fill in the gaps between rabbinic views of community and Christian ones, just as it helps fill in the missing steps between Jewish ritual immersion and Christian baptism. Because of the Dead Sea Scrolls we can now investigate the Qumran community's internal organization and see that they would score very high on all the scales Kanter develops for commitment. They were apocalypticists and committed members of their sect. They expected the end of the world imminently and the end of the arrogant dominion in Jerusalem. But they expected help from angels.

5. CONVERSION AMONG DIASPORA JEWISH GROUPS

Within the small area of Judea and the slightly larger area of the land of Israel, which included Samaria and the Galilee, we have evidence of a large number of hellenized Jews. These Jews produced the majority of the material evidence coming down to us from the first centuries. Josephus mentions the "representations of animals" which Herod Antipas put in houses in Tiberias (*Life* 65). Although the famous ruins of Galilean synagogues with their beautiful mosaics—containing zodiacs, the seasons, and depictions of Helios—date from the third century and later, they show the extent of Jewish acculturation to hellenism, the willing interplay of Jewish and pagan beliefs, one supposes, as long as some of the major tenets of Jewish belief were not endangered. In the Jewish Diaspora, where the synagogues were equally omnipresent and even more grand architecturally, acculturation can only have been all the more evident.

Philo, the spokesman for hellenistic Judaism, evinces a degree of cosmopolitanism and sophistication which parallels the acculturation evident in the material remains. Philo discusses the wisdom of the Greeks as one standard of truth in the world. Of course, he takes pains to show that everything good in Greek thought is paralleled by Jewish thought and that Judaism contains moral and philosophical truths only hinted at by the Greeks. However, he sometimes hints that Gentiles can attain to salvation, just as Jews attain to the philosophical mind. Though he mentions with pride that some Gentiles have even thought it fit to convert to Judaism, and goes out of his way to exhort Jews to accept them, he also seems to believe that there are some Gentiles who have the advantages of a moral and philosophical life without conversion to Judaism (*Spec Leg* 1.52, 1.308–9, *Virt* 103–4).[19]

This is a minor topic, however, compared to the *apologia* which Philo and

---

19. See A. Malherbe, *The Social Aspects of Early Christianity*, 2nd ed., enlarged (Philadelphia, 1983), pp. 51–52.

Josephus mount for proving the truth of Judaism in *Against Flaccus* and *Against Apion* respectively. Among the proofs of Judaism's truth are both its ancient history and its success in gaining converts, which was also noted by several prominent classical writers. Tacitus, the Roman historian, says of proselytes to Judaism: "The earliest lesson they receive is to despise the gods, to disown their country, and to regard their parents, children, and brothers as of little account" (*Histories* 5.5). Josephus and Philo answer these charges by showing that the Jews' dedication to monotheism is not atheism and that Jewish ethics do not disrupt family life; rather they build it up.

Such statements testify to the success which Judaism had in proselytism. But they also show something else important—the social threat which Judaism and Christianity presented to Greco-Roman society. A. Malherbe suggests quite cogently that both Philo's and Josephus' use of the so-called *Haustafel*, the idealized ethical portrait of a household which is so common in pagan ethical treatises, was partly an attempt to counter polemics and fears that Judaism was antisocial or would undermine pagan society.[20] The perception is even more important after the birth of Christianity, since both Jewish and pagan society shared exactly this distrust of Christianity. Jesus' message, according to the New Testament, did contain advice to leave parents and families. Needless to say, later Christianity found the same and greater need to apologize for possible family disruption as did Judaism, as, for example, the *Haustafel* in 1 Peter testifies.

Both before and after the rise of Christianity, Jews proselytized, and their proselytism gained them enemies. According to Valerius Maximus, the Jews were expelled from Rome in 139 B.C.E. because of their attempts to "transmit their holy rites to the Romans" (*qui Romanis tradere sacra sua conati erant*). Very likely this was the same reason for their expulsion under Tiberius in the first century, for according to Dio Cassius they were expelled because "they were converting many of the natives to their customs." In the first century B.C.E. the Maccabees were also known to have conquered the Idumeans and to have forced circumcision and conversion upon them.[21] Horace refers to the Jews' desire for non-Jews to join their group: *in hanc concedere turbam*.[22] Jewish proselytism was therefore both real and contro-

---

20. Philo, *Hypothetica*—see Eusebius, *Praeparatio* 8.6–7 355c–361b; Josephus, *Apion* 2.190.
21. Ptolemy the Historian, from Josephus, *Ant* 13.257, 318.
22. Seneca, *De Superstitione*—see Menachem Stern, *Greek and Latin Authors on Jews and Judaism*, 2 vols. (Jerusalem, 1974, 1980), pp. 127, 146, 147, 365. See also Valerius Maximus, *Facta et Dicta Memorabilia* 1.3.3; Horace, *Sermones* 1.4.142–43; Augustine, *De Civitate Dei* 6.11 and *Epistolae Morales* 108.22; Martial, *Epigrammata* 7.30.5–8, 35.3–4, 82.5–6, 9.94.1–8; Petronius, *Satyricon* 68.8; Dio Cassius, *Hist. Rom.* 67.14.1–3. See also M. Smallwood, *The Jews Under Roman Rule* (Leiden, 1976), p. 379 and n. 82. See also S. J. D. Cohen, "Conversion to Judaism in Historical Perspective: From Biblical Israel to Postbiblical Judaism," *Conservative Judaism* (Summer 1983), n. 15, and H. Green, *The Economic and Social Origins of Gnosticism*, SBLDS 77 (Atlanta, 1985), pp. 89f.

versial. Jews gained proselytes but did not overwhelm the pagan world because becoming a Jew was never merely a decision to join another religious club. Judaism was exclusive; it was deeply suspicious of other associations, for even the secular ones held perfunctory religious rites, which Jews found idolatrous. Because Jews despised other religious rites, even civic ones, as idolatry, they were seen as atheistic and intolerant. They did not participate in hellenistic society's easy pluralism of religious devotion. Joining Judaism was therefore primarily a decision to join another *ethnos*, which was a step not taken lightly and always accepted with some suspicion.[23]

That there were differing standards for the acceptance of converts to Judaism, perhaps attributable to the different orientations of the various sects, is clear not only from the rabbinic discussion but from a few precious reports from Josephus. Josephus claims that the Jews of Antioch "were constantly attracting to their religious ceremonies multitudes of Greeks, and these they had in some measure incorporated into themselves" (*War* 7.3.3.[45]). On the other hand, some Jews preferred that potential converts remain "God-fearers" or semi-proselytes because such in-between stages provoked fewer backlash incidents than did disrupting pagan families by converting wives, husbands, and children. The frequent charges of family disruption only underline that most conversions took place on a person-to-person level, spreading through organizations and families one member at a time. Such patterns are well known today, such as in Mormon preaching, and are a significant piece of evidence for the process by which Christianity spread as well.

Just as Jews received converts from pagan society, so many Jews, even those who wished to retain their Jewish identity, acculturated to pagan society. As in the modern period, the Jew's predicament as "marginal man" could be solved by leaving Judaism entirely, by downplaying the value of Judaism, or by reforming Judaism to make it more acceptable in Gentile eyes.[24] Obviously, some assimilated completely, losing their Jewish identity and often gaining citizenship in the Greek *polis*.[25] But there were many accommodations short of apostasy. While Philo believes that the special laws of Judaism

---

23. See B. J. Bamberger, *Proselytism in the Talmudic Period* (New York, 1968); S. Baron, *A Social and Religious History of the Jews* (New York, 1952), vol. 1, pp. 174f.; M. Hengel, *Judaism and Hellenism*, vol. 1, p. 307; S. Zeitlin, *The Rise and Fall of the Judean State*, vol. 3, p. 326; S. Applebaum, "The Social and Economic Status of the Jews in the Diaspora," in S. Safrai and M. Stern, eds., *The Jewish People in the First Century* (Philadelphia, 1976), vol. 2, pp. 622f.; J. R. Rosenbloom, *Conversion to Judaism* (Cincinnati, 1978); J. Z. Smith, "Fences and Neighbors: Some Contours of Early Judaism," *Imagining Religion: From Babylon to Jonestown* (Chicago, 1982), pp. 1–19; H. A. Green, "Jewish Identification and Assimilation: Continuities and Discontinuities in Roman Egypt," *Society of Biblical Literature 1985 Seminar Papers*, ed. K. H. Richards (Atlanta, 1985), pp. 505–13.

24. E. V. Stonequist, *The Marginal Man* (New York, 1937). In the latter case, secularized Jews themselves might be tempted to convert to other groups.

25. See 1Mac 1:11–15; 3Mac 2:31 and 7:10; also Philo, *Vita Mos* 1.130 and *Virt* 182.

had to be practiced literally, he also informs us in *Migr* 84ff. that some intellectual Jews did not practice them. Although they studied Torah, they understood the laws only as allegories illustrating moral principles, not seeing fit to observe them in their personal lives. This implies that a Jewish education was received by most of the community, though different Jews may have stressed different values. Philo does not agree with these "extreme allegorizers," but his criticism stops far short of real hostility. He is satisfied with satirizing them as persons who try to "live as souls without bodies, as though they were living by themselves in a wilderness" (89). Philo appears to mean by this that the customs of Judaism are designed to be practiced where they enforce moral standards within society. Philo essentially describes the "extreme allegorizers" as philosophers, misguided for having forgotten that universal values must be envisioned through particular material circumstances. [26]

The leniency of Philo's reproach of the "extreme allegorizers" can be seen in comparison with apostates, for whom Philo has less kind words: "being incontinent, . . . [they] have sold their freedom for luxurious food . . . and beauty of body, thus ministering to the pleasures of the belly and the organs below it" (*Virt* 34, 182). This discussion is reminiscent of 3 Maccabees where the apostates are called: "those who for their belly's sake had transgressed the divine command" (7:11). The apostates are not virtuous but merely indulge themselves in degradation. They make no attempt to live up to the virtues of Judaism, desiring complete assimilation, while the "extreme allegorizers" continued to consider themselves Jews and maintain the moral laws of Judaism, though they neglected the special customs.

These are hardly discussions of Jewish identity or conversion. But they show the range of choices available to Jews of the time. Conclusions about such modern analytic concepts as conversion can be teased out of the context, because across the myriad of differences separating the modern world from the Greco-Roman world, some of the social conflicts are quite similar.

Shaye Cohen among others has suggested that Jewish identity in this period resembles citizenship in that it was usually determined by birth and was not easily obtained otherwise. Indeed, the terms Ἰουδαῖος and *Iudaeus* like the Hebrew יהודי basically meant "Judean," retaining more geographical and national connotations than is true of the word "Jew" in modern languages. So a Jew could become a citizen of another place through naturalization, and often at the cost of his Jewish identity, which needed to be left behind like a previous citizenship.

But this is an overly simple comparison. For one thing, in the ancient

26. See J. J. Collins, "A Symbol of Otherness: Circumcision and Salvation in the First Century," *"To See Ourselves As Others See Us,"* ed. J. Neusner, *et al.* (Chico, Calif., 1986), pp. 163–86, and pp. 171–72.

world as in our own, many people were able to maintain more than one nationality; sometimes they could maintain conflicting nationalities. Though citizenship in Greek cities was zealously guarded, it was sometimes bestowed upon foreigners on the basis of habitation, property ownership, even religious rite, and primarily through local benefactions. Jews aspired to and obtained citizenship on an individual basis in Alexandria. As a result of the civil conflict between the Jews and the Greeks in that city, the best the *community* could receive was ἰσοπολιτεία, separate-but-(not so)-equal rights to citizenship.[27]

Some Jews were satisfied with such gains, content to develop independently; other Jews were not. Still other Jews, like Philo, came from families who had probably been part of the citizenry for generations. But citizenship was often bestowed on the basis of religious preference, rather than the other way around. Although one could own property in Athens without being a citizen, one way to become a citizen of Athens was to seek initiation into the Eleusinian mysteries.[28] One assumes that many foreigners gave up their previous allegiances to become landholders. The result is that Jewish identity in parts of the Diaspora was somewhat like foreign nationality, as it is today, though it is hardly identical with the ancient understanding of citizenship. On the other hand, Jewish identity in the ancient world could often be subject to the same stresses as it is in the modern secular American Jewish community, which has its many examples of apostasies to both established religion and the new religious cults, but also many different accommodations in which conflicts are minimized.

While we do not have many specific discussions of conversion from other hellenistic Jewish authors, John J. Collins has shown that there was among hellenistic Jews a very liberal attitude toward Gentile interest in Judaism.[29] A body of apologetic or "propaganda" literature was designed to inform Gentiles of the value of Jewish life. The Sibylline oracles praise the Jews as a race of most righteous men (3.219). Specific features proving Jewish moral superiority are enumerated: the practice of social justice (218–264) and the avoidance of idolatry and homosexuality (573–600). In a number of passages the sibyl speaks directly to the Greeks: "To what purpose do you give vain *gifts to the dead*[30] and sacrifice to idols? Who put error in your heart that you should abandon the fact of the great God and do these things?" (547–549). For the Sibylline oracles, salvation is sought in this world. Jews and Greeks alike may attain to a peaceful life free from war and subjugation. Hence,

---

27. A. Kasher, *The Jews in Hellenistic and Roman Egypt: The Struggle for Equal Rights* (Tübingen, 1985).

28. Plutarch, *Theseus* 33.2, G. E. Mylonas, *Eleusis and the Eleusinian Mysteries* (Princeton, N.J., n.d.), p. 77. My thanks to Holland Hendrix for this idea and reference.

29. J. J. Collins, see above, n. 26.

30. Italics mine. See M. Avodah Zarah 2:3.

salvation can be attained by Greeks if they abandon idolatry and offer sacrifice at the Temple of the great God in Jerusalem (624–634).

Likewise in the famous *Letter of Aristeas*, there is no direct appeal for conversion, but there is certainly an apologetic or propagandistic attempt to portray the merits of Judaism. The letter purports to be written by one Greek and sent to another, but scholars usually see a Jewish hand behind it. The God of the Jews is described as "the overseer and creator of all things, whom they worship, is He whom all men worship, and we too your Majesty, though we address him differently, as Zeus and Dis; by these names men of old not unsuitably signified that He through whom all creatures receive life and come into being is the guide and lord of all" (*Letter of Aristeas* 16). Judaism is presented as a nonviolent, nonaggressive philosophy and most especially not an exclusive or closed fraternity. Rather Judaism is a gift to all humanity, since God's providence is universal. It is not suggested that God will show special consideration for the Jews simply by virtue of their being Jews. Nor is there any hint of proselytization. The Jews follow their own rites, which attain a desirable religious end, but the same end can be attained by moral and God-fearing Greeks, though the rites be different.[31] It is clear that the most acculturated Jewish writers soft-pedaled conversion when it was viewed as threatening by the Gentile community, rather arguing that monotheism and virtue would be rewarded wherever it was found. These Jews asked Gentiles to worship the one true God, which entailed a rejection of idolatry or as it was often expressed, worship for the dead, and avoidance of sin, with emphasis on adultery and homosexuality as the two characteristic Gentile sins.

Of course, in spite of Jewish sensitivities to the charge of breaking up Gentile families, converts were welcomed. A brief mention of conversion occurs at the end of the book of Judith, which is probably to be dated to the hellenistic period. After Judith has killed Holofernes, the Ammonite general is so impressed with the saving acts of the Israelite God that he becomes a believer, even accepting circumcision, and is incorporated "in the house of Israel forever." No doubt this is meant to illustrate the highest possible form of pagan admiration for Judaism.

There is an account of Gentile conversion to Judaism in hellenistic writing, the romance of *Joseph and Asenath*, which is set during Joseph's sojourn in Egypt but is meant to be the model of proselytism in the hellenistic world. Since Asenath is a woman, the issue of circumcision does not arise. On the other hand, the ritual which is mentioned is completely puzzling. Joseph is described as eating the blessed bread of life, drinking the cup of immortality, and anointing himself with the blessed oil of incorruption. When Asenath converts, after she throws her idols away, she attains to these rites, which

31. M. Hadas, *Aristeas to Philocrates* (New York, 1951), p. 62.

are apparently symbolic of Jewish life in general, rather than representative of a specific conversion ritual.[32] The puzzling objects of Asenath's rites are known to be symbolic of Judaism in a general way. For instance, the b. Talmud Shabbat 17b forbids Gentile wine, bread, and oil: "the bread and oil of the heathen on account of their wine, and their win on account of their daughters, and their daughters on account of idolatry." Thus the symbols can be used to illustrate Asenath's entrance into the community. The context in *Joseph and Asenath* is apposite to the rabbis' warning, implying that the rules of commensality were broadly understood in the Judaism of this period as safeguards against the idolatry of Gentiles. We also learn that Joseph does not eat with the Egyptians, even though he is ruler of all Egypt (7:1; 20:9). Asenath is described as "dead" before her conversion, which represents her journey into life. In this document, immortality is the clear benefit of conversion.

Thus, the choices available to hellenistic Jews were manifold, implying many different kinds of adaptations to the Jewish-hellenistic cultural exchange, allowing for a variety of different opinions toward conversion in the Jewish community. Philo and the hellenistic Jewish writers give evidence of the liberal end of the spectrum of commitment to Judaism. Acculturated hellenistic Jews were still committed to Judaism, but their commitment was entirely different from that of the Essenes, who produced such a sectarian, inward-looking, and highly cohesive society, separate even from the majority of Jews. To the contrary, the acculturated Jewish community was intimately involved in many transactional relationships with the larger hellenistic world. Though the upper levels of hellenistic Jewish society may have felt deprived of the full rights of citizenship that many non-Greek or Roman Gentile hellenists had attained, most remained Jews and felt at some ease in hellenistic society and trade, seeking to remove as many nonessential boundaries as they could justify. They sometimes endeavor to remove a cause of suspicion between themselves and their Gentile neighbors by saying that all moral people could enjoy God's blessing by righteousness. It is likely that many did not seek to convert Gentiles, for this would have risked a backlash. But it just as likely that other Jews sought out Gentiles for conversion.

Of course, one cannot call the full spectrum of Jewish styles of commitment a unified policy in the way that a conversion community is. But this is precisely the point. Group commitment is built in hellenistic Judaism as a whole on a much wider series of models than in sectarian Jewish life of the first few centuries. It is quite probable that these hellenistic Jews, with a variety of differing accommodations to hellenism, were the majority of Jews

---

32. *Joseph and Asenath* may have some Jewish-Christian influence as the bread is marked with a sign that looks like the cross.

of that time. Yet, at the same time, they could not have felt the social cohesion which the Essenes developed. Furthermore, modern studies show that "liberal" positions do not grow as quickly as conservative ones, since some liberal members can be assumed to fall away, giving up any religious identification, while the more conservative positions are able, if they desire, to attract new highly committed members, in spite of their harsher lifestyle, indeed, on account of it. This can be summed up by noting that the Essenes were a highly cohesive group, while the hellenistic Jews were not a unified group at all.

6. THE GOD-FEARERS

"God-fearer" refers to those Gentiles with varying degrees of commitment to Judaism, who have been attracted to the synagogue but who are unwilling to become proselytes. Acts uses the term σεβόμενος, literally a *worshiper* (sometimes θεοσεβής and variants suggesting a worshiper of God most high), or φοβούμενος, literally a *fearer* of God. "Fearing God" is the normal Hebrew idiom for describing worshiping him, while the term *sebomenos* appears to translate the sense of the Hebrew idiom into Greek. The term "God-fearer" is used most obviously in Acts 10, where Cornelius is described also as a donor to the synagogue. But the term is not a Lukan invention, for Josephus uses it as well (*Ant* 14.110) to describe Gentiles and so does Julia Severa, a co-sponsor of the synagogue building in Acmonia.[33]

A. T. Kraabel has proposed that the presence of these people in the synagogues where Paul preaches are Luke's invention, introduced for the purpose of showing "how Christianity had become a Gentile religion legitimately and without losing its Old Testament roots."[34] Kraabel's skepticism was based upon the lack of any firm archeological or inscriptional evidence for the term "God-fearer" in any synagogue site, though he himself describes the synagogue at Sardis as designed to allow ample view by passers-by of the interior services in progress, so as to be a showplace of Jewish ritual for the Gentile world.[35] But the evidence is less one-sided than Kraabel suggests,

33. J. B. Frey, *Corpus Inscriptionum Ioudaicarum* (Rome, 1936), p. 766. The literature on this group is large. But see L. Feldman, "Jewish 'Sympathizers' in Classical Literature and Inscriptions," *TAPA* 81 (1950) 200; and H. J. Leon, *The Jews of Ancient Rome* (Philadelphia, 1960), pp. 247, 251. See esp. K. Lake, "Proselytes and God-fearers," in *The Beginnings of Christianity, Part I: The Acts of the Apostles*, ed. F. J. Foakes Jackson and K. Lake (Grand Rapids, Mich., 1966), vol. 5; Additional Notes to the Commentary, pp. 74–95. The arguments are clearly reviewed and critiqued in greater detail by J. Gager, "Jews, Gentiles and Synagogues in the Book of Acts," *Christians Among Jews and Gentiles: Essays in Honor of Krister Stendahl on His Sixty-fifth Birthday*, ed. G. W. E. Nickelsburg and G. W. MacRae (Philadelphia, 1986), pp. 91–99.

34. A. T. Kraabel, "The Disappearance of the 'God-fearers,'" *Numen* 28 (1981) 113–26; see also "The Roman Diaspora: Six Questionable Assumptions," *JJS* 33 (1982) 445–64.

35. Kraabel, "Sardis from Prehistoric to Roman Times," *Results of the Archeological Exploration of Sardis 1958–1975* (Cambridge, Mass., 1983), p. 184.

since the term does exist in a few inscriptions, where its meaning is moot, as it may refer to a Jew or a Gentile.

Two new, as yet unpublished inscriptions from Aphrodisias in Caria seem to settle the problem of the existence of God-fearers.[36] Besides identifying Jewish donors, with a mixture of Jewish, biblical, and hellenistic names, the texts identify a whole group of people as *theosebeis* who have exclusively Greek names, some with occupations likely to be Gentile, like city councillors. Within the list there is a sprinkling of people with biblical names who are described as proselytes. "God-fearer" thus appears to be a technical term, perhaps with a range of meanings, and is clearly to be distinguished from both Jews and proselytes. The inscriptions tend to support Luke's contention that some Gentiles were fellow travelers with Judaism, attending and aiding the synagogue but not formally converting. Thus, while Luke certainly construed the presence of God-fearers in the synagogues of the hellenistic world as consonant with his own theology, God-fearers actually existed, and possibly in large numbers. These people formed a reservoir of Gentiles interested in Judaism for whom Christianity would have had a natural appeal. Though one can imagine a number of purely political reasons why a Gentile would want to support a prominent local synagogue, among the God-fearers Philo would certainly have numbered some Gentiles who could achieve the status and privileges God had promised to the Jews. After all, benefaction was one of the accepted routes leading to adhesion with the group. These people were surely held in high respect by the community, since their gifts were accepted and recorded for posterity. We shall see that the rabbis held similar but not identical concepts of righteous Gentiles.

7. CONVERSION AMONG THE PHARISEES AND RABBIS

We can no longer be sure that the rabbinic reports about conversion come from the first century. Clearly they grew out of first-century practice, but because of the oral nature of rabbinic literature and extensive editing in subsequent centuries, we cannot be sure how the customs developed without outside corroboration. With regard to commitment, both Pharisaism and early Jewish Christianity would have fallen into intermediary positions between hellenistic Jews and the Essenes, the two extremes of commitment, since both Pharisees and Christians accepted converts, viewed themselves as a sect, but lived in the larger community rather than in isolation. It is

---

36. J. Reynolds and R. Tannenbaum, *Jews and God-fearers at Aphrodisias: Greek Inscriptions with Commentary* (Cambridge, 1986). Also see Gager, above, n. 33, who cites his indebtedness to Reynolds and Tannenbaum and to G. W. Bowersock, for his public lecture discussing the inscriptions. The substance of this paper was completed before the publication of the Aphrodisias inscription, though it is gratifying to see how well it substantiates the insights which come from social sciences.

probable from the description in the New Testament that Pharisees did not attain or need the same social cohesion which early Christianity evidenced. Conversion into the Pharisaic order of the first century seems to have involved a significant new level of cohesiveness, but limited to accepting rules of the *haburoth*—taking on the purity regulations at table, giving heave offerings, and being meticulous in observing the tithing regulations. The result of these regulations, as Jacob Neusner has pointed out so often, was to create a self-contained community defined by its ability to marry within its ranks, eat at its own houses and touch only its own implements. At first, the Pharisaic order would have been sectarian in nature; most of those who entered the order would already have been socialized to Judaism.[37] The later rabbis, reflecting on their traditions, idealized the legal situation in the first century and certainly held out high standards of entrance: "The rabbis say: 'If a proselyte takes it upon himself to obey all the words of the Torah except one single commandment, he is not to be received'" (Sifra, Kedoshim 8).

One supposes that these rules applied both to non-Pharisaic Jews and to Gentiles, for the rabbis never say anything which implies that proselytism was limited to other varieties of Jews. In today's society, conversion to Judaism is almost always embarked upon by people who want to marry a Jewish spouse. Because of the romance *Joseph and Aseneth*, we have evidence of the same motivation in the ancient world but no comparative statistics about other motivations.

When we study Gentile conversion to Judaism, we have to confront the problem that most of our information comes from the rabbinic evidence whose date and disinterestedness is a moot point. Here is the range of opinion, as idealized by later tradition:

A foreigner came to Shammai, saying, "Make a proselyte of me, on condition that you teach me the whole of the Torah while I stand on one foot."

Shammai drove him off with a measuring stick he had in his hand. Thereupon he repaired to Hillel with the same proposition.

Hillel received him as a proselyte and taught him: "What you do not like to have done to you, do not do to your fellow. This is the whole of the Torah; the rest is explanation of it. Go learn it." b.Shab 31a

This is one of three examples given at this place in Talmud of the difference between Shammai and Hillel, two early rabbis who lived just prior to Jesus, on the issue of conversion, but there is no way to be sure that the stories contain any historical value for the first century. The three Gentiles in the three examples are meant primarily to help display a difference be-

37. J. Neusner, *From Politics to Piety* (Englewood Cliffs, N.J., 1973).

tween the schools of Shammai and Hillel, which flourished later. They may also represent different positions in the group of potential proselytes. That is to say, the three stories in the rabbinic anthology emphasize the more lenient approach of Hillel, the dominant rabbinic sage, on the issue of conversion over the strict position of Shammai, who does not appear very interested in making converts. The three Gentiles may even represent varieties of opinions among converts to Judaism: those who convert to non-Pharisaic Judaism (no oral law and only of the laws of the Bible), those who convert out of ambition (to become the High Priest), and finally the one quoted above, who converts for the moral principles, and to whom is given the famous answer of Hillel: "What you do not like to have done to you, do not do to your fellow," but—and this is the important part for the rabbis—is immediately told to go out and study. The problem with the rabbinic evidence lies not only in what it means but also in the date it became the standard practice within Judaism.[38]

Even the lenient position of Hillel favored high commitment. Like the Essenes, the rabbis favored the slow, highly indoctrinated convert over the rapid, emotionally involved one. What became rabbinic doctrine may have been only a formalization of earlier general practice within the Jewish community, or it may have been the explicit beliefs of the first-century Pharisees. But it is quite clear that the effect of Hillel's answer is to encourage the convert to enter the stages of training to become socialized as a Jew. Now we see why gradual conversions are emphasized. Gentile conversions to Judaism were decisions to leave one kind of cultural milieu and enter another, moving from one socialization to another. They therefore demanded long training. So whether or not an emotional crisis was passed, the rabbis emphasized the process of education. Nor can we ignore that the rabbis here must mean study in whatever rabbinic schools of study then existed. The famous stories of Rabbi Akiba, who decided to become a rabbi late in his life, do not emphasize the suddenness of his decision so much as the stringent training he undertook so late in life. In later tradition, the cultic requirements of conversion were three, as the statement attributed to R. Judah the Prince (fl. 200 C.E.) makes clear:

> Rabbi says: Just as Israel did not enter the covenant except through three things—through circumcision, through immersion, and through the acceptance of a sacrifice—so it is the same with proselytes.   Sifre Num 108

---

38. For a fuller discussion of Jewish rules of conversion, see L. Schiffmann, "At the Crossroads: Tannaitic Perspectives on the Jewish-Christian Schism," *Jewish and Christian Self-Definition*, vol. 2, *Aspects of Judaism in the Hellenistic World*, ed. E. P. Sanders, with A. I. Baumgarten, and A. Mendelson (Philadelphia, 1981), pp. 122–56. Schiffman has expanded these thoughts into a book: *Who Was a Jew: Rabbinic and Halakhic Perspectives on the Jewish-Christian Schism* (Hoboken, N.J., 1985). See also S. J. D. Cohen, "Conversion to Judaism in Historical Perspective: From Biblical Israel to Postbiblical Judaism," *Conservative Judaism* 36 (Summer 1983).

The import of the story is clear: The rabbinic model of the acceptance of proselytes is the Sinai theophany. To the three ritual obligations one must add the fourth most important obligation: to know and practice the Torah of Israel, as interpreted and taught by the rabbis. It must be admitted that conversion per se was not much of an issue in preexilic times, hence neither the ritual nor the educational requirements of hellenistic conversion are clearly based in biblical law; rather they are derived from it in ways that are not self-evident. When the rabbis said Torah, they meant the written and the oral law, but other kinds of Jews may have practiced a less exacting Judaism. For purposes of this metaphor, all Israel is assumed to have been circumcised, to have been baptized, and to have made sacrifices before Sinai. By the end of the second century, the ideal of the rabbis was to insure that proselytes kept every single aspect of Torah (e. g. t. Dem 2:5) but there is no telling how close actual practice came to this ideal, nor when the rabbinic ruling became normative for the entire world community of Jews. Yet this statement does not contradict the practice of Hillel in first-century B.C.E. Judea. That Pharisaic Jews sought to make converts is evidenced outside of Jewish literature. Mt 23:15 reports that the Pharisees were zealous to make converts.

8. THE CONVERSION OF IZATES

The most famous of Josephus' conversion accounts, the conversion of the royal house of Adiabene (in *Ant* 20.2.3–4, 34–48), illustrates how important was the Pharisaic opinion in matters of conversion. But it also gives us a sense of how the differing views of conversion conflicted with each other in real cases. A Jewish merchant named Ananias (Hebrew: Hananiah) visited the royal house of Adiabene and taught the king's wives to worship the Jewish God. His efforts to convert began with the women and were carried out on a person-to-person basis. Through the harem, he won over the crown prince, Izates, but Izates' mother, Queen Helena, had already been won over by another Jew.

The issue of circumcision becomes problematic in this conversion account, since Izates is a male who needs circumcision to convert and, in fact, he wishes to be circumcised. But his mother disagrees, feeling that his subjects will reject him as king if he practices Judaism openly. Ananias takes the part of Queen Helena, not recommending circumcision under the circumstances. His words are very important. Josephus portrays him as recommending that Izates remain a God-fearer, since "he could worship the divine (τὸ θεῖον σέβειν) even without circumcision, if he had fully decided to be devoted to the ancestral customs of the Jews, for this was more important than circumcision." These words are Josephus' not Ananias', but they do show us how the problem of conversion was conventionally described, outside of the legal requirements discussed by the rabbis. It is a clear example that many Jews preferred to bypass formal conversion when a ticklish social situation was involved, relying on universal sentiments that all moral people are loved by God. Whether Josephus agreed with the practice or not, he implies that in common practice becoming a God-fearer was the functional equivalent of becoming Jewish. More importantly, it saved the sensitive hellenistic Jewish community from the ire of the relatives (or in this case, the irate subjects) of the convert.

Such a tolerant position can hardly have arisen from one of the Jewish sects. Rather it is another example of the kind of universalism characteristic of more acculturated Judaism. But this is not the end of the story. Later, Eleazar, a more pious Jew from Galilee, arrives and requires Izates to undergo circumcision, although the rite is performed by his physician, not by a *mohel*, the ritual circumciser, if such there were as yet. The story ends happily, in that Izates is circumcised, becoming a true convert. The populace also accepts Izates as king, whereupon he and Helena become famous as benefactors of Jerusalem, donating generously toward the improvement of the city, and again showing the importance of benefaction in establishing a new identity.

Possibly this story only evidences Josephus' own personal opinion about the correct way to enter Judaism, because Josephus claims to be Pharisaic and the rabbis demand circumcision for conversion. But Josephus may not have been much of a Pharisee, and his opinion about circumcision is far less strict than has been construed by the majority of scholars addressing the story of Izates' conversion:

> About this time there came to me from the region of Trachonitis two nobles, subjects of the king, bringing their horses, arms, and money which they had smuggled out of their country. The Jews would have compelled them to be circumcised as a condition of residence among them. I, however, would not allow any compulsion to be put upon them, declaring that everyone should worship God in accordance with the dictates of his own conscience (κατὰ τὴν 'εαυτοῦ προαίρεσιν τὸν θεὸν εὐσεβεῖν) and not under constraint, and that these men, having fled to us for refuge, ought not to be made to regret that they had done so. Having brought over the people to my way of thinking, I liberally supplied our guests with all things necessary to their customary manner of life.   (*Life* 113)

Granting that Josephus is only trying to prevent a forcible conversion, not trying to make a convert himself, and granting that he is certainly trying to ingratiate himself with his Roman audience, he still uses the vocabulary of God-fearing to describe the religious practice of the refugees.[39] After the war against Rome with its attendant conflicts and penalties, Josephus' testimony

---

39. Forced conversions, which were part of Maccabean policy, appear to have survived into Roman times, though they must have been an aberration.

implies that God-fearing must have increased as a strategy for gaining acceptance for Judaism.

These incidents in Josephus demonstrate that there were significant differences in entrance requirements throughout the Jewish community. They suggest not only that there were differences in definition of conversion throughout the Jewish community but that for acculturated Jews being a God-fearer was virtually the equivalent of being a Jew, especially since non-Jewish peoples could react with hostility to attempts at formal conversion. It also shows that while some Jews were content with making God-fearers, sensitive to the hostility that was generated by attempts at formal conversion, others risked themselves and possibly the welfare of the Jewish community to promote conversion. Although Eleazar comes from Galilee, he has some characteristics of the Pharisees since, like them and the rabbis after them, he was characteristically strict in the performance of ritual, whenever any possible doubt could be satisfied by punctiliousness (and probably characteristically lenient in the performance of punishment, where any doubt was satisfied by mercy, as Josephus says of the Pharisees in *Antiquities*). Furthermore, though nothing in the story specifically establishes the first-century historicity of the rabbinic traditions noted, the story does support the idea that something like the rabbinic practice was already in effect in first-century Pharisaism. Otherwise, the phenomenon of God-fearing or semiproselytism, which appears attractive to so many Jews and Gentiles for reasons we have already discussed, would have ended the matter. The really committed convert, as was Izates, wanted to undergo the stronger religious decision.

Rabbinic tradition illustrates how careful and sensitive the rabbis were to the issue of the intent and motivation of a convert. The following story does not have to be a first-century tradition to illustrate the issue we have clarified with Izates' conversion. On the other hand, it is consonant with the story which Josephus tells of Izates. Strong conversion experiences help to make more committed converts:

> Our rabbis taught: A proselyte who comes to convert at this time, we say to him: Why did you decide to convert? Do you not know that Israel at this time is afflicted, oppressed, downtrodden, and rejected, and that tribulations are visited upon them? If he says, "I am aware, but I am unworthy," we accept him immediately, and we make known to him a few of the lighter commandments and a few of the weightier commandments, and we make known to him the penalty for transgression of gleaning the forgotten sheaves, the corner, and the poor man's tithe (i.e., rules of charity, protecting the poor). And we make known to him the punishment for violating the commandments. . . . And just as we make known to him the punishment for violating the commandments, so we also make known to him their reward. . . . We are not too lengthy with him nor are we too detailed. If he accepts this, we circumcise him immediately. . . . Once he has recovered, we immerse him immediately. And two scholars stand over him and make known to him some of the lighter and some

of the weightier commandments. If he immersed validly, he is like an Israelite in all matters. In the case of a woman, position her in the water up to her neck, and two scholars stand outside and make known to her some of the lighter and some of the weightier commandments . . .   b. Yeb. 47a–b

This incident represents the practice of the rabbinic community, while the document and the reference to the fallen condition of Israel suggests a date later than the first war against Rome, which ended in the destruction of the Temple in 70 C.E. But it does underline the same motivations that seemed obvious in Josephus' story of Izates' conversion.

The rabbis were clearly not discouraging conversions; they were trying to make committed converts. Yet, if one looks at conversion within the broad context of the whole Jewish community, into which the convert fit when he or she finished training, is one justified in calling first- to fourth-century Judaism a high-conversion community? The answer is certainly less positive than in dealing with the Qumran community, a sect within first-century Judaism which was solely filled by conversion. Many Jews were born into Judaism, thus never consciously decided for it, but found it burdensome and avoided Jewish life. There were thus some very hellenized Jews who might almost be called adherents in Nock's terms. Finally, there were groups like God-fearers, who were fellow-travelers and attended synagogue but had not taken decisive steps to become Jews. In this case we would have to be satisfied with taking some measure of the average, saying that pockets of conversion experiences were correlated with high group coherence in various Jewish communities. They were not the only source of commitment. Nock's generalization might still be maintained but only in a carefully nuanced way. Within sectarian and apocalyptic Judaism, conversion was an important aspect of Jewish cohesion. In other parts of the community, the special laws functioned to keep community commitment high.

As we have seen, many varieties of both Judaism and Christianity proselytized, each using a method that was uniquely suited to itself—ranging from monastic social organization like the Dead Sea Scroll community to the Pharisees with their *haburah* fellowship communities to loose affiliations based on social class and sacral function in the wider hellenistic world. Within Christianity as well, different varieties of community sprang up, so we must characterize further the kinds of commitment that were built up by various communities within Judaism and Christianity. No single generalization will hold. The earliest Christian community contained both the most exclusive and the most open attitudes which were characteristic of Judaism of the day. Indeed, the Christian record is the best evidence that these attitudes existed in Judaism and should not be treated as unique examples of a Christian revolution in Jewish sensibilities.

The ancient world too knew both of highly emotional conversion experiences like the infusion of the spirit in the early Christian community, as well

as the ritual catechism of the Qumran community. Although the rabbis are
trying to make highly motivated and sincere converts, ecstatic experience is
never discussed. Circumcision, on the other hand, is quite fully discussed
and universally demanded. Unlike Christianity where emotional content
may be conventionally expected in some contemporary evangelism, the rabbinic community was uninterested in ecstasy. It had no legal ramifications
for conversion. The two communities differ in their conventional expectations about ecstasy. The frequently cited controversy between Rabbi Eliezer
and Rabbi Joshua (y. Yeb. 16a) does not imply that some rabbis accepted converts without circumcision; rather it underlines halakhic questions of some
importance for the convert—namely: When does a conversion take place?
and is a convert liable for all the responsibilities of a Jew?

Various pieces of Jewish literature which describe conversion lead us to
believe that ecstatic experience was not always absent in conversions to Judaism, though certainly revelations and ecstasy had other uses in the community, as our study of apocalypticism has already shown. In the story of
Joseph and Asenath,[40] the theme of conversion is blended with paranormal
and ecstatic experience. Asenath is valorized as a sincere Gentile convert to
Judaism. Her conversion and marriage to Joseph is viewed as a movement
toward new purity—even a holy marriage, (a ἱερὸς γάμος). The structures
of oppositions which frequently appeal to converts (because they eliminate
cognitive dissonance) are strongly present. The bread of life, immortality,
and incorruptability adhere to the true convert, the opposite to her detrac-
tors. This dualism is enforced by the visionary appearance of Michael the
chief captain of the Lord God and commander of all the host of the most High
(Joseph and Asenath 14:7). He is not only the morning star and a messenger
of light but amazingly is the twin of Joseph except that his features glow and
sparkle, conventional descriptions of heavenly beings. He appears to announce Asenath's glorification and underscore that she has, by virtue of entering the community, entered eternal life. After this, he returns to heaven
in his fiery chariot. Does this express the Jewish community's praise for a
man who sincerely takes a Gentile wife and converts her to a pious Jewess?
It seems to. Yet it might also express a Jewish Christian community's praise
for a conversion from paganism.

The visit from the heavenly being verifies the reward of the true convert
just as Enoch's heavenly ascent justifies continued belief in reward and punishment. There is a clear relationship between stories of heavenly journeys
and the concept of immortality in the ancient world. In many cultures of late
antiquity the journey itself confers a guarantee of astral immortality. Here
the messenger from heaven merely confirms that the ethical and spiritual

40. *Joseph et Asenath: Introduction, texte critique, traduction et notes*, ed. M. Philonenko
(Leiden, 1968). See the new English translation by C. Burchard, in *OTP*, vol. 2.

position of Asenath will be confirmed by astral immortality. Ecstasy, the motif of heavenly journey, the theme of conversion, and the resultant dualism will be important categories in analyzing Paul's experience.

Commitment in the ancient world was therefore formed in the same way it is formed in the modern world. There was an instrumental aspect, where a person develops willingness to carry out requirements of the group. These instrumentalities may start out as symbolic or ritual actions in which commitment is cemented and developed but end in moral or evaluative dimensions where a person continues to uphold the beliefs of the group outside of the ritual context. Behind this is, in Kanter's words, a cost/benefit ratio in which the individual invests psychological energy into the group. This seems to be the strategy of rabbinic conversion where the ritual qualifications yield both a highly cohesive group and a strong commitment to continue acceptable moral behavior. The special laws and the other rituals, rather than high conversion ratios, would have had the function of enforcing the belief.

The standard practice of the rabbis in trying to dissuade proselytes once they had signaled their desires had nothing to do with being opposed to proselytes in general. Rather rabbinic dissuasion was for the purposes of selecting highly motivated converts while discouraging others who might become immoral or lax and hence give to Judaism a bad name. Furthermore, we know from the New Testament among other places that the Pharisees were particularly zealous in trying to make converts (see Mt 23:15), in spite of the danger of inadvertantly admitting a Roman informer. All of rabbinic discussion about policy was accompanied by the most rigid instruction, change of lifestyle, circumcision for men, immersion and sacrifice for all, followed by a strict regime of purity and dietary prohibitions forever. The dangers of undergoing circumcision as an adult, given the state of medical knowledge, is reason enough to believe that conversion to Judaism was itself a high dissonance-producing situation (y. Yeb. 16a). But we also know that converts often faced social rejection from their previous friends and relations, an attitude which necessarily was fostered by the decision for a new faith.

9. PROSELYTISM AFTER THE WAR AGAINST ROME

After the war against Rome 68 to 70 C.E., Jews and Judaism went through a period of disfavor. The Emperor Domitian instituted a system of informers to ferret out anyone who converted to Judaism.[41] His successor Nerva seems to have abolished the system of denunciation. Later, Hadrian outlawed circumcision as a kind of castration, and possibly Jewish proselytism totally. Whether he did so before or after the second Jewish revolt against Rome is

---

41. A. M. Rabello, "The Legal Condition of the Jews in the Roman Empire," *ANRW* II, 13, pp. 665–762.

of great significance in weighing the causes for that unfortunate conflict. But the date of the edict has less significance to the history of proselytism, for its effect was uniformly to oppress the practice of Judaism, consequently stopping proselytism as well. Afterwards, under Antoninus Pius and thereafter, the penalties for circumcision were rescinded for Jews and presumably for Jews alone. Thus, while Jews could circumcise Jewish children again, circumcising Gentile proselytes still remained dangerous. No one knows precisely whether this was the force of Antoninus Pius' rules or whether they were enforced thereafter. But it is clear that becoming a God-fearer and indeed becoming a Christian rather than a convert to Judaism must have gained in attraction after the two revolts against Rome. We should not dismiss the effect of these second- and third-century facts as relevant to Christian missionary movements. Jewish proselytism and indeed Jewish Christianity remained a force in the Roman world long after the canonization of the New Testament. It was from this group of semiproselytes that many of Christianity's converts came, for they were an anomalous group, alienated from their Gentile past yet not fully Jews or fully accepted as such by the rabbinic definition. To take the final step into Judaism was a dangerous operation surgically and often politically most inexpedient. Such people were clearly attracted to the message of Paul during the first century. Thereafter they must have been yet more easily evangelized.

10. MESSIANISM AND CONVERSION

The best evidence about the close relationship between conversion and messianism is from Christianity. Here we must study both the Jesus movement in its Palestinian setting and the evidence of Paul in the Diaspora. A full study will have to await a later time.[42] Again we find that the Christian evidence not only supplements what we know from our fragmentary reports in Jewish literature but helps considerably in filling in gaps in our knowledge of first century Jewish life. Christianity is unique, but it also fits well within the spectrum of Jewish practice in the first century. It helps us better understand what that spectrum was.

In the Gospels we have specific evidence about two different related movements—the followers of John the Baptist and the followers of Jesus of Nazareth. Whether they were overtly political movements or not, the Romans interpreted them as a political threat, as evidenced by the martyrdom of the leaders of each movement. Both have been credibly described as apocalyptic, millenarian movements, though they surely contained other elements as well.

How they converted and initiated members is not very clear. In the case

---

42. See my book, *Paul, the Convert* (New Haven, 1990).

of John the Baptist, baptism was presumably a sign of greater commitment to John's time scheme for the coming of the end of time. The New Testament is an outside observer of John's movement, maintaining that John's mission was fulfilled in the teachings of Jesus. Thus we learn little of the internal structure of the group that followed John closely.

In the case of Jesus we learn a bit more. There is no question that the early church demanded an enormous commitment from the new member. Those who joined were warned that they may have to reorder and even give up previous family ties (Mk 3:31–35, Mk 10:28–31; also Lk 9:54–60). The early followers of Jesus must be considered converts into a new, dynamic movement within Judaism. But that counts as a conversion, according to modern use of the vocabulary. It is not clear whether the typical conversion was quick or slow, emotional or reasoned. The New Testament normally portrays the attraction of followers as quick, due to the power of Jesus' teachings and charisma. But without communal support and considerable teaching no conversion of that kind is effective. Whatever the system, the level of commitment of successful converts would necessarily have been high. The Jesus movement falls clearly into the Palestinian sectarian scene, where movements of politico-religious nature were common. That Christianity chose a passive political role did not mean that it would not be viewed by the establishment as an active political movement.[43]

11. THE KEY: CONVERSION IN PAUL

The language of conversion is explicitly present in Paul. Furthermore, and this is more important, we shall see that in the hands of Paul some phrases implying transformation reveal a conversion process as an internal, psychological event, hinting at the social factors behind conversion.

I take this to be a shocking and unexpected result, because the scholarship on Paul is dominated by the perception that Paul did not view himself to be a convert; rather he saw himself in the model of a prophet. One of the best summaries of this position, though certainly not the only one, is from Krister Stendahl.[44] Stendahl rightly attacks the portraits of Paul as a convert or as a man burdened with a guilty conscience when he practiced Judaism. He calls into question the whole idea of ascribing to Paul some modern understanding of existentialism. Yet, even with Paul's use of prophetic language to describe his mission, and his infrequent use of the traditional lan-

---

43. See *Rebecca's Children*, pp. 68–95.
44. "Paul and the Introspective Conscience of the West," originally a paper delivered before the annual meeting of the American Psychological Association and then published in *HTR* 56 (1963), 199–215. It has been reprinted in many places, most notably in Stendahl's own book, *Paul Among Jews and Gentiles and Other Essays* (Philadelphia, 1976).

guage of conversion in so many words, an extremely important and unappreciated language of conversion can be isolated in Paul's writings, provided one is open to looking at Paul's writings anew from the point of view of modern sociology.

Paul uses terms for conversion when he discusses the conversion of Gentiles:

> For they themselves report concerning us what a welcome we have among you, and how you turned (ἐπιστρέφεν) to God from idols, to serve a living and true God, and to wait for his Son from heaven, whom he raised from the dead, Jesus who delivers us from the wrath to come (1Thes 1:9–10).

Paul uses the term *"epistrephen"* to describe the pagan conversion from idolatry to service of the living God, which he identifies with faith in Christ.

> Formerly, when you did not know God, you were in bondage to beings that by nature are not Gods, but now that you have come to know God, or rather to be known by God, how can you turn back (ἐπιστρέφειν) again to the weak and beggarly elemental spirits whose slaves you want to be once more (Gal 4:8–9).

Here he uses the same term to discuss a counterconversion. It is clear, then, that this term for conversion is used by Paul to describe the boundary crossed from Gentile to Jewish religion.

Paul is even able to use this distinction to propound that Gentile conversion to faith in Christ is better than Jewish piety: "Yes, to this day, whenever Moses is read a veil lies over their minds, but when a man turns (ἐπιστρέφειν) to the Lord, the veil is removed" (2Cor 3:15–16). His language helps him make a polemical case against his Jewish-Christian opponents. The basic meaning of the word must involve repentance.[45]

That is not Paul's only term for religious conversion. He uses the term "metanoia" (μετανοία), again explicitly a term meaning "repentance" to discuss conversions to Christianity, although again a Gentile context of these words seems much clearer than any Jewish audience: 2Cor 7:9–10, 2Cor 12:21, Rom 2:4. In each of these places the connotation of repentance is strongly emphasized in Paul's polemic, as indeed μετανοία and ᾽επιστρέφειν appear to translate the Hebrew term תשובה.

However, there is a serious problem with these passages. They are not characteristic of Paul's discussion for entrance into Christianity, and they are never used to discuss his own entrance into the faith. Many scholars have rightly noted that these terms do not figure prominently in Pauline discussions.

Paul's reticence to apply these terms to himself, indeed his sparing use of

---

45. See D. Georgi, *Die Gegner des Paulus im 2. Korintherbrief* (Neukirchen-Vluyn, 1964), p. 49, and H. Koester, "The Purpose of the Polemic of a Pauline Fragment," *NTS* 8 (1962) 317–32.

the terms entirely, can be explained by adopting a single hypothesis: Paul's theory of conversion for Jew and Gentile comes from his own experience of transformation. The importance of this hypothesis is first observable in the way it supports Stendahl's hypothesis. Paul does not stress the traditional terms for conversion for exactly the reason that Stendahl says—because he does not view himself as a sinner, as Philippians 3 and Galatians 1 tell us so clearly. Paul claims to be blameless under the law, and there is no reason to doubt this statement as accurate to his personal feelings.[46] Indeed, he was a member of the one sect of first-century Judaism that was universally known for its piety, the Pharisees.

12. PAUL'S LANGUAGE OF TRANSFORMATION

Paul's language for discussing conversion is quite extended. In the first instance, Paul's consistent use of contrasts of darkness and light, flesh and spirit are suggestive of conversion, even today. But Paul uses another explicit language of transformation, which is a documentable part of Hellenistic spirituality.[47] That language is literally the language of transformation, which Paul expresses with the terms "μόρφωσις," "μεταμόρφωσις," and "συμμόρφωσις." Paul uses the term "transformation" not only to discuss the final judgment at the Parousia but also an experience that happens to Christian believers, in the act of believing, in their pre-Parousia existence. According to 2Cor 3:18 they are being changed (μεταμορφούμεθα) into Christ's likeness from one degree of glory to another. This concept has much in common with the hellenistic and magic concepts of deification (ἀπαναθανατισμός, as in the Paris Magical Papyrus). But the action does not work magically or by virtue only of having had a certain mystical experience.

These terms, clearly stated in Rom 12:2, for instance, imply not just renewal, as Koenig and Gaventa so cogently argue,[48] but something much more: "Do not be conformed to this world, but be transformed (μεταμορφοῦσθε) by the renewal of your mind." The interesting implication here is that Paul is suggesting that *everyone*, not just Gentiles, needs a psychic

---

46. Of course, the psychoanalytic question remains, because one can feel guilty without having committed a crime. The point is that we have no grounds for making a psychoanalytic analysis of Paul. Paul's writing does not yield us much evidence on these matters, as a comparison with St. Augustine makes clear. But see the fine book by G. Theissen, *Psychological Aspects of Pauline Theology*, trans. by J. P. Gavin of *Psychologische Aspekte paulinischer Theologie*, FRLANT 131 (Göttingen, 1983; Philadelphia, 1987), which combines psychiatric observations with cognitive and experimental psychology.

47. See my "Paul and Ecstasy," *1986 SBL Seminar Papers* (Atlanta, 1986), pp. 555–80 and chapter 1 of my book *Paul the Convert*.

48. See J. Koenig, *The Motif of Transformation in the Pauline Epistles: A History-of-Religions/Exegetical Study* (New York, Th. D. dissertation, 1970), pp. 65ff. Also B. Gaventa, *From Darkness to Light* (Philadelphia, 1986), pp. 17–52.

transformation to be part of the new community of believers. In context, conformity to the world means taking pride in circumcision and the other outward signs of piety. These are the claims of Paul's opponents, and they were also the pride of Paul himself when he was a Pharisee. Paul's new intuition is that the believers in Christ should not be so concerned to "fit in" with what others are doing. They do not define conversion as a matter of legal requirements. If so, they would merely be joining Judaism. Instead they belong to a heavenly group which is not afraid to "fit out" or nonconform. Such exhortations are extremely important to conversion groups today. The opposite of this worldly conformation is what Paul calls "transformation," and this transformation corresponds in important ways to the process which we today know as conversion, though it is not identical. But it is clear that he offers this definition in contrast to the more ordinary definition of conversion in Judaism.

In Rom 12:2, Christians are exhorted to be "transformed" (μεταμορφοῦ-σθε) by renewing their minds, as opposed to being conformed to ordinary Judaism where they must take pride in the things of the flesh. In 2Cor 3:18 Paul states that the *metamorphosis* involves being refashioned according to the εἴκων "image" of Christ, though the completion of this event he reserves for the Parousia (1Cor 15:49; Rom 8:18–29).

The differences between Pauline transformation and conversion have to do with the eschatological and mystical value of the process. The transformation is first of all a psychic event, but secondly it is an event that presages the coming eschaton. The transformation is a change to the likeness or image of Christ (2Cor 3:18), which is a mystical idea significantly related to Jewish apocalypticism and mysticism. There will be a further transformation of believers when Christ returns from heaven on the last day (1Cor 15:42–54; Phil 3:20f.; and Rom 8:23). But the process is already begun in the lives of believers and only the lives of *believers*, those who have faith. Anyone with any other style of identification with Christianity is not part of this process of transformation. For these reasons, I would suggest that Paul's language of transformation, not his language of repentance, should be seen as his basic language of conversion, together with his use of the terms "in Christ" and his use of the contrast between flesh and spirit, of course. While "repentance" is a term which largely characterizes Gentile entrance into Christianity, "transformation" is a term that should apply to all. Thus it can be said that conversion figures prominently in Paul's thought, even though he does not use the term "ἐπιστρέφειν" in important ways.

This has interesting implications within the world of Jewish and Jewish Christian life. First of all, Paul is suggesting that Jews as well as Gentiles need to undergo a significant transformation before they can enter the new community. This would contrast with the position attributed to James, in which the teaching of Jesus and his messianic mission can be added onto traditional Judaism with little extra effort. It means for Paul as it cannot mean for James that to be merely a Jew who has accepted Christ is not enough to be a Christian. For Paul even the Jew must be transformed by faith. Paul's new community is a new community of converts in every significant way.

On the other hand, Gentiles need not adopt the particular rules of Judaism in order to be in Christ. This has the social effect of recommending that God-fearing Gentiles may become one community with Torah-observant Christians. This is not an easy idea for either Gentiles or Jewish-Christians to adopt, as we know. But it is clear that it must be an attractive opportunity for God-fearers and other interested Gentile bystanders, who were seen as the equivalent of Jews by the most liberal sections of the community in all things but ritual purity. What Paul offers is not so much a chance for Gentiles to be saved, because they could already be "saved" as God-fearers by moral actions according to Judaism. He offers a chance for Gentiles to be a single, messianic community with Jews. This may seem a minor point compared to the promise of salvation, but to the first-century world it was an astounding claim, and one that took several generations even within Christianity to work out.

If the attraction of Gentiles to Pauline messianism is clear, so also must be the commitment which Paul envisions for his new messianic family. All must operate as a single community. This is brought about through justification, confirmed in the rituals of baptism and eucharist, and enforced in the moral behavior which all members of the community must exhibit.

Indeed, it is quite significant that Paul does resort to the terms for transformation to this single community. Philo, for instance, is also exceptionally interested in the process by which persons attain the qualities of divinity. In contrast to Paul, however, Philo almost always uses terms for gradual progress and maturation, terms which are occasionally used by Paul as well.[49] Philo has almost nothing to say about cosmic changes which are to happen in the future, although he speaks in a veiled way about a messiah and in *Praem* 168f. describes an ideal future.

Instead of metamorphosis, which may even be associated with decadence, as the reference to Caligula shows, Philo stresses the terms "progression" (προκόπτειν) and "perfection" (τέλειος). Both of these terms are part of conventional stoicism.[50] Of course, Philo's aims are not the explicit aims of Pharisaic Judaism. For Philo, the highest human existence is neither as God nor man but ". . . on the borderline between the uncreated and the perishing form of being" (*Somn* 2.234). The person making progress has not yet

---

49. Philo uses the term "metamorphosis" in three places: *Gaium* 95 describes how the emperor sought to change himself into Apollo, *Vita Mos* 1.57 describes Moses' inspiration as a prophet as a transformation, and in *Spec Leg* 4.147 virtue is transformed by the slightest alteration.

50. G. Staehlin, "Fortschritt und Wachstum," *Festgabe, Joseph Lortz*, vol. 2, *Glaube und Geschichte*, ed. E. Iserloh and P. Manns (Baden-Baden, 1957), p. 18.

come so far, but that is the goal. But, as an intellectual, Philo is not interested in quick-change transformations of the Gentile myths. Instead, the
transformation to divinity which he discusses is one of long education within
the meaning of the biblical text. And that, of course, is the same model of
conversion which the rabbis used. Though the rabbinic understanding of
education differed sharply from Philo's, both agreed that scripture was the
central curriculum.

Philo sees many degrees of progress from paganism to Judaism. There is
no need for radical transformation, because slow education brings about the
desired effect. It may even be that Philo feels the most educated, moral
persons of any group, Jew or Gentile, to be equal. The truly educated philos-
opher, who refrains from the unethical practices of paganism, would attain
perfection and see God as readily as an Israelite. Attaining that goal must
surely be rare. But, in any case, Philo is both an intellectual and the articulate spokesperson for gradual conversion and tolerance.

For Philo, the most significant transformations occur *after* conversion.
Men like Moses who are born with the highest capabilities and perfect them
through their lives are transformed into prophets and actually see the God of
Israel. This event is what transforms them into something between a man
and a god. And it happens after they are in Israel. Paul has a rather similar
notion, appearing (as Philo appears) to consider himself among those who
have seen God. His duty is to explain that vision to the faithful in Christ.

Paul has clearly retained the more sectarian and millenarian notion of conversion. And there are aspects of momentary and radical conversion in Paul's
formulation, though he repeatedly attacks the excesses of emotionalism
throughout Christianity (2Cor 11f.). Furthermore, after outlining the radical
sense of conversion, presumably in baptism or other Christian initiations,
Paul also talks about a period of training and growth, as we noted in 2Cor
3:18 when he speaks of being changed from one degree of glory to another,
through the action of the Spirit. Furthermore, Paul never forgets that the
new Christian must live in an unredeemed world (1Cor 5:10, for instance).
So no simple contrast between quick conversion and long training separates
Paul and Philo. Both see long periods of struggle and a similar goal. But they
have different views of the community borders. Philo sees conversion to Israel as a preliminary step to enlightenment, largely because God has given
Israel the Bible as a guide. Philo at least theoretically allows that philosophy
can bring about the same goals, because the process of intellection is the
same in both communities. The number of those Gentiles who actually see
God without becoming part of Israel must necessarily be limited to the
greatest philosophers. On the other hand, Paul sees a mixed group of believers of Israel and Gentiles; no one outside the community can be redeemed,
but taking up the ceremonial laws which would make one a convert to Judaism is unnecessary for those in Christ.

It does seem clear, however, that the impetus toward quick conversion is stronger in Christianity than it is in other sectarian forms of Judaism, where long training is generally stressed. But it is only quick in the sense that it can be accomplished by a reorientation of the mind. This puts even Pauline conversion in a more sectarian context, where sources of commitment come from strong religious decisions. The community must act as a holy temple, and those who seek to be part of it must learn what holy actions are.

Paul shares some of the attitudes of the Jewish Diaspora. He makes clear that Gentile God-fearers will share the future benefits of salvation if they become believers. Jew and Gentile are equal for him if their faith is equal. He differs in not accepting the purity distinctions between Jews and Gentiles as unbridgeable until conversion, which is characteristic of the Pharisaic world, within the new Christian community, because the rules of Jewish purity need no longer separate Christian from Christian. So he also appreciates the more acculturated notion that both Jews and Gentiles can know the truth, with or without the law (Romans 2)

13. PAUL'S ACCOUNT OF HIMSELF

We should not think of Paul as simply an apostate convert to Christianity; rather he remains a knowledgeable Jew representing, endorsing, and furthering the Gentile mission with all the Pharisaic acumen he had previously learned. In Rom 1:16 he speaks of salvation coming to the Jew first and then to the Gentile. But from his authentic letters we know only a few details of Paul's life. In Phil 3:4–8 he tells us that he was circumcised properly, that he was from the tribe of Benjamin, that he became a Pharisee, that he persecuted the church, and that he was blameless under the law. When Paul talks about his conversion to Christianity, it is in much more muted tones than Luke uses, but it is no less a conversion.

The central theme of Paul's autobiographical sections is the contrast between his previous life and his present one. As Paul says in Gal 1:23–24: "He who once persecuted us is now preaching the faith he once tried to destroy. And they glorified God because of me (Μόνον δὲ ἀκούοντες ἦσαν ὅτι ὁ διώκων ἡμᾶς ποτε νῦν εὐαγγελίζεται τὴν πίστιν ἥν ποτε ἐπόρθει, καὶ ἐδόξαζον ἐν ἐμοὶ τὸν θεόν)." Paul's life has come around suddenly upon him. His life is already proverbial in the community as a miraculous proof of the power of the spirit. Paul's experience is significant for the early church in that it is a mighty and unexpected conversion. Paul agrees with the characterization; indeed he uses himself as his best example of the power of the Spirit.

Whenever Paul relates his conversion he also reveals a central aspect of its meaning for him: His life as a Christian comes directly out of his conversion. Not only is his new self entirely dependent upon his conversion, his mission comes directly from his conversion as well: "But when he who had set me apart before I was born, and had called me through his grace, was pleased to reveal his Son to me, in order that I might preach him among the Gentiles" (Gal 1:16). His conversion causes his mission, coming directly out of God's revelation (*apokalypsis*, ἀποκαλύψις) of his son to him. The Greek is even more direct than the English, for the mission follows as a purpose clause (ἵνα) on the revelation: "for the exact purpose that I might preach him among the Gentiles—ἀποκαλύψαι τὸν 'υἱὸν αὐτοῦ ἐν ἐμοί, ἵνα εὐαγγελ-λίζωμαι αὐτὸν ἐν τοῖς ἔθνεσιν." In doing so, Paul collapses many years of learning within his newly found Gentile Christian community.

But we must also be aware of another overt agenda in the passage. Paul is displaying his credentials, because the other apostles do not recognize a person as apostle who did not know Jesus. His counterclaim is that his understanding of Christianity comes directly from a revelation of the resurrected Christ, not through the preaching of any human disciple—yet another reason for emphasizing the prophetic nature of the calling.[51] Like Jeremiah with his predestined mission from the womb of his mother (Jer 1:5), Paul claims to have received his mission before birth. Before his conversion, all is equally irrelevant for Paul. However, we shall see that his training in Pharisaism frequently affects his perception and analysis.

Though predestined for his task, Paul maintains that the radical change in his life is still a sign of the Spirit's activity. He makes this claim vivid by contrasting his former life as a persecutor of Christianity with his present one as an apostle. This contrast starts as a personal reflection on his conversion experience, which Paul sees both in terms of the commission of a prophet and a radical reversal of his previous life. Its personal meaning for Paul is not only his Christian commitment but his personal knowledge of Christ. Paul believes that he himself has met the Christ, though he never met the man Jesus. Although Paul may cast his mission to the Gentiles in terms of a prophetic commission, his explicit use of prophetic forms of speech is very restricted. He never explicitly calls himself a prophet either, preferring instead the term "apostle."[52] While there a some relationship between the term "apostle" and the term "prophet" in Christianity, the two terms are not identical. Rather, we shall see that Paul's great change of direction is better understood as a conversion.

Some of Paul's biography is evidently already known to his readers, for it has become a byword: "He who once persecuted us is preaching the faith he once tried to destroy" (Gal 1:23). But, as we shall see throughout our exploration of Paul's thought, this move is characteristic for Paul. Paul is not a systematic thinker. Rather he tries to understand a personal vision. He also feels that God's plan for world history is disclosed to him through his unex-

51. N. Habel, "The Form and Significance of the Call Narratives," *ZAW* 77 (1965), pp. 297–323.

52. See D. E. Aune, *Prophecy in Early Christianity and the Ancient Mediterranean World* (Grand Rapids, Mich., 1983), pp. 247–62.

pected personal experience, so he begins with his personal experience. His argument moves from personal experience to generalization, from his experience of personal salvation to a vision of world salvation. His personal experience is his key for understanding God's plan. This is equally true of modern converts, but the process has been insufficiently emphasized until recently. And if Paul uses his own experience to guide his understanding of world history, that is where we should start our analysis of him.

14. LUKE'S ACCOUNT

Both Luke and (less often) Paul describe Paul's conversion as a prophetic call, similar to the prophetic calls of the Old Testament.[53] Luke's accounts of Paul's conversion are deliberately patterned on Old Testament prophecy. Much can be made of the discrepancies between Luke's three accounts of Paul's conversion in Acts 9:1–19, 22:1–21, and 26:12–23. Like Paul himself in Gal 1:13 and possibly in 2 Cor 11:32, Luke's accounts of revelatory experience are incomplete narratives, for they do not describe the actual vision. All the passages in Acts say that Paul, then called Saul, was on the road to Damascus, that a bright light shone about him and that a voice called out: "Saul, Saul, why do you persecute me?" Saul inquires, "Who are you, Lord?" and is answered, "I am Jesus whom you persecute." Luke's Paul begins his career as a Christian by identifying Jesus as *Lord*. Although Paul uses "Lord" as a term of respect, it is also related to one Hebrew word for God and a significant *divine* title for Christ in Christianity. Paul is portrayed as applying the divine title before he knows the identity of the revealer, showing that accuracy to the historical events is not likely to be of first importance to Luke.

There the similarity between the three stories ends. In the first account, Paul's companions hear the voice but see nothing. In the second, they see the light but hear nothing. In the first two Paul falls to the ground while his companions stand. In the last they all fall to the ground. In the first account Jesus tells Paul to go to Damascus to await further orders.[54] But in the last account, the actual commission of apostleship to the Gentiles, Paul receives his commissioning directly from the revelation:

---

53. J. Munck, *Paul and the Salvation of Mankind* (Richmond, Va., 1959), pp. 24–35; M. Dibelius, *Studies in the Acts of the Apostles* (London, 1956), p. 158, n. 47, saw that the prophetic-call motif was also part of the literary purpose of Luke. See also E. Haenchen, *The Acts of the Apostles: A Commentary* (Philadelphia, 1971), pp. 107–10 and H. J. Cadbury, *The Making of Luke Acts* (London, 1968), pp. 213–38.

54. See K. Lake, "The Conversion of Paul and the Events Immediately Following It," *The Beginnings of Christianity*, Part I, *The Acts of the Apostles*, ed. F. J. Foakes Jackson and K. Lake (Grand Rapids, Mich., 1966), vol. 5, pp. 188–94; C. W. Hedrick, "Paul's Conversion/Call: A Comparative Analysis of the Three Reports in Acts," *JBL* 100 (1981) 415–32.

I am Jesus whom you are persecuting. But rise and stand upon your feet; for I have appeared to you for this purpose, to appoint you to serve and bear witness to the things in which you have seen me and to those in which I will appear to you, delivering you from the people and from the Gentiles—to whom I send you (τῶν ἐθνῶν, εἰς οὓς ᾽εγω ἀποστέλλω σε) to open their eyes, that they may turn from darkness to light and from the power of Satan to God, that they may receive forgiveness of sins and a place among those who are sanctified by faith in me (Acts 26:15–18).

Although these differences in detail show that the details of Paul's conversion were not well known, nor a carefully guarded literary tradition, most of the discrepancies are unimportant for us. But Paul's vocation, the command to proselytize the Gentiles, is a fundamental theme of Luke's narrative. We are left with the perplexing problem: Was it part of the vision itself (Acts 26:15–18) or did it come later, after Paul had learned more of the Christian message (Acts 9:1–19, 22:1–21)? Luke's reasons for placing the call to Gentile mission in his last description of the conversion may be partly literary. With deliberate intention and consummate artistry, Luke develops his theme slowly. Only in Luke's third version of Paul's commissioning do we find out that Jesus has entrusted Paul with a mission to the Gentiles. Probably this reticence to display the purpose of Paul's conversion in his earliest narration reflects Luke's idea that the Gentiles were evangelized only after the stubbornness of the Jews became manifest (see, e.g., 2 Corinthians 11). Paul himself often discusses his unhappy experiences while preaching within the Jewish community. He says in 1Cor 9:20f., for instance, that he lives as a Jew when he is in Jewish communities, in the hope of winning some of the Jews for Christ. In other words, while Luke sees Paul's destiny to be the apostle to the Gentiles, an evaluation which Paul himself shares, neither Luke nor Paul gives us an unambiguous report that Paul realized his destiny immediately. There are grounds for thinking that Paul's self-description as apostle to the Gentiles was the result of his experience of success among Gentiles and his rejection among Jews. Nevertheless, both accounts naturally portray the outcome as present in the original revelation, because in retrospect it must have seemed so. This is a reasonable enough assumption, but it also implies to a critical reader that modern observations about religious groups can be helpful in understanding the first century.

15. PAUL'S VISION OF THE *KAVOD* ACCORDING TO LUKE

While everyone acknowledges that Luke described Paul as a radical convert, Luke may have intended something more as well. When scholars emphasize Paul's description of himself as a prophet in contrast with Luke's description of Paul's radical conversion, they ironically are being unduly influenced by Luke's description, for Luke equally intended Paul's conversion to be understood as a prophetic call. Luke describes Paul's conversion as parallel to the commissioning of Jeremiah (Jer 1:5–11) and Isaiah (Isa 6:1–9). The encounter with God, divine commission with a "sending" formula, demur and resistance by the prophet, divine assurance, even preparation for the task by signs and wonders, are themes of prophetic calling from the Hebrew Bible. The contrast between conversion and prophecy is overdrawn. To the ancient world, they overlapped.

Yet Luke's portrayal of Paul's conversion is modeled on a specific prophet. The most provocative parallels with Luke's account are the commissioning of the prophet Ezekiel, whose call was special in several respects. First, Ezekiel was granted a vision of a human figure, shaped like a man, which is called "the likeness of the image of the Glory of God."[55] We shall see that for Luke, Paul has a revelation of the Glory of God. When Ezekiel beheld the Glory of God, he reported: "I fell upon my face, and I heard the voice of one that spoke" (1:28). Paul hears a voice speaking as well[56] and it is clearly a revelatory voice because Paul reacts in the same way as Ezekiel: He falls to the ground. When the Lord ordered Ezekiel to stand, Ezekiel narrated the words of Yahweh: "Stand upon your feet, and I will speak with you. . . . I send you to the people of Israel, to a nation of rebels, who have rebelled against me" (Ezek 2:1–3). Luke's Paul again reacts the same way, he rises, but with a significant modification: He rises and receives the charge to go to foreign lands to proselytize a nation of rebels, *Gentiles* rather than Jews as in Ezekiel. Moreover, to claim a prophetic appointment was not a commonplace in first-century Judaism. Many Jews in authority had already promulgated the idea that prophecy had ceased. To seek such a privilege was therefore to attract some powerful enemies in the Jewish community.

One of the unique aspects of Ezekiel's prophecy was that he envisioned what seemed to be a human figure, "the likeness of a man," on God's heavenly conveyance, pulled by the heavenly beasts (Ezek 1:26). This figure is called the *Kavod*, the Glory of God, by the prophet (Ezek 1:29).[57] By using this direct parallel, Luke is implying that the Glory of God was revealed to Paul. Such a claim is not merely a stylistic convention, for the idea has a deep prophetic, apocalyptic, and mystical meaning in Judaism. Furthermore, this

55. Indeed, it may be more exact to call the conversion a "discourse of heavenly appearance" or *Erscheinungsgespräch*, as does G. Lohfink, "Eine alttestamentliche Darstellungsform für Gotteserscheinungen in den Damaskusberichten: Apg. 9, 22, 26," *BZ* 9 (1965) 246–57 and *The Conversion of St. Paul* (Chicago, 1976), pp. 61–85. This perspective has been criticized by O. H. Steck, "Formgeschichtliche Bemerkungen zur Darstellung des Damaskusgeschehens in der Apostelgeschichte," *ZNW* 67 (1976) 20–28 and C. Burchard, *Der dreizehnte Zeuge: Traditions und kompositionsgeschichtliche Untersuchungen zu Lukas' Darstellung der Früzeit des Paulus* (Göttingen, 1970), pp. 54–55. See Hedrick, p. 416, n. 10.

56. See J. H. Charlesworth, "The Jewish Roots of Christology: The Discovery of the Hypostatic Voice," *SJT* 39 (1987) 19–41.

57. See G. Quispel, "Hermetism and the New Testament, Especially Paul," *ANRW* II.22, forthcoming.

identification is rare in exoteric Jewish literature, and it is characteristic of some kinds of Christianity, especially Justin Martyr's.

Christ is not explicitly given the title "the Glory of God" in the New Testament. But there are several New Testament passages in which *doxa* (glory) and, more relevantly, *the* Glory is attributed to Christ or the Son. In Jas 2:1, it is possible that we should translate "our Lord Jesus Christ, the Glory." In Eph 1:17 "the God of our Lord Jesus Christ, the Father of the Glory" appears. And Paul repeatedly uses the term "Glory" in a technical way to refer to Christ. In Phil 3:21 Paul speaks of Christ's "Body of Glory" (σῶμα τῆς δόχης) to which the believers' body is to be conformed.[58] Paul describes the "Glory of the Lord" (2Cor 3:16–4:6) in the very places where he describes his own conversion, which he also uses as a pattern for experience by which other believers come to be in Christ. Paul also talks of the faithful being changed or transformed into the "image of Christ" (Rom 8:29, 1Cor 15:49), which parallels some of Ezekiel's language and anticipates the technical terminology of Jewish mysticism. Central to Paul's idea is a theory of the transformation of believers at the consummation (1 Corinthians 15). Other passages bearing on this theme would include 1Cor 2:8, describing Christ as "the Lord of Glory," and the doubtfully Pauline Heb 1:3: "He reflects the Glory of God and bears the very stamp of his nature, upholding the universe by his word of power." Luke is not fabricating the relationship between Paul and Ezekiel, and he is not alone in seeing the identification between Christ and the Glory of the Lord.

In other words, the connection made by Luke between Paul and the call of Ezekiel is borne out by Paul's own writing. But the theological implications of this hypothetical identification are staggering. Does Paul's Christianity stem from the identification of Jesus with the Glory of God, the Hebrew *Kavod*, God's sometimes human appearance in the visions of the Hebrew Bible? Luke provides the first interpretation of Paul's conversion by figuring Paul's call in terms of Ezekiel's prophetic commissioning; viewing Paul's experience as a conversion, commissioning, or vocation, Luke interprets Paul's conversion as having been initiated by a revelation of the image of God's Glory. Although Luke never explicitly describes what, if anything, Paul saw, Luke's language both identifies Christ with the human figure of God and buffers that identification by means of the euphemistic words "likeness" and "image," exactly the words used by Ezekiel, apparently to protect the grandeur and dignity of the Jewish divinity. Ezekiel was not simply a prophet; these passages in Ezekiel are the foundation of Jewish apocalypticism and mysticism. This suggests that Paul and Luke's understanding of conversion to Christianity is influenced by Jewish apocalyptic mysticism.

---

58. G. Scholem has asked whether this phrase ought to be identified with the Merkabah term *guf hashekhina*, the body of Glory, which we find in Merkabah texts. See *Von der mystischen Gestalt der Gottheit* (Zürich, 1962), p. 276, n. 19. But Scholem did not exploit the implications of this perceptive intuition.

Although Luke may understand the sources for Paul's visions, he is interested in portraying Paul as a paradigmatic convert and missionary. Luke transforms Ezekiel's commission to the people of Israel into Paul's apostleship to all peoples, the earliest historical assessment of Paul's mission (see also Acts 9:15–16, 22:15). In this respect, succeeding generations of scholarship can find nothing to dispute in Luke. Paul's place in Christianity as *the* apostle to the Gentiles, par excellence, is assured. But the subtle ways in which Luke revalues Paul's own discussions are very significant for the study of conversion.

Even though Luke describes Paul explicitly as a new prophet, he also portrays Paul's experience as a radical conversion. It is a deeply disturbing and emotional experience, which turns Paul's life completely around, offered as a model for the experience of other believers. To call Paul's experience a conversion not only has the effect of authenticating an experience of great emotional power and mystery, it also recognizes that implicit within Paul's call to Christianity is a call to join and later define a new community. The best way to define Paul's conversion is in terms of the community he left behind and the community he joined. Paul left behind Pharisaic Judaism, and he joined Gentile Christianity. Indeed, we shall see that one of the most successful definitions of conversion merely describes a change of religious community. But certainly to make a change of the magnitude which Paul did necessitates a conversion.

16. PAUL AND LUKE COMPARED

There are many important differences between Paul and Luke, mostly stemming from their different purposes. Paul wants to vindicate his position as apostle, while Luke wants to portray the progress of the church from the Jewish community to the Gentile one. The sequence basic to Luke's history of the church is unemphasized in Paul's own writing. Paul tries to express the content of his revelation while Luke uses Paul's ecstatic experience as a model for Gentile conversions. Lastly and most importantly, although Paul certainly calls his conversion a revelation, Luke substitutes a revelatory audition unknown in Paul's writing.

Luke was writing with more historical perspective than Paul and, of course, less personal knowledge of the experience, but he understands the importance of Paul's conversion in ways which Paul himself perhaps did not fully realize. The most significant aspect of Luke's description is the radical distinction between Resurrection appearances of Christ and experiences of the spirit.[59] Neither Paul himself nor John distinguishes so clearly between "spiritual" and "Resurrection" appearances. In 1Cor 15:45, for instance, Paul

59. J. D. G. Dunn, *Jesus and the Spirit: A Study of the Religious and Charismatic Experience of Jesus and the First Christians as Reflected in The New Testament* (Philadelphia, 1975); pp. 104–109.

shows no sensitivity to Luke's interpretive categories when he conflates the appearance of the risen Jesus as "the life-giving spirit."

Luke, on the other hand, distinguishes Paul's experience from that of the original twelve apostles. For Luke, the authentic Resurrection appearances of Jesus in the Gospel and Acts are far more mundane and "realistic." Jesus walks and talks with travelers, blesses them, eats, and is even unrecognized at first. For Luke, these are not visionary appearances but meant to be descriptions of a physical presence experienced in ordinary consciousness. Luke understands the first sightings of Jesus as actual, physical manifestations. But the Resurrection appearances are brought to an end by the Ascension (Acts 1:9ff.).[60] For Luke, Paul's experience is simply a "vision" (ὀπτασία). Since Paul's experience was visionary in some way, it falls into a second category of sightings, an expression of the Spirit after Jesus' Ascension. Luke identifies the original twelve disciples as apostles, limiting apostolic status to those who had accompanied Jesus during the length of his ministry (Acts 1:21–26); by implication then, Paul falls into a secondary category.

Paul may accept the status of the twelve as special disciples, but he openly disputes his position. For him, the appearance of Christ to him vindicates his equal status as apostle, even though it occurred in a revelation and vision. Indeed, he includes himself in the list of those to whom Jesus' Resurrection was made manifest (Galatians 1; 1Cor 9:1, 15:8f.). Paul may recognize that he is "last of all" and "untimely born," but he will not give up his claim to be an apostle, because Christ appeared to him. He uses the same simple word, "see," to describe his and the other apostles' experience of the Christ. Paul therefore does not distinguish between the kind of appearance made known to him and those of his forebears.

Another way to express the difference between Luke and Paul's conception of the conversion is to rely on I. M. Lewis' sociological distinction between peripheral and central possession.[61] When claims for ecstasy occur in groups peripheral to power, they tend to function as bids to short-circuit the legitimate organization of power. In contrast, when possession or ecstasy occurs close to the center of a political movement, it is carefully controlled, usually by an established religious authority. Ecstatic religion represents a peripheral strategy in first-century Judaism; it was a kind of oblique attack against established order, as when the Qumran community practiced ecstatic ascent. They were priestly functionaries, locked out of their hereditary Temple functions. So they sought contact with the divine in the desert.

Within the Christian movement ecstasy carried different social distinctions. Though positing only two social strategies leaves out many intermedi-

---

60. Indeed, there are two different ascensions in his history. The Gospel implies an Ascension with the Resurrection, which is fulfilled at the beginning of Acts.

61. I. M. Lewis, *Ecstatic Religion: An Anthropological Study of Spirit Possession and Shamanism* (Baltimore, 1971).

ary ambiguous cases in early Christianity, one difference between Paul and Luke emerges from the way ecstatic experience functions in their writings. For Luke, ecstatic experience is already the established role model for the conversion of Gentiles because of Paul. But it is not the model for Resurrection appearances, which are treated literally and give a special status to the first apostles. For Paul, in contrast, the revelatory vision of the Christ functions as a bid for power, since he was a peripheral figure in Christianity, as his battle for apostolic acceptance shows.[62] The motif of realistic appearances in Luke is a Greco-Roman apologetic designed to impress critics and friends with the power of Jesus' Resurrection, whereas the ecstatic visions of Paul are more in line with the original Jewish apocalypticism out of which Christianity arose.

Luke and Paul's similar description of the risen Christ is significant in social ways as well. The contrast between them points to an incipient crisis in the church—between those mostly Jewish Christians, who based their new faith on an experience of Jesus in the flesh, and those mostly Gentile Christians championed by the ex-Pharisee Paul, who based their faith on a spiritual interpretation of the Christ, seen primarily in his Resurrection or spiritual body. The theology, in other words, parallels the social distinction in early Christianity between those who knew Christ in a fleshly way and those who knew him in his spiritual body. This vision and the subsequent success of the Gentile mission convinces Paul that the New Age is not only imminent but that it has already begun. It also convinces him that his Jewish opponents see the Christ in a fleshly rather than a spiritual way.

There is some interesting evidence that a language of personal and psychic transformation was used by two evangelists to describe Jesus' Transfiguration. It is quite possible that the language applied to Jesus in these passages is supposed to serve as a model for the eventual transformation of the believer.[63] According to Mark and Matthew, what happened to Jesus was a transformation (καὶ μεταμορφώθη ἔμπροσθεν αὐῶν; Mk 9:2; Mt 17:2). Luke probably wished to guard against the idea that Jesus had undergone a metamorphosis like a Greek hero, and so he avoids the term. Instead he says simply that the appearance of his countenance was altered (Lk 9:29).[64] These terms relate significantly to the heavenly journey motif in Jewish apocalypticism.[65]

---

62. Of course, one can take the distinction too far, for in 2 Corinthians 12, in the same passage in which Paul describes a revelation and ascent to the heavens, he argues against other Christians who claim yet more authority for ecstatic experiences. So Paul represents a compromise position between pure periphery and pure centrality in early Christianity. If he were more characteristic of a peripheral prophet, he would not oppose the charismatics so vigorously. On the other hand he feels that all have a proper place (1Cor 12:4–13).

63. See M. Smith, *Jesus the Magician* (San Francisco, 1978).

64. See J. Koenig, *The Motif of Transformation*, pp. 65ff.; and see above n. 48.

65. See my article, "Paul's Ecstasy," above n. 47.

17. ELIMINATING SOME FALSE DICHOTOMIES

The last decade has seen an enormous shift in emphasis in the study of conversion: Scholars have begun to rely on sociology more than psychology to understand the phenomenon of conversion, partly because sociological research is more easily quantifiable than psychological research. In L. R. Rambo's extremely helpful "Current Research in Religious Conversion,"[66] only twenty-five psychological studies are listed since 1970, while there are over one hundred sociologically oriented studies.

One major point of contemporary sociological research, as opposed to the previous psychological approach, is that there is no universal psychological definition of conversion. Each community defines what it means by conversion. For a long period psychological studies of conversion merely accepted one or another of western religion's definitions of conversion. Some researchers wanted to stress the emotional nature of conversion over against a rational decision. Others wanted to stress the speed of some conversions over against a long period of education in a new movement. Others have stressed other concepts: transformation, transcendence, typology, tradition, institution, affiliation, intensification, apostasy, context, crisis, or religious quest.

It turns out, however, that conversion is not a cultural universal. Each community evolves a definition of conversion which makes sense to itself. But if a universal definition of conversion is lacking, community definitions of the phenomenon are never absent. Conversions are almost always defined in some conventional way by each community, and most conversions in the community do conform to the community's evolving model.[67]

Many descriptive studies of conversion in special communities note a stereotypic character of the narration.[68] A conversion report idealizes and conventionalizes the conversion experience for the group that values it, guiding potential converts. We have already seen that Paul himself uses his conversion story to advance his gospel. This follows the expected pattern developed from modern data. When the reports are written down and collected, conventionalization becomes even more evident.[69]

---

66. *RSR* 8 (1982) 146–59.

67. See L. Rambo, "Conversion," *The Encyclopedia of Religion* (New York, 1987), vol. 4, pp. 73–79.

68. At a recent conference I heard one researcher remark, "Once you've read one Mormon conversion narration, you've read them all." The rather terse remark has nothing to do with Mormon literature, which is neither more nor less stereotypic than other devotional literature. Rather it is a comment about conversion literature in general.

69. See B. Taylor, "Recollection and Membership: Converts' Talk and the Ratiocination of Commonality," *Sociology* 12 (1978) 316–23; J. A. Beckford, "Accounting for Conversion," *British Journal of Sociology* 29 (1978) 249–62; D. Snow and R. Machalek, "The Convert as a Social Type," in *Sociological Theory*; see also their article "The Sociology of Conversion," *Annual Review of Sociology* 10:167–90; C. L. Staples and A. L. Mauss, "Conversion or Commitment? A Reassessment of the Snow and Machalek Approach to the Study of Conversion," *JSSR* 26 (1987) 133–47.

Paul's own experience may stand squarely within Jewish apocalypticism and mysticism. Luke's description is cognizant of that connection, but Luke is more taken with the issue of spirit possession in the later church. Luke's model for Paul's conversion reflects a more evolved definition of conversion within the church, a model for many converts to follow. For Luke, Paul's ecstatic conversion on the road to Damascus is the first of a large number of ecstatic conversions.

Paul's own narrative of his conversion experience is not free of editing itself, but his is not nearly so conventionalized, because the time period between the experience and his narration is shorter. Unlike Luke, Paul himself could scarcely have suggested that his emotional experience was typical of all believers. When we look at his ecstatic experiences, such as those narrated in 2 Corinthians 12, we shall see that it provides Paul with special credentials. It is not meant to be a universal experience, though it reveals to Paul a universal and hidden meaning to history. However, Paul's narrative is by no means coterminous with the events, either of his conversion or his subsequent revelations. A long period of time had passed between Paul's actual conversion experience and his account of himself. According to his autobiographical statements in Galatians 1, a minimum of fourteen and perhaps more than seventeen years must have passed, by our counting.[70] So Paul's own description is affected by his Christian calling.

This function of role modeling is even clearer in the pastoral epistles. 1Tim 1:12–17 purports to be Paul's own description of his conversion but has much more in common with Luke's ideas about Paul:[71]

> I thank him who has given me strength for this, Christ Jesus our Lord, because he judged me faithful by appointing me to his service, though I formerly blasphemed and persecuted and insulted him; but I received mercy because I had acted ignorantly in unbelief, and the grace of our Lord overflowed for me with the faith and love that are in Christ Jesus. The saying is sure and worthy of full acceptance, that Christ Jesus came into the world to save sinners. And I am the foremost of sinners; but I received mercy for this reason, that in me, as the foremost, Jesus Christ might display his perfect patience for an example to those who were to believe in him for eternal life. To the King of Ages, immortal, invisible, the only God, be honor and glory for ever and ever. Amen.

---

70. Hellenistic conventions for counting years give a different total than we might expect. Scholars have estimated on the basis of Hellenistic reckonings that from twelve to seventeen years could actually have passed. Since the counting could include the present year, even if it were a bare fraction of a year, as well as what we would consider the first year and the same inclusionary policy was possible at the end of the time period, a wider time span is possible than we would normally allow. See H. Koester, *Introduction*, pp. 101–6. Koester demurs from the use of the term "conversion" on the basis of Paul's self-understanding as a prophet. But once both the change and the mission are brought out, any differences in terminology are likely to be semantic.

71. See S. G. Wilson, *Luke and the Pastoral Epistles* (London, 1979) for the notion that the pastorals were written by Luke. His discussion of 1Tim 1:12–17 appears on p. 109.

This passage, in a letter of uncertain authorship, stresses the contrast between the two periods of Paul's life, before conversion and after it. But before conversion Paul is portrayed as the foremost of sinners (1:16) in this pastoral letter, while the Paul of the authentic letters asserts that he is blameless according to the law (Phil 3:6). Although Paul emphasizes his conversion and may even regret his former life as a persecutor of Christianity, he never considers himself to be the foremost sinner. This passage in 1 Timothy then has a distinctly post-Pauline character. As much or more than Paul himself, this conversion is depicted as a model (ὑποτύπος, 1:16) for the conversion of all nonbelievers. Rather, the theme of repentant sinners is appropriate to the Gentile mission, where repentance from a sinful life was a prominent theme. While the message is mostly Pauline, and the narrative reflection upon it comes from the historical distance, it is closer to Luke's than to Paul's authentic voice. And it points out how, by means of Luke's narrative, Paul's life came to be a model for Christian conversion. Thus we have at least three distinct stages of development in the early church's understanding of ecstatic conversion: (1) Paul's own ecstatic, emotional experience, which is intensely personal, special, and visionary, and equivalent to the disciples' experience of the Christ; (2) Luke's contention that Paul's experience is typical of conversions but not equivalent to the experience of the disciples; and (3) the deliberate attempt to make Paul into a paradigm for Gentile conversion experiences.

Although the Pauline community lacks the commitment which circumcised converts to Judaism must exhibit, it presumably was able to develop different sources of commitment, based on the quick coming of the Messiah and the moral rules of community which that coming entailed. The commitment in Pauline communities of Jews and Gentiles was different from the commitment generated by more typically Jewish communities. Unlike Judaism, which built commitment by means of God's commandments, the new Pauline Christian community of messianists built commitment on conversion experience, the tearing down of some traditional ritual actions which separated parts of the community. It did not, however, do without ritual. Rather it changed the symbolic value of rituals like baptism and blessings over food in Judaism so that they signified the hopes of a messianic community and the goal of a single body of believers. Later generations accomplished that goal, but they forgot what Paul knew about Judaism. In the process, the Christian community used Paul's experience to create a new definition of conversion for itself.

16

"THERE SHALL COME FORTH A MAN"
Reflections on Messianic Ideas in Philo

INTRODUCTION

The problem of method is a critical issue in Philonic studies. What then should be an adequate approach for analyzing messianic expectations in Philo? It would seem natural to identify relevant passages and discuss them in detail, drawing at the same time on ideas and passages elsewhere in Philo. Certain specific questions might be addressed to these passages, such as: Do the eschatological and the messianic expectations play a central or peripheral role in Philo's understanding of Judaism?[1] Is there an interconnection between the Messiah and the Logos? Is there a tension between universalism and nationalistic particularism?

These and other questions easily lead to an attempt to understand the messianic expectations as an element in Philo's thoughts conceived as a comprehensive philosophical system. This approach is taken by H. A. Wolfson. In Wolfson's presentation of Philo's philosophy of religion, a chapter is devoted to his political theory; Wolfson sees Philo's ideas of a messianic age as

---

1. A central role: E. R. Goodenough, *The Politics of Philo Judaeus* (New Haven, Conn., 1938, repr. Hildesheim, 1967), pp. 115–19; G. Bertram, "Philo als politisch-theologischer Propagandist des spätantiken Judentums," *Theologisches Literaturblatt* 64 (1939) 193–99; see H. A. Wolfson, *Philo*, 2, 2nd ed. (Cambridge, Mass., 1948), pp. 395–426; P. Borgen, "Philo of Alexandria," in M. Stone, ed., *Jewish Writings in the Second Temple Period* (Assen and Philadelphia, 1984), pp. 233–80; idem, "Philo of Alexandria: A Critical and Synthetical Survey of Research Since World War II," *ANRW* II.21.1, pp. 98–154.

A peripheral role, alien to Philo's philosophy, etc.: A. Gfrörer, *Philo und die alexandrinische Theosophie*, 1 (Stuttgart, 1831), pp. 471–534; P. Volz, *Die Eschatologie der jüdischen Gemeinde*, 2nd ed. (Tübingen, 1934), p. 59; W. Bousset and H. Gressmann, *Die Religion des Judentums*, 3. Aufl. (Tübingen, 1926), p. 443, etc.; E. Bréhier, *Les Idées philosophiques et religieuses de Philon d'Alexandrie* (Paris, 1908), pp. 3–10; Y. Amir, *Die hellenistische Gestalt des Judentums bei Philon von Alexandrien* (Neukirchen-Vluyn, 1983), pp. 31–37; R. Barraclough, "Philo's Politics, Roman Rule and Hellenistic Judaism," *ANRW* II.21.1, pp. 480–81; U. Fischer, *Eschatologie und Jenseitserwartung in hellenistischen Diasporajudentum* (Berlin, New York, 1978), pp. 184–213.

a solution to the tension between his conception of the ideal state and the present condition of the Jewish nation.[2]

Wolfson goes too far, however, in making Philo into a systematic theologian. Much more emphasis has to be placed on the fact that Philo was an exegete whose aim was to interpret the Laws of Moses.[3] Even so, it seems possible to avoid the opposite extreme—that of understanding Philo as an eclectic with no uniting core at all. In *On the Life of Moses* I and II, and in the *Exposition of the Law* (= *Op, Abr, Jos, Decal, Spec, Virt, Praem*) Philo informs us about the outline and about the basic concept of these two works.[4] The first part of this study will analyze the aspects of particularism, universalism, and eschatology in these two works. Against this background the main "messianic" passages (*Vita Mos* I:289–91, *Praem* 91–97 and 163–72) will receive further discussion. Some other relevant passages in Philo's writings will be included in this discussion.

This study has led to the following conclusion: In *On the Life of Moses* and the *Exposition of the Law*, "eschatology" means the realization of the universal aspect of Moses' kingship and of the universal role of the Hebrew nation. This universal realization of Moses' kingship did not take place in Moses' lifetime. It would be accomplished in the future by "a man" who would be commander-in-chief of the Hebrew army and would conquer the enemies and be emperor of many nations—i.e. of the world. Moses' and the Hebrew army's battles with the Phoenicians and with Balak and his people are events which point forward to the Hebrew people's future "eating up" of its enemies. The eschatological blessings are conditioned upon the people's obedience to the commandments in the Laws of Moses and the virtues present in them. Philo prefers a peaceful ideological warfare but accepts, if necessary, military war, led by "a man" as commander-in-chief. The messianic prophecy about "a man" thus is a natural and integral element in Philo's interpretation of the Law of Moses, but the central and basic idea is the eschatological role of the Jewish nation as being the head of all nations.

The following analysis will demonstrate the basis for this conclusion.

PARTICULARISM, UNIVERSALISM, AND THE ROYAL ESCHATOLOGICAL LEADER

Particularistic Universalism

What is the relationship between particularism, universalism, and eschatology in the two treatises *On the Life of Moses* and the several treatises

---

2. H. A. Wolfson, *Philo*, 2, 2nd ed., pp. 395ff.
3. See P. Borgen, *ANRW* II.21.1, pp. 141–42.
4. See P. Borgen, CRINT, II.2, pp. 233–41; E. R. Goodenough, "Philo's Exposition of the Law and His De Vita Mosis," *HTR* 26 (1933) 109–25; P. Borgen, *Philo, John, and Paul: New Perspectives on Judaism and Early Christianity* (Atlanta, 1987), p. 20; B. L. Mack, "Philo and Exegetical Traditions in Alexandria" in *ANRW* II.21.1, p. 266.

which form the *Exposition of the Law*? Philo indicates that this question determines the outline and perspective of these two works.

In *Praem* 1–3, Philo divides the *Exposition of the Law* into three main parts: the story of creation, the historical part, and the legislative part. Accordingly, the *Exposition* consists of the treatise *On the Creation (Op)*, the historical part which covers the biblical story from the events after Adam and Eve to the death of Joseph (preserved treatises are *De Abrahamo [Abr]* and *De Iosepho [Jos]*), and the legislative part, which starts with a summary of the laws in *On the Decalogue (Dec)* to be explained in detail in *On the Special Laws (Spec Leg)*. The two final works—*On the Virtues (Virt)* and *Rewards and Punishments (Praem)*—tie the whole of the *Exposition of the Law* together.

In *On the Virtues* 52, Philo refers to the two books which he had written on the life of Moses, and in *Praem* 53, he summarizes the scheme of these books in the same way as he does in *Vita Mos* II:3. Moses is seen as a king, legislator, prophet, and high priest. Thus the two treatises *On the Life of Moses* are to some degree expanded versions of the sections on Moses, *Virt* 51–71 and *Praem* 52–56. In *Virt* 51–71 Moses serves as illustration of a person who practiced philanthropy and piety. His life was to serve as a paradigm (*Virt* 51 and 70). According to *Praem* 52–56, Moses was the winner of the crown in the sacred contest of virtues against vices. Moses had the queen virtue of piety in a special degree for his own, and through it he gained the four special rewards of the offices of king, legislator, prophet, and high priest.

This understanding is supported by *Vita Mos* II:45–52, where the whole perspective of the *Exposition of the Law* is given. The sacred books of Moses consist of two parts, the historical and the legislative. The historical part is divided into the story of the creation of the world and the genealogical section. Beginning with an account of the creation of the universe, Moses wished to show that the Father and Creator was in the truest sense also its Lawgiver, and that he who observes the laws lives in accordance with the ordering of the universe. Thus the particular enactments of the Laws of Moses seek to attain to the harmony of the universe and are in agreement with the principles of eternal nature. In this way the Laws of Moses differ from the laws of other nations, according to Philo.[5]

Three important points can be made from these passages: (1) The distinctive and particular role and life of the Jewish nation are based on universal principles. Philo here stresses that the God-given cosmic principles are the foundation of Jewish existence. (2) Since the general, universal principles are

---

5. See H. A. Wolfson, *Philo*, vol. 2, pp. 189–92; D. Winston, "Philo's Ethical Theory," *ANRW* II.21.1, pp. 386–88; For par. ideas in other Jewish writings, see GenR 1:1 (the Torah is God's model in his creation of the world); Josephus, *Ant* 1.24 (everything in the Mosaic Law is set forth in keeping with the nature of the universe). See R. Barraclough, *ANRW* II.21.1, pp. 507–8. See esp. *Quaes Ex* II:42 and also *Abr* 1–6.

made manifest in the specific laws of the Jewish nation, this nation is the center and the head of all nations. (3) All nations, hopefully, will recognize God's universal laws revealed in the Laws of Moses, and recognize the leading role of the Jewish nation. Philo's eschatology means that this universal claim for the Laws of Moses and the Jewish nation is effectuated, in what in a seeming contradiction must be called particularistic universalism.[6]

On the Life of Moses. Against this background, the contexts of *Vita Mos* I:289–290; *Praem* 91–97, and 163–72 should be examined. First, the context in the two treatises *On the Life of Moses* will be given. Moses' role as king is described in the first treatise. Moses gave up the hegemony of Egypt to which he was heir. God bestowed him with the kingship of a nation more populous and mightier than Egypt, a nation destined to be consecrated above all others to offer prayers forever (αἰεί) on behalf of the human race (ὑπὲρ τοῦ γένους τῶν ἀνθρώπων) that it may be delivered from evil and participate in what is good (*Vita Mos* I:149). God judged him worthy to appear as a partner of His own possessions, and gave into his hands the whole world as his portion (155–57).

Philo's interpretation of the biblical stories runs as follows: The Israelites marched as a military army from Egypt through the desert, and came within sight of the confines of habitable land and the outlying districts of the country in which they proposed to settle. They entered into confrontations with the peoples who lived in that area. In the encounter with the Phoenicians, the superior and universal call of the Hebrew nation was made manifest. Moses mounted the neighboring hill, and when they were about to engage in the fight his hands became very light and very heavy alternatively. Whenever his hands rose aloft, the Hebrews were strong, but whenever his hands were weighed down the enemy prevailed. By such symbols, God showed that earth and the lowest regions of the universe were the portion assigned to the Phoenicians and the ethereal, the holiest region, to the Hebrews. Just as heaven holds kingship in the universe and is superior to earth, so the Hebrew nation should be victorious over its opponents in war (*Vita Mos* I:217).

Another confrontation took place with Balak and his people. Balak hired Balaam to curse the Hebrew army. Instead, Balaam invoked blessings on them:

---

6. Scholars have often regarded particularistic nationalism and universalism (and individualism) as mutually exclusive alternatives and, accordingly, they find an inner conflict running through Philo's works between his Jewish nationalism and his individualistic universalism. As an example, see U. Fischer, *Eschatologie*, pp. 184–213, and the criticism of his work by U. B. Müller, "Rez. Ulrich Fischer, Eschatologie . . . 1978," in *TZ* 26 (1980) 238–40, and by M. Hengel, "Messianische Hoffnung und politischer 'Radikalismus' in der 'jüdisch-hellenistischen Diaspora,'" in D. Hellholm, ed., *Apocalypticism in the Ancient Near East and the Hellenistic World* (Tübingen, 1983), pp. 657–58.

The View of the Hebrew Army

So, setting his face to the wilderness,
he looked upon the Hebrews encamped in their tribes,
    and, astounded at their number and order
    which resembled a city rather than a camp,
he was filled with the spirit and spoke as follows:

The Seer's Self-Introduction; His Visionary Experience

Thus saith the man who truly sees,
    who in slumber saw the clear vision of God
        with the unsleeping eyes of the soul.

Praise of the Hebrew Army (Army addressed in second person)

How goodly are thy dwellings, thou army of the Hebrews.
Thy tents are as shady dells,
                as garden by the riverside
                as a cedar beside the waters.

The Appearance of a Universal Emperor (Army addressed in second person)

There shall come forth from you one day a man,
and he shall rule over many nations
and his kingdom spreading every day shall be exalted on high.

The Conquering Nation and Those Conquered

This people, throughout its journey from Egypt, has had God as its guide,
    who leads the multitude in a single column.
For that very reason, it shall eat up many nations of its enemies
    and take the fatness of them right up to the marrow,
    and destroy its foes with its far-reaching bolts.
It shall lie down and rest as a lion,
        or a lion's cub,
    full of scorn, fearing none but putting fear in others.
Woe to him who stirs up and rouses it.

Blessing and Curse

    Worthy of benediction are those who bless thee;
    worthy of cursing those who curse thee.   (*Vita Mos* I:289–91)

The end result of the conflict with Balak and his people was that Moses selected the best of his men of military age, one thousand from each tribe. The
Hebrew soldiers made a slaughter of their opponents and returned themselves all safe and sound without a single one killed or even wounded (*Vita
Mos* I:306–11).

Philo thus interprets the oracle of Balaam in Numbers 24 within the context of Moses' office as king and primarily as a warrior king. As king of the Hebrew nation, Moses and his people had a universal call from God, and their victory over the other peoples was partial fulfillment of this divine call. Consequently, when Philo quotes Num 24:7ff. in *Vita Mos* I:290—"There shall come forth from you one day a man and he shall rule over many nations"—he pictures a Hebrew emperor who will bring to its full realization the universal charge of Moses and the Hebrew nation.

It must be added that the same universal and eschatological perspective is applied to Moses' offices as legislator (*Vita Mos* II:12–65), high priest (II:66–186) and prophet (II:187–291). It has already been pointed out that according to Philo the Laws of Moses are the specific laws of the Hebrew nation and are at the same time the eternal principles of the universe (*Vita Mos* II:45–52). Accordingly, it was an event of redemptive history when the Laws of Moses were translated into Greek, ordered by King Ptolemy Philadelphus and done in Alexandria by Jewish scholars. In this way the Laws were not only made known in the "barbarian" half of the world, but were also revealed to the Greek half of the human race (*Vita Mos* II:25–40). According to Philo, the Jewish Laws have received wide acceptance already and Philo expects that the eschatological era will come when all nations cast aside their ancestral customs and honor the Laws of Moses alone (II:43–44).[7] Moses as high priest established the priesthood in Israel, and the priestly tribe was the nucleus of all mankind as an anticipation of the blessed eschatological life to come (II:66–186). As prophet he defended the Jewish religion and foretold the future of the nation (II:187–291, esp. 288). Thus the central role of the Jewish nation as the head (and ruler) of all nations is a fundamental element of Philo's eschatological hope.

The Exposition of the Law. The outlook of Philo's comprehensive work called the *Exposition of the Law* is the same as that in *On the Life of Moses.* The Hebrew nation is seen as the center and as the head of all nations and of the universe. Abraham's marriage with Sarah is seen within this context of particularism and universalism: ". . . that marriage from which was to issue . . . a whole nation, and that the nation dearest of all to God, which, as I hold, has received the gift of priesthood and prophecy on behalf of all mankind" (*Abr* 98).

The high priest makes prayers and gives thanks not only on behalf of the whole human race, but also for other parts of nature, such as the earth,

---

7. This shows that Philo held the view that all nations would become proselytes and worship the One God of the Jews. U. Fischer, *Eschatologie*, p. 186, performs forced exegesis when he thinks that *Vita Mos* II:44 champions a spiritual and universal eschatology, not a national Jewish eschatology. Philo here rather stresses the universal role of the Jewish nation when he says that by its prosperity together with the Mosaic Law, the Jewish nation will darken the light of other nations and laws.

water, air and fire (*Spec Leg* I:97). The Jewish nation uses its prayers, festivals, and first-fruit offerings as a means of supplication for the human race in general as well as for itself, as a means of making its homage to the truly existent God in the name of those who have evaded the service which it was their duty to give (*Spec Leg* II:167, cf. *Gaium* 3).

Just as stated in *Vita Mos* II:45–52, the treatise *On the Creation of the World* introduces the Laws of Moses, "implying that the world is in harmony with the Law, and the Law with the world, and that the man who observes the Law is thereby constituted a loyal citizen of the world, regulating his doings by the purpose and will of Nature, in accordance with which the entire world itself also is administered" (*Op* 3).

The lives of the patriarchs are interpreted by Philo within this context of general cosmic principles and the particular laws. Patriarchs are living laws—that is, they are an embodiment of the divine cosmic laws. Conversely the specific laws given on Mount Sinai are memorials of the life of the ancients and commentaries on it (*Abr* 1–6).[8]

Again, Philo's view is to be characterized in a paradoxical way as particularistic universalism, such as is formulated in *Quaes Ex* II:42—"And it is fitting that it should have a worthy author of law and legislator, since among men (God) appointed the contemplative race (i.e. Israel) in the same manner (as the law) for the world. And rightly does he legislate for this race, also prescribing (its laws) as a law for the world, for the chosen race is a likeness of the world, and its Law (is a likeness of the laws) of the world." Just as the Hebrew nation epitomizes the world, so the Laws of Moses epitomize the laws of the world.[9]

As already stated, in *Praem* 1–3 Philo outlines the whole work called the *Exposition of the Law:* the story of the creation is followed by the historical part, the legislative part, and then the two final works, *On the Virtues* and *Rewards and Punishment*. The two final works tie the whole *Exposition of the Law* together: the virtues are needed for all commandments, and those who are schooled in the laws are called to make a practical exhibition of what they have learned by bringing such knowledge into the sacred arena to be tested. The true athletes of virtue will gain victory and rewards, while the unmanly will suffer defeat and punishment. Furthermore, the carrying out of the laws brings blessings, and disloyalty results in curses. While *On the Decalogue* and *On the Special Laws* give an exposition of laws in Exodus, Leviticus, Numbers, and Deuteronomy, the blessings and curses cover

8. Jewish and Platonizing motifs are woven together here. The Jewish motif is the correspondence between the practices of the Patriarchs and the Mosaic Law. For example, according to the Book of Jubilees, Noah, Abraham, and others observed and enjoined the laws inscribed on heavenly tables which were later given to Moses. A similar correlation is found in Philo, but here the Platonizing element makes the lives and words of the Patriarchs archetypes and the Mosaic Laws copies. See P. Borgen, CRINT, II.2, p. 238.

9. See R. Barraclough, *ANRW* II.21.1, pp. 508, 541.

other sections in these books, with main emphasis on Leviticus 26 and Deuteronomy 28.

The section on rewards and punishments (*Praem* 7–78) refers to the experiences of persons in the biblical past, while the section on blessings and curses (*Praem* 79–172) points to the rewards and punishments decreed for the future, depending on man's obedience or disobedience to the laws.[10] The first blessing is victory over enemies, i.e. over wild beasts and men. When men keep the commandments, the beasts will be tamed and wars will come to an end (*Praem* 79–94). War will either never come or, if some people are still mad enough to attack the Jewish nation, "'there shall come forth a man' (Num 24:7 LXX), and leading his host to war, he will subdue great and populous nations . . ." (*Praem* 95). The second blessing is wealth, the third long life, and then freedom from disease (98–126). The curses are famine, cannibalism, slavery, business failures, diseases and wars (*Praem* 127–51). If the Jewish nation in this way is for a while rejected, proselytes take over the role of the native citizens. Then, finally, restoration and return will take place and the curses will be turned upon the persecutors of the nation (*Praem* 152–72).

The two passages most important for our discussion are *Praem* 79.93–97 and 163–72. *Praem* 79.93–97 belong to the section on blessings:

The Condition

(79)   If, he says, you keep the divine commandments . . . ,

The Blessing

the first boon you will have is victory over your enemies.

The Blessing Is Specified: Victory
Alternative 1 (the enemy will give in peacefully)

(93)   Either, then, as he says, the war will not pass through the land of the
       godly at all, but will dissolve and fall into pieces of itself when the
       enemy perceives the nature of their opponents, that they have in
       justice an irresistible ally. (For virtue is majestic and august and can,
       unaided and silently, allay the onsets of evils, however great.)

Alternative 2 (futile attack)
a. Victory by superior strength

(94)   Or if some fanatics whose lust for war defies restraint or remonstrance
       come careening to attack, till they are actually engaged, they will be

---

10. E. R. Goodenough, *HTR* 26 (1933) 118ff., attempts to separate the section on blessings and curses (*Praem* 79–172) from Philo's larger work, the *Exposition of the Law*. His hypothesis has not commanded assent among scholars. See F. H. Colson (ed., trans.), *Philo* 8 (Loeb, Cambridge, Mass., 1960), pp. xix–xx; P. Borgen, CRINT, II.2, p. 241; J. Morris, "The Jewish Philos-

full of arrogance and bluster, but when they have come to a trial of
blows, they will find that their talk has been an idle boast,
as they are unable to win.
Because, forced back by your superior strength, they will fly headlong,
companies of hundreds before handfuls of five,
ten thousands before hundreds
by many ways for the one by which they came.

b. Some stricken by fear

(95)   Some, without even any pursuer save fear,
  will turn their backs and present admirable targets
to their enemies so that it would be an easy
matter for all to fall to a man.
For "there shall come forth a man," says the oracle,
  and leading his host to war he will subdue great and populous nations,
because God has sent to his aid the reinforcement
which befits the godly,
and that is dauntless courage of soul
and all-powerful strength of body,
either of which strikes fear into the enemy,
and the two if united are quite irresistible.

c. Some defeated by swarms of wasps

(96)   Some of the enemy, he says, will be unworthy to be defeated by men
He promises to marshall against them to their shame and perdition
swarms of wasps to fight in the van of the godly.

d. The victory

(97)   They will win not only a permanent and bloodless victory in the war,
  but also a sovereignty which none can contest
bringing to its subjects the benefit which will
accrue from the affection or fear or respect which they feel.
For the conduct of their rulers show three high
qualities which contribute to make a government
secure from subversion, namely dignity, strictness, benevolence,
which produce the feelings mentioned above.
For respect is created by dignity, fear by strictness, affection by
benevolence, and these when blended harmoniously in the soul render
subjects obedient to their rulers.

The final passage is *Praem* 163–72. *Praem* 163–72 follows after the section
on curses, which they will suffer who disregard the holy laws, 127–62. Then

---

opher Philo," in E. Schürer, *The History of the Jewish People in the Age of Jesus Christ*, a new
English version rev. and ed. by G. Vermes, F. Millar, and M. Goodman (Edinburgh, 1987), vol.
3.2, pp. 853–54.

those Jews who confess their sins and turn back to virtue will experience restoration and their enemies will in turn suffer punishment.

Praem 163–72, quoted in part, shows us this:

The Condition: Conversion

If however they accept these chastisements
    as a warning rather than as intending their perdition,
if shamed into a whole-hearted conversion they reproach themselves for going
    thus astray,
        and make a full confession and acknowledgment of all their sin,
            first within themselves with a mind so purged
        that their conscience is sincere and free from lurking taint,
            secondly with their tongues to bring their hearers to a better way,
then they will find favour with God the Savior, the Merciful,
    who has bestowed on mankind that
        peculiar and chiefest gift of kinship with His own Logos,
        from whom as its archetype the human mind was created.

From Slavery to Liberty

    (164) For even though they dwell in the uttermost parts of the earth,
        in slavery to those who led them away captive,
        one signal, as it were, one day will bring liberty to all.
    This conversion in a body to virtue will strike awe into their masters,
        who will set them free,
        ashamed to rule over men better than themselves.

Return Under Guidance

(165) When they have gained this unexpected liberty,
        those who but now were scattered in Greece
            and the barbarian world over islands and continents,
    will arise and post from every side with one impulse to the one
        appointed place,
        guided in their pilgrimage by a vision divine and superhuman,
        unseen by others
        but manifest to them as they pass from exile to their home.

Three Intercessors

(166–67) Three intercessors they have . . .

The Change from Ruin to Prosperity

(168)   When they have arrived, the cities which but now lay in ruins
        will be cities once more; . . .

The Reversal

(169)   Everything will suddenly be reversed,
        God will turn the curses against the enemies of these penitents,
            the enemies who rejoiced in the misfortunes of the nation
            and mocked and railed at them,
            thinking that they themselves would have a heritage which nothing
                could destroy
            and which they hoped to leave to their children and descendants
                in due succession;
            thinking too that they would always see their opponents
                in a firmly established and unchanging adversity
                which would be reserved for the generations that followed them.
(170)   In their infatuation they did not understand . . .
(171)   But these enemies who have mocked at their lamentations,
            proclaimed public holidays of their misfortunes,
            feasted on their mourning,
            in general made the unhappiness of others their own
                happiness,
        will, when they begin to reap the rewards of their cruelty,
        find that their misconduct was directed
            not against the obscure and unmeritable
            but against men of high lineage,
                retaining sparks of their noble birth,
                which have to be but fanned into a flame,
            and from them shines out the glory
                which for a little while was quenched.

New Growths from the Roots

(172)   For just as when the stalks of plants are cut away . . .

ANALYSIS OF *VITA MOS* I:289–91, *PRAEM* 93–97 AND 163–72

The passages *Vita Mos* I:289–91 and *Praem* 93–97 draw on the biblical story of Balak and Balaam. In *Vita Mos* I:263–305, Numbers 22–25 and 31 are interpreted. In addition to using the story about King Balak and the seer Balaam in Numbers 22–24, Philo (on the basis of Num 31:15–16) ascribes to the advice of Balaam the sins of adultery and idolatry which the Israelites committed (Numbers 25). Philo here represents a broad Jewish exegetical tradition.[11]

Parts of the story about Balak and Balaam are used by Philo at various places in his works.[12] Of these, *Virt* 34–46 is of special interest for our discussion.

---

11. See G. Vermes, *Scripture and Tradition in Judaism* (Leiden, 1961), pp. 169ff.
12. *Leg All* III:187.210; *Cher* 32–36; *Sacr* 94; *Quod Det* 71; *Quod Deus* 52–69.181–83; *Conf* 64–66.72, 98.159; *Migr* 113f.; *Mut* 202f.; *Somn* I:234–37; *Virt* 34–46.

The passages *Praem* 93–97 and 163–72 belong to the section on blessings and curses, *Praem* 79–172. They render the blessings and curses spoken by Moses in Leviticus 26 and Deuteronomy 28. Philo does not elsewhere draw on Leviticus 26 and Deuteronomy 28 in such an extensive and concentrated manner, but parts of these two Old Testament chapters are found scattered in various of his writings.[13]

When the oracle spoken by Balaam in *Vita Mos* I:289–91 is examined in detail, we see that Philo paraphrases the Septuagint text of Num 24:1–9 closely. The paraphrase as such is similar to the way of rendering the Old Testament text in the targums.[14]

The Septuagint translation of Num 24:7 differs from the Hebrew text in a puzzling way. It is not within the scope of the present paper to discuss this problem, although it is of great importance in itself.[15] Our task is to examine *Vita Mos* I:289–90 on the basis of the Septuagint text. In Philo's paraphrase of Num 24:1–9, the following distinctive emphases can be seen:

1. Philo stresses that the Hebrews had a well-organized army. He says that the camp of the Hebrews resembled a city rather than an encampment (ὡς πόλεως ἀλλ' οὐ στρατοπέδου), although he explicitly states that the Hebrews were an army, στρατιὰ Ἑβραίων. Moreover, according to him the Hebrews went away from Egypt in the kind of military formation called a column. He interprets the Septuagint μονοκέρωτος (unicorn, Num 24:8) to mean ἓν κέρας and reads καθ' ἓν κέρας ἄγοντι. The words κατὰ κέρας ἄγειν is a technical phase for leading an army in marching order as a column, as over against ἐπὶ φάλαγγος ἄγειν, to lead an army in the line of battle.[16]

2. Philo clearly places the appearance of "a man" (Num 24:7) some time in future, by adding ποτέ: ἐξελεύσεταί ποτε ἄνθρωπος (there shall come forth *one day* a man). In this way he distinguishes in time the universal reign pictured in Balaam's oracle from the present conflict with Balak. At the same time he makes a clear connection by adding τοιγαροῦν "for that very reason": ὁ λαὸς οὗτος ἡγεμόνι τῆς ἀπ' Αἰγύπτου πάσης ὁδοῦ κέχρηται θεῷ καθ' ἓν κέρας ἄγοντι τὴν πληθύν. τοιγαροῦν ἔδεται ἔθνη πολλὰ ἐχθρῶν . . . (*Vita Mos* I:290–91) "The people has used God as leader on the whole journey from Egypt, God who leads the multitude (as an army) in (the marching order of) a single column; for that very reason, it shall eat up many nations . . ." God's leadership of the Hebrew army in the Exodus of the past

---

13. Lev 26:5 in *Virt* 47; 26:10 in *Sacr* 79 and *Heres* 279; 26:12 in *Sacr* 87, *Mut* 266, and *Somn* I:148f., II:248; 26:41 in *Spec Leg* I:304; Deut 28:1.2.7 in *Virt* 47–48; 28:12 in *Leg All* III:104, *Quod Deus* 156, and *Heres* 76; 28:14 in *Post* 102; 28–29 in *Heres* 250; 28:49–57 in *Spec Leg* I:313; 28:65–66 in *Post* 24f.; and 28:67 in *Flacc* 167.
14. See G. Vermes, *Scripture and Tradition*, pp. 155–61.
15. Cf. M. Hengel, in D. Hellholm, ed., *Apocalypticism*, pp. 679–80.
16. See Xenophon, *Institutio Cyri*, 1.6.43; H. G. Liddell and R. Scott, *A Greek-English Lexicon*, new ed. by H. S. Jones (Oxford, 1958), pp. 941, 1913.

is the guarantee for the people's military success in the future encounter with many nations. This line of reasoning is in accordance with Moses' words at the time of his death, *Vita Mos* II:288: "Then, indeed, we find him [Moses] possessed by the spirit, no longer uttering general truths to the whole nation but prophesying to each tribe in particular the things which were to be and hereafter must come to pass. Some of these have already taken place, others are still looked for, since confidence in the future is assured by fulfilment in the past." [17]

3. Philo pictures "a man" in Num 24:7 as an emperor who shall rule over many nations, and, after he has appeared, his kingdom will spread gradually:

Philo: "There shall come forth from you one day a man.
LXX: "There shall come forth from his seed a man
Philo: and he shall rule over many nations
LXX: and he shall rule over many nations,
Philo: and his kingdom advancing every day
LXX: and the kingdom of Gog shall be exalted
Philo: shall be exalted."
LXX: and his kingdom shall be increased."

This concentration on "a man" as a glorious emperor is stressed by Philo since he omits the Septuagint reference to the eschatological enemy king Gog. Thus "a man" rules over many nations, without one particular enemy being named.

On the basis of this analysis of *Vita Mos* I:298–91, how should Philo's eschatology be characterized? It is to be defined in this way: (a) From God's action in the past, Moses' prophecies for the future receive a firm basis. (b) Moses' call to kingship made him king of the Hebrew nation, the center of all nations. God judged him worthy to appear as a partner of His own possession, the world, and the Law given through Moses was at the same time the universal cosmic law.

Eschatology means then the realization of the universal aspect of Moses' kingship and the universal role of the Hebrew nation and its worship and its laws. This universal realization of Moses' kingship did not take place in Moses' lifetime. It will be accomplished in the future by "a man" who will be emperor of many nations, i.e. of the world. This "man" is not a new Moses, but an emperor who, on the basis of the exodus, will continue Moses' work and bring it to its complete fulfillment. Moses' and the Hebrew army's

---

17. See *Virt* 77. See the same method of reasoning by Josephus in *Ant* 4.125—"And from these prophecies having received the fulfillment which he predicted one may infer what the future also has in store"; cf. *Ant* 10.210.

battles with the Phoenicians and with Balak and his people are events which point forward to the Hebrew people's future eating up of many nations of its enemies.

As the eschatological emperor, the "man" carries the features of the Messiah, in accordance with the messianic interpretation of Num 24:7 in the Targums.[18]

Moreover, the universal role of the Jewish people is a central theme in Jewish literature in Egypt. So also was the militaristic war-tradition important, since a large number of the Jews were soldiers in the Ptolemaic army. The transfer into Roman rule brought a change; the Jews were eliminated as a military factor together with the Ptolemaic army as a whole. The military tradition of warfare was carried on, however, and led to an armed uprising by the Alexandrian Jews at the death of Emperor Gaius Caligula in 41 C.E., the uprising in 66 C.E. and the large-scale revolution of Jews in Cyrene and Egypt in the years 115–117 C.E.

Philo's picture of Abraham (Abr 225–35) and Moses partly as warrior kings, and his characterization of the Hebrews in Vita Mos I:289–91 as a well-organized army, and his quotation of the hope for a Jewish eschatological emperor in Num 24:7, reflect this militaristic stream of Egyptian Jewry.[19]

As we turn from the analysis of Vita Mos I:289–91 to Praem 93–97, we notice that Philo here paraphrases the Septuagint text in a freer way. Although the passage is based on the blessings and curses in Leviticus 26 and Deuteronomy 28, a quotation of Num 24:7 is included, and there seems to be allusion to Is 11:1–5 and Exod 23:28 (Deut 7:20). Again, this treatment of the Septuagint is similar to the use of the Old Testament text in the Aramaic Targums, in this case the freer use of the text in the Fragmentary Targum to the Pentateuch and the Targum Pseudo-Jonathan to the Pentateuch.[20]

If the divine commandments are kept, then victory over the enemies follows as a blessing. This theme is developed in two alternatives in Praem 93–97: (1) victory will be won without war, or (2) if some attack, they will be defeated. In alternative (1) §93, Lev 26:5 is quoted and elaborated upon:

---

18. G. Vermes, Scripture and Tradition, pp. 159ff.; cf. the messianic interpretation of Num 24:17.24 in the Targums, the Dead Sea Scrolls, TI2P, SibOr, and in R. Akiba's application of Num 24:17 on Simon bar Kokhba. See G. Vermes, Scripture and Tradition, pp. 165f.; M. Hengel, in Apocalypticism, pp. 679–80; D. Dimant, "Qumran Sectarian Literature," in CRINT, II.2, pp. 505, 518, and 540; J. Neusner, Messiah in Context (Philadelphia, 1984), pp. 241–47; P. Volz, Die Eschatologie der jüdischen Gemeinde, 2. Aufl. (Tübingen, 1934), pp. 180–84, 189, 193, 210, 400; G. F. Moore, Judaism (Cambridge, Mass., 1927), vol. 2, pp. 329–30; W. A. Meeks, The Prophet-King (Leiden, 1967), pp. 71–72.

19. M. Hengel, in Apocalypticism, pp. 655–85; P. Borgen, "The Jews of Egypt," in The Anchor Bible Dictionary (forthcoming).

20. See S. H. Levey, The Messiah: An Aramaic Interpretation—The Messianic Exegesis of the Targum (Cincinnati, 1974), p. 1. Similar paraphrastic exegesis is found in the "rewritten" Bibles the Book of Jubilees, the Genesis Apocryphon, and the Biblical Antiquities of the Pseudo-Philo. See P. Borgen, in CRINT, II.2, pp. 233–34, and idem, Philo, John, and Paul, pp. 20, 52.

"and war shall not go through your land." In alternative (2) §§94–97 there is first a general description of the futility of the attack by the enemy (§94). They will be forced back by "your superior strength." Philo here paraphrases words from Lev 26:8 and Deut 28:7. Then two groups and cases are specified, as indicated by "some" (ἔνιοι) in §§95 and 96.

The first case deals with "some" who flee due to fear. The fear will be caused by the military leader. Here Num 24:7 is quoted and elaborated upon, corresponding to the use of Lev 26:5 in Praem 93: "For there shall come forth a man, says the oracle, and leading his army and doing battle, he will subdue great and populous nations, because God has sent to his aid the reinforcement which befits the godly, and that is dauntless courage of soul and all-powerful strength of body, either of which strikes fear into the enemy and the two if united are quite irresistible."

The second case deals with "some" who are unworthy to be defeated by men. They will be conquered by swarms of wasps, Praem 96. Here, as in Praem 93, Philo refers to a saying by Moses (φησιν). The reference is to LXX Ex 23:28 (or Deut 7:20): "I will send the wasp before thee . . ."

The concluding part, Praem 97, says that the godly ones will not only win victory, but gain ruling power of the enemies subsequent to the war.[21] Praem 97 then gives a brief catalogue of three virtues which contribute to the ruling power, dignity, strictness, benefaction.

Some observations are of importance for the understanding of Praem 93–97. (1) A comparison with the presentation of the virtue courage (ἀνδρεία) in Virt 34–48 is illuminating. From the story about the victory in the war which the Hebrew army fought against the Midianites (the Arabians), Num 25:1–18 and 31:1–18, Philo sees demonstrated the blessings of Deut 28:1, 2, and 7, and Lev 26:5. The connection is made by ὅθεν, whence, therefore," in Virt 47: "Therefore, he says in his Exhortations, 'If thou pursuest justice and holiness and the other virtues, thou shalt live a life free from war and in unbroken peace, or if war arises, thou shalt easily overcome the foe under the invisible war-leader God, who makes his care mightily to save the good.'"

Since in Virt 34–48 the victorious wars fought by the Hebrews during the exodus from Egypt to Canaan served as the basis for Moses' words about the blessing of peace or victory in wars—provided that they pursue the virtues—then those events are also presupposed as background for Moses' words in Deuteronomy 28 and Leviticus 26 about the blessings of peace or victory in war, Virt 93–97. Thus it is natural that the prophecy about the future "Man," Num 24:7, uttered during the Hebrew army's conflict with

---

21. The τοῦτο with which Praem 97 begins must be changed into τούτους, esp. due to the plural subject of ἐπιτηδεύουσι later in the paragraph. The word τούτους then refers back to τῶν ὁσίων in §96. Goodenough, Cohn and Colson read τούτους, while Bréhier reads τούτον (i.e. the "man" §95). See E. R. Goodenough, The Politics of Philo Judaeus, pp. 115–16.

Balak and his people, has been included in the blessings, *Praem* 93–97, based on Leviticus 26 and Deuteronomy 28.

Both in *Virt* 47 and in *Praem* 95, the Hebrew army is led by a warrior king. The same word is used, στρατάρχεω, "command an army." In *Virt* 47 the commander-in-chief is God, and in *Praem* 95 it is the "man." This double leadership corresponds to the double royal leadership of God and Moses during the exodus, with Moses' kingship derived from that of God (cf. *Vita Mos* I:149–59).

Since Philo in this way has brought the oracle about the "man," Num 24:7 into Moses' description of blessings in Leviticus 26 and Deuteronomy 28, he has not just in a mechanical way accepted a word about Messiah from Scripture. He has deliberately placed Num 24:7 into the new context. The corresponding passage in *Virt* 24 has God as commander-in-chief, a fact which shows that Philo could have excluded the prophecy about the "man" if he had wanted to. These points speak against the scholars who in different ways hold that Philo only pays lip service to Num 24:7 as a word from Scripture, without placing any importance on it in his own thinking or expectations.[22]

(2) U. Fischer states that instead of the enemy being killed in the war, Philo in *Praem* 97 talks of a bloodless (ethical?) victory by the godly people. And they will reign on the basis of the virtues σεμνότης (dignity), δεινότης (shrewdness), and εὐεργεσία (doing good deeds), and not on the basis of military superiority.

Several points speak against Fischer's interpretation. First, the term "bloodless" (ἀναιμωτί) does not exclude the possibility that the enemies were killed, since the Hebrews won a bloodless victory when the Egyptians drowned in the sea when they pursued the Hebrews, *Vita Mos* I:180, cf. *Virt* 38. Bloodless means therefore that the soldiers were not involved in a direct fight. Victory was won by other means, such as through drowning or through wasps (*Praem* 96)[23] or through terror (*Praem* 95), with killing involved, or without.

Moreover, Fischer sees ethical virtues and military warfare as mutually exclusive entities. This is not Philo's view. He applies ethical virtues to the pursuits of war as well as to peacetime activities. Thus some of the examples given in the treatise *On Virtues* are taken from warfare (*Virt* 22–50; 109–18) just as also is the case in the discussion of the virtue "justice" in *Spec* IV:219–25. And the virtues of σεμνότης, δεινότης, and εὐεργεσία (*Praem* 97) are

---

22. Against U. Fischer, *Eschatologie*, pp. 199–202, and J. Drummond, *Philo Judaeus* 2, (London, 1888), p. 322; cf. W. Bousset, *Die Religion des Judentums*, 3. Aufl., p. 439. R. Barraclough, *ANRW* II.21.1, pp. 480–81. In his section on "Die messianische Erlösung," Y. Amir (*Die hellenistische Gestalt*, pp. 31–37) does not discuss *Praem* 95 at all.

23. See Philo's interpretation in *Quaes Exod* II:24 of Ex 23:28 about the assistance of wasps in warfare.

attributes associated with rulers without excluding their military engagements.[24]

In *Praem* 93–97 Philo does not soften the thought that the Hebrew people and its "man" as general-in-chief were to enter into warfare against the enemies. Corresponding to the divine help in the wars fought under the leadership of Moses during the exodus from Egypt God also sent aid to the "man" and made him awe-inspiring and irresistible.

The conclusion of our analysis above of *Vita Mos* I:289–91 harmonizes well with the results of our study of *Praem* 93–97. Three distinctive features of *Praem* 93–97 stand out: (1) While the "man" in *Vita Mos* I:289–91 is seen chiefly as the eschatological emperor who shall rule over many nations and whose kingdom will be spreading every day, he is in *Praem* 95 chiefly seen as the commander-in-chief in the eschatological war, who brings the Hebrew nation to be rulers of the conquered enemies. (2) The eschatological blessing is in *Praem* 93–97 conditioned upon the loyalty and obedience of the Hebrew nation to the commandments in the Laws of Moses and the virtues present in them.

(3) Most important, Philo in *Praem* 93 states clearly that the possibility of eschatological victory might be won by peaceful means, without war. At several places Philo indicates that he favors a peaceful ideological "warfare" rather than a victory won through military war. Even when war was to be fought, the aim was peace for Abraham: "So, then, the man of worth was not merely peaceable and a lover of justice but courageous and warlike, not for the sake of warring . . . but to secure peace for the future . . ." (*Abr* 225).

Thus Philo's preferred approach is indicated by the statement in *Virt* 119–20: "This is what our most holy prophet [Moses] through all his regulations especially desires to create, unanimity, fellowship, unity of mind, blending of dispositions, whereby houses and cities and nations and countries and the whole human race may advance to supreme happiness. Hitherto, indeed, these things live only in our prayers, but they will, I am convinced, become facts beyond all dispute, if God, even as He gives us the yearly fruits, grants that the virtues should bear abundantly. And may some share in them be given to us, who from well-nigh our earliest days have carried with us the yearning to possess them."

The regulations and virtues in Moses' Laws contained, however, stories about wars fought under the leadership of Abraham and Moses, and sections on virtues and divine assistance in wars, extensive sections on kingship, and ideas about the Hebrew nation as the head of all nations, and about a univer-

---

24. Concerning σεμνότης, see for example *Jos* 165 and *Flacc* 4. Concerning δεινότης, see for example *Gaium* 33. Concerning εὐεργεσία, see for example *Vita Mos* I:199 and *Gaium* 148, 284, 323.

sal acceptance of the Mosaic and cosmic laws, and the final reign of the Hebrew nation and its "man," commander-in-chief and emperor, over mankind.
If necessary, this goal would be accomplished through divine intervention in
future wars. The conclusion is this: without using the term "Messiah," Philo
looks for the Messiah to come in the form of "a man" who is seen as a final
commander-in-chief and emperor of the Hebrew nation as the head of the
nations.

Philo puts the emphasis on the cosmic order of the world made manifest
in the biblical events of the past, however, and expresses the conviction that
these events of the past give certainty for the fulfillment of prophecies in the
future. Philo and his fellow Jews hope for shares also now in the blessings to
come. Here lies a motivation for Philo's peaceful ideological warfare to bring
the Law of Moses and its virtues to all nations.

In *Vita Mos* I:289–91 and *Praem* 93–97 a royal warrior is mentioned in an
explicit way. As we turn to *Praem* 165 we find a reference to "a vision divine
and superhuman." Some scholars believe that this also is a reference to the
Messiah. For this reason, and for other reasons, some comments need to be
made on *Praem* 163–72. Some features in this section make an interesting
connection with the two historical books of *To Flaccus* and *On the Legation
to Gaius*, and the central notion of return has important parallels in parts of
Philo's allegorical commentary.

The section 163–72 is based on Lev 26:40ff. and Deut 30:1–7. Lev 26:14–
39 tells about curses which will come upon the Israelites if they do not obey
God and his commandments, after which restoration will take place. According to Deut 30:1–7, the people, when they return to God, will be gathered
to their land from their dispersion among the nations and the curses which
they have suffered will be brought upon their enemies.

Into his paraphrase of Lev 26:40ff. and Deut 30:1–7, Philo brings in much
from Jewish eschatological traditions, as has been shown by several scholars.[25]

In *Praem* 163 the condition for the restoration is conversion. Then the
change from slavery to liberty follows in §164, and the return of the diaspora
will take place, under supernatural guidance (§165). Three intercessors
plead for their reconciliation with the Father (§166–67). The restoration will
lead to new prosperity (§168). A reversal will take place: God will turn the
curses against the enemies of the penitents (§169–71). Finally, new growths
will shoot up from the root of the Hebrew nation (172).

Praem 165 reads: "When they have gained this unexpected liberty, those
who but now were scattered in Greece and the outside world over islands

---

25. See W. Bousset, *Die Religion des Judentums*, 3. Aufl., pp. 236–37; U. Fischer, *Eschatologie*, pp. 202–13.

and continents will arise and post from every side with one impulse to the
one appointed place, guided in their pilgrimage by a vision divine or superhuman unseen by others but manifest to them as they pass from exile to their
home."

The phrase πρός τινος θεοτέρας ἢ κατὰ φύσιν ἀνθρωπίνην ὄψεως, "by
a vision more divine than according to human nature," means, according to
E. R. Goodenough, a vision of a "Man" who is beyond human nature and
will lead them together. L. Cohn states: "Hier findet sich bei Philo auch die
etwas unklare Andeutung von der jüdischen Erwartung eines persönlichen
Messias . . ."[26]

This interpretation is not probable, since the "man" in *Vita Mos* I:289–91
and *Praem* 93–97 is not characterized as a divine vision, θεία ὄψις. In *Vita
Mos* II:252 it is said, however, that there was a divine vision (θεία τις ὄψις)
in the cloud that guarded the Hebrews when they left Egypt. The θεία ὄψις
at the eschatological return then corresponds to the cloud-vision at the exodus, and means the future completion of the exodus to the promised land.[27]

The general conclusion reached in the discussion of *Vita Mos* I:289–91
and *Praem* 93–97 is supported by the several agreements between thoughts
in *Praem* 163–72 and the treatises *To Flaccus* and *On the Legation of Gaius*.
Fischer has pointed out several of these similarities: (a) According to *Praem*
165, Hebrew people were scattered in Greece and the barbarian world over
islands and continents. The same general picture of the Diaspora is found in
Flacc 45–46; *Gaium* 214 and 281–83.

(b) The descriptions of the enemies in *Praem* 169–71 are largely the same
as points found in *To Flaccus* and *On the Legation to Gaius*: enemies rejoiced
in the misfortunes of the nation, *Praem* 169 and *Gaium* 122, 359, 361, 368;
Flacc 34; their cruelty, *Praem* 171 and *Flacc* 59–66; they rejoiced in their
misfortunes, *Praem* 169 and *Gaium* 137 (353–54); lamentations, *Praem* 171
and *Gaium* 197, 225; the enemies proclaimed public holidays on the days
of their misfortunes and feasted on their mourning, *Praem* 171 and *Flacc*
116–18.

It should be added that the principle of reversal is stated both in *Praem*
169 and *Flacc* 170. In *Praem* 169 it says that reversal of all things will take
place, for God will turn the curses against the enemies of the penitent Hebrews. Correspondingly, Flaccus says in *Flacc* 170: "all the acts which I
madly committed against the Jews I have suffered myself." The use of the
curse of Deut 28:67, both in *Praem* 151 and in *Flacc* 167, illustrates this
point. Deut 28:67 reads "In the morning you shall say, 'Would it were eve-

26. E. R. Goodenough, *Politics*, p. 117; L. Cohn, *et al.*, *Philo von Alexandria* (Die Werke in
deutscher Übersetzung, 2. Aufl. 2.; Berlin, 1962), p. 382.

27. See W. Bousset, *Die Religion des Judentums*, 3. Aufl., p. 237; F. H. Colson, *Philo with an
English Translation*, 8 (Loeb, Cambridge, Mass., 1934, repr. 1960), p. 418; Y. Amir, *Die hellenistische Gestalt*, pp. 33–34; U. Fischer, *Eschatologie*, p. 205.

ning!' and at evening you shall say, 'Would it were morning!' because of the dread which your heart shall fear, and the sights which your eyes shall see." In *Praem* 151 the verse is paraphrased and applied to the disobedient Hebrews, while in *Flacc* 167 it is applied to Flaccus.

These agreements show that the principles at work according to *Praem* 127–72 were already at work in historical events of Philo's own time. Moreover, they support the view that the national and nationalistic motifs present in *On the Life of Moses* and the *Exposition of the Law* were central to Philo himself. U. Fischer is therefore mistaken when he tries to isolate *Praem* 162–72 from the rest of Philo's writings.[28]

Finally, a comment should be made on the question of allegorization. Since the specific laws and the special position of the Hebrew people reflect and are in harmony with cosmic law and cosmic citizenship, then the heavenly reality, and the general cosmic philosophical, ethical, and psychological principles are the foundation and the dynamic force at work in the life of this people and in its relationship to the rest of the world. Accordingly, when a non-Jew becomes a Jewish proselyte, he secures for himself a place in heaven, while the Jewish apostates are dragged down to hell, to Tartarus (*Praem* 152).

The various interpretations may be illustrated by Philo's use of Deut 30:4 in *Praem* 115, 164–65 and *Conf* 197: those who dwell in the uttermost parts of the earth (in Greece and the barbarian world) in slavery to those who led them away captive (*Praem* 164–65) live in the spiritual dispersion which vice has wrought (115) and have been living in exile for many a day under the ban of folly's tyranny (*Conf* 197), they will arise and travel from every side with one impulse to the one appointed place (*Praem* 165), not despair of a restoration to the land of wisdom and virtue (115); they shall receive their recall under a single proclamation, even the proclamation enacted and ratified by God, as the oracles show, in which it is declared that "'if thy dispersion be from one end of heaven to the other he shall gather thee from thence' [Deut 30:4]. Thus it is a work well-benefitting to God to bring into full harmony the consonance of the virtues. . . ."

Since the foundation of the Hebrew nation and its native land is the cosmic and national laws of Moses, their divine virtues and wisdom, it follows that the return to these laws, virtues, and wisdom is the basis of the national and geographical return to Palestine. Thus the literal and allegorical interpretations are interwoven, and the concrete national and "messianic" eschatology and the general, cosmic principles belong together. To Philo, the special theological role of the Jewish nation is central, both on the historical and the cosmic/universal level, a well as within the context of futuristic eschatology. The expectation of a messianic emperor is not as central, but it

28. U. Fischer, *Eschatologie*, pp. 202–13.

forms *a natural and integral part* of the thinking of Philo, since he emphasizes the role of Moses as king and entertains an ideology of kingship as part
of the Jewish legislation. Accordingly, the concept of a future messianic emperor is not an alien element in his exegesis and in his expectations for the
future.

PART FIVE

"THE MESSIAH" AND JESUS OF NAZARETH

J. D. G. DUNN 17

MESSIANIC IDEAS AND THEIR INFLUENCE ON THE JESUS OF HISTORY

INTRODUCTION

Jesus was a Jew. It is inconceivable that he was *not* "influenced" by Jewish "ideas." This uncontroversial *a priori* conceals potentially explosive issues. In particular, it leads naturally to a whole sequence of follow-up questions. To what extent was Jesus' whole message and ministry shaped and determined by particular ideas which came to him as part of his Jewish upbringing, character, and context? To what extent was the movement which sprang from Jesus shaped and determined by these same Jewish ideas, and to what extent by other (non-Jewish) forces? Does Jesus belong more to the Judaism from which he emerged or to the Christianity which resulted from his ministry? Did Jesus inject something new and different into his ancestral faith and practice, and can he therefore be credited (or blamed) for the consequent transformation which within two or three generations led to the schism between (rabbinic) Judaism and Christianity?

Such are the wider issues with still wider ramifications which surround the more specific issue. Was Jesus influenced by current Jewish messianic ideas? Did he see himself or his ministry as the fulfillment of his people's hopes and aspirations for the future? Even this topic is huge, and impossible to tackle at more than an overview level within the scope of a single paper. Nevertheless the issue is potentially of immense significance and it is important that such a summary treatment be attempted as part of the wider inquiry of this colloquy.

Definitions

The terms used need to be defined with some care, lest we find ourselves arguing at cross purposes: (a) What do we mean by "messianic ideas"? Are we referring to: (i) Specific figures of whom the word "messiah" is used—in Jewish circles prior to Jesus or also in the first century C.E. as a whole? (ii) "Messiah" as redefined within earliest Christianity, not the least by drawing

365

in other motifs and passages of the OT not previously regarded as "messianic"? (iii) The range of Jewish eschatological expectation (the "messianic age"), including expectations where no figure as such is specified, as well as the whole range of revelatory or redemptive or judgmental figures who feature within the kaleidoscope of diverse Jewish hopes and visions? In short, what can we say *might* have influenced Jesus (or any of his contemporaries) on the theme of "messiahship"? Since the issues are mutually entangled and a too narrow definition could shut off possible sources of influence too quickly, I will try to keep the inquiry as broad as possible within the constraints of the paper.

(b) "The Jesus of history" as popularly used denotes the Jesus who ministered within Palestine during the late 20s and/or early 30s of the common era—"the historical Jesus," "Jesus as he actually was." NT scholars sometimes disparage this more popular usage and insist on a more restricted definition—"the Jesus of history," in some antithesis to "the Christ of faith/dogma," or Jesus insofar as he may be reconstructed by the tools of historical criticism. The problem with the former is that it makes too sharp a distinction between the "before and after" of Easter; it will hardly be disputed that Jesus made a considerable impact during his ministry—that is, before Good Friday and Easter. It would be unwise to predetermine what that impact could have involved in terms of "messianic ideas" or to assume that talk of either "Christ" or "faith" before Easter is inadmissible. The problem with the latter is that methodological presuppositions may impose a grid upon the text and prevent us from including within our evidence matter which is highly relevant. For the purposes of this paper I prefer to attempt a more open-ended inquiry into what "messianic ideas" we can say with some historical probability actually did influence Jesus in his ministry and in what he said about it.

Both these areas, of context and of methodology, need some fuller exposition before we proceed. To avoid overextending this study, however, I will restrict the discussion of Jewish "messianic ideas" chiefly to those sources and Jewish writings which most probably predated or were contemporary with Jesus. This is not to deny that later documents may contain earlier traditions, but the need to demonstrate the earlier form of any tradition would involve some complex analysis and disrupt the form of the overview here offered. Besides which the undisputedly pre-Jesus traditions already provide substantial material and a relatively clear perspective on the range of options which must certainly have been "available" to Jesus and his contemporaries.[1]

---

1. For a more extensive survey, see J. H. Charlesworth, "The Concept of the Messiah in the Pseudepigrapha," *ANRW* II.19.1 (1979), pp. 188–218.

What "Messianic Ideas" Were in Current Use or Available As Categories of Possible Definition at the Time of Jesus?

(a) The category of "messiah" itself.

(i) Most important here is the hoped-for Davidic or *royal* messiah—so designated explicitly in the Psalms of Solomon 17 (see esp. 17:32; cf. 18:57), and *Shemoneh 'Esreh* 14, and almost certainly in view in the DSS's designation of the "messiah of Israel" (1QSa 2.12, 14, 20; also 1QS 9.11; cf. CD 12.23f.; 14.19; 19.10; 20.1).[2] This more specific language is clearly part of a richer strain influenced both by other "messiah" references with eschatological overtones (1Sam 2:10; Pss 2:2, 89:51, 132:17; Dan 9:25–26); and by specific promises regarding the Davidic dynasty—David's son/God's son (2Sam 7:12–4; 4QFlor 1.10–13), the royal "branch" (Jer 23:5 and 33:15; 4QPat 3–4 and 4QFlor 1.11), and the Davidic "prince" (Ezek 34:24 and 37:25; CD 7.20, 1QSb 5.20, 1QM 5.1, 4Q161); see also Isa 11:1–2; Hag 2:23; Zech 3:8, 4, 6:12; Sir 47:11, 22; 1Mac 2:57. We may conclude that these passages must have nurtured a fairly vigorous and sustained hope of a royal messiah within several at least of the various subgroups of Israel at the time of Jesus, and that that hope was probably fairly widespread at a popular level (such being the symbolic power of kingship in most societies then and since).[3] Talk of an expected "coming of the Messiah" would have been meaningful to first-century Jews and represented a major strand of Jewish eschatological expectations.[4]

(ii) "Messiah" is also used of a hoped-for *priest* figure. This is explicit in the same "messiahs of Aaron and Israel" references from Qumran (1QS 9.11 etc.) and in TReu 6:8 (ἀρχιερεὺς χριστός)—the high priest being also an anointed office (Lev 4:3, 5, 16; 6:22; 2Mac 1:10; cf. Ps 84:9). But it is closely modeled on the Moses-Aaron and Zerubbabel-Joshua (Zechariah 4) dual role, with T12P showing a similar concern to rank the priestly figure above the royal figure (particularly TJud 21:2–5), such as is also evident in 1QSa 2.11–22. The influence of this double expectation is indicated in the possible association of the priest Eleazar with Bar Kokhba in the leadership of the second revolt.[5] We should note also here TMos 9:1—the expectation regard-

---

2. L. H. Schiffman's cautions (during the colloquy) on identifying the Messiah of Israel as Davidic are methodologically commendable, but since a clear Davidic hope is entertained in the DSS [see (i) above], and since the Messiah of Israel associated with a Messiah of Aaron (1QS 9.11) would most naturally be understood as a reference to a royal messiah [see (ii) above], it is hard to know how else the "Messiah of Israel" would be understood other than as a way of designating the hoped-for Davidic branch or prince.

3. See further R. A. Horsley and J. S. Hanson, *Bandits, Prophets, and Messiahs: Popular Movements in the Time of Jesus* (Minneapolis, 1985), ch. 3.

4. See further E. Schürer, *The History of the Jewish People in the Age of Jesus Christ*, rev. G. Vermes *et al.* (Edinburgh, 1979), vol. 2, §29.

5. Schürer, *History*, vol. 1, p. 544.

ing Taxo, "a man from the tribe of Levi." A further element which should be reckoned within the total picture is the promise of a "covenant of perpetual priesthood" made to Phinehas (Num 25:10–13), which evidently fascinated and influenced more than one branch of early Judaism (Sir 45:23–24; 1Mac 2:54; *LAB* 48:1), not the least the Zealots.[6]

(b) When the category of "messiah" broadens out, the first to be considered is the *prophet*, not least since anointing can be associated also with prophets (1Kgs 19:16; Isa 61:1–2; Joel 3:1; CD 2.12, 6.1; cf. Ps 105:15). But beyond that, the expectation becomes diverse and unclear, with various strands or fragments evident whose relation to each other is far from clear. (i) Least problematic is the anticipated return of Elijah (Mal 4:5; Sir 48:9–10; see also 1En 90:31, Rev 11:3); but whether this was confined to the thought of Elijah's personal return (he had never died) or included the idea of a further prophet, Elisha-like, "in the spirit and power of Elijah" (Lk 1:17: cf. 2Kgs 2:15), remains uncertain. (ii) The hope of a prophet like Moses (Deut 18:15, 18) might have been expected to generate considerable expectation, but the only clear evidence of its influence in pre-Christian Judaism comes in the Qumran Testimonies (4QTestim 5–8); though we should note that according to Josephus, *Ant* 20:97, 169–70, Theudas and the Egyptian saw themselves both as "prophet" and as successor to Moses (dividing Jordan, and causing city walls to fall down). (iii) For the rest there is a scattering of evidence difficult to correlate: "the prophet" (1QS 9.11 = the Moses prophet of 4QTestim?; cf. Jn 6:14; 7:40, 52; how different from 1Mac 4:46 and 14:41?; cf. Josephus, *War* 6:285); the anointed one of Isa 61:1–2 (used in 1QH 18:14–15 and 11QMelch); "a prophet" (Mk 6:15, 8:28) or "one of the old prophets risen" (Lk 9:8; cf. Mt 16:14); Samaritan expectation focused particularly on a prophet figure, but our evidence does not enable us to reach a firm conclusion on whether such a hope was already entertained at the time of Jesus.[7]

Whether these are diverse expressions of a single broad but vague conviction that some prophet figure was bound to be part of any eschatological climax is impossible to say. And how this variegated expectation related to the hopes of one or more messiahs (§1.2a) is also obscure—even in the one text which mentions all three together (1QS 9:11); perhaps it was simply an expression of a similarly imprecise conviction that the three main offices in Israel's salvation-history (king, priest, prophet) must surely be represented in any new age. In particular there is no indication that the idea of Elijah coming as the precursor or forerunner of another (*the* Messiah?) was already current in pre-Christian Judaism outside Christian sources (particularly Mk

6. M. Hengel, *The Zealots* (Edinburgh: T. & T. Clark, 1989), pp. 171–77; Schürer, *History*, vol. 2, pp. 598–606.

7. Schürer, *History*, vol. 2, p. 513.

9:11); the relevance and point of Mal 3:1 is unclear (the forerunner of God?);[8] and though a forerunner role could have been claimed by the Baptist (cf. Jn 1:23 with 1QS 8:13–14, 9:19–20 and Mk 1:3 par.), the question both of Christian editing and of whom he might have meant by "the one stronger than me" (Mk 1:7 pars.) remains open.

(c) When we turn to OT motifs and passages which seem first to have been given a messianic significance by application to Jesus, the focus of the discussion shifts. For in this case we cannot speak properly of "messianic ideas" already abroad at the time of Jesus; though since, in the event, a messianic significance has been claimed by Christianity, we should presumably allow a category of "potentially messianic ideas," which might within the constraints of the Jewish history of revelation, tradition, and hermeneutics be candidates for application to a putative messiah. Here the whole range of interest in the suffering righteous man would have to come under consideration,[9] including not the least the "suffering servant" of Second Isaiah. It is beyond doubt that Isaiah 53 in particular played an important role in earliest Christian apologetic on behalf of a crucified Messiah (Acts 8:32–33; Rom 4:25; 1Pet 2:22–25; etc.); the real question for us would be whether it was Jesus himself who first drew the passage as such, or the motif in general, into play, or whether its potential as a messianic proof text only became evident in the wake of Jesus' death.

Under this heading should also be mentioned the figure of Daniel 7, "one like a son of man." The continued fecundity of this theme in NT scholarship is remarkable,[10] though too much of the debate is repetitive. I continue to see no evidence for the existence of a pre-Christian/pre-Jesus Son of Man expectation within Judaism. Daniel 7 is not itself evidence of such speculation,[11] though clearly it is a "potentially messianic" passage. The Similitudes of Enoch, which do make messianic use of Daniel 7 cannot be dated to the period before Jesus' ministry with any confidence; they appear to be making a fresh interpretation of Daniel 7 (as also 4 Ezra); and probable influence on

---

8. See the brief review of the evidence in J. Jeremias, *TDNT*, vol. 2, pp. 931f.

9. See particularly G. W. E. Nickelsburg, *Resurrection, Immortality, and Eternal Life in Intertestamental Judaism* (Cambridge, Mass., 1972).

10. For example, R. Leivestad, "Jesus-Messias—Menschensohn: Die jüdischen Heilandserwartungen zur Zeit der ersten römischen Kaiser und die Frage nach dem messianischen Selbstbewusstsein Jesu," *ANRW* II.25.1, pp. 220–64; B. Lindars, *The Son of Man* (London, 1983); S. Kim, *"The Son of Man" as the Son of God* (WUNT 30; Tübingen, 1983); M. Müller, *Der Ausdruck "Menschensohn" in den Evangelien* (Leiden, 1984); C. Caragounis, *The Son of Man* (WUNT 38; Tübingen, 1986); D.R.A. Hare, *The Son of Man Tradition* (Minneapolis: Fortress, 1990).

11. At this point I should register my cordial disagreement with colloquy colleagues M. Black and A. Yarbro Collins: I do not see the manlike figure of Dan 7:13–14 as an "angelic representative" of Israel, but as a symbolical representation of Israel, in which the creation myth is reworked (Dan 7:2ff.) by depicting Israel's enemies as the beasts (beastlike figures) over which man (the manlike figure, Israel) is given dominion.

the Synoptic tradition is confined to the later strata. The lack of any clear
confessional or apologetic identification of Jesus with "the [well-known] Son
of Man" would be very surprising if such a powerful image was already in use
at the time of Jesus (contrast 1En 71:14, Knibb).[12] Here too then the question
is not of influence on Jesus of already recognized and established ideas or
categories. The question is rather whether an innovative use of Daniel 7 can
be ascribed to Jesus himself or can be traced back only as far as the first
Christians in the post-Easter Palestinian conventicles. Here too earliest
Christian thought (including Jesus?) has to be seen itself as *part* of the development and transformation in the messianic ideas of the period, and not
merely as reactive to ideas already in existence.

(d) Beyond this, the category of "messianic ideas" becomes too ill-defined
to be of much use. Should we include glorification of heroes like Phinehas
(Ps 106:30–31; Sir 45:23–24; 1Mac 2:54; 4Mac 18:12), or the idea of a human
translated to heaven without death (Enoch—Jub 4:23, 1En 12:4, TAb 11) or
after death (Ezra and Baruch—4Ezra 14:9; 2Bar 13:3, 25:1; etc.) or given
roles in the final judgment (Enoch, Elijah, Abel—1En 90:31; TAb 11; Melchizedek (?)—11QMelch)? Should we include heavenly intermediaries—
angels (e.g. Dan 10:13, Tob 12:15, 1En 9:1–3, TLevi 3:5, 1QH 6:13) or the
vigorous poetic imagery used of divine wisdom (e.g. Prov 8:30; WisSol 9:4;
Sir 24:5)?[13] For myself I think not. The full spectrum of eschatological expectation within Judaism, so far as we know it, should be borne in mind, including the visions in which no recognized or potential messianic figure appears.
For any or all of it could have influenced Jesus, and have interacted in his
teaching and ministry with more specifically "messianic ideas" to evolve a
new formulation or idea. But in that case we are talking of the eschatological
or apocalyptic context of the messianic ideas more than the ideas themselves. In view of the limitations of the paper, therefore, I do not propose to
go into any detail on this broader area of interest.

Methodology and Perspective

A final word of introduction must be said about the perspective from
which I approach the Jesus tradition of the Synoptics, where the debate must
obviously focus most intensively. Such a declaration is necessary since it is
very clear from the study of the Synoptic tradition during the past sixty years
that the critical tools do not of themselves provide clear verdicts on most
debated passages. Agreed criteria for determining redaction simply do not

---

12. See further my *Christology in the Making* (London, Philadelphia, 1980), pp. 67–82. My
point is unaffected even if there is an emerging consensus on a pre-70 date for the Similitudes
(Charlesworth), since the other evidence just indicated would still point to a post-Jesus, post-
earliest Christian date for the document or its ideas coming to public attention.

13. See further J. D. G. Dunn, "Was Christianity a Monotheistic Faith from the Beginning?"
SJT 35 (1982) 303–36; *The Partings of the Ways Between Christianity and Judaism* (London:
SCM; Philadelphia: T.P.I., 1991), ch. 10.

exist beyond a few general principles—and when it becomes a question of distinguishing multiple layers of tradition, the argument becomes increasingly circular and the subjectivity factor unacceptably high. Probability judgment in most individual cases therefore depends on a broad presuppositional perspective bolstered by a few key examples.[14]

In my own work, not specializing on the Synoptics so thoroughly as many of my colleagues, I have become increasingly persuaded that the best *starting* point for study of the main body of the Synoptic tradition is to view it as the earliest churches' memories of Jesus as retold and reused by these churches. The importance of teachers and of tradition is well attested in the earliest documents of the NT (e.g. teachers—Acts 13:1, 1Cor 12:28, Gal 6:6; tradition—1Cor 11:2, Col 2:6, 1Thes 4:1, 2Thes 2:15 and 3:6). The Synoptics themselves conform surprisingly closely to the ancient (not modern) biography (*bios* or *vita*);[15] and the *a priori* probability that the earliest groups cherished and rehearsed the memories of the one whom they now counted as Lord (*mar*, κύριος), that is, the traditions which gave them reason for their distinctive existence, must be regarded as strong. This perspective differs significantly from the characteristically *literary* model which has exercised far too much influence on tradition-history analysis of the Synoptic tradition. The literary model envisages strata of tradition, and the task as tracing the linear descent of a tradition down through successively elaborated layers, each one dependent on the previous exemplar—much as one does in textual criticism or in tracing the history of translations of the Bible. But in *oral* transmission that model is inappropriate, for in oral tradition we have to do with themes and formulae and core material which often remains constant while quite a wide range of variations are played on them. The point is that one variation need not necessarily lead to another; subsequent variations may be derived directly from the central theme or core. Consequently tradition history analysis seeking to penetrate back to Jesus himself need not consist solely of pressing back through different variations but can focus immediately on the more constant material. For the probability is that the more constant material is the living heart of the earliest recollections of Jesus which has maintained the vitality of the tradition in all its variant forms.

In short I see the earliest tradents within the Christian churches as preservers more than innovators, as seeking to transmit, retell, explain, interpret, elaborate, but not to create *de nova*. All of which means that I approach the Synoptic tradition with a good deal more confidence than many of my New Testament colleagues. Through the main body of the Synoptic tradition, I believe, we have in most cases direct access to the teaching and min-

---

14. E. P. Sanders, *Jesus and Judaism* (London, 1985), despite his trenchant criticism of his predecessors, provides a classic example.

15. D. Aune, *The New Testament in Its Literary Environment* (Philadelphia, 1987, ch. 2).

istry of Jesus as it was remembered from the beginning of the transmission process (which often predates Easter), and so also fairly direct access to the ministry and teaching of Jesus through the eyes and ears of whose who went about with him.

So much by way of introduction. What then of the issue itself: what messianic ideas influenced Jesus and how?

JESUS WITHIN A CONTEXT OF ESCHATOLOGICAL EXPECTATION

We can start by noting the likelihood that Jesus would have been aware of such messianic ideas as were current at the time. The strong eschatological note which is an undeniable feature of his preaching is of a piece with the broader stream of eschatological and apocalyptic expectation which served as the seed bed within which messianic ideas flourished during the various crises of Israel's history in the two centuries prior to Jesus' ministry. No one, I think, would dispute either that Jesus' proclamation of the kingdom of God was central to his preaching, or that his remembered utterances on the subject are essentially eschatological in character. We need not even go into the still contested question of whether he saw the kingdom as a future good ("the restoration of Israel")[16] or present reality, or both, though I would have to contest any attempt to argue that Jesus saw it as a timeless symbol (and therefore, properly speaking, noneschatological).

Given this eschatological context and emphasis, it would be utterly astonishing if Jesus had not come into some sort of interaction with the messianic ideas which thrived in that same context. Without making any prejudgment on the question of whether Jesus saw a role for himself with regard to the kingdom, it nevertheless remains highly likely that one who proclaimed the kingdom of God in the way Jesus did would be faced with the issue of how his eschatological ideas related to the other (messianic) ideas cherished by others.

Moreover, we must accept that Jesus made a substantial stir, even if only for a short time, and that he gained a fair amount of publicity and/or notoriety, however local or regional—he was, after all, condemned to death for causing some sort of trouble. In such circumstances his fellow Jews (or Galileans) were bound to attempt to categorize him, to fit him into an appropriate slot in their perspective. And the available categories would have included the ones reviewed above: was he one of the looked-for anointed figures? was he a/the prophet? In other words, the tradition of popular speculation and questioning which we find in Mk 6:15, 8:28, and Jn 1:19–22 is just what we might have expected.

---

16. Sanders, *Jesus*, part one; Dunn, *Partings*, pp. 47–49.

But can we be more specific? More important, can we say whether Jesus reacted to these suggestions and questions? And if so, *how* he reacted? Only thus will we be able to speak of any influence of such messianic ideas on him. We naturally start with the messianic idea most narrowly defined as such in the above review—Jesus as messiah.

ARE YOU MESSIAH? A QUESTION JESUS MUST HAVE FACED

We can dismiss at once the second of the two messiah figures described above—the *priest* messiah. There is no indication whatsoever that this was ever canvassed as a possibility or seen as an option in the case of Jesus. Presumably Jesus was known to lack the basic qualification of belonging to the tribe of Levi, and so it was a nonstarter even for (or particularly for) those who would have regarded the priestly messiah as more significant than the royal messiah. Significantly when the attempt is subsequently made to present Jesus as High Priest, it is done by using the quite different and extraordinary order of Melchizedek rather than that of Aaron (Heb 5:7).

The picture is quite different, however, in the case of the *royal* messiah. The fundamental fact here is that Jesus was put to death as a claimant to such a role—executed as a messianic pretender for claiming to be king of the Jews (so all four Gospels—Mk 15:26 par.). Since "king of the Jews" is not a Christian title and probably caused the Christians some political embarrassment, there is a general agreement that this much at least must be historical of the passion narratives. But once that is granted, along with the fact of Jesus' crucifixion as a royal messianic pretender, a sentence carried out as a formal legal act on the authority of the Roman governor (cf. Tacitus, *Ann* 15.44.3),[17] we have established the core of the hearing before Pilate described in Mk 15:1–4. And when we press further backward to the issue of some sort of preliminary Jewish hearing, we find ourselves with an equally plausible historical core—where an accusation that Jesus said something about the destruction and rebuilding of the temple results in the question, "Are you Messiah, son of the Blessed?" (Mk 14:57–61). For it was precisely this association of ideas which the messianic prophecy (4QFlor 1:10–13) of 2Sam 7:13–14 would suggest—the son of David (royal messiah) who would build the temple and who would be God's son.[18] In short, the evidence is strong that at the end of his life Jesus was confronted with the question, certainly implicitly but probably also explicitly as well: Are you Messiah, son of David?

It is also unlikely that this was the first or only time in the course of Jesus' ministry that this question was put to him or the issue confronted him. Assuming that Jesus did say something about the future of the temple, on

---

17. See further particularly A. E. Harvey, *Jesus and the Constraints of History* (London, 1982), chap. 2.

18. O. Betz, *What Do We Know About Jesus?* (London, 1968), pp. 88–89.

which the later accusation was based (Mk 14:58 par.; cf. esp. Mk 13:2, Jn 2:19, Acts 6:14), and that Jesus engaged in some sort of symbolic act in the temple (Mk 11:15–17 pars.),[19] the same correlation (Messiah = temple builder) probably occurred to him and to others (hence the subsequent accusation). Given too the excitement he engendered as a successful healer, it would be of no surprise that one such as Bartimaeus should seek to attract his attention or ingratiate himself with Jesus by hailing him as "Son of David" (Mk 10:47–48 par.).[20]

The confession of Peter at Caesarea Philippi is a much contested pericope (Mk 8:27ff. par.) whose detail we can hardly enter into here. Suffice it to say its basic content carries with it a strong degree of probability: Jesus had engaged for some time in what had evidently been overall a highly successful and popular teaching and healing ministry. It would have been odd indeed if none of those who had invested their lives in following him had not asked themselves whether Jesus might be the hoped-for leader from the house of David and in due course expressed the belief or hope to Jesus himself.

To mention only one other episode. If we allow that behind the "feeding of the five thousand" (Mk 6:30ff. par.) lies the memory of some symbolic meal in the desert, such a meal would probably have evoked a very potent mix of messianic ideas—Moses and manna, the shepherd king feeding his flock (Ezek 34:23), perhaps the same association of eschatological banquets presided over by the messiah(s) which we find in 1QSa. It is not surprising then that John's Gospel contains the testimony that the crowd wanted to make Jesus king by force (Jn 6:15), which meshes well in an uncontrived way with the unexpected note in Mark's Gospel that Jesus brought the occasion to an end by *forcing* the disciples to leave by boat, *before* he dismissed the crowd. There is a strong suggestion here of a crowd caught up on a wave of messianic enthusiasm which affected also the immediate circle of Jesus' disciples. Here too, in other words, Jesus was probably confronted in effect with the same stark question, "Are you Messiah, son of David?"

This brief review of the most directly relevant evidence must suffice. In my judgment it presents us with the very strong probability that Jesus was confronted with the category of royal messiahship and was forced, whether he liked it or not, to respond to it. The more important question for us is: how did he respond? What sort of influence did the prevailing or dominant expectation regarding the royal messiah have on him?

The answer which emerges is consistent and striking. He reacted more negatively than positively to it. As a possible role model he was more hostile than welcoming to the idea of the royal messiah. The evidence can be reviewed briefly.

19. See particularly Sanders, *Jesus*, ch. 1.

20. The argument here is not dependent on an early date for TSol or for the traditions behind it; David was already regarded as a healer (ἰατρός) and exorcist in the case of Saul, as Josephus, *Ant.* 6:166–68, indicates.

A basic fact is that nowhere in the Synoptic tradition is Jesus remembered as having laid claim to the title or role of messiah on his own initiative (only Jn 4:26). Since the earliest Christians certainly wanted to claim the title for him, the silence of the Synoptic tradition is striking: it confirms an unwillingness to retroject material beyond what Jesus was remembered as teaching back into the Jesus tradition; and since the claim to such a role was certainly a possibility for Jesus (as in principle for many first-century Jews), the fact that no such claim is remembered suggests at least an unwillingness on the part of Jesus to associate his mission with that particular role.

This inference gains strength from some of the episodes touched on above. The "feeding of the five thousand" pericope has two points of interest. First, it confirms that there was abroad, in Galilee at least, a popular conception of the messiah as a kingly, political figure—the sort of king of the Jews, we might say, that Pilate felt justified in crucifying. Second, it indicates that Jesus reacted *against* this role and rejected it. The lesson learned there, about the inflammability of the Galilean crowd, would certainly help explain Jesus' reticence in other situations.

In the Caesarea Philippi episode the earlier account of Mark shows Jesus as neither welcoming nor denying the confession of Peter (though Matthew understandably develops the tradition to give Jesus' response a warmer note—Mt 16:17–19). The command to silence of Mk 8:30, so often taken as part of a theological motif later imposed on the tradition,[21] makes very good sense if the category "messiah" used by Peter was the same as that cherished in the Psalms of Solomon and among the Galileans. Since that indeed *was* what Messiah, son of David meant, the only content of the category "royal messiah" as then understood, we may assume that in any such historical confrontation this *would* have been the prospect offered to Jesus. The ambivalence of his immediate response thus becomes indicative of a certain unwillingness on the part of Jesus to entertain such a political role. And if the immediately appended teaching on the prospect of his suffering and rejection (Mk 8:31–33) belongs to the same sequence as remembered by those involved, as is certainly arguable, then we would have to begin speaking of an attempt by Jesus to redefine the category of messiahship.

Finally with the hearing and trial of Jesus the interest again focuses on Jesus' reply in each case. To the High Priest's question Jesus is shown as answering "I am" (Mk 14:62). But the more weakly attested longer reading has a strong claim to originality—"You say that I am."[22] In which case it

---

21. I refer of course to "the Messianic secret"; see e.g. C. Tuckett, ed., *The Messianic Secret* (London, Philadelphia, 1983).

22. The longer reading explains the Matthean and Lukan versions better than the shorter:

Mark	σὺ εἶπας	ὅτι ἐγώ εἰμι
Matt	σὺ εἶπας	
Luke	ὑμεῖς λέγετε	ὅτι ἐγώ εἰμι.

And it is more likely that the equivocal longer text was abbreviated to the strong affirmation (ἐγώ εἰμι) rather than the reverse.

matches more closely the reply to the equivalent question by Pilate, "Are you the king of the Jews?" To which Jesus is said to have responded, σὺ λέγεις (you say so) (Mk 15:2). In each case, therefore, the answer probably was ambivalent—"You could say so"; "that is your way of putting it." In other words, we can see here a further indication of an unwillingness on the part of Jesus to accept the title of royal messiah, at least as understood by his questioners. For our enquiry the exchanges are important since they exemplify the dilemma which constantly must have confronted Jesus: could he accept or use categories which, however desirable in themselves, were usually understood to describe a role he did not or could not see himself as fulfilling?

In short, if the question is "Did the hope of a royal messiah influence Jesus in shaping and executing his mission?" the evidence points to a fairly negative answer. Jesus seems to have reacted against rather than to have been influenced by the idea of a royal messiah as then conceived. The only qualification we would have to add is that this title "messiah" was too potent and resonant with theological significance for it to be rejected outright. And Jesus may have attempted to redefine the content of the title in terms of the role he saw himself as filling. The first Christians were certainly in no doubt that Jesus was Messiah and that the title had to be understood in the light of what had actually happened to Jesus ("Christ crucified"). But the extent to which we can say that the process of redefinition began already with Jesus himself depends on our evaluation of other material within the Jesus tradition which at the time of Jesus would not have been regarded as "messianic" in the stricter sense.

THE ESCHATOLOGICAL PROPHET

In terms of messianic categories properly so called at the time of Jesus, the only other category of significance is that of *prophet*. Of all the categories available, it seems to have been the one which was used most often. It was evidently applied to the Baptist (Mk 11:32; Mt 11:9; Lk 7:26); it was the category canvassed most frequently for Jesus, according to Mk 6:15 and 8:28 (cf. 14:65; note also particularly Mt 21:11, 46 and Lk 24:19); and there seems to have been no lack of claimants to the role of prophet during that whole period (Josephus, *Ant* 18:85–87; 20:97–98, 167–72, 188). Given the relative prominence of Jesus as preacher and healer, it is wholly to be expected that he would have been regarded by many as at least *a* prophet.

Jesus himself is remembered as accepting the designation for himself in at least some degree (see particularly Mk 6:4 par. and Lk 13:33). But more important is the evidence that he, like the Qumran sect, made use of Isa 61:1–2, as providing a program for his mission. The primary evidence is not Lk 4:18–19, which looks too much like an elaboration of the briefer account of Jesus' preaching in the synagogue at Nazareth as recalled by Mark. It is rather the emphasis which comes out both from the first beatitude (Lk 6:20/ Mt 5:3), and from Jesus' response to the question of the Baptist in prison (Mt 11:5/Lk 7:22)—viz. that Jesus saw one of his priorities as proclamation of the good news to "the poor."[23] If this recalls one of Jesus' own repeated assertions, as seems likely, then the implication is strong that he drew on Isa 61:1–2 to inform his own mission. This also makes best sense of the Lukan account of Jesus' preaching in Nazareth, for Lk 4:16–30 is then best seen not as a complete fabrication by Luke but as the sort of midrashic elaboration of a basic claim made by Jesus which we would expect in the course of oral retelling of the memories regarding Jesus, with Luke of course setting it at the beginning of his account of Jesus' ministry to give it programmatic significance for his own retelling of the Jesus story.

Relevant here too is the fact that Jesus is remembered as having spoken on more than one occasion of his sense of commission in prophetic terms— as one "sent" by God (Mt 10:40/Lk 10:16; Mk 9:37 par.; Mt 15:24; Lk 4:43).[24] Also that Jesus evidently undertook what might be called a self-consciously prophetic role—both in terms of his championing "the poor," and in terms of such prophetically symbolical actions like the entry into Jerusalem, the clearing of the temple, perhaps the meal in the desert, and certainly the Last Supper.

All this is significant, for so far as the Evangelists were concerned, the category of prophet was not particularly helpful and certainly not of sufficient weight to embody the significance of Jesus. Part of the point of the Caesarea Philippi episode in all the Synoptics is that prophet categories canvassed by the crowds are less satisfactory (even that of Elijah) than the title ascribed by Peter—"You are the Messiah" (Mk 8:28–29 par.). The point of Mt 12:41 (and Lk 11:32) is that something *greater* than Jonah is present among them. According to Lk 16:16, the time of the law and the prophets has been left behind by the new era in which the kingdom of God is preached. And most striking of all, the category of prophet, even *the* prophet, has been completely relegated by the Fourth Evangelist to the status of one of the less than satisfactory opinions of the fickle crowd (particularly Jn 4:19, 6:14, 7:40, 8:52–53, 9:17). The implication is plain: it is unlikely that the category of prophet was first applied to Jesus after Easter. In the wake of Easter even the category of eschatological prophet would have been regarded as inadequate to express his status and its significance. From this it follows that the attribution of a prophetic role to Jesus and the use made of Isa 61:1–2 in describing his mission is likely to go back to the pre-Easter period; also that Jesus himself probably accepted the category of "prophet" as a more ade-

---

23. The passages are discussed in more detail in my *Jesus and the Spirit* (London, Philadelphia, 1975), pp. 55–60.

24. For the prophetic significance of the claim, cf. e. g. Ps 105:26; Jer 1:7; Mic 6:4; Lk 4:26, 20:13.

quate description of his role (than messiah) and took Isa 61:1–2 as at least to some extent programmatic for his ministry.

To sum up: Of the range of options within the more diverse expectation of a prophetic figure, the prophet like Moses has left least trace in the Synoptic Gospel accounts (Mk 9:7 par.; Jn 12:47–48; cf. Acts 3:22; 7:37). And though others may have proposed the category of Elijah for Jesus (Mk 6:15, 8:28), Jesus himself is remembered as referring that designation to the Baptist (Mt 11:10/Lk 7:27; Mk 9:13). It is only of the less specific categories of prophet and eschatological prophet that we can speak with some confidence. But there it does seem possible to speak of an influence and a positive influence on Jesus of the Jewish expectation that a prophet figure would be involved in the last days.

THE SUFFERING RIGHTEOUS MAN

Of those reviewed in the first section, the only other category which calls for consideration is that of potential messianic ideas, in particular the suffering righteous man. The prominence of the motif in the Psalms and the Wisdom of Solomon and the variations on it in Daniel 7 and the martyr theology of the Maccabean literature are sufficient to indicate the strong probability that wherever those of faith found themselves in a situation of oppression, the theme of the suffering righteous man would be one which proved fruitful for consolation and encouragement. Under the Roman occupation it must be judged likely therefore that this strand of theologizing was still being actively pursued in Jewish circles and was available to Jesus, or at least near to hand for Jesus to use if he so chose.

That he did so choose is strongly attested in the Synoptic tradition. Unfortunately this testimony has become for the most part inextricably bound up with the much more specific issues of whether Jesus was influenced in his own self-understanding by the suffering servant passage in Isaiah 53 and the vision of the manlike figure in Daniel 7. I say unfortunately, because the more contentious features of these more specific debates have tended to obscure the fact that both Isaiah 53 and Daniel 7 are quite properly to be seen as particular expressions and outworkings of the broader and more pervasive reflection in Jewish thought of the sufferings of the righteous.[25] It may very well be the case therefore that what we should be looking for in the Jesus tradition are indications of whether Jesus was influenced by that broader stream of Jewish theologizing; and, moreover, we should bear in mind the possibility that any use made of Isaiah 53 and Daniel 7 in particular in the Synoptic tradition is a Christian elaboration of a less specific strand within the earliest memories of Jesus' teaching. Alternatively, of course, the possi-

25. See above n. 9.

bility equally should be borne in mind that it was Jesus himself who saw the value and importance of these particular crystallizations of the broader movement of thought and saw their appropriateness to his own mission.

The debate on these issues is much too complex to allow a satisfactory treatment here. I must confine myself to three observations. First, it must be judged highly likely that Jesus anticipated suffering and rejection for his message and himself—that is, that Jesus saw himself in the tradition of the suffering righteous. The expectation is clearly attested, apart from any influence of Isaiah 53 and Daniel 7, in Mark 10:38–39 par. and 14:36 par.; the facts that the prophecy of John suffering the same martyrdom was apparently not fulfilled and that the anguish of Jesus in the garden is depicted in most unmartyrlike terms (contrast Mk 14:33 with 2Mac 7:14) strongly suggest that these formulations are based on firsthand memory of what Jesus himself said. Moreover, as one who saw himself in the prophet tradition, Jesus must have anticipated the possibility of rejection, as a firm strand of tradition confirms (Mk 6:4 par.; 12:1–9 par.; Mt 23:29–36/Lk 20:47–51; Lk 13:33; Mt 23:37/Lk 13:34); the fate of the Baptist provided precedent and warning enough; and the opposition which Jesus roused must have confirmed the strong likelihood that he would meet a similar fate. Moreover, if Jesus did see the full consummation of the kingdom of God as imminent (Mk 1:15 par.; 9:1 par.; 13:29–30 par.; Mt 10:7/Lk 10:9,11; Mt 10:23), he would probably be aware of the apocalyptic expectation of a period of extreme tribulation prior to the final climax (Dan 12:1–2; Mt 3:7–12/Lk 3:7–9; 16–17)[26] and indeed probably shared it (cf. Mk 13:5–8, 17–20 par. with Mt 5:11–12/Lk 6:22–23; Mt 6:13/Lk 11:4; Mk 10:39 par.; etc.). That he himself would be caught up in that extreme suffering must have been recognized as at least a real possibility. And when we add in the other strands just referred to, the probability begins to become rather strong that Jesus anticipated his own death, and indeed saw it in positive terms as somehow redemptive—as an eschatologically (or messianically) intensified expression of the martyr theology which comes to expression elsewhere in 2Mac 7:38 and 4Mac 17:22. Certainly it must be judged improbable that Jesus saw his likely death as a complete defeat (otherwise he could have stayed out of harm's way), and probable that he would see it as bound up with the coming of the kingdom. The famous passage of Schweitzer, its rhetorical flourish notwithstanding, looks more and more like a justifiable restatement of Jesus' own hope and expectation—"Jesus' purpose is to set in motion the eschatological development of history, to let loose the final woes, the confusion and strife, from which shall issue the par-

---

26. Sanders notes that the "dogma" that suffering *must* precede the coming of the kingdom is difficult to document before 135 c.e. (*Jesus*, p. 124). But the idea flows directly from Dan 7 and 12:1–2, and is already implicit in such passages as Jub 23:22–31, TMos 5–10, 1QH 3:28–36, and SibOr 3:632–56.

ousia, and so to introduce the supra-mundane phase of the eschatological drama."[27]

All this strengthens the likelihood that behind the passages influenced more explicitly by Isaiah 53 and Daniel 7 stand utterances of Jesus himself, remembered either as expressing his expectation of suffering by himself drawing in these passages, or as expressing an expectation of rejection which was illuminated and readily elaborated by the first Christians who themselves drew in these passages. In fact it is difficult to demonstrate use of Isaiah 53 at the earliest level of the Synoptic tradition: Lk 22:37, although found in an obviously ancient context, does look as though it has been inserted into preexisting material; Mk 10:45 is as likely to have been influenced by Daniel 7 as by Isaiah 53; and the earliest form of the cup-word in the Last Supper is disputed (Mk 14:24 par.; 1Cor 11:25). And it is certainly arguable that behind the three Son of Man passion predictions (Mk 8:31 par.; 9:31 par.; 10:33–34 par.) lie בר אנשא sayings which of themselves contained no specific reference to Dan 7:13;[28] in which case they would quite likely have used the Jewish recognition of human frailty (as in Ps 8:4) as the means of expressing expectation of the brevity of life and the expectation of it being soon cut off.[29] But even if our critical tools and methods do not permit firm conclusions that Jesus himself made use of (and therefore was influenced by) Isaiah 53 and Daniel 7, the probability remains strong that Jesus entertained an expectation of rejection, suffering, and death, which was of a piece in his own perspective with the suffering of the righteous man and the final eschatological tribulation, and which would play a positive role therein.

CONCLUSION

It would seem then that we can speak of the influence of messianic ideas on Jesus in several ways. (1) Some ideas he reacted *against*. In particular, the current view of the royal messiah was one which he did not find helpful as a means of understanding or informing his mission. (2) Some he drew on and used to inform his own vision of what he had been called to. This may not be the same as saying that he applied clearly defined *roles*, let alone clearly defined *titles* to himself. It would be more accurate to say that particular elements within a much more variegated spread of messianic ideas were taken up by him. Isa 61:1–2 is a good case in point. (3) Even those he did respond to favorably and found inspirational or informative for his own mission he adapted and molded by his own conception of his mission. This

---

27. A. Schweitzer, *The Quest of the Historical Jesus* (London, 1910), p. 369.

28. See P. M. Casey, *The Son of Man: The Interpretation and Influence of Daniel 7* (London, 1980), pp. 232–33; Lindars, *Son of Man*, ch. 4.

29. See esp. J. Bowker, "The Son of Man," *JTS* 28 (1977) 19–48.

would apply in greater or lesser degree to all the categories and motifs discussed above.

In every case, in fact, we have to avoid any impression of a fixed category which Jesus filled (or fulfilled), of a sequence of clear-cut "messianic ideas" which provided the agenda for Jesus' mission. It would appear that Jesus was as much shaping the messianic ideas of the time as being shaped by them. Certainly that has to be said of the totality of the Christ-event as reflected on in earliest Christian theology; but it would be surprising if Jesus himself had not begun the process of redefining the categories either by deliberate teaching or simply by the very shape of his ministry and its undoubted significance for many. In other words, Jesus is in no sense a tailor's dummy draped convincingly or otherwise in the robes of Jewish messianic hope. Rather he himself must be seen as part of the stream of Jewish messianic reflection and one of the most important currents within that stream during the first half of the first century C.E. broadening the stream and quite soon becoming the occasion of it splitting into two different channels.

A final point worth pondering is that the brief review of the Jesus tradition just completed has by no means encompassed the full sweep of that tradition. We have had insufficient occasion to comment on other aspects of the Jesus tradition which certainly have christological if not messianic significance. I think of the question of the unusually high degree of authority Jesus evidently claimed—as a spokesman for God who could pronounce authoritatively on the eschatological meaning of the Torah without having undergone proper training. Or of the significance of his sense of intimate sonship evidenced in his "Abba" praying to God—a lived-out "claim" to divine sonship which seems surprisingly independent of any messianic son of God claim (2Sam 7:14). The point is that if we are to have any hope of seeing Jesus adequately, we cannot confine the discussion to the question of the influence of messianic ideas on him. That there was some such influence can be strongly affirmed, but the impact of Jesus and his own part in redefining several of these ideas has other roots as well.

MESSIANIC IDEAS AND THE CRUCIFIXION OF JESUS

INTRODUCTORY REMARKS

The crucifixion of Jesus is a historical fact beyond any reasonable doubt. Messianic ideas are just that—ideas. The relationship of ideas to facts is a key question in any attempt to reconstruct the history of Jesus and the origins and early history of Christianity, especially the roots of christological doctrine.

Until the beginnings of modern biblical scholarship Christian theologians tended to assume that Jesus was the Messiah whose coming was announced by the "messianic prophecies" of the Old Testament. Even Jewish messianic ideas were to a large extent read in light of, and in contrast to, faith in Jesus Christ, the true Messiah. This concept made a lasting impact even upon scholars, both those who reacted against it and those who tended to retain it in a modified, more historical form.

Throughout the 19th century—and to a considerable degree even in this century—NT scholars have approached the origins of Christology primarily in terms of the history of ideas (concepts, titles, or myths) and/or of religious experience (attitude, "self-consciousness"). Up until the last decades this has remained the case even in spite of otherwise opposite approaches. Conservative scholars have, as far as possible, traced NT Christology back to Jesus himself; liberals regarded the identification of Jesus as the Messiah as a time-conditioned expression of his singular religious significance; radicals denied that Jesus regarded himself as the Messiah and thought that the concept was only applied to him after Easter. "Moderates" have argued, and still argue, that NT Christology, including the doctrine of incarnation, is an organic and legitimate development of what was implicit in the person and ministry of Jesus.

A number of scholars have either assumed that Jesus radically reinterpreted the traditional concept "the Messiah" or that he rejected (or at least avoided) this title because of its political connotations, while he identified himself with some other "messianic" figure, such as the apocalyptic "Son of Man" and/or the suffering "Servant of the Lord," or the "eschatological prophet." The discussion still continues but has become more complicated. The Qumran texts have shown that Jewish messianic doctrines were open to greater variation than earlier assumed, and Jesus' use of the term "the Son of Man" and the whole question of a pre-Christian concept of the apocalyptic Son of Man are under debate.

H. S. Reimarus and a minority of scholars, mostly outsiders, have taken the fact that Jesus was crucified by the Romans as their point of departure, arguing that Jesus initiated a more or less militant movement of liberation and that the Gospels and other early Christian writings have covered up this original zealotism in order to propagate Christianity as a politically innocent religion. Historical reconstructions along this line have rightly been rejected by Jewish as well as by Christian scholars. Their recurrence does, however, represent a challenge: Any genuinely historical attempt to understand the origins of the faith in Jesus the Christ must take account of the historical events that led to and followed after his crucifixion.

While the theories of W. Wrede and A. Schweitzer were influential and have been actively discussed in our century, the view of J. Wellhausen that the crucifixion of Jesus caused a radical alteration of the concept "Messiah" was largely neglected until I restated the main thesis in an article on "The Crucified Messiah" in 1960 (now available in *Jesus The Christ* [Minneapolis: Fortress Press, 1991]). The main point has been accepted by a number of fellow scholars (e.g., M. Hengel) while others have criticized or neglected the article. The Princeton symposium has given me a welcome opportunity to return to the theme. "The Crucified Messiah" was written as a contribution to the discussion of "The historical Jesus and the kerygmatic Christ" which was especially lively in the 1950s and 60s. In the present paper I take a more strictly historical approach. It can only be a sketch without full documentation. For various reasons I have not been able to take account of recent literature to the degree that would have been desirable. I will, however, include new elements, namely, the attention given to the interplay of prophetic and royal messianic categories (see for example the work of W. C. van Unnik, K. Berger, and M. de Jonge in this area), and the discussion of the collection of sayings and other texts in which the term "Christ" and the Messiahship of Jesus play little, if any, role (see especially the work of H. Koester).

THE MESSIAH AND MESSIANIC IDEAS

The terms "Messiah" and "messianic" have often been used in a broad sense without sufficient discrimination. Some clarification is therefore necessary.

All four Gospels presuppose that "the Anointed One" was in common use as a designation of the man whom God was expected to make king of his people at the end of times. The use of the term is also attributed to Jews in Mk 14:61 and 15:32, and more frequently in Matthew, Luke, and especially in John, where even the Samaritan woman refers to the coming of *Messias* (Jn 4:25). Later Christian sources report that adherents of John the Baptist supposed that he was the Christ and that the Samaritan Dositheus claimed to be the Christ (Origen, *CCels*, I 57, etc.). At least to some extent non-Christian terminology was construed in analogy with and in contrast to Christian usage.

The designation "the Anointed" (Aram. *mešîḥā*, Heb. [*ha*] *māšîaḥ*) and "the King, the Anointed" are common both in the Targumim and in rabbinic literature as a designation of the mighty and righteous king for whose coming Jews were hoping and praying.

The use of "the Anointed One" with the definite article presupposes the designation of the coming king or ruler as "YHWH's (my, his) Anointed." The Qumran writings contain some terms which may illustrate the transition from biblical to later terminology: "The Anointed of Israel" (1QSa 2.14, 20) and "the Anointed of Righteousness" (or "the right, legitimate Anointed," 4QPBless 3). Other biblical terms which refer to the Messiah (to use the later but common term) are the "branch" (*ṣemaḥ*) and the "offspring" (*zeraʿ*) of David (4QPBless 3, 4; 4QFlor 1.10, 11). The designations "son of David" and "king of Israel" occur in *PsSol* 17.21, 42. The Qumran texts, however, avoid the royal title and use the designation "prince (*nāśî*) of the congregation" (e.g., 1QSb 5.20; CD 7.20).

The promises to David and his house (2Sam 7:4–17, etc.), oracles about a future Davidic prince (Isa 11:1–10 etc.), and royal psalms provided the basis for the messianic hope. The borderline between hope for the restoration of the Davidic kingdom and expectation of one Davidic prince, who might or might not be called *the* Anointed One, may long have remained fluid. The Messiah was not a necessary feature of the hope for a better future, and by and large the presence of the messianic ruler may simply have been included in the blessings which would come when God redeemed his people. When described as an active agent of redemption, his main task is to gather, purify, and rule over a holy people. Even when he is described as a conqueror, the Messiah was often assumed to perform the destruction of hostile forces by his word (or breath, Isa 11:4) rather than with military force.

While the core concept of "the Messiah" was shaped by scriptural passages that spoke about a descendant of David, other passages were also associated with the messianic descendant of David, though not necessarily so. This applies, of course, especially to passages in the Pentateuch, among which Gen 49:10 and Num 24:7(–9a) and 17–19 are most important. The Balaam oracles were important in the eschatology of the Samaritans which apparently was complex but did not include hope for a Davidic Messiah. Neither Philo nor the Sibylline Oracles use the term "the Anointed One," but their expectation does seem to be based upon the Greek text of Numbers

24 (see esp. Philo, *Praem* 94–97; SibOr 5.256, 414–19). The oracle about a world ruler from Judea, which according to Josephus (*War* 6.312–13) was of importance for the insurrection, is more likely to be derived also from Numbers 24 (or Gen 49:10) than from Daniel 7, which could hardly be applied to Vespasian. Josephus himself certainly did not consider Vespasian to be "the Messiah" (*War* 3.400–402). Simon b. Kosiba, the "prince of Israel" during the second war against Rome, was hailed as the star from Jacob (Num 24:17) and renamed "Bar Kokhba." There is no evidence that he was a descendant of David, but Talmudic texts report not only that R. Akibah said, "This is the king, the Anointed," but also that he made the same claim himself (y. Ta'an. 4., 68d; b. Tann. 93b).

Since Aristobulos (104–103 B.C.), and at least since Alexander Jannaeus (103–76 B.C.), the Hasmonean high priests used the title *king* (see especially the inscription "Alexander the King of the Jews," quoted by Josephus, *Ant* 14.36, from Strabo). This has to be understood primarily in the context of the political conditions of the time with a variety of minor kingdoms, city-states, etc., in the frontier area between the Black Sea and the Caspian Sea and the Persian Gulf and Egypt. The Hasmoneans and their adherents are likely to have argued that their zeal for the Law made them the legitimate successors of Phinehas for the foreseeable future and made up for the lacking genealogy (1Mac 2:25–26, 52–58; 14:41; cf. Num 25:6–13; Ps 106:28–31). Whether they also found some biblical warrant for their kingship remains uncertain, but it would be strange if they did not. The eulogy of Simon in 1Mac 14:4–15 celebrates the (partial) fulfillment of God's promises (see e.g., Micah 4:4) in his time, but even so terms like "(realized) eschatology" and "messianic" would not be appropriate.

Among the freedom fighters during the tumults after the death of Herod, some claimed royal dignity for themselves, e.g., Judas, son of the "archrobber" Hezekiah, Simon, and Athronges (Josephus, *War* 2.55–65; *Ant* 17.271–82, cf. 17.285). At the beginning of the Jewish war Menahem entered Jerusalem like a king, and later Simon b. Giora was welcomed in a similar way (*War* 2.433–48, 574–76). Unfortunately Josephus gives no information about the particular biblical passages involved (the "ambiguous oracle" to which he refers in *War* 6.5.4 [312f.] might be Daniel 7, Num 24:17f., or Gen 49:10), and his accounts of the sequence of events do not make clear which, if any, of the alleged kings were anointed and considered a Davidic Messiah. Still it is more likely than not that messianic ideas in a wider sense of the term played a role for the freedom fighters.

Among the texts for which a messianic interpretation was optional, of special interest are some of the *'ebed YHWH* passages in (Second) Isaiah and the vision in Daniel 7. These have been the topic of long debates which have centered on the "Son of Man" in the Similitudes in 1 Enoch 37–71. In this vision he is described, not as an earthly king, but as a heavenly figure as in the vision of Daniel, and is typologically more like the angelic prince (Mi-

chael, or Melchizedek in 11QMelch) who acts as God's agent of eschatological redemption. However, in the Ethiopic text, he is designated as "His (the
Lord's) Anointed" (1En 48:10; 52:4) and several passages about the Davidic
Messiah (e.g., Isaiah 11) and the Servant (e.g., Isa 42:6; 49:1) have been
applied to him.

It has become increasingly clear that Jewish expectations did not always
concentrate on the Davidic Messiah but left room for a plurality of persons
who would play a role at the time of salvation or shortly before. In all cases
some biblical passage provided the basis or could be used as a warrant for
these expectations.

The idea of one such figure, that of an eschatological high priest, "the
Anointed of Aaron," also called "the anointed priest" (?), was based upon the
blessing of Levi in Deut 33:8–11 and the promise to Phinehas in Num
25:10–13 (see also 1Sam 2:35; Mal 2:4–7; Sir 45:23–24). In Qumran texts,
"the Anointed of Aaron" ranks higher than "the Anointed of Israel," but neither of them is a Savior figure, as they were possibly in the Testaments of the
Twelve Patriarchs prior to their Christian adaptation. In rabbinic writings
the future high priest (or *kohēn ṣedek*) is simply mentioned.

The expectation of another such person, that of a prophet like Moses, was
based upon Deut 18:15–19 and/or upon the expanded text of Ex 20:19–22 in
the Samaritan Pentateuch and 4QBibParaph (= 4Q158). In 11QMelch 18–
20 the messenger of peace in Isa 52:7 is called "the Anointed of the Spirit"
and is probably associated with the prophet like Moses (cf. 1QS 9.11 and
4QTestim).

Elijah was still another figure whose coming was expected. The hope for
his return was based upon Mal 4:5–6 (cf. 3:1–4; Sir 48:10 and later texts).

One could also mention the expectation of "the Anointed One, the son of
Ephraim" or "of Joseph." However there is no certain evidence before C.E.
135 for such an expectation. Here Deut 33:13 was the main warrant, but
other passages, including Zech 12:10, were also applied to him. In this case
the translation "Messiah" may be appropriate. The designation "Messiah of
War" suggests some—but which?—relation to the priest in Deut 20:2.

The number and functions of "eschatological persons" were open to considerable variation, as were the passages adduced.

For example, the expectation of two leaders, a (Davidic) ruler and a Levitical (Aaronitic) priest must be considered normal (see e.g., Jer 23:5–6;
Zech 3:6–8; 4:13–14; 6:9–13). This dual pattern reappears in Qumran writings and the Testaments of the Twelve Patriarchs, and also at the beginning
of the insurrections in C.E. 66 and 132. Other pairs occur in later, mostly
rabbinic texts: the Davidic Messiah and Moses or Elijah, Moses and Elijah,
or Elijah and Enoch.

The triad consisting of (the) prophet and the Anointed Ones of Aaron and
Israel is attested by 4QTestim as well as by 1QS 9.11. John 1:20–21 has the
Christ, Elijah, and the prophet. TargYer I Ex 40:9–11 relates the royal Mes-

siah, the high priest Elijah and the Messiah from Ephraim to the triad "the kingdom of the house of Judah," Aaron, and Joshua. In interpretations of Zech 2:3 (ET 1:20) the number was extended to four, who in b.BBat. are identified as the two Messiahs (the Son of David and the Son of Joseph), Elijah, and the high priest, kohēn ṣedek. In most cases, though not all, the warrior Messiah is supposed to fight and to die before the coming of the Davidic Messiah, but there is little evidence that Elijah was considered the precursor of the Messiah, as presupposed in Mk 9:11.

The number of eschatological persons could be diminished as well as increased. In the textual transmission of Zech 6:11–13 the name of Zerubbabel may have been eliminated, but there are traces of the notion of the Davidic "Branch" at his side. The Damascus Document does not mention the eschatological prophet, and the Anointed Ones of Aaron and Israel may have merged and become one person (CD 12.23, etc.). In rabbinic texts, the prophet like Moses plays no independent role; the Messiah was rather considered to be the second redeemer and to be like the first redeemer, Moses. The eschatological high priest could be identified with the returning Elijah, whom some rabbis assumed to be the same person as Phinehas.

The same texts and the same functions may be applied to more than one of the persons to come. For example, the identity of the měbaśśēr of Isa 52:7 was left anonymous by some rabbis while others supposed him to be Elijah or the Messiah. Yet the Melchizedek fragment from Qumran may imply that he is to be identified with the prophet like Moses. In another text, the Balaam oracle (Num 24:17), the "star from Jacob" and the "scepter" (LXX: "man") might refer to one or two persons.

The expectations were normally derived from scriptural promises and predictions, or supported by passages which were assumed to refer to some person whose coming they announced. Selection, combination, and interpretation of the texts were contingent upon social setting, cultural environment, political structures, historical circumstances, etc. To some degree it is possible to trace the various forms of expectations to specific areas or groups.

The expectation of a Davidic Messiah was contingent upon the recognition of the former and later prophets and the Psalms as sacred Scriptures. Thus Samaritan eschatology included several figures, but no Davidic prince. Even in parts of the Greek diaspora the promises to David and his offspring were of little, if any, importance (see, e.g., Philo). What is more remarkable is that this also seems to be the case in the Jewish-Christian traditions preserved in the Pseudo-Clementine Homilies and Recognitions. This may indicate that there also existed some other Jewish circles whose "messianic ideas" were almost exclusively warranted by the Pentateuch.

The Qumran documents make it possible to get a fairly clear picture of the correlation between the structure and aspirations of the sect and the roles assigned to the "messianic figures." They are also likely to provide a model which should be applied to cases where we lack information about the social setting of the writings or about the ideology of liberation movements. The conflicts between the secessionist priest at Qumran and the Hasmonean high priests are well known. Tensions between the priestly aristocracy and Levites in or outside Jerusalem are likely to have continued and may have endured for some time. They may be reflected in expectations for the future, affecting whether Levi, Aaron, Phinehas, or Zadok was seen as the more important ancestor and model. I must, however, leave this question open.

Outside priestly and levitical circles, the inclusion of the "prophets" and other writings favored the hope for the restoration of the Davidic kingdom and a Davidic Messiah, both because of the number of passages which supported it and because it was most closely linked to the general hope for the liberation from foreign rulers and other evils. Already from the time of Zerubbabel onward the hope could be actualized and again projected into a more distant future. Probably composed briefly after Pompey's conquest of Jerusalem, Psalms of Solomon 17 and 18 draw heavily upon biblical passages to portray the promised Son of David as the ideal king, in explicit contrast to the illegitimate and corrupted Hasmoneans. Under the impact of the destruction of Jerusalem the apocalyptic visions of 4Ezra and 2Baruch give a more or less prominent place to the Messiah, who at his coming will bring an end to the last period of tribulation, judge the wicked nations and the last empire (Rome), and inaugurate a time of salvation which, however, at least in 4Ezra 7:26–44, is to be followed by the end of the world, the last judgment, and the renewal of creation. Other than these four texts we have little literary evidence for the expectation of a Davidic Messiah that is contemporary with the New Testament writings. Synagogue prayers for the kingdom of the house of David or for the coming of the Messiah may, however, go back to this period. The redactor(s) of the Mishnah had other concerns and may consciously have kept silent about the Messiah, but in the Targumim and Midrashim and in both Talmuds the intimate correlation of messianic ideas and exposition of Scripture is clearer than ever.

In principle, but not always in praxis, scholars recognize that Jewish "messianic ideas" have to be studied on their own premises and that neither the Davidic Messiah nor any of the other persons who were expected to come were necessary features of the hope of redemption. Not only the controversy between Christians and Jews (viz., whether Jesus was the Messiah or the Messiah is yet to come), but also the special interest in messianic ideas that were applied to Jesus, or were already applied by him, have too often resulted in an approach that failed to do justice to the complexity of the data. The aim of the preceding survey has been to show that the diversity of expectations is, in some cases obviously, in other cases probably, due to the use of a shifting number of biblical passages within various, often conflicting groups and under changing historical circumstances.

My insistence upon the scriptural basis of messianic ideas should not be misunderstood as an argument in favor of the view that external influence made little or no impact upon their development in Judaism and early Christianity. Indeed, the notion of an ideal Savior-King was from the outset related to the notion of sacred kingship in the ancient Near East, and since antiquity interpretation and reinterpretation of Scriptures have remained a main tool for the integration of contemporary trends into the biblical religions.

At the time of Jesus there existed no normative doctrine of the Messiah. Hence, distinctions between national, this-worldly, eschatological, and apocalyptic expectations have only limited value as tools of classification. An overarching unity was, however, provided by the common faith in the one God, the God of Israel and the entire world, who had given the Law and would keep His word and do what He had promised. The divergent, or even conflicting, "messianic" ideas and movements operated within this framework. For that reason, even chronologically later texts may contribute to a better understanding of the history of the Jesus movement and the origin of Christology. Under certain circumstances, even a radical reinterpretation of all traditional ideas could take place. As Gershom Sholem has pointed out, the story of the apostate Messiah, Sabbatai Zevi (1625–1676), provides the most illuminating analogy to the story of the crucified Messiah, Jesus of Nazareth.

The main point of this paper, as of some of my earlier essays, is that the interpretation of events and experiences in light of the Scriptures and the corresponding reinterpretation of scriptural passages were essential for the formulation of Christological doctrines, and that Jewish analogies to such interpretive interplay contribute more to a genuinely historical understanding of the origin of these Christological doctrines than any specific ideas about the Messiah and other eschatological figures. Detailed study of titles, concepts, and traditions remains important but does not provide any satisfactory explanation of the historical origin of Christological doctrine. The basic facts that need explanation are: (1) that the "Prophet from Nazareth," who performed miracles but also was a sage and a teacher, was crucified by the Romans, and (2) that he was, nevertheless, after his death proclaimed as the (royal) Messiah who was vindicated by God, who raised him from the dead. This makes the relationship between, and the interpenetration of, prophetic and royal categories a question of primary importance for the theme of this paper.

THE CRUCIFIXION OF JESUS

The debate about the trial and crucifixion of Jesus is as lively as ever. I shall not attempt to make a contribution to the vexed questions but simply assume that some basic historical facts were retained both in the fluid oral tradition and in the literary composition of the Gospels. Most important among them are: (1) that only Jesus and none of the disciples was arrested,

(2) that one or two hearings took place in the presence of the high priest and a council gathered by him, and (3) that whatever the legal competence of this body, and whether or not a formal sentence was passed, the outcome was that Jesus was handed over to Pilate, who sentenced him to death and let him be crucified. The increasing tendency to exculpate Pilate served as apologetic purpose, but from early on, Jews who believed in Jesus are likely to have placed special blame upon the Jewish leaders who delivered him into the hands of Gentiles. The meager evidence at hand makes it likely that other Jews responded by maintaining that Jesus did indeed deserve death.

All four gospels agree that Jesus was sentenced and crucified as an alleged king of the Jews and that the charge was stated on a placard which, at least according to Matthew and John, was placed upon the top of the cross. It is highly unlikely that Christians introduced this title into the narrative since it was otherwise used in clearly political contexts (see Josephus, Ant 14.36; 15.373; 16.311; War 1.282). It is also quite probable that Roman soldiers in fact saluted Jesus as a mock king. "The King of the Jews" occurs also in the mouth of Pilate, in his interrogation of Jesus (Mk 15:2 par.) and in the Barabbas scene (Mk 15:9, 12; Jn 18:39). These occurrences may be derivative, as the use of direct speech is probably due to the narrators, but they confirm that the title itself was at the basis of the developing tradition.

The later evangelists tended to substitute more biblical and Christian designations for the political title "King of the Jews": "The King of Israel" (GPet 3.7, 11; cf. Mt 27:42), "an anointed king" (Lk 23:2), or "Jesus who is called Christ" (Mt 27:17, 22). The first three Gospels also tell about how Jesus was mocked while he was hanging upon the cross, but in this context they all used terms that would be appropriate in the mouth of Jews and/or Christians: "The Christ, the king of Israel" (Mk 15:32, cf. Mt 27:42), "the Anointed of God, the Chosen One" (Lk 23:35), "the Anointed One" (Lk 23:39), or "the Son of God" (Mt 27:40, 43). The terms used by Matthew and Luke correspond to their own usage, whereby Luke consciously makes the persons of his narrative employ a vocabulary that would fit the historical context (see Lk 23:37 and also 23:47 compared with Mk 15:39; Mt 27:54, and GPet 11.45, 46). The reviling, which no doubt took place, became important because of the testimonies in Pss 22:6–8 and 69:7–11, 19–22 (see also the "messianic" Psalm 89, esp. vss. 39–42, 50–51). The words which narrators attributed to the mockers reflect that ongoing conflict between those who believed in the crucified Jesus and other Jews who found the idea of a crucified Messiah repugnant and ridiculous.

The resurrection experiences would not have led the disciples to affirm that Jesus was the promised Messiah unless he had been crucified as an alleged royal Messiah. Post-mortem appearances, an empty tomb, and assumption to heaven were not aspects of messianic ideology, and the messiahship of Jesus plays little, if any, role in the resurrection stories, with the exception of Luke 24 where vss. 18–27 and 44–49 represent Luke's own theology. The conjecture that the stories of the transfiguration and possibly the confession of Peter were originally resurrection stories and later projected back into the earthly life of Jesus is based upon the theory which they are assumed to support. The appearances of the risen Christ were, no doubt, of crucial importance for the radical Christian transformation of the concept "Messiah," but they can only have had this effect because they convinced the disciples that God had vindicated the crucified King of the Jews. The narratives about the life and the death of Jesus are all informed by this conviction.

THE EARLIEST EVIDENCE

The conclusions that may be drawn from an analysis of the passion stories are confirmed by the letters of Paul, our earliest sources for the application of the title *Christos* to Jesus. Yet the argument could just as well proceed from the Pauline evidence. In fact, the thesis which I first presented in "Der gekreuzigte Messias" (1961) drew the consequences of further reflections on the theme "Die Messianität Jesu bei Paulus" (1953). (An English translation of both articles is now available in *Jesus The Christ*, 15–25, 27–47).

In the letters of Paul *(ho) Christos* always refers to Jesus Christ. Only the informed reader will be aware of the rich connotations of the honorific name. Paul uses the name "Christ" in a variety of contexts and constructions, often with reference to the living and present Christ, to whom Christians belong and with whom they have communion. Traditional formulations tend to use *Christos* in statements about Christ's death and/or resurrection. On the basis of his own experience, Paul accentuates the offensive contrast between the crucified Christ and current messianic ideas (see esp. Rom 9:32–33, 1Cor 1:19–25; Gal 3:13, 5:11). His own understanding of Christ is shaped by the Christian faith much more than by messianic ideas which he may have had before his conversion.

The phrase "according to the Scriptures," appears twice in the summary of the gospel which Paul received and handed on: "Christ died for our sins according to the Scriptures . . . and he was raised on the third day according to the Scriptures" (1Cor 15:3–4). In his letters Paul does not find it necessary to persuade his audience that Jesus is the Messiah, but he uses messianic testimonies drawn from the Scriptures to support his arguments. For example, Romans contains several quotations from the Psalms or Isaiah (Rom 9:33; 11:9–10, 26–27; 15:3, 8–12). Further, in 1Cor 15:25–27 he paraphrases and comments upon Pss 101:1 and 8:6. Other allusions are more veiled, as in Rom 4:25 (Isa 53:5, 11) and Gal 3:19 (Gen 49:10 combined with 2Sam 7:12). The most explicitly messianic text is the summary in the prescript of Romans in which Paul introduces himself as an apostle who was set apart to preach the same gospel other Christians had heard and believed. The summary is best understood as a paraphrase and interpretation of the promise to David in 2 Samuel 7, esp. vss. 3 and 4a: "According to the flesh"

Jesus descended from David, "according to the spirit of holiness," by virtue of God's promise and action (cf. Gal 4:23, 29), he was "designated Son of God in power."

Relative to the rest of the NT, in Pauline letters the messiahship of Jesus is seldom clearly visible at the surface but is present at a deeper level and shapes the entire theology. Paul's Christological language and ideas are shaped by the Greek-speaking Christian environment in which he lived, in Antioch and elsewhere, as well as by his own experience and thought. There can be no doubt, however, that God's vindication of the crucified Messiah was at the center of the faith which he had once tried to destroy but later proclaimed (Gal 1:23). At least in intention, the persecution was directed against the *ekklesia tou theou*, a term that must have included the church in Jerusalem in which Peter at that time was the most prominent leader. Paul explicitly affirms that in spite of their different commissions, he and the authorities in Jerusalem where in full agreement about the substance of the gospel (1Cor 15:1–7, 11; Gal 2:1–10). Peter and others did not draw the same consequences as did Paul from the common gospel they shared with him (Gal 2:11–16). Nor is their thinking and preaching likely to have focused on the crucifixion of Christ to the same degree as Paul's. Even so, the transformation of Jewish messianic ideas to faith in the crucified, risen, and enthroned Messiah is likely to be due to Peter more than to any other individual.

THE DIVERSITY OF CHRISTOLOGICAL VOCABULARY AND CONCEPTS

The passion stories of the Gospels and the letters of Paul provide a double foundation for the thesis that the designation of Jesus as "the Messiah" was primarily connected with his crucifixion (and vindication). The question remains how well the thesis stands up in view of the diachronic development and the synchronic diversity of christological concepts which a number of first-rank scholars have stressed and overstressed.

The common opinion that *Christos* gradually lost its titular force and became a proper name is only part of the truth. As *christos* was a verbal adjective ("to be smeared") and not applied to persons outside the biblical sphere, uninitiated Greeks may from the beginning have understood *Christos* as a proper name or byname. Both the word *christianos* and the designation *Iesous ho legomenos Christos* (Josephus, *Ant* 20.200 as well as Mt 27:17, 22) may support this. A confusion of *Christos* with the adjective and name *Chrestos* was also possible. Instruction about the meaning of the name may have followed later.

All NT authors use the double name Jesus Christ (or Christ Jesus) and presuppose that it was familiar to the readers, but their writings mostly clarify the connotations of the honorific name *Christos*. The Johannine Apocalypse may be the most obvious example. The form "Jesus Christ" is used in the epistolary framework, but the apocalyptic visions make a rich and varied use of biblical terminology (e.g., "the Lord and his Anointed"), metaphors, and imagery to convey the message that God, who has vindicated the crucified Messiah, will also soon vindicate his suffering followers.

Three of the four evangelists use the familiar name in the beginning of their narratives (Mt 1:1; Mk 1:1; Jn 1:17). The titular use of *Christos* is part of the narratives which gradually clarify the identity of Jesus Christ and the sense in which Jesus was and was not the expected Messiah, until the mystery of his messiahship finds its solution in the passion and resurrection stories. Especially the Fourth Evangelist shows some familiarity with Jewish messianic ideas, but he uses them to point out that "the Jews" failed to understand the deeper meaning of their Scriptures and of their own traditions. With regard to the Fourth Gospel there is little room for doubt that the titular use of *ho Christos* in the discussions of Jews among themselves and with Jesus belong to the later layers of the complex prehistory of the Gospel (see esp. 7:26–27, 31, 40–43; 10:24–26; 12:34).

In the Gospel of Luke *Christos* is always a title, but Acts makes it clear that the name Jesus Christ was current at his time. The story of Jesus the Christ is told with great literary and historical art, to a considerable extent in a biblical and archaizing style. For instance, the announcement to Mary restates the biblical promises (Lk 1:32–33, cf. 1:67–75), and, anointed by the Spirit at his baptism, Jesus begins his public ministry by reading Isa 61:1–2 (Lk 4:18–21, cf. Acts 4:27; 10:38). This latter scene in Nazareth is programmatic for the following narrative, but it is not until the risen Christ appears to his disciples that he fully discloses the meaning of what was written about the Anointed One. The kerygmatic discourses in Acts may contain some early traditions, but in the narrative sequence they presuppose and unfold the explanation of Scripture in Lk 24:25–26, 44–47. Luke's preference for the titular use of *Christos* is related to his interest in the proof from prophecy. Individual testimonies to Christ are integrated into a coherent "Old Testament concept of the Messiah" which exactly corresponds to the story of Jesus.

Even writings which use only *Christos* as a designation of Jesus Christ can, like Paul, retain and elaborate the meaning which the term "Messiah" received when it was applied to the crucified Jesus (see e.g., 1Pet 1:10–11; 2:21–25). In Hebrews "Jesus" is a personal name while *Christos* is used with reference to Christ's rank and work as king and high priest. The entire Christology of the epistle is based upon interpretation of Scripture and also mentions that Christ was anointed (Heb 1:9).

The more general use of *Christos* as an appelative (= "the Messiah") was kept alive and re-actualized by continuing contact and controversies, and even dialogues, between Christians and Jews, as well as by the ongoing elaboration of the proof from prophecy. This is especially clear in the writings of

Justin, who in greater detail than Luke constructs an Old Testament doctrine of the Messiah in order to prove that Jesus is the promised Christ. Justin goes beyond Luke in making the Logos-doctrine an integral part of this proof. As in Hebrews, Ps 45:7–8 provides the proof that Jesus was "the Anointed One." Justin explicitly understands *Christos* to imply that Jesus was (high) priest as well as king.

Like Justin, Tertullian and other authors after him associated the name Christ with the sacerdotal as well as the royal office, but also assumed that other Old Testament names and titles were to be applied to Jesus. As far as I know, the observation that kings, priests, and prophets were anointed was applied to Jesus' baptismal anointing before the concept *munus triplex Christi* was developed. The chief patristic witness to this idea is Eusebius of Caesarea, according to whom the heavenly Logos is "the only high priest of the universe and the only king of creation and the Father's only archprophet of prophets" (*HE* 1.3.8, see also the entire chapter and *DemEvang.*, proem book 2 and book 8.15). The connection between the name Christ and the offices of kings, priests, and prophets is also attested in writings such as the following which show some affinity to Jewish legends and concepts: Aphrahat (*Hom.* 17.3, cf. 4.8), Pseudo-Clementine Recognitions (1.44.3–46, esp. the Syriac version), and the Syriac Cave of Treasures. It was, however, apparently only since Calvin that this interpretation of the name *Christos* became the standard doctrine and was popularized in catechisms and other textbooks.

When *Christos* had become a name for Jesus as a Savior who only had the name in common with the Jewish Messiah, it became possible to take a further step and distinguish between Jesus, a human being, and Christ, the heavenly redeemer. The heretics of 1 and 2 John are likely to have taken this step. Later sources report that Cerinthus and some gnostics thought that the Christ had come down upon Jesus at his baptism (see e.g., Irenaeus, *Adv Haer* 1.26.1, 7.11, 30.12). Epiphanius attributes a similar doctrine to the Ebionites (*Haer* 30.16.3, 18.5). The basic idea that Jesus became the Messiah when the Holy Spirit came down and anointed him at his baptism almost certainly originated among Jewish Christians, upon whom also Luke may be dependent.

Both the Pauline and the later evidence suggests that Christians who spoke Aramaic may have used *mĕšîḥā* in a way that was similar to the Greek use of *Christos* as an honorific title and byname of Jesus. Several of the early Christian leaders, and the outsider Josephus too, were bi- or trilingual, and the Aramaic form was retained in Christian Syriac. The Odes of Solomon uses "the Anointed of the Lord" and "(our Lord) the Anointed One" as a designation of Jesus, but contains few, if any, echoes of New Testament texts or explicitly messianic testimonies. Among gnostic writings, the Gospel of Philip shows a special interest in the names of Jesus and explains that "Messiah" has two meanings: "the Christ" (the Anointed One), and "the Measured

One" (62.8–18). Although I fail to understand the deeper meaning of the second etymology, it confirms my suspicion that "Messiah" as well as "Christ" could be used as a byname of Jesus.

At this point it should be clear that the common idea that *Christos* gradually lost its titular force and became a proper name is only part of the truth. I now want to move on and show that the very widely accepted theory that the title "Messiah" was first applied to Jesus as a "Messias designatus" (i.e., in view of his expected royal return) rests on very shaky foundations.

In preserved documents the title *Christos* is only seldom used with special reference to the glorious coming of Christ, or to his reign during the millennium (Rev 20:4). The passage about "the Christ appointed for you, Jesus" in Acts 3:20–21 is so intertwined with typical Lucan terms and ideas that I find it hard to believe that it preserves a very early tradition.

Early Christians will from the beginning have expected that the crucified Jesus would soon be publicly vindicated, redeem his own people, and judge his and their adversaries. The delay of the parousia, however, should not be made the major factor in the development of Christology. Expectations that Christ would return in the very near future waned and were rekindled on several occasions in the early history of the Church, as they have been subsequently. A unilinear decline in expectation is most improbable.

Some messianic testimonies were taken to include the future coming or revelation of Jesus as the Christ, but not exclusively so. The parousiological interpretation of Psalm 110 presupposes the enthronement of Christ (see 1Cor 15:23–28; Heb 10:12–13, cf. Mk 14:62). The application of Zech 12:10 presupposes that the "pierced one" was identified with the crucified Jesus (Jn 19:37; Rev 1:7, cf. Mt 24:30). The affinity to common messianic ideas is obvious in the allusion to Isa 11:4 in 2Thes 2:8 and in Rev 19:15, where Isa 11:4 is combined with the "rod of iron" in Ps 2:9. The vision in Rev 19:11–16 does not, however, merely draw upon messianic images, it ascribes titles and attributes of God to the glorious and conquering Christ.

The terms and images that were applied to the "second coming" of Christ were to a very large extent derived from strictly *theo*logical, not messianic, language. "The day of the Lord" became the "day of our Lord Jesus (Christ)." The use of *parousia* as the term for the future coming of (the) Christ is Christian; in Jewish texts it only occasionally refers to the coming or presence of God. The more detailed descriptions of Christ's glorious coming, accompanied by the holy ones, the angels, the sound of trumpets, etc., are to a considerable extent modeled upon Old Testament texts which describe the coming of Yahweh to Mount Sinai or to judgment (1Thes 3:13; 4:15–16; esp. 2Thes 1:6–10, but also Mk 13:24–27). The Messiah was expected to execute judgment upon the nations who oppressed Israel and upon sinners within the people. Judging individuals according to their works was God's privilege, but even this function was ascribed to Christ (e.g., Mt 16:27; 2Cor 5:10; Rev 2:23; 22:12). I see here no basis for the assumption that the transfer of "God-language" to Jesus was conditioned by the fading of the hope of his near *parousia*.

Already Luke assumed that the earliest disciples expected that Jesus would become the messianic redeemer and restorer of Israel (Lk 24:21; Acts 1:6), but he realized, better than many modern critics, that the concept "Messiah" was radically changed after the crucifixion and resurrection of Jesus. Modern critics have often, and with many variations, reconstructed the earliest history according to a model which to a large extent depended upon the agreement of A. Schweitzer and W. Bousset that the point of departure was the identification of Jesus as the coming "Son-of-Man-Messiah" in earliest Palestinian Christianity. This construction combines the Pauline evidence for "Messiah" with the "Son of Man" sayings in the synoptic tradition and proceeds on the assumption that there was an apocalyptic Son of Man figure who was identified with Jesus and was supposed to come from heaven to earth. I suspect that the entire construction was wrong but shall not enter into any detailed critique as my ambition has been to offer an alternative.

The development of early Christology did not follow any single line, and the language used drew upon many and diverse sources. Jesus not only was identified as the royal Messiah, but what was written or said about other eschatological figures could also be applied to him. Scriptural passages which had never been read as messianic in any sense became christological testimonies. Jesus was also depicted as a "holy man," a man of God (or a *theios aner*): a prophet, sage, miracle worker, and exorcist, the suffering righteous one. The language used of heavenly beings, of the hypostatized Wisdom and the Logos, or of the highest of angelic princes (and also language used about God) was transferred to Jesus, long before it became customary to call Jesus "God." The main titles, such as "Lord," "Son of God," contained several components.

Whatever the close or remote sources, the titles received new meanings when they were applied to Jesus Christ and used in a new context. Within the main stream of tradition which is represented by the New Testament writings, the various titles and concepts were based upon or integrated with the conviction that the crucified Jesus was the promised Messiah to whom the Scriptures bore witness. While this does leave room for great flexibility and diversity, it also calls for caution in that one should not unnecessarily postulate a plurality of different Christologies, perhaps centered around one title located in more or less separate congregations. Even so, the absence of the word *Christos* and "messianic ideas" in some writings and types of texts does indeed raise a genuine historical problem.

With few exceptions—and most of them secondary—*Christos* does not occur in the sayings of Jesus and collections of such sayings. This observation calls for an explanation.

Christos in Mk 9:41 and "Jesus Christ" in Jn 17:3 are redactional additions. The saying about the Christ as the one master in Mt 23:10 is important for the Christology of Matthew but is formulated in analogy with the preceding sayings about God as the one rabbi and father. This means that *Christos* was absent from the sayings common to Matthew and Luke (whether Q was ever a published book or not), and also from the Johannine *rhemata*-tradition and the sayings peculiar to Matthew and to Luke, with the possible exception of Mt 23:10.

Christos does not occur in the Gospel of Thomas nor in the sayings collections in the Dialogue of the Savior. Neither does it occur in dialogues between the risen Christ and some of his disciples which have been preserved in the Nag Hammadi library (see e.g., the *Apocryphon of James*, the *Book of Thomas the Contender*, and also the *First* and *Second Apocalypse of James*. Sayings of Jesus are introduced with "Jesus," "the Lord," "the Savior," or occasionally, "the Son of Man said." This is not a gnostic peculiarity, however.

Paul refers to sayings of Jesus as sayings of the Lord or of "the Lord Jesus," not as sayings of Christ. The "Freer Logion" (inserted after Mk 16:14 in cod. W) has "Christ said to them," but Justin seems to be the first to make a fairly frequent use of formulas like "Christ, our teacher, said."

Christos occurs only once in Didache (9.4, "through Jesus Christ"); the Shepherd of Hermas contains a single allusion to *Christos* in the wordplay *to Theo euchrestoi* (14.6 = *HermVis.* 3.6). Its occurrence in connection with miracle stories in the Gospels is likely due to the evangelists (Mt 11:2; Lk 4:41; Jn 7:31; 9:22, possibly also 11:27). Its absence may be due to genre and style, to the environment of traditions and writings, or to a combination of both factors.

I see no reason to doubt that the disciples quoted sayings of Jesus and that they, and possibly others, told stories about him during his own lifetime. They did not, of course, use the title Messiah, and the same habit of speech was preserved in later tradition, which continued to let Jesus refer to himself as the "Son of Man" and to introduce important sayings with "Amen, I say unto you." This simple explanation must be part of the truth since writings which otherwise frequently use *Christos* avoid linking the word to sayings of Jesus. This allows for the reversed conclusion, namely, that collections of sayings of Jesus may well have emerged in communities that were familiar with and shared the faith in the crucified and risen Christ.

The Gospel of Thomas contains "sayings of the living Jesus," and the revelatory discourses and dialogues report what Jesus, the Lord and Savior, taught his disciples after his resurrection. What brings knowledge, life, and salvation is, however, not cross and resurrection as saving events, but the sayings of Jesus, as is indicated in GThom 1: "Whoever finds the interpretation of these sayings will not experience death." The Johannine Jesus says: "The words which I have spoken to you are spirit and life" (Jn 6:63). Even Q attributes the highest importance to the reaction to the words of Jesus, but emphasizes hearing and doing (Mt 7:24–27 par.).

Whether or not the sayings tradition had its setting in some local community or, more likely, in the preaching of itinerant charismatics may be left an open question. My aim has simply been to show that the absence of *Christos* in sayings collections confirms that the crucifixion and the messiahship of Jesus belong inseparably together in the early Christian tradition.

The problem of the relationship between the Jesus-tradition and the gospel of the crucified and risen Christ is a problem within the early church and not simply to be subsumed under the question "the historical Jesus and the kerygmatic Christ" or, in the earlier and more popular formulation, "Jesus and Paul." The distinction between the ongoing tradition (i.e., teaching and preaching of sayings of Jesus) and the proclamation of the crucified Christ cuts across the distinction between "orthodoxy" and heresy. The first type is attested by "Q," the Gospel of Thomas, and other writings, while Valentian doctrines about Christ (or several "Christs") to a much higher degree presuppose and transform a more "Pauline" proclamation of the crucified and vindicated Christ.

Within orthodox and within more or less heretical circles both the Jesus-tradition and the Christ-kerygma were subject to variations, alterations, and development. A main difference was that the mainstream development which was canonized in the emerging collection of the New Testament retained and, to an increasing degree, emphasized the notion that it was "the God of the Fathers," the Creator of the world, who had sent Christ and raised him from the dead. The emphasis upon the "messianic promises" and the contact with messianic ideas remained important, while the radical gnostic and Marcionite distinction between two deities caused a distinction between two or more Christs.

KING AND PROPHET

Within the mainstream of development, the sayings tradition and the conception of Christ as the revealer of true knowledge could be related to and integrated with faith in the crucified Messiah in several ways. For the sake of simplicity I will offer a brief overview of the use of royal and prophetic categories.

For Paul the saving gospel is the "word of the cross." The sayings of the Lord are authoritative rules of conduct and order in the church, but otherwise the ministry of Jesus as prophet, healer, and sage seems to be of little importance. The "Q" type of tradition presents Jesus as the teacher of wisdom and of the knowledge of God and his will, who will, as the Son of Man, be a witness at the celestial court, be enthroned in glory, and/or be revealed on his day. It is presupposed that he will be persecuted and die in the succession of prophets, but there is no reference to his crucifixion.

In the Johannine Apocalypse, Jesus is the heavenly revealer; John and other prophets are his witnesses. The crucifixion and vindication of the Christ, the slain lamb and the lion of Judah, is at the center of the apocalyptic visions, however, as in no other apocalypse.

The four Gospels all integrate the story of Jesus' public ministry as a teacher and prophetic figure with his crucifixion as a messianic king, but do so in different ways.

For John, Jesus is the prophet-king (Meeks) whose kingdom is not of this world but who bears witness to the truth. Upon the cross he is elevated from earth to the Father; he is no longer limited by space and time, and all who are "of the truth" will hear his voice. The portrait has more in common with the Moses-figure of Philo and of some rabbinic and Samaritan sources than with traditional messianic ideas.

For Matthew, Jesus is the Christ, not only a royal Messiah but also one who performed mighty works and was the one master and teacher. An analogy to Moses is already apparent in the story of the Magi in ch. 2, and continues through the authoritative interpretation of the law in the Sermon on the Mount and further. Future disciples are to be taught all that Jesus had commanded the eleven, as the Israelites were to observe the commandments of God through Moses.

To Luke, Jesus is both the Anointed One to whom the promises of David apply, and the prophet like Moses (Acts 3:22–23; 7:37). Anointed by the Spirit, Jesus acts as a prophet, whose work recalls that of Elijah as well of Moses, and has to face opposition, persecution, and suffering like the prophets before him. But God has enthroned him at his right hand and appointed him to restore the people and judge the quick and the dead.

Mark makes less explicit use of prophetic categories than the three other evangelists and draws no attention to an analogy between Jesus and Moses. Jesus' parables, however, are considered an esoteric revelation of the mystery of the kingdom of God, and prophetic predictions of his own fate, the fate of the disciples, the destruction of the temple, and the events of the last days are constitutive elements of the story. Jesus is condemned as claiming to be "Christ, the Son of the Blessed One," and reviled as a prophet, but his predictions turn out to be true (Mk 14:55–72).

These summaries, while highly superficial, are only meant to illustrate that all the Gospels combine the messiahship of Jesus with "prophetic" features. They do not, however, follow a common pattern. Matthew, Luke, and John all make some use of the analogy of, and contrast between, Jesus and Moses, but they do so in different ways. This indicates that the combination of royal messianic categories with prophetic categories is due to historical events (viz., the public ministry of Jesus as a sage and prophet and his crucifixion as king of the Jews) and only secondarily to a given set of messianic or other ideas.

PROTOTYPES

"Messianic ideas" and "early Christologies" were formed by the use of promises and predictions, but important in that process were also prototypes and precedents of the past, as retold in contemporary settings. Both the Hebrew Scriptures and later writings attest several configurations of royalty or charismatic leadership with prophecy and other offices and functions which may vary from case to case (e.g., priesthood, judging, military command or action, miracles and, often, wisdom). The figures may belong to the remote past from Adam to Moses, to the premonarchial period and later epochs, or to the heavenly world. Both the variability of combinations and interrelations of myth, legends, historical events and circumstances, and the hopes for the future have analogies in the Ancient Near East, in the Greco-Roman world, and in other cultures as well. In several cases, we can observe both correlation and contrast between biblical and later figures (who may be either contemporaries or persons expected to come in the future).

Kings

David was considered an inspired prophet and composer of Psalms, at least some of which referred to his offspring, the Messiah. The fights of the young David and his men may have served as a model for freedom fighters who aspired to kingship after the death of Herod and later. Christians tended to stress that Jesus was not a king like David, even though the promises to David and David's own prophetic words applied to him (e.g., Mk 12:35–37; Jn 7:40–42; Acts 2:29–32). Solomon was the prototype of the wise king, the son of David who built the temple, and a great exorcist. I am not aware of any Jewish evidence that he was considered a prototype of the Messiah, but some similarity between Solomon and Jesus as "Son of David" may be more than fortuitous.

High Priests

In postexilic times the high priest was also civil leader. The priests had administered the lot oracle, and prophetic inspiration could be ascribed to Aaron and his descendants, including Caiaphas. Prophetic gifts as well as priesthood and militant zeal were ascribed to Levi and to Phinehas. The promises to them and their descendants may have been applied to later "savior" figures, but not to a royal Messiah. Samuel was a priest, but could be called "the greatest of prophets and kings" (Philo, *Ebr* 143). He does not, however, seem to have been regarded as a prototype of a "messianic" figure.

Prophet

Moses was the mediator of redemption from Egypt and the giving of the Torah. Philo and others regarded him as king and priest, but the idea of succession and the hope for a man like Moses was linked to Moses the prophet (Deut 18:15–19, cf. 34:9–12). The Mosaic model was important both for Philo (see Borgen) and for Samaritan hopes for the future (e.g., the Samaritan who promised to recover the sacred vessels which Moses had buried on Mount Gerizim [Josephus, *Ant* 18.85–86]). The Mosaic model contributed not only to the picture of Jesus as the Christ but also (later) to rabbinic ideas about the Messiah, the "second redeemer."

As the first successor of Moses, Joshua is depicted as a charismatic leader and prophet, the shepherd of the congregation (Num 27:15–23). As such, he was a model, not for the Messiah but for Theudas, the Egyptian prophet, and possibly for others who gathered a crowd around themselves in the expectation that God would intervene in such a way that a miraculous crossing of Jordan or the fall of the walls of Jerusalem would inaugurate redemption.

Elijah is depicted as a zealous prophet who performed miracles and interfered in both political and religious affairs. In hopes for the future, the coming Elijah was generally a separate figure who was to restore the tribes of Jacob, to whom later rabbis ascribed various functions. The evidence for the identification of Elijah with the eschatological high priest is slim, but several scholars have assumed that the juxtaposition of "the priest Elijah" and "the high priest John (Hyrcanus)" in *TargPsJon* Deut 33:11 goes back to a very early tradition. Otherwise there are few, if any, Jewish analogies to the opinion that John the Baptist or Jesus himself was Elijah in Matthew and Mark (Mt 11:14; Mk 6:15; 8:28; 9:12) or to Luke's use of Elijah (and Elisha) in the Gospel narrative. At the very least, however, one can draw the conclusion that both John and Jesus were regarded as eschatological prophets.

THE HISTORY OF JESUS

I cannot deal with the history of Jesus in any depth, but the preceding survey allows for some conclusions and suggestions.

Jewish messianic ideas and movements at the time of Christ must primarily be studied within the setting of Jewish political, social, and religious history and not as antecedents of or contrasts to Christology.

Like messianic ideas, even christological conceptions were diverse, but the divergency should not be exaggerated as easily happens when diverse titles, genres, or concepts are postulated to represent different Christologies cultivated in different social groups. It is possible, however, to distinguish between a type of preaching and teaching that centered on the crucified and vindicated Christ and another type which mainly understood Jesus as teacher, sage, and revealer of the saving truth. Both types were subject to diverse developments depending upon time, upon the cultural, local, and social setting, and upon individual teachers and writers, but they were not completely separated at the outset and, in fact, could later be integrated with one another.

While it is possible to trace Christological terms back to their roots within or outside Judaism, it is also possible—and perhaps more important—to observe that the elaboration of faith in the crucified Messiah and of messianic ideas both worked by means of interpretation (and reinterpretation) of Scriptures in light of historical events, experiences, and situations, and vice versa.

Our knowledge of the history of Jesus is dependent upon the memories of the disciples as handed on and altered in the generation(s) after them. Any attempt to recover that history must therefore be critical, and what can be established with approximate certainty is more important than impressive reconstructions. Detailed analysis of the history of tradition is often conjectural, however, and the "criterion of dissimilarity" isolates Jesus from his environment. Both approaches are to some extent dependent upon general paradigms and can easily result in new forms of modernizing Jesus. A genuinely historical approach cannot isolate Jesus but must rather employ a "criterion of similarity" in order to relate the history of Jesus to the history of his environment. The real history must have been a history of action and reaction of Jesus, his disciples, and his opponents and adversaries, and the outcome was the crucifixion of Jesus and the disciples' faith in the crucified and risen Messiah.

In terms of the reaction of Jesus' opponents to him, the question of E. Rivkin, "What crucified Jesus?" is more fruitful than the traditional question "Who crucified Jesus?" The traditional problem "Jesus and the Zealots" might be reformulated "Jesus and the Fourth Philosophy." Judas the Galilean was a "sophist," not the leader of an insurrection. Opponents must have found several similarities between Judas and his followers and Jesus and those who followed him: affinity to yet distance from the Pharisees; a radical insistence upon the sovereignty of God and a radical interpretation of God's will, without any accommodation to what was necessary to retain social order and religious life in an occupied country; and willingness to endure persecution and death. Not paying taxes to the Romans was an act of passive resistance, but the "Fourth Philosophy" could also supply terrorists and, later, freedom fighters with an ideology (as the philosophy of Marx has done!). Given the circumstances of first-century Palestine, the teachings of Jesus would, like those of Judas, seem to threaten the delicate coexistence of Jewish and Roman authorities as much as they would seem to threaten Roman power itself.

Jesus acted as a teacher, prophet, exorcist, and healer, but the role of king and prophet might overlap. He acted as an agent of God, with an authority which did not quite fit any category. Both followers and opponents may have thought of him as a potential messiah, even though he himself did not claim to be *the* prophet or the Messiah. I strongly suspect that Jn 6:15 is an addition to the story of the feeding miracle, but some sayings in "Q" would suggest that what was now taking place in Jesus surpassed the presence of kings and prophets (see esp. Lk 10:24; 11:30–32;). Especially Jesus' entry into Jerusalem and his action in the temple must have provoked the priestly aristocracy and could be construed as evidence that a messianic movement was taking shape. If Jesus was also supposed to have said that he would, by a miracle, destroy the temple and build it up again, that would also be proof that he claimed something appropriate only to a king.

The crucifixion of Jesus as king of the Jews is a necessary condition but not a sufficient cause of the faith in Jesus as the Christ. The same must be said about the Easter experiences of the disciples. They must have been convinced that God had acted through Jesus and that the kingdom of God was at hand. They may even have thought of Jesus as the Messiah, but if so their messianic ideas had undergone a radical transformation.

The historian can only know anything about Jesus' intentions to the degree that they correspond to his actions, words, and experiences. Thus the question of whether or not Jesus had a messianic self-consciousness will, of necessity, elude the historian.

The Gospels are testimonies of faith, not historical reports, and their narratives may be biased. They do, however, reveal a historical sense that a political power play was a feature of the events that led to the crucifixion of Jesus. They distinguish between the surface happenings that everyone could observe and the deeper dimension at which God was realizing his hidden plan through these events. To this extent, they exhibit a historical realism which is absent in many critical attempts to explain the transformation of messianic ideas to Christology in terms of the history of ideas.

CHRISTIAN PROPHECY AND THE
MESSIANIC STATUS OF JESUS

THE PROBLEM

Jesus of Nazareth was regarded by his followers as the Messiah of Jewish eschatological expectation, if not during his lifetime, then certainly within a very short interval after his crucifixion and resurrection.[1] Jesus was executed for treason, after all, for pretending to be "the King of the Jews" (Mk 15:26). One of the first and most significant stages in the development of the christology of earliest Palestinian Christianity was the conviction that through his resurrection, understood as his exaltation or enthronement at the right hand of God,[2] Jesus had become both Lord (Aram.: *mar;* Gk.: *kyrios*) and Messiah (*Christos*).[3] Ps 110:1, the single OT passage most quoted and alluded to in the NT, played a key role in facilitating such a belief,[4] though it is also probable that 2Sam 7:12–14 may have played an even more significant role in the development of the so-called two-stage christology, from son of David to son of God (Rom 1:3–4).[5]

---

1. This statement is intentionally formulated in such a way that the problem of the messianic consciousness of Jesus is avoided.

2. B. Lindars, *New Testament Apologetic* (London, 1961), p. 42; W. O. Walker, "Christian Origins and Resurrection Faith," *JR* 52 (1972) 44.

3. Acts 2:32–36, 13:33; Rom 1:3–4; Phil 2:9–11; cf. Heb 1:3–13; cf. J. H. Hayes, "The Resurrection as Enthronement and the Earliest Church Christology," *Int* 12 (1968) 333–45; R. H. Fuller, *Foundations of New Testament Christology* (New York, 1965), pp. 184–86.

4. See the important study with an extensive bibliography by D. M. Hay, *Glory at the Right Hand: Psalm 110 in Early Christianity* (Nashville, 1973). For an updated bibliography, see T. Callan, "Ps 110:1 and the Origin of the Expectation That Jesus Will Come Again," *CBQ* 44 (1982) 625, n. 11. There are five quotations of portions of Ps 110 in the NT (Mk 12:36 = Mt 22:44 = Lk 20:42–43; Acts 2:34–35; Heb 1:13), two quotations in the Apostolic Fathers (1Clem 36:5; EBar 12:10), and nineteen allusions to Ps 110:1 in the NT (Mk 14:62 = Mt 26:64 = Lk 22:69; Mk 16:19; Acts 2:33; 5:31; 7:55, 56; Rom 8:34; 1Cor 15:25; Eph 1:20, 2:6; Col 3:1; Heb 1:3, 8:1, 10:12–13, 12:2; 1Pet 3:22; Rev 3:21).

5. E. Schweizer, "Röm. 1:3f. und der Gegensatz von Fleisch und Geist vor und bei Paulus," *Neotestamentica* (Zürich, Stuttgart, 1963), pp. 180–89; D. C. Duling, "The Promises to David and Their Entrance into Christianity—Nailing Down a Likely Hypothesis," *NTS* 20 (1973–74) 70–77.

In the seven undoubtedly genuine letters of Paul, the earliest extant Christian literature, the term *Christos* occurs 266 times. It is used in two primary ways: as a proper name for Jesus and as a name for a specific Messiah, Jesus (cf. Rom 9:5). According to N. A. Dahl, *Christos* is *never* used in these letters as a general term but always as a designation for Jesus—it is *never* used as a predication of Jesus (e.g. "Jesus is the Christ"), is *never* accompanied by a genitive (e.g. "the Christ of God"), and the form "Jesus *the* Christ" is not found in the oldest text of the epistles.[6] The situation is virtually the same in the six disputed Pauline letters which were probably written during the generation following Paul's death (Ephesians, Colossians, 2 Thessalonians, 1 Timothy, 2 Timothy, Titus), in which the term *Christos* occurs 113 times, always as a proper name for Jesus. In the seven general epistles, *Christos* occurs 50 times and again is consistently used as a name for Jesus. In 1 John, however, *ho Christos* is used 2 times as a title predicated of Jesus. 1Jn 2:22 speaks of those who deny "that Jesus is the Christ," and 1Jn 5:1 mentions the benefits possessed by one "who believes that Jesus is the Christ."[7] *Christos* occurs 12 times in Hebrews, 3 times in the traditional form "Jesus Christ" (10:10; 13:8, 21), and 9 times alone, usually with the article, as designations for Jesus (3:6, 14; 5:5; 6:1; 9:11, 14, 24, 28; 11:26). In Revelation, an apocalypse in an epistolary framework, *Christos* occurs 7 times—3 times in the traditional formulation "Jesus Christ" (1:1, 2, 5), 2 times in the articular form "his [i.e. God's] Christ" as a title for Jesus (11:15, 12:10), and 2 times in the articular form as a name for Jesus (20:4, 6).[8] In the heterogeneous group of texts comprising the Apostolic Fathers, *Christos* occurs 213 times, usually as part of the compound name "Jesus Christ," once as a general designation for the Jewish Messiah (EBar 12:10 alluding to Mk 12:35–37 and par.), and just twice in the titular form "Jesus *the* Christ" (1Clem 42:1, Ignatius *Eph* 18:2). In summary the messiahship of Jesus is assumed in the NT epistolary literature, and with the exception of 1Jn 2:22 and 5:1, little or no interest is shown in the problem of specifically demonstrating the messianic status of Jesus.

The situation is completely different in the Gospels and Acts, where the issue of the messianic status of Jesus is a matter of central concern. The term *Christos* is found 80 times in the gospels and Acts—16 times as a proper

---

6. Dahl, "Die Messianität Jesu bei Paulus," *Studia Paulina in Honorem Johannis de Zwaan* (Haarlem, 1953), p. 83.

7. R. E. Brown in *The Epistles of John* (AB 30 [Garden City, N.Y., 1983], p. 172) observes that in Christianity the titles Christ and Son of God were more than just messianic titles derived from Judaism but were used to express the divinity of Jesus. Therefore the problem reflected in 1Jn 2:22 and 5:1, in Brown's view, is that the "secessionists" apparently refused to identify the earthly, human Jesus with the divine Messiah, the Son of God (Brown, *Epistles of John*, p. 352). According to Brown, "the opponents so stress the divine principle in Jesus that the earthly career of the divine principle is neglected" (*The Community of the Beloved Disciple* [New York, 1979], p. 112).

8. M. De Jonge, "The Use of the Expression *ho Christos* in the Apocalypse of John," *L'Apocalypse johannique et l'Apocalyptique dans le Nouveau Testament*, ed. J. Lambrecht (Leuven, 1980), pp. 267–81.

name for Jesus (e.g. Mk 1:1; Jn 1:17, 17:3) and 64 times as a title, either as a general designation for the eschatological Davidic king,[9] or less frequently but more importantly as a title predicated of Jesus (Mk 8:29 = Mt 16:16 = Lk 9:20; Mk 14:61 = Mt 26:63 = Lk 22:67; Jn 9:22; 11:27; 20:31; Acts 5:42; 8:5; 9:22; 17:3b; 18:5, 28). Statements such as "Jesus is the Christ" (Acts 17:3b, Jn 11:27), or "Jesus is the Christ, the Son of God" (Jn 20:31) are often and correctly categorized as short creedal statements or confessions.

This brief survey of the use of the *Christos* designation in the NT presents a problem. The earliest surviving Christian literature, the genuine letters of Paul (written over a fifteen-year period, 49–64 C.E.) do not suggest either directly or indirectly that the messianic status of Jesus was a matter of particular concern during Paul's career. In Acts, on the other hand, Paul is presented as arguing that Jesus was the Messiah (9:22; 17:2–3; 18:5, 28). The simplest (though not the most satisfying) explanation is that Paul expressed different concerns when addressing Christian congregations on the one hand and unconverted Jews on the other. On the whole, the Gospels and Acts, written during the generation following the death of Paul, show a vital concern with the problem of Jesus' messianic status. This is peculiar since one would expect that the period during which the issue of Jesus' messiahship would be most prominent and controversial would be the years immediately following the crucifixion and resurrection of Jesus, the period when Christianity was a group within early Judaism. Aside from the Gospels and Acts, the messianic status of Jesus does not come up for serious discussion again until second-century apologists, such as Justin Martyr, engage in Jewish-Christian dialogue. Why do the Gospels and Acts, written ca. 70–100 C.E., exhibit a seemingly anachronistic concern with the problem of Jesus' messianic status?

THE PROPOSAL

Preoccupation with the ultimate religious significance of Jesus of Nazareth was not the only striking feature of early Palestinian Christianity. Christians consciously constituted an elect community living in the last days. They experienced the presence and power of the Spirit of God in their midst, externalized and verified through prophesying and miracles of healing. In addition to his messianic status, Jesus was also, perhaps alternatively, categorized as a prophet or even as the eschatological Mosaic prophet.[10] One significant aspect of the continuity between the early community and Jesus was that

---

9. Mt 2:4, 24:5; Mk 12:35 = Mt 22:42 = Lk 20:41; Mk 13:21 = Mt 24:23; Mk 14:61 = Mt 26:63 = Lk 22:67; Mk 15:32 = Lk 23:35; Lk 3:15; 4:41; 23:2, 39; 24:26, 46; Jn 1:20, 25; 3:28; 4:25, 29; 7:26, 27, 31, 41b, 42; 10:24; 12:34; Acts 2:31; 3:18, 17:3a.

10. The evidence is summarized in D. E. Aune, *Prophecy in Early Christianity and the Ancient Mediterranean World* (Grand Rapids, Mich., 1983), pp. 153–57.

both were filled with the Spirit of God.[11]

In this paper I wish to link the two topics of Jesus' messianic status and the prophetic character of early Christianity by posing a question of potentially great significance, though one which is very difficult to answer: Is there any evidence to suggest that the recognition of Jesus' messianic status (however defined) was legitimated by prophetic speech or prophetic visions by early Christians during the period ca. 30–50 C.E.?

The prophetic legitimation of the messianic status of Jesus is a possibility which coheres well with ancient Israelite kingship ideology, since there is abundant evidence in the OT to suggest that prophets played a significant role in the prophetic identification and anointing of prospective kings. Samuel anointed Saul (1Sam 10:1–8), and David (1Sam 16:1–3); Ahijah anointed Jeroboam I (1Kgs 11:29–39; 14:7); Jehu ben Hanani anointed Baasha (1Kgs 16:1–2); an unnamed prophet anointed Jehu (2Kgs 9:1–6). It is also likely that prophets participated in coronation ceremonies, perhaps declaring the new status of the king as son of God. Ps 2:7 and Ps 110:4 probably originated as prophetic oracles proclaiming the royal status and divine sonship of prospective kings.[12] During the late fifth century B.C.E., Sanballat and Tobiah accused Nehemiah of hiring prophets to declare "There is a king in Judah" (Neh 6:7). Josephus, who considered himself a clerical prophet,[13] reportedly announced to Vespasian that he was Caesar: "You are Caesar, Vespasian, and emperor, you and your son here" (Josephus War 3.400–2), a role also attributed to Yohanan ben Zakkai in rabbinic literature: "Behold, you are about to be appointed king" (ARN [Rec. A], 4.5; b. Gitt 56a–b).[14] Of the many popular messianic movements in Palestine from the death of Herod the Great in 4 B.C.E. to the second Jewish revolt of 132–35 C.E. led by Simon Bar Kosiba,[15] it was only Bar Kosiba who apparently made an explicit messianic claim. This claim was publicly recognized and announced by Rabbi Akiba.[16] According to y. Ta'an 68d, "Again, when R. Akiba saw Bar Kosiba [Kokhba], he cried out, 'This is King Messiah,'" using the typical form of the recognition oracle.[17] Akiba reportedly referred to bar Kosiba as bar Kokhba, "son of a star," referring to Simon's messianic status by an allusion to the messianic

11. H. Windisch, "Jesus und der Geist nach synoptischer Überlieferung," Studies in Early Christianity, ed. S. J. Case (New York and London, 1928), pp. 209–36; C. K. Barrett, The Holy Spirit and the Gospel Tradition, rev. ed. (Philadelphia, 1966).

12. H.-J. Kraus, Theology of the Psalms, trans. K. Crim (Minneapolis, 1986), pp. 111–19.

13. J. Blenkinsopp, "Prophecy and Priesthood in Josephus," JJS 25 (1974) 239–62.

14. A. Schalit, "Die Erhebung Vespasians nach Flavius Josephus, Talmud, und Midrasch: Zur Geschichte einer messianischen Prophetie," ANRW 2.2, pp. 208–377.

15. For a survey, see R. A. Horsley and J. S. Hanson, Bandits, Prophets, and Messiahs: Popular Movements at the Time of Jesus (Minneapolis, 1985), pp. 88–134.

16. E. Schürer, The History of the Jewish People in the Age of Jesus Christ (175 B.C.–A.D. 135), rev. and ed. by G. Vermes and F. Millar (Edinburgh, 1973), vol. 1, pp. 543–52.

17. Schürer, History of the Jewish People, vol. 1, p. 543, n. 130. J. Fitzmyer, "The Bar Cochba Period" in Essays on the Semitic Background of the New Testament (Missoula, Mont., 1974), pp. 314–15.

prophecy of Num 24:17. Yet the title which Bar Kosiba preferred, according to numismatic and papyrological evidence, was not Messiah, but *Nasi* ("prince"), a traditional title of the Israelite king.

Yet in the final analysis, the ultimate religious significance of Jesus could not be confined to messianic categories. When fewer and fewer Jews and more and more pagans were attracted to Christianity, christological motifs derived from Israelite kingship ideology inevitably became less functional. Thus while it is probable that in the very early period of Aramaic-speaking Palestinian Christianity the messianic status of Jesus was of paramount importance, messiahship became a decreasingly less useful way of conceptualizing the ultimate significance of Jesus.

AMBIGUITIES IN THE TERM "MESSIAH"

While various and sometimes contradictory reconstructions of Israelite enthronement ritual have been proposed on the basis of the two OT coronation accounts (1Kgs 1:32–48; 2Kgs 11:12–20),[18] and the important enthronement Psalms 2 and 110,[19] it was the *unction* of the new king (representing his election by Yahweh)[20] which was the most important feature of coronation. Consequently the nominal form *māšîaḥ* ("anointed one") is often used in the OT with various modifiers, with the connotation "the king who has been consecrated through unction with oil."[21] The rite of unction was closely associated with possession by the Spirit of God (cf. 1Sam 10:1, 9; 16:13; Isa 61:1; Zech 4:1–14), an association also reflected in the NT (Acts 10:38; 1Jn 2:20, 27). In the NT, the Gk. term *Christos* ("anointed") is a translation of the Heb. term *māšîaḥ* (twice transliterated as *messias* in Jn 1:41 and 4:25). When used in the Gospels and Acts as a general designation, it unambiguously refers to the ideal future Davidic king of Jewish eschatological expectation (Mk 15:32, Jn 7:42). There is little indication of the ambiguity which surrounded the notion in early Judaism. The reasons why the title *Christos* became the

18. R. de Vaux, *Ancient Israel: Its Life and Institutions*, trans. J. McHugh (New York, 1961), pp. 102–7, suggests five stages of Israelite enthronement rituals: (1) investiture with insignia, (2) the anointing, (3) the acclamation (e.g. "Long live the king!"), (4) the enthronement, and (5) the homage.

19. Basing his findings primarily on Ps 110 and Ps 2:7, H.-J. Kraus, *Theology of the Psalms*, pp. 111–19, suggests that the protocol for bestowing authority on the new king consisted of three distinct phases: (1) A prophetic speaker declared that the king was the "son of God" (Ps 2:7, 110:3). (2) The king was then told to ascend the throne and sit at the right hand of God (Ps 110:1). (3) After ascending the throne the king was declared the legitimate heir (Ps 110:4).

20. Halpern, *The Constitution of the Monarchy in Israel* Harvard Semitic Monographs, 25 (Chico, CA, 1981), p. 14.

21. Cf. such phrases as 'Yahweh's anointed" (1Sam 16:6; 24:6, 10; 26:9, 16; 2Sam 1:14, 19:21; Lam 4:20), "my [i.e. Yahweh's] anointed" (1Sam 2:35; 1Chr 16:22; Ps 105:15, 132:17), "thy [i.e. Yahweh's] anointed" (2Chr 6:42; Ps 84:9; 89:38, 51; 132:10; Hab 3:13), and "his [i.e. Yahweh's] anointed" (1Sam 2:10; 12:3, 5; 2Sam 22:51; Ps 2:2, 18:50, 20:6, 28:8; Isa 45:1).

central way of defining the ultimate religious significance of Jesus in early Palestinian Christianity is problematic since his career did not fit early Jewish messianic expectations.[22]

It has become increasingly evident that the conception of "*the* Jewish Messiah" is in reality a synthetic construct which masks the variety of messianic figures in early Jewish eschatological expectation.[23] The absolute form "the Messiah," without an accompanying genitive or possessive pronoun, occurs rarely and primarily in late first-century texts (1En 48:10; 52:4; 2Bar 30:1; 70:9; 4Ezra 7:28, 29; 12:32).[24] When it does occur, it usually refers to the eschatological Davidic king. Yet a priestly Messiah and a royal Messiah, with the latter subject to the former, are mentioned in both the Dead Sea Scrolls (1QS 9.10–11; 1QSa 12–13; cf. CD 19.10–11; 20.1) and the Testaments of the Twelve Patriarchs (TReu 6:5–12; TLevi 18:2–9). Prophets could also be called "Yahweh's anointed" (e.g. Samuel in 1Sam 24:6, 10; 26:16; 2Sam 1:14, 16), or "anointed ones" (Ps 105:15; CD 2:12, 6:1; 1QM 11:7–8; 11QMelch 18). In the Mishnah (codified ca. 200 C.E.), the Davidic Messiah is mentioned only twice and the designation "the anointed one" is used of the high priest.

The messianic role of Jesus was not limited to the traditional though ambiguous title Messiah, but was also conveyed through other titles such as Son of God, Son of David, King, and Son of man. Since the king of Israel was occasionally designated as the Son of God (2Sam 7:12–14, Ps 2:7), that title was also appropriate for the Messiah once those passages were understood in a messianic sense (cf. 4QFlor 1.10–13; cf. 4Ezra 7:28: "my son the Messiah"; cf. 13:32, 37).[25] Even though there were many ways of referring to the royal descendant of the Davidic dynasty, the specific title "son of David" occurs in pre-Christian Jewish texts only in PssSol 17:23.[26] Similarly the term *kyrios* could be understood in a messianic sense in hellenistic Jewish Christianity on the basis of Ps 110:1 (Mk 12:35–37; Acts 2:33–36; EBar 12:10–12), a passage which was probably interpreted messianically in early Judaism by the first century C.E.[27] The Son of man designation is the most problematic

22. It is this problem which concerned W. C. van Unnik in "Jesus the Christ," *Sparsa Collecta: The Collected Essays of W. C. van Unnik*, part 2 (Leiden, 1980), pp. 248–68. Van Unnik proposes that for early Christians messiahship did not consist in the outward activity of a king but in a person who possesses the Spirit of God (p. 266).

23. See R. A. Horsley, "Popular Messianic Movements Around the Time of Jesus," *CBQ* 46 (1984) 471–95; Horsley and Hanson, *Bandits, Prophets and Messiahs*; R. A. Horsley, "'Like One of the Prophets of Old': Two Types of Popular Prophets at the Time of Jesus," *CBQ* 47 (1985) 435–63.

24. M. de Jonge, "The Use of the Word 'Anointed' in the Time of Jesus," *NovT* 7 (1966) 132–48; idem, *TDNT*, vol. 9, pp. 511–17.

25. E. Schweizer, "The Concept of the Davidic 'Son of God' in Acts and Its Old Testament Background," *Studies in Luke-Acts*, ed. L. E. Keck and J. L. Martyn (Nashville, 1966), pp. 186–93.

26. See the evidence assembled by Duling, "The Promises to David," pp. 55–69.

27. Hay, *Glory at the Right Hand*, pp. 19–33.

of all. In recent years it has become increasingly clear that in pre-Christian Judaism there was no concept of "the Son of man" as an eschatological heavenly redeemer figure. The Jewish and Christian texts which use the Son of man designation in a titular sense all date from the last half of the first century C.E. Though Jesus very likely used the "Son of man" idiom as an indirect way of referring to himself, its transformation into a messianic title based on Dan 7:13 was probably accomplished by the early church.

The evangelists and their sources used these titles to define the person and function of Jesus. By the time the traditions of Jesus were incorporated into Q (ca. 50 C.E.) and particularly into Mark and the other Gospels (ca. 70–100 C.E.), the more significant eschatological titles and titles of honor found in them had become, at least to some extent, synonymous with one another by virtue of their common application to Jesus.[28] Because the meaning of such titles varied from context to context in Jewish eschatological scenarios, the specific application of each title to a particular historical figure such as Jesus necessarily resulted in the transformation of the titles in light of the historical particularity of Jesus and the transformation of the historical image of the Jesus to whom they were applied. The transformation of the titles themselves was unavoidable since the varied and even contradictory associations with which they were associated could not be applied to a historical figure without eliminating some connotations in favor of others. The transformation of the historical image of Jesus himself was also inevitable in view of the power and resiliency which many of these eschatological titles carried with them.

The meaning of the title Messiah or *Christos* when applied to Jesus, however, was determined primarily by *Christian* conceptions of Jesus rather than by conventional *Jewish* messianic notions.[29] That means that the Christian conception of the *heavenly* coronation of Jesus as Messiah represents a spiritualization of the traditional Jewish understanding of an *earthly* coronation of the ideal king of the future. It was the death of Jesus, however, which the early church regarded as the primary obstacle preventing the general Jewish recognition of Jesus as the Messiah of Jewish expectation. The church therefore tried to revise the Jewish conception of the Messiah by arguing

28. The complex relationship between the christological titles in Mark, for example, has recently been treated by J. D. Kingsbury, *The Christology of Mark's Gospel* (Philadelphia, 1983). In a recent book by S. Kim, *The Son of Man as the Son of God* (Grand Rapids, Mich., 1985), the author intends to show that Jesus consciously used the title Son of man as a discrete way of revealing himself as the Son of God. He has really only succeeded in achieving the obvious—i.e. that the designations "Son of man" and "Son of God" are synonymous by virtue of their application to Jesus.

29. S. J. Case, "The Rise of Christian Messianism," *Studies in Early Christianity,* ed. S. J. Case (New York and London, 1928), p. 313; W. Manson, *Jesus the Messiah* (London, 1943), p. 12; N. A. Dahl, "Die Messianität Jesu" p. 86; W. C. van Unnik, "Jesus the Messiah," p. 259; M. De Jonge, "The Earliest Christian Use of *Christos*: Some Suggestions," *NTS* 32 (1986) 321.

from OT proof texts that both suffering and death were integral aspects of
the divinely ordained role of the Messiah (Lk 24:46; Acts 3:18, 17:3, 26:22–
23; 1Cor 15:3). For this reason early creeds or confessions placed the motif
of the *death* of Jesus in close association with *Christos*, which already tended
to be used as a proper name for Jesus in pre-Pauline hellenistic Jewish Christianity (cf. 1Cor 15:3).[30] The problem of identifying Jesus as the Messiah,
however, did not simply center on the fact of the Messiah's death (which in
itself was not so problematic, cf. 4Ezra 7:29), so much as the fact that he died
before accomplishing the tasks traditionally associated with the ideal future
Davidic king. However, early Palestinian Christianity did not *deny* the traditionally messianic role to Jesus, but simply *postponed* that role into the
imminent (though indefinite) eschatological future (Acts 1:6; 3:20–21; Rev
11:15; 12:10; 20:4, 6).

ORACULAR LEGITIMATIONS OF ROYAL STATUS

Introductory Considerations

The focus of this section is on one particular feature of sacral legitimation,
the prophetic or oracular recognition of the king as one divinely ordained to
rule. In an earlier study, I called attention to the recognition oracle, a form
of prophetic speech found in many parts of the ancient Mediterranean
world.[31] The basic function of this oracular form was to provide both super-
naturally guaranteed identification and divine legitimation for individuals of
singular importance. Sacral legitimation was an important feature of ancient
coronation rituals and ancient kingship ideologies. While all kings are "sacred" in one way or another, in the ancient Mediterranean world all kingships were sacred kingships.[32] The essential feature of sacral kingship is the
special connection thought to exist between kings and the divine world, by
virtue of which the king is accorded the status of a superior human being. In
the cultures of the ancient Near East and the ancient Mediterranean world,
sacral kingship was conceptualized through two very different royal ideologies. The king could either be accorded divine quality or divine descent, or
he could be regarded as divinely chosen or elected. One of the primary concerns of usurpers who interrupt dynastic succession and found new dynasties
is sacral legitimation of their rule. Israelite kingship ideology saw the sacral-
ity of the king in terms of the tradition of divine election. Since the eschatological fantasies of messianism in the ancient Near East were based on the

---

30. W. Kramer, *Christ, Lord, Son of God*, trans. B. Hardy (SBT 50; Naperville, Ill., 1966),
pp. 38–44.
31. Aune, *Prophecy in Early Christianity*, pp. 68–70.
32. C. Grottanelli, "Kingship: An Overview," *Encyclopedia of Religion*, ed. M. Eliade (New
York, 1987), vol. 8, p. 313.

hope of the reestablishment of native kingship, it was inevitable that sacral legitimation in particular should play a significant role in authorizing the ideal future savior-king.

The Example of Alexander the Great

Alexander the Great was interested in promoting his divine descent in order to legitimate his status as ruler over the many formerly independent kingdoms which he conquered and attempted to unify through the imposition of hellenistic language and culture. Callisthenes, the official eyewitness historian and propagandist of Alexander's expedition (in a fragment of a lost work preserved in Strabo 17.1.43), mentions oracles revealing Alexander's divine origin. The most famous were reportedly pronounced by an Egyptian prophet at the oracle of Zeus-Ammon at the Oasis of Siwah, the oracle of Apollo at Didyma, and the prophetess Athenais. Though nothing further is known of the oracles of Didymaean Apollo and Athenais (cf. Strabo 14.1.34), several fragmentary versions of Alexander's visit to Siwah survive (Arrian, *Anabasis Alexandri* 3.3–4; Plutarch, *Alexander* 27.5–11; Diodorus 17.49.2–51; Q. Curtius Rufus 4.25–30).[33] The most likely historical reconstruction is that the priest of Ammon greeted Alexander as a "son of Zeus" (following the conventional *interpretatio Graeca,* Zeus was identified with Ammon, and Alexander's recent conquest of Egypt had made him the successor to the pharaohs, who were considered to be incarnations of the god Horus and sons of Amun Ra). The form of this greeting is variously preserved as [*su ei*] *Dios hyios* (Strabo 17.1.43), or *O pai Dios,* "O son of Zeus," a phrase which, according to one ancient rationalizing tradition, was based on a mispronunciation of *O paidos,* "My son" (Plutarch, *Alexander* 27.9). At all events, while Alexander did enter into the innermost shrine of Amun to pose questions to the oracle, he never revealed either his questions or the answers he received. It was Callisthenes, doubtless with Alexander's approval, who turned the priest's greeting into an oracular announcement of Alexander's divine sonship.[34] Following Callisthenes, the many popular accounts of Alexander's visit to Siwah tended to repeat and amplify the fiction of an oracular recognition of Alexander's divine status as son of Zeus.

Gospel Accounts of Jesus

The historical Jesus, in a manner characteristic of charismatic leaders of thaumaturgical movements,[35] used various strategies to legitimate his mis-

---

33. For a review of the literature on the question of Alexander's visit to Siwah and the oracle of Ammon, see J. Seibert, *Alexander der Grosse* (Darmstadt, 1972), pp. 116–25. See also the reconstruction by R. L. Fox, *Alexander the Great* (London, 1973), pp. 200–14, 523–24. More recently, see P. A. Brunt, trans., *Arrian* (Cambridge, Mass., London, 1976), vol. 1, pp. 467–80 (Appendix V: "The Visit to Siwah").

34. Fox, *Alexander the Great,* pp. 211–12; Brunt, I, pp. 471–72.

35. B. R. Wilson, *Magic and the Millennium: A Sociological Study of Religious Movements of Protest Among Tribal and Third-World Peoples* (New York, 1973), pp. 102–95.

sion and message as ultimate and transcendent. The historical core of the miracle tradition, though later embellished and amplified, certainly functioned in this way. Equally important was Jesus' confident proclamation of the imminent arrival of the kingdom of God. Further, his prophetic actions (e.g. the cleansing of the temple, the triumphal entry) and his prophecies of the fate of Jerusalem and the temple, though also modified in the tradition, constituted another form of legitimation.[36] There is, however, no historically reliable evidence to suggest that either Jesus himself or those around him appealed to revelation to specifically identify or legitimate his person and work.[37] Whether or not his intention was to legitimate his role as *a* prophet, *the* Prophet, or the Messiah, or he did not consciously play any scripted role, it is clear that the early Palestinian church regarded the designation *Messiah* as so central for conceptualizing the significance of Jesus that it was quickly transformed into a proper name in pre-Pauline hellenistic Jewish Christianity.

There are many instances in the synoptic gospels in which the messianic status of Jesus is affirmed through supernatural means. (1) Using the form of the recognition oracle, on the occasion of the baptism of Jesus a heavenly voice declares, "Thou art my beloved Son; with thee I am well pleased" (Mk 1:11 = Mt 3:17 = Lk 3:22; cf. Jn 1:34), and in the episode of the transfiguration a heavenly voice announces, "This is my beloved Son; listen to him" (Mk 9:7 = Mt 17:5 = Lk 9:35).[38] (2) Demons, speaking through those in whom they reside, are depicted as providing supernatural confirmation of Jesus' identity.[39] An important example is the Markan summary (3:11): "And whenever the unclean spirits beheld him, they fell down before him and cried out, 'You are the Son of God.'" This is a significant passage because Mark, in summarizing the demonic identification of Jesus, casts his summary in the form of a recognition oracle. (3) Peter's confession to Jesus that "You are the Christ" (Mk 8:29 = Mt 16:16 = Lk 9:20) also exhibits the form and content, if not the function, of a recognition oracle in Mark and Luke. Yet that defect is rectified by Matthew, who specifically emphasizes the revelatory character of Peter's pronouncement in Mt 16:17: "Blessed are you, Simon Bar-Jona! For flesh and blood have not revealed this to you, but my Father who is in heaven." (4) Particularly in Luke a series of angelic disclosures and prophetic utterances reveal various aspects of the messianic status of Jesus.[40] Two

36. D. E. Aune, *Prophecy in Early Christianity*, pp. 171–88.

37. The revelatory discourses in the fourth gospel, in which the "I am" predications of Jesus occur, did not originate with the historical Jesus.

38. Aune, *Prophecy*, pp. 271–72.

39. Demonic identifications of Jesus are found in Mk 1:24 (= Lk 4:34); 3:11 (= Lk 4:41); 5:7 (= Mt 8:29 = Lk 8:28).

40. C. H. Talbert, "Promise and Fulfillment in Lukan Theology," *Luke-Acts: New Perspectives from the Society of Biblical Literature Seminar,* ed. C. H. Talbert (New York, 1984), pp. 91–103; idem, "Prophecies of Future Greatness: The Contribution of Greco-Roman Biographies to an Understanding of Luke 1:5–4:15," *The Divine Helmsman,* ed. J. L. Crenshaw and S. Sandmel (New York, 1980), pp. 129–41.

oracles are attributed to the aged Simeon, who functions as a prophet in recognizing the messianic status of the infant Jesus (2:25–35). Luke then introduces the prophetess Anna, who also recognizes Jesus as the one who will redeem Jerusalem (2:36–38). To this should be added the angelic message to Mary (1:26–38) and the aged Zechariah's prophecy (1:67–79).

An extensive instance of the remolding of Jesus traditions in line with messianic motifs is found in the gospel accounts of the baptism of Jesus mentioned above (Mk 1:9–11, Mt 3:13–17, Lk 3:21–22; cf. Jn 1:29–34). While the event itself is certainly historical, and perhaps even functioned as a prophetic call for Jesus, tradition has overlayed the narrative with imagery appropriate to the preliminary divine designation of a future Israelite king as a *nagid*, usually understood as a private anointing ritual.[41] While the ritual washing practiced by John has nothing in common with the practice of anointing with oil associated with Israelite royal designation and confirmation rituals (two separate but related stages),[42] the author of Luke-Acts understood the baptism of Jesus as his divine unction with the Holy Spirit (Lk 4:18; Acts 4:27, 10:38). Luke is very careful in his version of the baptism of Jesus to dissociate John from that event. According to Luke, John had already been arrested (Lk 3:20) before the baptism of Jesus took place (Lk 3:21–22). Similarly Acts 10:38 refers to "the baptism which John preached" and the fact that "God anointed Jesus of Nazareth with the Holy Spirit" without explicitly equating the two events, though they can hardly be understood otherwise.

Another legendary embellishment of the baptismal scene, the heavenly voice or *bat qol* either proclaiming *to* Jesus, "You are my beloved Son; with you I am well pleased" (Mk 1:11; Lk 3:22), or proclaiming *about* Jesus, "This is my beloved Son; with whom I am well pleased" (Mt 3:17), a conflated allusion to Ps 2:7 and Isa 42:1.[43] Psalm 2 is a coronation hymn, and the declaration in vs. 7, "You are my son," is an oracular adoption formula spoken to the king by a prophetic participant in the consecration ritual. A further step in the embellishment of the baptism episode is found in the fourth gospel, where the baptism of Jesus is by John the Baptist himself. The baptismal scene is described as a revelation to John, probably modeled after scenes in which God enables Samuel to recognize Saul and later David as the Lord's anointed in 1Sam 9:15–17 and 16:1–13. John claims that God had revealed to him that "'He on whom you see the Spirit descend and remain, this is he who baptizes with the Holy Spirit'" (Jn 1:33). He therefore concludes: "'And I have seen and have borne witness that this is the Son of God'" (Jn 1:34).

---

41. See Z. Weisman, "Anointing as a Motif in the Making of the Charismatic King," *Bib* 57 (1976) 379–82; Halpern, *Monarchy,* pp. 125–48.

42. Halpern, *Monarchy,* p. 125.

43. But see B. Chilton, *A Galilean Rabbi and His Bible* (Wilmington, Del., 1984), pp. 125–31.

The Primitive Confession "Jesus Is Lord"

1Cor 12:3 has provoked a great deal of discussion among NT interpreters:

> Therefore I want you to understand that no one speaking by the Spirit of God ever says "Jesus be cursed!" and no one can say "Jesus is Lord!" except by the Holy Spirit.

It is possible that the negative confession "Jesus be cursed!" represents a Pauline construct formulated as the antithesis to the positive confession "Jesus is Lord!" Though this confession was widely used throughout early Christianity (Jn 20:28, Rom 10:9, Phil 2:11), only here is it evident that it was (or could be) an inspired oracular utterance. The title "Lord" (*mar*) was already used of Jesus in Aramaic-speaking Palestinian Christianity (cf. the famous *marana tha* prayer in 1Cor 16:22).[44] The title "Lord" is closely linked to the messianic status of Jesus, since the Christian confession "Jesus is Lord" can be understood as an affirmation that Jesus is the royal Messiah at the right hand of God (Acts 2:34, Rom 8:34, 1Cor 15:25, Eph 1:20, Col 3:1), i.e. the Lordship of Jesus is the result of the completion of his saving work, not the presupposition for it. In hellenistic Jewish Christianity, "Lord" was the title which replaced "Messiah," which had been the centrally significant title for Jesus in Palestinian Christianity. While the form of this prophetic saying or confession is that of the recognition oracle,[45] any specific allusion to Jewish messianic ideology is missing.

Conclusions

In the gospels the oracular legitimations of the ultimate religious significance of Jesus abound. Yet without exception they appear to be *literary dramatizations* of the messianic status of Jesus overlayed on the Jesus traditions. With the single possible exception of 1Cor 12:3 (a problematic passage with many possible interpretations), there is no evidence that Christians exercised prophetic speech to legitimate the messianic status of Jesus. However, that does not mean that such prophetic legitimation did not occur, since it appears that very few authentic examples of Christian prophetic speech have been preserved.

VISIONARY REVELATIONS OF JESUS' MESSIANIC STATUS

When Paul claimed that God "was pleased to reveal his Son to me" (Gal 1:16), he was very likely referring to his experience on the road to Damascus in which he saw and recognized that the exalted Jesus was the Messiah. In

---

44. J. Fitzmyer, "The Semitic Background of the New Testament *Kyrios*-Title," *A Wandering Aramaean: Collected Essays* (Missoula, Mont., 1979), pp. 115–42.
45. Aune, *Prophecy in Early Christianity*, pp. 86, 140–41, 256–57, 270–74.

Gal 1:16 he uses the designation *Son*, while in 1Cor 9:1 he refers to the object of his Damascus experience as *Lord:* "Have I not seen Jesus our Lord?" He never connects the term *Christos* with his Damascus experience. For Luke, Paul's Damascus experience was linked to his recognition of the Messianic status of Jesus (cf. Acts 9:20, 22; 26:22–23). Similarly in 1Cor 15:8, after a list of various appearances of the risen Jesus, Paul claims that "he appeared [*ōphthē*] also to me." The fact that Paul used the same verb *ōphthē* three times in connection with five earlier resurrection appearances (1Cor 15:5–7) indicates that he regarded resurrection appearances (whether to Peter or to himself) as revelatory visions.[46] Yet neither Paul himself, nor the three later accounts in Acts 9, 22, and 26, reveal very much about the character of visionary revelations of the messianic status of Jesus. There are two important passages in the NT, however, which may provide more information about the form and content of such visionary revelations, Acts 7:55–56 and Rev 1:12–16.

Acts 7:55–56: The Vision of the Enthroned Son of Man

Acts 7:55–56 is an account of Stephen's own prophetic witness to the messianic status of Jesus, i.e. the enthroned Son of man at the right hand of God. It could well have been the kind of visionary experience mentioned by Paul but never described. Acts 7:55–56 is one of several passages in early Christian literature which reflect the exegetical permutations of Dan 7:13 combined with Ps 110:1 (cf. Mk 14:62 = Mt 26:64 = Lk 22:69).[47] Mk 14:62 and Acts 7:55–56, in addition to their common allusions to Dan 7:13 in combination with Ps 110:1, share two other features. They are both introduced with a verb of seeing (though two different Gk. verbs are employed), and they are both presented as revelatory sayings (Mk 14:62 is presented as a prophecy of Jesus regarding a future vision by the high priest, while Acts 7:55–56 presents a visionary experience of Stephen when he is at the point of death). The hypothesis that I wish to explore is that the tradition behind both Mk 14:62 and Acts 7:55–56 reflects a vision by a Christian prophet (rather than simply a *pesher* tradition formulated by a Christian exegetical school), confirming the heavenly messianic status of Jesus.

---

46. R. H. Fuller, *The Formation of the Resurrection Narratives* (New York, 1971), pp. 31–32, 49, 170. It is perhaps going too far beyond the evidence to suggest that Paul realized that the resurrection was true on the basis of his Damascus experience, as S. Kim proposes in *The Origin of Paul's Gospel* (Grand Rapids, Mich., 1982), p. 72. Regarding the Damascus experience, W. Marxsen observes that "Paul therefore fails to indicate whether it was that experience which convinced him of Jesus' resurrection" (*The Resurrection of Jesus of Nazareth* [Philadelphia, 1970], p. 101).

47. A similar tradition combining Dan 7:13 with Ps 110:1 is found in Hegesippus in a quotation from a lost work preserved by Eusebius (*HE* 2.23.13):

And he answered with a loud voice, "Why do you ask me concerning the Son of Man? He is sitting in heaven on the right hand of the great power, and he will come on the clouds of heaven."

A review of the relevant texts is an important first step in our discussion. Mk 14:62 (and Mt 26:64) has a clear reference to both the *Sessio ad Dextram Dei* and the Parousia:

> And Jesus said, "I am, and you will see the Son of man seated at the right hand of Power, and coming with the clouds of heaven."

In the parallel in Lk 22:69 the reference to the Parousia is not found:

> "But from now on the Son of man shall be seated at the right hand of the power of God."

The Parousia motif is also missing from Acts 7:55–56:

> But he [Stephen], full of the Holy Spirit, gazed into heaven and saw the glory of God, and Jesus standing at the right hand of God; and he said, "Behold, I see the heavens opened, and the Son of man standing at the right hand of God."

Since Luke knew Mk 14:62, he may have deleted the reference to "coming with clouds" for theological reasons. Yet he may have been familiar with a combination of Dan 7:13 and Ps 110:1 which lacked the Parousia motif. In Dan 7:13 itself, the "one like a son of man" comes on clouds *to* the Ancient of Days who is enthroned in heaven. This interpretation of Dan 7:13, when combined with Ps 110:1, is found in three other texts—the *Apocalypse of Peter* (ca. 135 C.E.), Book 2 of the Christian Sibylline Oracles (c. 150 C.E.), and the Odes of Solomon (c. 125 C.E.). The first text is in the Apocalypse of Peter 6 (trans. Hennecke-Schneemelcher, II, 671–72):

> And all will see how I come upon an eternal shining cloud, and the angels of God who will sit with me on the throne of my glory at the right hand of my heavenly Father.

Here allusions to Dan 7:13 and Ps 110:1 are placed on the lips of Jesus in the form of a prophecy very similar to Mk 14:62. The second text is found in the Christian Sibylline Oracles 2.241–44 (trans. Hennecke-Schneemelcher, II, 715–16):

> There shall come on a cloud to the eternal, eternal himself, Christ in glory with his blameless angels, and shall sit on the right hand of Majesty, judging on his throne the life of the pious and the ways of impious men.

Finally, the third text is found in the Odes of Solomon 36:3 (trans. Charlesworth), which retains a two-stage christology with allusions to Dan 7:13 and Ps 110:1, and is presented in terms of a report of a visionary ascent to heaven through the eyes of Jesus himself; as in Acts 7:55–56, there is no mention of the Parousia:

> [The Spirit] brought me forth before the Lord's face, and because I was the Son of Man [Syr. *br nš'*], I was named the Light, the Son of God [Syr. *brh d'lh'*].

In OdesSol 36:1–2, the speaker claims that the Spirit lifted him to heaven "And caused me to stand [Syr. *w'gymtny*] on my feet in the Lord's high place." This motif of "raising up"[48] can be seen in connection with the two-stage christology derived from 2Sam 7:12–14 and expressed in the pre-Pauline confession preserved in Rom 1:3–4.

There are three major solutions to the tradition-critical problem presented by Mk 14:62 and Acts 7:55–56 in the light of these texts: (1) The Parousia motif found in Mk 14:62 could have been added by the evangelist to a tradition similar to that reproduced in Acts 7:55–56 (B. Lindars).[49] (2) The absence of the Parousia motif in Acts 7:55–56 could be due to the fact that Luke consciously deleted it from Mk 14:62 or a similar tradition known to him from another source (H. Tödt).[50] (3) Mk 14:62 and Acts 7:55–56 represent independent developments and combinations of earlier stages of exegetical developments (A. J. B. Higgins, N. Perrin).[51] While the second possibility is the simplest, the first is more convincing since the absence of the Parousia motif from allusions to Dan 7:13 suggests that Luke had access to a more primitive tradition. The real problem is to account for how the Parousia motif was first associated with Dan 7:13.[52] Since Jesus was the Son of man, and the enthronement of the Son of man is implied in Dan 7:13–14, he is therefore the Messiah, since the enthronement of the Messiah is testified to in Ps 110:1. In Lk 22:69 the visionary character of the saying is changed by the omission of "you will see," a phrase which has been added to Acts 7:56 in the modified form "I see," though a verb different from that in Mark 14:62 is used.[53]

The tradition history of Acts 7:55–56 is much more complex than that of Mk 14:62. First, vs. 56 is a doublet of vs. 55 and was either composed by Luke himself or (in my view more likely) was an independent prophetic logion which the author modified and inserted at that point.[54] The reference to "Jesus" standing at the right hand of God" in vs. 55 is changed to "the *Son of*

---

48. Duling, "The Promises to David," pp. 70–77.

49. Lindars, *New Testament Apologetic*, pp. 48–49.

50. H. E. Tödt, *The Son of Man in the Synoptic Tradition*, trans. D. M. Barton (Philadelphia, 1965), pp. 304–5; Lindars changed his earlier opinion (see n. 30) to the view that Luke has modified the saying found in Mk 14:26, cf. B. Lindars, *Jesus Son of Man* (Grand Rapids, Mich., 1984), p. 142.

51. A. J. B. Higgins, *Jesus as the Son of Man* (Philadelphia, 1964), pp. 143–46; N. Perrin, "Mk 14:62: The End Product of a Christian Pesher Tradition?" in *A Modern Pilgrimage in New Testament Christology* (Philadelphia, 1974), pp. 16–18; idem, *Rediscovering the Teaching of Jesus* (New York, 1967), pp. 179–80.

52. Though this specific problem is addressed by T. Callan, "Psalm 110:1 and the Origin of the Expectation That Jesus Will Come Again," *CBQ* 44 (1982) 622–36, his solution is unsatisfactory.

53. Luke tends to replace *horaō* with other verbs for seeing; see H. J. Cadbury, *The Style and Literary Method of Luke* (Cambridge, Mass., 1920), pp. 175–76.

54. See the discussion in R. Pesch, *Die Vision des Stephanus* (Stuttgart, 1966), pp. 50–54, and G. Schneider, *Die Apostelgeschichte* (Freiburg, 1980, 1982), vol. 1, 473–75.

man standing at the right hand of God" in vs. 56, to make the identification of Jesus with the Son of man absolutely clear. In vs. 55 the narrator reports that Stephen "saw [*eiden*] the glory of God, and Jesus standing at the right hand of God." This may simply be a literary dramatization of an exegetical tradition based on Ps 110:1 and Dan 7:13. In my view it is a literary dramatization of a brief vision report which circulated independently (perhaps originally introduced with a verb of seeing used in a past tense, e.g. "I saw [*eidon*]"), conceptually influenced by Ps 110:1 and Dan 7:13. In either case, the point is that Jesus of Nazareth is now enthroned in heaven as Lord and Messiah (cf. Acts 2:34–36). In Acts 7:56 there are only two possible allusions to Dan 7:13; the Son of man designation and (less probably) the participle "standing" (*hestota*), since the Son of man, like angels, could be imagined as standing in the presence of God.[55] The unique feature of this vision report is that *the vision is narrated as it is experienced.* Though without parallel in the NT, very close parallels are found in Philo (*Vita Mos* 2.250–52, 280–81) and Pseudo-Philo's *Liber Antiquitatum Biblicarum* 28:6–10, which include a description of the visionary's inspired state followed by a vision report using a verb of seeing in the present tense.[56] Without exception these *visionary announcements of judgment* are literary productions in which future events are seen as though present by the visionary.

Though the precise exegetical reasons for combining Dan 7:13 with Ps 110 are now obscure,[57] it is likely that they were used to interpret the resur-

---

55. On this dubious point see E. Haechen, *The Acts of the Apostles* (Philadelphia, 1971), p. 292, n. 4. The unique reference to "the Son of Man *standing* at the right hand of God" (Acts 7:56) has never been satisfactorily explained, and sometimes for that very reason has been considered a feature of pre-Lukan tradition. However, the reference makes sense as part of an indirect piece of anti-Simonian polemic. Luke knew a great deal about Simon and Simonianism, perhaps more than he chose to reveal. In the Clementine literature it is said that Simon "intimates that he is the Messiah by calling himself the Standing One (*ho hestōs*). He uses this title to indicate that he shall always stand, and that there is no cause of corruption which can make his body fall" (PseudClemHom 2.22; cf. PseudClemRec 2.7). In Samaritan and gnostic texts, "standing" can be used as a divine attribute referring to the eternality of God, and it can also be used in Samaritan texts of the eschatological Mosaic prophet (J. E. Fossum, *The Name of God and the Angel of the Lord* (Tübingen, 1985), pp. 120–24; R. M. Grant, *Gnosticism and Early Christianity*, rev. ed. [New York, 1966], pp. 90–93). Simon reportedly claimed "I am the Son of God standing to eternity" ("filius dei stans in aeternum") (PseudClemRec 3.47). The prophet whom God will "raise up" (Acts 7:37, alluding to Deut 18:15, 18), can be thought of as "standing"; R. M. Grant suggests the parallel in Deut 5:31 in which God addresses Moses and says, "You stand with me, and I will tell you all the commandments" (Grant, *Gnosticism*, p. 92). This is supported by the fact that the variant tradition in which an allusion to Dan 7:13 and Ps 110:1 is attributed to the dying James the Just by Hegesippus (Eusebius, *HE* 2.23.13), the phrase "the Great Power," meaning God, is found only in Samaritan sources apart from this one fragment of Hegesippus; see Fossum, *The Name of God*, p. 169.

56. For a formal analysis of these and similar texts, see Aune, *Prophecy in Early Christianity*, pp. 148–52, 270.

57. W. O. Walker, "The Origin of the Son of Man Concept as Applied to Jesus," *JBL* 91 (1972) 482–90, argues that the missing link is provided by Ps 8:6b (LXX 8:7b): "thou hast put all things

rection of Jesus in the Aramaic-speaking Palestinian church,[58] though some contend on philological grounds that Ps 110:1 could only have been applied to the resurrection in hellenistic Jewish Christianity.[59] Dan 7:13 was used to identify Jesus, who probably used the 'Son of man" idiom as an indirect way of referring to himself, as the vicegerent of God; none of the Son of man sayings which allude to Dan 7:13 have a strong claim to authenticity.[60] If that is so, then Mk 14:62 (which, introduced with "you will see," is awkward in its present context) cannot be regarded as authentic and must be considered a later addition to the narrative of the trial of Jesus.[61] Since Ps 110:1 may have been understood messianically in first-century Judaism, it was probably used in combination with Dan 7:13 to understand Jesus' resurrection in terms of heavenly enthronement of the Son of man as Messiah. The combination of Dan 7:13 with Ps 110:1 clearly identified Jesus, recognized as the Son of man, with the Messiah, a necessary step since there was no concept of an apocalyptic Son of man in pre-Christian Judaism. Since the designation "Son of man" was not used as a title of Jesus in christological confessions (a fact made obvious by Mt 16:13: "Who do men say that the Son of man is?"),[62] the primary purpose of combining Dan 7:13 with Ps 110:1 must have been to identify Jesus the Son of man with the Messiah.

---

under his feet," since vs. 4 uses the expression "son of man," the whole Ps was applied to Jesus. The no less probable suggestion of N. A. Dahl is mentioned by Hay, *Glory at the Right Hand*, p. 26, n. 32, namely Ps 80:17: "But let thy hand be upon the man of thy right hand, the son of man whom thou hast made strong for thyself!" The same solution is proposed by O. J. F. Seitz, "The Future Coming of the Son of Man: Three Midrashic Formulations in the Gospel of Mk," *Studia Evangelica* 6 (1973) 482–88. The simplest solution, however, is to note the mention of thrones, on one of which the Ancient of Days took his seat in Dan 7:9. In a Messianic interpretation of the Son of Man figure quite separate from that found in the gospels and Acts, the enthronement of the Son of Man is a conclusion also drawn in 1En 62:5, though without the aid of Ps 110:1: "and pain shall seize them when they see the Son of man sitting on the throne of his glory" (*OTP*, vol. 1, p. 43); see 1En 61:8, 69:29. Slightly later than the Similitudes of Enoch (1En 37–71, dated ca. A.D. 90) is the rabbinic tradition attributed to Akiba that the two thrones of Dan 7:9 were for God and the Davidic Messiah (b.Hag 14a; b.Sanh 38b); cf. Andre LaCocque, *Le livre de Daniel* (Neuchatel and Paris, 1976), p. 108, n. 6. A very similar tradition is found in Mt 19:28: "the Son of man shall sit on his glorious throne," a passage which exhibits no influence from Ps 110:1, a fact made clear by the parallel in Mt 25:31: "When the Son of man comes in his glory, and all the angels with him, then he will sit on his glorious throne."

58. G. Loader, "Christ at the Right Hand—Ps. CX. 1 in the New Testament," *NTS* 24 (1977–78) 200. Without mentioning Ps 110:1, J. Fitzmyer argues that the absolute use of the *kyrios* title for Jesus originated within a Palestinian-Semitic religious background ("The Semitic Background of the New Testament *Kyrios*-Title," pp. 115–42).

59. Fuller, *Foundations of New Testament Christology*, pp. 184–86.

60. W. O. Walker, "The Son of Man: Some Recent Developments," *CBQ* 45 (1983) 595–98; M. Casey, *Son of Man*, p. 237.

61. Tödt, *The Son of Man*, pp. 36–40; Leivestad, *Jesus in His Own Perspective: An Examination of His Sayings, Actions, and Eschatological Titles*, trans. D. E. Aune (Minneapolis, 1987), p. 159; Lindars, *Jesus Son of Man*, pp. 110–12; A. J. B. Higgins, *The Son of Man in the Teaching of Jesus* (Cambridge, 1980), pp. 77–79.

62. D. G. Dunn, *Unity and Diversity in the New Testament* (Philadelphia, 1977), pp. 35–40; R. Leivestad, *Jesus in His Own Perspective*, pp. 153–54.

Rev 1:12–16: The Heavenly Son of Man

Rev 1:9–20 is a vision report of John's divine commission to write messages dictated by the exalted Christ for transmission to the seven churches. The seer John describes the supernatural being he saw as "one like a son of man" (vss. 13–14), clearly alluding to Dan 7:13 without suggesting any awareness of the extensive use of the title in the gospels. It does maintain the primitive Christian identification of Jesus as Son of man with the Jesus of heavenly exaltation. The figure is presumably standing, a posture explicitly mentioned when John describes the Lamb in Rev 5:6. In the MT of Dan 7:13 the "one like a son of man" is presented to the Ancient of Days, thus clearly distinguishing the two figures. Yet in Rev 1:13–14, the "one like a son of man" is described *as if he is identical* with the Ancient of Days (whose hair is white as wool according to Dan 7:6; cf. Rev 1:14). This identification was not original with John. It is already presupposed by the LXX version of Dan 7:13: "He came like a son of man, and like the Ancient of Days was present, and those who were near were present with him." This reading is found in the only two LXX manuscripts of Daniel, the Codex Chisianus (Ms. 88), and the incomplete Chester Beatty papyrus codex 967 (late second- or early third-century C.E.). Ms. 88 and the Syro-Hexaplar version of Daniel are both dependent on Origen's Hexapla; Ms. 967 is one of the earliest extant copies of parts of the LXX and constitutes an important independent witness to the reading of Ms. 88.[63] Wherever and however it originated, this text intentionally identifies the "one like a son of man" with the Ancient of Days.[64] Thus despite the problematic relationship between the Apocalypse of John and the rest of the Johannine corpus, they do share an emphasis on the divinity of Jesus, an emphasis that goes beyond Jewish messianic categories. It is not John's purpose to provide divine legitimation for the messianic status of Jesus, but rather to provide legitimation for his own status as a prophet for the revelatory book he was composing.

Summary

The earliest revelatory visions of the resurrected Jesus probably involved revelatory perception of his heavenly messianic status. The prophetic tradition standing behind the series of texts we have examined, all of which allude to a combination of Dan 7:13 with Ps 110:1, may have originated as a pro-

---

63. This reading is neither the result of accident nor error (F. F. Bruce, "The Oldest Greek Version of Daniel," OTS 20 (1977) 25; J. Lust, "Daniel 7:13 and the Septuagint," *ETL* 54 (1978) 62–69), as J. Ziegler, who corrected it to agree with the MT, presumed (*Susana-Daniel-Bel et Draco* [Göttinger Septuaginta 16.2; Göttingen, 1954] *ad loc.*), though it probably does not preserve a variant Hebrew reading (against Lust, "Daniel 7:13," p. 68).

64. The precedent for this exegetical step taken by the LXX translators may have been Ezek 1:26, in which Ezekiel saw God as one "in the likeness of a man" sitting on the "likeness of a throne."

phetic vision of the messianic status of Jesus, the Son of man, enthroned at the right hand of God. The following arguments support this view: (1) The earliest combination of Dan 7:13 with Ps 110:1 lacked any reference to the Parousia and instead focused on identifying the Son of man as the enthroned Messiah. (2) The combined allusions to Dan 7:13 and Ps 110:1 tend to occur in literary contexts as a prophecy or as a vision report, a usage in harmony with the hypothetical original revelatory function of the saying. (3) Sayings combining Dan 7:13 with Ps 110:1 are usually introduced with a verb of seeing, a feature appropriate to an original vision report with the introductory formula "I saw." (4) Acts 7:55–56 coheres with what is known of visions of the resurrected Jesus known from 1Cor 15:5–8, from Acts 9, 22, 26, and allusions in Paul's letters to his Damascus experience. (5) The conceptual character of revelatory visions exhibits a marked dependence on canonical visions (e.g. Paul understood his Damascus vision in terms of Jeremiah's inaugural vision; cf. Gal 1:15, Jer 1:5), and an OT interpretation (e.g. Rev 1:9–20). (6) There is evidence to suggest that other short oracular and visionary forms were circulated orally in early Christianity (e.g. Rev 1:7).[65]

CONCLUSIONS

In this paper we have explored the issue of whether or not the problematic issue of the messianic status of Jesus was legitimated by the inspired speech or revelatory visions of early Christian prophets. The fact that early Christian prophetic speech and visionary experiences have survived only fragmentarily has made the task very difficult. It appears that the messianic status of the earthly Jesus was a concern of central importance for the transmitters of the Jesus traditions to the extent that the portrait of Jesus took on greater and greater messianic significance. The evidence for this literary transformation of the Jesus tradition is evident in all of the Gospels, though we have focused only on the literary use of oracles and prophecies of the true status of Jesus. In discussing the brief vision report reflected in Acts 7:55–56 and Rev 1:14–16 (and several related texts), we discovered in them a major concern with affirming the messianic status of Jesus as the exalted and enthroned Son of man. We further proposed that these texts have made use of a primitive prophetic vision report which both confirmed and legitimated Christian perceptions of Jesus as Messiah. While this hypothesis is necessarily speculative, given the paucity of the evidence, there is nevertheless a strong possibility that both the reception and transmission of such revelatory visions made a major contribution to the spread of faith in the fact that Jesus had not only risen from the dead but had also been exalted to the right hand of God as Messiah and Lord.

---

65. See Aune, *Prophecy in Early Christianity*, pp. 247–338.

PART SIX

"THE MESSIAH," "THE CHRIST," AND THE NEW TESTAMENT

CHRISTOLOGICAL TITLES IN EARLY CHRISTIANITY

THE CRUCIFIED SON OF GOD[1]

Between 110 and 112 C.E., in his well-known letter to Trajan, Pliny the Younger, then governor of Bithynia, describes a worship service of Christians. They gather together, "on a certain day before sunrise in order to sing an antiphonic hymn to Christ, as though he were their God" (*carmenque Christo quasi deo dicere secum invicem*).[2] As judge, therefore, he demands that those charged with being Christians curse Christ, their God (*Christo maledicere*).[3] Pliny does not clarify who this *Christus* is whose followers sing a hymn to him *quasi deo*. He presupposes that Trajan already has accurate information concerning the sect. However, we learn it a little later from his friend Tacitus in the well-known description of the persecution by Nero: "The founder of the Christian sect, Christus, was executed by the procurator Pontius Pilate,"[4] i.e., he died for crimes against the state in the notoriously

---

1. This paper is a thorough reworking of a lecture given in Tübingen in an interdisciplinary series of lectures entitled "The Name of God." See M. Hengel, "Die christologischen Hoheitstitel im Urchristentum," in *Der Name Gottes*, ed. H. v. Stietencron (Düsseldorf, 1975), pp. 90–111. I wish to thank my doctoral students—Paul Cathey for the English translation, Ulrike Richert-Mittmann for preparing the manuscript, and Dr. Christoph Markschies for a number of valuable suggestions—and Professor Charlesworth for polishing the discussion and editing the notes.

2. *Ep.* 10, 96, 7. See A. N. Sherwin-White, *The Letters of Pliny* (Oxford, 1985, 3rd ed.), pp. 702–10 (esp. 704ff.); see also the forthcoming dissertation in WUNT of Dr. J. C. Salzmann on *Der frühchristliche Wortgottesdienst*. A short contribution of his dealing with the Christian worship service in the letter of Pliny appeared in *Studia Patristica* 20 (1989) 390–95. For early Christian hymnody see M. Hengel, "Das Christuslied im frühesten Gottesdienst," in *Weisheit Gottes—Weisheit der Welt: Festschrift für Joseph Kardinal Ratzinger zum 60. Geburtstag* (St. Ottilien, 1987), vol. 1, pp. 357–404 (esp. 382f.); see n. 16 of this essay.

3. Pliny, *Ep.* 10, 96, 5–6. See R. Freudenberger, *Das Verhalten der römischen Behörden gegen die Christen im 2. Jahrhundert* (MBPF 52; Munich, 1969²), pp. 145ff.; *MartPol* 9, 3; Bar Kokhba also demanded that Christians curse Jesus Christ: Justin, *Apol* 1.31, 6. See n. 10 of this essay.

4. *Ann* 15, 44: *Auctor nominis eius Christus Tiberio imperitante per procuratorem Pontium Pilatum supplicio affectus erat.* In his lost book VII of the *Ann*, Tacitus probably reported on the

unruly province of Judaea. Pliny and Tacitus are at one in their brusque condemnation of this sect: This *superstitio*, according to Pliny, is "depraved and insolent" (*prava et immodica*), and according to Tacitus, "pernicious" (*exitiabilis*).[5]

These two ancient Roman witnesses to Jesus Christ describe the offense that the early Christian message caused for the ancient world. An uneducated craftsman from the despised Jewish people, condemned to a disgraceful death by Roman authorities—was this man supposed to be the divine Revealer of God's truth and the coming Judge of the world? Were not reason, pious sensibility, and national interest here equally challenged?[6] A visible example of this is offered in that caricature discovered in the Palatine of a crucified man with an ass's head with the inscription, "Alexamenos worships his God."[7] The Platonist, Celsus, speaks for all the educated: "How can we regard him as God, who . . . delivered nothing of what he promised, and who—after we exposed him, found him guilty, and determined to execute him—hid himself and fled, but nevertheless was captured in disgrace . . . ? Although he pretended to be God, he could neither escape, nor be freed from his chains, and still less should he who was regarded as Savior (*sōtēr*), as Son and Messenger of the highest God have been abandoned and betrayed by his comrades!"[8] Celsus deliberately puts this indictment on the lips of a Jew; on this common front Jews and Greeks were at one. The charges of the Jew, Trypho, in Justin's *Dialogue* sound very similar: "It is just *this* that we cannot comprehend, that you set your hope on one crucified." "Prove to us that (the Messiah) had to be crucified, and had to die such a shameful and

---

events under Pilate in Judaea; see R. Syme, *Tacitus* (Oxford, 1985), vol. 1, p. 449, n. 7; vol. 2, p. 469.

5. See Suetonius *Nero* 16, 2: *afflicti suppliciis Christiani, genus hominum superstitionis novae ac maleficae*. According to Tacitus, *Ann* 11, 15, Claudius tried to revive the old haruspicy, *quia externae superstitiones valescant*. In 57 C.E. a woman of the Roman nobility, Pomponia Graecina, was accused before the senate because of *superstitio externa*, *Ann* 13, 32. R. Hanslik (PRE 1st Series XXI, 2; 1952, 2351, no. 83) supposes "Anhängerschaft an das Christentum," but it could also be an inclination to Judaism, for the reproach of superstition was frequently made by Roman authors against Jews as well; see M. Stern, *Greek and Latin Authors on Jews and Judaism* (Jerusalem, 1984), vol. 3, p. 149, s.v. "superstition." See also L. F. Janssen, "Die Bedeutungsentwicklung von *superstitio/superstes*," *Mnemosyne* 27 (1974) 135–88; idem, "'Superstitio' and the Persecution of the Christians," *VC* 33 (1979) 131–59; A. N. Sherwin-White, *Racial Prejudice in Imperial Rome* (London, 1967, 1970), p. 38: ". . . *superstitio*, a bad word in Flavian writers" (Tacitus about Germanic tribes). For the identification of superstition and the accusation of mental disorder, see M. Hengel, *Crucifixion in the Ancient World and the Folly of the Message of the Cross*, trans. J. Bowden (London, Philadelphia, 1977), pp. 2f.: Horace, *Satires* 2, 3, 79f.; Minucius Felix, *Octavius* 9, 2; 11, 9.

6. See W. Bauer, *Das Leben Jesu im Zeitalter der neutestamentlichen Apokryphen* (Tübingen, 1909 [reprint 1967]), pp. 452–86; Hengel, *Crucifixion*, pp. 1–10; 15ff.; 84ff.

7. For the so-called "Spottkruzifix" (mock-crucifix) from the ruins of the "Paedagogium Palatini," see H. Riemann, "Paedagogium Palatini" (PRE 1st Series XXXVI, 1, 1942, 2211ff.) and I. Opelt, "Esel" (RAC VI, 1966); cf. E. Dinkler, "Signum Crucis" (Tübingen, 1967), pp. 150ff.; Hengel, *Crucifixion*, p. 19 n. 12; M. Smith, *Jesus the Magician* (San Francisco, 1977), pp. 61ff.

8. Origen, *Contra Celsum* 2. 9; cf. 2. 35, 68; 6. 10, 34, 36 [translation mine].

dishonorable death, cursed by the Law. We could not even consider such a thing!"[9] It was therefore thoroughly consistent that the Jewish messianic pretender, Simon bar Kosiba, in 132 C.E.—as did the Roman authorities—required the Jewish Christians within this sphere of power to curse Christ and punished with death those who refused to do so.[10] Paul's program, already formulated in 1Cor 1:23, and confirmed by years of mission experience, is illustrated by numerous ancient witnesses: "We preach Christ crucified, a stumbling block to Jews, and folly to Gentiles." Goethe's protest in the "West-Eastern Divan," when Chosru discovered a cross on his Armenian mistress's pearl necklace, shows that this scandal was not restricted to antiquity:

> You would that I hold him to be
> God—this wretch upon the tree![11]

9. Justin, *DialTrypho* 10. 3; 90. 1.

10. Justin, *Apol* I. 31.6; cf. *DialTrypho* 11. 3; 133. 6. For Bar Kokhba's messianic claims, see M. Hengel in *Gnomon* 58 (1986) 329ff.

11. From his posthumous poems to the "West-Eastern Divan," see J. W. Goethe, *Poetische Werke, Gedichte und Singspiele III* (Berlin [East], 1979, 3rd ed.), pp. 341–42. I cite the verses in the context:

> Jesus fühlte rein und dachte
> Nur den *einen* Gott im Stillen;
> Wer ihn selbst zum Gotte machte,
> Kränkte seinen heil'gen Willen.

> Und so muß das Rechte scheinen
> Was auch Mahomet gelungen;
> Nur durch den Begriff des *einen*
> Hat er alle Welt bezwungen.

> Wenn du aber dennoch Huld'gung
> Diesem leid'gen Ding verlangest,
> Diene mir es zur Entschuld'gung,
> Daß du nicht alleine prangest. —

> Doch allein!—Da viele Frauen
> Salomonis ihn verkehrten,
> Götter betend anzuschauen,
> Wie die Närrinnen verehrten.

> Isis' Horn, Anubis' Rachen
> Boten sie dem Judenstolze,
> *Mir willst du zum Gotte machen*
> *Solch ein Jammerbild am Holze!* [italics mine]

> Und ich will nicht besser scheinen
> Als es sich mit mir eräugnet,
> Salomo verschwur den seinen,
> Meinen Gott hab' ich verleugnet.

> Laß die Renegatenbürde
> Mich in diesem Kuß verschmerzen:
> Denn ein Vitzliputzli würde
> Talisman an *deinem* Herzen.

Like the indignation of the "Olympian of Weimar," the voices of protest from the ancient world strike the very *nervus rerum* of the Christian faith, emphasizing sharply the scandal as the secret of Christology. There were innumerable crucifixions in the Roman Empire: slaves, robbers, rebels (all criminals from the lower strata), and notably the freedom-loving Jews.[12] Against this background, a *crucified Son of God*—i.e., a crucified God, Kyrios, Soter or Messiah—*was an offense without analogy.*

It is the peculiarity, indeed uniqueness, of earliest Christianity that the development of Christology and its titles remained inextricably bound to the offense of the crucified Jesus of Nazareth. For wherever Christians yielded to the pressure of the religious and philosophical premises of prevailing contemporary thought and therefore explained the humanity of the suffering and dying Jesus as mere *"appearance"* or dismissed it as unimportant for salvation, contending that the heavenly Christ was separated from the man Jesus before his death, christological thinking deteriorated into gnostic speculation.[13] In this light, it was entirely consistent with ancient thinking when Celsus' Jewish source argued thus: If it had been important to Jesus to prove his divinity, he would have had to become invisible on the cross (and be carried back to Heaven).[14] This is similar to Ovid's depiction of Caesar's apotheosis during the *fasti*, when he has Caesar carried away by Vesta just before the attack, so that only his naked image or shadow is pierced by the murderous daggers.[15] The appropriate Christology for the educated in an-

---

Sulpiz Boisserée noted in his diary: "Too acerbic, too callous and one-sided; I counseled him to discard."—ibid., p. 770; cf. the sixty-sixth Venetian epigram:

Wenige sind mir jedoch wie Gift und Schlange zuwider;
Viere: Rauch des Tabaks, Wanzen und Knoblauch und †.

12. See Hengel, *Crucifixion, passim*, at several points enlarged upon in the French translation, *La crucifixion dans l'antiquité et la folie du message de la croix* (Lectio Divina 105; Paris, 1981). For the crucifixion among the Jews see Hengel, *Crucifixion*, pp. 84–85; idem, *The Zealots* (Edinburgh, 1988); idem, "Rabbinische Legende und frühpharisäische Geschichte," *AHAW.PH* (1984) 27–36; and H. W. Kuhn, "Die Kreuzesstrafe während der frühen Kaiserzeit," *ANRW* II 25, 1 (1982) 648ff.

13. For "docetic" christologies, see 1Jn 4:2; 2Jn 7; Ignatius, *Smyr* 2; 4, 2; 5, 1f.; *Trall* 10; Irenaeus, *AdvHaer* 1, 24; 2, 4; 25, 1; 26, 1; 3, 18, 7; 4, 33, 5; characteristic for Basilides a generation after John (1, 24, 4): *"et non oportere confiteri eum qui sit crucifixus, sed eum qui in hominis forma uenerit et putatus sit crucifixus et uocatus sit Iesus et missus a Patre . . . Si quis igitur . . . confitetur crucifixum, adhuc hic seruus est et sub potestate eorum qui corpora fecerunt; qui autem negauerit, liberatus est quidem ab his, cognoscit autem dispositionem innati patris."* See J. G. Davies, "The Origins of Docetism," in *Studia Patristica* 6 (TU 81; 1962) 13–25, who stresses the Jewish influence in early docetism; K. Koschorke, *"Die Polemik der Gnostiker gegen das kirchliche Christentum,"* (NHS 12; Leiden 1978) 20–26, 36, 44–48; K. W. Tröger, "Doketische Christologie in Nag-Hammadi-Texten," *Kairos* 19 (1977) 45–72. For the importance of docetism and antidocetism for early christology, see A. Grillmeier, *Jesus der Christus im Glauben der Kirche* (Vienna, 1979), p. 820 and esp. pp. 187–89; A. Orbe, "Christologia Gnostica," *BAC* 384/385 (Madrid, 1976) 380–412. The term "docetism" should not be used in too narrow a sense or restricted only to the later Valentinians. It includes, rather, various conceptions.

14. Origen, *Contra Celsum*, 2. 68.

15. Ovid, 3, 701f. (ed Bömer): *ipsa virum rapui simulacraque nuda reliqui; quae cecidit ferro,*

tiquity was the "docetic," which declared the humanity of Jesus and, above all, his passion to be unimportant for salvation, since a heavenly being could not suffer and die at all.

Which hymn might those Christians in Bithynia have sung *Christo quasi deo?* It is futile to speculate about this, since we have few fragments from the rich early Christian liturgy. Most of the christological hymn fragments,[16] however, have just this *quasi deo* as theme, often counterpointed with the cross motif.[17] This is no accident, since the unfolding of the titles of divine dignity of the Crucified One and his saving offices occurred not so much in the prose of theoretical speculation or missionary preaching, as in the poetic, inspired language of hymn and confession; i.e., they had their place in the *worship service.* Here, in overflowing praise to Christ, the early Christian churches formulated their thanks for the gifts of salvation they had received. In worship, however, the spontaneously formulated, enthusiastic expressions of the spirit were bound together with the trustworthy older, and now binding, "apostolic" or "Jesus" tradition, as well as with the charismatic exposition of scripture. The working together of these three apparently opposite components gave to christological development its specifically inner dynamic.[18]

In what follows, I would like to take three hymns from different periods and communities as a point of departure and to consider each in turn in its

---

Caesaris umbra fuit. See E. Bickermann, "Consecratio," in *Le culte des souverains dans l'Empire romain, Entretiens sur l'Antiquité classique* 19 (Vandoeuvres-Genève, 1973) 15f. Ovid, *Metamorphoses* 15, 840ff., has the Greek alternative: Venus translates Caesar's soul from his murdered body and brings it up to the stars, where it is transformed into the fiery *sidus Iulium,* which can admire without envy the even greater deeds of his son Augustus. See also the commentary of F. Bömer: *P. Ovidius Naso. Die Fasten,* ed. F. Bömer (Heidelberg, 1957), vol. 2, p. 192: "Das Vorbild für das *simulacrum* Ovids ist das εἴδωλον der Helena bei Eur. El. 1281ff." Cf. already Homer, *Odyssey* 11, 601ff.: Odysseus sees in Hades only the εἴδωλον of Hercules: (αὐτὸς δὲ μετ' ἀθανάτοισι θεοῖσι τέρπεται ἐν θαλίῃς καὶ ἔχει καλλίσφυρον Ἥβην (He himself is feasting with the gods . . .). Docetism presupposed higher education, the influence of popular philosophy, and some knowledge of Greek literature.

16. For early Christian hymnody, see R. Deichgräber, *Gotteshymnus und Christushymnus in der frühen Christenheit* (SUNT 5; Göttingen, 1967); J. T. Sanders, *The New Testament Christological Hymns* (SNTS MS 15; Cambridge, U.K., 1971); K. Wengst, *Christologische Formeln und Lieder des Urchristentums* (StNT 7; Gütersloh, 1973³); M. Hengel, "Hymnus und Christologie," in *Wort in der Zeit: Festgabe für K. H. Rengstorf zum 75. Geburstag* (Leiden, 1980), pp. 1–23; trans. J. Bowden in *Between Jesus and Paul* (London, Philadelphia, 1983), pp. 78–96; 188–90; idem, *Das Christuslied im frühesten Gottesdienst,* see n. 2 in this essay.

17. See Phil 2:6–11; Col 1:15, 20; Heb 1:2f.; 1Pet 2:21; Rev 5:9; Ignatius, *Trall* 9; *Smyr* 1; and Eusebius, *HE* 5, 28, 5: "τὸν λόγον τοῦ Χριστοῦ ὑμνοῦσιν θεολογοῦντες."

18. For the development of christological thought, see F. Hahn, *Christologische Hoheitstitel* (FRLANT 83; Göttingen, 1964²); R. H. Fuller, *The Foundations of New Testament Christology* (New York, 1965, 1967); M. Hengel, "The Son of God," *The Cross of the Son of God,* trans. J. Bowden (London, 1986), pp. 1–90; C. F. D. Moule, *The Origin of Christology* (Cambridge, U.K., 1977); J. D. G. Dunn, *Christology in the Making* (London, Philadelphia, 1980). For the Jewish background see J. E. Fossum, *The Name of God and the Angel of the Lord* (WUNT 36; Tübingen, 1985); L. W. Hurtado, *One God, One Lord* (Philadelphia, 1988); see also J. H. Charlesworth, "From Jewish Messianology to Christian Christology: Some Caveats and Perspectives," in *Judaisms and Their Messiahs,* ed. J. Neusner et al. (Cambridge, 1988), pp. 225–64.

greater christological context. The *carmen Christo quasi deo* of Pliny applies
to them all, and indeed, each gives voice anew in a different way to the
"worthiness" of Jesus and his offices.

1. This *quasi deo* appears in its fullest form in the Prologue of the Gospel of
John, likely written a bit earlier (between ten and twenty years) than Pliny's
letter. We will therefore concentrate our most detailed examination on John
1:1–18.[19]

"In the beginning was the Word, and the Word was with God (*pros ton
theon*), and the Word was God (*theos ēn ho logos*)." The Logos has not only
created all that is; it is also the power that embodies the "true life" and the
light that illuminates the darkness. This light first breaks in the Old Testament salvation history and bursts forth fully in Jesus of Nazareth. In him the
impossible paradox happened. The divine Logos became a mortal man: "And
the Word became flesh and dwelt among us, and we beheld his glory." He
brings "grace and truth" in contrast to the Law of Moses. In accordance with
the rules of style of the *inclusio*,[20] the key word "God" appears again at the
end of the Prologue: *monogenēs theos*, "the only-begotten, God, by nature,
who is in the bosom of the Father, he has made God known" (1:18).

This enigmatic Logos appears only in the Prologue of the Gospel of John
and twice elsewhere in the New Testament. It is certainly not the "universal
reason" of the Stoics, nor, as was thought in Germany for a long time, the
heavenly redeemer of a gnostic sect. Behind it stands the creative Word of
God of the Old Testament, that in ancient Judaism had merged with Wisdom, and thereby was able to assume the office of Creator and bringer of
salvation.[21] The three variants of Faust's translation, *Wort* (word), *Sinn*
(sense), and *Tat* (deed), all delineate the effecting work of the divine Logos.
We encounter the designation of Christ as *theos*, "God," in only one other
place in the Gospel of John, at its end in the confession of the unbelieving

---

19. From the abundant literature I mention those authors from whom I have learned most:
W. Eltester, "Der Logos und sein Prophet," in *Apophoreta: Festschrift für Ernst Haenchen*
(BZNW 30; Berlin, 1964), pp. 109–34. He stresses the OT background of the Prologue over
against R. Bultmann's exegesis of Jn 1:9–11: "Soll dem Evangelisten wegen seiner zeitgenös-
sischen Judenpolemik eine positive Beziehung zum Alten Testament und der darin enthaltenen
Geschichte Gottes mit seinem Volk bestritten werden? . . . Es scheint, dass die gnostische
Brille die Augen nicht unbedingt schärft" (pp. 131f., n. 40); see A. Feuillet, *Le prologue du
quatrième évangile* (Paris, 1968); K. Barth, "Erklärung des Johannesevangeliums (Kapitel 1–8),"
(ed. W. Fürst), *Karl-Barth-Gesamtausgabe*, 2nd section; *Akademische Werke* (Zürich, 1976), pp.
12–163; E. Ruckstuhl, "Kritische Arbeit am Johannesprolog," in *The New Testament Age: Essays
in Honor of Bo Reicke*, ed. W. C. Weinrich (Macon, Ga., 1984), vol. 3, pp. 443–54; O. Hofius,
"Struktur und Gedankengang des Logoshymnus in Joh 1, 1–18," ZNW 78 (1987) 1–25. Reviews
of research: H. Thyen, *ThRu* NF 39 (1974) 53–69, 222–52; J. Becker, *ThRu* NF 47 (1982) 317–
21; 51 (1986) 12f., 32, 64, 69f.; M. Theobald, *Die Fleischwerdung des Logos* (NTA NF 20; Münster, 1988), pp. 6–161. To the author, see M. Hengel (below n. 32).
20. J. A. Bengel and also O. Hofius in ZNW 78 (1987) 12 n. 64 have drawn attention to the
inclusio.
21. See J. Jeremias, "Zum Logos-Problem," ZNW 59 (1968) 82–85.

Thomas before the Risen One (20:28)—"My Lord, and my God!" This carefully formulated second inclusio is *not* an allusion to the *dominus et deus* of the contemporary Caesar, Domitian,[22] but rather—as the first-person singular possessive pronoun shows—intends that personal faith and its confession be shown as the goal of the entire Gospel. This is made clear by what immediately follows: "These things have been written that you might believe . . ." (20:31). The confession of the divinity of Christ stands thus at the beginning and end of the Fourth Gospel, and, with the self-declaration of Jesus at 10:30, determines the middle as well: "The Father and I are one." This accords with the hint that the Johannine Jesus gives to his preexistence in 8:58: "Before Abraham was, I am."

The christological statements of the earliest Church thus reach their climax in the Fourth Gospel. Elsewhere we find the title *theos* only in the related letter, 1 John, in the conclusion formula: "This One is the true God and eternal life" (5:20), and in two or three very late New Testament texts (Tit 2:13, 2Pet 1:1, and perhaps 2Thes 1:12), and then numerous times in the letters of Ignatius, written after 110 c.e.[23] With this title, and the statement in 10:30, then, the Gospel of John provides the most important basis for the further christological reflection of the ancient Church.

It is therefore clear that the Christianity of the first century—like contemporary Judaism—was reluctant to transfer the term "God" directly to a heavenly mediator figure, although it did not rule it out completely. It was expressed as a kind of "upper limit" statement, similar to those of Philo, who—in contrast to the definite *ho theos*, which was reserved for God alone—could describe the Logos with the indefinite *theos*, indeed even *deuteros theos*.[24] Later the Rabbis charged the Christians unjustly with "ditheism." Yet even rabbinic mysticism knew godlike mediators such as Metatron, who was named "the little Yahweh," and the Essenes of Qumran dared to refer a passage such as Isa 52:7, "*Your* God has become King," to the heavenly redeemer of the Sons of Light, Michael-Melchizedek.[25]

---

22. Suetonius, *Domitian* 13.2; see Cassius Dio 67.4, 7; 13.4. This, however, was not an official title for Domitian. See J. R. Fears, "*Princeps a diis electus*" (PMAAR 26; Rome, 1977) 190f., 223f.; idem, "The Cult of Jupiter and Roman Imperial Ideology" in *ANRW* II 17, 1 (1981) 3–141 (74–80), and already A. Harnack, *Lehrbuch der Dogmengeschichte* (Tübingen, 1909⁴), p. 209, n. 1. This fact is overlooked by B. A. Mastin, "The Imperial Cult and the Ascription of the Title to Jesus," in *Studia Evangelica* 6 (TU 112; Berlin [East], 1973) 352–65; see idem, "A Neglected Feature of Christology of the Fourth Gospel," *NTS* 22 (1975/76) 32–51: "These three verses (Jn 1:1, 18; 20:28) describe the preexistent Logos, the incarnate Logos, and the risen Christ as 'God,' and so they complement each other to provide an outline of the church's understanding of Jesus. The fact that each of these verses is placed at a significant point in the Gospel emphasizes the importance of what they say" (p. 51).

23. Ignatius, *Rom* prol, 3:3, 6:3; *Eph* prol, 1:1, 7:2, 15:3, 18:2, 19:3; *Smyr* 1:1, 10:2; *Trall* 7:1; cf. 2Clem 1:1; see also Heb 1:8f. = LXX Ps 45:7.

24. *QuaestGen* 2, 62; *leg. all.* 3, 207; *Som.* 1, 229f., 238f.

25. 3En 12:5 in *Synopse zur Hekhalot-Literatur*, ed. P. Schäfer (Tübingen, 1981), §15; cf. the "Commentary" in *3 Enoch or the Hebrew Book of Enoch*, ed. and trans. with Introduction, Commentary, and Critical Notes by H. Odeberg (repr. New York, 1973) p. 33; J. Fossum, *The*

Indeed, one might think that especially in the Fourth Gospel the apotheosis of Jesus had become a speculative end in itself, and had pushed the salvation event—above all his suffering and dying—to the side. The inference, however, would be incorrect. For already in the Prologue the accentuation of the *Father* (1:14, 18) and the "only-begotten" Son, as well as the goal of the Gospel, stated at the end, "in order that you might believe" (20:31), show that Jesus as the *Son* (i.e., in his relation to the Father and in his role as Savior for those who believe) is the controlling christological motif of the whole Gospel. The task of the *monogenēs theos*, the "only-begotten," God by nature, is to communicate God's innermost nature to humankind, and this nature is love: "For God so loved the world that he gave his only-begotten Son, that whoever believes in him should not perish but have eternal life" (3:16).

The first letter of John, which takes the intentions of the Gospel further, defines this precisely: "Whoever does not love does not know God; *for God is love*. In this the love of God was made manifest among us, that God sent his only-begotten Son into the world, that we might love through him" (4:8ff.). This means that in the Son who has become human, God's love, his very nature, has become manifest for humankind; God himself comes to them. The *incarnation of the love* of God, not the deification of Christ, is the main theme of Johannine theology. This means at the same time that its goal is the salvation of humankind.[26] "And from his fullness have we all received . . ." (Jn 1:16). Therefore "Son" is the most frequent christological title, and not "God" or "Logos," and this not in the dyadic form as "Son of God," but rather as *the absolute ho huios, the Son*, in his continual relatedness to the Father, whose nature he reveals. In John the Father himself, *ho patēr*, appears more often than all the christological titles put together, and it is in the very unity with him that the Son remains always subordinated to the Father: the Son can do nothing without the Father (5:19).[27] To sharpen

---

Name of God and the Angel of the Lord (WUNT 36; Tübingen, 1985), pp. 300ff.; 11QMelch Col. II, 16 in "Milkî-ṣedeq et Milkî-rešaᶜ dans les anciens écrits juifs et chrétiens," J. T. Milik, *JJS* 23 (1972) 98; see M. Hengel, "The Son of God" (n. 18), p. 81; P. J. Kobelski, *Melchizedek and Melkîrešaᶜ* (*CBQ* MS 10; Washington, D.C., 1981), pp. 59ff.: Melchizedek as ʾLHYM; cf. F. L. Horton, *The Melchizedek Tradition* (*SNTS* MS 30; Cambridge, U.K., 1976), pp. 64–82 (77f.); 167ff.

26. Gese correctly understands "χάρις καὶ ἀλήθεια" in 1:14 as "overflowing of salvation"; see H. Gese, "Der Johannesprolog," in *Zur biblischen Theologie: Alttestamentliche Vorträge* (Tübingen, 1983²), pp. 186ff.

27. Concerning the discussion on Johannine christology, see E. Käsemann, *Jesu letzter Wille nach Johannes 17* (Tübingen, 1966, 1980⁴); U. B. Müller, *Die Geschichte der Christologie in der johanneischen Gemeinde* (SBS 77; Stuttgart, 1975); Jan-A. Bühner, *Der Gesandte und sein Weg im 4. Evangelium* (WUNT; Tübingen, 1977); C. K. Barrett, *Essays in John* (Philadelphia, 1982), pp. 1ff., 19ff., 37ff. Against the widespread opinion that John was a "naïve docetist" (E. Käsemann), see now G. Johnston, "*Ecce Homo*: Irony in the Christology of the Fourth Evangelist," in *The Glory of Christ in the New Testament: Studies in Christology in Memory of G. B. Caird*,

the point even further, one could say that the "Word" from Jn 1:1 contains nothing except the one word Abba, "dear Father," and communicates this to humankind.[28]

The Johannine Son christology is therefore misunderstood when regarded as a syncretistic-speculative alienation of the simple message of Jesus or the early Church. It is, rather, the final, mature conclusion of a spiritual development that, along with the messianic preaching of the kingdom of God and Jesus' unique relationship to God, introduces a relationship that manifests itself in Jesus' prayer address, "Abba," "dear Father."

The christology of the Fourth Gospel is not a foreign element introduced from gnosticism, but represents rather the completion of the tradition within the Church of the person and work of Christ. This is clearly shown by the intentional occurrence of nearly all other important christological titles side by side, much more so here than in the Synoptic Gospels. The list also contains the absolute *"Lord"* (*ho kyrios*), *"Savior of the world"* (*sōtēr tou kosmou* [4:42]), *"Son of Man," "Elected of God"* (1.34), *"Holy of God"* (6:69),[29] *"Christ,"* and its Hebrew equivalent, *"Messiah,"*[30] and even the simple Palestinian form of address for the master, *"Rabbi,"* or *"Rabbouni."* The *"I am" sayings* are specifically Johannine expressions of the "worthiness," or more precisely, the revelation of Jesus: "I am the Bread of life," "the Light of the world," "the Good Shepherd," "the Resurrection and the Life," "the Way, the Truth, and the Life," "the True Vine."[31] Recent so-called critical investigation is fond of conjecturing about early Christianity generally, and in John particularly, different, conflicting christologies lie behind this richness of christological titles. But is not this accumulation of extremely different titles from "Rabbi" and "Son of Man" to "Logos" and *"theos"* an expression of the dialectic between Jesus' humanity and his divinity? It is just the diverse and numerous titles and names that express Jesus' unique "worthiness" which at the

---

ed. L. D. Hurst and N. T. Wright (New York, 1987), pp. 125–38. Of all New Testament writers, the author of the Fourth Gospel was the most subtle and least naïve, but I agree with Lietzmann, who says: "Es konnte sich aus dieser Logoschristologie ein naiver Doketismus *entwickeln*" (*Geschichte der Alten Kirche*, vol. 2, *Ecclesia catholica* [Berlin, Leipzig, 1936], p. 117); K. Wengst clarifies Käsemann's position: see *Bedrängte Gemeinde und verherrlichter Christus* (BTS 5; Neukirchen-Vluyn, 1983[2]), p. 14, n. 11. See also M. Hengel (n. 32:57ff, 68ff).

28. Joachim Jeremias was therefore quite correct when he put this one word at the center of his *New Testament Theology;* see his *Neutestamentliche Theologie*, vol. 1, *Die Verkündigung Jesu* (Gütersloh, 1979[3]), pp. 67ff.

29. The title ὁ ἐκλεκτός appears in Isa 42:1, but also in the Parables of Enoch 39:6, 40:5, 45:3, 49:2–5, 51:3 (cf. 55:4, 72:1), and 52:6, 9; 53:6, 61:5. Jn 6:69 and Mk 1:24 show that ὁ ἅγιος τοῦ θεοῦ is probably an archaic title and represents an early stage of christological development.

30. See M. de Jonge, "Jewish Expectations About the 'Messiah' According to the Fourth Gospel," *NTS* 19 (1972/73), pp. 246–70.

31. E. Schweizer, *Ego Eimi* (FRLANT 56; Göttingen, 1939, 1965[2]). A Feuillet, "Les Ego Eimi christologiques du quatrième Évangile," *RSR* 54 (1966) 5–22, 213–40; P. B. Harner, *The "I Am" of the Fourth Gospel* (Philadelphia, 1970); H. Klein, "Vorgeschichte und Verständnis der johanneischen Ich-bin-Worte" in *KuD* 33 (1987) 102–36.

same time demonstrates the intensity of the early Christian experience of salvation. Therefore, we should not try to isolate the titles of Jesus in John; it is their manifold interplay which makes John's christology so fascinating and full of tension and power.

The Fourth Evangelist articulates at the same time unmistakably the *paradox of the Passion of the Son of God*. Although this is unfolded—true to the confession in the Prologue, "and we beheld his *glory* . . ." (1:14)—in a rather unhistorical development of the words and works of Jesus, whose divine *glory* shines through continually, the road he travels is still one that, from the very beginning, leads to the cross. Already John the Baptist bears witness to him as "the Lamb of God who takes away the sin of the world" (1:29, 36), and, in connection with an old tradition already retained in Mark, the title "Son of Man"—literally, "the man"—is inseparably bound with Jesus' death on the cross: "Just as Moses lifted up the serpent in the wilderness, so must the Son of Man be lifted up, that whoever believes in him may have eternal life" (3:14ff.). Here "lifted up" (in Aramaic *'ezd'qef*) is code for "being crucified" (see also Isa 52:13 LXX), but it also means "lifted up" from the earth (12:32). Jesus' very claim to divine revelation provokes the attempt on his life: in answer to "I and the Father are one," his listeners ". . . took up stones . . . to stone him" (10:31). Pilate brings him scourged and thorn-crowned before the crowd: "Behold, the man!" (*idou ho anthrōpos*), but they demand his death: "because he has made himself the Son of God" (19:5, 7). R. Bultmann's comment here is correct: "The *ho logos sarx egeneto* ('and the Word became flesh') has become visible in its most extreme consequence."[32] Very similar to the Synoptics, the—deadly—messianic claim of Jesus is a thread that runs through the trial narrative to the title on the cross: "Jesus of Nazareth, *basileus tōn Ioudaiōn*" (19:19; cf. Mk 15:26).

The uniqueness of the Fourth Evangelist reveals itself, however, in that, in contrast to Mk 15:34 and Mt 27:46, the Son does not end his life with the cry of dereliction, but with the shout of the victor—"It is finished!"—which signifies the finishing of the work of *new* creation, at the eve of the sixth day.[33] The confession "and we beheld his glory" (1:14) from the Prologue

32. *Das Evangelium des Johannes* (KEK; Göttingen, 1986[21]), p. 510: "So muss denn Jesus heraustreten (. . .) als die Karikatur eines Königs, und Pilatus stellt ihn vor mit den Worten: . . . das ist der Mensch! Da seht die Jammergestalt! Im Sinne des Ev[an]g[e]listen ist damit die ganze Paradoxie des Anspruchs Jesu zu einem ungeheuren Bilde gestaltet. In der Tat: solch ein Mensch ist es, der behauptet, der König der Wahrheit zu sein! Das ὁ λόγος σάρξ ἐγένετο ist in seiner extremsten Konsequenz sichtbar geworden." See now M. Hengel, *The Johannine Question* (London/Philadelphia, 1989), pp. 68–72.

33. Jn 19:30—see already the first τετέλεσται in 19:28 and the unique ἵνα τελειωθῇ ἡ γραφή. Jn 1:1ff.: ἐν ἀρχῇ . . . corresponds to Gen 1:1; the two τετέλεσται in 19:28, and 30 to Gen 2:1f.: way'kullū and way'kal (LXX: καὶ συνετελέσθησαν . . . καὶ συνετέλεσεν ὁ θεὸς . . . τὰ ἔργα αὐτοῦ), see Jn 4:34 and the translation of the RSV Jn 19:30: "it is finished"; Gen 2:1f.: ". . . was finished" and: "God finished his work." On Friday evening, just before nightfall, Gen 2:1ff. is read as a part of Shabbat-qiddūsh—see b.Shab 119b; GenR 10. 8 (to Gen 2:2). For John the

points ultimately to the Dying One. The single—ideal—eyewitness of the Gospel stands at the foot of the cross of Jesus (19:35). The crucified Son of God and his way into suffering—the severest challenge for ancient polemic—is thus a basic theme in the Fourth Gospel, and not only in the passion story (cf. 2:4, 17, 21; 3:14; 5:17f.; 6:51–58; 7:19f., 33, 39; 8:59; 10:11, 15; 11:50ff.; 12:24, 31f.).

2. The Letter to the Hebrews, written about two decades before the Gospel of John, has likewise assimilated a Christian hymn into its introduction. The letter—actually an early Christian sermon—begins with a reminder of how God has spoken. Once he spoke through the prophets, but now, in the last days, through the Son. Through this One he created the worlds and appointed him "heir of all things." Here the actual hymn begins:

> He reflects the glory of God
> and bears the very stamp of his nature.
> He upholds the universe by his word of power,
> He has made purification for sins
> and sat down at the right hand
> of the Majesty on high.

The scribal argument follows: "He has become as much superior to angels as the name he has obtained is more excellent than theirs. For to what angel did God ever say, 'You are my son, today I have begotten you' (Ps 2:7)? Or again, 'I will be to him a father, and he shall be to me a son' (2Sam 7:14; 1Chr 17:13)?" (Heb 1:3–5).[34] Despite the difference in language, the substantive points of contact with John's Prologue are striking: here as well *the Son appears as God's Word of revelation*, and here as well he is *Mediator of the Creation*. Since, however, the beginning of time corresponds to the end of time, the Son, as the *eschatological representative of God*, is the "heir of al!

---

following Shabbat, when Jesus was "resting" in the tomb, was a "great" Shabbat day (19:31). In Jn 20:21f., at the evening of the first day, when the resurrected Christ is breathing the Holy Spirit to his disciples, the Evangelist uses the same word, ἐνεφύσησεν, as in Gen 2:7, where God is breathing a "breath of life" to Adam. At the beginning and at the end of the Fourth Gospel, we therefore have distinct allusions to Genesis 1 and 2 combining the old and new creation. See M. Hengel, "Die Schriftauslegung des 4. Evangeliums," *Jahrbuch für biblische Theologie* 4 (1989) 249–88 (pp. 284–86).

34. See O. Hofius, *Der Christushymnus Philipper 2, 6–11* (WUNT 17; Tübingen, 1976²), pp. 75–92; Hengel, "The Son of God" (n. 18), pp. 82–85. The text of Hebrews is already quoted in 1Clem 36:2ff. Strong relations also exist to the older hymn in Phil 2:6–11. I put the question hypothetically, whether the letter could not have been written from Rome to Christians in Palestine in the early sixties C.E. before the destruction of the Temple. Is it conceivable, had it been composed shortly after 70 C.E., that this would not have been mentioned at all? It probably belonged to the first collection of the Pauline letters. See its interpolation between Romans and Corinthians in P⁴⁶ and other MSS mentioned by W. H. P. Hatch, "The Position of Hebrews in the Canon of the NT," *HTR* 29 (1936) 133ff. The inscription was then deleted because the letter was not Pauline. These are mere reflections, not solutions!

things." As in the Prologue to John, we meet statements here that, in their boldness and universality, completely transcend the possibilities of pagan-polytheistic apotheoses, whether those of the Roman Caesars, or an Alexander, or a Hercules.[35] The preexistence and mediator of creation functions attributed to the crucified Messiah, Jesus of Nazareth, have no real analogy here. The ultimate intention of these statements is not the deification of a superhuman wielder of power, but the summing up of God's final revelation. The language of the hymn fragments touches the predicates of the *divine Wisdom* as we meet them, for example, in the Jewish-hellenistic Wisdom of Solomon. Thus concepts such as "reflection of His glory" (*apaugasma tēs doxēs*) and "very stamp of his nature" (*charaktēr tēs hypostaseōs*) interpret the mediating work of the Preexistent One,[36] who gives divine light and true being to the creatures threatened by Chaos. But this is not yet enough: this mediation becomes really concrete in the atoning death of Jesus: "He has made the purification for sins" and thereby spanned the gulf that separates God and his creatures. Following his deepest mortification comes the exaltation: "He has sat down at the right hand of the majesty on high." And here we meet the real theme of the letter in which Jesus is several times described as *"Mediator of the new covenant"* (*diathēkēs kainēs mesitēs*, 9:15; cf. 8:6, 12:24).[37]

35. *Alexander:* F. Taeger, *Charisma* I (Stuttgart, 1957), pp. 171–233; C. Schneider, *Kulturgeschichte des Hellenismus* II (Munich, 1969), pp. 891ff., 1102; J. Tondriau, "Alexandre le Grand assimilé à differentes divinités," *RPh* 23 (1949) 41–52; J. P. V. D. Balsdon, "The 'Divinity' of Alexander the Great," *Hist* 1 (1950) 363–88; C. Habicht, *Gottmenschentum und griechische Städte* (Zetemata 14; Munich, 1956, 1970²), pp. 222–42; J. Straub, "Divus Alexander—Divus Christus," in P. Granfield and J. A. Jungmann, eds., *Kyriakon: Festschrift J. Qua.ᵢₑ.* (Münster, 1970), vol. 1, pp. 461–73.

Heracles: F. Pfister, "Herakles und Christus," in *ARW* 34 (1937) 42–60. Pfister suspects an influence of the Hercules myth upon the gospels; see also C. Schneider, *Geistesgeschichte des Antiken Christentums* I (Munich, 1954), p. 57. A critical stance against this position is taken by H. J. Rose, "Heracles in the Gospels," *HTR* 31 (1968) 113–42; see also M. Simon, *Hercule et le christianisme* (Paris, 1955); M. Mühl, "Des Herakles Himmelfahrt," *RMus* 101 (1958) 106–34; R. Flacelière/P. Devambez, *Héraclès* (Paris, 1966); N. Robertson, "Heracles' Catabasis," *Hermes* 108 (1980) 274–300. Against a precipitate parallel between Hercules and Christ, see also E. Käsemann, *Das wandernde Gottesvolk* (FRLANT 55; Göttingen, 1938, 1959³) pp. 65f., contra H. Windisch; idem, *Exegetische Versuche und Besinnungen* II (Göttingen, 1964), vol. 2, p. 50, contra H. Braun, *Gesammelte Studien zum N.T. und seiner Umwelt* (Tübingen, 1967²), p. 265 (= *ZTK* 54 [1957] 362f.).

36. Cf. WisSol 7:26 about the preexistent divine Sophia:

> For she is an effulgence (ἀπαύγασμα)
> from everlasting light,
> and an unspotted mirror of God's working,
> and an image (εἰκών) of his goodness.   (trans. Charlesworth)

37. This formulation makes Jesus an antitype to Moses as the "mediator of the Old Testament." Philo, *Vita Mos* 2.166, calls Moses μεσίτης καὶ διαλλακτής, mediator and reconciler (with God). TMos 1:14: καὶ προεθεάσατό με ὁ θεὸς πρὸ καταβολῆς κόσμου εἶναί με τῆς διαθήκης αὐτοῦ μεσίτην (Gk. text according to Gelasius Cyzicenus, *HE* 2.17, 17 (GCS 28; 1918; see A.-M. Denis, ed., *Fragmenta pseudepigraphorum graeca* [Leiden, 1970], p. 63). In rabbinic texts, too, Moses is "mediator" (*sarsôr*)—see A. Oepke, *TWNT* 4 (Leiden, 1942), vol. 4, pp. 619ff., and Strack-Billerbeck III, 556, to Gal 3:19. The angelic mediator is μεσίτης θεοῦ καὶ

Still further observations are important in this context: Christological reflection, both in Hebrews and in early Christianity generally, was stimulated by the charismatic exposition of the Old Testament understood as the prophetic Word, i.e., it was more prophetic than learned, rabbinic, and scribal. The author of the letter therefore cites two texts following the hymn that are of major importance for the transmission of the title "Son" to Jesus. One of these concerns the appointment of the Davidic king, the *"Anointed" of Yahweh*, to *Son of God* in Ps 2:7 (cf. 2:2): "You are my Son, today I have begotten you." The importance of this citation for the Letter to the Hebrews becomes clear when it is repeated later (5:5).[38] At the same time, however, it is one of the most important Old Testament messianic proof texts in the entire New Testament; it helped shape the heavenly voice at Jesus' baptism in Mk 1:11, as well: "You are my beloved Son; with you I am well-pleased."[39] Together with the second citation, Nathan's prophecy to David (2Sam 7:14), "I will be a father to him, and he shall be to me a son," this text shaped one of the oldest confessions in the New Testament. This is the two-part formula with which Paul introduces himself to the community at Rome (unknown to him), and which, in its pre-Pauline form in the earliest Palestinian community, read as follows:

Jesus Christ, descended from the seed of David,
appointed as Son of God
Since his resurrection from the dead.[40]

Here there is still nothing about a Being before time, about the preexistence of the Son. Rather, the Son of David seems to be "adopted" as Son of God only through the *resurrection*, and the title "Son of God" is an interpretation

---

ἀνθρώπων καὶ ἐπὶ τῆς εἰρήνης τοῦ Ἰσραηλ κατέναντι τῆς βασιλείας τοῦ θεοῦ (or ἐχθροῦ?) στήσεται (TDan 6:11). About angelic mediators see A. F. Segal, *Two Powers in Heaven* (SJLA 25; [Leiden, 1977]); idem, "Ruler of This World: Attitudes About Mediator Figures and the Importance of Sociology of Self-Definition," in E. P. Sanders, ed., *Jewish and Christian Self-Definition* (Leiden, 1981), vol. 2, pp. 245–68, 403–12 (esp. with regard to the Fourth Gospel, see pp. 251ff.). Concerning the "mediator" in the hellenistic Roman world, see Reinhold Merkelbach, *Mithras* (Königstein, 1984), p. 27; regarding the Persian Mithras as μεσίτης, see also Plutarch, *De Iside* 46 (p. 369E), and the seminal essay of M. P. Nilsson, "The High God and the Mediator," *HTR* 56 (1963) 101–20: "It is the great achievement of Christianity . . . introducing a mediator between the High God and man" (p. 118): "The gap was bridged by the mediator Christ. Christianity presented the mediator in his most concrete form, as God's son and as suffering man."

38. According to O. Michel, *Der Brief an die Hebräer* (KEK 13; Göttingen, 1984¹⁴), p. 110, the second citation of Ps 2:7 in 5:5 is situated at the beginning of the second principal section of the letter.

39. Here also we find the secondary influence of the "Servant of God" tradition from Isa 42:1. See the quotation of Isa 42:1 in Mt 12:18 and J. Jeremias, *Abba* (Göttingen, 1966), pp. 192ff.

40. Cf. Rom 1:3f. Concerning the oldest form see M. Hengel, "The Son of God" (n. 18), pp. 57f.; H. Schlier in *Neues Testament und Geschichte: O. Cullmann zum 70. Geburtstag*, H. Baltensweiler and Bo Reicke, eds. (Zürich, 1972), pp. 207–18; U. Wilckens, *Der Brief an die Römer* (EKK 6.1; Zürich, 1977, 1987²), pp. 56ff.; 64ff.

of the title "*Christos*," the Messiah from the house of David, and expresses his unique relation to God. Already in the pre-Christian period these two texts, 2 Samuel 7 and Psalm 2, appear together in a collection of messianic prophecies from the Essenes in Qumran.[41]

The earliest Church drew on these passages in order to explain theologically the resurrection event upon which it was founded. But less than two generations later as well, with a much more widely developed christology such as we find in Hebrews, these Old Testament texts still retained their constitutive significance. Indeed, one was able with their help to answer burning christological questions, such as how the Exalted One stands in relation to the angels.

Speculation was extensive in Early Judaism over the hierarchically ordered angel world. Outstanding human beings such as Enoch and Elijah, who had been taken up into Heaven, could be changed into angelic figures as well. What could have been more natural for the Jewish Christian circles than that they should see in the exalted Christ one of the highest of the angels? It is curious that this problem surfaces only here in the letter to the Hebrews and is at once tersely rejected. Not until later writings, to some extent in the Apocalypse of John and more so in the Shepherd of Hermas and other second-century texts, does it again become virulent. "*Angel Christology*" was apparently not a live option for earliest Christianity. The Son, lifted up and seated at the right hand of God, was from the beginning set *above* all angels.[42] The argumentation of the unknown author of our letter is correspondingly uncomplicated: the citations prove Christ to be the Son; his utterly unique relation to God cannot be compared to that of the angels who occupy a subordinate position as *leitourgika pneumata*, ministering servants (1:14).

As a final support for his argument, the author uses a third citation from the most important Old Testament text for all christology, a text already alluded to in the Christ hymn: "He has sat down at the right hand of the maj-

---

41. 4Q Flor = 4Q 174; see E. Lohse, *Die Texte aus Qumran* (Darmstadt, 1964, 1981³), pp. 256ff.; J. M. Allegro, *Qumran Cave 4* (DJD 5; Oxford, 1968), pp. 59ff.; and the corrections of J. Strugnell, *RQ* 7 (1969/71) 220ff. For the importance of 2Sam 7:10–15 for NT christology, see O. Betz, *What Do We Know About Jesus?* (Philadelphia, 1968), pp. 88ff., 95ff. D. Lührmann is incorrect in saying, ". . . in der Auslegung—soweit erhalten—wird aber der Sohnestitel nicht auf den דוד צמח angewendet." Idem, *Das Markusevangelium* (HNT 3; Tübingen, 1987), p. 38. But see 4QFlor 1.11: והוא יהיה לי לבן הואה צמח דויד.

42. Contra M. Werner, *Die Entstehung des christlichen Dogmas* (Bern, Tübingen, 1953²), pp. 302ff.; see J. Barbel, *Christos Angelos* (Theoph 3, Bonn, 1941); J. Daniélou, *Théologie du judéo-christianisme. Histoire des doctrines chrétiennes avant Nicée* (Tournai, 1958), vol. 1, pp. 167–98; R. N. Longenecker, *The Christology of Early Jewish Christianity* (London, 1970), pp. 26ff.; A. Grillmeier (see n. 13), vol. 1, pp. 150–57; J. E. Fossum (see n. 18) *passim;* R. Williams, "Christologie II, 1," *TRE* 16 (1987) 726f. The angel christology has only a very reduced importance in the earliest and most important New Testament texts. Probably in a Jewish-Christian and popular milieu, angelogical traits were secondarily introduced in christology. Thus H. Leclercq, "Anges VII: Culte des anges," *DACL* (Paris, 1924), vol. 1.2, cols. 2144–2150.

esty on high." The angels stand before God like the ministers before the great king;[43] it is only the Son for whom the word of Ps 110:1 is meant: "The Lord [i.e., God himself] said to my Lord [Christ]: '*Sit at my right hand*, until I make your enemies a footstool for your feet.' "[44]

It is not only the formula entrusted to us in the Apostles' Creed of Christ's sitting, or rather being enthroned at the right hand of God that we have from this verse. It probably encouraged as well the introduction of the title "Lord," "*Kyrios,*" in the earliest Church. This is already in use in the oldest Palestinian community, in a prayer to him who is exalted to the right hand of God: "Our Lord, come!"—in Aramaic: *Maran 'atā.*[45] The Greek form appears as the concluding prayer in the Apocalypse of John: *erchou kyrie Iēsou* (22:20).

Now it is striking, indeed paradoxical, that the Son who is exalted to God's right hand, separated from the angels and completely bound to God, is portrayed at the same time in his full humanity.[46] For this purpose the author takes over a title from older tradition with whose help he develops the saving effectiveness of Christ: Jesus is the true *High Priest.* The Essenes already expected for their two Messiahs a high priest figure and a ruler-warrior figure, although the messianic high priest from the line of Aaron was superior to the Davidic prince from Israel.[47] In the Jewish-hellenistic Testament of Levi the messianic high priest reveals himself from heaven (18:3; a text which I believe to be Jewish). For the Letter to the Hebrews, Christ is the high priest, because he presents himself as the atoning sacrifice: "Therefore he had to be made like his brethren in every respect, so that he might be-

43. See b.Hag 15a: ". . . on high there is no sitting [no jealousy and] no emulation of the angels before the throne of God." Cf. 3En 16 in *Synopse zur Hekhalot-Literatur* (see n. 25) §20 and A. F. Segal (see n. 37), pp. 60ff. For the text see D. J. Halperin, *The Merkabah in Rabbinic Literature* (AOS 62; New Haven, Conn., 1980), pp. 168 and 87. Three manuscripts read: "there is no standing and no sitting . . . ," but the original story "presupposes that heavenly beings would normally stand, not sit" (so Rashi and two manuscripts). The addition of "standing" seems to be an antianthropomorphic "philosophizing" interpretation. See idem, *"The Faces of the Chariot"* (TSAJ 16, Tübingen, 1988), 149ff. For the "standing" of the angels see y.Ber 1:1, 2c, l. 23ff.; GenR 65, 21: they have according to Ez 1:7 and Dan 7:16 no knees, so they cannot sit. Only Moses was allowed to sit before God on Mount Sinai in contrast to the angels. ExR 34:4; Tanh B b^eṣallaḥ 13 to Ex 15:1: "There is in the high no sitting, rather they are all standing. . . ." The rabbis were very reluctant to speculate about heavenly enthronizations.

44. For 1:13 and Ps 110:1 in earliest Christianity, see D. M. Hay, *Glory at the Right Hand* (SBLMS 18; Missoula, Mont., 1973); M. Gourges, *À la droite de dieu* (EtB; Paris, 1978); cf. Hengel, "The Son of God" (see n. 18), p. 78.

45. 1Cor 16:22; *Did* 10, 6; for the linguistic problems see H. P. Rüger, *ZNW* 59 (1968) 120f. and idem, "Aramäisch II im Neuen Testament," *TRE* 3 (1978) 607. The prayer *maran 'atā* has a possible connection as well with the messianic Ps 118:26 Targ Teh: *bārîk d^e'ātê b^eṣûm mêmrā* . . . ; and Dan 7:13: *k^ebar 'e nāš 'ātê h^ewā*; see Mt 23:39 = Lk 13:35 (= Q).

46. Concerning the "full humanity," see Heb 2:17: "κατὰ πάντα τοῖς ἀδελοῖς ὁμοιωθῆναι"; 2:11: "κατὰ πάντα καθ' ὁμοιότητα" 4:15 and 5:7f.

47. See A. J. B. Higgins, "The Priestly Messiah," *NTS* 13 (1966/67) 211–39. For Qumran see J. Starcky, *RB* 70 (1963) 481–505; E. M. Laperrousaz, *L'attente du Messie en Palestine* (Paris, 1982).

come a merciful and faithful high priest in the service of God, to make expiation for the sins of the people. For because he himself has suffered and been
tempted, he is able to help those who are tempted" (2:17ff.). "In the days of
his flesh, he offered up prayers and supplications, with loud cries and tears,
to him who was able to save him from death. . . . Although he was a Son, he
learned obedience through what he suffered; and being made perfect he became the source of eternal salvation to all who obey him . . ." (5:7–9); ". . .
who for the joy that was set before him endured the cross, despising the
shame . . ." (12:2). "Therefore let us go forth to him outside the camp and
bear the abuse he endured. For here we have no lasting city (*polis*), but we
seek the city which is to come" (13:13ff.). The obedient sacrifice of the Son,
the self-sacrifice of the true high priest, summons to discipleship.[48]

3. The last hymn is at least a decade or two older than the Letter to the
Hebrews. We find it in the letter of Paul to the church at Philippi (Phil 2:6–
11),[49] to whom it was written approximately in the middle of the fifties C.E.,
if it came from Ephesus, or at the beginnings of the sixties, if it came from
Rome. The composition of the hymn was possibly much earlier.

> Have this mind among yourselves, which was also in Christ Jesus,
> who, though he was in the form of God,
> did not count equality with God a thing to be grasped,
> but emptied himself,
> taking the form of a servant,
> being born in the likeness of men.
> And being found in human form
> he humbled himself
> and became obedient unto death,
> even death on a cross.
>
> Therefore God has highly exalted him
> and bestowed on him the name which is above every name,
> that at the name of Jesus every knee should bow,
> in heaven and on earth and under the earth,
> and every tongue confess
> that Jesus Christ is Lord,
> to the glory of God the Father!   (2:5–11)

---

48. The Jewish background of Hebrews, related to Merkabah mysticism, is demonstrated by
O. Hofius in *Der Vorhang vor dem Throne Gottes* (WUNT 14; Tübingen, 1972); see also
W. R. G. Loader, *Sohn und Hoherpriester* (WMANT 53; Neukirchen-Vluyn, 1981).

49. See Hengel (see n. 18), pp. 1f.; O. Hofius (see n. 34); L. W. Hurtado, "Jesus as Lordly
Example: On Philippians 2:5–11," in *From Jesus to Paul: Studies in Honour of F. W. Beare*, ed.
P. Richardson and J. C. Hurd (Waterloo, Ont., 1984), pp. 113–26; C. A. Wanamaker, "Philippians 2:6–11: Son of God or Adamic Christology," *NTS* 33 (1987) 179–93. U. B. Müller's recent
essay ("Der Christushymnus Phil 2:6–11," *ZNW* 79 [1988] 17–44) betrays a complete misunderstanding of Hofius. This often-discussed text is surely in its first part related to the preexistence
of Christ—see 1Cor 8:6, 10:1ff.; Rom 8:3; Gal 4:4.

First, it is striking that the hymn occurs not in a context of dogmatic argumentation, but within ethical exhortations from the apostle. The hearers of the letter should live in spiritually gifted conformity like Paul himself (cf. 2Cor 1:7 sharing in his sufferings) to the way and work of Christ. The statements about humiliation and exaltation have concrete application in life. Secondly, this oldest of the three hymns is the most well-balanced of all. He who is preexistent and like God regards his divine form of existence not as "a thing to be snatched," but empties himself, becomes human, and dies the shameful death of a slave on the cross. Therefore God has exalted (*hyperhypsōsen*) him above every comparable power, and given him his own name of majesty, "*Kyrios*," that he might be Lord over all Creation, the heavenly (i.e. the angels), the earthly (i.e. humanity), and the underworld (i.e. the dead—or the demons?), in order that they all confess him as "*Kyrios*"—not to his own glory, but to the glory of God the Father.[50]

The first thing to consider here is that "*Kyrios*" in the hellenistic synagogue—as a substitute (*qᵉrê*) for the Hebrew name for God, YHWH, the tetragrammaton—was the most important appellation for God. Early on, the Greek-speaking community referred Old Testament statements in which "Kyrios" meant the God of Israel to the "Kyrios Jesus." For example, Joel 3:5, "Everyone who calls on the name of the Lord (i.e. Yahweh) shall be saved," was so understood in the sense of the saving appeal made to the *kyrios Iesous*) (Rom 10:13; cf. Acts 2:21). Philo could already occasionally refer an Old Testament "Kyrios" to the "Archangel," i.e. the Logos, in whose form God himself appears.[51] However, early Christianity was establishing here the theological principle which expresses the eschatological identity of the revelation of God, the "Kyrios" and "Father," and Jesus, the "Kyrios" and "Son." The absolute *ho kyrios*, and *kyrios Iēsous*, is far and away the title of majesty most used by Paul, appearing in the genuine letters 184 times. "Son of God" by contrast appears only 15 times. The apostle expresses thereby the personal connection of the Church, as well as the individual, with the Exalted One. "Son of God," on the other hand, emphasizes primarily Jesus' relation with the Father. One may safely dismiss the derivation of the title "Kyrios" from the hellenistic-oriental cults of the "Kyria Isis" and other oriental "Kyrioi."[52] An important preliminary stage of the Pauline usage was formed

---

50. Cf. Rev 5:8–14. I see no reason to assume that the original hymn was enlarged by Paul. It is, as we have it, perfect. The "anadiplosis" (cf. O. Hofius, n. 34, p. 10), θανάτου δὲ σταυροῦ is as necessary as the εἰς δόξαν τοῦ θεοῦ πατρός, so already M. Dibelius, *An die Philipper* (HNT 11; Tübingen, 1937³), p. 81. Most probably the hymn was created by Paul himself. Its special language, which is somewhat different from Paul's prose, is the language of pneuma-inspired hymnic poetry.

51. *Somn* 1:157ff. to Gen 28:13; see Fossum (n. 18), pp. 110, 292ff. and Segal, *Two Powers* (n. 37).

52. Against the hypothesis of W. Bousset, *Kyrios Christos* (Göttingen, 1913, 1965⁵), influential and often repeated in Germany, but in many ways misleading, Bousset tried to derive the title "Kyrios" from pagan oriental Kyrios cults in the gentile-Christian community in Antioch. See

from the practice of using scripture as proof with the help of the above mentioned Ps 110:1: "The Lord said to my Lord . . ." The roots for this were
basically the respectful form of address to Jesus himself with *marî* or *rabbî*,
which could with no problem be translated with *kyrie*, "Lord." Paul can
therefore call Jesus' physical brothers—James, for example—simply "the
brothers of the Lord" (1Cor 9:5; Gal 1:19). On the other hand, the most
important confession formula of acclamation is for him *kyrios Iēsous*, "Jesus
is Lord," the confession in which according to the conclusion of our hymn,
all creation joins.

That the acclamation, "Jesus is *Kyrios*," is made "to the glory of God the
Father" shows that the title "*Kyrios*" and the title "Son" are connected in the
closest possible way. This acclamation is the goal of creation and history,[53] or
more precisely, the goal of the self-disclosure of God through the Son:
"When all things are subjected to him, then the Son himself will also be
subjected to Him who put all things under him, that God may be all in all"
(1Cor 15:28). If the Son returns to the Father at the end of all things, it is,
after all, because he came forth from him. Therefore the beginning of the
Philippian hymn speaks of *divine* "nature" and the *divinity* of the Son. The
morphē theou, divine nature, is in this regard closely related to the *eikōn
theou*, the image of God. According to 2Cor 4:4ff., Christ, as God's *eikōn*,
radiates the glory of God, preached in Paul's gospel, into the hearts of believers. This metaphor as well is taken over from Jewish Wisdom theology.[54]

---

the protest already by P. Wernle, "Jesus und Paulus: Antithesen zu Boussets Kyrios Christos,"
ZTK 25 (1915) 1–92, and the seminal but often overlooked investigations by W. Foerster, *Herr
Ist Jesus* (NTF 2nd Ser.; Gütersloh, 1924), pp. 69ff., 201ff.; idem, *Kyrios*, *TWNT* 3 (1938) 1045ff.
(p. 1049); R. N. Longenecker (n. 42), pp. 120ff.; Hengel, "The Son of God" (see n. 18), pp. 23ff.,
75ff.; idem, *Between Jesus and Paul* (Philadelphia, 1983), pp. 41ff.; J. A. Fitzmyer, "The Semitic
Background of the New Testament *Kyrios* Titles," in *A Wandering Aramean: Collected Essays*
(Missoula, Mont., 1979), pp. 115–42; L. W. Hurtado, *One God, One Lord* (Philadelphia, 1988),
passim. Hurtado's important summary of research, especially of the last twenty years, seems to
me to be fundamental for further investigation. The old assertions of the *Religionsgeschichtliche
Schule*, still given in some circles today, are no longer tenable. It underestimated *the richness
and creative power of Palestinian Judaism*, the intermingling of Jewish and hellenistic thought
in Jewish Palestine, and the importance of bilingualism in the Palestinian Jesus Movement in
Galilee and Jerusalem. The resurrected and exalted Son of Man was the lord of the community
and so Ο ΚΥΡΙΟΣ became very early—astonishingly enough, apparently with no difficulties—
the appellation for the man Jesus himself, and the words of the man Jesus were called λόγοι
κυρίου; cf. 1Thes 4:15 and 1Cor 7:10, 9:14, and 11:23. See now M. Hengel, *The "Hellenization"
of Judaea in the First Century after Christ* (London/Philadelphia, 1989), esp. pp. 54ff.
        53. Cf. O. Hofius (n. 34), pp. 41ff.; 65: "Der Christushymnus Phil 2,6–11 besingt die Offen-
barung der eschatologischen Königsherrschaft Gottes in der Erhöhung des gekreuzigten Jesus
Christus."
        54. F. W. Eltester, *Eikon im Neuen Testament* (BZNW 23; Berlin, 1958); J. Jervell, *Imago Dei*
(FRLANT 76; Göttingen, 1960), pp. 197–231. A gnostic background of this important Jewish-
hellenistic term cannot be presupposed. Cf. B. Mack, *Logos und Sophia* (SUNT 10; Göttingen,
1973), pp. 166–71, and index p. 220; G. Schimanowski, *Weisheit und Messias: Die jüdischen
Voraussetzungen der urchristlichen Präexistenzchristologie* (WUNT 2nd Ser. 17; Tübingen,
1985), pp. 336–40.

The Son, however, renounces divine nature and divine glory; he takes the form of a human being, comparable with a slave, subject to weakness, temptation and death, and lets himself be crucified. Although Paul knows the function of mediation of the Creation by the Preexistent One and his revelation already in the Old Testament history of Israel (1Cor 8:6; 10:1ff.; cf. Col 1:15), this theme appears in his writings only peripherally: it is not the Preexistent One or the Exalted One in his glory whom he preaches, but the Crucified. This one is the center of his christology (1Cor 1:17ff.; 2:1ff.). The apostle himself characterizes his message as *logos tou staurou*, "word of the cross." The scandal this must have created for people of antiquity, both Jews and Greeks, and us, with our domesticated Christianity, can hardly be estimated. The polemic of Celsus against Jesus as a crucified criminal and deceiver can give us a notion of it.[55]

4. With this we come to our real problem. The comparison of the three hymns in the Johannine Prologue, the Letter to the Hebrews and the Letter to the Philippians shows, first of all, that christological thinking between 50 and 100 C.E. *was much more unified in its basic structure* than New Testament research, in part at least, has maintained. Basically, the later developments are already there in a nutshell in the Philippian hymn. This means, however, with regard to the development of *all* the early Church's christology, that more happened in the first twenty years than in the entire later, centuries-long development of dogma.[56] Secondly, it is clear that the glorification of Christ, the doctrines of his preexistence, creation mediation and exaltation, did not remove the scandal of his shameful death, but rather deepened it. A crucified Jewish martyr, a martyred innocent, a second Socrates could have appealed to Jews and Greeks as an edifying example; a crucified *God* was for every educated person in antiquity a shameless impertinence, indeed, an absurdity.

The basic question of New Testament christology is[57]: How did it come about that in the short space of less than twenty years the crucified Galilean Jew, Jesus of Nazareth, was elevated by his followers to a dignity which left every possible form of pagan-polytheistic apotheosis far behind? Preexistence, Mediator of Creation and the revelation of his identity with the One God: this exceeds the possibilities of deification in a polytheistic pantheon;

55. Origen, *Contra Celsum* 2.33ff., 37–39, 47, 55, 61, 68, 72f.; 5.64; 6.10 (κεκολασμένος αἴσχιστα); 6.34, 74—etc. See C. Andresen, *Logos und Nomos: Die Polemik des Kelsos wider das Christentum* (AKG 30; Berlin, 1955), pp. 176; 232ff.; Hengel, *Crucifixion*, pp. 7f., 17; see above nn. 6–8.

56. Hengel, *Between Jesus and Paul*, pp. 30–47; 156–66; M. Casey, "Chronology and Development of Pauline Christology," in *Paul and Paulinism: Essays in Honour of C. K. Barrett*, M. D. Hooker and S. G. Wilson, eds. (London, 1982), pp. 124–34.

57. Hengel, "The Son of God" (n. 18), pp. 1f. For the soteriological interpretation in the earliest community, see M. Hengel, *The Atonement* (London, Philadelphia, 1981), pp. 65ff.

here we have a new *religions-geschichtliche* category before us that must be explained from the first Christian experience itself, or as the case may be, from its Jewish background.[58]

In order to answer this basic question with the required brevity, we turn to two titles that, as titles, already for Paul no longer played an important role, and which we have until now barely touched. In 1Cor 15:3ff. Paul cites a formulaic summary of the salvation event, which he held to be the basis for the founding of the church in Corinth around 49 C.E.: "For I delivered to you as of first importance what I also received"—i.e. probably after his conversion in the mid-thirties C.E.—: "that *Christ* died for our sins in accordance with the Scriptures, that he was buried, that he was raised on the third day. . . ." It is disputed whether "Christos" here is still a messianic title,[59] or—as otherwise almost always in Paul—used as a proper name.[60] This ambivalence results from the fact that the Jewish title for the eschatological ruler promised in the Old Testament, the "Messiah," *mašiaḥ*, i.e., the "Anointed," would hardly have been understood in pagan circles outside Palestine. A *personal* understanding was restricted to the Septuagint and a Jewish milieu, since for Greeks "*christos*" is an adjective never used for persons, meaning something that was "to be rubbed in" or "used as ointment or salve";[61] "*neochristos*" had the meaning "newly plastered."[62] The early Christian confession "Jesus is Messiah," *Christos Iesous*, was quickly changed therefore into a proper name.[63] Already by the end of the thirties the members of the new Jewish sect in Antioch were called "Christians" (Acts 11:26). For the later Roman authors, Suetonius, Pliny and Tacitus, it was taken for granted that "Christos" was a proper name that was confused with the common slave name "Chrēstos."[64] Without doubt, however, "*Christos*" originally had titular significance in the confession of 1Cor 15:3ff. The intent was to say,

---

58. "Jewish" includes the Jews who spoke Greek—"hellenistic" and pagan should no longer be identified!

59. J. Jeremias, *Die Abendmahlsworte Jesu* (Göttingen, 1967⁴), pp. 97f.; cf. idem, "Artikelloses Χριστός," *ZNW* 57 (1966) 211–15.

60. Hengel, *Between Jesus and Paul*, pp. 65–77, 179–88.

61. Liddell and Scott, *A Greek-English Lexicon*, col. 2007; see Stephanus and Dindorf, *Thesaurus Graecae Linguae* IX, col. 1688: φάρμακα χριστά sunt omne genus unguenta et olea quibus aegri inunguntur, vel etiam pigmenta et fucamenta quibus illitis color emendatur.

62. Liddell and Scott, col. 1170; Stephanus and Dindorf, VI, col. 1447: οἶκον or οἴκημα νεόχριστον; see ἀρτίχριστος/ον in Liddell and Scott, col. 250: fresh-spread φάρμακον. See the inimitable G. Zuntz's amusing description of possible reactions of pagan readers: "Ein Heide las das Markusevangelium," in *Markus-Philologie. Historische, literargeschichtliche und stilistische Untersuchungen zum zweiten Evangelium*, ed. H. Cancik (WUNT 33; Tübingen, 1984), p. 205.

63. For the use of "Christos" in Judaism and the NT, see A. S. van der Woude, M. de Jonge, and W. Grundmann, χριστός, *TWNT* 9 (1973) 482–576.

64. Suetonius, *Divus Claudius* 25.11: "Iudaeos impulsore Chresto assidue tumultuantis Roma expulit." For the use of "Chrestiani" in Tacitus, *Ann* 15.44, see H. Fuchs, "Der Bericht über die Christen in den Annalen des Tacitus," in *Tacitus*, ed. V. Pöschl (WdF 97; Darmstadt, 1969), pp. 558–604 (esp. see pp. 563f.).

"that the *Messiah* died for our sins."[65] This declaration about the Messiah dying for us (*hyper hēmōn*) is for Paul the basis for numerous formulaic expressions.[66] These sounded strange to Jewish ears, for in the Judaism of Jesus' time, the "Anointed" was above all a victorious ruler; the suffering Messiah in Jewish literature appears unequivocally only from the second century C.E. on.[67] The historical roots of this formulaic expression of the dying of the Messiah lie in the Passion of Jesus. According to the unanimous witness of all four gospels the messiah question ruled not only the trial of Jesus, but could also be read on the cross itself as the *causa poenae*, the reason for execution: "The King of the Jews" (Mk 15:26, par.).[68] After the resurrection event upon which the Church was founded, the early Christian proclamation could not do otherwise than concentrate on this point which so

---

65. Hengel, *The Atonement*, pp. 34–47. For the OT understanding of sacrifice and atonement and its importance for the early interpretation of the death of Jesus see H. Gese, "Die Sühne," in *Zur biblischen Theologie* (see n. 19), pp. 85–106; see also his pupil B. Janowski, *Sühne als Heilsgeschehen* (WMANT 55; Neukirchen-Vluyn, 1982); for Rom 3:25 see pp. 350ff.

66. Cf. W. Kramer, *Christos Kyrios, Gottessohn* (ATANT 44; Zürich, 1963), pp. 22ff.; W. Popkes, *Christus Traditus* (ATANT 49; Zürich, 1967), pp. 153ff.; K. Wengst, *Christologische Formeln und Lieder im Urchristentum* (SNT 7; Gütersloh, 1973²), pp. 55ff.; A. J. Hultgren, *Christ and His Benefits* (Philadelphia, 1987), pp. 47ff.

67. TBen 3:8, often quoted in his respect, is, even in its shorter Armenian form, probably a Christian enlargement; the original form was perhaps related to Joseph. Certainly there was no reference to a suffering Messiah. But the late Abbé Starcky, *RB* 70 (1963) 492, mentions an unpublished fragment of "a Testament of Jacob (?)" from Cave 4 of Qumran with references to messianic (?) suffering. Abbé Starcky graciously sent me a transcription. In this text an eschatological person seems to play an atoning and a suffering role:

> he atones for all sons of his generation, and to all sons [. . .] it will be sent [remission of sins? his word] will be like the word of heaven and his teaching like the will of God.

Later on he will be attacked and defamed:

> and in falsehood and violence he will be, (and) the people will go astray in his days.

In a further fragment, perhaps from the same column, there is mention of a persecuted person (probably the same one). In the first line appears *wmk'byn; ngdy mk'bykh* is all that is left on the third. As *mak'ob* is relatively rare in the OT, appearing twice in close succession in Isa 53:3 and 4, a reference to this chapter here is probable. May the text be published soon! For the older discussion about the suffering Messiah, see the critical opinions of G. Dalman, *Der leidende und sterbende Messias* (Berlin, 1888); S. Hurwitz, *Die Gestalt des sterbenden Messias* (Zürich, 1958); K. Hruby, "Die Messiaserwartungen der Talmudischen Zeit mit besonderer Berücksichtigung des Leidens des Messias," *Judaica* 20 (1964) 6–22, 73–90, 193–212; 21 (1965) 100–22; J. Heinemann, "The Messiah of Ephraim and the Premature Exodus of the Tribe of Ephraim," *HTR* 68 (1975) 1–15; positive: J. Jeremias, *Abba*, pp. 191–216; Jeremias, παῖς θεοῦ, *TWNT* (1954⁴) 680ff.

68. J. Blinzler, *Der Prozess Jesu* (Regensburg, 1969), pp. 351, 362: Suetonius, *Caligula* 32; *Domitian* 10; Cassius Dio 54.3, 7; 73.16, 5; Eusebius, *HE* 5.1, 44: This information from antiquity about delinquents sentenced to death carrying a signboard with the *causa poenae* on their way to the place of execution presupposes that after the execution the board remained on the cross for public deterrence. Together with the suffering of the victims, surely it had a strong effect on the spectator. The inscription "king of the Jews" is in keeping with the personal anti-Judaism of Pilate.

radically contradicted the prevailing Jewish hope: "Was it not necessary that the Messiah must suffer these things and enter into his glory?" (Lk 24:26).[69]

5. While we possess no text in the Synoptic Gospels besides the trial in which Jesus confesses himself to be the Messiah, the other title, "Son of Man,"[70] with one exception (Acts 7:56), appears only in the gospels, and then only as self-declaration on the lips of Jesus. One can, in my judgment, explain its importance in the gospel tradition only if one concedes that Jesus had already used it himself. Indeed, it is probably more a veiled code word than an actual title. The word "Son of Man," in Aramaic, bar ᵃⁿāš, basically has the simple meaning, "man," or "anyone"; it is—in an eschatological or messianic sense—found outside the gospels only in a very few Jewish apocalyptic texts where it also obscures more than illuminates.[71] In at least two places "the Son of Man" is directly identified with "the Messiah."[72] The Synoptic Jesus uses this cipher with three meanings: for the heavenly figure of the coming Judge, for his present work, and for his future suffering. In the latter two cases it could be no more than a circumlocution for the first person. We need not go deeper into the hotly disputed problem of the Son of Man title, for one thing is certain: with the first appearances of the Risen One, the identity of the Crucified with the heavenly Son of Man was, for the disciples, certain; they could pray for his quick return with the call, maran ᵃta, "Our Lord, come!" From here then, the one yielded to the other. If God had confirmed his crucified Messiah through the resurrection and exalted him to his right hand, it was thus fitting, not the least of all because of Ps 2:7

---

69. N. A. Dahl, *Jesus the Christ* (Minneapolis, 1991), chap. 1; Hengel, *Atonement*, pp. 41ff., 65ff.

70. The literature on his "cipher" is endless. The article by C. Colpe, υἱὸς τοῦ ἀνθρώπου, *TWNT* 8 (1969) 403–81, is still basic; idem, *Kairos* NF 11 (1969) 241–63; 12 (1970) 81–112; 13 (1971) 1–17; 14 (1972) 241–57; see J. Jeremias, *Neutestamentliche Theologie*, vol. 1, pp. 245ff.; see also F. H. Borsch, *The Son of Man in Myth and History* (Philadelphia, 1967); S. Kim, *"The Son of Man" as the Son of God* (WUNT 30; Tübingen, 1983); C. C. Caragounis, *The Son of Man* (WUNT 38; Tübingen, 1986).

71. The starting point is the enigmatic comparison of Dan 7:13: kᵉbar ᵃⁿāš; beyond this we find only the slightly altered formula in 1En 46:2–4; 48:2; 62:5f.; 62:9, 14; 63:11; 69:26–29; 70:1; 71:14; see also 60:10 and in 4Ezra 13; see also TAb A 12:5: the ἀνὴρ θαυμαστὸς ἡλιόρατος ὅμοιος υἱῷ θεοῦ residing on a throne as judge of the souls of the dead (12:11) who is identified with Abel. For the Parables of Enoch see J. Theisohn, *Der auserwählte Richter* (SUNT 12; Göttingen, 1975) and the invaluable commentary of M. Black, *The Book of Enoch or 1 Enoch: A New English Edition with Commentary and Textual Notes* (SVTP 7; Leiden, 1985), pp. 206f.

72. 1En 48:10, 52:4; see U. B. Müller, *Messias und Menschensohn in jüdischen Apokalypsen und in der Offenbarung des Johannes* (SNT 6: Gütersloh, 1972); Black, *The Book of Enoch*, p. 212. Of the two possibilities which Black is considering I would prefer the last: the author "reserves the term to the climax of this vision, and is sparing in its use simply because it is a special term of majesty with royal as well as high-priestly and prophetic associations." "Son of Man" is not only "elect" and "just," but also the title of the hidden one, the Messiah, after his revelation to Israel. Late rabbinic tradition could call the Messiah, alluding to Dan 7:13, ᶜᵃⁿānî, Strack-Billerbeck I, 486, 957; see Justin, *Dial.* 32:1.

and 2Sam 7:14, that he receive the title of honor "Son of God," which clearly emphasized his relation to the Father, instead of the obscure term "Son of Man." Had he not, after all, taught his disciples to call on God as the kind Father, to address him without any fear as "Abba" (Rom 8:15; Gal 4:6; cf. Mk 14:36)?[73] Already Paul confesses in connection with his vision of Christ, which took place some two or three years after Jesus' death, that it pleased God *"to reveal his Son to me"* (Gal 1:16). According to the old confession of Rom 1:3ff., Jesus, the Son of David, was appointed as the Son of God through the resurrection. If God himself had revealed himself ultimately and once for all time in the life and death of Jesus, the One Exalted to the Son and the Lord of the Church, then the Son of God stood not only in rank above all the angels—at the same time his relation to the revelation at Sinai and to Moses as the Lawgiver had to be determined anew. For according to the common Jewish view, God had given the people of Israel in the Torah his universal, final revelation through Moses at Sinai. All the later words of the prophets—indeed, even the Messiah—were expositions of this Torah. Against this, the absoluteness and unsurpassability of the final word of God in his Son Jesus could not have been expressed more clearly or unequivocally than in the message that this crucified Messiah was a preexistent Being, identified before creation and before time with the wisdom of God, a privilege which until then had been the prerogative of the Torah. This situation is still discernible in the Prologue of John: "For the Law was given through Moses, grace and truth came through Jesus Christ" (1:17). Thus the unity of the word and work of God in creation and history was restored, and his eschatological revelation in Jesus of Nazareth obtained the rank which could not be surpassed. The Crucified and Exalted One was now, as the preexistent Mediator of Creation, identical with the divine Word of revelation of the Old Covenant. Through this the certainty was obtained that in Jesus, God himself had disclosed his complete salvation—i.e. his love for human beings. This thoroughly bold, dynamic way of thinking took place in the astonishingly short space of hardly more than fifteen years. As Paul began his great missionary journeys toward the end of the forties, it was already complete. In his letters no further christological development can be seen.

The unfolding of New Testament christology, however strange it may appear to us today, was certainly not idle speculation or haphazard mythological "wild growth." We find rather an amazing inner consistency from the oldest Christian confession to the Prologue of the Fourth Gospel. The earliest Christians attempted with the contemporary Jewish thought-forms, which were passed on to them, to so formulate God's self-disclosure in the crucified

---

73. Jeremias, *Abba,* pp. 15–67; idem, *Theologie,* pp. 45, 67ff.; G. Schelbert, "Sprachgeschichtliches zu 'Abba," in *Mélanges Dominique Barthélemy* (OBO 38; Fribourg, Göttingen, 1981), pp. 395–447. See also S. Kim, *"The 'Son of Man'" as the Son of God.*

Galilean, Jesus of Nazareth, that neither the human reality of the life and suffering of Jesus would be abandoned, nor the absolute ultimateness of God's revelation in Jesus, which gave them certainty of salvation. In the irresolvable dialectic between the two poles lies the truth and the power of the Christian faith.

THE ORIGIN OF MARK'S CHRISTOLOGY

The first task in a paper such as this must be to establish what is meant by "Mark" in the expression "Mark's christology." That may seem rather obvious. In view of the most recent decades of scholarship, however, some clarification is in order. Let me state first, then, that by "Mark" I refer to the implied author of the book known as the Gospel According to Mark. The implied author is the personality—the sum total of the perspectives and judgments—that emerges from the overall work. We may or may not be able to establish some link between the anonymous narrator and an identifiable, flesh-and-blood person from the early Christian movement. We can presume the work was written by one individual and not a group, and it is even possible that some of the traditions about the author, beginning with the testimony of Papias, are reliable. On the other hand, interpretation cannot await a scholarly consensus regarding so speculative a matter as the identification of the author of the Gospel, who chose to remain anonymous. Even without a consensus regarding the flesh-and-blood writer, however, we can still speak of the "author" (in the sense of the "implied author") as the personality behind the overall perspective of the gospel. By "Mark" then I mean that implied author. I am personally dubious about the historical reliability of the tradition that views the composer of this work as an intimate of Peter, but that will not be a major factor in interpreting the finished product.

As a matter of equal importance, I wish to distinguish this "implied author" from the "Mark" isolated by redaction critics. Particularly since the work of Willi Marxsen, scholars have identified "Mark" as the editor responsible for shaping and modifying traditional material, whose hand is clearest in summaries and seams. The perspective of this redactor has been derived by redaction critics largely from the small group of summaries and the obvious modifications of tradition. Redaction critics have consequently seen their primary interpretive task as the distinguishing of tradition and redaction. Such an approach tends to suggest that the author's perspective is known only to the degree he disagreed with and modified the tradition.

What is "Markan" comes to be identified with a small portion of the work. Not only does such an approach presume an unrealistic ability to distinguish tradition from redaction; it also must discount most of the literary work as relevant for describing the perspective of the author. Ii believe such a procedure is highly misleading. Distinguishing "Markan" christology from the views of earlier tradition expressed in the sources of his Gospel will not be the primary goal of this study. "Markan christology" refers to the perspective of the work as a whole—presuming that such a perspective can be identified.

I wish to limit my work further by focusing on the theme of the conference, i.e. messianism. While it is not necessary to know Mark's sources to understand his work, it is helpful, even necessary, to understand the historical/traditional setting of the language he employs. Mark, like other Christians, sought to offer an assessment of Jesus and his ministry in terms of traditional imagery drawn from the Jewish scriptures as they were understood in the first century. I will argue that the fundamental category in Mark's view of Jesus is that of Messiah (Gk. "Christ"), a conception that has roots in the Jewish Bible but that had a history in postbiblical Jewish circles prior to its use by Jesus' followers. We should be clear about the relationship between New Testament exegesis and historical reconstruction. Demonstration of the importance of the concept "Messiah" ("Christ") in Mark requires exegetical argument. Historical studies regarding the previous history of "Messiah" cannot establish the significance of the term for Mark, though they have an important role to play in interpretation. What the title meant in the tradition available to Mark and his readers, and what the traditional meaning contributes to our understanding of Mark, are matters of considerable importance for our exegesis.

We should recognize, of course, that for the task of historical reconstruction of postbiblical messianic tradition, Mark's Gospel is a significant piece of evidence. In his story a variety of characters offer their assessment of Jesus. Particularly in the passion sequence, religious and political leaders provide a sense of how the title "the Christ" sounds as an epithet for Jesus. Their views, which to a considerable extent clash with those of the narrator and his readers, may offer important clues to the meaning of "Messiah" in postbiblical Jewish tradition. Other postbiblical Jewish literature can confirm or disconfirm such clues as historically helpful. I assume my task is to examine Mark; I leave the examination of other postbiblical Jewish literature for other contributors to this volume.

I. "THE CHRIST" IN MARK

A brief survey of the concordance indicates that the title "the Christ," though used relatively infrequently, might well qualify as the preeminent title in this Gospel. It occurs with about the same frequency as "the Son of God" (or related terms like "Son of the Most High" or "My Son"), a title whose significance has long been recognized, and which appears in crucial situations. Particularly significant are two passages: the "confessions of Peter" in 8:29 and the question of the high priest in 14:61. The latter passage provides something of a climax to the story. The chief priest asks the decisive question, using titles that appear together only in the opening sentence of Mark's gospel (if we are to adopt the reading of Nestles' twenty-sixth edition): "Are you the Christ, the Son of the Blessed?" Jesus—for the first and only time in the story—gives an unambiguous statement about his identity: "I am" (14:62). The exchange between Jesus and the high priest surely provides one of the story's climaxes, ensuring Jesus' death and forcing the Jewish court to make a decision about the alleged Christ. The place of the title "the Christ" in such a passage is reason enough to pay particular attention to the epithet.

The expression "the Son of man" is of course the most frequent epithet in the Gospel. It ought not, however, be considered a title in the same way as "Christ" and "Son of God." It never appears as a predicate in a statement like "You are the Son of man." It occurs exclusively on the lips of Jesus. And whatever one may think of pre-Markan tradition, in Mark "the Son of man" is always to be understood as Jesus' self-designation; he uses the expression to refer to himself. Its absence in any assessment of Jesus and its exclusive use as a self-reference by Jesus ought to caution against speaking of a "Son of man" christology. There is little exegetical warrant for such an alleged "Son of man christology," which must rely almost exclusively on (often fanciful) historical speculation. In 14:62, Jesus' promise that his judges "will see the Son of man sitting at the right hand of power and coming with the clouds of heaven" does not represent a qualification of the messianic epithets but a promise that the claim will be vindicated. It is similar in function to 13:26, where the return of the Son of man will be the occasion for vindicating those who have ignored the "false Christs and false prophets" (13:22) and remained faithful to the true Christ. On that occasion, all "will see."

Exegetical data suggest the importance of the concept "Messiah" for understanding Mark's christology. The data also exhibit patterns that require interpretation:

a. "Christ" appears in 1:1, then (apart from the variant reading in 1:34) not again until Peter's confession in 8:29. Virtually the whole of Jesus' public ministry passes without the suggestion that he is the Messiah. Herod fears that he is John the Baptist raised from the dead (6:14 and 8:28); the common people regard him as a prophet, perhaps Elijah. It is not until Peter's confession, which is probably to be understood not so much as an assessment of what Jesus has done as an anticipation of what he is yet to do, that anyone uses the title "the Christ."

b. The greatest concentration of the use of the term "Christ" is in the last section of Mark, in particular the passion story, where Jesus is interrogated as "the Christ, the Son of the Blessed," and is mocked as "the Christ, the

King of Israel." The latter phrase, used by the chief priests and the scribes in 15:32, identifies "the Christ" as a royal figure. The Jewish use of the term "the Christ" is related to the Roman phrase "the King of the Jews." It seems obvious from the passion account that "the Christ" is understood as a royal epithet, whatever scriptural possibilities may have existed for speaking about "anointing."[1] If "the Christ" and "the King" are to be understood as synonymous, it becomes clear that the passion narrative is dominated by "messianic"—i.e. royal—imagery. The word "Christ" is used twice, "King of the Jews" five times. Jesus is tried, mocked, and executed as "the Christ, the Son of the Blessed," "the Christ, the King of Israel," and "the King of the Jews."

c. Though there is some ambiguity about Jesus' attitude toward the title "Christ" in 8:30, there can be no doubt that according to Mark, Jesus regards the title as an appropriate designation. When the high priest asks Jesus the decisive question, "Are you the Christ, the Son of the Blessed," he replies with an unambiguous answer: "I am, and you will see. . . ." The promise that his judges will see him enthroned and returning with the clouds in no sense modifies his claim to be the Christ but rather promises that there will be a spectacular vindication of that claim. The promise is couched in scriptural language, specifically drawn from Daniel 7 and Psalm 110. From the vantage point of the narrator, the confession that "Jesus is the Christ" is true.

d. The Gospel provides ample evidence that calling Jesus "the Christ" involves some difficulty. Characters in the story tell us how the confession sounds. After Peter confesses Jesus as "the Christ," he responds to Jesus' forecast of rejection, death, and resurrection by rebuking him. Peter is in turn rebuked, since his mind is focused on human rather than divine ways (8:31–33). Peter finds the combination of messiahship and suffering incongruous.

The chief priest offers the next estimate. "Are you the Christ, the Son of the Blessed?" he asks. At Jesus' response, he tears his robes—suggesting that the claim is blasphemous.[2] The mockery of the guards, including the taunt, "Prophesy!" suggests that the messianic claim and the attendant promise of vindication strike the court as outrageous.

The Roman soldiers offer an estimate of how the confession sounds to non-Jews. They understand that Christ means "King." As befits their status as non-Israelites, they speak of this kingship exclusively in political terms. They call him "the King of the Jews," appropriately employing the term "Jew" to refer to Israelites. They dress Jesus in royal garb and pay him mock

---

1. On the use of "the Christ" as a royal epithet in Mark, see my *Messiah and Temple: The Trial of Jesus in the Gospel of Mark* (SBLDS 31; Missoula, Mont., 1977) and F. Matera, *The Kingship of Jesus* (SBLDS 66; Chico, Calif., 1982).

2. The relationship between the charge of blasphemy and Jesus' statements has been a matter of considerable scholarly debate. For a discussion of the problem, see my *Messiah and Temple*, pp. 95–106.

homage. It is as "King of the Jews" that Pilate executes Jesus. The soldiers' behavior and Pilate's formulation of the charge indicate that the claim Jesus is the King is—from the Roman perspective—both seditious and comical.

The mockery of Jesus as he hangs on the cross plays on his name (Jeshua = Savior), but the claim to be "the Christ, the King of Israel" also appears in the taunt (15:31–32). Jesus' inability to save himself and to descend from the cross is taken as evidence that he is not the promised king and deliverer.

Even if we had access to no postbiblical Jewish literature, like the seventeenth and eighteenth Psalms of Solomon, we could hazard a guess as to the meaning of "the Messiah." It is a royal term and its associations in postbiblical Jewish tradition suggest that to claim Jesus is the Messiah is absurd. Mark does nothing to minimize the problem; he plays on it.

There have been various attempts to derive "Messiah" from nonroyal traditions in postbiblical Judaism and thus avoid the problem posed by the nonmessianic character of the career of Jesus the Messiah.[3] When such alleged nonroyal messianic tradition is used to interpret Mark, however, the passion narrative makes no sense, for Mark's story is predicated on the tension between what everyone thinks and expects of the Messiah and what is in fact the case. Mark's story is deeply ironic, and the irony is bound up with the royal imagery that dominates Mark's narrative of the passion. As readers we know that Jesus is the Christ (1:1, 14:62, inter alia). The great irony is that it is Jesus' enemies who "invest" him as king and "pay homage." They offer testimony of what the reader knows to be the truth. Of course Jesus' enemies, whether Jewish or Roman, do not understand in what sense the words they speak are true. Jewish leaders regard the claim to be blasphemous and absurd; Romans view the claim as seditious and outrageous. Nevertheless they speak the truth—contrary to their intentions and beyond their ability to understand. The irony in the story is pronounced, but it only works if Jesus is the Christ—and if the religious and political leaders speak for the tradition and common sense. Even if it were possible to demonstrate that "the Messiah" could be used in the first century to refer to a prophetic and not a royal figure, such a derivation could not explain the way Mark's passion narrative employs messianic tradition.

The Controversy Regarding the Messiah as David's Son

The claim that the traditional title "the Messiah" is central to Mark's christology must deal with a problematic passage in 12:35–37, where Jesus seems to take issue with traditional messianic categories:

---

3. Those who have attempted to derive "Messiah" from prophetic tradition include K. Burger, "Zum Problem der Messianität Jesu," ZTK 71 (1974) 1–30, and "Die Königlichen Messiastraditionen des Neuen Testaments," NTS 20 (1973–74) 1–44; and A. E. Harvey, Jesus and the Constraints of History (Philadelphia, 1982).

And as Jesus taught in the temple, he said, "How can the scribes say that
the Christ is the son of David? David himself, inspired by the Holy Spirit,
declared,

"The Lord said to my Lord,
Sit at my right hand,
till I put thy enemies under thy feet."
David himself calls him Lord; so how is he his son?"

These verses have been included in Mark within a section of controversies that precede Jesus' arrest, trial, and death. His opponents are religious
officials—the scribes, chief priests, and elders. The issues that provide the
focus of controversy were of considerable import to the Jewish community
in the later decades of the first century—and presumably to Mark's audience.

If we assume that these verses are consonant with the rest of Mark's Gospel—and we ought to make such an assumption until every effort to understand a particular passage within its narrative setting has failed—we should
first observe that nowhere else in this gospel is there a suggestion that Jesus
is not the "Son of David." The confession of blind Bartimaeus in 10:47 suggests that the title is quite appropriate. The blind man, who is commended
for his faith, sees what Jesus' disciples (and his enemies) do not. The crowds
acclaim Jesus as he rides into Jerusalem on a donkey with a line from Psalm
118—"Blessed is he who comes in the name of the Lord!"—followed by
"Blessed is the kingdom of our father David that is coming" (Mk 11:9–10). To
argue that Jesus could accept the designation "the Christ, the Son of the
Blessed" from the high priest (14:61–62) while insisting that he is not "the
Son of David" is improbable, whether we are considering the actual words
of Jesus or Mark's story world. The little evidence that Jewish tradition knew
of a non-Davidic Messiah is relatively late, and the notion of a Messiah ben
Joseph would do little to clarify Jesus' comments in Mark 12. Attempts to
prove that "the Christ" could refer to a priestly or a prophetic figure are
likewise unconvincing, and in any case such a derivation would also do little
to clarify the problem Jesus poses for his opponents by quoting Psalm 110.

The comments are enigmatic, but it seems best to view the juxtaposition
of "the Son of David" and "Lord" in Jesus' comments within the category of
alleged scriptural contradictions familiar from rabbinic tradition.[4]

In this case, the view of the scribes that "the Christ is David's son" may
be a shorthand substitution for the actual citation of a passage like 2Sam
7:12–14. This scriptural view is juxtaposed with another, the opening verse

---

4. Representative interpretations of this passage are discussed in E. Lövestam's "Die Davids-
sohnsfrage," SEÅ 27 (1962) 72–82. In the essay he convincingly argues the case I am presenting.
See also the comments on Mk 12:35–37 in W. Lane, The Gospel According to Mark (Grand
Rapids, Mich., 1974), ad loc.; and N. A. Dahl, "Contradictions in Scripture," Studies in Paul
(Minneapolis, 1977), pp. 159–77.

from Psalm 110, which seems to call into question what the Bible says elsewhere. (Jesus' question presumes his learned audience knows that Ps 110:1 refers to the Messiah; that interpretation does not have to be argued.) Though the form of the pericope differs from that of the surrounding controversies, we must assume that Jesus' concluding question implies an answer to the problem he poses. Some point has been scored that would make sense to the audience.

It seems most likely, as Evald Lövestam has argued, that the implied solution to the problem Jesus has posed—a possible contradiction within the scriptures—is provided by events the readers know will soon follow. Jesus, the Son of David, rejected by the temple authorities, will be raised from the dead and enthroned at God's right hand (cf. Jesus' promise in 14:62, alluding to Ps 110:1). It is appropriate for David to call his messianic son "Lord" in view of Jesus' installation at God's right hand. In fact, only if Jesus, the Son of David, has been elevated to that position does the alleged scriptural contradiction disappear. As in rabbinic tradition, the alleged contradiction is used to score a point—here, that death and resurrection are not incompatible with what the scriptures have to say about the Christ. Since tradition knew nothing of a crucified Messiah, it could hardly have any conceptions of a resurrected king. The use of Psalm 110 to construct a scriptural image of a dying and rising Messiah is an example of creative Christian exegesis.

The advantage of this interpretation is that it is compatible with what we know of postbiblical messianic tradition and does not result in contradictions within Mark. The passage presumes no distinction between an earthly and a heavenly deliverer. Rather, as in Acts, Ps 110:1 becomes part of an argument according to which God's promise to David of a "seed" to sit on his throne forever (2Sam 7:12–14, Ps 89:3–4) is fulfilled only with the installation of the risen Christ in heaven. It is as the enthroned "Lord" that Jesus is Son of David.

II. "SON OF GOD" AS A MESSIANIC EPITHET

Related to Mark's use of "Messiah" is the use of the title "the Son of God." Though there may be other components in the title, royal overtones are unmistakable. The most obvious connection is in the question of the high priest, where "the Christ" and "the Son of the Blessed" are in apposition.[5] There are two other occurrences that are equally convincing. In both the baptismal story and the transfiguration, God himself addresses Jesus as "Son"—using language from the messianic oracle in Psalm 2, where God calls the anointed king "my son" (see also 2Sam 7:14). Though evidence from the Qumran Scrolls that "Son of God" could function as a messianic title in

---

5. On "Son of God" as a royal title in Mark, see *Messiah and Temple*, pp. 108–14.

postbiblical Jewish circles is not absolutely convincing, it does demonstrate that 2Sam 7 (and probably Psalm 2) was regarded as a messianic oracle prior to Christianity—and that "son" was a designation for the Messiah-king used by God. Milik's now famous fragment from Cave 4 at least demonstrates that "Son of God" and "Son of the Most High God" were titles appropriate to royalty.[6]

All this suggests that one of the components in the title "Son of God" in Mark is royal. The prominent place of the title in the passion narrative, which tells the story of the trial and death of the "Christ," the "King of the Jews," confirms the royal associations of the title. There may be additional components and associations. The demons know that Jesus is "the Son of God" and "the Son of the Most High God" (3:11, 5:7), while they never call him "Christ" (see, however, Lk 4:41, where the narrator views "Son of God" and "Christ" as synonymous). The use of the title "my Son" by God, however, in contexts where there are strong reminiscences of royal psalms (esp. Psalm 2) makes it likely that even the supernatural knowledge of Jesus' sonship by demons should be understood as part of royal—i.e. messianic—tradition.

The Baptism of Jesus

The passion narrative is constructed in such a way as to exploit the tension between messianic tradition and Jesus' messiahship. The account of Jesus' baptism in the opening chapter of the Gospel plays on the same tension. Central to appreciating the messianic overtones is the use of "my Son." The climax of the brief narrative is a *bat kol*, which employs biblical language. The most prominent image is from Psalm 2: "You are my son." As in the psalm, it is God himself who calls the anointed his son. Messianic interpretation of Psalm 2 in pre-Christian tradition is nearly certain (see above).

It is also possible, as is well known, that the voice includes an allusion to Isa 42:1 (in nonseptuagintal form). It is likewise conceivable that the reference to a "beloved son" presumes an allusion to Genesis 22. There is ample evidence in Paul that a link between Jesus and the "beloved son" of Abraham had been established prior to Mark; the mechanism for the link is even clear: the use of "seed" in 2Sam 7:12 and Gen 22:18 would be sufficient justification for arguing that God's promise of a "seed" to David represented the fulfillment of his promise of a "seed" of Abraham in whom all the nations would be blessed. A similar logic, predicated on the confession of Jesus as Messiah, led Jesus' followers to the "servant poems" in Isaiah as potentially messianic texts.[7] It is possible, in other words, that the voice at Jesus' baptism is for-

6. The fragment has now been published by J. Fitzmyer in "The Contribution of Qumran Aramaic to the Study of the New Testament," *A Wandering Aramean* (SBLMS 25; Chico, Calif., 1979), pp. 102–13.

7. See my "The Servant-Christ," *Southwestern Journal of Theology* 21 (1979) 7–22, and ch. 5 in my *Messianic Exegesis: Christological Interpretation of the Old Testament in Early Christianity* (Philadelphia, 1987).

mulated from scriptural passages that have become important features of Christian messianic exegetical tradition.

There are likewise possible associations between the whole baptismal scene in Mark and scenes depicted both in the Testament of Levi (ch. 18) and the Testament of Judah (ch. 24). Separating Christian redaction from earlier narratives in the Testament of the Twelve Patriarchs is notoriously difficult at this point, but it is not impossible that the "confirmation" scene in which the heavens open and God pours out his Spirit on an eschatological office holder (in the Testament of the Twelve, either the priest or the king) was traditional.

The most striking feature of the baptismal story emerges from within the narrative setting. The more one knows about the background of the imagery in Mark, the more striking is the account. Jesus is introduced as the one greater than John who will baptize with the Holy Spirit—the Christ, the Son of God. Yet when Jesus appears, it is not as the conquering warrior fitted with the appropriate trappings of a savior. The occasion for his confirmation by God and his anointing by the Spirit is John's baptism—which is a washing for the forgiveness of sins. The tearing of the heavens, the descent of the Spirit, the authoritative declaration of God—all seem fitting testimony to the stature of the promised deliverer. The setting is all wrong, however. Jesus should be among the mighty, in the great city that served David as his citadel, not among sinners who have come to repent for their sins.

The story opens with a great shock. The promised deliverer has been confirmed and anointed for his appointed tasks. Yet he looks nothing like what was expected; he is in the wrong place, associating with the wrong people. Jesus' career begins with a tension between what is expected of God and what he actually provides. As the narrative progresses, the tension increases rather than decreases. The ministry that begins with a dramatic tearing of the heavens concludes with the tearing of the Temple curtain, as Jesus dies condemned, ridiculed, and executed as "the King of the Jews" and as "the Christ, the Son of the Blessed."

The baptismal scene introduces tensions into the narrative which will be developed into a story that seeks to depict the reality of the "gospel about Jesus Christ." And the tension central to the narrative arises from the difference between Jesus the Christ and traditional messianic speculation. The messianic associations of "Son of God" are central to this narrative strategy.

III. THE ORIGIN OF MARK'S CHRISTOLOGY

One of the basic motifs in Mark's portrait of Jesus is the unprecedented nature of his ministry. He is the expected one, the one for whom God has prepared, the one whose career is "in accordance with the scriptures"; his ministry likewise does not fit established patterns or expectations. He associates with the wrong sorts of people, threatens the tradition, and, at the climax of his ministry, is executed as a would-be king, rejected by the religious and political authorities, deserted by his followers, abandoned even by God. The tension is not a simple misperception but is in fact constitutive of the gospel Mark knows. God's truth is disclosed only by way of confrontation with established tradition and human institutions. There is a tension between "God's ways" and "human ways" (Mk 8:33). "New skins for new wine" stands as a useful summary of this feature of Mark's portrait of Jesus. And for precisely this reason, irony is the only suitable vehicle for narrating the climax of the story. Truth is not identical with appearance but must in some way be in tension with it. Jesus is a hero who does not look like a hero—and thus conventional ways of narrating stories about heroes are not sufficient as vehicles for the evangelists.

The tension between Jesus and the tradition is made concrete in the story in terms of his messianic office. The tension is between the royal title and his ignominious death on the cross. The inordinate amount of space devoted to the story of Jesus' trial and death testifies to the importance of this tension for understanding Jesus (and, for that matter, for understanding the will of God). It is not just that Jesus must die, but that he must die as "king." Scholars have frequently noted the prominence of biblical imagery in the passion narrative, particularly allusions to Psalms 22 and 69. The Psalms, certainly in Mark, are enlisted in the task of telling the story of the death of Jesus, the "King of the Jews." They do not provide an alternative view of Jesus (say, of Jesus as the paradigmatic righteous sufferer), nor do they provide an alternative derivation of Mark's christology. As M. Hengel has stated, the Psalms are used to speak of Jesus as king.[8] Royal conceptions dominate Mark's passion narrative.

The origin of Mark's christology cannot be found in postbiblical Jewish tradition, though it cannot be understood apart from such a tradition. Jesus is indeed the Messiah—the only Messiah known by Jewish tradition prior to Bar Kokhba. But his career does not correspond to that of the promised Christ. Thus the adage formulated by Nils Dahl: the confession of Jesus as Messiah is the presupposition for NT christology, but not its content.[9]

The origin of Mark's christology lies first of all in the events that climaxed

8. M. Hengel, *The Atonement,* trans. J. Bowden (Philadelphia, 1981), p. 41: "For Mark, the few psalms of suffering which illuminate individual features of the suffering and death of Jesus, like Psalms 22 and 69, are exclusively *messianic* psalms, such as Psalms 110 and 118." Among those who have sought to derive the Markan passion from the psalms without reference to messianic tradition are C. Peddinghaus, "Die Entstehung der Leidensgeschichte: Eine traditionsgeschichtliche und historische Untersuchung des Werdens und Wachsens der erzählenden Passionstradition bis zum Entwurf des Markus" (unpublished Heidelberg dissertation, 1965), and J. von Oswald, "Die Beziehungen zwischen Psalm 22 und dem vormarkinischen Passionsbericht," *ZKT* 101 (1979) 53–66. Their views are discussed in Matera, *The Kingship of Jesus,* pp. 125–30.

9. N. A. Dahl's approach is detailed in the variety of essays published in *The Crucified Messiah* (Minneapolis, 1974), now republished in a revised and expanded edition by Fortress Press under the title *Jesus The Christ: The Historical Origins of Christological Doctrine* (Minneapolis, 1991).

Jesus' ministry in Jerusalem—his arrest, trial, death, and vindication as "Christ, the Son of the Blessed," "the king of the Jews." The events provided Mark and the early Christian movement with an agenda. What does it mean that the Messiah had to die? One alternative was to redraw OT tradition until the scandal of the cross disappeared: "Was it not necessary that the Christ must suffer and on the third day rise?" The end product of such an approach is the Epistle of Barnabas and its apologetic. The alternative chosen by Mark (and Paul, and to a degree John) is to use the tension between Jesus the crucified Christ and messianic tradition as an interpretive key for understanding not only Jesus but God and the human situation. To overstate the matter somewhat, Mark used the tradition available to him to make sense of the career of one who died as the king of the Jews—one whose vindication by God on the third day not only resulted in the tearing of the temple curtain and the ripping wide of the heavens but in a new conception of what royalty must mean.

The origin of Mark's christology is to be sought in the history of Jesus of Nazareth, principally in the events that brought his career to an end and offered a whole new beginning. His christology is firmly anchored there, in the cross of the one who died as "the king of the Jews." The relationship between Jesus' messianic death and his nonmessianic career, so essential to Albert Schweitzer's construction of the life of Jesus, remains a central problem for theology. Mark does not solve the problem. It seems unlikely to me, as some commentators have suggested, that Mark tells the story of Jesus the exorcist and healer only to reject the relevance of such notions.[10] The crowds are not completely wrong in their assessment of Jesus as a prophetic (i.e. eschatological) figure. But they do not grasp the whole truth, which is focused in the confession of Jesus as the promised Christ—the Christ, of course, who died and was raised after three days.

Questions remain. A thorough interpretation of Mark must show how the tradition of Jesus' ministry is integrated into his "messianic" career. Luke is farther along in that development, as is clear principally in the narrative of Luke 4, where the passage from Isaiah 61 about "anointing" provides a bridge between messianic and prophetic functions (Lk 4:18–19). Because this paper intends to deal with the origin of Mark's christology and not its full explication, I willingly leave the remaining questions for another occasion.

POST-CONFERENCE REFLECTIONS

The conference made available an enormous amount of data that will not easily yield to systematic organization. There were important disagreements

---

10. Such is the view, for example, of scholars like T. Weeden, *Mark—Traditions in Conflict* (Philadelphia, 1971).

(e.g. on the assessment of evidence for the traditional interpretation of "the Son of Man" as a christological title) and significant consensus. I will confine my remarks to studies directly relevant to the theme of my paper.

I must confess that I found the conference largely confirming of my position. There was no significant challenge to the notion that "the Christ" is a royal title. Studies on the historical origin of messianism seemed rather to support the notion. All seemed to agree that "the Messiah" was only one of several salvation figures encountered in postbiblical Jewish eschatological tradition, that he was by no means the dominant figure, and that there was no uniform eschatological pattern encountered throughout the wide variety of Jewish texts. Such views seem to confirm the argument made by Nils Dahl that New Testament christology cannot be explained solely on the basis of the history of ideas. There is no "trajectory" within postbiblical Judaism that can account for the widespread confession of Jesus as Christ. There is something historically contingent about the confession—something that seems to call attention to those events during the procuratorship of Pontius Pilate that culminated in the execution of Jesus as the "king of the Jews."

I am certain that many of the participants at the conference have not drawn such conclusions from our collective efforts. I offer my contribution regarding the origin of Mark's christology with the conviction that my exegetical results fit well the historical data provided by other papers presented at the conference.

SACRED VIOLENCE AND THE MESSIAH:
The Markan Passion Narrative as a Redefinition of Messianology

The Davidic ideology of Zion produced the concept of the messiah[1] and placed the Temple at the center of the national life. Accordingly, Mark's presentation links the concept of the messiah so closely to the Temple that one cannot understand the one without the other. By rejecting the whole order of sacred violence that the Temple symbolized, by which the traditional idea of a messiah was defined, Mark rejects the traditional idea. The rejection of the Temple may represent the history of Jesus,[2] who in an act of prophetic symbolism drove out the money changers.[3] In any case, Mark presents the Temple as the focal point for a rejection of the messiah of sacred violence and the revisioning of the messianic idea in a nonviolent form. Therefore we shall read the Markan passion narrative in which the process of revisioning is most evident,[4] as a narrative redefinition of the concept of the messiah.

We shall read the text as a literary artifact that has been generated by a deep structure. This does not mean that we shall neglect the historical context of the gospel—the war with Rome in 66–70 C.E.[5]—but only that we are

---

1. See S. Talmon's contribution to this volume.

2. E. P. Sanders, *Jesus and Judaism* (Philadelphia, 1985), p. 75, "Thus we conclude that Jesus publicly predicted or threatened the destruction of the temple, that the statement was shaped by his expectation of the arrival of the eschaton, that he probably also expected a new temple to be given by God from heaven, and that he made a demonstration which prophetically symbolized the coming event." Sanders does not believe that Jesus opposed sacrifice itself. We intend to show that the tradition deposited in Mark does oppose sacrifice as such.

3. Ibid., pp. 69–71; M. Borg, *Conflict, Holiness and Politics in the Teachings of Jesus* (Studies in the Bible and Early Christianity 5; New York and Toronto, 1984), pp. 171–73.

4. D. Juel, *Messiah and Temple: The Trial of Jesus in the Gospel of Mark* (SBLDS 31; Missoula, Mont., 1977). See also J. H. Elliott, "Social Scientific Criticism of the New Testament: More on Methods and Models," *Semeia* 35 (1985) 1–33, esp. 21, who, in criticizing Theissen's reconstruction of the social situation of the gospels, points out that Theissen neglects the role of the tension between the temple and various groups, "Patterns in the evidence brought to light by the matrix, furthermore, reveal how the temple was a focal point of tension (political, economic, social, cultural, and ideological)."

5. W. Kelber, *The Kingdom in Mark* (Philadelphia, 1974).

concerned neither to isolate the level of tradition that can be assigned to the historical Jesus, nor to trace the history of that tradition within the Markan sources. We see the text as having been structured by the impact of Jesus on the deep structure of human existence, an impact that can be discerned through the text without certifying any single event or saying as from the historical Jesus himself. Through the text one sees the general imprint of his work on human consciousness in his time and in subsequent times down to our own.

Our reading is guided by the thought of R. Girard.[6] We can give only a very brief and therefore inadequate account of his theory here. It is based on the premise that human beings are in imitative thrall to one another. Ethological evidence shows that this compulsion to imitate goes back to our pre-human ancestors. Imitation becomes rivalrous because we imitate one another's desire for an object, and as the imitation becomes successful we become the rivals of our models. At this stage Girard prefers to speak of mimesis rather than imitation; rivalry is, therefore, mimetic rivalry. Since the imitation is the imitation of desire, one may also call it mimetic desire.

Mimetic rivalry escalated in the primitive hominid hordes to a point of violent crisis. This escalation of rivalry can probably be correlated with the growth of the brain; in bands of apes mimetic rivalry does not reach the point of crisis because the simian brain does not generate the same amount of mimetic energy as the larger human brain. Therefore patterns of dominance are relatively easily established in animal groups. Humans, however, cannot establish patterns of dominance without the presence of some new ordering factor. This ordering factor is the surrogate-victim mechanism that arises spontaneously from within the mimetic crisis. Mimetic enthrallment with the model/rival diverts attention from the object; the surrogate-victim mechanism rediscovers the object as something to be destroyed rather than possessed. The killing of the victim (object) spontaneously unites the rivals, and this spontaneous unity provides the primary basis of culture. Therefore the surrogate-victim mechanism, as a spontaneous change in a self-organizing phylogenetic system that transforms the system dramatically from disorder to order, is the foundation of culture. All culture comes out of the victim.

In the moment of peace that follows the killing, the mob mislocates the cause of this miraculous peace in the victim rather than in themselves. They transfer to the victim the mimetic rivalry and surrogate victimage of their own violence. Thus they make the victim, who is at most a catalyst for the process, into the active cause of it. They attribute to him the mimetic rivalry that escalates to crisis and metamorphoses spontaneously into surrogate victimage, and thus they declare themselves innocent of violence and conceal from themselves the violent origin of their order. This mislocation of responsibility starts the process by which the victim becomes a god, and religion, in the form of the primitive sacred, comes into being. The double transference explains the double valency of the sacred, threat and promise corresponding to the mob phenomena of mimetic rivalry and surrogate victimage. Transference to the victim is facilitated by the fact that disorder pertained when he was alive and order came when he died—therefore he must have been the cause of both states.

The sacred is this ambivalent energy of transformed violence that congeals around the victim-become-god. It is the primal energy of culture and takes the form of prohibition, ritual, and myth—the three building blocks of religion. Prohibition issues from the mimetic rivalry pole of the sacred to forbid any behavior that might cause that rivalry to break out again; thus cultural differentiation comes about. Ritual comes about as the controlled repetition of the surrogate-victimage pole in the form of ritual sacrifice, with a view to renewing the ordering energy of surrogate victimage. Myth comes into being as the account of the founding murder told from the point of view of the murderers, as part of the transformation of the murder into a culturally organizing act.

The victim is, therefore, the first transcendental signifier. The sudden peace that followed his death made him the first object of noninstinctual attention, the first "other" from whom we are distinct and to which we can point, and from which we can receive signification. The signified is the mimetic violence and surrogate victimage of the mob that goes out to the victim-signifier as violence and comes back as prohibition, ritual, and myth, that goes out as disorder and comes back as religious order. Thus differential thought originates in the logic of the exception, of the one who is different, rather than the logic of conventional structuralism's binary opposites. The sacred is, therefore, the rich source of signification.

This culturally fruitful "sacred" is, however, based on the lie that the energy of the system is not our violence but the violence of the god. Religion, which is another term for the primitive sacred, pretends that the god demands sacrifice to prevent the outbreak of mimetic violence in the form of his vengeance against us. The truth is that religion is a disguise for our own violence thrown from us not into the unconscious but into the sociopsychological order of religion. Religion is violence transformed into culture, and religious institutions exist to perform the work of this transformation.

In the realm of texts, the founding mechanism, which is the term we shall use for the process of the double transference and its religious result, generates myth. Myth is the narrative version of the sacred lie. It portrays the victim as guilty, or willing, and the killers as benefactors. It also portrays culture as coming from the victim's death and thereby declares the necessity and goodness of that death. This is the mechanism that the gospel text uncovers because the gospel is generated by a different mechanism, one that uncovers the lie that the sacred tells. This uncovering is a mechanism of revelation and truth-telling. It is the Gospel in the gospels and generates the structural opposite of myth.

We shall consider the passion narrative while being on the lookout for the founding mechanism. To anticipate our results, we shall show that the generative process at work in the gospel is the opposite of the process of the founding mechanism. It is a process of demythification that works by uncovering the founding mechanism, rather than a process of mythification that disguises it by transformation. The death of Jesus reveals that the victim is innocent and the founding mechanism is a lie. This gives one the opportunity to locate the responsibility for violence where it belongs, namely within the human group, to identify and deal with its mimetic expressions and to renounce the use of scapegoats.

We use the terms "founding mechanism" or "the sacred" to designate the generative level of the text and the term "sacrificial system" to designate the sacrificial practice that Mark presents as taking place in the Temple in Jerusalem. The latter is the thematic expression of the former; it is not a revelation of it but rather a veiling, because it pretends that the violence of sacrifice is a necessary and good thing. We shall be looking for the way the text unveils the mechanism behind the system. In general, a sacrificial text for Girard is one that is generated by the founding mechanism (produced by the sacred), and that is why he can argue that the passion narrative is not a sacrificial text, even though it deals thematically with sacrifice and the sacrificial system. It is important to bear in mind the distinction between the thematic and the generative level of the text. In the passion narratives sacrifice is vividly present as a theme; Jesus is being driven out and killed as a sacrificial victim and scapegoat, but the generative mechanism is nonviolent. This is precisely why the theme of sacrifice is so vivid; by the way it treats this theme the new generative mechanism of the gospel discloses the old mechanism of the sacred.

However, we must also take into account the possibility that at the thematic level these texts are scapegoating the Jews for the death of Jesus.[7] In that case the passion narratives would be generated by the same founding mechanism as other myths and would be charters for Christian persecution of the Jews. At times in Christian history they have functioned in that way, but Girard claims that that has been a sacred misreading. He claims emphatically that the passion narratives are not myth because they are not generated by the sacred, but rather are the revelation of the sacred, the very opposite of myth.

There are, therefore, two levels in any text; the level at which the sacred

---

7. B. Mack, "The Innocent Transgressor: Jesus in Early Christian Myth and History," *Semeia* 33 (1985) 135–65.

founding mechanism is lodged in the collective mind of the society out of which the text comes (the generative level) and the level on which it comes to expression in the text (the thematic level). The nature of the coming to expression can be of several kinds. At one end of the spectrum is myth, a text that is structured by the mechanism and in which it comes to veiled and transformed expression. At the other end of the spectrum is a text that is formed by another mechanism and in which the sacred is unveiled. The gospels are the clearest instances to date of this kind of text. The mechanism that generates such texts is called Gospel. Gospel is the opposite of the sacred as the gospels are the opposite of myths. In between these limits are the various possibilities of revelation and concealment. "In history we are always between the gospel and myth."[8] Whether the gospels are indeed Gospel in this sense remains to be seen. We turn now to that question in the gospel of Mark. We shall ask, "To what extent is the formative power of the sacred founding mechanism of mimetic violence and surrogate victimage revealed or concealed in the text?" That is, "To what extent is it *gospel* and to what extent *myth?*"

We shall not pay much attention to the idiosyncrasies of the author, actual or implied, because we are treating the text as a deposit of a consciousness shared by a community. We want to discern the understanding of existence conveyed by the whole configuration of events in the pericopes we shall consider, and in this regard our endeavor is formally like that of the Bultmannian school. Our thesis is that the text unveils the mechanism of sacral violence that forms and maintains the society of which it is a part, and that it does so because it is generated by another mechanism, which the gospel calls love.

The Temple in Jerusalem stood as the effective sign of the human need for victims; every day it offered both public and private sacrifice to change society. It was a ritual expression of the founding mechanism. Since the mechanism uses the victim to unify the mob, and since the power of that unification, the force that holds the mob together, is represented by the political and religious leaders, those sacral figures that control the institutions founded on the sacred, we have chosen to begin our probe of the text with the pericopes that feature the mob and its representatives hunting the victim. These are the pericopes in chs. 11–13 of Mark. Then we shall read the pericopes that tell of the killing of the victim. These are the passion narrative proper, in chs. 14–15. We shall interrogate them firstly on the manifest level to see whether they do disclose the founding mechanism; at the same time we shall be asking whether they are themselves sacrificial texts, like all other religious texts that derive their energy from scapegoating and victimage, in this case the scapegoating of the Jews. Since the mechanism orders society,

---

8. R. Girard in *Violent Origins: Walter Burkert, Rene Girard, and Jonathan Z. Smith on Ritual Killing and Cultural Formation*, ed. R. G. Hamerton-Kelly, with an introduction by B. Mack and a commentary by R. Rosaldo (Stanford, 1987), p. 145.

we shall refer to its product as an "order." Our thesis is that the gospel text presents a vision of a new order generated by a new mechanism structured not by violence as the old order is, but by something that the text calls love and describes by means of the narrative of the innocent victim who gives his life to found the "Kingdom of God."[9]

THE NEW HUMAN ORDER—CHS. 11–13

The Entry of Jesus into the Temple—11:1–11

The point of this pericope is not the entry of Jesus into Jerusalem in general but into the sacred precincts of the Temple in particular.[10] It presents the victim coming to the place of sacrifice. The pericope begins with a statement linking the city and the Temple. "Into Jerusalem into Bethphage" in vs. 1 does so because Bethphage was, according to the Talmud, the outermost limit of the sacred precinct. Shewbread consecrated there was validly consecrated, but beyond Bethphage the consecration was no longer valid.[11] The pericope ends with "And he went into Jerusalem into the Temple" (vs. 11). This is parallel in form to vs. 1 and restates the point of the foregoing narrative, which is to locate Jesus in the Temple. Thus he is positioned to interact with the sacrificial system in all its ramifications, which stands as the ritual expression of the founding mechanism. He is about to reveal the mechanism behind the system.

The account of the procession has been influenced by Zech 9:9 in a messianic direction—"Behold your king comes to you meek and riding upon an ass"—but it is presented predominantly as a festal procession of entry into the Temple. Palm branches are associated with the feast of Tabernacles which entailed a procession around the altar, and with the cry "Hosanna" in Psalm 118. Indeed, in the Talmud, the palm branch used at Tabernacles was called the "Hosanna."[12] The use of Psalm 118 here and in Mk 12:10–11, where the passage about the rejected stone becoming the head of the corner is cited, shows that the associations of Jesus' entry to the Temple with his

---

9. G. W. E. Nickelsburg, "The Genre and Function of the Markan Passion Narrative," *HTR* 73 (1980) 153–84, argues plausibly that the Markan passion narrative is patterned on a well-attested generic model of a story of the persecution and vindication of a righteous person. Examples from the same tradition as Mark are: the Joseph story in Genesis 37ff., the story of Ahikar, the book of Esther, Daniel 3 and 6, the story of Susanna, and (with some qualifications) Wisdom of Solomon 2, 4–5. All of these are stories that are eminently susceptible to a Girardian reading. Nickelsburg begins his characterization of the passion narrative with Mk 11:15–18 in order to make it fit the genre.

10. Juel, *Messiah and Temple*, p. 127: "From the moment Jesus enters Jerusalem, the story focuses on Jesus and the temple."

11. H. L. Strack and P. Billerbeck, *Kommentar zum Neuen Testament aus Talmud und Midrasch*, 6 vols. (Munich, 1926), vol. 1, p. 839 (hereafter cited as S-B).

12. S-B 1, p. 850.

rejection and the building of a new "Temple" with him as the cornerstone, are already in mind here and intended to be seen by the reader. The messianic victim is in the Temple and positioned to interact with the sacrificial system in all its manifestations.

The Attack on the Sacrificial System Narrated and Symbolized by the Cursing of the Barren Fig Tree—11:12-25

The key to an understanding of the two incidents narrated here is that the one is placed within the other, the attack on the traders is placed within the account of the attack on the fig tree. The tree is a symbol of the sacrificial system whose time is now passed ("It was not the season for figs," vs. 13), and the command "May no one eat fruit of you ever again" (vs. 14) is interpreted by what follows immediately. Jesus "began to drive out those who sold and bought in the Temple, and overturned the tables of the money changers and the seats of those who sold pigeons; and he would not allow anyone to carry anything through the Temple precinct" (vss. 15-16). These functionaries were essential to the operation of the sacrificial system. They provided the currency and the victims necessary for the offering of individual sacrifices. The reference to prohibiting the carrying of anything does not mean that Jesus is especially concerned about the sanctity of the Temple, but rather that he wishes to bring its functioning to a standstill.[13] Because it does not bear fruit, does not feed the religiously hungry (vs. 12), the system is to stop.[14] So there is no question of a "cleansing" of the Temple, as if the presence of holy trade somehow polluted it; such a judgment is a parochialism and an anachronism, arising out of the Protestant delicacy about the association of money with religion, and a far cry from an ancient Temple devoted to animal slaughter, in which the exchange of money was perhaps the least offensive thing to a modern Protestant sensibility. No, the attack on the traders was a prophetic symbolic act advocating and foretelling the destruction of the sacrificial system.[15] Sanders considers it an act of the historical Jesus; it may indeed have been so, but that is not of concern to our argument. The Markan community understood it to signify and authorize the destruction of the Temple and the inauguration of a new form of piety.

The texts cited, from Isa 56:7 and Jer 7:11 (vss. 9-10), repudiate the exclusiveness based on sacrifice. Mauss, Harrison, and van Gennep associate initiation and sacrifice together as the primordial religious rites, and Mauss suggests that the link between the two is the rules governing the entry to

---

13. Kelber, *Kingdom*, p. 101.
14. Juel, *Messiah and Temple*, p. 131, focuses on the rejection of the leaders of the Temple. We hope to show that they function only as representatives of the system, so that it is the system as a whole that is being rejected, because it represents the mechanism.
15. See n. 2.

and exit from the sacrificial precinct.[16] The quotation from Isaiah comes from a context that tells of the admission of foreigners to the cultic community, and the passage from Jeremiah repudiates a superstitious notion that the ritual will defend the Temple from destruction despite the moral failure of those who rely on its sanctity. We may also hear in the phrase "a bandits' cave" (σπήλαιον ληστῶν) an allusion to the zealot takeover of the Temple in the latter days of the Roman war, when it became quite literally a refuge of bandits and a place of open violence (λησταί is Josephus' word for the military opponents of Rome).[17] Thus the text identifies the Temple as a place of violence and shows that the exclusion of the stranger is an expression of this violence. In the Jeremiah passage there is a clear prophecy of the destruction of the Temple, and we take it that our text intends us to hear an echo of it, to reinforce the idea that some new nonviolent opportunity is to be provided for the stranger to draw near to God. This complex of ideas recalls the Pauline struggle with the Jewish law about initiation into the covenant community and his affirmation of the primacy of faith. The understanding of faith in the text is the same as Paul's; indeed, Paul makes the same case theoretically that our text makes by means of narrative.

The sacrificial system is to be replaced by faith and prayer, founded on the renunciation of vengeance (vss. 17, 22–25), and a new generative mechanism is to be installed. We are being shown that sacrifice is violence in the form of vengeance deflected and monopolized by the religious institution.[18] The mimetic reciprocity of violence is essentially vengeance that is rationalized in the legal manifestation of the sacrificial system. Vengeance is the heart of the mechanism, and that is why the injunction "Whenever you stand praying, forgive if you have anything against anyone, so that your father in heaven may forgive you your trespasses" (vs. 25) is set off in a position of emphasis at the end of the teaching on faith and prayer. If faith and prayer are to replace the sacrificial mechanism, vengeance must be renounced; to renounce vengeance and to break with the mechanism of sacrifice is the same thing.

There is another aspect of the narrative to be illuminated by the Girardian hermeneutic, namely the interplay between religion and magic in the text, the movement in the text from public to private religion, from the Temple cult to faith and prayer. On a Durkheimian reading, magic comes out of reli-

16. D. O'Keefe, *Stolen Lightning: The Social Theory of Magic* (New York, 1982), pp. 167–72, 251 n. 21; H. Hubert and M. Mauss, *Sacrifice: Its Nature and Function* (Chicago, 1964), pp. 19–49.

17. Borg, *Conflict*, p. 174.

18. S. P. Stetkevych, "Ritual and Sacrificial Elements in the Poetry of Blood-Vengeance: Two Poems by Durayd ibn Al-Simmah and Muhalhil ibn Rabi'ah," *JNES* 45 (1986) 31–43, and "The Ritha' of Ta'abbata Sharran: A Study of Blood-Vengeance in Early Arabic Poetry," *JSS* 31 (1986) 27–45, give a good account of the link between vengeance, sacrifice, and initiation according to the theories of van Gennep, Hubert, and Mauss.

gion as the appropriation of religious instrumentalities for private ends. The religious feeling is the individual's awareness of the group, experienced initially in those group activities in which he feels swept up in the spirit of the group and carried beyond himself. This is well known in our time as mob hysteria. The Temple kills surrogate victims on behalf of the mob so that the mob might remain united as a mob and not fall apart into private vendettas. The Temple (state) must have a monopoly on violence. (This was the impulse behind the Deuteronomic reform that closed down the provincial places of sacrifice and centered it in Jerusalem; a step on the way to the elimination of sacrifice altogether, which is the subject of our text, and not just as a contribution to the humane treatment of animals but as a step on the road of civilization.) But the individual is always in danger of being destroyed by the group; Durkheim is unable to explain how this might take place, but Girard has made plain that it is the threat of mimetic violence that the individual feels. Thus in order to establish and defend an individual self over against the group, the individual (mis)appropriates the public religious symbols for private ends. The problem that magic seeks to solve is the problem of individual existence in the face of the power of the group.

Our text puts a remarkable emphasis on the ability of the individual to do for himself what formerly only the system could do. It expresses an extraordinary confidence in the individual and urges an energetic resistance to the group. "Have faith in God. Truly I say to you, whoever says to this mountain, 'Be taken up and cast into the sea,' and does not doubt in his heart but believes that what he says shall come to pass, it shall happen for him. For this reason I say to you, whatever you pray for and seek, believe that you have received it, and it shall be yours" (vss. 22–24). By means of hyperbole our text tells us that the antidote to the mob is an individual self-confidence founded on the renunciation of vengeance. The Durkheimians call this magic; but that is a misunderstanding, for it is not the appropriation of the religious act of sacrifice for private ends—that would be the vendetta that is properly prohibited by the state's monopoly on violence—rather it is the replacement of the religious system with something else, the coming to his own of the violence-renouncing individual. It is faith, not magic, a new and potentially liberating end to religion as transfigured violence. The individual, hitherto constituted by mimetic membership in the group and nonexistent apart from it, is now to be constituted by "faith in God" (vs. 22).

It should be clear at this point that we are not arguing that the historical Jesus was a rationalist who purified his ancestral religion of the atavistic system of animal sacrifice. It is not a matter of purification, but of replacement, of the uprooting of the mountain and its casting into the sea. For the system of ritual sacrifice was merely the outward and visible sign of a universal mechanism of human relations founded on mob violence generated by mimetic rivalry. Our text focuses on the Temple as the most vivid symbol of the mechanism, but the mechanism itself is much more pervasive than just the

Jerusalem cult; it is expressed in all the mythic, legal, military, and status manifestations of the power of violence as epitomized by the state and its representatives.

These representatives come upon the scene at the end of the incident in the Temple. They are carefully designated, and we must pay attention to this designation because our text intends to show Jesus in conflict with every one of the established authorities. Indeed, as the narrative progresses every class of authority is introduced by name. Here we meet "the chief priests and the scribes"—that is, the administrative and legal managers of the Temple. We also meet that source of all authority, the mob (ὄχλος).[19] We are told that the authorities were afraid of Jesus because the mob was hypnotized (ἐξεπλήσσετο) by his teaching (vs. 18). This is a revealing statement that is usually understood to mean that the mob was on his side, a misunderstanding that causes a further misunderstanding when later the mob appears as his opponent and causes knowing comments about the fickleness of the crowd. The mob in this text is, on the contrary, remarkably consistent in its role as the source of the authority of the leaders.

The reason why the leaders fear Jesus is because his teaching has hypnotized the mob, and thus, for the moment, taken the mob away from their control; a more powerful hypnotist has come on the scene. The text does not say that the mob was on the side of Jesus but only that it was not available to the Temple managers. The term ἐκπλήσσω means literally "to strike out, to drive away from, to expel" and here seems to bear the metaphorical meaning of "to strike out of one's senses, to be overwhelmed with desire." But what if we include the literal meaning of the word in this context and read it as a double entendre? Then the teaching of Jesus,[20] that is, the deeds and the words just reported, have caused the mob to be overwhelmed with desire, because the institution which channels that desire has been impugned. The teaching has expelled them from the womb of sacrificial violence where they are shielded from the truth by the Grand Inquisitor, and the mob is on the verge of chaos; the managers cannot control it; no wonder they fear Jesus. But there may also be a memory trace of the leader as scapegoat here, as the one who stands in a relation to the mob of having been expelled, and now, having been sacralized, generates the unanimity which makes group life pos-

19. R. A. Horsley, *Jesus and the Spiral of Violence: Popular Jewish Resistance in Roman Palestine* (San Francisco, 1987), pp. 90–120, gives an account of the Jerusalem crowd and its political importance based on Josephus. His treatment is of interest, but only indirectly relevant to our concern, which is the role of the crowd in Mark. That social history has shown that the crowd is more than the mob of misfits and criminals that Taine and Le Bon identified does not make a difference to our portrayal of the mob in Mark, because it is not the defects but rather the strengths of the members of the mob that are dangerous. The mob does not have to be made up of criminals to be dangerous. Mimetic contagion affects the best of us.

20. In Mark "teaching" refers to "the rule of God and the destruction of evil powers," V. Taylor, *The Gospel According to St. Mark* (London, 1957), p. 172.

sible. By a reversal of the direction of the action of the verb, on the grounds that at the generative level the power of myth formation has reversed the proper order to make it appear that it is the mob which is being scapegoated and not Jesus, Jesus appears as the victim who provides order; the mob is in a manner of speaking "on his side"; it has already identified him as the victim whose power to form the group is greater than the power of the Temple's ritual sacrifice. Soon he is to meet the mob's demand; in the meantime, for a brief moment he usurps the Temple's power. A hint from the generative level; a mythic moment in which the victim appears as the victimizer and the mob as the victim. This situation involves the leaders in a crisis of authority.

Authority and the Mob—11:27–33

All political and social authority derives from the mob as transfigured mimetic violence. The religious institutions were the original structures of violence; subsequently law and the state emerged as religious forms in this sense. The gospel discloses this state of affairs by making violence and constituted authority a stupefyingly obvious theme of its narrative. If there is any doubt about the theme of the narrative so far, it is removed by the present pericope.

Jesus is presented "walking about in the Temple" (vs. 27) in the style of the peripatetic teacher, and the authorities approach him with a question. They are carefully identified as "the chief priests, the scribes, and the elders." They represent violence in three of its most respectable disguises—respectively, the religious, the legal, and the political dimensions of established power. The question is "By what kind of authority do you do these things? Or who gave you this authority to do these things?" (vs. 28). It is the question about the legitimacy of power, and they ask both about its nature and its source. What kind of authority is it, and who gave it to you?

We assume from the context that the "things done" is the attack on the sacrificial system. The question, therefore, implies that if Jesus attacks the system from which all authority derives, he leaves us all exposed to chaos. It is the "law and order" argument for political repression, and the Grand Inquisitor's reason for maintaining the religious institutions. Jesus uncovers the bias of the question by asking them in his counter-question to describe the nature of the noninstitutional authority of John the Baptist. They refuse to do so "because they feared the mob" (ἐφοβοῦντο τὸν ὄχλον—vs. 32). Thus we arrive at the point of disclosure of the whole narrative, namely, the mob as the source of authority.

In the counter-question Jesus limits the options to two mutually exclusive sources of authority, from men or from heaven. The established leaders do well from a tactical point of view to refuse to answer on these narrow grounds, because they presumably wish to argue that their authority is both from heaven and from men, the former being mediated through the latter.

The mob, however, has a vague notion of prophetic authority as the authority that comes from heaven. The Weberian categories of "charismatic" and institutionalized authority might classify the two types, but they do not explain them. The key to an explanation is the fact that the authority of John is the authority of the expelled victim, as the immediately following parable of the wicked husbandmen who expel and kill the emissaries of God indicates. A parallel is drawn between John and Jesus, they are doubles of a different kind than the doubles of the sacrificial crisis when disorder erases distinctions. Their doubling is the doubling of the victim; both are cast out and killed, and both manifest a different kind of power in and because of that situation.

On the surface the dilemma of the leaders is obvious. The mob took John for a prophet and the leaders killed him. If they admit that he was a prophet, they show themselves to have acted against God; if, on the other hand, they deny that he was a prophet they risk losing credibility in the eyes of the mob that took him as such. At the deeper level the text recognizes that the authority of the leaders depends entirely on the acquiescence of the mob; they cannot risk antagonizing it. The mob, be it noted, did nothing to prevent the powers from killing John. They merely took him for a prophet; they did nothing indeed to take the part of the prophetic victim at the time of his need, and they do not do so now. They are easily put off by the prevarication of the powers. The mob remains the explosive but manipulable source of the authority of the powers, and the exchange ends inconclusively. Nevertheless, we have been shown that there is another kind and source of authority than the sacrificial system that operates by unifying the group through expelling and killing victims. It is the authority of the victim, and it is hinted that it is at least conceivable that the mob could take the part of the victim and find another kind and source of authority, "from heaven."

The word "authority" (ἐξουσία) shows something of its rootage in sacrifice and victimage, by the fact that it can mean both power or authority in the sense of the intrinsic ability and legal right to do something, on the one hand, and the abuse of power in the sense of arrogance and license, on the other. It means both order and its opposite, disorder, just as the primitive sacred exudes both succor and threat because the victim is perceived as the source of order and the cause of disorder. [21]

The Authority from Heaven—12:1–12

Jesus refuses to give a direct answer to their question about authority, but he does not leave it entirely unanswered. His answer takes the form of the parable of the wicked husbandmen and it is doubly appropriate. It takes up the theme of the relationship between Jesus and John, and it carries forward

---

21. It is used in parallel with ὕβρις in Thuc. 1.38, 3.45, and in OGI 669.51 there is an example of this usage from the first century C.E. Josephus uses it with this meaning: ὁ πᾶς ὄχλος ἐπ' ἐξουσίας ὕβριζεν ἀλήθελεν, Ant 10.103.

the explanation of the new form of authority that the gospel is recommending. In its reference to John and Jesus, it is equivalent to the sayings from Q, in Lk 7:33–35 (par. Mt 11:18–19), and Lk 11:49–51 (par. Mt 23:34–36), that link the two of them together in the chain of the rejected prophets of the divine wisdom. The point of the parable is clear; the religious establishment is opposed to God, and it shows that opposition by killing the representatives of God. The sacrificial victims are the representatives of God! The issue is defined for us by what has preceded as the question of the two kinds of authority—that from men and that from heaven. The authority from men operates by expelling and killing victims; the authority from heaven operates by taking sides with the victims and vindicating them.

The role of Psalm 118 is central to this argument. It was first introduced at the beginning of the section we are reading to herald the entry of Jesus into the Temple, to announce the coming of the victim to the place of sacrifice. Here it is invoked to explain the destruction of the Temple, alluded to in vs. 9 as the vindication of the victim (Ps 118:22–23 quoted in vss. 10–11, cf. Acts 4:11, 1Pet 2:7). The theme of the rejected stone that becomes the head of the corner probably gave rise to the image of the resurrected Christ as the cornerstone of the metaphorical new Temple of the Christian community,[22] thus explaining the much discussed "false accusation" in 14:58 that he had threatened to destroy the Temple made with hands and replace it in three days with one not made with hands. The whole idea is a metaphor, and the text clearly intends it as such and intends us to see that the "falsehood" of the accusation lodges in the attempt to present a metaphor as a literal threat.

The force of the metaphor is that the sacrificial system of the Temple that symbolizes and actualizes the founding mechanism with its violence and scapegoating is replaced by a system that takes its point of departure from the stone that the builders rejected, from the victim, and exercises the authority of heaven. The conclusive sign and seal of this new order is the destruction of the Temple in the Roman war, an event of which the text is aware.

The Temple managers perceive that Jesus has told the parable "against" them and would like to arrest him on the spot, but once again their fear of the mob inhibits them. Thus we are brought back as by a refrain to the source of all authority that is "from men," in the mob. By now it should be clear that the dominant interest of our text is political in the deep sense of the nature and source of the authority that brings order to human groups. The ground and roots of that authority is the violence of the group that is channeled in various institutions. Having dealt with the religious institu-

22. Juel, *Messiah and Temple*, p. 57, "The church is characterized as a spiritual temple made without hands and is viewed as replacement of the Jewish temple."

tions, symbolized by the Temple, the text now proceeds to consider the authority of the state, the law, the messiah, and the individual, culminating in the vision of the end of all human institutions and modulating into the presentation of the new order based on the death and vindication of the victim.

The Right Attitude Toward the State—12:13–17

His antagonists from the Temple now withdraw and act through representatives. They send to him certain Pharisees and Herodians to trap him into saying something indiscreet and show him to be a revolutionary. It is important to note that the religious antagonists from the Temple remain the force behind the opposition, signifying that the founding mechanism remains the source of the authority from men, no matter what form it takes. The roll of antagonists is lengthened here by the introduction of "some of the Pharisees," carefully designated so as to leave open the possibility that some other members of that persuasion did not oppose him and the Herodians. The latter are the agents of the Roman puppet king of Galilee and Peraea, Herod Antipas, within whose jurisdiction Jesus as a Galilean fell. The Herodians are the symbol of collaboration with Caesar, whereas the Pharisees probably represent the zealous opposition to Roman rule. The strategy is to trap Jesus one way or another with reference to the two parties represented. If he forbids the paying of taxes he falls afoul of the Herodians, and if he advocates it he falls afoul of the Pharisees. In any case the roll of all the possible representatives of established power is being called and arrayed against Jesus.

They flatter him as part of the stratagem, and with delicious irony they speak the truth. Jesus is, indeed, the one who "is true and does not concern (himself) with anyone nor look upon the face of men but teach(es) the way of God in truth" (vs. 14). "The way of God" is probably a reference to the halakah, which is literally "the way of the law" and the kind of phrase one would expect from the Pharisees. The phrase "to regard the face of" is Hebraic (LXX 1Kgs 16:7, Ps 81:2, Lev 19:15) and, together with the statement that he does not concern himself about any man, makes a striking disclosure of what it is precisely that causes men to behave untruly, namely the concern for others in the sense of the influence of the mob upon the individual.

O'Keefe[23] presents evidence for "our dizzying susceptibility to one another" and tells of Hilgard's theory that hypnotism arises out of our susceptibility to light trances in response to one another. From the cognitive dissonance studies of Festinger, which show that individual perception cannot withstand group influence, to the work of Bandura on "modeling," which shows that it is impossible not to learn behavior that we see engaged in by others, the Girardian idea of mimetic contagion receives widespread ratifi-

---

23. O'Keefe, *Stolen Lightning*, p. 92.

cation. Here we are told significantly that Jesus does not concern himself with others nor look into the face of another man. Looking into the face of another is the surest way of being entranced by him, and precisely this is what Jesus avoids. For this reason he is able to resist mimetic contagion and to be "true." Thus, ironically, the antagonists tell us the secret of his integrity: to resist mimetic involvement and stick to the way of God.

Jesus' reply expresses this noninvolvement perfectly. The currency belongs to the state, so let the state have it. The important things are those that belong to God, and they should be given to him. Jesus refuses to be drawn into either a negative or a positive opposition to the state. If he were to involve himself in such opposition, he would become a part of the violence of either the state or the counter-state, and that would be to succumb to the founding mechanism. Jesus withholds all cooperation from that mechanism. The net result is that rather than he being entranced by the system represented by his antagonists, they are entranced by him (καὶ ἐξεθαύμαζον ἐπ' αὐτῷ—vs. 17).

The attitude toward the state advocated here is the same as the one recommended by Paul in Rom 12:19–13:10, where the apostle, probably in opposition to a zealotic impulse to withhold cooperation from the state,[24] urges the renunciation of vengeance and the giving of due honor to the established powers. The context of the early Christian debate about the right attitude to the state is the Jewish resistance to Rome that led to the war and the destruction of the Temple in 70 C.E. Jesus and Paul are presented in the texts as standing aloof from revolution, because, we suggest, counter-violence is as much a part of the sacrificial mechanism as the violence of the established order, and one cannot fight the devil with his own weapons. A totally new and different approach is needed, which begins with the taking of the side of the victim and refusing all collaboration with violence. But how is this mode of action to succeed? The answer is the vindication of the victim in the resurrection; and so the next challenge is to the concept of resurrection.

"You Are Completely Mistaken!"—12:18–27

This strong refutation with which the pericope ends shows that something of major importance is at stake here. The roll of official opponents is extended once again, this time to include the Sadducees, who are the party that denies the possibility of the resurrection of the dead. They are also the priestly aristocracy whose power is centered on and derives from the hereditary prestige of the priestly caste that maintains the sacrificial system. We have, therefore, a head-to-head confrontation between a society structured by the sacred mechanism on the one hand and the possibility of a new society

---

24. R. Jewett, "The Agitators and the Galatian Congregation," *NTS* 17 (1971) 198–212; M. Borg, "A New Context for Romans 13," *NTS* 19 (1973) 205–18.

based on the vindication of the victim on the other. This vindication is called resurrection, and the Sadducees seek to ridicule it by an artificial *reductio ad absurdum* based on the Levirate law of marriage.

In response Jesus takes up the argument in the terms proposed by his antagonists and refutes it trenchantly. They do not understand the scriptures or the power of God. Both testify clearly to the resurrection. This is the first time that Jesus accepts the terms of an argument proposed. In the case of the question about authority and the question of taxes to Caesar, he bypasses the opponent's terms. That he takes them up in this case shows again that something of special and substantive importance is under consideration. Other matters might be bypassed, but this one is of the essence and it is vital that the validity of the resurrection be shown to be established both by tradition and the current working of the divine power. Those who deny the possibility of the resurrection must be shown to be "completely mistaken," because they deny the possibility of a new order based not on the sacrifice of victims but on their vindication.

The Essence of the New Order: Love Is More Than Holocausts and Sacrifices—12:28–34

The religious and the secular powers have been shown to be transcended by the new order of the victim called "resurrection." What then shall be the power of the new order? How shall it be preserved from chaos if not by holocausts and sacrifice? And what shall be the basis of law (prohibition is one of the three results of the primal murder) in the new order?

A lawyer who has been impressed by the astuteness of Jesus' answers hitherto asks him what is the fundamental principle underlying the law. Jesus answers with the Shema, the principle of all of Israel's religious life, the prohibition on idolatry. If there is to be a new order, it must be founded on the renunciation of the primitive sacred, of the victim made into a god by transfigured violence. This entails the renunciation of vengeance. The full quotation from Lev 19:18 is: "You shall not take vengeance or bear any grudge against the sons of your own people, but you shall love your neighbor as yourself: I am the lord." It is clearly a proscription of vengeance, the fundamental principle of law as reciprocity. The web of reciprocity must be broken and replaced by a network of love if there is to be a new order, and for that to happen the idol which is the primitive sacred must be forsworn. The passage rejects the whole panoply of sacred violence in its idolatrous first principle and its social manifestation in mimetic violence and vengeance. The lawyer is the one who expresses this fact when he is made to say, "You spoke elegantly and truly, teacher, when you said that God is one and there is no other besides him, and that to love him with a whole heart and a whole mind and a whole strength and to love the neighbor as oneself is more than holocausts and sacrifices" (vss. 32–33). Jesus did not speak the words about holocausts and sacrifices; the lawyer added them, and we can only understand them as a summary of all that has gone before in the section beginning with the incident in the Temple and the ensuing questioning of Jesus. We are told at the outset of the pericope that the lawyer had been listening to the exchanges and was impressed by Jesus' answers. He is not far from the kingdom because he understands the import of Jesus' teaching on the nonsacrificial nature of the new order.

The antagonists are silenced. "No one dared to question him anymore." It is now clear that a society based on monotheism and love, apart from the law of reciprocity, apart from the order based on the driving out of the innocent victims, a new order called "resurrection" is at hand. Jesus represents something more than the order of holocausts and sacrifices; he represents a new and different mechanism based on love. No one dares to question him any longer; now it is his turn to ask the question.

A Different Kind of Messianic Hope—12:35–40

We are told again, for the first time since the discussion about authority in 11:27, that Jesus is in the Temple. Although we should understand that all these debates take place there, the fact that at this point we are explicitly reminded of the venue tells us that what follows has special pertinence to the Temple and what it stands for. Psalm 110 is invoked to make the point that Jesus is not the Davidic messiah, that he stands for a different messianic hope. The psalm was widely used in early Christianity (Acts 2:34–35; 1Cor 15:25; Heb 1:13, 5:6, 10; 7:1, 10–17) to identify Jesus as the one who transcends the hope both for the political and the priestly messiah. The location of this incident in the Temple makes it likely that an allusion to the figure of Melchizedek is in the background here, and that the text is arguing that Jesus represents an order that makes both the religious and the secular political hope obsolete. The letter to the Hebrews spells out the theme of the transcendence of the cultus and the priesthood in terms of the Platonic world of ideas. Here it is expressed in terms of a new nonsacrificial order in which the violence of the Davidic hope and the scheme of religiopolitical status that it supports is transcended. As David's lord he is to bring in a kingdom that is ordered by a principle different from the one that entitles the scribes to the privileges of position, "greetings in the marketplace, the foremost seats in the synagogue, and the choice places at banquets" (vs. 39). Such a system devours the weak and encourages hypocrisy. The new order is to be one in which the individual is affirmed on the basis of inner integrity; the violent political dreams of the messianic age, hitherto imagined according to the memory of the territorial extent and political prestige of the Davidic kingdom, are set aside by the nonviolent kingdom based on the vindication of the victim by resurrection.

Here for the first time the mob seems to be on his side. "The whole mob heard him gladly" (vs. 37). What has he said to evoke this positive response from the people? Why should the rejection of the Davidic version of the messianic hope cause such gladness? If we read the text within the context of the war against Rome, we might hear a sigh of relief on the part of those who did not want to be swept up in the violence of an armed resistance inspired by the political vision of the Davidic hope. We might, however, also hear an echo of the old ambivalence about the appropriateness of a monarchical form of government for Israel expressed in the accounts of the establishment of the monarchy in 1 Samuel 8–10; and we certainly hear an echo of the humble messiah of the opening scene who comes to the Temple riding on an ass, in step with the prophecy of Zech 9:9, which, although it is not mentioned explicitly by Mark, is in the background and is brought to the fore by the other evangelists.

The pertinence to the Temple of this line of reflection is well expressed in the words of Archbishop Lord to King James at the height of the debate about the form of governance of the church of England in the seventeenth century, "My Lord, no bishops, no king!" The monarchy and the priesthood are natural allies and mutually dependent. It was David who first assayed to build the Temple, who purchased the threshing floor from Araunah the Jebusite, and who brought the ark to Jerusalem (2Sam 24:18–25, 6:1–15). It was he who established the system of status based on sacred prestige that excluded the bulk of the populace from positions of power in the state. The message that the common people, the mob, heard gladly was that this order was to be ended not repristinated, replaced not refurbished.

The Individual Is Worth More Than the System—12:41–44

The inclusion of this pericope here might have been motivated by the reference to the devouring of widows' households in vs. 40, but that is not the only or sufficient reason for its inclusion. We must read it as part of the ongoing exposition within the context of the announcement of the advent of the new order. We see the mob in thrall to the Temple, casting their money into the treasury. Then we see an example of the way the establishment devours the individual, a concrete instance of the rapacity referred to in vs. 40. The text is usually read as a moral comment on the relatively greater importance of intention compared to action. Because of the total commitment of the gift, it is worth more than all the other gifts that cost their givers less. But we are left wondering about the fate of the widow, now that she has given her all to the system. How will she live? Is this sort of prodigality really being commended, or are we being shown an example of why the crowd heard with gladness the announcement of the passing of so rapacious an institution? We think that the latter is the more likely message of the passage. We are not told that the crowd understood the positive side of the equation, only that they rejoiced in the negative, in the removal of their oppression.

This story picks up the theme with which our section on the Temple began, the theme of the faith of the individual over against the barren system (11:22–25), and shows how the demands of the system make the life of the individual difficult if not impossible. It tells us that the intention of the individual, misguided and betrayed as it is, is nevertheless worth more than all the mob's participation in this oppression. It presents the culminating indictment of the system and prepares for the climactic announcement of its destruction.

Not One Stone Upon Another—13:1-2

Now he leaves the Temple. The center of God's presence with his people moves to a place "apart from Law" (Rom 3:21). We are reminded of the vision of God's departing from the Temple in Ezekiel 10 and taking up position "upon the mountain which is on the east side of the city" (11:23) as a prelude to the destruction of the city and the departure into exile. We have arrived at the climax of the rejection of Jerusalem and the Temple. A disciple draws his attention to the pretentious size of the Temple buildings, a marvel that can still be appreciated today from the size of the Herodian stones visible *in situ*. Jesus solemnly pronounces the prophecy that not one of these great buildings will remain standing, not one stone will remain upon another.

Discouraging Words—13:3-36

Dieter Lührmann[25] sees this passage as a portrayal in the apocalyptic style of a typical war situation, presenting the position of the Christians caught between the Jews and the Romans in the war of 66–70 C.E. Kelber sees it as an expression of the anti-Zion theology that was "forced upon" Mark by the Roman destruction.[26] We shall follow the main outline of Kelber's interpretation. The interpretive context of the passage is the war and its aftermath, especially the eschatological hopes aroused by it in the minds of certain Christians. Mark refutes their version of the hope and argues for his own.

Jesus answers the private question of the four disciples about the time and the sign of the destruction of the Temple. The answering speech refutes one interpretation and proposes another. It is organized into three sections: (1) A revision of an account of past history, vss. 5b–23; (2) the Parousia, vss. 24–27; and (3) the nearness of the Parousia, vss. 28–37. Each section has three subsections: (1a) the war, vss. 5b–8; (1b) persecution and the Gentile mission, vss. 9–13; (1c) the abomination of desolation and the destruction of Jerusalem, vss. 14–23; (2a) the cosmic drama, vss. 24–25; (2b) the coming of the Son of Man, vss. 26; (2c) the gathering of the elect, vs. 270; (3a) the parable of the fig tree, vss. 28–29; (3b) three sayings, vss. 30–32; (3c) the parable of the doorkeeper.[27] Its purpose is to refute the interpretation of the fall of Jerusalem as the eschatological event, while holding fast to the

---

25. "Markus 14.55–64, Christologie und Zerstörung des Tempels im Markusevangelium," *NTS* 27 (1981) 457–74, esp. 467.
26. Kelber, *Kingdom*, pp. 106 and 109–28.
27. Kelber, *Kingdom*, p. 126.

conviction that that event is nevertheless near. The references to the false messiahs and the false prophets (vss. 6 and 22) point to rival Christian prophets who interpreted the war as the end of the world and the time of the coming of the Son of Man.[28]

To be sure, the discourse is delivered within the context of eschatological thought; these events of the war are eternally significant, but they are not the end of the age. They are merely the beginning of the messianic tribulation (vs. 8c), and they are starkly historical. They are narrated in apocalyptic terms because they are indeed a negative apocalypse. The "abomination of desolation" set up in the Temple probably refers to the triumph of Roman violence signified by the installment of some pagan symbol, an altar, or the standards of the legions in the sacred precinct. Kelber points out that the "abomination" is construed as a person, the masculine participle ἑστηκότα giving a personal identity to the neuter βδέλυγμα (vs. 14). This enables him to talk of it as Satan. Satan has taken over the Temple, and thus it is disqualified forever as the place of the Parousia.[29]

The presence of Satan in the Temple is an unveiling of the violence that has always been the secret of its life. The negative apocalypse that reaches its climax here has been coming from the moment that Jesus entered the Temple. It is not just a historical reference to the Roman desecration but an unveiling of the mechanism that drives the Temple. There is a deep consistency in the violent destruction of a violent system. There is also a consistency in Mark's presentation of this speech at this point. Kelber sees it to reside in the historical circumstances of the conflict between the Galilean and the Jerusalemite Christian communities; the speech is the climax of the argument made by the former against the position of the latter. This may, indeed, be a part of the explanation for its occurrence here; but it can only be a part, because it does not account for the linkage of this passage with what comes after it in the succeeding chapters, namely, the outbreak of Satanic violence emanating from the Temple against the innocent victim Jesus.

What the reader must understand (vs. 14) is that the "abomination" is a symbol of the violence that is to come in the narrative, when "the chief priests and the scribes sought to take him by stealth and kill him" (14:1). The conclusion of the speech points directly to the Gethsemane scene, where the Lord finds the disciples sleeping (vs. 36; cf. 14:37–41) and utters the same warnings to stay awake and watch (vs. 33). The mention of the crowing of the cock (ἀλεκτοροφωνία—vs. 35; cf. ἀλέκτωρ ἐφώνησεν—14:72; cf. 30), recalls the same element in the account of Peter's denial. The frequent references to being "handed over" or betrayed (παραδίδωμι vss. 9, 11–12) recall

---

28. Lührmann, NTS 27 (1981) 467.

29. Kelber, Kingdom, pp. 119–20. "The ἐρημώσεως was fulfilled in its most radical, literal sense, and the βδέλυγμα was impersonated by Satan himself. Satan had taken possession of the holy temple" (p. 120).

the betrayal of Jesus and especially the handing over of the Son of Man at the conclusion of the Gethsemane pericope (14:41), which takes place as the disciples sleep. The threefold organization of the speech also recalls the three times Jesus comes and finds the disciples sleeping in Gethsemane, and the three denials of Peter.[30] All of this causes the reader to understand that the revelation of the "Abomination" is the unveiling of the founding mechanism that is about to break out against Jesus; it is the clue to the sacred energy that generates the action from now on. Chapter 13 is not merely the climax of what has gone before but also an introduction to what is to come.

The role of the section on the Parousia (vss. 24–27) in this chapter is analogous to the role that the question about the resurrection plays in the discourses in the Temple. It introduces the note of miraculous intervention and signals that the fulfillment of the hope for a new order can only take place through the action of God. It is as if for a moment the veil is lifted and we are shown the real agent in the history that is being recounted. The Temple is to be replaced not with another sacrificial system but with the community of those chosen by the Son of Man. We cannot take up the whole matter of the meaning of the Son of Man in Mark, but we can refer to the fact, demonstrated by Morna Hooker,[31] that the figure symbolizes in Daniel the community of the truly human one, who with the restoration of the right order of creation takes the place of the beasts as the ruler of humanity. Sin caused the beasts to rule over Adam in contradiction to the intended order of the creation. Now the right order is restored and the human one rules in the human community.

At this point the section on the replacement of the Temple ends. We have been shown how the messiah replaces the order of the founding mechanism with the order of the truly human one, the new order founded on the inclusion rather than the exclusion of the victim. With ch. 14 there begins a new section that we have chosen to call "The Expulsion of the Scapegoat," which discloses with simple clarity the basis of the new order in non-cooperation with violence and reveals once and for all the nature of the old order founded on the sacred mechanism of the surrogate victim.

THE EXPULSION OF THE SCAPEGOAT AS THE
BASIS OF THE NEW ORDER—CHS. 14–16

As we approach the reading of this section, we bear in mind the challenge posed by Burton Mack to the Girardian reading of the passion narrative. Far from being a demythification of the sacrificial mechanism, Mack avers, the

---

30. On Mark's use of a triadal pattern of composition see Nickelsburg, *HTR* 73 (1980) 177–78, and N. R. Petersen, "The Composition of Mark 4:1–8:26," *HTR* 73 (1980) 185–217.

31. M. D. Hooker, *The Son of Man in Mark: A Study of the Background of the Term "Son of Man" and Its Use in St. Mark's Gospel* (Montreal, 1967), pp. 15–17.

passion narrative is a diabolically subtle complexification of the generative power of that system. It seems to reveal the mechanism, and at one level it does, but that revelation serves only to blind the reader to the fact that the narrative is being generated by that very mechanism, with the Jews as the scapegoats and Jesus as a spurious innocent. This is a complicated argument for a number of reasons: it goes behind the text to the historical context and on that basis judges that Jesus was in historical fact not innocent but guilty of some crime;[32] it assumes, on the same grounds, that the Jews were not responsible for his death, but rather the Romans alone, and that the whole element of Jewish participation was introduced to shift the blame from the Romans because the church rapidly became a Greco-Roman organization and wanted to justify itself in terms of its origins.

The evidence for these conjectures is the gospel texts themselves and the well-known technique of comparing one with another to show that there is an escalation of the attribution of Jewish blame from one to the other; but such comparison is based on a thematic reading without attention to the deep structure. Furthermore, the paucity of sources makes going behind the gospels for anything more than general impressions a very uncertain procedure. Josephus is virtually our only source, and it is astonishing how willing we are to accept him as a reliable witness while we withhold the same confidence from the gospels. He was after all an ardent apologist. This is not to suggest that we read the gospels as naively as we read Josephus, but rather that we read Josephus with the same sophistication as we read the gospels. In that case it would be impossible to use Josephus to prove the nonhistoricity of any item in the gospels. That the passion narratives were read at later times as sacrificial texts that justified persecution of the Jews tells us not about the gospels so much as about the enthrallment of the subsequent readers to the sacrificial mythology. We shall confine our discussion to the text before us for present purposes and ask whether Mack is justified on the basis of this text alone in calling it a "myth of innocence."

We bring to a consideration of the passion certain impressions formed by our reading so far. The list of opponents of Jesus is a roll call of the Jewish leadership; the chief priests, the scribes, the elders, the Pharisees, the Herodians, and the Sadducees; and always in the background, providing the power of the leaders, is the mob. The clear impression given is that the opposition between Jesus and these powers is motivated not by the fact that

---

32. Horsley, *Violence*, pp. 149–66 argues in very general terms that the charges against Jesus were not entirely false. He points to the same evidence that we have remarked to the effect that Jesus posed some kind of a threat to the Temple. The truth is that in the eyes of the defenders of the system and its mechanism he is guilty but that his guilt is precisely a function of the system of violence, the duplicity of which consists in its portraying its victims as worthy of the death it inflicts. Thus the logic of guilt and innocence is confused in this discussion. Jesus is neither the first nor the last person to have been judicially murdered.

they are Jews, but by the fact that they are the powers of this world sustained by the founding mechanism. At issue is not the inadequacy of the Jewish religion by comparison with the new Christian religion but rather the deadly effect of the sacrificial order that feeds on self-deception, compared to a new order based on self-knowledge and determined to renounce the sacrificial way by taking the part of the victim.

The Priests Buy a Victim—14:1–2

At several points in the narrative the powers have indicated a desire to apprehend Jesus; now they fulfill that desire. The Temple authorities take the lead again as they did at the beginning of the previous section, in the aftermath of the driving out of the traders; "the chief priests and the scribes sought to take him by stealth and kill him," but once again they are inhibited by the mob (14:1–2). A vignette announces his impending death (vss. 3–9), and then we are told how the chief priests arrange with Judas to have Jesus betrayed to them. They promise to give him money. Money is a theme in the narrative. Jesus came to the hostile attention of the powers by driving the money changers from the Temple; the issue of his relation to the state was posed in terms of money, and an actual coin was part of the narrative; the throng and the widow acknowledged their thrall to the system by casting money into the Temple treasury, and now the chief priests offer money in return for his life.

Money is one of the most powerful symbols of the value of life, from the old Germanic *Wergeld* to the modern awards of punitive and compensatory damages. Indeed, we are told that the widow cast her whole life into the treasury (12:44). The power of money derives from the sacrificial origins of symbolism, rooted in the discovery that one thing, the victim, can stand for another, the group. The sacrificial victim is essentially a form of currency, representing the life of the offerer.[33] Judas takes the life of Jesus from the hands of the priests, in an essentially sacrificial exchange. Matthew makes more of this fact than Mark, actually calling it "blood money" (27:6) and treating it as polluted and hence unworthy of being returned to the Temple treasury. He also puts it in the context of a prophecy from Zechariah (11:12–13), in which the money was cast into the Temple treasury in order to make the point of its not being so deposited in this case more poignant by contrast. In

---

33. E. Gans, *The End of Culture, Toward a Generative Anthropology* (Berkeley, 1985), p. 34, who proposes a formally similar but significantly different explanation of the origin of culture to Girard's, makes the system of exchange that begins with the sharing of the desired object among the participants in what he calls the "originary scene of designation"—the central ethical, and therefore constitutive, act of culture. Money originates in this primal sharing of the victim; cf. B. Laum, *Heiliges Geld* (Tübingen, 1924); W. Desmonde, *Magic, Myth and Money* (Glencoe, Ill., 1962) and, for a more general treatment of the role of the sacrificial mechanism in economics, P. Dumouchel and J.-P. Dupuy, *L'Enfer des Choses: René Girard et la Logique de L'Economie* (Paris, 1979).

any case, in Matthew, to return it to the treasury would pollute the Temple by interfering with the logic of sacrifice. An offering has been made, a victim purchased and slaughtered; to take back the price of the sacrifice would be to contradict the logic of the sacrifice by taking back the offering, and that would annul its efficacy. So they bought with it a field for the burial of foreigners. The reference to foreigners underlines the scapegoat associations of the transaction; the foreigner, the stranger, is the typical scapegoat. To take back the money would be to take back the scapegoat and so return the violence that they had sought to expel. To be sure, all this is not spelled out in Mark, but it is there *in nuce,* as Matthew indicates. Money is a sacrificial symbol of life taken and offered.

The New Form of Religion—14:12–26

The pericope of the last supper recalls the entry into the Temple in ch. 11. The same mystery attends the locating of the appropriate room as attended the finding of the ass for the triumphal entry. Disciples are sent on ahead to meet a man marked by the fact that he is carrying a jar of water. This is unusual in a society in which water is usually carried by women. Once in the room, which by the analogy with ch. 11 is a counterpart of the temple, the talk turns to the "handing over" of Jesus as a sacrificial victim to the chief priests, who, like the patrons of the Temple traders have bought but not yet paid for him. Judas is in the role of the offerer of sacrifice and as such is condemned by all the poignancy of a scene in which a friend and fellow diner betrays the host. The power of this condemnation and the efficacy of this narrative can be measured by the deep impression it made on subsequent Christian imagination. Dante puts Judas along with Brutus, the betrayer of Caesar, in the nethermost pit of hell, welded to the icy air machine that is the devil himself.

The term παραδίδωμι, which in general means simply "to hand over," takes on the meaning, in this context, of the handing over of a victim, since the recipients are the priests. There is some precedent for this usage in the literature on martyrdom, and in Eph 5:25 we find precisely such a meaning. In Mark it is used in the passion predictions (9:31, 10:33), the predictions of persecution (13:9, 11, 12), at the conclusion of the Gethsemane scene (14:41), and more importantly for present purposes, at the handing over of Jesus to Pilate by the Sanhedrin (15:1, 10), and of Pilate's handing him over to the soldiers to be crucified (15:15).

The institution of the eucharist is intended as a parallel to and a replacement for the Temple sacrifices, just as the room is a counterpart to the Temple. Jesus "gives" (δίδωμι) his body and blood to them as symbols of the covenant and pledges of the "new" (καινός—vs. 25) kingdom. The usual direction of the sacrificial offering is reversed; instead of the worshipper giving to the god, the god is giving to the worshipper, in what amounts to a trenchant refutation of the sacrificial order. This is precisely what makes the new kingdom new. It is a disclosure of the deep structure of the old order founded on violence and self-deception, and a replacement of it with a new order founded on self-giving. The parallel to the Temple scenes is confirmed by the concluding indication that after leaving the room they go to the Mount of Olives, just as they did when they finally left the Temple (13:3).

Peter Succumbs to Mimetic Desire and Rivalry—14:27–43

In the foretelling of Peter's denial (14:27–31) we encounter the theme of mimetic desire.[34] The analysis of the meaning of "scandal" in the gospels belongs among Girard's most brilliant achievements.

> In the Gospels, the skandalon . . . is always someone else, or it is myself to the extent that I am alienated from other people . . . scandal invariably involves an obsessional obstacle, raised up by mimetic desire with all its empty ambitions and ridiculous antagonisms . . . it is the model exerting its special form of temptation, causing attraction to the extent that it is an obstacle and forming an obstacle to the extent that it can attract. The skandalon is the obstacle/model of mimetic rivalry; it is the model in so far as he works counter to the undertakings of the disciple, and so becomes for him an inexhaustible source of morbid fascination.[35]

Scandal is an essential feature of what Girard and his collaborators call interdividual psychology. This psychology is patterned by the mimetic relationship between persons in which rivalry develops as the imitator becomes like the imitated and begins to threaten the model's access to the object. Then the double message, "Be like me, do not be like me," begins to sound, and the model becomes both attractive and revolting. The imitator has a vested interest in the superiority of the model because that is what makes him a model, and so ensues the morbid fascination of masochism, of the obstacle that one obsessively stumbles against, the source of hurt that one cannot turn away from.

In 8:32–33, Peter objects to the prediction of the passion and Jesus rebukes him as Satan for thinking "as men think and not as God thinks." Matthew (16:23) introduces the term "scandal" into this context as the equivalent of Satan, showing that Satan is nothing more than the mythological representation of mimetic rivalry. This is another instance of Matthew's making explicit what is only implicit in Mark. Nevertheless in Mark it remains clear that Peter's relationship to Jesus is enmeshed in the coils of mimesis, because he cannot tolerate the diminution of his model through rejection and death.

Peter stands for all the disciples and for all the readers of the gospel of Mark; he misunderstands on behalf of us all. He shows that we want our model to be part of the violent order of sacred prestige, a greater warrior and

34. Girard has treated this incident in *The Scapegoat*, pp. 149–64.
35. R. Girard, *Things Hidden from the Foundation of the World*, p. 416.

a more sacred god than those of others. He shows that we need to be "put down" by our model, because that is the way he assures us that he is a worthy model. Peter represents our need for an *alter Iago!*

Peter's boast that he will not be among those who are scandalized and flee expresses all the bravado and self-deception of mimetic rivalry. He does not see that the mechanism destroys with particular ease those who deny that they are subject to it. His boast reveals that he and all the disciples are locked in rivalry for the affection of Jesus, that they have made him a sacred object, that they idolize him. His impending death, unadorned by the pretense that it is a good thing, will remove him as a sacred object and thus subvert the Jesusolatry of the disciples and all subsequent Christians. He dies not as a contributor to the sacrificial system, not as a hero or martyr whose blood consecrates the violent order, but as an innocent victim of a lynch mob that cloaks its desire with the costumes of culture and slakes its thirst for mythic prestige with the blood of slandered victims.

The mysterious reference to the crowing of the cock suggests that Jesus has divine foresight, whereas not divine foresight but only human insight is needed to see that the mimetic rivalry expressed in the boast to be the only one that will not deny him is bound to lead to such denial. The fact that the text presents this insight as a miracle shows that at one level it still does not understand the operation of the founding mechanism. It does and does not understand. It understands the outcome, but it does not see how or why it will come about. That remains a mystery and a miracle. How shall we explain this facet of the text? Girard suggests that we have here a trace of the difference in understanding between the writer of the text and the luminous intelligence that inspired it. The latter is a trace of the historical Jesus, and the text shows how his interpreters failed to understand him fully. The fact that the text does not obscure the truth entirely, however, shows that there is a significant measure of historical verisimilitude in the report, which recounts even that which it does not fully understand.

The incident ends with all the disciples solemnly asseverating that they will not be scandalized by him; and in the very next scene they are shown up for the nincompoops that they are, when their representatives fall asleep in Gethsemane. They fail to understand their hero's human need for companionship in his hour of temptation. Confident that the great leader has everything, including his own emotions, under control, they doze off in the moment of terror. They could not stand to hear that he was sorrowful in his soul to the point of death. Even if they must resort to unconsciousness, they will maintain their sacred illusion about him.

The theme of the disciples asleep is emphasized by being narrated three times. The first time Jesus directs his rebuke at Peter for not being strong enough to stay awake to all that is going on. He warns Peter to be alert and on guard. The second time we are not told what the content of the rebuke was, but rather that the disciples were unable to answer him; they are confused and ashamed for not having heeded the first rebuke. They lack the strength needed to go through the ordeal with their eyes open. They were silenced by shame. Jesus' concluding verdict on their sleep is enigmatic and plagued by textual uncertainty. We do not know whether it is a question or a command; we do not know whether or not to read τὸ τέλος after ἀπέχει in vs. 41, and we do not know precisely how to take ἀπέχει.

The textual evidence does not seem to us to favor the inclusion of τὸ τέλος, and the most likely meaning for ἀπέχει seems to be the commercial one known from the papyri, "he has been paid." If we take the verse as a command, not a question, we may construe the concluding statement as follows: "Stay asleep for the rest of the time (i.e. for the rest of the drama about to be played out), and take your rest. He (Judas) has (now) been paid. The hour has come, behold the Son of man is handed over into the hands of sinners." The weary and biting irony of the saying "Stay asleep for the rest of the time" conveys to us that we are not able to stand the truth about the founding mechanism and would rather not witness its uncovering. We prefer nescience; we are asleep most of the time, and that is how we are able to endure the violence of the sacrificial order. The fact that it is immediately followed by the urgent and contradictory "Get up! Let's go! See, my betrayer is near!" (vs. 42) confirms that we are intended to read the ironic command to sleep on as a metaphor. "Sleep on for the rest of the time" means, therefore, "you do not have the strength to go through this with your eyes open, so you might as well remain asleep." We the readers are expected to hear the irony and be convicted by it and thus motivated to "stay awake and watch!" so as to see the truth unfold before us in the text and all around us in the violent world of sacrificial order.

Thus a sequence of action that begins with Jesus telling the disciples that they will all be scandalized by him in the sense that they will be able neither to support him nor to reject him, but will be bound to him in a bond of morbid fascination, ends with the irony of their sleeping through the revelation of the scandal of mimetic rivalry and surrogate victimage. All the important action takes place while they (we) dream of a heroic denouement in which violence overcomes violence, Beelzebub drives out Beelzebub. In the world of reality, however, the finger of God is driving out violence, in the shape of the unheroic victim of a commercial transaction. He has been bought, and now he has been paid for, and the one who attacked the traders in sacrificial animals has become an item of their trade. Not by the whip of his prophetic action, but by exposing to the light their violent complicity, Jesus ends the trade in victims, destroys the Temple made with (blood-stained) hands, and founds the metaphoric new Temple, not made with hands. But alas, his disciples (we, the readers) sleep through it all and awake refreshed, with renewed enthusiasm, to rebuild the order that he has just brought down by idolizing Jesus and installing him in the place of honor in a new sacrificial system.

The Traitor and the Mob—14:43–52

The mob returns to the scene led by the traitor and armed to the teeth. Treachery and violence come unmasked upon the stage. The same trio we have dealt with from the beginning—the chief priests, the scribes, and the elders—sent them. They act through surrogates, thereby preserving the fiction of their uninvolvement with mob violence. So we have a full representation of the powers of this world, a traitor, an armed mob, and religious, legal, and political functionaries behind a veil of surrogates. The act of treachery takes the form of a tender kiss, the intensity of it expressed by κατεφίλησεν.[36] Friendship and affection are suborned in the service of church, state, law, and order. There follows a burlesque of resistance when one of the bystanders—we are not told that it is a disciple—draws his sword and cuts off a little piece of a servant's ear.[37] Then Jesus denies that he is a ληστής likely to put up a violent resistance. The authorities have cast him in their own violent image, but he is different, and as soon as the disciples see this, they forsake him and flee (vs. 50).

Among those who fled was a youth who ran away naked leaving his garment behind. We can think of no plausible way to integrate this incident into the logic of the text, except to regard it as an emphasis on the fact that absolutely everyone forsook him and fled. Morton Smith thinks it is a historical reminiscence of the initiatory rite that Jesus required of those who wished to join his group.[38]

Jesus and Peter on Trial—14:53–72

As the attack on the traders in the Temple is set within the account of the cursing of the fig tree and the teaching on faith and forgiveness, in 11:12–25, so here the account of the hearing before the high priest is set within the account of Peter's denial. The scene is set; Jesus is led away to the high priest, and the trio of priests, scribes, and elders goes with him. Peter follows at a distance and sits with the servants warming himself at their fire. We have thus the scene of a contrasting rather than a similar pair. The mimetic effect is reversed; the two become not similar but increasingly different for the time being.

The witnesses against Jesus are all false, especially the construal of the threat against the Temple as a threat of literal violence. Once more the alter Iago principle is at work, and they cast Jesus in their own image of violence. We have already seen that the text intends the reference to the new Temple as a metaphor for a new order of society. But it is significant that the one

36. Taylor, *St. Mark*, p. 559.
37. Ibid., p. 560.
38. M. Smith, *Clement of Alexandria and a Secret Gospel of Mark* (Cambridge, Mass., 1973), pp. 167ff. See also M. Smith, "Clement of Alexandria and Secret Mark: The Score at the End of the First Decade," *HTR* 75 (1982) 449–61.

accusation made concerns a literal threat to the Temple; that confirms our reading hitherto.

The introduction of the messianic confession and the reference to the coming Son of Man has the same suddenness about it as we observed in connection with 13:24–31. The juxtaposition of the messianic identity of Jesus with the destruction of the Temple has no counterpart in a Jewish belief that the messiah would destroy the Temple. Lührmann rightly points out that the evidence for that belief in the Targums to Isa 53:5 and Zech 6:12, and the reference in Lev.R.9:6, is from the time after the destruction of the Second Temple.[39] Thus the interpretation of Jesus' dignity by relating it to the destruction of the Temple is original with the gospel, showing its understanding of him as the one who displaces the sacrificial system.

The scene before the Sanhedrin is the key to the passion narrative and to the whole gospel.[40] Here the innocence of the victim is revealed. The scene is carefully prepared for in all that precedes (e.g. 3:6, 19; 10:33; 11:18, 27; 12:12; 14:3–9, 21, 25, 32–42), and referred back to in what follows (15:10, 14). The reference in 15:10 to the φθόνος of the Sanhedrin underscores the unfairness of the trial, ". . . die Beschuldigung βλασφημία, die das Todesurteil begründen sollte, lediglich φθόνος, (ist) wohl der schwerste Vorwurf, den man gegen ein Gericht erheben kann!"[41] The point is made and underlined that the victim is innocent; the verdict has been decided beforehand (14:55), the judges collude, and no viable evidence is presented; the witnesses are suborned and contradict each other (vs. 56), and even the quotation that they attribute to him is inaccurate because although he spoke of the destruction of the Temple, he never said that he personally would be the one to destroy it.[42]

Peter is outside while all this is taking place, included in the cozy circle of the group around the primordial fire. Suddenly someone turns on him and begins the process of expelling him from the group by identifying him with the criminal. Now the figures of Jesus and Peter begin to converge, but as they do so they diverge dramatically at another level. Whereas Jesus was silent before his accusers and did not defend himself, Peter resists with three fierce denials that correspond to the three warnings in the garden of Gethsemane. Three times Jesus had found them asleep; three times Peter fulfills the prophecy of 14:30–31 by denying Jesus. All takes place as in a nightmare; one of those around the fire turns on him, and his denial causes him to leave that circle of primordial human fellowship; in the courtyard a maid challenges him, and he denies Jesus a second time; later all the bystanders, the whole group, turn questioningly on him, ganging up to drive him out. Con-

---

39. Lührmann, *NTS* 27 (1981) 465.
40. Ibid., p. 461.
41. Ibid.
42. Ibid., p. 459.

fronted by the group, he resorts to oaths and anathemas in an attempt to change the mob into a conjuration, a group united in an oath. All to no avail; and then the cock crows and Peter wakes from his trance; at last it dawns on him! "And he fell down and wept."

Jesus and Barabbas on Trial—15:1–15

As Peter was the counterpart to Jesus in the action before the high priest, so Barabbas is the counterpart in the action before Pilate. They are not doubles but opposites, showing how distinctions are made by the sacrificial mechanism. Once again the authorities are named, in a slightly different order, the chief priests, the elders, the scribes, and the whole Sanhedrin. They bind Jesus, lead him away, and hand him over to Pilate. With the advent of Pilate the roll call of the powers of this world is complete.

The counterposition of Jesus and Barabbas makes the point of the contrast between the two orders so vivid that it is almost a caricature. Barabbas is an insurrectionist and a murderer, a creature and a leader of the mob. We are reminded of the situation of the war that we saw clearly in ch. 13. We are told that Pilate sees the envy (φθόνος) of the priests. Envy is the essence of mimetic desire and rivalry; it reveals the extrinsic nature of values with especial clarity in that it is the urge not so much to have the object oneself as to deprive the other of it; the possession of the object is not the important thing, the rivalry with the other is. The condemnation of Jesus arises only indirectly out of the Sanhedrin's envy in that they do not desire something Jesus has, but rather that their own inner-group rivalry can only be contained by the unanimous condemnation of the victim. Jesus attracts their envy to himself and so enables them to survive as a group. He has done this all along, as the roll of all the leaders shows; leaders who otherwise would have been in competition with one another act in concert for a change. The solidarity between the collaborationist Sanhedrin an the insurrectionist Barabbas trumpets the truth of the uniformity of violence across political divisions.

The priests incite the mob to choose Barabbas. The text now rubs our noses in the fact that we prefer the murderer to the man of peace, the sacrificial order to the order of nonviolence. Pilate tries to withstand the demands of the mob, knowing that Jesus is innocent; but truth is the first casualty of violence. He cannot, because his power, like that of the priests, arises out of the mob and must respect its source. And so he sacrifices Jesus to the mob. The text is quite explicit on this; it reads ὁ δὲ Πιλᾶτος βουλόμενος τῷ ὄχλῳ τὸ ἱκανὸν ποιῆσαι . . . The phrase ἱκανον ποιῆσαι is the Latinism *satisfacere alicui*;[43] "to satisfy the mob" means to propitiate it by throwing it a victim.

---

43. W. Bauer, *A Greek-English Lexicon* (Chicago, 1979) *ad loc.*

The very language of the text, therefore, shows that it understands the mechanism that is at work between Pilate and the mob.

Far from Pilate being exonerated, he is shown to be in exactly the same boat as the Jewish authorities, only somewhat weaker than they are because he is unable to manipulate the crowd. His one attempt to do so, by offering to release a prisoner on the occasion of the feast, fails because the Sanhedrin owns this particular crowd. So Pilate is coerced by the mob, like every politician before or since, and has to give it the victim it demands. There is no attempt to exonerate Pilate, only a demonstration of the fact that those who control the mob control the source of power; Pilate's weakness reflects only this relative disadvantage, that it is not his mob. If this were an attempt on the part of the text to ingratiate itself with the Roman state, it would be ludicrous; it shows political opportunism instead of due process of law. To be sure it condemns the Jewish authorities, but not because they are Jews but because they are, like Pilate, the agents of violence. The text sees no essential difference between Pilate and the Jews at the level of the mechanism.

Jesus Mocked, Crucified, and Killed—15:16–47

The soldiers' treatment of Jesus shows this essential solidarity of the Romans and the Jews in violence, for their mockery parallels the Sanhedrin's (14:65). The question that Pilate asked him, whether he was "king of the Jews," seems to have been answered in the ironic affirmative by his adversaries, for he is mocked as such by the soldiers and on the cross. The irony of the title for the reader is that we know him to be the king of a new order. A further irony is that the only one truly to reject the mechanism of violence is ranked with two men of expressed violence, hanged with two λῃσταί. He rejects the Davidic interpretation of the messiah conclusively by failing to come down from the cross in response to the challenge "Let the messiah the king of Israel come down from the cross, so that we might see and believe" (vs. 32). The chief priests and the bandits join in this taunt; they demand the only kind of proof they can understand, an act of violent self-affirmation; the priests want a miracle and the λῃσταί want the king of Israel to leap down from the Roman cross and lead the armed resistance. Jesus is not the Davidic messiah of violence but the Son of God (vs. 39)[44] and the suffering servant (compare Isa 53:9, 12).

As if in response to the taunt, Jesus speaks the words of the sufferer in Ps 22:1. The role of the Old Testament scriptures in the composition of the passion narrative is well known. Both Psalm 22 and Isaiah 53 tell of a righteous sufferer who is at present humiliated but in the future to be vindicated

---

44. Lührmann, NTS 27 (1981) 462–63, points out that the background of the title in Mark is not the Davidic tradition of 2Sam 7:14 or Ps 2:7, but rather the tradition that goes back to the servant songs of 2 Isaiah and is mediated through sources like WisSol 2:12–20 and 5:1ff.

by God. The cry of dereliction is, therefore, not to be interpreted psychologically but as an expression of the rejection of the way of violent self-assertion in favor of a trust in God to vindicate him in the future. This is of a part with the instruction in ch. 13 not to take part in the apocalyptic hopes associated with the war, but to wait patiently for the future vindication of Jesus as the Son of Man.

At the moment of his death the veil of the holy of holies is torn and the most sacred place exposed (vs. 38). There has been much discussion of the significance of the rending of the veil in the gospels.[45] The mention of it here seems to interrupt the flow of the narrative from vs. 37 to 39; it has the same "suddenness" that we have noted in the juxtaposition of christological and Temple sayings, and it is, indeed, another example of the juxtaposition of those two interests. For the verse preceding it is the culmination of the identification of Jesus as the suffering servant, and the verse following it a culmination of the revelation and recognition of Jesus as Son of God. These two vital interests in Mark's gospel therefore receive a symbolic summary presentation in the rending of the Temple veil. The incident is in the nature of a summary symbol of the significance of the work of Christ.

It is not necessary in the light of all that Mark has told us of the displacement of the sacrificial system to search for any more *recherché* significance of the torn veil; neither is it necessary to ascertain whether the curtain is the one before the holy of holies or the penultimate one before the vestibule of the altar of the incense, the shewbread, and the Menorah.[46] The message is in any case clear; the holy of holies has been exposed to public view, its mystery has been removed; the system has been demystified and so deprived of the efficacy that depended on its operating behind a veil. We all now know what it sought to hide, the mechanism behind the system, the foundation of the present order in the murder of innocent victims. That much the cross of Jesus shows us; and when the veil of sacred violence is lifted we see that there is nothing there, no blood-sucking idol, no devouring mouth that craves "the fruit of my body for the sin of my soul" (Micah 6:7b)! It was all a bad dream, and with the crowing of the cock we awake to the bitter truth of our own denial and complicity. Is it any wonder that we "fall down and weep" (14:72)?

---

45. See D. D. Sylva, "The Temple Curtain and Jesus' Death in the Gospel of Luke," *JBL* 105 (1986) 239–50; see esp. p. 241, n. 7, where he lists representative scholars who have argued respectively for its significance as a sign that Jesus' death has opened up a way to God for humanity, a sign of the destruction of the Temple and a sign of the abrogation of the Temple cultus. See also H. L. Chronis, "The Torn Veil: Cultus and Christology in Mark 15:37–39," *JBL* 101 (1982) 97–114. Chronis makes the unlikely suggestion that the temple is a symbol for the person of Jesus throughout Mark, so that the temple to be destroyed and rebuilt is his body, and the torn veil is the veil of his flesh that tears to reveal the face of God.

46. Juel, *Messiah and Temple*, pp. 140–42.

"He goes before you . . ."—15:42–16:8

We saw that in the previous section the pericopes on the resurrection and the great commandment present a hint of the nature of the new order. It is to be the work of God and it is to be characterized by love. Now the whole gospel culminates with the resurrection; but it is not so much a presence as an absence. The announcement is not "Here he is!" but rather "He is not here!" (vs. 6). What the resurrection symbolizes is not part of the present order, but something that belongs to the future. In the proclamation of his absence from the grave, the resurrection announcement symbolizes hope for new order and a good future.

The message is directed specifically to Peter, that is, to us who have wakened from our dream of violence and need reassurance of forgiveness for our former denial. "He goes before you into Galilee" means that Jesus leads us away from Jerusalem, the place of sacrifice, to Galilee, the place of peaceful fellowship with himself. The "theological geography" of Mark has been recognized ever since Lohmeyer and confirmed by subsequent studies in redaction criticism.[47] So the promise of a new nonsacrificial order is expressed in the phrase, "He goes before you . . ."

It would be comforting if these were the last words of the gospel, but they are not. The actual last words are more somber and portentous: ἐφοβοῦντο γάρ . . . "for they were afraid." Afraid of what? We can only conjecture. Afraid perhaps of leaving the shelter of the founding mechanism, afraid of disorder and chaos. Can it be that the gospel ends on the note of the Grand Inquisitor? If so, it is not yet fully *Gospel*, but only on the way from myth to *Gospel*, somewhere in the time between fear and hope, bondage and freedom. The fact that it was later read as a sacrificial text to justify the persecution of the Jews shows that, to some extent, it is "in between"; but it shows much more the status of those later readers, in thrall to the founding mechanism. Perhaps the best construction one might place on this final note of fear is to see it as an expression of realism at the prospect of life in the old sacrificial order without sacred defenses, and the rueful realization that such a life is not yet possible. Nevertheless, our eyes have been opened, we have once been awake, and so forevermore, when we lapse back into sleep our dream, like the dream of Yeats's Sphinx, will be "vexed to nightmare by a rocking cradle."[48]

---

47. Kelber, *Kingdom*, bases his study on the opposition between Jerusalem and Galilee, and W. Marxsen, *Mark the Evangelist: Studies in the Redaction History of the Gospel* (Nashville, 1969), includes a study of "The Geographical Outline," pp. 54–111. See E. Lohmeyer, *Galiläa und Jerusalem* (Göttingen, 1936) and *Lord of the Temple* (Richmond, Va., 1962).

48. W. B. Yeats, "The Second Coming" (1920).

THE JEWISH SOURCES OF MATTHEW'S MESSIANISM

To my former colleague Louis H. Martyn, on his retirement, in admiration and gratitude.

The term "messianism" in the title of this chapter needs careful definition since it can easily be confused with "christology." Is Matthew's "messianism" a christology? Traditionally in Christian theology, the term "christology," in its strict sense, designates the doctrine about the way in which God became man "in Christ"—that is, the mode or, if one may so crudely put it, the mechanics of the Incarnation in Christ. Recently, L. J. Kreitzer has urged that the Messiah was regarded as a divine or divinely begotten being in some passages in Jewish sources.[1] However, most of the evidence of those sources points unambiguously to the Messiah as purely human. Is the same true of Matthew's understanding of Jesus?

Certain verses have been taken to indicate that God became man in Jesus, his Son, in the story of the virgin birth in Mt 1:18–25. But that story begins with τοῦ δὲ Χριστοῦ ἡ γένεσις οὕτως ἦν, not with τοῦ δὲ υἱοῦ τοῦ θεοῦ ἡ γένεσις οὕτως ἦν, and the role of the Son of God christology in the strict sense, so emphasized by Kingsbury[2] in his influential and important studies, is not foremost in the birth narratives as a whole. This should warn against overemphasizing its significance. Similarly, to read any later trinitarian significance into "the spirit" in Matthew is unjustifiable. In the virgin birth narrative, the "spirit," a term neuter in Greek and feminine in Hebrew, is best understood as the invasive power of God; there is no suggestion of the spirit as the second person of a trinity. But what of vs. 23 in Matthew 1: ἰδοὺ ἡ παρθένος ἐν γαστρὶ ἕξει καὶ τέξεται υἱόν, καὶ καλέσουσιν τὸ ὄνομα

---

1. L. J. Kreitzer, "Theocentricity and Christocentricity in Paul's Eschatological Thought," Dissertation, London University, June 1985. See now *JBL* 108, 3, pp. 534–36.

2. See J. Kingsbury, *Matthew: Structure, Christology, Kingdom* (London, Philadelphia, 1975), p. 75, and *Jesus Christ in Matthew, Mark and Luke*, pp. 64–73.

αὐτοῦ Ἐμμανουήλ, ὅ ἐστιν μεθερμηνευόμενον, μεθ' ἡμῶν ὁ θεός? There
are those who have taken Matthew to equate Jesus with God in this verse.
(cf. Jn 1:1–5; 20:28). This view appears as early as Irenaeus (*AdvHaer* 3.21.4:
"carefully, then, has the Holy Ghost pointed out, by what has been said, His
birth from a virgin, and His essence, that He is God [for the name Emman-
uel indicates this].") In recent scholarship, many have placed 1:23 in parallel
with 28:20. It is claimed that the words "Lo, I am with you" at the end of the
Gospel most naturally refer to God and recall the presence of God in Jesus
in 1:23. The argument is that μετά with the genitive usually means "in company with." But usually in Matthew, God is referred to as being "in heaven."
To be "with men" would be more appropriate to the Son than to God, the
Heavenly Father: the Son has here become God with us.[3]

But all these considerations (and they are not very cogent) do not out-
weigh others. Apart from 1:23, even by implication there, Matthew never
refers to Jesus as God, as is the case with most of the New Testament. If
Matthew had intended to identify Jesus with God, we should have found in
1:23 Ἐμμανουήλ . . . ὁ θεός μεθ' ἡμῶν rather than μεθ' ἡμῶν ὁ θεός. Here
the order of words makes ὁ θεός adverbial. The passage is not a statement of
the Incarnation—that is, it is not strictly christological—although in a general sense it does indicate that for Matthew in Jesus' coming God's spirit has
become uniquely present among men. The trinitarian formula in the canonical text in 28:19 poses such textual difficulties that it cannot be taken to
invalidate the rejection of a strictly christological aspect in the messianism of
Matthew. The most that could be claimed is that the messianism of Matthew
offers an inchoate christology, its raw materials as it were. The use of the
term "Lord," important and possibly primary as it is for Jesus in Matthew,
does not invalidate our position.[4]

We can now turn to the origins of the teaching about Jesus, the Messiah,
in Matthew. But before we do so, three other preliminary notes are necessary. First we take Matthew to have been a Jew who had accepted the Christian belief that Jesus was the Messiah. Everything points to his having been
a sophisticated sage, possibly a trained Pharisee, rooted in Judaism, although familiar with the Hellenistic mentality and language. Hellenism and
Judaism had deeply intermingled in Matthew's day, but it is to the Jewish
sources that we most naturally turn for the signs of his thought. "Messianic"
ideas in the form of an expectation of a future deliverer were not peculiar to
Judaism, but they were certainly prominent in the first-century Jewish
world. Hellenistic and other parallels, though interesting, are peripheral to
our purpose: they cannot be allowed to govern our exegesis.

---

3. See W. D. Davies and D. C. Allison, *A Critical and Exegetical Commentary on the Gospel
According to Saint Matthew* (ICC; Edinburgh, 1988), vol. 1, p. 217. The reader is referred for
exegetical data and secondary literature pertinent to this chapter to this work.
   4. For details, see Kingsbury, *Matthew: Structure*, pp. 103–13. Pertinent texts include Nah
1:1; Tob 1:1; TJob 1:1; ApAb, title; 4Ezra 1:1–3; Sepher Ha-Razim, preface.

A second preliminary is this. The title of this chapter speaks of origins in the plural. We are not seeking a single origin. If we were, our task would be concentrated on the historical Jesus of Nazareth. The ultimate origin of Matthew's messianism is the historical Jesus and the influence he had on those who first believed. He is the *fons et origo* of Matthew's messianism; in this sense, there is one origin to it, whether Jesus himself claimed to be the Messiah or not. The elusiveness of that one origin, however, we need not emphasize.

Thirdly, owing to limitations of space we can here only deal with broad central aspects of our theme: we cannot follow every twist and turn in the origins of Matthew's messianism. Because of this we shall concentrate on the beginnings of Matthew's Gospel, the prologue. Fortunately much that is most pertinent in the rest of the Gospel is there foreshadowed. To examine the prologue will provide a guide to most, though, as we shall see, not all, of Matthew's emphases; and because the prologue, that is chapters 1 and 2, is replete with quotations and allusions to the origins of those emphases as well.

What then are the broad outlines of Matthew's messianism and what are their origins?

THE NEW CREATION

We begin where Matthew began. His messianism is from the beginning cosmic in scope: the coming of Jesus is comparable with the creation of the universe. The evidence is clear in the first verse. Scholars have treated Mt 1:1, βίβλος γενέσεως Ἰησοῦ Χριστοῦ υἱοῦ Δαυὶδ υἱοῦ Ἀβραάμ, as introducing either the genealogy in 1:2–17, or the genealogy and the virgin birth in 1:2–25, or 1:2–2:23 down to the coming of Jesus to Nazareth. Or, again, the whole section from 1:2 to 4:16, which ends with the settling of Jesus in Capernaum before he began his ministry. But as early as Jerome, the first verse was understood to refer to the entire Gospel: it is a title for the whole of the Gospel of Matthew. The word γένεσις was understood to mean either "genesis" or "history." This seems to us to be the intent of Matthew in this first verse; it is twofold at least. In the first place, he quite deliberately begins his Gospel with the words βίβλος γενέσεως to suggest a parallel with the first creation described in Genesis 1 and 2, a parallel with the creation of the Universe and Adam and Eve, on the one hand, and the new creation brought by Jesus, the Messiah, on the other. In using the term βίβλος, which is anarthrous, he is doubtless following prophetic, didactic, and apocalyptic conventions: the evidence is abundant.[5] But there is more to it than this. Matthew intends his βίβλος γενέσεως to recall the first book of the

5. See Davies and Allison, *Matthew*, pp. 151–52.

Tanak. (Compare the function of the title "Little Genesis" in many MSS of Jubilees.) The title "Genesis" had already been given to the first book of the Tanak in the earlier MSS of the LXX and other sources: but when I wrote *The Setting of the Sermon of the Mount* in 1963, I had not proved that it was so used when Matthew wrote. However, Dale C. Allison has referred me to passages in which Philo uses "Genesis" for the first book of the Tanak (viz. *Post* 127, *Abr* 1, *Aet* 19). The word "Genesis" in Mt 1:1 would, we conclude, naturally evoke that book. Jesus is the initiator of a new creation parallel with the first: the genitive in 1:1 is subjective.[6] We might speculate further. Like the Hebrew text at Gen 1:1, so Mt 1:1 begins with the letter *beth* or *beta*. Later sages made much of the initial *beth* in בראשית of Gen 1:1. Some interpreted it as indicating "blessing" (ברכה), some (because *beth* is the numerical two) as connoting two worlds of space and time. One interpretation claimed that the first letter was *beth* because *beth* (ב) is not circular and, therefore, closed, but open-ended: the creation is open-ended and looks to the future. (See GenRab. 1:10 on Gen 1:1.) Did such speculation, which is not dateable but is apparently early, influence Matthew to begin his Gospel with *beta?* Such speculation, fantastic to us, would be congenial to Matthew.[7]

But even if the significance assigned to the initial *beta* is too speculative, there is much in Matthew besides the initial words to suggest a new creation. It has been claimed with some degree of probability that the role of the Holy Spirit in the virgin birth in 1:18 recalls the activity of the Spirit in Genesis 1 at the creation; Matthew takes up from Q reference to the Spirit of God descending as a dove on Jesus at his baptism in Jordan in 3:16. There have been differing interpretations of the dove, but the most probable is that which points to the new creation motif. The calming of the raging of the Sea in 8:23–27 recalls passages in the Old Testament (Job 38:8–11; Pss 89:9, etc.) indicating God's cosmic control. The discussion of divorce in 19:3–9 directs Matthew's hearers to Genesis 1 and 2. As the synoptic parallels to some of the passages referred to indicate, Matthew was not alone in the New Testament in thinking in this way. There were Jewish-Christians before him who had thought so. The relationship between Matthew and the Pauline epistles is unresolved, but certainly Paul had understood the Christian dispensation in terms of a new creation and Jesus in terms of the Last Adam; it was he who may have been the first to develop the interpretation of Jesus as the Last Adam. One of the direct sources of Matthew, Mark probably implies the new

6. W. D. Davies, *The Setting of the Sermon on the Mount* (Cambridge, 1963), pp. 67–72.

7. The speculations are introduced by R. Jonah in R. Levi's name; they were probably widespread. Hengel informed me orally that he found these natural for Matthew. On the notion of "newness" in early Christianity, see the rewarding discussion by G. Vahanian—"'Ni Juif, Ni Grec . . .': "L'Utopisme Chrétien comme prélude à La Modernité" in *Embraismo, Ellenismo, Christianesimo* (*Archivio Di Filosofia* 53.2–3 [Rome, 1985] 443–68).

creation in its use of ἀρχὴ τοῦ εὐαγγελίου in its very first verse and in the evocation of Adam in its account of the temptation. The prologue of the Fourth Gospel is no stranger to the notion of a new creation. Jewish and other Christians before and after Matthew were familiar with it (Epistle of Barnabas 6). Its ultimate source is clear: Judaism.

Gunkel long ago established the parallelism between the cosmic beginnings in Genesis and the anticipated messianic beginnings: as he put it, *Urzeit* parallels *Endzeit*. This is given prominence in Matthew from the very first words of his Gospel. The interpretation of Jesus as the Messiah who inaugurates a new creation is fundamental for him. He embraced the conviction explicitly expressed in 4Ezra 7:30, but with a long history before his day, that with the coming of the Messiah the world would once again be as it was in the beginning." As did sages, he connected the beginning, the *rēʾšît* of Gen 1:1, with the Messiah and accepted the principle τὰ ἔσχατα ὡς τὰ πρῶτα, that messianism has a cosmic dimension. Jesus sets in motion a γένεσις, a new creation. I emphasized that the title of this chapter concerns origins, but there is a caveat to be uttered: there *is* one origin—in the inaugurator of the new creation, Jesus.

A scientific analogy may help here. Modern physicists and astronomers have sought to find a common center from which the totality not only of this universe but of all universes is to be derived. Through intricate mathematical calculations they have been able to locate this center in space and time. They concluded that there was a kind of ball of fire which originally exploded. There was a "Big Bang," an explosion, at or of this central core from which all else has evolved. For Matthew, we may argue, Jesus as Messiah was comparable with this "Big Bang" in that he explosively inaugurated a new creation.[8] But the matter is not so simple. According to the scientists, we cannot go behind the "Big Bang" to any space or any time. Unimaginable as this is to common sense, before the "Big Bang" there was no space and there was no time: these are concepts relative only to the "Big Bang." Space and time only came into being in relation to each other with or as a result of the "Big Bang," which has no origin or origins. To speak of any purpose or will of God behind the "Big Bang" is inadmissible. Oddly enough, some of the rabbinic sages *mutatis mutandis* said the same of the beginning of Gen 1:1. "Just as the *beth* is closed at the sides but open in front, so you are not permitted to investigate what is above and what is below, what is before and what is behind" (Genesis Rabbah on 1:1). This is explained in b. Ḥag 11a as referring either to space or time, or both.

---

8. The use of such scientific analogy as suggested is often rejected and the author is fully aware of its dangers. It is used here with apologies and acknowledgments to Sir Brian Pippard. A reading of G. Steiner's "Black Holes," *Bulletin of the American Academy of Arts and Sciences* 41 (1987) 12–38, confirms its appropriateness.

THE SON OF DAVID

But for Matthew's understanding of Jesus as the inaugurator of the new creation, things are different. Certainly he is the Big Bang, so to put it. But he emerged at a particular time and space and he has an origin and origins. Much as Matthew by implication emphasized the newness of the Messiah, Jesus is no novelty for him, and the centrality of Jesus' initiatory power connects him with a past in time and space. We can and must go behind him to the history of his people in time and to the land of Israel in space. The very term "Messiah" is incomprehensible without that people and their understanding of their own existence and of the world's.

Again we turn to the title of the Gospel. The term βίβλος γενέσεως not only refers to the creation in Gen 1:1. As elsewhere in Matthew, one word or group of words can have more than one connotation and function. So here βίβλος γενέσεως refers not only back to Gen 1:1 but also forward to the genealogy of Jesus. The term γένεσις in 1:18 refers to the birth of Jesus, and it can also refer to the history or life of Jesus. βίβλος γενέσεως recalls the first creation and past history and simultaneously points forward to the emerging new creation and new history, and Matthew finds in the first creation and in the past history of God's people, Israel, the type or pattern of events in the life of Jesus and his people, the Church.

Let us first look at the genealogy particularly, but also at the whole of 1 and 2. Matthew inherited the belief endemic to Judaism that the creation embodied a divine intention and that God is the Lord of history. God is divinely sovereign over all things. History is in the hands of God and is the sphere of his purposeful activity. Looking for redemption (to use Luke's prologue [2:38]) rose out of this belief. Messianism for Matthew is the corollary of the Jewish certainty about God—that He was responsible for creation and committed to history and, if so, committed not only in the past but in the future—hence the messianic hope. In fact, for Matthew history had a messianic pattern. Each stage of Jewish history suggested the Messiah to him. The pattern leading to Jesus, the Messiah, is threefold. Each stage is composed of fourteen generations. From Abraham to David the king in 1:2–6; from David to the deportation to Babylon and the Exile (7–11); from the Exile to Jesus—in each of these divisions there were fourteen generations: this is expressly stated by Matthew in 1:17. According to the tradition of gematria, well established in first-century Judaism, fourteen, as a number, spells the name of David. By explicitly pointing to "fourteen" in 1:17, Matthew indicates that history is messianic in form and leads to Jesus as the Messiah. Objections raised to the use of gematria in the genealogy are not cogent, as I have argued elsewhere.[9] There is precedence for the use of gematria in 1:1–7 in Gen 46:8–27, where gematria occurs in a genealogy.

---

9. See Davies and Allison, *Matthew*, pp. 163–65.

Knowing that the Old Testament listed fourteen names from Abraham to David, Matthew probably set himself to look for fourteens and constructed his own Davidic messianic genealogy on this pattern. In his text the name David is named immediately before the genealogy, is placed in the four-teenth spot in the genealogy itself and twice at its conclusion. At the four-teenth spot David is uniquely honored with the title "King": τὸν βασιλέα. The very first name after Ἰησοῦ χριστοῦ in 1:1 is David.

Historically the term Son of David as a standard messianic title is attested in the Rabbis in b. Sanh 97a–98a and may already be present in the Psalms of Solomon, 17:21–35, cf. 18:5–9, in the first century B.C.E. It developed out of Old Testament passages such as Isa 11:10 (the root of Jesus), Jer 23:5, 33:15. By the first century it had become a major, if not dominant, Jewish expectation. Possibly it was the shortcomings of the monarchy historically, and especially of the non-Davidic Hasmonaeans, that furthered the process which led to this. The messianic king "who was to come" was conceived as a Son of David who would fulfill the promises of 2Sam 7:16, where the prophet Nathan is commanded by God to tell David: "Your family shall be established and your kingdom shall stand for all time in my sight, and your throne shall be established for ever" (2Sam 7:16). Already, before Matthew wrote, Chris-tian circles recognized the Davidic connections of Jesus (Rom 1:3–4; cf. Acts 2:29–36, 13:22–23; 2Tim 2:8; Rev 5:5, 22:16). But of all New Testament writ-ers it is Matthew who most emphasizes that Jesus is of Davidic ancestry. "Son of David" occurs nine times in Matthew, as against three times in Mark; it never occurs in Luke. It was apparently Matthew's most characteristic des-ignation for the earthly Jesus, the Messiah. In the prologue, which refers to Bethlehem, the city of David (2:1, 6, 8, 16), there is a clear intent to set forth Jesus as qualifying through his father Joseph (1:16) as the royal Messiah of the Davidic line. It agrees with this that in the genealogy in 1:2–17, unlike Luke in 3:31, Matthew traces the descent of Jesus through Solomon, a Son of David, who later became famous as a mighty healer, exorcist, magician (Josephus, *Ant* 8:45–49). It is significant that Matthew connects Jesus as Son of David precisely with healings and exorcisms (9:27; 12:23; 15:22; 20:30, 31).

So far we have noted two aspects of Matthew's messianism—it affirms a new creation, and it traces a pattern in history which leads to the emergence of a Son of David as Messiah. In all this he draws upon the Tanak and tradi-tions within Judaism. But one thing already makes it clear that he draws upon both selectively. In view of the reference to Genesis, one would expect a parallel to be indicated between Jesus and Adam in the genealogy, as was the case with Luke. One scholar has found Adam to be the key to the chais-mus he finds in 1:1–16.[10] But although Adam is probably in Matthew's mind,

---

10. See Davies and Allison, *Matthew*, p. 149.

as in Mark's, in the Temptation narrative the name is not found in Matthew's genealogy and does not appear even once in his Gospel. Paul was probably an innovator here, but Matthew, if he knew of Paul's thought, ignored it. His concentration is on the divine activity in so guiding history as to lead to Jesus as the Son of David. Matthew's thought smacks of "determinism." The note of purpose and its fulfillment is strong: history seems inevitably to have led to Jesus as Messiah. But it is a "determinism" that allows for human error and perversity. Individuals are always free to dispute and thwart the divine purpose, at least temporarily. As in the Joseph saga, man may mean evil and do it, and God may mean it for good (Gen 50:20), so in Matthew's genealogy there are sinners, but they subserve the divine purpose. Matthew is Pharisaic in his understanding of the paradox that everything is determined and free will given (*Aboth*), and for him the determination of history is messianically aimed: the emergence of Jesus, the Son of David, is its climax.

THE SON OF ABRAHAM

In all that we have said about the Son of David, it is clear that Matthew has drawn upon the kingship ideology of ancient Israel. This ideology was grounded on that of the Ancient Near East, and Mowinckel urged that this was the source of the messianic idea as it emerged in Jewish sources, the Tanak and the extracanonical literature. However, S. Talmon is right when, in his invaluable *King, Cult, and Calendar in Ancient Israel*, he writes that "in attempting to elucidate pivotal aspects of ancient Israel's conceptual universe, pride of place is given to the Hebrew Scriptures, in full agreement with Henri Frankfort's dictum: 'the borrowed features in Hebrew culture, and those which have foreign analogies, are least significant.'"[11] Notice that the Davidic messianic hope was essentially a hope of and for Israel: it was unmistakably ethnic. As 2 Samuel 7 makes clear, the choice of David to be king had been inextricably bound in the tradition to the choice of Israel to be God's people. In 2Sam 7:23 David asks, "And thy people Israel to whom can they be compared? Is there any other nation on earth whom thou, O God, hast set out to redeem from slavery to be thy people? Any other for whom thou hast done great and terrible things to win fame for thyself?" In the Hebrew tradition on which Matthew drew, messiahship had grown out of a particular people's history. It could be and often was read exclusively in terms of that people's history—it involved Israel's peoplehood and territory and history. The source and condition of the messianic yearning which Matthew had indicated were the words "I will be their God and they will be my people." There was and is in the Jewish messianic hope what K. Cragg has called the

---

11. S. Talmon, *King, Cult, and Calendar in Ancient Israel: Collected Essays* (Jerusalem, 1986), p. 7.

perspective of an "inherent privacy": it was the hope of God's own chosen.[12] With this "privacy" or, to use the more usual term, "exclusiveness," Matthew had to come to terms. He does so in the very first verse by asserting that Jesus is not only the son of David, but the son of Abraham also. Here the meaning of "son of Abraham" is probably dual: first, Jesus is the son of David and, through him, he is personally and biologically the son of Abraham; he is the son of Abraham, as are all Jews whose father is Abraham. The term "son of Abraham" is not to be taken automatically as "messianic." In Mt 1:1 it certainly means that Jesus is one of Jewish blood or one worthy of the father Abraham. But second it may also be that "son of Abraham" is here a messianic title or, at least, is messianic in intent. Outside Matthew, in Luke (1:30–33, 55, 69–73; Acts 3:25, 13:23) the promises concerning the seed of David and the seed of Abraham are brought together. Paul takes Jesus to be of the seed of Abraham (Gal 3:16). And in the Tanak, Jer 33:21–22, and later in the targum on Ps 89:4, Gen 17:7, the promise to Abraham and his seed is associated with 2Sam 7:12, the promise to David and his seed. The first verse of Matthew then, we suggest, means not only that Jesus is Messiah as son of David—indicating the fulfillment of the strictly private Jewish hope, but also as son of Abraham. What does this signify?

The figure of Abraham in Jewish tradition needs scrutiny. He is certainly, like David, of the highest significance for the Jewish people as such. It was with him that God had made a covenant with Israel (Gen 12 and 15); in the Testament of Jacob 7:22 he is the "father of fathers"; descent from him constituted the ground for membership in the Jewish people (Judg 12:24, 13:3; 4Ezra 3:13–15). Thus as son of Abraham, Jesus is in Mt 1:1 an Israelite indeed, a true member of the people of Israel. Matthew makes him bring to its culmination the history which began with Abraham: the genealogy underlines his Jewishness. But there is another side to Abraham and his significance. He had a particular relevance to those who were not Jews by birth, that is, to those not within the covenant made between God and Israel through him. God had called Abraham before God had established the covenant with him—before there were Jews, so to put it. Another way of stating this is to claim that by birth Abraham was a Gentile, and the covenant that God had initiated through him was to be a blessing not only to Jews but to all nations (Gen 12:3, 18:18). Abraham came to be portrayed as the father of all nations (Gen 17:5, 1Mac 12:19–21). The promise to Abraham could therefore be exploited to further the Jewish mission. One Tannaitic sage saw in him the first proselyte (b. Ḥag. 3a). Paul therefore could naturally use the figure of Abraham as the true father of all who have faith, both Jews and

---

12. See K. Cragg, *The Christ and the Faiths* (Philadelphia, 1986), p. 99; from which I have in this article borrowed some phrases and to which I am much indebted. But on particularism and universalism, see also S. Talmon, *King, Cult, and Calendar in Ancient Israel*, pp. 142–43.

Gentiles (Rom 4:1–25; Gal 3:6–29). Likewise Matthew, in 8:11–12, and possibly in 3:9 and 1:1, appeals to an Abrahamic strain in Judaism itself to serve his Gentile interests. Franz Rosenzweig defined Judaism as follows: "[It is a life which one possesses by birth in] the eternal self-preservation of procreative blood . . . through shutting the pure spring of blood off from foreign admixture . . . Descendant and ancestor are the live incarnation of the eternal people, both of them for each other. . . . We experience our Judaism with immediacy in elders and children." [13] This has an ancient ring. We suggest that while Matthew in 1:1 includes Jesus, as Messiah, among the people of Israel by calling him a son of David and a son of Abraham, at the same time by calling him a son of Abraham he intends to redefine that people to include Gentiles. And just as the motif of the new creation reemerged in the prologue in the story of the virgin birth (1:18ff.), and the significance of the son of David is pointed to 1:2–17, so too the evocation of the Gentiles in the term son of Abraham in 1:1 finds confirmation in the disconcerting introduction into the genealogy itself of women of foreign origin—Tamar, a Canaanite or an Aramaean; Rahab, a Canaanite; Ruth, a Moabitess; and Bathsheba, a Hittite; and also in the story of the Magi. In thus connecting Jesus, son of David, the king of the Jews, with the Gentile Abraham, Matthew was not innovating. In some Jewish sources Abraham was regarded as a king, and the advent of the Messiah was to witness the incoming of the Gentiles. [14] There were elements in Jewish apocalyptic, as well as in the Old Testament, of universalism, as well as of exclusivity or privacy, especially the prophecies of Deutero-Isaiah, which provided a hope for the final redemption of Gentiles. Doubtless Matthew was aware of these, and doubtless they were being neglected in the renewed apocalypticism after 70 C.E. And so he called Jesus, the son of Abraham, that is, one who was relevant to the crisis in Jewish-Gentile relations which three centuries of the exposure of Jews to Hellenism had produced, the Savior of the world, "not only of Israel." Was he not opposing the narrow exclusiveness of the nationalism of his day, alive even after the collapse of Jerusalem, in calling Jesus the Son of Abraham?

THE GREATER MOSES

We now go beyond the title and the genealogy in the prologue to another figure or rather presence which the birth narratives in chapters 1 and 2 evoke quite unmistakably, though not explicitly, for the interpretation of Jesus: that of Moses. In his genealogy Matthew does not mention Moses at all among the ancestors of Jesus. The reason is simple. In that part of the ge-

---

13. Cited by Cragg, *The Christ and the Faiths*, p. 125 from *The Star of Redemption* (New York, 1970); ET: pp. 341, 346.

14. For the evidence see W. D. Davies, *Jewish and Pauline Studies* (Philadelphia, 1984), p. 318, nn. 71, 78.

nealogy which covers the period up to the exile, Matthew largely follows the genealogy provided for him in 1 Chronicles. Up to 1:13 he copies an Old Testament genealogy. All the names in 1:13–15 occur in the LXX. But after this for the five hundred years between Zerubbabel and Joseph, the father of Jesus, he has only nine names. The names in 1:2–6 occur in 1Chr 1:28, 34 and 2:1–15 (cf. Ruth 4:18–22). The name Moses is not in these passages, and Matthew, while innovative in the formulation or pattern of his genealogy, does not choose to depart from the substance of the Scriptures where he is drawing upon them and so omits Moses or rather does not insert his name. However, the influence of the figure of Moses in Matthew's interpretation of Jesus as Messiah has long been recognized, although in different degrees. The evidence is clear. Here I note the bare bones.

1. The infancy narratives recall the circumstances at the birth of Moses, especially as recorded in Josephus, and the *Liber Antiquitatum Biblicarum.* I note only the peril at the birth of Jesus and Moses, the exile of both into Egypt, the flight at night.[15]

2. The events in chapters 3–4, immediately following the birth narratives, recall the story of the Exodus from Egypt. The baptism of Jesus at Jordan is parallel to the passing of Israel through the Red Sea; the sojourn for forty days in the desert to fast and to be tested is comparable with the forty years of Israel's wandering in the wilderness where she was tempted. As Israel was tempted by the worship of the golden calf, so Jesus was tempted to idolatry. The temptations of Jesus are a reliving of the temptations of Israel and are understood by Matthew in the light of Deut 8:2–3.

3. Following on chapters 3–4 comes the sermon on the mount. Probably most scholars have seen here a delineation of Jesus as a New Moses giving his new Torah from a new Sinai. For many reasons, not the least of which was the desire not to read into Matthew what was congenial, I long resisted this direct parallel. In a recent study, T. L. Donaldson[16] has dismissed the parallel with Mount Sinai in favor of a parallel with Mount Zion, which von Rad taught us to consider as the mount of the assembly of the nations at the end and of which Jeremias wrote so approvingly. After examining every mountain scene in Matthew, Donaldson comes to the conclusion that in Matthew, "The mountain motif is a device used by the evangelist to make the christological statement that Christ has replaced Zion as the center of God's dealings with his people: in him all the hopes associated with Zion have come to fruition and fulfillment."[17] This fits into the deterritorializing of Judaism in much Early Christianity, but it overlooks two things: the data to which I have earlier referred pointing to a well-marked Mosaic motif in Matthew and also

15. See Davies and Allison, *Matthew,* pp. 190–95.
16. T. L. Donaldson, *Jesus on the Mountain* (JSNT Supplement Series 8; Sheffield, 1985).
17. *Ibid.,* p. 200.

the very convincing data presented by D. C. Allison.[18] Allison deals with the nature of the introduction to the sermon on the mount and its conclusion. First, after Jesus has gone up to the mountain from which he gives his "sermon," he sits down on it. His "sitting" has suggested to commentators that Jesus here simply assumes the role of a teacher. Teachers and sages and rabbis and others sat when they taught. In 5:1–2 Jesus has his yĕšîbā (yĕšîbā means "sitting"; cf. Sir 51:23). But this does not go far enough. Mt 5:1–2 recalls Deut 9:9 (which may well have been alluded to in 4:2). Deut 9:9 reads: "When I went up to the mountain to receive the tablets of stone, the tablets of the covenant which the Lord made with you, I remained on the mountain forty days and forty nights. I neither ate bread nor drank water" (RSV). The Hebrew word, translated as "remained" in the RSV, is wā'ēšēb, from yāšab. To this verb the BDB gives three meanings—the second and third are "remain" and "dwell," but the first is "sit." The Jewish sages made much of this. In b. Meg 21a we read: "One verse says, 'And I sat in the mountain' [Deut. 9:9], and another says, 'And I stood in the mountain' [Deut. 10:10]. Rab says: He [Moses] stood when he learnt and sat while he went over [what he had learnt]. R. Ḥanina said: He was neither sitting nor standing but stooping. R. Joḥanan said: 'Sitting' here means only staying, as it says, 'And ye stayed in Kadesh many days' [Deut. 1:46]. Raba said: The easy things [he learnt] standing and the hard ones sitting?" The same text appears in b. Soṭa 49a. The verb wā'ēšēb was, then, ambiguous. The dating of the rabbinic texts is uncertain, but there were some sages who took Deut 9:9 to refer to Moses *sitting* on Mount Sinai, as Jesus did according to Matthew on the mount of the sermon. Matthew not only knew the Hebrew text of the Tanak but was probably acquainted with the Jewish exegetical traditions. This is further indicated by another simple datum. Jesus in 5:1–2 "goes up to the mountain." The Greek is simple: ἀνέβη εἰς τὸ ὄρος. This phrase occurs in the LXX twenty-four times, eighteen of these are in the Pentateuch and most refer to Moses. The phrase ἀναβαίνω + εἰς + ὄρος occurs in Deut 9:9.

But, further, the close of the sermon also recalls Moses on Sinai. In 8:1 we read: "when he had gone down from the mountain." This is a redactional verse. The Greek is καταβάντος δὲ αὐτοῦ 'απὸ τοῦ ὄρους. This is identical with the LXX(A) at Ex 34:29 of Moses' descent from Sinai (cf. Ex 19:14; 32:1, 15). The construction cited occurs only once in the LXX (LXX[B] has ἐκ— for ἀπό). The beginning and closing of the sermon linguistically recall Moses on Sinai. I have elsewhere, in *The Setting of the Sermon on the Mount*, 1963, pp. 25–108, indicated that the figure of Moses lurks behind the Matthean Jesus in other passages outside the sermon and the prologue: they cannot be

18. D. C. Allison, "Jesus and Moses (Mt 5:2–12)," *ExpT* 98 (1987) 203–5.

discussed here. We can safely assert that the figure of Moses had drawn into itself messianic significance for Matthew, and his Jesus and his messianism have inescapable Mosaic traits. Even 11:27–30, usually interpreted in terms of Sirach 51, almost certainly should be understood in terms of Moses: Allison has made this convincingly clear in an article in *JTS*.[19] He refers to Ex 33:12–13, where there is reciprocal knowledge between God and Moses which Jews took to be exclusive. This is implicit in the context (cf. 33:7–11, 17–23); Deut 34:10 makes it explicit. Paul reveals echoes of Ex 33:12–13 in 1Cor 13:12ff., and Allison finds the Exodus passage to be the background of Mt 11:27 as well. In addition, the reference to "rest" in 11:28 has its parallel in Ex 33:14; Ex 33:12–13 sheds light on the order of the mutual knowledge presented: "the order of the Father knows the Son and the Son knows the Father" in 11:27 may have been influenced by the fact that God's knowledge of Moses comes first in the Exodus passage. Finally the attribution of meekness to Jesus (11:29) has its parallel in Moses' characterization in Judaism. Num 12:3 reads: "Now the man Moses was very meek" (πραΰς σφόδρα) in the LXX. If Allison is followed—and his case is strong—there is no need to go outside the Exodus tradition to any Hellenistic Jewish syncretism, to the DSS, to the mystical philosophical literature of the East, or, as Professor Suggs has no forcefully urged, to the wisdom tradition, to account for 11:27–30.

Up to this point we have noted four strands in the messianism of Matthew. First, it is informed by the interpretation and realization in Jesus of a new creation. Second, it is Davidic: Matthew drew upon the kingship ideology of the Ancient Middle East, which Mowinckel long ago argued was the source of the messianic idea and which Professor S. Talmon has emphasized in his many studies. Third, there is the Mosaic strand: Jesus is the greater Moses who has wrought a new Exodus and brought a new Law. That is, Matthew's messianism drew upon the Exodus tradition, which Joseph Klausner emphasized as the determinative element in messianism, and which had also drawn to itself creation motifs. Then, fourth, there is the Abrahamic strand, which had struggled to break through the privacy of the Davidic and Exodic traditions to reach out to the larger world. But here I must issue a warning. While preparing this lecture I came across words by William Blake, who refused to go to school because "Education," he wrote, "produces straight lines but life is fuzzy." (I quote from memory.) The differentiation of these four strands—four straight lines, if you will—I have suggested in Matthew is almost certainly too clear. As in modern science, our messianic models tend toward a conceptual clarity which belies the "fuzziness" of all the data with which we have to deal. The four strands I noted are inseparable; they intermingle and

19. D. C. Allison, "Two Notes on a Key Text: Matthew 11:25–30," *JTS* 39 (1988) 472–80.

are evoked not in isolation but all together to produce a complexity of messianic presentation which belies the clarity and simplification of our neat divisions. Of one thing we can be certain. All the strands have their ground in the Tanak. I shall not attempt to prove this statement. The familiarity of Matthew with the Tanak I have indicated elsewhere. The formula quotations, which are from his hand, and not drawn from a distinct preexistent source, alone establish that he knew the Hebrew Bible as well as the LXX: there is other massive evidence for this, but, as has already appeared and will later appear, it was not the MT and the LXX in their isolation or textual nudity that he knew; he knew them as they were understood and interpreted in the Judaism of his day. The Apocrypha and Pseudepigrapha and other Jewish sources here claim their inescapable due.

This leads to at least two other dimensions of Matthew's messianism which are most important. I can only touch upon them here. Matthew applies the term "Messiah" to Jesus of Nazareth, who had endured the most ignominious and painful death, crucifixion—a form of death which Jews especially regarded as under the curse of God. Nor does Matthew regard the suffering of Jesus as confined to the cross. It was foreshadowed with trials at his birth, the political opposition of Herod the King, the calumny of his origin. The temptation narrative points to his encounter with unseen powers of evil and Satan; there was constant opposition from religious leaders. To use another scientific metaphor, Matthew has throughout fused the messianic with suffering. The crucified messiah seems a contradiction in terms: it constitutes a fusion, to use another scientfic term, the opposite of a fission. Was it a revolution?

It has been claimed that it was, that Judaism knew nothing of a suffering Messiah. I here refer to my discussion in *Paul and Rabbinic Judaism* and note in addition certain facts. Apart from the presence of the great enigma of Isaiah 53, so important for Matthew, I suggest that the presentation of Jesus as the Greater Moses probably itself carries within it the notion of suffering. Moses certainly knew suffering—in the flight from Egypt as a refugee and fugitive, in the suffering with and for his people in the wilderness, where he faced the difficulties of idolatry and rebellion. Moses was a man of sorrow and acquainted with grief and disappointment, culminating in his failure to enter the land of promise. Not surprisingly some scholars discovered his lineaments in Isaiah 53. The first redeemer was a suffering redeemer. And so too the prophets, especially Jeremiah, were suffering figures as the righteous in Israel often were. Not surprisingly and not unrelated to all this is the high evaluation of suffering in Judaism. I refer here to *Paul and Rabbinic Judaism*, pp. 264ff. The difficulties in connection with the place of Isaiah 53 in Matthew and in the rest of the New Testament I can only refer to.

And then there is the enigma of the meaning of the Son of Man and his relation to the Messiah. Some have traced the figure to Ezekiel, others to Enoch, others to Daniel 7, where he suffers. The debate continues, even though some have refused to contemplate a definite figure, the Son of Man, but simply find a personal reference in the term. The literature on all this is familiar. For our purposes what needs to be emphasized is that in determining the sources of Matthew's messianism we have to consider not only the Tanak but the Apocrypha and Pseudepigrapha and other extracanonical literature, which include the apocalyptic strands of Judaism. It is clear that there was a futuristic as well as a realized dimension to the messianism of Matthew and the future was associated with the coming of the Son of Man. This demands that we recognize the inadequacy of the analogy of the Big Bang, which we used at the beginning. That analogy cannot be accepted uncritically and unmodified, and not only for the reason pointed out on page 498. Like all analogies, it should not be unduly pressed. Useful in evoking the significance of Jesus as the one who set in motion for Matthew the New Creation, the term "explosion"—a purely inorganic or physical one in the Big Bang theory—bears connotations and evocations inappropriate to personal dimensions. Although Jesus did bring fire to the earth, the change he wrought was physically invisible; it was not accompanied—except symbolically—by blinding, thunderous, destructive phenomena: it was the silent work of a man of sorrow, acquainted with grief and disappointment. Moreover, if the Big Bang is thought of as a single unrepeated event (some scientists think of more than one Big Bang), the analogy breaks down (despite the undertone of ἐφάπαξ ["once for all"] in the New Testament). In one passage at least, Matthew indicates apparently two stages in the history of the creative beginning wrought by Jesus. In 19:28 he refers to a *palingennesia* as if he contemplates another second "creation," marked by the coming of the Son of Man on his throne of glory, accompanied by the twelve who also will sit on twelve thrones judging the twelve tribes of Israel.[20] This is another *genesis*, though not exactly a repetition of that indicated in 1:1. The words in 19:28 may be Matthew's own redactional words or, more likely, a tradition he had received and modified, possibly going back to Jesus himself. Their exact force is unclear. For our purposes we can claim that they at least signify that Matthew or the tradition he had preserved had a further *genesis* in mind in which the *genesis* of 1:1 would issue and find its interpretation at the judgment of the Son of Man and his own over Israel. (The theme of judgment, as Matthew Black has so strongly insisted, is inseparable from that of the Son of Man.) The relationship of this futuristic element to Matthew's messianism as a whole we cannot pursue here.

With these bare statements we must leave the role of suffering and of the Son of Man in Matthew. Nor can we here deal with the Wisdom tradition. Some concluding thoughts are in order. We have emphasized that the origins

---

20. On this see Davies, *The Gospel and the Land: Early Christianity and Jewish Territorial Doctrine* (Berkeley, Los Angeles, London, 1974), pp. 363–65.

of Matthew's messianism, essentially governed as it was by the figure of Jesus of Nazareth, are in the Old Testament, which was Matthew's chief quarry both in Hebrew and Greek. But now we have to recognize that his use of it was both governed by interpretations current among his contemporaries in Israel and very selective. He took over much from the Jewish tradition; he cast off much. In two areas especially he may have abandoned or neglected what he found in Judaism. First, it is not clear that he retained the political territoriality of Jewish messianism and, second, he ignores the priestly elements in the messianic hope. That he did not embrace the territorialism of Judaism is consonant with his emphasis on Abraham and the Gentiles: he is not governed by Jewish privacy. Moreover, his distance from the discredited Zealots and the apocalyptic fervor that was probably reemerging in his day would reinforce his aloofness from territorialism. Similarly his indifference to priestly elements in messianism, which could have been speculatively exploited by Christians and which were so exploited, as for example in the Epistle to the Hebrews, is also understandable. His dialogue was with Pharisaism; the Temple was in ruins, the priesthood having been made unnecessary and surviving only in the shadow of Pharisaism. And in the dialogue with Judaism in its Pharisaic form (although Pharisaism was not without its territorial devotion and not to be separated sharply from apocalyptic), it was the messianic Torah—a notion at least inchoate in first-century Judaism—and the greater Moses that immediately concerned Matthew. There *were* elements in the ministry of Jesus that could have fostered the notion of Jesus as Priest in Matthew, but given the climate after Jamnia, which was not conducive to this, they were insufficiently powerful to do so. Nevertheless, despite its emphasis on the new creation, Matthew's messianism, because of its restraint, is not utopian but restorative.[21] This is largely because its sources are not simply the Jewish tradition in the Tanak and in the Apocrypha and Pseudepigrapha, but also, indirectly, the actualities, social, political,

---

21. At this point S. Talmon (*King, Cult, and Calendar*, p. 206) needs to be questioned and his position modified. He writes: "For Christianity, the 'Utopian' element, seemingly freed from the fetters of actual history, became the most prominent trait of its *Messianism.*" We prefer the position indicated in the text and also urged by Hengel. In a forthcoming essay, "The Old Testament in the Fourth Gospel," Hengel rightly emphasizes the Mosaic role of Jesus in Matthew as the ultimate expounder of Torah; Jesus is the superior *antitype* to Moses, not only to the New Moses. He contrasts the strong emphasis on the commandments of Jesus in Matthew with that on the Spirit in the Fourth Gospel. In the latter, the Spirit—pneumatic experience—is emphasized. In Matthew moral obedience to the commandments of Jesus is stressed. "On this point," he writes, "the fourth Gospel is radically different from its direct opposite, Matthew." Was Matthew reacting against "enthusiasm," or is it that we are simply dealing with two distinct and very different communities behind John and Matthew? John urges his community to emphasize the Spirit as the expounder of Jesus' words which the earliest disciples had misunderstood and which needed explaining: Matthew, whether in reaction to this emphasis or independently, urged his community to keep the commandments of Jesus as they had been given by him and handed on by the disciples. However, in both Matthew and John (who mentions Moses more often than the Synoptics and even Paul) the appeal to the Lawgiver of Sinai is unmistakably significant.

and religious, of the situation he faced after the collapse of Jerusalem and the rise of rabbinic Judaism. The necessity to formulate a parallel attraction to Pharisaism at Jamnia was among the factors which led to his presentation of a new Moses with a new messianic torah; the necessity to break the chrysalis of an increasingly privatized Judaism, when Judaism turned in more and more on itself to develop into its rabbinic form, brought forth the Abrahamic emphasis; the presentation of the Son of Man as judge and of the Suffering Messiah, whose words are in the sermon on the mount, was possibly not unrelated to a recrudescent triumphalist apocalyptic which was finally to lead to Bar Kokhba, although it was endemic to parts of the tradition Matthew had received.

At the same time, while Matthew was aware of the demands of Judaism and deliberately honored them through the emphasis on Jesus as Son of David, in a period when many Christians were doubtless tempted to revert to Judaism, he also preserved the radical newness of the Gospel in terms of the new creation. In sum, any treatment of the origins of Matthew's messianism must recognize at least three dimensions: first, the actuality of the messianic ministry of Jesus; second, the illumination brought to the presentation of that messianic ministry from Jewish sources in the Tanak, the Apocrypha, and Pseudepigrapha; and third, the social, political, and religious conditions within which the messianism of Matthew came to be formulated. This last element of the context does not *determine* the content of Matthew's messianism—Jesus and Judaism did that—but we suggest that the context does help to *define* the emphases with which he presents it. Perhaps this is the best point at which to refer to a most significant final aspect of Matthew's messianism.

Messianism, as Scholem reminded us (for him it is endemically revolutionary), has its dark side—it can lead to unrealistic, visionary enthusiasms which prove destructive. Doubtless much in Early Christian messianism was of this nature. Paul had to combat it and even more so did Matthew shy away from it. In my work on *The Setting of the Sermon on the Mount,* I traced a *gemaric,* cautionary note in Matthew, in which he tempered the radicalism of the Early Christian movement and began to adapt its more perfectionist, extreme expressions to the actualities. There is evidence, pointed out especially by Kilpatrick and Kingsbury, that Matthew's Church was probably more comfortably situated than those where Mark and Paul found themselves and that he was more prepared than Christian enthusiasts to come to terms with the well-to-do. How far Early Christian thinking was under the constraint of the disappointment caused by the postponement of the Parousia is in dispute. Matthew at any rate seems to have come to terms with that postponement and seems to contemplate a future on earth for the Church of an indefinite duration, although he retains the sense of urgency. In such a situation his messianism became tempered, not to say modified. His emphasis on the commandments of Jesus as the greater Moses is not unrelated to this, as those aspects of his Gospel which might be labeled as traces of "early-catholicism." And so it is that, opposed as it is to Pharisaism, paradoxically the messianism of Matthew is rabbinically sober: it is "Mosaic." Matthew pricks the balloons of enthusiasts by fashioning a messianism in which the figure of Moses is as prominent as the figure of David: and the figure of the Son of Man comes especially as judge. His messianism, in short, is a corrective messianism, corrective of excesses and illusions, even as it recognizes ethnic privacy (or particularity) and at the same time affirms universalism.

THE JEWISH ANTECEDENTS OF THE CHRISTOLOGY IN HEBREWS

The cultic and ritualistic language which features so prominently in Hebrews makes it seem remote and alien to most lay people today. On the other hand, its very strangeness in relation to the rest of the New Testament canon has, from the first century until now, lent it a particular fascination for scholarly interpreters. The scholar who has read even only a relatively small part of the voluminous literature on Hebrews recognizes clearly how numerous and complex are the still largely unresolved problems presented by this puzzling, and I think we can say, highly original document, despite its several affinities with certain New Testament and extrabiblical writings.

Regarding the authorship, date, destination—who were the addressees and what was their life situation? What contact if any did they have with the Qumran sect? What of the author's hermeneutical methods? Did he treat the Old Testament text with reserve and caution or with great freedom? How are we to understand the literary structure of the work as a whole or of such shorter segments as 3:1–6? Is chapter 13 a later addendum? Above all, there is what has come to be commonly known as the "riddle" of Hebrews—that is, the perplexing question of how we are to determine the cultural, intellectual, religious, or literary-interpretive factors which influenced or motivated the author in the composition of a work which, in its structure, literary style, thought process, and theological or christological formulations, differs considerably from other New Testament writings.

The difficulties are compounded by the fact that nearly all of these issues are closely or indeed organically interrelated. It is virtually impossible to isolate any one specific area of inquiry. That is certainly true of Hebrews' conception of the person and work of Jesus Christ, especially since this writing may be characterized as an essay in christology *not in any abstract, speculative, or purely doctrinal sense*, but with the direct, practical aim of reviving the flagging zeal of an apparently somewhat jaded Christian group or groups. In short, christology stands here in the service of parenesis, and any deemphasizing or neglect of the latter will inevitably produce an imbalance in our perception of the former. Respect for the extraordinary intellectual prowess and imaginative genius of the author among commentators—an entirely justifiable respect—has in my judgment sometimes led them to do less than justice to his urgent pastoral concerns.

Our primary interest is in the intellectual background of Hebrews. How are we to "explain" him and his thought, in particular his thought on Christ and its relevance to the *Sitz im Leben* of the people he seeks to reach and touch effectively? I believe we may appropriately attempt some ground clearing by offering a few general observations on the larger question of tracing the originating religiocultural categories involved in the working out or formulation of the theology or christology of different New Testament writers.

The History of Religions school, as is well known, enjoyed great prominence in the earlier part of this century, and left a strong imprint on subsequent scholarship. The *Babel und Bibel* controversy that had raged around the Old Testament found its analogy in the school's supposition that through contact with pagan religious and mythological antecedents in the Greco-Roman world, the Christianity of the Diaspora transformed the human Jesus of Palestine into a heavenly divine figure. In other words they posited a radical shift or dislocation from the ministry and message of the man Jesus to the Church's presentation of Christ as a cult God. W. Bousset, for instance, contended that in order to commend Christ as Lord and Savior to residents of the great centers of pagan learning, Christian missionaries simply had to clothe him in the raiment of the celestial Son of Man, the Cosmocrator. In so doing, in shaping up his christology, Paul drew very heavily on the pagan mysteries for his doctrine of the Eucharist and the sacrament of baptism, and on broader pagan cultural trends for his teaching on "wisdom" and "knowledge," and "flesh and spirit."[1] Under the influence of the "*Religionsgeschichtliche Schule*," R. Bultmann, consistently with his (as we now see, extremely questionable) notion of the existence of a pre-Christian Gnostic Redeemed-Redeemer myth, felt able to envisage a remarkably rapid Hellenization of the Jesus-message by maintaining the emergence of a pre-Pauline Hellenistic kerygma.[2]

In recent years the History of Religions school's idea of a sharp dichotomy between Palestine and Palestinian Judaism on the one hand and the Hellenistic cultural context and hellenistic Judaism on the other has been seriously challenged and, as many would hold, overcome. Ever since the conquests of Alexander the Great, for over three centuries the Jewish homeland of Palestine, and not the least the Galilee of the Gentiles, was pervaded by Hellen-

---

1. W. Bousset, *Kyrios Christos*, trans. J. Steeley (Nashville, 1970), pp. 119, 11–21, 317f.
2. R. Bultmann, *Theology of the New Testament*, vol. 1, trans. K. Grobel (London, 1952), pp. 33ff.

istic influence, as a result inter alia of the presence of Greek immigrants and the return from the Diaspora of Jews well acquainted with Greek thought.[3] The main arguments adduced in support of this view may, at the risk of over-simplification, be set out as follows:

(a) Extensive archaeological discoveries as well as the unearthing of extremely important literary remains, notably at Qumran, indicate that the Greek language was widely known and used in Palestine in the first century C.E. Inscriptions on the dedication stone of a Jerusalem synagogue as well as on ossuaries and tombs reveal popular knowledge of Greek. In regard to commerce in Palestine, some would claim that Jews could not possibly have conducted business without Greek.[4]

(b) The gravest mistake of the "*Religionsgeschichtliche Schule*" was to underestimate or disavow altogether the amazing development that had taken place in christological conceptualization within the Christian movement as early as twenty years after the death of Jesus. Paul's christology, for instance, as exemplified in Phil 2:6–11 and Rom 10:9, 13, was already complete before 48 C.E., so it is claimed. Accordingly, since terms like "son of God" or "Lord" have a history of their own entirely within a Semitic context, the rise of christology can be understood on *Jewish* presuppositions.[5]

It would be foolish to deny that these arguments do carry weight. Nevertheless, in my judgment the pendulum has swung too far in the direction of upholding the essential unity of Diaspora Judaism and Palestinian Judaism. Take the language situation in Palestine. Widespread knowledge and employment of Greek among Palestinian Jews, to the extent of their being bilingual is, I believe, not yet proven.[6] Greek inscriptions on Jewish tombs and ossuaries fall short of such proof and denote only that *some* Jews in Palestine knew *some* Greek. In any case, even if the populace at large did have some acquaintance with the Greek language, it does not automatically follow that they took over Greek thought forms lock, stock, and barrel. For centuries the Jews in Palestine had struggled valiantly to stem the tide of foreign invasion and foreign domination. Such resistance and the continuing sense of election and exclusivity that went with it should caution us against overesti-

3. M. Hengel, *Judaism and Hellenism*, 2 vols. (Philadelphia, 1974), *passim*.

4. E. L. Sukenik, *Ancient Synagogues in Palestine and Greece* (London, 1934), pp. 69ff. J. N. Sevenster, *Do You Know Greek? How Much Greek Could the First Jewish Christians Have Known?* (Supplements to *NovT* 19 [Leiden, 1968]).

5. M. Hengel, *The Son of God: The Origin of Christology and the History of Jewish Hellenistic Religion*, trans. J. Bowker (Philadelphia, 1976).

6. Contrast A. W. Argyle, "Greek Among the Jews of Palestine in New Testament Times," *NTS* 20 (1973) 87ff. He claims that it would be as foolish to suppose that a Welsh boy in Cardiff would not know English as to suppose that a Jewish youth in Palestine would not have known Greek. Perhaps not, however, if in spite of their proximity to England, the Welsh had remained exclusively Welsh in respect of their Celtic culture.

mating the extent of the infiltration of Greek ideas into the minds of the Jewish people.[7]

It is more pertinent to our interest in christology to notice here how easily the importance of the twenty years after the death of Jesus can be exaggerated, as I think it is in Professor Martin Hengel's statement that "more happened in this period of less than two decades than in the whole of the next seven centuries, up to the time when the doctrine of the early church was completed.[8] It is not difficult to see why Hengel can say this. In defending the case for a one-to-one relationship between Jesusology and christology, he argues for the consistent development and completion of early christological concepts as a phenomenon of Jewish religious history. Like C. F. D. Moule, Hengel wants to insist that all the "dignities" which the church subsequently attributed to Christ were *from the very outset* present *in nuce* in the life and person of Jesus of Nazareth. Scholars such as Moule and Hengel emphasize the fluidity and interpenetration of Hellenistic and Jewish categories even in Palestine, before Christianity had ever reached out to the Greek and Roman world.[9] It is rather odd that they should at the same time contend that in the period of some twenty years after the death of Jesus christology flowered organically from the soil of *basic Jewish presuppositions*. But we must not forget that the christological perceptions of the Apostle Paul were those of a Hellenized Jew of the Diaspora (even if he was trained in Jerusalem at the

7. See now, however, F. Gerald Downing's interesting if adventurous suggestion that Cynic models may have been influential for the people of Galilee and indeed for Jesus himself: "Cynic ideas and the Cynic life-style (in its considerable varieties) could well have been available for Jesus to adopt and adapt and for his first followers to recognize and make sense of." See his "The Social Contexts of Jesus the Teacher," *NTS* 33 (1987) 449. He adds that "if Jesus grew up in Nazareth, it was 6 km from Sepphoris, Herod Agrippa's 'thriving Hellenistic capital city' (R. A. Batey)." But Downing makes the following concession: "For all the increased willingness of some scholars to consider that 'hellenisation' may have widely affected first century Palestine, there is still a strong preference for seeing Jesus in terms of a continuing 'pure' Judaism. There are few stories of encounters between Jesus and Gentiles, and none of contact being chosen. The tradition that Jesus forbade entry into Gentile towns (in Mt 10:5) can be generalized into a rejection of everything Gentile. My suggestion may well not be itself immediately persuasive in terms of the wide consensus within which most scholarship operates its discussion. I propose it at this stage primarily as a test case." See further below my statement on C. F. D. Moule and M. Hengel. In general, one wonders whether the felt necessity to search for models or prototypes, especially in the case of Jesus as teacher (and healer) does not limit excessively the possibility of the emergence of the new in history.

8. M. Hengel, *Son of God*, p. 2. Professor Hengel informed me in private conversation that his statement was intended to apply specifically to christological development. While we acknowledge how remarkably early is the sublime christological hymn in Phil 2:5–11, reservations remain. "An idea or cause in history becomes known only as it develops. Time is usually required before its essential features and forces are fully understood, even by its own adherents," J. Moffatt, *The Thrill of Tradition* (New York, 1944).

9. M. Hengel, *Between Jesus and Paul: Studies in the Earliest History of Christianity*, trans. J. Bowden (London, 1983), ch. 2. Cf. C. F. D. Moule, *The Origins of Christology* (Cambridge, 1972), p. 2: "Jesus was, *from the beginning*, such a one as to be appropriately described in the ways in which, sooner or later, he did come to be described in the N.T. period."

feet of Rabbi Gamaliel [Acts 23:3]). And we should respect the fact that just as Judaism in the first century C.E. was no monolith, but a richly colored tapestry of varied religious experiences, confessions, traditions, and interpretations, so there were in fact dissimilarities between Diaspora Judaism and Palestinian Judaism. While acknowledging that we cannot now draw rigid lines of separation between these, Professor W. D. Davies once wisely stated that there *is a difference* between Philo and, say, R. Joshua ben Hananiah or Rabbi Simeon ben Gamaliel.[10]

In regard to the narrowly historical perspective of Moule and Hengel on the genetic development of the church's christology from Jesus himself, I find myself in agreement with L. E. Keck: "If the legitimacy of christology depends on establishing historically the continuity between the historically-reconstructed Jesus and the christology of the church, then the turn to history alone has not only made suspect all christology which goes beyond that which was in the mind of Jesus, but continued historical work is unable to resolve the dilemma."[11] Nor need we any longer subscribe to the old fallacy that whatever in the New Testament can be traced back to purely Hebraic or Jewish roots is necessarily superior to those elements in Early Christianity where mutations have occurred through the intrusion of extraneous Greek ideas.

We can now say then that Hellenized Jews of the Diaspora, like Philo or the author of Fourth Maccabees or the author of Hebrews, were not quite the same as their Palestinian contemporaries. The intricate intermingling of Greek philosophy and Jewish religious thought we find in their works would scarcely have been possible in Palestine.

Concerning the christology of Hebrews, the question of the moment is not whether it represents an admixture of Greek and Jewish categories. It undoubtedly does. The question is rather whether we can gauge where the balance of his christological perspective lies, or alternatively his basic intel-

---

But to posit that kind of continuity is to presuppose that the historian can know precisely what Jesus was *from the beginning* and then go on to compare it with what the early church said about him in its confessional christological statements! In support of Moule and Hengel, J. H. Charlesworth holds that there were already highly developed ideas in the 30's C.E., and even in Jesus' ministry, and what was needed for the extension of christology was *transference* to Jesus of Jewish notions of the Lord God and his messengers, and *specification* of Jesus as the Coming One, Messiah, Son of God, and Son of Man. See Charlesworth, *The Old Testament Pseudepigrapha and the New Testament* (SNTS Monograph Series 54; Cambridge, 1985), p. 81.

10. W. D. Davies, Review of H. J. Schoeps, *Paulus, Die Theologie des Apostels im Lichte der jüdischen Religionsgeschichte* (Tübingen, 1959) NTS 10 (1964) 301. See, however, G. Thyen, *Der Stil der Jüdisch-Hellenistischen Homilie* (Göttingen, 1955). Thyen counsels caution about whether Hebrews was without qualification a Hellenistic-Jewish homily, and suggests there are Palestinian elements in it. Cf. J. Swetnam, *NovT* (1969) 261ff. See also W. Horbury, "The Aaronic Priesthood in the Epistle to the Hebrews," *JSNT* 19 (1983) 44f.—the writer is not, as in the view of Käsemann and Moffatt, "a scholarly Hellenist *tout court*, but one who was in living touch with a living contemporary Jewish faith."

11. L. E. Keck, "Toward the Renewal of New Testament Christology," NTS 32 (1986) 368.

lectual framework, or the religiocultural *point de départ* for his portrayal of the High Priestly person and work of Christ.

Broadly speaking, six different answers have been given: (1) Hebrews has a Gnostic background; (2) the thought world is that of Middle Platonism as mediated through Philo of Alexandria; (3) the principal determinant is Jewish eschatology-apocalyptic; (4) it offers its author's interpretation of the Old Testament; (5) it is dependent on internal Christian traditions; (6) it is influenced by or has affinities with extrabiblical literature. We shall consider these in turn, noting in advance that most space will be devoted to (2), the much controverted issue of the Philonism of Hebrews, which needs to be taken in conjunction with (3), and finally that (4), (5), and (6) need not cancel each other out.

HEBREWS EMANATES FROM A GNOSTIC MILIEU

So contended Professor E. Käsemann in his provocative early book on Hebrews. In the focus of Hebrews on the concepts of "wandering," "pilgrimage," "rest," and the heavenly High Priestly figure of Christ, Käsemann found a patent Gnostic proclivity—in much the same fashion as he later located the Fourth Gospel in a Gnostic conventicle in Ephesus on the basis of his investigation of John 17.[12] But the motifs of "wandering," "pilgrimage," and "rest" in Hebrews belong to the general *Zeitgeist* of late antiquity. Only because he identifies Gnosticism very broadly with that general spirit is Käsemann able to classify Hebrews as Gnostic.[13] And we have to remember that he was writing before the discovery and subsequent study of the Nag Hammadi Coptic and Gnostic texts enabled us to discern more accurately the actual contours of Gnosticism. It is worth noticing that Käsemann regards Hebrews much more as a document of *"kosmisch-metaphysische Spekulation"* than as a *Gelegenheitschrift* addressed out of empirical concern to a concrete situation. I shall shortly argue that in Hebrews there is in fact, in respect of his references to the life, suffering, and death of Christ, a marked historical realism quite foreign to the dualistic speculation of Gnosticism.

---

12. E. Käsemann, *Das Wandernde Gottesvolk* (FRLANT 55; Göttingen, 1938). Käsemann found support latterly in E. Grässer, "Der Hebräerbrief 1938–63," *ThRu* N.F. 30 (1964) 186.

13. H. M. Schenke, *"Erwägungen zum Rätsel des Hebräerbriefes,"* in *Neues Testament und christliches Existenz,* ed. H. D. Betz and L. Schottroff (Tübingen, 1973), p. 423, states that only Käsemann's identification of Gnosticism with the general spirit of late antiquity enables him *"sozusagen alles in einem Topf zu werfen."* Cf. J. W. Thompson, *The Beginnings of Christian Philosophy: The Epistle to the Hebrews,* CBQMS 13 (Washington, D.C., 1982), p. 3.

THE THOUGHT WORLD IS THAT OF MIDDLE PLATONISM AS MEDIATED THROUGH PHILO; THE CONTRARY VIEWPOINT: THE PRINCIPAL DETERMINANT IS JEWISH ESCHATOLOGY

At the center of the debate about Hebrews stands the sharp division of opinion about the author's fundamental intellectual framework. Was he so deeply imbued with Philonic ideas and the philosophical principles of Hellenistic thinkers in the Neo-Platonic stream that he can be regarded as primarily an exponent of a metaphysical dualism of the Alexandrian type? Or was his basic viewpoint more in keeping with biblical perspectives on salvation-history, and so with typical Jewish eschatological expectations of the New Age or the end time?

That the author of Hebrews was familiar with and dependent upon the writings of Philo at first hand cannot be proven. That the author shared the same thought world as Philo and that he drew on the same Greek rhetorical and philosophical sources for much of his vocabulary and many of his ideas is irrefutable.[14]

Obviously we cannot here rehearse the parallels which it takes C. Spicq some fifty pages to cover,[15] a number of which are lucidly set forth by J. W. Thompson in his effort to show that Hebrews represents the "beginnings of Christian philosophy." There is no denying that such notions in Hebrews as "wandering," "rest," "perfection," the contrast between the "A B C" and mature learning, that is the progress from "milk" to "solid food" in *paideia* ("instruction"), between the world of sense perception and the invisible world, between earth and heaven, all these are normative concepts in the Philonic corpus. However, we are not justified in deducing simply from their occurrence in Hebrews that they carry in the new context of Hebrews the same import as they did for Philo, and that the thought of Hebrews is therefore structured first and foremost on the speculative metaphysical dualism of Philo and the ontological categories of Neo-Platonic philosophy.[16] Our submission is that many of the passages in Hebrews which are taken to support that thesis are capable of viable alternative interpretation. Unfortunately we have space to make only one or two soundings.

It is claimed that Heb 5:11–14 conforms closely to the Platonic distinction

---

14. We do well to keep in mind S. Sandmel's famous strictures against "Parallelomania," *JBL* 81 (1962) 1 and 5f., with special reference of course to Paul and the Gospels vis-à-vis the Qumran Scrolls.

15. C. Spicq, *L'Épître aux Hébreux*, vol. 1 (Paris, 1952), pp. 39–91. Spicq lists a host of parallels between Hebrews and Philo and holds that the author was "*un philonien converti au christianisme.*"

16. See e.g. U. Luz, "*Der alte und der neue Bund bei Paulus und im Hebräerbrief,*" *EvT* 27 (1967) 331–33. It is easy to forget that, unlike Philo, the author of Hebrews had entered the fold of a new faith, which focused upon the life and death of a real person within actual history.

between the two stages of *paideia* ("instruction"), and that it provides an excellent key to grasping "the theological assumptions and intention of the author," serving as it does as a sort of frontispiece to the crucial section 7:1–10:18.[17] The argument is that *nōthroi* in 5:11 denotes both intellectual sluggishness and spiritual lassitude, and that the *nōthroi* therefore need to be lifted up to the higher learning that would enable them to grasp the heavenly food and acquire the *parrēsia* ("confidence") of those who are disfranchised from the present world of change and are given to enter the stable world of God.[18] Further the heavenly food is in fact identical with the *logos dysermē-neutos* ("a word which is hard to explain") of 5:11, which is in turn an expansion of the foundational confession found in 3:1, 4:14, 10:21–23, and in part in 1:3.[19] Finally the "word which is hard to explain" comes in 7:1–10:18, and in this line of argumentation that major section of Hebrews is intended to demonstrate the *metaphysical dignity* of Christ the High Priest: access to the stable world of God is achieved through the *heavenly work* of Christ. We take careful note of the stress on the adjectives "metaphysical" and "heavenly."[20] If we focus narrowly on the heavenly exaltation of Christ, we can readily enough discover in passage after passage that the author of Hebrews constantly witnesses in good Platonic-Philonic fashion to the infinite superiority of the eternal, heavenly world to the world of flesh and earthly reality.

Throughout his otherwise very informative study of Hebrews, J. W. Thompson constantly transfers our gaze prematurely, so to speak, to the heavenly sphere. We restrict ourselves to the following four examples and to a brief response to each:

(1) Heb 5:5–10, it is argued, demonstrates that the exaltation of Christ is the foundation of the author's understanding of the High Priesthood of Christ.[21] That seems to me to be a very surprising claim, indeed, since in fact in these verses it was only through his obedience to the will of God in his human weakness and suffering that Christ was "perfected."[22]

(2) What next of the suggestion that it was entirely because of his heavenly ministry that Christ could be depicted in Hebrews as "a High Priest after the order of Melchizedek,'" or the assumption that the terminology of 7:3 comes from the Hellenistic world and points up the eternal nature of the *taxis* ("or-

---

17. J. W. Thompson, *Beginning of Christian Philosophy*, p. 18, speaks of the *unique language* of 5:11–14, but on p. 30 he does allude to 1Cor 3:1–3 (cf. 1Pet 2:2) and suggests now that it is the *emphasis* of Heb 5:11–14 that is unique.

18. Ibid., pp. 29ff. See below, pp. 17f. for further discussion of the term *nōthroi*.

19. But in 3:1, 4:14, and 10:21–23 there is an unequivocal stress on the lowliness of Jesus' way through sharing our human weakness and through the cross, which is the sole ground of his exaltation. In the case of 1:3 the affirmation of Christ's heavenly status stands in close proximity to 1:1–2, which reflects a biblical salvation-history perspective.

20. Thompson, *Beginning of Christian Philosophy*, p. 32.

21. Ibid., p. 117.

22. See H. Anderson, *Jesus and Christian Origins* (New York, 1964), pp. 280ff.

der") to which both Melchizedek and Christ belong?[23] But in the extended midrash of Heb 7:1–10:18, particularly in 7:1–11, the eternal superiority of Melchizedek arises from what purports to be a historical narration of Gen 14:18–20. Although we have to concede that Christ's exalted status is highlighted in these chapters, it is inseparably bound up with testimony to Christ's sacrifice on the cross, which runs like a refrain through the whole section (7:27; 9:12–17; 9:26, 28; 10:10, 12, 14). Accordingly the *dysermēneutos logos* of 5:11 is not after all the heavenly ministry of Christ *per se* but the scandalous notion that the exalted one is the one who died a shameful death on the cross.

(3) Most surprising of all is the attempt to force the distinctive *ephapax* ("once for all") of Hebrews into a Platonic mould: the *hapax*—*ephapax* is in line with the Platonic conception of the once-for-allness of eternity, while time and sense perception are in the realm of "becoming" and are never completed. In contrast with the ministrations of the Levitical priesthood in the earthly sphere of "becoming," Christ *offered himself in the heavenly sphere*, and so his work is final (*eis to panteles;* Heb 7:25: RSV "for all time") and therefore *ephapax*, its once-for-allness being an inference from the author's metaphysical understanding of Ps 110:4.[24]

Even if it is conceded that the death and exaltation of Christ together constitute one event in Hebrews (1:3, 5:8–9, 12:1–2),[25] in the foregoing line of argumentation, if I am not mistaken, the historical actuality of the death of Christ is obscured or altogether lost from sight. Are we not really confronted with a gnosticizing interpretation of the role of Christ which has been, wittingly or unwittingly, influenced by the *Religionsgeschichtliche Schule* hypothesis of an existing Revealed Revealer myth (Bousset, Reitzenstein, and later Bultmann and Käsemann)? The same tendency is surely in evidence when it is proposed on the basis of Heb 4:16 that what brings enabling *charis* ("grace") to the believing community is *Christ's work in the heavenly sanctuary.* But if we take the *oun* ("therefore") of 4:16 seriously, as we must, then access to the throne of grace is the *consequence* of Christ's oneness with us in our humanity: "We have not a high priest who is unable to sympathize with our weaknesses, but one who in every respect has been tempted as we are, therefore let us boldly . . ."

(4) Finally the disputed phrase *exō tēs pylēs* ("outside the gate"), Heb 13:12, has been understood to refer to Christ's passing beyond the sphere of the *sarx* ("flesh") to his *sacrifice in the heavenly sanctuary*—what gives stability to the heart is the heavenly character of Jesus' death (Heb 13:9; cf. 6:19).[26]

23. Thompson, *Beginnings,* pp. 117, 120.
24. Ibid., p. 126.
25. Thompson does concede this, *Beginnings,* p. 147.
26. "When Moses took the tent and pitched outside the camp, he left the whole array of bodily things." So Christ's offering was in the heavenly sanctuary. See Thompson, *Beginnings,* p. 148.

In the immediate context of 13:9, however, the writer by no means allows the heavenly to blot out the earthly reality of Christ's death. Similarly the verse that follows 6:19 portrays Jesus as the *forerunner* on our behalf. In Hebrews Jesus is the *archēgos* ("forerunner") of our salvation (2:10), not by any arbitrary divine fiat or miracle-working power in himself, but by his life of obedience and suffering, culminating in death.

Plainly, in locating the death of Jesus "outside the gate," the writer was aware that Jesus was crucified outside the wall of Jerusalem. Whereas it is true that our author summons his readers to a vision of Christ's ministry at the heavenly altar, his exhortation to the believers to "go forth to Jesus outside the camp bearing abuse for him" (13:13) indicates that he has in mind the shame of the cross, and reflects his kinship here with Paul's testimony to the *skandalon* ("stumbling block"). The words *ek tēs parembolēs* are of course a notorious *crux interpretum*. Are they to be interpreted in the Philonic mode as an appeal to Jesus' followers to separate themselves from worldly things in general and to attain to a lofty spirituality? Or are they aimed at Gentile Christians as an entreaty to break completely with the worldly allurements of paganism?[27] Or again in the light of Heb 13:14, is there an anti-city, anti-Jerusalem polemic and an implicit request to withdraw into the wilderness, as the Qumran sectarians had done?[28]

Against these proposals there stands the fact that there is nowhere in Hebrews any hint of the attractions of paganism to which the readers might be turning back. Nor is there any counsel of withdrawal from city or world toward the attainment of a pure and perfect religion. Rather is the whole thrust of the parenetic sections a call for steadfastness, obedience, and endurance (which Christ himself manifested) *in the world*, inspired and supported to be sure by the vision of the shining goal of the city of God to come. Where else than *in the world* could anyone "bear the shame of Jesus"?

In the submissions we have made, we have sought to show that the basic tendency of Hebrews is not toward the neo-Platonic/Philonic contrast between an impure earthly form and a perfect spiritual and heavenly form. Of course the vocabulary and categories the author employs in his christological and soteriological statements are largely derived from Hellenistic philosophy. But they are baptized into a new mode of reckoning and made subser-

---

27. See J. Moffatt, *The Epistle to the Hebrews* (ICC; Edinburgh, New York, 1924), p. 235.

28. The hostility to the Temple at Qumran was not any hatred for the Temple and its worship in themselves, but a reaction to the corruption of the priestly leadership. Cf. W. H. Brownlee, "Messianic Motifs of Qumran and the New Testament," *NTS* 3 (1957) 203. The sectarians did hope, however, that in the Messianic Age the Temple would be repossessed and its worship renewed under the direction of the Chief Priest (1QM 2). Cf. TestLevi 18:2ff. W. Manson claimed that Hebrews extended the message of Stephen (Acts 7), which verged on universalism (Manson, *The Epistle to the Hebrews* [London, 1953], pp. 27–36).

But L. W. Barnard correctly notes that Stephen's polemic against the Temple is completely radical, whereas Hebrews affirms that what in terms of the Old Covenant was valid for the Hebrew people, has been superseded by Christ: "St. Stephen and Early Alexandrian Christianity," *NTS* 7 (1980) 31ff. Heb 5:1–4 seems to me to support Barnard's viewpoint.

vient to a strong grasp of the meaningfulness of time and history. "The disclosure of the Word of God [see 1:1] takes its shape as a history, a history which
has a past and a present (and indeed a future)." [29] If we accept that, then we
can consider the hinge of the christology of Hebrews to be a series of relationships: Christ the Pioneer / High Priest; humiliation / exaltation;[30] old
covenant and the Levitical ordinances integral to it / new covenant inaugurated through Christ's once-for-all sacrifice by which the old is superseded;
and then / now / yet, or yesterday / today / tomorrow.

The historical realism reflected in these relationships gives credence to
the view that "the thought of Hebrews is consistent, and . . . in it the eschatological is the determining element." [31] The imagery conjured up by such
terms as *katapausis, epangelia, polis* ("rest," "promise," "city") in Hebrews
has an element of concreteness in it that is quite untypical of the static, abstract conceptualization of the metaphysical dualism of the Alexandrian type.
The "rest" (Heb 3:11, 18; 4:1, 3, 5, 10f.) is identified with the "sabbath rest"
of God (*sabbatismos*, Heb 4:9), and is envisaged as the ultimate goal of the
wandering people of God. The following words of Jürgen Moltmann are not
inapposite to these verses: "The sabbath opens creation for this true future.
On the sabbath the redemption of the world is celebrated *in anticipation*.
The sabbath is itself the presence of eternity in time, and a foretaste of the
world to come." [32] As to the "promise" the people of the old covenant, by
reason of their disobedience, did not lay hold upon it, and so the readers of
Hebrews are encouraged to see that the promise is still open and lies ahead
of them in their worldly way into the future (4:1–10, 6:11–20).[33] Similarly the
author exhorts his readers to realize that despite hardship and tribulation (of
which they have already had their share, 10:32–34), there is in store for
those who, like Christ, are obedient to God's will, the final destination of
another, higher city. He does so by appealing to their imagination and holding up before their eyes "Mount Zion, the city of the living God, the heav-

29. G. Hughes, *Hebrews and Hermeneutics* (SNTS MS 36; Cambridge, 1979), p. 36.

30. G. Johnson, "Jesus As Archēgos," *NTS* 27 (1981) 381ff. wants to take *archēgos* as a Messianic title designating Christ as *Prince*, derived from the *nasī* of Num 13:2–3 and 16:2, or the
sēr of 1Chr 26:26. But there is precious little messianology in Hebrews, and we rather think of
archēgos as Pioneer, Trail-Blazer, or *Bahnbrecher*, whose life of obedience to the will of God is
the ground of his exaltation.

31. C. K. Barrett, "The Eschatology of the Epistle to the Hebrews," *The Background of the
New Testament and Its Eschatology*, ed. W. D. Davies and D. Daube (Cambridge, 1956), p. 366.
See B. Klappert, "The prevalence of the futuristic-apocalyptic conceptualization precisely in the
paraenesis, which provides the point for the dogmatic, christological sections, shows that
the Alexandrian dualism . . . stands in the service of . . . the establishing of a new basis for
the futurist eschatology." *Die Eschatologie des Hebräerbriefes* (Munich, 1969), p. 49. Cf.
also R. Williamson, *Philo and Hebrews* (Leiden, 1970), pp. 142–59: "Time, History and Eschatology."

32. J. Moltmann, *God in Creation*, trans. M. Kohl (London, 1985), p. 276.

33. The future is no very distant prospect: see 9:27f., 10:25.

enly Jerusalem" (12:22).[34] The perfect tense *proselēlythate* ("you have come to Mount Zion") may be regarded as a proleptic or prophetic perfect, since in 13:14 the city is described as "the city which is to come."

If we are persuaded that the framework of the author's thought was primarily eschatological, we may think of him as resembling those apocalyptic writers an essential part of whose makeup was the visionary gift. Like them, in view of the preeminent place given to parenesis in his work, he was less interested in stimulating "*kosmische-metaphysische Spekulation*" than in renewing in his readers' confidence, hope, and courage amid the practicalities of their existence.[35]

In this whole field of investigation, the question of the identity, circumstances, posture, or demeanor of the group addressed in Hebrews is of paramount importance. It is worth noting that the scholars who favor the theory of a gnostic or neo-Platonic/Philonic provenance for Hebrews are usually content to be rather unspecific in describing the life situation of the readers.[36] Our own appraisal of the primacy of the temporal-eschatological in Hebrews should help us to identify more precisely the predicament and theological malaise of the group addressed.

There is nowhere any express evidence that the group, whose troubles the author urgently wishes to remedy, had become apostate or were on the verge of apostasy. The verb *parapiptein* in Heb 6:6 may denote any kind of transgression (cf. WisSol 6:9, 12:2; Ezek 22:4), and not necessarily "apostasy." Similarly the *hyposteilētai* (RSV "shrink back") of Heb 10:38b does not refer to apostasy, but to the group's acceptance of Isa 26:20 ("shut your doors behind you; hide yourselves for a little while until the wrath is past") as a pretext for defeatism and withdrawal.[37] Nor is there evidence of their being schismatics of heretical bent, evidence of the kind we find in Colossians or 1 John, for instance.[38]

---

34. The language is of course reminiscent of that of Paul (Gal 4:26) and the Seer of Patmos (Rev 3:12, 21:1, 10).

35. See L. Hartman, "The Functions of Some So-called Apocalyptic Timetables," *NTS* 22 (1975) 13f., maintains that the time factor in itself was very much secondary to the practical function: "the timetables were aimed less at the brain than at the heart and hands."

This emphasis is developed in a rather refined and sophisticated way in so-called rhetorical criticism. See e.g. E. Schüssler Fiorenza, "Rhetorical Situation and Historical Reconstruction in I Corinthians," *NTS* 33 (1987) 387: "Unlike poetic works, actual speeches, homilies or letters are a direct response to a specific historical-political situation and problem. . . . They come into existence because of a specific condition or situation which invites utterance. The situation controls the rhetoric in the same sense that the question controls the answer."

36. See e.g. E. Käsemann, *Gottesvolk*, although he does concede that the parenesis in Hebrews is of paramount importance. See W. G. Kümmel, *Introduction to the New Testament*, trans. A. J. Mattill, Jr. (Nashville/New York, 1966), pp. 279ff.; he thinks of the addressees of Hebrews as Gentile Christians or Christians *as such*, against whose "general weaknesses" Hebrews is directed.

37. See T. W. Lewis ". . . And if he shrinks back, *hyposteilētai* (Heb 10:38b)," *NTS* (1975) 88ff.

38. Of the many theories concerning the recipients of Hebrews, we note only the following: (1) Addressed to no one in particular but rather a general treatise—H. Windisch, *Der Hebräer-*

The exact relationship of the circle of Christians addressed in Hebrews to the Qumran sect has proven very difficult to determine. But ever since Yigael Yadin's erudite article on the subject, it has seemed likely that this circle did indeed have some affinities with Qumran.[39] Certainly the author's argumentation in the early chapters concerning Christ's superiority to all angels, to Moses, and to the Aaronic priesthood would possess all the greater cogency if his readers shared the developed Qumran angelology (and thought perhaps of Christ as an archangel), or if they held in common with the sectarians the expectation of the appearance in the endtime of an eschatological prophet like Moses and a priestly Messiah of the house of Aaron. The complexity of the subject is too great to permit detailed discussion here. Suffice it to say that, despite obvious resemblances, the evidence does not justify regarding the readers of Hebrews as converts from Qumran. At one strategic point in fact they differed greatly. Although the Qumran covenanters appear to have anticipated the reconstitution of the Temple and its worship in the New Age (1QM2), they remained altogether aloof from the actual Jerusalem Temple because of the corruption of its priesthood. The addressees of Hebrews would appear on the contrary to have had a profound interest in the Temple and sacrificial cultus, for why otherwise should the author of Hebrews go to such great length to convince them that the old *nomos* ("law") of the Levitical ordinances under the old covenant had been superseded by Christ?[40]

At this juncture the question of the date of Hebrews cannot be avoided. Among the sizable number of scholars who accept a date prior to the destruction of Jerusalem in 70 C.E., the late J. A. T. Robinson has very stoutly defended it. Like C. F. D. Moule,[41] Robinson opts for a setting in the crisis years of 66–70 C.E., which witnessed the outbreak of a fervent Jewish nationalism: but he specifies further a synagogue of Jewish Christians within the church of Rome, whose apostasy was caused by their permitting racial and economic factors to overcome their Christian commitment (1:2, 4, 14; 6:12, 17; 9:15; 11:7f.; 12:17). Whereas these Jewish Christians were in fact guilty of some kind of defection, it is very hard to detect in these verses an accusation against their *commercialism*. Nor is there evidence of racial bitterness;

---

brief (HNT 2 Auflage; Tübingen, 1931). (2) Christians from a "dissenting" Hebrew background, whose naive and undeveloped view of Jesus is too incoherent to sustain their faith in Judaism— R. Murray, S.J., "Jews, Hebrews and Christians," *NovT* 24 (1982) 194ff. (3) A group who bore some relationship to esoteric merkabah mysticism—O. Hofius, *Der Vorhang vor dem Thron Gottes* (Tübingen, 1972). I have not been able to obtain a copy of O. Hofius' work entitled *To Katapetasma*, to which professor Hengel drew my attention. For other options, see below.

39. Y. Yadin, "The Scrolls and the Epistle to the Hebrews," *Scripta Hierosolymitana* 4, pp. 36ff.

40. Cf. F. F. Bruce, "'To the Hebrews,' or 'To the Essenes,'" *NTS* 9 (1963) 217ff.

41. J. A. T. Robinson, *Redating the New Testament* (London, 1985), pp. 207, 212. Cf. C. F. D. Moule, *The Birth of the New Testament* (London, 1981), p. 68.

the words *Ioudaios* ("Jew") and *ethnē* ("Gentiles") nowhere occur in Hebrews. The present tenses, which are a distinctive feature of Hebrews' descriptions of the Temple ordinances and practices (5:1–4; 8:3–5; 9:6f.; 10:1–4, 11, 18), need not mean that the sacrificial cultus of the Temple is still operative.[42] Rather they serve very well the author's design to draw a stark contrast between a ritual that needs ("needed") to be repeated day in, day out, and so is futile, and the once-for-all perfect sacrifice of Christ, which ensures that "we *have*" (*echomen*) a high priest (Heb 8:1), and an altar (13:10), which have superseded the former ritual and alone are efficacious for salvation.

Again it is not necessary to suppose that if the writer of Hebrews had been active after 70 C.E. the termination of the High Priestly office at that date must have found its way into his argument in 7:11–28, or that if the "first tent" had actually disappeared, he must have referred to it in 8:13.[43] Not at least if we may suppose, as a plausible alternative conjecture, that the very cessation of the Priesthood succession and Temple worship had been a prime factor in causing the malaise now afflicting the Jewish-Christian group addressed in Hebrews. We picture them as a circle of former devotees of the Temple converted to Christianity, but now, with the Temple's destruction, longing nostalgically for its restoration and the renewal of the sacrificial ritual. Even if they were located in Rome or Corinth, Ephesus or Antioch, distance from Jerusalem would not have diminished such longing.[44]

Reverting to the *nōthroi* ("sluggish") of 5:11 and 6:12, undoubtedly a key word in relation to the life situation of the readers of Hebrews, we now suggest that in 5:11 *nōthroi tais akoais* does not refer to intellectual inertia or loss of an otherworldly spirituality, but to the fact that they are now disposed toward the Word of God as if it were static and not a living and dynamic reality forever on the move through history.[45] It is surely significant that in 6:12 the word *nōthroi* by itself occurs in a context where the emphasis is on "sure hope until the end" and on "the faith and patience which inherit the promises." The failure or "falling away" of the addressees of Hebrews consists therefore of their attachment to an irrecoverable past and their resultant lack of vision, faith, and hope in that promised city of the future, the way to which God has opened up through everything he has revealed in his Son, our Pioneer and High Priest. If all those who died in faith had been thinking

42. Robinson, *Redating*, p. 202, admits that many of the present tenses are timeless and that long after the destruction of the Temple, Josephus gives a long account in the same terms. *Ant* 3:224.

43. Ibid., p. 203.

44. See Dan 9:16–19, Ps 137:2. In the period 70–135 C.E. the Tannaim frequently expressed their hope for the rebuilding of the Temple and the renewal of the sacrificial cultus. See e.g. b.Mes 28b: "May it speedily be rebuilt in our time." Cf. m. Ta'an 4.8 and m.Tam 7.3.

45. See G. Hughes, *Hebrews and Hermeneutics: The Epistle to the Hebrews as a New Testament Example of Biblical Interpretation* (SNTS MS 36; Cambridge, 1979), p. 45.

of that land from which they had gone out, they would have had opportunity to return. But as it is, they desire a better country, that is, a heavenly one (we take *epouranios* here to signify the country bestowed as a gift by God in the endtime). "Therefore God is not ashamed to be called their God, for he has prepared for them a city" (Heb 11:15f.).

We may summarize the author of Hebrews' appeal and challenge to his ailing readers in the following paraphrase:

> Do not turn the clock back! Imagine the Levitical ordinances and sacrificial ritual are *still* in full force, and realize that they would be no more effectual today than they were throughout the duration of the old covenant. Christ the Pioneer and High Priest has opened up once and for all a new and living way toward the coming consummation of God's purpose. Look forward then and move on as pilgrims with eager expectation in full assurance that salvation is secure for believers against the "Day now drawing near" (10:25), through Christ the one Mediator between God and humanity.

We maintained previously that the exhortation to "go forth outside the camp bearing the shame of Jesus" (Heb 13:13) is not a call out of the world, but a call to costly discipleship for Jesus' sake *in the world,* in the profane place.[46] The term *parembolē* ("camp") would then be synonymous with Israel and all that the name Israel stood for, her life and worship, traditions and rites and practices: Jesus' suffering and death "outside the camp" represented a complete break with the old order. That is consistent with the life situation we have envisaged for the Jewish Christian addressees of Hebrews, who in a time after 70 C.E. were feeling the pull of their Jewish heritage,[47] were yearning for a restoration of the sacrificial ritual and had to be urgently reminded that this was not at all viable since they now had a great High Priest over the house of God (Heb 10:21).[48] For such a group the best or only medium of persuasion was a fresh exposition of biblical and extrabiblical traditions.

---

46. H. Koester, "Outside the Camp," *HTR* 55 (1962) 305f., interprets it in this way.

47. F. V. Filson, *Yesterday, A Study of Hebrews in the Light of Chapter 13* (Studies in Biblical Theology, 2nd Series 4; London, 1967), pp. 67ff. W. Horbury, in "Aaronic Priesthood," p. 49, notes the abiding importance of the priesthood as attested by the attention paid to priestly genealogy in Mishnah *Nashim;* also later Palestinian inscriptions of the priestly courses show the importance of the priesthood for synagogue worshippers.

48. F. L. Horton, *The Melchizedek Tradition* (*SNTS* MS 30; Cambridge, 1976), pp. 152ff., argues that Reull-Ruel Jethro in Exodus and Numbers appears without mention of his birth, death, or genealogy, and that he figured much more prominently in the Pentateuch than Melchizedek: yet Hebrews opts for Melchizedek as the type of Christ—on the ground that he is the *first* priest mentioned in the Pentateuch. But it is difficult to see how the all-important notion of the permanence of Melchizedek's priesthood could be adduced simply from being the *first* priest mentioned. Moreover Melchizedek speculation was rife in our author's time (see below).

THE AUTHOR OF HEBREWS' INTERPRETATION
OF THE OLD TESTAMENT

Hebrews is permeated with scriptural quotations. In calling up so many Old Testament texts, the author has one great aim in view: to instruct his readers on the High Priesthood of Christ and on its saving benefits. The pivot of his treatment is the biblical description of Melchizedek. In this certainly lies one of the main roots of his christology. In 1:5, Hebrews quotes Ps 2:7 in support of his defense of the superiority of Christ over all angels. In 5:5f. he picks up again the designation of Christ as Son in Ps 2:7, and now connects it closely with Ps 110:4: "Thou art a priest forever after the order of Melchizedek." The largely hortatory section 5:11–6:20 closes with yet another allusion to Jesus as "a high priest forever after the order of Melchizedek," and this is followed in 7:1–10:18 by a rather elaborate midrash on Gen 14:17–20 intended principally to assert the supremacy of Christ as High Priest over the Aaronic priesthood. Christ's superiority resides in the abiding character of his priestly ministry grounded in the "once-for-all" of his sacrificial death, in contrast with the priests of the old covenant who had to succeed each other constantly "because they were prevented by death from continuing in office" (7:23). Clearly Hebrews' focus is on the *forever* of Christ's Priesthood "after the order of Melchizedek." Being "without father or mother or genealogy," Melchizedek "continues a priest forever" (7:3). It is commonly supposed that our author derived his notion of the permanence of Melchizedek's priesthood by applying the hermeneutical principle *quod non in thora non in mundo* (or *typologia e silentio*) to Gen 14:17–20: the complete silence of the text on Melchizedek's origins means he is *agenealogētos* ("without genealogy") and so a "priest forever." [49]

It is, however, unlikely that the author of Hebrews built up his whole imposing christological edifice from Ps 110:4 and Gen 14:17–20. We restrict ourselves then to the question of how he does approach the texts he employs, what presuppositions he brings to bear upon them. It is best to think of him as engaged in a "triangular interaction."

At the apex of the triangle are the Jewish Christian group addressed by the writer. We cannot be sure whether they are already familiar with Melchizedek speculation, or perhaps even, in confession and liturgy, with the attribution to Christ of "High Priesthood after the order of Melchizedek." [50] But if we are right in supposing that parenesis was of the most urgent concern to the author, and that as directed to a situation in which his addressees

---

49. Käsemann, *Gottesvolk*, pp. 107f., does think the idea was present in the homologia in the church's liturgy.

50. I owe the phrase to T. H. Robinson, *The Epistle to the Hebrews* (MNTC; London, 1941), p. 22.

had become backward-looking and were longing for a renewal of the sacrificial cultus, then he would have had a springboard for delineating the person and work of Christ in cultic-priestly terms.

At the first lower point of the triangle stands the author himself. Like nearly all New Testament writers, he had no doubt reflected in depth in his own personal way on how it was that Jesus became the bringer of salvation. Crucial to his soteriology is his stress throughout on Christ's *suffering* and *sacrificial* death, through which and through which alone he could enter completely into the human condition. In the section 2:10–18 we have an early clue as to how Hebrews' doctrine of "Atonement by Sympathy"[51] was associated with the priestly function: "He had to be made like his brethren in every respect, so that he might become a merciful and faithful high priest in the service of God, to make expiation for the sins of the people" (2:17). The follow-up to this is the remarkable dialectic of 5:1–10, where in accord with Pss 2:7 and 110:4 Christ is designated for the first time in Hebrews as Son and High Priest *for ever*, and is also compared in his humanity and humility with the priests of the old covenant, "beset with weakness" (5:2); he too is a priest in lowliness, but also, through his suffering and death, in exaltation.

At the third point of the triangle are the texts of Ps 110:4 and Gen 14:17–20, from which the author builds up the large midrashic section 7:1–10:18. He did not, I believe, impose upon these texts an already clearly defined and fully formulated doctrine of Christ's abiding High Priestly ministry. We think rather of two-way traffic: the author brings to the old texts christological and soteriological ideas in the process of formation in his mind, and the texts in turn inspire in him a broadening of the horizons. That does not mean that we minimize the newness of the Christ event nor the dramatic and revolutionary impact it had upon Hebrews and indeed the whole New Testament. But we are also eager to uphold the tremendous impact the Jewish Scriptures made on the christological formulations of skilled and imaginative exegetes like the writer of Hebrews.[52] Hence our paradigm of "triangular interaction."

DEPENDENCE ON INTERNAL CHRISTIAN TRADITIONS

It is sometimes claimed that there are sufficient resemblances between Hebrews and other New Testament writings to justify the thesis that the

---

51. P. Katz, "The Quotations from Deuteronomy in Hebrews," *ZNW* 49 (1958) 213–23, reminds us that the LXX was undergoing extensive revision in the early Christian centuries and the quotations in Hebrews may represent the Hebrew text current in its time. See G. Howard, "Hebrews and the Old Testament Quotations," *NovT* 10 (1968) 208ff.; also J. C. McCullough, "The Old Testament Quotations in Hebrews," *NTS* (1980) 363ff., see esp. p. 379.

52. See C. Spicq, *L'Épître*, vol. 7 (Paris), pp. 102–38.

matrix of the author's theology/christology was internal Christian tradition or at least ideas, possibly extraneous, mediated through Christian tradition.[53] It is certainly quite possible to list a fairly large number of affinities, especially with John and Paul and Luke-Acts. In John 17 there is what is commonly called the "High Priestly" prayer of Jesus, where the way of Jesus as the one sent by God into the world and as uniquely the Sanctified is the indispensable precondition of the sanctification of the disciples and their sending out to all the earth (cf. Jn 17:17–19 and Heb 2:10ff.). As in Hebrews, so in Paul the continuing ministry of the exalted Christ is based upon his once-for-all act of obedience on the cross (e.g. Rom 6:10). Luke's Gospel closes with the risen Christ lifting his hands in priestly blessing over his disciples (Lk 24:50). These are only a very few examples of parallel concepts as between Hebrews and other canonical works.

It is tempting, in order to bring Hebrews into canonical line, so to speak, to overestimate the imprint on his mind of a shared stock of Christian tradition.[54] But if we turn from a reading of any New Testament document in its entirety to a reading of Hebrews in its entirety, we cannot but be struck by the singularity and strangeness of the latter. This has much to do with the *unique* manner in which, within the limits of the New Testament canon, he construes the Melchizedek texts of Ps 110:4 and Gen 14:17–20, and incorporates them in his witness to the eschatological High Priesthood of Christ. The inference is that *extracanonical* sources need to be reckoned with in any attempt to "explain" Hebrews. That we have postponed consideration of these until now is no reflection on our appraisal of their significance.

HEBREWS AND EARLY JEWISH
EXTRABIBLICAL LITERATURE

Professor J. H. Charlesworth has sought resolutely to free us from the shackles of a too narrowly canonical perspective in the investigation of Early Judaism and Christian origins. In the case of Hebrews he very rightly claims that it "should be read in the light of all documents anterior to and contemporaneous with it."[55] There are of course a number of passages in Hebrews which have long been widely recognized as possible allusions to documents

53. C. J. Hickling, "The Background of Hebrews 2:10–18," *NTS* 29 (1983) 112ff., lays great stress on the indebtedness of Hebrews to other canonical writings and points out the "striking frequency" of similarities between a single passage such as 2:10–18 and the Fourth Gospel (e.g. 2:10—Jn 3:14f.; 2:11—Jn 17:19; 2:12—Jn 17:6 and 28; 2:14b—Jn 12:31; 2:15—Jn 8:32). We must not overlook, however, the weighty influence on Hebrews of extracanonical factors.

Still under the influence of the biblical theology movement, I overstated the case for the unity of Hebrews with the rest of the NT in the early 1960s. Anderson, *Jesus and Christian Origins*, p. 288.

54. Charlesworth, *The Old Testament Pseudepigrapha and the New Testament*, p. 82.

55. *OTP*, vol. 2, pp. 811ff., "Ezekiel the Tragedian," trans. R. G. Robertson.

of the Apocrypha and Pseudepigrapha, and Charlesworth lists the following: 1En 70:1–4, Heb 11:5; Sir 25:23, Heb 12:12; Sir 44:16, Heb 11:5; Sir 44:21, Heb 6:14; WisSol 4:10, Heb 11:5; AscenIs 5:11–14, Heb 11:37. None of these, however, really sheds much light on the intellectual background of Hebrews, since the writer of Hebrews is merely dependent on a common treasury of traditions that circulated in various forms.

More promising is the dream vision of Moses in the *Exagōgē* of Ezekiel the Tragedian to which Charlesworth calls attention (EzekTrag 2:68–89). On the peak of Sinai, Moses sees a throne stretching right up to the heavens and seated on it a *phōs* (which is a poetic term for "man" but by which Ezekiel here means "God"). Moses is invited to mount the throne and is handed a scepter and crown, whereupon God himself withdraws from the throne. His father-in-law then interprets the dream as a sign of Moses' coming heavenly majesty: "You shall cause a mighty throne to rise/and you yourself shall rule and govern men." In Heb 3:1–6 the author strives to convince his readers of the supremacy of Christ, whose greatness far exceeds the greatness of Moses.

Legends about Moses did abound in early Judaism. Conceivably the group addressed in Hebrews had some knowledge of a tradition of Moses' exaltation like the one embedded in the dream vision of the *Exagōgē*. In that case we could the more readily see the force of the argument in 3:1–6: Christ is superior even to the Moses whom the readers continue to revere. But I am not sure that such a tradition may have been a spur for the author of Hebrews' witness to God's appointment of Christ as the enthroned High Priest (5:5–10; 6:20; 7:23–28; 8:1), as Charlesworth conjectures.[56] The *sessio ad dextram*, the heavenly enthronement or exaltation of Christ, is expressly mentioned in a good many places in the New Testament where there is no hint of a comparison with Moses.[57] One possible source may have been a configuration of ideas around the "Son of Man." Again there is nothing whatever *priestly* about the figure of Moses in the dream vision of the *Exagōgē*. He appears to be described rather in terms of an imperial, even secular, majesty. Yet it is the idea of High Priesthood which is uppermost in the mind of the author of Hebrews, as his opening invitation clearly shows ("Consider Jesus, the apostle and *high priest* of our confession," 3:1), when he compares Moses and Jesus, and embarks on his brief midrashic exegesis of Num 12:7. Accordingly, perhaps the most we should say is that a tradition somewhat similar to that in the Tragedian's account of Moses' vision may lie vaguely in the background of Hebrews.

To turn again to Melchizedek, scholars have long been well aware from

---

56. Charlesworth, *The Old Testament Pseudepigrapha and the New Testament*, p. 84.
57. See e.g. Mk 14:62, Lk 22:69, Phil 2:9, Col 3:1, a number of passages in Rev; cf. Acts 2:33, 5:31.

references in Philo and Josephus that this mysterious figure was a subject of interest in early Jewish writers very different in location, aim, and intention. Philo refers to Melchizedek in three different passages. In the first of these he takes the narrative data of Gen 14:18–20 simply as supporting the institution of tithing, although he makes fleeting mention of Melchizedek's "self-tutored" and "instructive" priesthood. The second is an amplification of the encounter between Melchizedek and Abraham. The third is the most extensive, describing Melchizedek as a "righteous king," but going beyond that to an allegorizing interpretation of Melchizedek as "divine," as the Logos, probably by way of inference from Philo's concept of his underived, untutored priesthood (cf. Heb 1:1–2). Josephus tells us little more than that he was a "righteous king," the first priest before God and founder of the Temple. The Melchizedek traditions represented in Philo and Josephus do not appear to be very close to Hebrews, possibly least of all Philo's allegorical treatment.[58]

Recent research on early Jewish pseudepigraphical works (some hitherto unknown) has opened up a richer vein of Melchizedekian speculations. However, the Genesis Apocryphon from Qumran, which alludes to Melchizedek at 22:14 can hardly be said to illumine the theme. Of indeterminate date, it is little more than a paraphrastic translation into Aramaic of Gen 14:18–20.

The much disputed 11Q Melchizedek, also from Qumran, is another matter. The text is unfortunately fragmentary and difficult to reconstruct. But it would seem that there is nowhere explicit reference to Melchizedek's High Priesthood.[59] Whether or not the "angelic warrior soteriology" in 11Q Melchizedek constitutes a sort of backdrop for the reference in Heb 2:14b and 17 to the Son's conflict with the devil (commonly the agent of evil and death in Jewish tradition) is hard to say. Certainly there is a striking contrast between the angelic warrior Melchizedek wrestling with Belial in 11Q Melchizedek and the Christ whose victory is won through suffering and death in Hebrews.

Again, there is considerable ambiguity in the use of the term 'elōhīm in 11QMelch, especially in lines 9–11. Apparently the obedient angels and even the powers of Belial are called by that name. But most probably in line 10 it means a divine figure or heavenly being, with whom Melchizedek is identified, so that he appears here as a Redeemer. One of the central issues raised by 11QMelch, therefore, is whether in presenting Melchizedek as a

---

58. Philo, *De Congressu*, 99; *Abr* 235; *Legum Allegoriae* III 79–89; Josephus *War* 6.438; *Ant* 1.180–81. For a concise discussion of these passages, see F. L. Horton, *The Melchizedek Tradition*, pp. 54ff.

59. For different renderings of the text, see M. de Jonge and A. S. van der Woude, "11Q Melchizedek and the New Testament," *NTS* 12 (1966) 306; J. A. Fitzmyer, "Further Light on Melchizedek from Qumran Cave 11," in *Essays on the Semitic Background of the New Testament* (London, 1971), pp. 245–67; F. L. Horton, *The Melchizedek Tradition*, p. 74.

divine Redeemer, 11QMelch confronts us with a tradition radically different from the testimony of Hebrews.[60]

If we accept that for the author of Hebrews, Melchizedek is the antitype of Christ, then we might think of the contrast Hebrews draws as being between the eternal heavenly priesthood of Christ and the earthly perpetual priesthood of Melchizedek.[61] The difficulty with that is its inappropriateness to the real contrast made throughout chapters 7 and 8, which is that between Christ's everlasting priesthood founded on his once-for-all perfect sacrifice (7:27) and the continual day-to-day sacrifices of the earthly priests of the old covenant. The likeness between Melchizedek and Christ therefore is that they share an everlasting or permanent priesthood. Consequently a certain correspondence between the tradition of a divine redeemer figure in 11QMelch and the elevated status accorded Melchizedek in Hebrews is not an unreasonable hypothesis, although one might have serious reservations about accepting the suggestion of Professors M. de Jonge and A. S. van der Woude that Hebrews regarded Melchizedek as an (arch-) angel who appeared to Abraham long ago.

We proceed now to a quite different brand of Melchizedek legend. Slavonic Enoch or 2 Enoch, as we now have access to it in the most recent English translation, contains at the end in chapter 73 a highly mythical report of the miraculous birth of Melchizedek, which together with chapters 69–72 was left out of the longtime standard edition of *The Apocrypha and Pseudepigrapha* by R. H. Charles.[62] The report has Noe (and Nir) place Sothonim, the dead wife of Nir (who had had no sexual contact with her), on the bed before leaving for the sepulcher. Then a child came out of the dead Sothonim and sat on the bed, and the glorious badge of priesthood was on his breast. Noe and Nir called him Melchizedek. And the Lord told Nir he would send the archangel Gabriel to take the child and place him in the paradise of Edem.

2 Enoch is a passing strange work. F. I. Andersen, the leading expert on it, justly comments that "there must be something very strange about a work when one scholar, Charles, concludes that it was written by a Hellenized Jew of Alexandria in the first century B.C., while another, J. T. Milik, argues that it was written by a Christian monk in Byzantium in the ninth century A.D."[63] The work is extant only in Slavonic; its textual history is very complicated; no known manuscript goes back earlier than the fourteenth century C.E.; it

60. F. L. Horton, *The Melchizedek Tradition*, p. 162, suggests that the divine figure of Melchizedek in 11QM could, *inter alia*, have given rise to the later Melchizedekian heresies which subordinated Christ to Melchizedek.

61. See F. L. Horton, *The Melchizedek Tradition*, p. 162. See E. Riggenbach, *Der Brief an die Hebräer* (Leipzig-Erlangen, 1962), p. 186.

62. J. H. Charlesworth, *Old Testament Pseudepigrapha and the New Testament*, p. 85.

63. F. I. Andersen, in *OTP,* vol. 1, p. 95.

has been subjected to extensive interpolations and revisions, some by Christian scribes; the original language, most probably Semitic, can no longer be determined. In my view it is reminiscent in some places of some features of the Mandean literature, but it could of course have emanated from any Gnostic or quasi-Gnostic source. If it does go back, as it perhaps may, to around the first century C.E., "it is a source of the highest importance for the history of syncretism of selected parts of the Jewish faith and cosmological speculation." [64]

As to the legend of the miraculous birth of Melchizedek, it cannot possibly be either strictly Jewish or Christian, contradicting as it does the Jewish conviction of the Aaronite or Zadokite lineage of the priesthood, and blasphemous as it would be as a secondhand copy by any Christian of the birth stories of Jesus in Matthew and Luke. If such a legend were "in the air" in the time of Hebrews, the author of Hebrews surely brought Melchizedekian speculation of that order "down to earth," by his own sober and restrained handling of the theme. Drawing a bow at a venture, we conjecture that the story of the miraculous birth of Melchizedek from a dead mother could be a highly fanciful midrash on the *amētōr* ("without mother") of Heb 7:3a, with intermingled echoes of the dying and rising again of the fertility deities in the Mysteries, of the death and resurrection of Christ, of Abraham-Sarah, and the notion of the Messianic birth pangs. In the syncretistic world of 2 Enoch, such a congeries of ideas is only to be expected. Even if one posits for the myth of Melchizedek's birth in 2 Enoch a Jewish substratum,[65] a significant *parallel* between the 2 Enoch passage and Heb 7:3a cannot be lightly assumed.

We come finally to affinities of a broader kind between Hebrews and early Jewish extrabiblical literature. The language and imagery of Hebrews resemble those of such apocalypses as Fourth Ezra and the (Syriac) Apocalypse of Baruch. For instance, the plainly Christian introduction to the Jewish apocalypse of Fourth Ezra depicting Mount Zion (peopled by an innumerable company clad in immortal clothing and crowned by the Son of God whom they confessed in the world, 4Ezra 2:42–48) is very much reminiscent of Heb 12:22–24. The great fourth vision (4Ezra 9:26–10:59) portrays a woman bewailing the death of her son on the very day of his wedding, but then suddenly transformed into Zion itself, the city of God to come (cf. Heb 12:12 and 13:14). The fact that the woman is promised *"rest"* (4Ezra 9:24) in the context of this apocalyptic vision suggests that the parallel tradition of the *katapausis* ("rest") in Hebrews refers not so much spatially, in the Greek philosophical manner, to the transcendent world at God's side as the place of

64. Ibid., p. 96.
65. See A. Caquot, "La pérennité de sacerdoce," *Paganisme, judaisme, christianisme: Influences et affrontements dans le monde antique. Melanges offerts à Marcel Simon* (Paris, 1978), pp. 109–16. See Charlesworth, *The Old Testament Pseudepigrapha and the New Testament*, p. 175, n. 65.

rest, but to the *coming* place of rest entered by the believers at the endtime when the old world is dissolved and the new world appears.[66]

Recent study of Fourth Maccabees persuades me that its author and the author of Hebrews have a good deal in common. Both were Hellenized Jews of the Diaspora (the latter of course become Christian), conversant with Greek philosophical principles and Greek rhetoric, which they took up and applied in the service of their respective faith standpoints. Fourth Maccabees suggests that the cardinal Greek virtues are subsumed under what is called (in a remarkable fusion of Greek and Hebrew ideas) "the pious reason" (*ho eusebēs logismos*), which alone enables human control of the passions or emotions, and in the case of the Maccabean martyrs manifests itself as *hypomonē* ("endurance") under the most horrendous tortures, in steadfast loyalty to the Law of Moses. The author of Hebrews also is preoccupied with the theme of human suffering and persecution, and frequently turns Greek philosophical terminology to the primary purpose of encouraging in his addressees *hypomonē* and *pistis* ("faith") which can keep them going amid the hardships of the world toward the final goal.[67]

In both treatises the "end" or "goal" can be identified with death itself as the ultimate perfection (Heb 12:23, 13:14). Compare 4Mac 7:15, where in the panegyric on Eleazar we read: "O blessed old age, revered gray head, life loyal to the Law, and perfected by the faithful seal of death."[68] One can scarcely turn from a reading of the eleventh chapter of Hebrews to Fourth Maccabees without being impressed by the correspondence between the rhetorical form of "the roll-call of the faithful" in Hebrews and the glory attributed to martyrdom in the latter (in what is surely a more florid and less sophisticated rhetoric).[69] Again the Greek notion of the immortality of the soul replaces the prevalent Jewish doctrine of the resurrection of the body in Fourth Maccabees (9:22, 14:5f., 16:13, 17:12, 18:23). In Hebrews there is no mention either of the resurrection of the dead. Here at least both authors capitulated to their Greek cultural environment—but so did many others without forfeiting their elemental Jewishness.

Again and again we have emphasized how extremely significant for Hebrews is the human anguish, suffering, and death of Jesus in obedience to the will of God, as a once-for-all act of atonement. In Fourth Maccabees, Eleazar prays: "Make my blood their purification and take my life as a ran-

66. See 4Ezra 4:27, 5:40, 7:119; 2Bar 5:3. See also O. Hofius, *Katapausis: Die Vorstellung von Endzeitlichen Ruheort im Hebräerbrief (WUNT,* Tübingen, 1970), pp. 91ff.

67. H. Anderson, "Fourth Maccabees," *OTP,* vol. 2, p. 540. A. Deissmann's description of 4 Maccabees as a bestseller well known to the Apostle Paul ("Das Vierte Makkabäerbuch," *APAT,* vol. 2 [Tübingen, 1900], pp. 151f., 160, 174) is probably an exaggeration.

68. In 4 Maccabees the aged Eleazar is apostrophized thus: "O priest worthy of your priestly office" (4Mac 7:6–8). Priesthood and martyr death are here in very close proximity.

69. H. Windisch, *Der Hebräerbrief (HNT;* Tübingen. 2 Auflage, 1931), p. 81, thinks of a Jewish source for Hebrews 11.

som for theirs" (6:29), and we read later: "Through the blood of these righteous ones and through the propitiation of their death the divine providence rescued Israel" (17:22). But we cannot read much into this parallel between the two works—the idea of vicarious redemption had a long history in Israel and is virtually omnipresent in the New Testament.

The "riddle" of Hebrews is many-sided. It will surely continue to be discussed, despite or perhaps to a large extent because of the additional material at our disposal through contemporary research in the extrabiblical literature. We have tried to show that it is impossible to discuss the writer's christology as if he were a philosophically minded formulator of doctrine. Since it is agreed on all sides that his christology/soteriology is designed to serve the interest of the urgent parenesis which runs through the whole document, it should follow that any attempt to "explain" the author depends on the way we construe the life situation of the addressees and the way he interprets Scripture in meeting it. Hence our "triangular interaction."

Our own theory, which will not commend itself to the many who favor an early (pre-70) date for Hebrews, hinges on the argument that the primary determinant of his thought is eschatology. He is confronting a Jewish-Christian group, who are "perishing" from the loss of vision, of a strong sense of eschatological urgency, and are refusing, in their nostalgia for a Jewish past, to lay hold of the *promise*. He exhorts them and challenges them to recapture the visionary gleam, to get on the march again toward the goal. So he confronts them with an imagery, Mount Zion, the city of God to come, "outside the camp," calculated to rekindle their waning imagination. We see the author of Hebrews as an image maker in the apocalyptic mold.[70]

70. Contrast W. Horbury, "There are no accounts of visions in Hebrews, whether apocalyptic or Philonic" ("Aaronic Priesthood," p. 47). See J. Moffatt, "Hebrews," LV. There are certainly no accounts of visions as in Revelation, but there is a visionary element and a vivid series of appeals to the readers' imagination.

THE "SON OF MAN" TRADITION AND THE BOOK OF REVELATION

The book of Revelation contains several sayings which allude to Daniel 7:13[1] and two which are variants of sayings in the synoptic tradition which, in one or more forms, refer to the Son of Man (ὁ υἱὸς τοῦ ἀνθρώπου).[2] The purpose of this paper is to clarify how these sayings relate to Daniel 7 and the synoptic tradition. These clarifications, it is hoped, will contribute to the understanding of an early form of christology and how this christology was indebted to Jewish tradition.

THE PROPHETIC SAYING OF REV 1:7

The book of Revelation begins with a prologue in the third person which characterizes the book as a revelation (ἀποκάλυψις) and as words of prophecy (1:1–3). This prologue is followed by an epistolary introduction (1:4–6). In 1:9 the vision account proper begins. Between the epistolary introduction and the vision account are two prophetic sayings. One is spoken anonymously (vs. 7) and one is attributed to God (vs. 8).

The anonymous saying of 1:7 alludes both to Dan 7:13 and to Zech 12:10–14. Apparently the only other first-century text which conflates these two passages from older scripture is Mt 24:30. Zech 12:10 is quoted as scripture in Jn 19:37.[3] The texts are laid out below for comparision.[4]

Mt 24:30
καὶ τότε φανήσεται τὸ σημεῖον
τοῦ υἱοῦ

Rev 1:7
ἰδοὺ ἔρχεται μετὰ τῶν νεφελῶν,
καὶ

---

1. Rev 1:7a, 1:13, and 14:14.
2. Rev 3:3b/16:15a is related to Mt 24:43–44/Lk 12:39–40, and Rev 3:5c is related to Mt 10:32/Lk 12:8.
3. See also EBar 7.9–10.
4. The table of texts which follows is based on that of K. Stendahl, *The School of St. Matthew* (Acta Seminarii Neotestamentici Uppsaliensis 20; Lund, 1954), pp. 212–13.

τοῦ ἀνθρώπου ἐν οὐρανῷ, καὶ τότε
κόψονται πᾶσαι αἱ φυλαὶ τῆς γῆς καὶ
ὄψονται τὸν υἱὸν τοῦ ἀνθρώπου
ερχομενον επι των νεφελων του ουρανου
μετα δυναμεως και δοξης πολλης.

ἐν οὐρανῷ] τοῦ ἐν οὐρανοῖς D

ὄψεται αὐτὸν πᾶς ὀφθαλμὸς καὶ
οἵτινες αὐτὸν ἐξεκέντησαν, καὶ
κόψονται ἐπ᾽ αὐτὸν πᾶσαι αἱ φυλαὶ τῆς γῆς.

μετὰ] ἐπὶ C pc
ὄψεται] ὄψονται X al.

Jn 19:37
ὄψονται εἰς ὃν ἐξεκέντησαν.

Zech 12:10, 12, 14 LXX[B]
καὶ ἐκχεῶ ἐπὶ τὸν οἶκον Δαυιδ καὶ ἐπὶ
τοὺς κατοικοῦντας Ιερουσαλημ πνεῦμα
χάριτος καὶ οἰκτιρμοῦ · καὶ ἐπιβλέψονται
πρός με ἀνθ᾽ ὧν κατωρχήσαντο καὶ
κόψονται ἐπ᾽ αὐτὸν κοπετὸν ὡς ἐπ᾽
ἀγαπητῶ, καὶ ὀδυνηθήσονται ὀδύνην ὡς
ἐπὶ πρωτοτόκῳ . . . καὶ κόψεται ἡ γῆ
ὑπολελειμμέναι φυλαὶ . . .

MT
ושפכתי על בית דויד ועל יושב
ירושלם רוח חן ותחנונים
והביטו אלי את אשר דקרו וספדו
עליו כמספד על היחיד והמר עליו
כהמר על הבכור;

וספדה הארץ משפחות . . .
וספדה הארץ משפחות משפחות . . .
כל המשפחות הנשארות . . .

ἀνθ᾽ ὧν κατωρχ.] εἰς ὃν ἐξεκέντησαν Lucian Theod.—ἐπ᾽ αὐτόν] αὐτόν Aq. Symm. Theod.

Dan 7:13a LXX	Theodotion	MT
ἐθεώρουν ἐν ὁράματι τῆς	ἐθεώρουν ἐν ὁράματι τῆς	חזה הוית בחזוי
νυκτὸς, καὶ ἰδοὺ ἐπὶ τῶν	νυκτὸς, καὶ ἰδοὺ μετὰ τῶν	ליליא וארו עם ענני
νεφελῶν τοῦ οὐρανοῦ	νεφελῶν τοῦ οὐρανοῦ	שמיא כבר אנש אתה
ὡς υἱος ἀνθρώπου	ὡς υἱὸς ἀνθρώπου	הוה.
ἤρχετο.	ἐρχόμενος	

μετὰ] ἐπὶ Q.
ἐρχόμενος] add. ἦν A.

Relation to Dan 7:13

The first question to be addressed is how Rev 1:7 relates to the texts of Dan 7:13. It is well known that the book of Revelation never explicitly quotes scripture. It is equally well kown that it is permeated by the language, forms, and ideas of older scripture, especially the prophets. In spite of the lack of explicit quotation (i.e. with a formula), many scholars have believed it possible to discern what text or texts of scripture the author was using. R. H. Charles concluded that the author translated directly from the Hebrew or Aramaic of the biblical text, although he was sometimes influenced by the Old Greek and by another, later Greek version. This later Greek version was a revision of the Old Greek,[5] according to Charles, which was later revised and incorporated into his version by Theodotion.[6] H. B. Swete concluded that the author of Revelation "generally availed himself of the Alexandrian version of the Old Testament."[7] L. P. Trudinger has argued that a substantial number of quotations and allusions in Revelation have their closest affinity with the Palestinian Aramaic Targumim.[8]

With regard to Rev 1:7, Charles concluded that the author of Revelation used a Semitic text of Dan 7:13 similar to the text used by Theodotion in translating his version. Charles argued further that he translated directly from the Hebrew of Zech 12:10, 12.[9] Bousset simply noted that the preposition μετά of Rev 1:7 agrees with the reading of the Masoretic text[10] and of Theodotion.[11] Grelot, following Montgomery, linked Rev 1:7 to Theodotion because of the μετά.[12] Swete concluded that in Rev 1:7 the author made use of a collection of prophetic testimonies in Greek.[13]

Recent text-critical discoveries and studies have changed the scholarly view of the text of the Jewish Bible in comparison to the time of Charles and Swete. Although Swete acknowledged that the author of Revelation may have used a text of the OG different from that which is found in the surviving

---

5. Hereafter, OG.

6. R. H. Charles, *A Critical and Exegetical Commentary on the Revelation of St. John* (ICC; New York, 1920), vol. 1, pp. lxvi–lxxxi.

7. H. B. Swete, *The Apocalypse of St. John*, 3rd ed. (London, 1909, repr. 1917), p. clv.

8. L. P. Trudinger, "Some Observations Concerning the Text of the Old Testament in the Book of Revelation," *JTS* 17 (1966) 82–88. Although he points out that Rev 1:7b reads against the OG, Trudinger does not find any particular affinity between Rev 1:7 and the Palestinian Targumim (85, n.3 and 86, n.1). The article by H. M. Parker ("The Scripture of the Author of the Revelation of John," *The Iliff Review* 37 [1980] 35–51) is concerned with the implicit canon of the Apocalypse, not with the text or version of the Old Scripture used by the author.

9. Charles, *The Revelation of St. John*, vol. 1, pp. 17–18.

10. Hereafter, MT.

11. W. Bousset, *Die Offenbarung Johannis* (Kritisch-exegetischer Kommentar über das Neue Testament [Meyer] 16; rev. ed.; Göttingen, 1906, repr. 1966), p. 189.

12. P. Grelot, "Les versions grecques de Daniel," *Bib* 47 (1966) 386; J. A. Montgomery, *A Critical and Exegetical Commentary on the Book of Daniel* (ICC; Edinburgh, 1927, repr. 1979), p. 304.

13. Swete, *The Apocalypse of St. John*, pp. 9–10.

manuscripts,[14] too often earlier scholars neglected to distinguish between the original OG and the mixed textual witnesses which reflect modifications made by Origen in his attempt to reconstruct the Septuagint.[15] Further, it was too often assumed that the *Vorlage* of the OG was identical to the Hebrew and Aramaic of the MT.[16]

Recent discoveries which contribute to our knowledge of the text of the Jewish Bible in the first century C.E. are the biblical manuscripts from Qumran (and elsewhere in the Judean wilderness) and Papyrus 967, which contains OG versions of Esther, Ezekiel, and Daniel.[17] The Qumran manuscripts at times provide evidence for a different Hebrew or Aramaic text from the MT. Papyrus 967 is a witness to the OG which may antedate Origen. At least it is non-Hexaplaric.[18]

A study which has had great impact on current thinking about the history of the Greek version is D. Barthélemy's analysis of the Greek Scroll of the Minor Prophets which was discovered in Wadi Khabra in 1952.[19] The manuscript has been dated to the second half of the first century B.C.E. Barthélemy has persuaded many scholars that this manuscript represents a revision of the OG in order to bring it more into line with the MT or its prototype. This recension is an early example of the enterprise reflected in the recensions attributed to Theodotion and Aquila, which went further in the direction of literalness of translation and consistency in translating a particular Hebrew/Aramaic word with a particular Greek word. The consensus now appears to be that the works attributed to Theodotion, Aquila, and their predecessors should be called recensions rather than versions, because they seem to have been revisions of the OG rather than fresh translations.[20]

These recent studies reopen the following question: what were the original reading(s) of Dan 7:13 and with what reading(s) was the author of Revelation familiar? The major witnesses are given below for comparison.

---

14. Ibid., p. clv.

15. See S. Pace Jeansonne, *The Old Greek Translation of Daniel 7–12 (CBQ* MS 19; Washington, DC: CBA, 1988), p. 2.

16. Ibid, pp. 2–3.

17. In Pap. 967 the order of episodes is different from that in MT. P.-M. Bogaert has argued that the order in Pap. 967 is secondary ("Relecture et refonte historicisante du Livre de Daniel attestées par la première version grecque [papyrus 967]," in *Études sur Le Judaïsme Hellénistique* [Lectio Divina 119; Paris, 1984], pp. 197–224).

18. A. Geissen, *Der Septuaginta-Text des Buches Daniel Kap. 5–12, zusammen mit Susanna, Bel et Draco sowie Esther Kap. 1, 1a–2, 15* (Papyrologische Texte und Abhandlungen 5; Bonn, 1968), p. 18.

19. D. Barthélemy, "Redecouverte d'un chainon manquant de l'histoire de las Septante," *RB* 60 (1953) 18–29; see also his *Les devanciers d'Aquila* (VTSup 10; Leiden, 1963). Subsequent investigation has led to the conclusion that the scroll was actually found at Nahal Hever in 1953. See now the definitive publication of this manuscript by Emanuel Tov, with the collaboration of R. A. Kraft and a contribution by P. J. Parsons, *The Greek Minor Prophets Scroll from Nahal Hever (8HevXIIgr)* (DJD 8; Oxford, 1990).

20. Pace Jeansonne, *The Old Greek Translation of Daniel 7–12*, pp. 19–23.

MT Biblia Hebraica Stuttgartensia 1967/77 (Aramaic)

חזה הוית בחזוי ליליא
וארו עם ענני שמיא
כבר אנש אתה הוה
ועד עתיק יומיא מטה
וקדמוהי הקרבוהי

OG

Ziegler 1954[21]

ἐθεώρουν ἐν ὁράματι τῆς νυκτὸς καὶ ἰδοὺ ἐπὶ τῶν νεφελῶν τοῦ οὐρανοῦ ὡς υἱὸς ἀνθρώπου ἤρχετο, καὶ ἕως τοῦ παλαιοῦ ἡμερῶν παρῆν,
καὶ οἱ παρεστηκότες προσῆγαγον αὐτόν.

Codex Chisianus (MS. 88; Chigi MS.; 9th/11th C.E.; Origen's Hexaplaric
recension) and Syh (the Syro-Hexaplar; early 7th cent. C.E.[22]

ἐθεώρουν ἐν ὁράματι τῆς νυκτὸς καὶ ἰδοὺ ἐπὶ τῶν νεφελῶν τοῦ οὐρανοῦ ὡς υἱὸς ανθρώπου ἤρχετο, καὶ ὡς παλαιὸς ἡμερῶν παρῆν, καὶ
οἱ παρεστηκότες παρῆσαν αὐτῷ.

Kölner Teil des Papyrus 967 (2nd–early 3rd cent. C.E.)[23]

ἐθεώρουν ἐν ὁράματι τῆς νυκτὸς καὶ ἰδοὺ ἐπὶ τῶν νεφελῶν τοῦ οὐρανοῦ ἤρχετο ὡς υἱὸς ἀνθρώπου καὶ ὡς παλαιὸς ἡμερω(ν) παρῆν καὶ
οἱ παρεστηκότες προσῆγαγον αὐτῷ.

Theodotion[24]

ἐθεώρουν ἐν ὁράματι τῆς νυκτὸς καὶ ἰδοὺ μετὰ τῶν νεφελῶν τοῦ οὐρανοῦ ὡς υἱὸς ἀνθρώπου ἐρχόμενος καὶ ἕως τοῦ παλαιοῦ τῶν
ἡμερῶν ἔφθασε καὶ προσήχθη αὐτῷ.

Of the portion of Dan 7:13 which is employed in Rev 1:7a, the only word
of the MT which is disputed is the preposition עם. It is possible that it was in
the *Vorlage* of the OG. If it was, the translator may have misread על for עם.
Another possibility is that the translator used ἐπί to translate עם in an attempt to render the sense. The use of prepositions in the OG of Daniel is
not standardized and επι is the most common preposition. It is unlikely, as

---

21. The text cited is Ziegler's critical edition of the Old Greek (σ′) from J. Ziegler, *Susanna,
Daniel, Bel et Draco* (Septuaginta: Vetus Testamentum Graecum 16.2; Göttingen, 1954), pp.
169–70.

22. This reading is reconstructed from Ziegler's apparatus. It is also the reading printed by
A. Rahlfs, *Septuaginta* (Stuttgart, 1935), vol. 2, p. 914, as the reading for the Old Greek (OG).

23. This reading is taken from Geissen, *Der Septuaginta-Text*, p. 108.

24. The text cited is Ziegler's critical edition of Theodotion (θ′) from Ziegler, *Susanna, Daniel, Bel et Draco*, pp. 169–70.

some have argued, that the translator's choice of επι was theologically motivated. It is also possible that the *Vorlage* of the OG was different from the MT.[25]

Attention may now be turned to the relation of Rev 1:7a to Dan 7:13. Notable is the fact that Rev 1:7a differs from the MT and all the Greek forms of the text in the order of words. In Rev 1:7a, the verb follows immediately after ἰδού. In the other texts, the verb comes later in the clause, after the prepositional phrase regarding clouds. The Aramaic of the MT has as a verbal form a participle (אתה) with the perfect tense of the finite verb (הוה). The OG translates this verbal phrase with the simple imperfect (ἤρχετο). In Theodotion the participle only is used (ἐρχόμενος).[26] Rev 1:7a differs from all the other texts in having the present finite verb (ἔρχεται). These two differences are most likely due to the author's free citing of old scripture by way of adapting it to his own concerns and to the context of his work. The placement of the verb ἔρχεται before the phrase about the clouds tends to emphasize the verbal action. The use of the past tense in Dan 7:13 is due to the context: the relating of events in a vision seen in the past. The new context in Rev 1:7a is a prophetic saying or oracle. In such a shift from vision to oracle, a shift from past to future tense would be expected. Here the present is used to express a vivid, realistic confidence in the speedy fulfillment of the oracle.[27]

The use of μετά rather than ἐπί may be an indication of what text of Daniel was known to the author of Revelation. Those who argue that the author of Revelation was quoting or alluding to scripture from memory are probably correct.[28] Charles envisioned the author writing with a number of manuscripts at his disposal.[29] Recent studies have tended to view the author as an itinerant charismatic leader or prophet.[30] This view makes it unlikely that the author carried scrolls with him. If one assumes, however, that the use of μετά is not simply an oral variant of the tradition, but accurately reflects the text remembered by the author, it follows that in this case, he was not dependent on the OG. Either he himself translated a remembered Aramaic text or he recalled a Greek recension closer to the MT than to the OG.

One of the most significant differences between Rev 1:7a and the various forms of Dan 7:13, as well as the allusion to the Daniel verse in Mt 24:30, is that the allusion in Revelation lacks any explicit reference to the figure de-

---

25. On these points, see Pace Jeansonne, *The Old Greek Translation of Daniel 7–12*, pp. 65, 109–114.

26. Alexandrinus and the minuscules 106 and 584 add ην.

27. See Blass-Debrunner-Funk, § 323.

28. For example, L. A. Vos, *The Synoptic Traditions in the Apocalypse* (Kampen, 1965), p. 52.

29. Charles, *The Revelation of St. John*, vol. 1, pp. lxv, lxxxiii.

30. See A. Yarbro Collins, *Crisis and Catharsis: The Power of the Apocalypse* (Philadelphia, 1984), pp. 34–49, and the literature discussed there.

scribed as "one like a son of man" in Daniel and as "the Son of Man" in
Matthew. This point will be discussed below.[31]

Relation to Zech 12:10–14

The MT of Zech 12:10 reads "and they [the house of David and the inhabitants of Jerusalem] will look at me whom they pierced."[32] The OG reads,
"and they will look at me because they treated (me) despitefully."[33] Apparently the translator of the OG misread דקרו as רקדו.[34] The OG follows the
MT or its prototype closely in translating והביטו with ἐπιβλέψονται. The OG
follows the MT also in having a first person singular object of the looking.

The MT continues, "and they will mourn over him [vs. 10] . . . The land
will mourn, family by family, separately [vs. 12] . . . All the surviving families (shall mourn), each family separately and their wives separately [vs.
14]."[35] The OG rendering of this portion of vs. 10 is very similar in meaning
to the Hebrew. In both there is a shift from looking at "me" to mourning over
"him." As does הארץ, ἡ γῆ can mean "the land," as in the land of Israel, or
"the earth" in vs. 12. The word used (φυλή) to translate משפחה has much the
same meaning, at least by the hellenistic period.[36]

The allusion to Zech 12:10 in Rev 1:7b differs considerably in wording
from both the MT and the OG. Instead of referring at first to a specific group
of people, the house of David and the inhabitants of Jerusalem, the text of
Revelation says that "every eye will see him." Not only is the subject different, but the verb is simply "will see" (ὄψεται), rather than "will look at"
(ἐπιβλέψονται or the equivalent). The change in subject is due to the author's adaptation of the scripture for his own purposes. The reference to
"every eye" makes the appearance of the one coming with the clouds an
event of universal significance. The difference in the verb may be due to
paraphrasing of the original.

Rev 1:7b continues "including those who pierced him." In this allusion to
Zech 12:10, Revelation differs from both the MT and the OG in having the
third person rather than the first person singular object. This change may
have been made in order to render the sense of Zech 12:10, under the assumption that the prophetic, oracular "I" is the voice of Christ.[37] Revelation

---

31. T. Holtz (*Die Christologie der Apokalypse des Johannes* [TU 85; Berlin, 1962], pp. 135–
36) tried to explain the lack of the title Son of Man in Rev 1:7 as deliberate, because in the book
of Revelation, the title was reserved for the expression of the relationship of Christ to the community. This argument fails to take into account the fact that the *title* Son of Man does not occur
in the messages (chs. 2–3) either.

32. See the Heb. text given above.

33. See the Gk. text given above and labeled as LXX[B].

34. So, for example, argues D. J. Moo, *The Old Testament in the Gospel Passion Narratives*
(Sheffield, 1983), p. 210.

35. See the Heb. text given above.

36. See LSJM, p. 1961.

37. Cf. Moo, *The Old Testament in the Gospel Passion Narratives*, p. 211.

agrees with the MT, however, against the OG, in having a verb meaning "pierced" (ἐξεκέντησαν). Swete suggested that this non-Septuagintal reading was current in Palestine at the time the fourth gospel was written, since it appears also in Theodotion.[38] This agreement could be explained either by the author's knowledge of the prototype of the MT or of a Greek recension which had corrected the error in the OG on this point.

In the beginning of the next clause of Rev 1:7b, Revelation is very close to both the MT and the OG; in fact, the wording is identical to the OG: καὶ κόψονται ἐπ' αὐτόν. However, the subject of the clause, which comes at the end, is quite different: πᾶσαι αἱ φυλαὶ τῆς γῆς. This expression may be seen simply as a paraphrase of the more elaborated subject of the MT and OG and translated "all the tribes of the land." Alternatively, and this seems more likely in light of the phrase "every eye will see him," it may be seen as a universalizing adaptation and translated as "all the tribes of the earth."

Relation to Mt 24:30

Matthew and Revelation agree in the universalizing subject of the mourning: πᾶσαι αἱ φυλαὶ τῆς γῆς. They also agree in using a form of the verb ὄψομαι, rather than ἐπιβλέψομαι or another verb close to והביטו in meaning. Very significant also, as noted above, is the fact that these two passages are the only two of the first century which conflate Dan 7:13 and Zech 12:10–14.[39]

A number of differences are noteworthy as well. Only Matthew links the mourning of all the tribes of the earth with the appearance of the sign of the Son of Man.[40] Indeed, only Matthew explicitly mentions the Son of Man. Matthew has ἐρχόμενον rather than ἔρχεται and ἐπὶ τῶν νεφελῶν rather than μετά.

As noted above, Swete explained the similarity between Rev 1:7 and Mt 24:30 in terms of their common dependence on a collection of prophetic testimonies.[41] In this suggestion, Swete may have been dependent on the thesis of J. Rendel Harris that there was a widely used "testimony-book" in the early church, made up of quotations from the Jewish Bible.[42] C. H. Dodd

38. H. B. Swete, *An Introduction to the Old Testament in Greek* (2nd ed., rev. by R. R. Ottley; Cambridge, U.K., 1914), p. 398. See also Moo, *The Old Testament in the Gospel Passion Narratives*, pp. 210–11.

39. The same conflation is found also in Justin Martyr, *DialTrypho* 14.8; cf. *DialTrypho* 64.7 and *First Apology* 52.11. See B. Lindars, *New Testament Apologetic* (London, 1961), p. 127; Vos, *The Synoptic Traditions in the Apocalypse*, p. 62.

40. *Did* 16.6 may refer to the same or a similar tradition.

41. Swete, *The Apocalypse of St. John*, p. 9.

42. For a summary of Harris' thesis and a discussion of responses to it, see D. M. Smith, Jr., "The Use of the Old Testament in the New," in *The Use of the Old Testament in the New and Other Essays: Studies in Honor of W. F. Stinespring*, ed. J. M. Efird (Durham, N.C., 1972), pp. 25–30. Alternatively, Swete may have been influenced by one of Harris' predecessors, such as E. Hatch (see Stendahl, *The School of St. Matthew*, pp. 208–9).

effectively refuted the hypothesis of the testimony-book in his work *According to the Scriptures: The Substructure of New Testament Theology.*[43] Dodd explained the repeated use of the same and neighboring texts from the older scripture in early Christian writings in terms of an oral consensus about which older texts were significant in expressing the Christian message.[44]

At the time Dodd wrote, the Dead Sea Scrolls were becoming known. Krister Stendahl suggested that the formula-quotations in Matthew should be understood as analogous to the use of old scripture in the Pesher on Habakkuk discovered by Qumran.[45] He suggested that the peculiarities of the text reflected in these quotations were due to the fact that members of the school made their own translations which were interpretive and actualizing.[46] Stendahl rejected the hypothesis of a collection or book of testimonies.[47] He argued that the "methods of the synagogue in dealing with the texts of the OT, both in liturgical reading and in teaching, account for most of the features that Harris wanted to explain by his Book of Testimonies."[48] With regard to the relation of Mt 24:30 and Rev 1:7, he concluded that the combination of Zechariah 12 and Daniel 7 must have been "a common matter, either understood as a *verbum Christi* or as belonging to the church's basic teaching in Christology."[49]

In 1961, seven years after Stendahl's book was published, Lindars' book *New Testament Apologetic* appeared. He attempted to flesh out Dodds' picture of the early Christian use of Scripture and to pursue the analogy with Qumran pointed out by Stendahl. Lindars argued that the early Christian use of the Bible was fundamentally apologetic and that the church's apologetic needs changed over time. The earliest concerns were to demonstrate that Jesus was the Messiah and that he had been raised from the dead. Soon followed the need to explain Jesus' ignominious death. In this "passion apologetic," the book of Zechariah played a prominent role. He argued further that the use of Zechariah in the Gospel of John better represented the older passion apologetic than its use in Matthew.[50]

On the issue of the relations among Rev 1:7, Mt 24:30, and Jn 19:37, Lindars claimed that Stendahl went too far in minimizing the verbal agreements among the three versions. He did so, according to Lindars, to avoid

43. Smith, "The Use of the OT," pp. 27–29.

44. Smith says that Dodd's book appeared in 1957 (ibid., p. 27). This seems to be incorrect, since it is cited by Stendahl with a publication date of 1952 (*The School of St. Matthew*, pp. 52, n. 1 and 225).

45. Stendahl, *The School of St. Matthew*, pp. 183–202; for a summary, see Smith, "The Use of the OT," pp. 44–45.

46. Stendahl, *The School of St. Matthew*, pp. 200–1.

47. Ibid., p. 214.

48. Ibid., p. 217.

49. Ibid., p. 214.

50. See the summary in Smith, "The Use of the OT," pp. 31–34.

the conclusion that there was a written testimony book in the early days of the church. Lindars thinks it probably better to imagine a living apologetic tradition, oral rather than written, in which the practical usefulness of the abbreviated text helped to preserve its identity.[51]

The verbal similarities among these three passages led Lindars to conclude that behind Mt 24:30, Rev 1:7, and Jn 19:37 is a common original text, not quite the same as the standard LXX text, abbreviated for its apologetic purpose before its later employment in Christian apocalyptic:

καὶ ὄψονται εἰς ὃν ἐξεκέντησαν
καὶ κόψονται ἐπ' αὐτὸν πᾶσαι αἱ φυλαὶ τῆς γῆς.[52]

Lindars comments that the original context in Zechariah describes the restoration of Jerusalem after devastating warfare, and then, when the new life of the city begins, the inhabitants are expected to "look upon me whom they have pierced." The sight will evoke mourning in liturgical order. The very obscurity of the text is the apologist's opportunity to demonstrate the correct meaning: the apologetic point is that the messiah was bound to be "pierced," i.e., crucified.[53]

Lindars argued further that the brief form of the quotation then came into the Christian apocalyptic tradition by way of the identification of the moment of vindication with the parousia, the revealing of the Son of Man. Then the unbelievers will have good cause to mourn (Rev 1:7). This version of the text contains a deliberate modification: the distinguishing of all the tribes and the ones who pierced him. The modification is due to the placement of the passage in an apocalyptic framework. The Son of Man will come in judgment to vindicate the righteous and condemn the wicked, namely, whose who crucified him.[54] According to Lindars, Mt 24:30 has much the same motive. The gospel of John "retains the strict reference to the Passion."[55]

In his treatment of the problem, Louis Vos argued against those who had argued for independent use of older scripture by the authors of Matthew and Revelation.[56] He follows one of Stendahl's suggestions, namely, that the combination of the two older passages goes back to a *verbum Christi*. He thus concludes that the author of Revelation in this passage is dependent on an aspect of the *logion* tradition which, in this case, is uniquely shared with Matthew.[57]

---

51. Lindars, *New Testament Apologetic*, p. 127. In support of this view, Lindars cited the false ascription to Hosea of the very free précis of Zechariah 12 in Justin's *First Apology* (52.11), when he alludes to it in *DialTrypho* 14.8, as another sign that it belongs to living tradition.
52. Lindars, *New Testament Apologetic*, pp. 123–24.
53. Ibid., pp. 124–25.
54. Ibid., pp. 125–26.
55. Ibid., p. 126.
56. Vos, *The Synoptic Traditions in the Apocalypse*, pp. 63, 67–71.
57. Ibid., p. 71.

Norman Perrin accepted Lindars' overall thesis. He also accepted Lindars' reconstruction of the common source of Rev 1:7, Mt 24:30, and Jn 19:37 (see the reconstructed Gk. text above) with one reservation. Perrin argued that the text (oral or written) probably opened with καὶ ἐπιβλέψονται rather than with καὶ ὄψονται.[58] He saw this text as a selection from some Gk. version of Zechariah. The ἐπιβλέψονται of the source was then, according to Perrin, changed in the formation of the Christian pesher through a play on words with κόψονται. This original form of the pesher Perrin found in Jn 19:37. Perrin agreed with Lindars in concluding that Rev 1:7 represents the second stage in the development of this pesher tradition and in seeing the combination of Zech 12 with Dan 7:13 as characteristic of this stage. Perrin added the idea that the word ἰδού was added at this stage as a further play on words: ἰδού is connected with ὄψομαι. The ἰδού then became ὄψονται in Mk 13:26. He argued that the addition in Mt 24:30 of the quotation from Zech 12 to the saying taken from Mk 13:26 supports his thesis about the evolution of the word play: the addition makes explicit what was implicit in the ὄψονται of Mk 13:26.[59]

The attempt to reconstruct a source common to all three passages is very precarious, since there is not a single word common to all three. All three share the root ὄψομαι, but Revelation has the third person singular, whereas Matthew and John have the plural. Revelation and John both have ἐξεκέντη-σαν, but the verb is lacking in Matthew. The similarities in wording, form, and function are greatest between Matthew and Revelation.[60] The similarities warrant the conclusion that there is a connection between the two texts. The lack of close similarities in wording precludes the conclusion of literary dependence of one upon the other and any attempt to reconstruct a common source. The most defensible conclusion is that the conflation of Zechariah 12 and Dan 7:13 was known to both of the authors, but not as a saying with fixed wording. The variants ἐπί/μετά may simply be oral variants, or they may reflect familiarity with different recensions of Daniel.

The argument of Lindars and Perrin that the conflation of Zech 12 and Dan 7:13 in Matthew and Revelation represents a second stage in the development of this particular tradition fits in well with the hypothesis that Jesus himself was perhaps eschatological, but non- or even anti-apocalyptic, and that certain groups in the early church apocalypticized older non-apocalyptic traditions. The community which produced and used the Synoptic Sayings

58. N. Perrin, "Mark 14:62: The End Product of a Christian Pesher Tradition?" *NTS* 12 (1965–66) 150–55; repr. with a postscript in *A Modern Pilgrimage in New Testament Christology* (Philadelphia, 1974), pp. 10–22; the discussion above relates to p. 14 in the reprinted form of the article.

59. Ibid., p. 15.

60. Vos has made this case in greatest detail (*The Synoptic Traditions in the Apocalypse*, pp. 60–71).

Source (Q) and the milieu of the gospel of Mark are so presented by Perrin in his *The New Testament: An Introduction*.[61] It is at least equally plausible that Matthew and Revelation represent the oldest recoverable form of this tradition. Philipp Vielhauer suggested that the earliest christology was an articulation of an experience of the resurrection conceived in terms of the crucified Jesus' exaltation and identification with the heavenly being described as "like a son of man" in Dan 7:13.[62] According to Daniel 7, this heavenly figure was to be given "dominion and glory and kingdom, that all peoples, nations, and languages should serve him" (vs. 14, RSV). The use of the pesher method at Qumran was combined with eschatological expectation. Eschatologically minded Christians, especially if their expectations involved political and cosmic elements, would naturally expect this awarding of dominion to involve public events with social implications. Such Christians, reading Zech 12, would connect the mourning of the tribes, and their looking at or seeing the one whom they had pierced, with the revelation of the dominion of the humanlike figure of Daniel 7. Rather than preserving the original use of Zech 12, then, Jn 19:37 may be seen as a reinterpretation of the significance of that passage for Christian faith. Rather than a prophecy of a future event with a cosmic or apocalyptic character, Zech 12 is presented as already fulfilled in the death of Jesus. Such a reinterpretation is consistent with the present-oriented eschatology of the gospel of John[63] and with the statement of Jesus in Jn 18:36: "My kingship is not of this world" (RSV). The parousia of Jesus seems to be reinterpreted in Jn 14:18–24 in terms of the Father's and Jesus' coming to and dwelling in those who keep Jesus' word(s).[64] In Jn 19:37 a passage which other Christians had used to point to the parousia (Zech 12) was used in close connection with a symbolic portrayal of the present significance of the death of Jesus: the blood and water which flow from his side symbolize baptism and eucharist, which have their salvific power through the saving death of Jesus.[65]

The fact that Rev 1:7 does not use the phrase ὁ υἱός τοῦ ανθρώπου is an indication of the antiquity of the tradition which it shares with Mt 24:30. This point will be discussed below.

61. N. Perrin and D. Duling, *The New Testament: An Introduction* (2nd ed.; New York, 1982), pp. 424–25; in general, contrast chs. 3, 4 and 8 with ch. 13. This point of view also characterized the first edition of this work (1974) and Perrin's *Rediscovering the Teaching of Jesus* (New York, 1967).

62. Vielhauer, "Gottesreich und Menschensohn in der Verkündigung Jesu," in idem, *Aufsätze zum Neuen Testament* (Theologische Bücherei, Neues Testament 31; Munich, 1965), pp. 90–91.

63. See R. E. Brown, *The Gospel According to John (i–xii)* (AB 29; Garden City, N.Y., 1966), p. cxvii.

64. See E. Haenchen, *John 2: A Commentary on the Gospel of John Chapters 7–21* (Hermeneia; Philadelphia, 1984), p. 126.

65. So Haenchen, *John 2*, p. 201; another interpretation is that the water (and blood) symbolizes the gift of the Spirit made possible by Jesus' death; see R. E. Brown, *The Gospel According to John (xiii–xxi)* (AB 29A; Garden City, N.Y., 1970), pp. 949–51.

THE EPIPHANY OF ONE LIKE A SON OF MAN

In Rev 1:9–3:22, an epiphany of one like a son of man is described, who dictates to John, the author of Revelation, seven messages for "the seven congregations which are in Asia" (1:11; cf. 1:4). The designation "one like a son of man" in an early Christian context suggests to the reader that the risen Christ is meant. But the description of the figure includes also some characteristics ascribed elsewhere to angels and some elsewhere attributed to God. The reader's assumption that the figure in the epiphany is the risen Christ is confirmed when he says, "I became dead and behold! I am living forever and ever" (1:18).

Angelic Attributes

In terms of form and content, Rev 1:9–3:22 seems to have been modeled on Dan 10:2–12:4. Both passages describe the epiphany of a heavenly being to a human visionary. In both the author identifies himself by name and gives the time and place of the experience. In both texts the visionary says that he looked and then gives a description of the heavenly being. Following the description, both passages relate that the seer is overwhelmed by the apparition and falls to the ground senseless. The heavenly being then comforts or strengthens the seer. After this exchange, the heavenly being conveys to the seer a long verbal revelation which is associated with a book.[66]

Significant similarities occur in the descriptions of the heavenly revealer-figures. The figure in Revelation is described as dressed in a robe reaching to the feet (ἐνδεδυμένον ποδήρη—1:13). In the MT the figure of Daniel 10 is depicted as לבוש בדים (vs. 5). The OG renders this description as ἐνδεδυμένος βύσσινα, Theodotion as ἐνδεδυμένος βαδδιν. The same Heb. phrase appears, however, in the MT of Ezek 9:2, which is translated as ἐνδεδυκὼς ποδήρη in the OG. The author of Revelation may have known the prototype of the MT of Dan 10:5 and translated it similarly to the way the phrase is translated in the OG of Ezek 9:2; he may have known a Gk. recension which read something like ἐνδεδυμένον ποδήρη in Dan 10:5; or the OG of Ezek 9:2 (cf. vss. 3,11) may have been an influence on this aspect of Rev 1:13.

The heavenly figure of Revelation 1 is also described as girded on the breast with a golden girdle (περιεζωσμένον πρὸς τοῖς μαστοῖς ζώην χρυ-σᾶν—vs. 13). The figure in Daniel 10 is depicted as girded around the loins with gold of Uphaz. The MT reads ומתניו חגרים בכתם אופל (vs. 5). Theodotion reads similarly: ἡ ὀσφὺς αὐτοῦ περιεζωμένη ἐν χρυσίῳ Ωφαζ. According to the OG, his loins were girded with linen. Here Revelation is closer to the MT and Theodotion.[67] In Rev 15:6 the seven angels with the seven

---

66. In Daniel the book is the heavenly book of truth (10:21); in Revelation it is the book which John is to write (1:11, 19).

67. According to the OG of Ezek 9:2, the angel who marked the faithful in Jerusalem wore a sapphire girdle around his loins (cf. vs. 11 OG).

plagues are described as girded around their breasts with golden girdles (περιεζωσμένοι περὶ τὰ στήθη ζώνας χρυσᾶς).

The heavenly figure in Revelation 1 is said to have eyes like a flame of fire (οἱ ὀφθαλμοὶ αὐτοῦ ὡς φλὸξ πυρός—vs. 14).[68] The being in Daniel 10 has eyes like torches or flames of fire (ועיניו כלפידי אש—vs. 6). The OG and Theodotion read οἱ ὀφθαλμοὶ αὐτοῦ ὡσεὶ λαμπάδες πυρός. Φλόξ is a possible translation of לפיד, but Revelation differs from the MT in having the singular.

According to Rev 1:15, the feet of the heavenly being were like "χαλκο-λιβάνῳ, as in a furnace of burnished brass,"[69] or "as when it is smelted (or refined) in the furnace."[70] Χαλκολίβανον is the name of a metal or alloy, the exact nature of which is unknown, since the word does not appear independently of Rev 1:15 and 2:18.[71] It means something like "gold ore," or "fine brass" or "bronze."[72] The figure in Daniel 10 has arms and legs like the appearance[73] of burnished bronze (MT—וזרעתיו ומרגלתיו כעין נחשת קלל). The OG reads οἱ βραχίονες αὐτοῦ καὶ οἱ πόδες ὡσεὶ χαλκὸς ἐξασ-τράπτων; Theodotion, οἱ βραχίονες αὐτοῦ καὶ τὰ σκέλη ὡς ὅρασις χαλκοῦ στίλβοντος. The passage in Revelation is closest to the OG and is most probably a free citation or paraphrase of it or a similar Gk. recension.[74]

The voice of the figure in Revelation 1 is like the sound of many waters (ἡ φωνὴ αὐτοῦ ὡς φωνὴ ὑδάτων πολλῶν—vs. 15). In Daniel 10, the sound of the words of the heavenly figure is said to be like the sound of a multitude (MT: וקול דבריו כקול המון—vs. 6). The OG reads φωνὴ λαλιᾶς αὐτοῦ ὡσεὶ φωνὴ θορύβου; Theodotion, ἡ φωνὴ τῶν λόγων αὐτοῦ ὡς φωνὴ ὄχλου. In this passage in Revelation, Ezek 1:24 or 43:2 has had an influence, as well as Dan 10:6. In Ezek 1:24, the wings of the four living creatures make the sound of many waters (MT: כקול מים רבים). The OG reads ὡς φωνὴν ὕδατος πολλοῦ. According to Ezek 43:2, the sound of the coming of the glory of God was like the sound of many waters (the MT has the same phrase as in 1:24). The OG differs from the MT in 43:2.

In Rev 1:16, the face of the heavenly being is said to shine like the sun (ἡ ὄψις αὐτοῦ ὡς ὁ ἥλιος φαίνει ἐν τῇ δυνάμει αὐτοῦ). Although the wording of Revelation here may have been influenced by Judg 5:31, the description corresponds to that of the figure in Daniel 10 whose face was like the appearance of lightning (MT: ופניו כמראה ברק, vs. 6). The OG and Theodotion read το προσώπον αὐτοῦ ὡσεὶ ὅρασις ἀστραπῆς.

68. The same attribute is associated with Christ as the Son of God in Rev 2:18 and as the Word of God in 19:12.

69. So Hort and Swete, cited by Charles, *The Revelation of St. John*, vol. 1, p. 29.

70. So Charles, ibid.

71. See BAGD, p. 875.

72. Ibid.

73. Or "gleam, sparkle"; see BDB, pp. 744–45.

74. In Ezek 1:7 the soles of the feet of the four living creatures are said to sparkle like the appearance of burnished bronze (MT, ונצצים כעין נחשת קלל). The OG reads σπινθῆρες ὡς ἐξασ-τράπτων χαλκός.

The similarities between Rev 1:12–16 and Dan 10:5–6, as well as the analogies between their respective contexts, suggest that the "one like a son of man" in Revelation 1 is an angelic figure.[75] This impression is reinforced by the association of some of these attributes with angels elsewhere in the book of Revelation. The reappearance of the golden girdle around the breast in 15:6 was mentioned above. Angels are not explicitly associated with the voice or sound of many waters, but the song of the 144,000 is so described (14:2). This group may be humans exalted to angelic status. The heavenly hymn of 19:6–8 is likened to a voice or sound of many waters (vs. 6). The mighty angel of 10:1 has a face like the sun. Significantly, "one like a son of man" (ὅμοιον υἱὸν ἀνθρώπου in both passages) is closely associated with angels, if not identified as an angel, in 14:14–20.

The fact that "one like a son of man" in Revelation 1 is described with angelic attributes is not surprising in light of the angelic character of the figure in Dan 7:13 to whom allusion is made with that phrase. A convincing case has been made that the "one who was ancient of days" and the "one like a son of man" of Daniel 7 are Jewish adaptations of Canaanite mythic traditions concerning El and Baal.[76] In their present context—i.e. from the point of view of the composition of the book of Daniel between 164 and 167 B.C.E.—the ancient of days is a representation of God and the one like a son of man is the angelic patron of Israel, namely, Michael.[77]

It is likely that the author of the book of Revelation understood the one like a son of man of Dan 7:13 as an angel. Since the author was familiar with Jewish apocalyptic traditions, it is likely that he knew traditions like those preserved in the Testament of Moses and in the sectarian documents from Qumran. In the Testament of Moses 10, the manifestation of the kingdom of God is closely associated with the consecration or appointment of an angel as chief who avenges the people of God against their enemies.[78] In the War

---

75. Rowland has explored the angelic elements of the description of Christ in Revelation 1 ("The Vision of the Risen Christ in Rev. i. 13ff.: The Debt of an Early Christology to an Aspect of Jewish Angelology," *JTS* N.S. 31 [1980] 1–11; *The Open Heaven: A Study of Apocalyptic in Judaism and Early Christianity* [New York, 1982] pp. 100–1, 103). See also R. Bauckham, "The Worship of Jesus in Apocalyptic Christianity," *NTS* 27 (1981) 322–41.

76. J. A. Emerton, "The Origin of the Son of Man Imagery," *JTS* 9 (1958) 225–42; A. Bentzen, *Daniel* (HAT 19; Tübingen, 1952), pp. 59–61; C. Colpe, "ὁ υἱὸς τοῦ ἀνθρώπου," *TDNT*, vol. 8, pp. 415–19; F. M. Cross, *Canaanite Myth and Hebrew Epic* (Cambridge, Mass., 1973), pp. 16–17; J. J. Collins, *The Apocalyptic Vision of the Book of Daniel* (HSM 16; Missoula, Mont., 1977), pp. 99–106; J. Day, *God's Conflict with the Dragon and the Sea* (University of Cambridge Oriental Publications 35; Cambridge, U.K., 1985), pp. 157–67.

77. N. Schmidt was the first in recent times to propose this view ("The Son of Man in the Book of Daniel," *JBL* 19 [1900] 26). Others who have held this view include T. K. Cheyne, W. E. Barnes, G. H. Box, F. Stier, J. A. Emerton, U. Müller, J. J. Collins, and J. Day. For bibliographical references and discussion of the issues, see Collins, *Apocalyptic Vision*, pp. 144–47, 149 n. 7; Day, *God's Conflict*, pp. 167–77.

78. See the translation of R. H. Charles, revised by J. P. M. Sweet under the title "Assumption of Moses" in *The Apocryphal Old Testament* (ed. H. F. D. Sparks; Oxford, 1984), pp. 612–13; cf. the translation by J. Priest in *OTP*, vol. 1, pp. 931–32.

Scroll from Qumran, the victory of God is described in terms of the establishment of the kingdom or dominion of Michael in heaven and of the people of Israel on earth (1QM 17.7–8). 11QMelchizedek is an eschatological midrash[79] or a Pesher on the Periods of History.[80] In it the Melchizedek who is mentioned in Genesis 14 and Psalm 110 is reinterpreted as an angelic being, the counterpart of Belial, who will exercise judgment and bring salvation in the end time. There is evidence that this Melchizedek was identified with Michael by the community at Qumran.[81]

Although it is likely that the author of Revelation understood the "one like a son of man" in Dan 7:13 as an angel, it is not necessarily the case that he identified him with Michael. In Daniel 8, after he saw the vision of a ram and a he-goat, the seer sought to understand it. Then he saw before him one with the appearance of a man (MT: כמראה גבר—vs. 15). The OG reads ὡς ὅρασις ἀνθρώπου; Theodotion, ὡς ὅρασις ἀνδρός. This being is identified in the next verse as Gabriel. The seer's reaction (vss. 17–18) is similar to that described in 10:9, 15. The designation of this being as a "man," especially in the reading of the OG (ἀνθρώπου), may have suggested to the author of Revelation that the "one like a son of man" in Dan 7:13 is the same as the revealing angel in Daniel 8. The similarity of the revealing function of the angel and the seer's response to him in ch. 8 to the corresponding parts of ch. 10 may have suggested to our author that the angels of chs. 8 and 10 were the same—namely, Gabriel.[82] The relationship of Gabriel to Christ for the author of Revelation will be discussed below. If our author identified the "one like a son of man" in Dan 7:13 with the revealing angel of Daniel 10, this identification explains why elements from Dan 7:13 and Dan 10:5–6 are conflated to describe the heavenly being of Rev 1:12–16.

Divine Attributes

The most obviously divine attribute, at least from the point of view of the probable original meaning of Dan 7:9, is the statement "his head and hair were white like white wool, like snow" (ἡ δὲ κεφαλὴ αὐτοῦ καὶ αἱ τρίχες λευκαὶ ὡς ἔριον λευκὸν ὡς χιών—Rev 1:14). The MT of Dan 7:9 says that the garment of the ancient of days was white as snow and that the hair of his head was like pure wool (לבושה כתלג חור ושער ראשה כעמר נקא).[83] Rev 1:14

79. So G. Vermes, *The Dead Sea Scrolls in English* (2nd ed.; New York, 1975), p. 265.

80. Following J. T. Milik, so P. Kobelski, *Melchizedek and Melchiresa* (*CBQ* MS 10; Washington, D.C., 1981), pp. 50–51.

81. Ibid., pp. 71–74.

82. Some modern scholars have made this identification—namely, Z. Zevit, "The Structure and Individual Elements of Daniel VII," *ZAW* 80 (1968) 385–96; J. Fossum, "The Name of God and the Angel of the Lord" (D. Theol. dissertation, University of Utrecht, 1982), p. 92 (cited by Segal; see next reference); Fossum's dissertation has now appeared as idem, *The Name of God and the Angel of the Lord* (WUNT 36; Tübingen, 1985); and A. Segal, *Two Powers in Heaven* (SJLA 25; Leiden, 1977), p. 201, n. 54.

83. According to Ziegler, the original readings of both the OG and Theodotion were equivalent to the MT (*Susanna, Daniel, Bel et Draco*, p. 168). In Rahlfs' edition, the text of OG lacked

may reflect a Jewish apocalyptic tradition, based on Dan 7:9 ultimately, but
varying in wording. 1En 46:1 mentions a "head of days" and says that "his
head was white like wool."[84] The Apocalypse of Abraham says that the hair of
the head of Iaoel was like snow.[85]

Certain literary echoes in Rev 1:10, 12–13 may also be hints that the heavenly figure of 1:12–16 has divine status. In vs. 10 the seer says, "I heard
behind me a great voice like a trumpet" (ἤκουσα ὀπίσω μου φωνὴν μεγάλην
ὡς σάλπιγγος). This passage seems to be an echo of Ezek 3:12, which links
the glory of God with the prophet's hearing the sound of a great earthquake
behind him (MT: גדול רעש קול אחרי ואשמע). The OG reads καὶ ἤκουσα
κατόπισθέν μου φωνὴν σεισμοῦ. Rev 1:10 also echoes Ex 19:16. The great
sound or voice like a trumpet of Rev 1:10 (see the Gk. text above) recalls the
theophany on Mount Sinai, which involved sounds or voices (MT: קלת) and
a very powerful sound (blast) of a trumpet (MT: מאד חזק שפר וקל). The OG
reads: . . . φωναὶ . . . φωνὴ τῆς σάλπιγγος ἤχει μέγα (cf. also Ex 20:18
OG). Finally, the "one like a son of man" in Rev 1:12–13 is depicted in the
midst of seven golden lampstands. These lampstands echo the description of
the menorah in Ex 25:31–40, esp. vss. 35 and 31. In this passage and others,
the menorah is a symbol of the divine presence.[86]

James Charlesworth has suggested recently that καὶ ἐπέστρεψα βλέπειν
τὴν φωνὴν ἥτις ἐλάλει μετ᾽ ἐμοῦ (Rev 1:12a) should be translated literally
as: "And I turned around to see the Voice who spoke with me. . . ."[87] He has
argued further that this "Voice" should be understood as a heavenly being,
namely, a "hypostatic creature," related to the Bath Qol known from rabbinic
literature.[88] It is more likely that the peculiarity of the reference to seeing a
voice in vs. 12a is to be explained in literary terms. The use of the word
"Voice" here may be seen as synecdoche, the part, "Voice," being used to
stand for the whole, "the one like a son of man" described in the following
verses. Such a figure of speech fits well with the style of the apocalyptic
genre, since visionary and auditory experiences are often presented as mysterious, vague, or partial; in a word, dreamlike. At first the seer has only the
sound or voice to go by and thus refers to his experience as such.

---

the λευκήν modifying "snow" and had a λευκόν modifying "wool" (*Septuaginta* 2, p. 913). Ziegler seems to think that the text of Revelation influenced the readings of Pap. 967 and 88-Syh;
see his apparatus to o′ on 7:9.

84. Translation by M. A. Knibb in *The Apocryphal OT*, p. 227. Cf. 1En 71:10, which says
that the head of the ancient of days' head was white and pure like wool.

85. ApAb 11:2 (*OTP* 1, p. 694).

86. C. L. Meyers, *IDBS*, pp. 586–87. The menorah also appears in Zech 4:2, 11. There the
seven lamps are interpreted as the seven eyes of God. This tradition seems to be behind Rev
1:4, 3:1, 4:5, and 5:6, where the seven eyes of God are attributes of the Lamb.

87. J. H. Charlesworth, "The Jewish Roots of Christology: The Discovery of the Hypostatic
Voice," *SJT* 39 (1986) 20–23.

88. Ibid., pp. 22–25.

The Relation of the Angelic and Divine Attributes

How is the interpreter to explain the juxtaposition of angelic and divine attributes in the description of the heavenly being in Rev 1:12–16? Most Christian readers downplay or ignore the angelic elements. They see no problem in the risen Christ being described as divine. Traditional Christians connect this attribution of divinity with the doctrine of the incarnation. More historically minded Christian readers understand it in terms of the divinity of the exalted Christ and link this passage with others like Rom 1:3–4, Phil 2:6–11, and Acts 2:32–36. Some scholars have tried to explain this state of affairs textually, proposing a hypothesis about the relation of Revelation 1 and Daniel 7.

In his critical edition of the Septuagint, Rahlfs followed MS 88 and Syh in reading ὡς παλαιὸς ἡμερῶν in Dan 7:13. J. A. Montgomery, however, had suggested that this reading is an ancient error for ἕως παλαιου ἡμερῶν, but a pre-Christian error, as the citation of it in Rev 1:14 shows. He rejected W. Bousset's suggestion that the reading reflected a Septuagintal notion of a pre-existent messiah, suggesting that the reading was accidental.[89] He reasoned that ἕως was misread as ὡς and that this error resulted in the correction of παλαιου to παλαιὸς. The result of the compounded error was the transformation of the "one like a son of man" into the "ancient of days."[90] Since Rev 1:14 seems to identify the two figures, Montgomery assumed that the author of Revelation read the error, namely, ὡς παλαιὸς, in his text. In his critical edition of the OG of Daniel, J. Ziegler followed Montgomery's suggestion and printed ἕως παλαιου ἡμερῶν as the reading of o΄.[91]

In preparing his critical edition of the OG of Daniel, Ziegler was unable to make use of the portion of Pap. 967 which contains Dan 7:13. This manuscript reads ὡς παλαιὸς ημερῶ(ν).[92] J. Lust argued that this reading is the original OG reading and that the text of Rahlfs did not need to be corrected on this point.[93] He argued further that the intention of the OG was to identify the "one like a son of man" and the "ancient of days." In this intention, according to Lust, the translator was following a Hebrew *Vorlage*, which was prior to the Aramaic text preserved in the MT. The identity of the two figures in Daniel 7 is supported, in his opinion, by the similarities between the son of man in Dan 7:13 and the human figure (God) on the throne in Ezek 1:26, which was the inspiration of vs. 13.[94]

---

89. Montgomery, *Daniel*, p. 304. See also his "Anent Dr. Rendel Harris's 'Testimonies,'" *Expositor* 22 (1921) 214–17.
90. See the citation of the argument from "Anent," p. 214 by J. Lust, "Daniel 7, 13 and the Septuagint," *ETL* 54 (1978) 62–63.
91. This reading is supported by Justin, Tertullian, Cyprian *et al.*
92. See the Gk. text cited above as Kölner Teil des Papyrus 967.
93. Lust, "Daniel 7, 13," p. 63.
94. Ibid., pp. 64–69.

Although he apparently had not seen the reading of Dan 7:13 in Pap. 967,
F. F. Bruce took a position similar to Lust's in some respects.[95] Bruce argued
that the editor of the OG version intended ὡς παλαιὸς ἡμερῶν παρῆν to
convey a definite meaning. He listed the following possibilities:

1. "as (when [ὡς taken temporally]) the Ancient of Days arrived, then
   (καὶ) the bystanders were present beside him."
2. "[as (when) the Ancient of Days arrived,] then (καὶ) the bystanders
   presented him," i.e. presented the "one like a son of man" to the Ancient of Days.
3. "[the one like a son of man appeared] as (the) Ancient of Days."[96]

Bruce found support for (3) in the book of Revelation, in which the opening
vision records the appearance of "one like a son of man," but whose description is based on the vision of the ancient of days (hair white like wool). Bruce
admitted, however, that since the only witnesses to the OG of Daniel are of
Christian provenance, the possibility of Christian influence on this particular
rendering of Dan 7:13 cannot be ruled out.[97]

Sharon Pace Jeansonne follows Ziegler in arguing that ἕως in 7:13 was
corrupted in the transmission of the OG to ὡς because of the preceding ὡς
(υἱὸς ἀνθρώπου) and the immediately preceding καὶ. The genitive παλαιοῦ would have been "hyper-corrected" to the nominative παλαιὸς in order for the phrase to be grammatically "correct."[98] She argued further that
the reading in 88-Syh, παρῆσαν αὐτῷ (later in vs. 13), is a secondary corruption of the original OG προσήγαγον αὐτόν attested in the 88-Syh margin
and in Justin. The secondary substitution of πάρειμι for προσάγω was
prompted by the preceding use of πάρειμι (παρῆν). Once προσήγαγον was
altered to παρῆσαν, the corruption of αὐτόν to αὐτῷ follows from sense.[99]
According to Pace Jeansonne, the differences between the OG of Dan 7:13
and the MT and other Gk. recensions are due not to the theological tendency
of the translator of the OG, but to secondary scribal errors in the course of
the transmission of the OG.

Pace Jeansonne discusses another passage in Daniel in which she argues a
similar case. She concludes that the original OG reading in 7:6 was πετεινοῦ
(agreeing with Ziegler). In the course of the transmission of the OG, a scribe
read πετεινόν instead of πετεινοῦ. Perceiving the form as verbal rather than

---

95. F. F. Bruce, "The Oldest Greek Version of Daniel," in H. A. Brongers *et al.*, *Instruction
and Interpretation* (OTS 20; Leiden, 1977), pp. 22–40; see the comment by Lust, "Daniel 7,
13," p. 62, n. 2.
96. Bruce, "The Oldest Greek Version," p. 25.
97. Ibid., p. 26.
98. Pace Jeansonne, *The Old Greek Translation of Daniel 7–12*, pp. 97–98.
99. Ibid., p. 98.

adjectival, this scribe must have assumed that the initial *epsilon* had mistakenly been omitted. Therefore, he "hyper-corrected" πετεινόν to ἐπέτεινον.[100]

This type of argument is convincing both for Dan 7:6 and 7:13. It is better to explain variants as mechanical errors when such an explanation is credible. The reading ὡς παλαιὸς ἡμερῶν is most likely a secondary scribal error rather than a deliberate change by the translator of the OG. As Montgomery suggested, this error may be very ancient. Pap. 967 provides evidence that the error occurred in the second century or earlier. As an inadvertent error, it may have been made by a Jewish scribe as easily as by a Christian scribe. It is possible that once this reading was in circulation, a theological meaning was attached to it. It is not necessarily the case that Christians were the first or the only ones to find theological meaning in the reading ως παλαιος ημερων. Before discussing this possibility, it would be well to review the reading in context as it appears in Pap. 967:

ἐθεώρουν ἐν ὁράματι τῆς νυκτὸς καὶ ἰδοὺ ἐπὶ τῶν νεφελῶν τοῦ οὐρανοῦ ἤρχετο ὡς υἱὸς ἀνθρώπου καὶ ὡς παλαιὸς ἡμερῶ(ν) παρῆν καὶ οἱ παρεστηκότες προσήγαγον αὐτῷ.

The passage may be translated:

I was observing in a vision of the night and behold! Upon the clouds of heaven there came one like a son of man, and as (the)[101] ancient of days he came, and the bystanders approached him.[102]

MS 88 (supported by Syh) agrees with Pap. 967 with two exceptions. It has the verb ἤρχετο after ἀνθρώπου rather than before ὡς υἱός. Instead of προσήγαγον αὐτῷ, it reads παρῆσαν αὐτῷ. The meaning of the two forms is basically the same.[103] The last clause of Dan 7:13 in MS 88 should be translated, "and the bystanders came to him."[104]

The question arises as to how those who used these manuscripts understood Dan 7:13 in the form in which it appears there. The possibility is worth considering that this form of the text played a role in the controversy over two powers in heaven. Alan Segal has pointed out that the subject of the two

100. Ibid., p. 93. Rahlfs printed ἐπέτεινον in his edition of the OG (*Septuaginta*, 2. 912).

101. According to Pace Jeansonne, "the OG does not consistently translate the construct chain, which has the *nomen rectum* in the emphatic state with the article." She also points out that the OG may have been influenced by the previous reference to the ancient of days in the poetic section of vs. 9, which does not have the article (*The Old Greek Translation of Daniel 7–12*, pp. 98–99).

102. According to LSJM, προσάγω can apparently be used intransitively, meaning "approach." The person approached may appear in the dative (here, αὐτῷ; see LSJM, p. 1499).

103. Unless καὶ οἱ παρεστηκότες προσήγαγον αὐτῷ is to be translated "and the bystanders presented (him) [the one like a son of man] to him [the ancient of days]."

104. Another possibility is Bruce's translation, "And the bystanders were present beside him" ("The Oldest Greek Version," p. 25).

powers is introduced in the Mekhilta of R. Simeon b. Yohai, Bashalah 15, as an exegetical comment on the two statements made about Yahweh in Ex 15:3.[105] The exegesis notes and explains the repetition of the name YHWH. "YHWH is a man of war" describes YHWH's manifestation at the Red Sea as a young warrior. "YHWH is his name" refers to the manifestation of YHWH at Sinai as an old man, showing mercy. The same God is present in both manifestations, even though they look different. The proof-text is Dan 7:9–10, which describes a heavenly enthronement scene involving two manifestations. The "thrones" of vs. 9 is interpreted as two thrones. This interpretation relates to the appearance later in the text of one like a son of man. The context suggests that the exegesis implies that God may be manifested either as a young man (one like a son of man) or as an old man (the ancient of days).[106] That the one like a son of man is young and merciful, the ostensible point of the exegesis, is not evident from Dan 7:9–10. Therefore, Segal concludes that the text was probably as important for the "heresy" as it was for the defense against it. Since this text appears to be a fairly late summation of a considerable amount of argumentation over time, it is probably not the earliest version of the tradition; it is rather an epitome.[107]

Another version of this tradition is found in the Mekhilta of R. Ismael, Bahodesh 5, Shirta 4.[108] This text uses Dan 7:10 to demonstrate that Daniel 7 does not describe two powers in heaven: a fiery stream . . . came forth from *him* (singular).[109]

The Babylonian Talmud, Hag. 14a, describes a debate between R. Akiba and R. Yosi the Galilean on how to explain the seeming contradiction between Dan 7:9a ("thrones") and 7:9b ("his throne"). Akiba said, "One (throne) for Him, and one for David." Yosi said, ". . . one for justice and one for grace." The anecdote ends with the remark that Akiba accepted Yosi's interpretation.[110] Segal concluded that the controversy over the messianic read-

---

105. The criticism of S. Cohen (review in *AJS* 10 [1985] 114–17) that the exegesis of Ex 15:3 is entirely theoretical and bears no relation to actual heretics has been shown to be mistaken by J. Fossum (*The Name of God and the Angel of the Lord*, pp. 228–29). The Samaritan *Malef* 3:5 contains traditions of mediation attached to Ex 15:3: "The Glory too seemed to be saying: 'O congregation, keep yourself from me, for is there not before me a mighty deed? I slew, I oppressed, I destroyed, I made alive; and with you, I did all this when I was at the sea and showed you every wonder and made you cross with great marvels by the mighty power of God.'" This tradition may not be an old one, but it is an actual heretical one. The Samaritans, of course, did not canonize the book of Daniel, which was so important to the Christian interpretation. I am grateful to Alan Segal for this reference.

106. Segal, *Two Powers in Heaven*, p. 35. Segal suggests that the reading ως παλαιος ημερων may have been created as a defense against a form of the "heresy" of the two powers (ibid., pp. 201–2).

107. Ibid., p. 36.

108. Ibid., pp. 37–38.

109. Ibid., p. 40.

110. Ibid., p. 47. In the next interpretation in b. Hagigah, Eleazar b. Azariah states that the two thrones are actually a throne and a footrest, referring to Isa 66:1 (ibid., n. 21).

ing of Dan 7:9–10 probably occurred during Akiba's time; the revision in terms of mercy and justice probably derives from the time of his students.[111]

Segal concludes that rabbinic opposition to theories about two powers in heaven can be dated as early as the second century and suspects that it was even earlier. According to Segal, the rabbis opposed the ideas that (1) a principal angel may be seen as God's primary or sole helper and as sharing in God's divinity; (2) a human being could ascend and become one with this figure, as Enoch, Moses, or Elijah had.[112]

The prototypes of the MT and of Theodotion and the earliest recoverable form of the OG as reconstructed by Ziegler may be read as revealing that alongside God (the ancient of days) there is a primary angel or there will be an exalted messiah (the one like a son of man). This point of view apparently was opposed by certain rabbis in the second century C.E. who argued exegetically that the ancient of days and the one like a son of man were two different manifestations of the one and only God. Greek-speaking Jews of this persuasion would have welcomed the reading of Pap. 967 and Ms 88-Syh as support for their point of view. Such readers would probably have taken vss. 9–12 and vss. 13–14 as parallel accounts of the same event. The appearance of the one like a son of man and the establishment of his kingdom is a description from a different point of view of the same complex of events portrayed earlier in terms of the session of the ancient of days with his court in judgment and the destruction of the four beasts. What is characteristic of this point of view is its close association of both figures with God as manifestations of him.

The question arises as to how the opponents of the point of view described above would have understood the reading ὡς παλαιὸς ἡμερῶν, if it were current among them, or if they were confronted with it in a debate. Jews of a "two powers" persuasion may have responded with the argument that neither the ancient of days nor the one like a son of man is God himself. The two descriptions should be interpreted rather as variant manifestations of the principal angel, a hypostasis who is God's agent in anthropomorphic form.[113]

If the form of Dan 7:13 known to the author of Revelation is ὡς παλαιὸς ἡμερῶν, how did he understand this phrase in context and in relation to Christ? It is likely that the author of Revelation interpreted *both* the ancient of days *and* the one like a son of man as hypostatic manifestations of God. In other words, the ancient of days is not actually God, but a distinguishable manifestation of God as a high angel. The ancient of days and the one like a

111. Ibid., p. 49.
112. Ibid., p. 180.
113. This hypothesis is supported by the interpretation of Dan 7:9–10 implied by the Visions of Ezekiel, an early Merkavah text. The text seems to identify the ancient of days with the heavenly prince of the third heaven (see I. Gruenwald, *Apocalyptic and Merkavah Mysticism* [AGAJU 14; Leiden, 1980], p. 140).

son of man from this point of view are angelic beings, and thus creatures, but creatures of a special kind.[114]

For the author of Revelation, God could be described as seated on his heavenly throne. He is so described in ch. 4. Since this passage draws on Isaiah 6 and Ezekiel 1, those passages were probably understood as descriptions, however inadequate, of God. Other passages, such as those which refer to the מלאך יהוה and apparently Dan 7:9–10, were interpreted as descriptions of the principal angel. In Rev 3:31 the risen Christ says that he has conquered and sat with his father on his throne. The vision of Dan 7:9–10 may have been understood by the author of Revelation as a prophecy of that event. These verses depict the exaltation of Christ (and his identification with the angelic ancient of days), whereas vss. 13–14 predict his second coming (cf. Rev 1:7). Thus the two figures of Daniel 7 represent for the author of Revelation the same being, namely Christ exalted to the status of the principal angel.

It was suggested earlier that the author of Revelation probably identified the one like a son of man in Daniel 7 with the revealing angel of ch. 10, whom he interpreted as Gabriel.[115] This identification is not incompatible with understanding the one like a son of man as the principal angel. Gabriel appears in some texts as simply one of several important angels or archangels. Often, however, one of these angels is depicted as the chief or principal angel and this is sometimes Gabriel.[116] J. Daniélou gathered considerable evidence that traditions linking Gabriel and Michael with the name of God were incorporated into Christian writings, often with the titles transferred to Christ.[117] In ch. 8 of the Pistis Sophia, the risen Christ says that he appeared to his mother Mary in the form (τύπος) of Gabriel.[118] Although this conclusion must be tentative, the evidence suggests that the author of Revelation considered Gabriel to be God's principal angel and the risen Christ to be identified with Gabriel.

---

114. Although the world view of the author of Revelation is different, there is an analogy between this reconstruction of his understanding of the relation of the principal angel to God and Philo's notion of the relation of the Logos to God. See the discussion in Segal, ibid., pp. 161–81.

115. Gabriel is explicitly named as the revealing angel in Dan 8:16 and 9:21. J. Comblin points out that John identifies the "man" of Daniel 10 with the Son of Man of Daniel 7 and draws out the implication that the Son of Man is the envoy of God not only at the final judgment, but also in the present as revealer and instructor (*Le Christ dans l'Apocalypse* [Bibliothèque de Théologie; Paris, 1965], p. 63).

116. Segal, *Two Powers in Heaven*, p. 187.

117. Cited by Segal, ibid., p. 200.

118. See the Coptic text in C. Schmidt, *Pistis Sophia* (Coptica 2; Copenhagen, 1925); a German translation may be found in C. Schmidt and W. C. Till, *Koptisch-gnostische Schriften I* (2nd ed.; rev. W. C. Till; GCS 45; Berlin, 1954), p. 8. English translations have been provided by G. R. S. Mead, *Pistis Sophia* (2nd ed.; London, 1921) and V. MacDermot, *Pistis Sophia* (NHS 9; Leiden, 1978).

A SARDIAN THREAT AND A PROMISE TO THE CONQUEROR

The body of the message to Sardis contains a prophetic admonition to "remember therefore how you received and heard, and keep (that which you received and heard), and repent" (Rev 3:3a). This admonition is followed by a threat: "If then you do not awake, I will come like a thief, and you shall surely not know at what hour I shall come upon you" (3:3b). The formulation of the threat has been identified as a direct use of a saying of Jesus by Louis Vos and by M. E. Boring.[119] This saying is similar to a saying of Q which was adapted by Matthew and Luke (Mt 24:43–44 and Lk 12:39–40). In the synoptic variants of the saying, the coming of the thief is compared with the coming of the Son of Man. The variants of the saying, however, which were known to Paul and to the author of 2 Peter, compare the coming of the thief to the coming of the Day of the Lord (1Thes 5:2, 2Pet 3:10).[120] The statement "I will come/am coming" of Rev 3:3 and 16:15 may be a variant of the form of the saying "The day of the Lord is coming/will come." It is a short step, especially in an oral context, from "the Day of the Lord is coming" to "the Lord is coming" to (in an oracular, prophetic/apocalyptic context) "I am coming" (Christ speaking). Thus the similarity between Rev 3:3/16:15 and Mt 24:43–44/Lk 12:39–40 is not necessarily evidence that the author of Revelation knew a form of this saying which mentioned the Son of Man.

Also in the message to Sardis, the following promise is given to the conqueror: "The conqueror will be clothed thus in white garments and I will surely not blot his name out of the book of life and I will confess his name before my father and before his angels" (Rev 3:5). The verse actually contains three promises. The last one is similar to a Synoptic saying. The closest parallels are laid out below.[121]

Rev 3:5c	Mt 10:32–33	Lk 12:8–9
καὶ ὁμολογήσω τὸ ὄν-	πᾶς οὖν ὅστις ὁμο-	πᾶς ὃς ἂν ὁμολογήσῃ
ομα αὐτοῦ ἐνώπιον	λογήσει ἐν ἐμοὶ ἔμ-	ἐν ἐμοὶ ἔμπροσθεν
τοῦ πατρός μου καὶ	προσθεν τῶν ἀν-	τῶν ἀνθρώπων, καὶ ὁ
ἐνώπιον τῶν ἀγγέλων	θρώπων, ὁμολογήσω	υἱὸς τοῦ ἀνθρώπου
αὐτοῦ.	κἀγὼ ἐν αὐτῷ ἔμπρο-	ὁμολογήσει ἐν αὐτῷ

---

119. Vos, *The Synoptic Traditions in the Apocalypse*, pp. 75–85; M. E. Boring, "The Apocalypse as Christian Prophecy," cited by D. Aune, *Prophecy in Early Christianity and the Ancient Mediterranean World* (Grand Rapids, Mich., 1983), p. 421, n. 80. The saying is used again in Rev 16:15; on the latter passage, see Aune, pp. 283–84 and Vos, ibid.

120. In a variant of the saying attested by the Gospel of Thomas, the coming of the thief is compared to the temptations of "the world" (21.3; cf. 103).

121. See also Mt 16:27, Mk 8:38, Lk 9:26, 2Tim 2:12b, 2Clem 3:2. The remark in Rev 3:8 that "you did not deny my name" is in a different message, namely the one to Philadelphia; nevertheless, it may be evidence that the author of Revelation knew the double form of this saying which mentioned acknowledging in one clause and denying in the other (so Vos, *The Synoptic Traditions in the Apocalypse*, p. 94).

σθεν τοῦ πατρός μου   ἔμπροσθεν τῶν ἀγ-
τοῦ ἐν [τοῖς]   γέλων τοῦ θεοῦ· ὁ δὲ
οὐρανοῖς· ὅστις δ᾽ ἂν   ἀρνησάμενός με
ἀρνήσηταί με ἔμπρο-   ἐνώπιον τῶν ἀν-
σθεν τῶν ἀνθρώπων,   θρώπων ἀπαρνήθησε-
ἀρνήσομαι κἀγὼ αὐ-   ται ἐνώπιον τῶν ἀγ-
τὸν ἔμπροσθεν τοῦ   γέλων τοῦ θεοῦ.
πατρός μου τοῦ ἐν
[τοῖς]οὐρανοῖς.

Literary dependence of Rev 3:5c upon Mt 10:32 or Lk 12:8 or vice versa is ruled out by the lack of a close similarity in wording. The only word which all three accounts have in common is the root of ὁμολογεῖν.[122] The lack of close verbal similarities between Rev 3:5c and the two passages cited above from Matthew and Luke also rules out the possibility that Revelation is here dependent on the form of the saying in Q. The wording of the saying in Matthew and Luke suggests that it has been translated from Aramaic. Ev αὐτῷ and ἔμπροσθεν have been pointed out as semitisms, possibly reflecting Aramaic.[123]

An important aspect of the debate on the original form of this saying has been the question of whether the form "I will acknowledge/deny" or the form "the Son of Man will acknowledge/deny/be ashamed" is original. Bultmann argued that the form "the Son of Man will acknowledge" is the older form. He concluded that behind the variants was an authentic saying of the historical Jesus, in which he referred to a coming, apocalyptic Son of Man from whom he distinguished himself, but with whom he linked his teaching and activity.[124] H. E. Tödt followed Bultmann in this conclusion.[125] Philipp Vielhauer agreed with Bultmann that the form of the saying with the Son of Man is the older form, but did not agree that the saying originated with the historical Jesus.[126] Vos argued that the form of the saying in Revelation is the original form, mainly because it has both "before my/the Father" and "before the/his angels."[127]

Norman Perrin argued that behind Lk 12:8–9 is an authentic saying of the historical Jesus, namely, "Everyone who acknowledges me before men, he

122. So also Vos, *The Synoptic Traditions in the Apocalypse*, pp. 87–89.
123. Ibid., p. 90.
124. R. Bultmann, *The History of the Synoptic Tradition*, trans. J. Marsh (rev. ed.; New York, 1968), pp. 112, 128, 151–52.
125. H. E. Tödt, *Der Menschensohn in der synoptischen Überlieferung* (Gütersloh, 1959), pp. 50–56. See also the ET, *The Son of Man in the Synoptic Tradition*, trans. D. M. Barton (London, 1965); references in this paper are to the German.
126. Vielhauer, "Gottesreich und Menschensohn," pp. 76–79.
127. Vos, *The Synoptic Traditions in the Apocalypse*, pp. 91–92. Both audiences appear also in Lk 9:26; cf. Mt 16:27a, Mk 8:38b.

will be acknowledged before the angels of God." He accepted this saying as authentic because it contains a "double Aramaism" and because it "is a saying on the basis of which all other variants found in the tradition are readily explicable."[128] The earliest form was the one using the passive in the apodosis as a circumlocution for the activity of God. As the tradition developed, an increasing christological emphasis led to the ascription of God's activity to Jesus. This happened in two ways. In one group of variants, "I" was used for the subject of the action in the apodosis. In another group, "the Son of Man" was used. The result was the double tradition we now find in Lk 12:8–9 par.[129] This argument suggests that Mt 10:32 and Rev 3:5c are related variants of a saying of Jesus which had been transformed in a post-Easter situation.

Vielhauer had argued that Lk 12:8–9 was probably not a saying of Jesus, because it presupposed a forensic situation. A situation in which followers of Jesus would be asked to acknowledge him in a court setting is more likely to have occurred after Jesus' death than before.[130] The same observation must be made about Perrin's reconstruction of the earliest form of the saying. Ὁμολογεῖν is a term commonly used of testimony in court.[131] Even if the term includes the metaphorical meaning, such meaning is most understandable if the literal meaning is a real possibility. It seems best, therefore, to consider the earliest form of the saying as reconstructed by Perrin, to have originated in a post-Easter situation. The earthly courts faced by Christians are placed in the perspective of the heavenly court in which God passes judgment. It would have been a short step from that simple perspective to a conception of the heavenly court in which the risen Christ served as the advocate (παράκλητος) of his faithful followers.[132] The forms of the saying which mention the Son of Man connect this conception with Daniel 7 and identify Jesus as heavenly παράκλητος with the one like a son of man. The sayings without reference to the Son of Man do not make this connection (at least not intrinsically). Thus Mt 10:32 and Rev 3:5c (at least prior to their incorporation into Matthew and Revelation) are as close to 1Jn 2:1 in their basic conception of the heavenly court as they are to Lk 12:8–9.[133]

This discussion suggests that one should not assume that the author of Revelation was familiar with a form of the saying in 3:5c which referred to

---

128. N. Perrin, *A Modern Pilgrimage in New Testament Christology* (Philadelphia, 1974), pp. 35–36. The argument is presented in more detail in idem, *Rediscovering the Teaching of Jesus* (New York, 1967), pp. 185–91.

129. Perrin, *Rediscovering*, p. 189.

130. See n. 126 above.

131. O. Michel, "ὁμολογέω. κτλ . . . " *TDNT*, vol. 5, pp. 200–2.

132. On the notion of the παράκλητος in early Judaism and early Christianity, see J. Fossum, "Jewish-Christian Christology and Jewish Mysticism," *VC* 37 (1983) 275.

133. The notion of an angelic παράκλητος was an important one at Qumran; see Otto Betz, *Der Paraklet* (Leiden, 1963).

the Son of Man. "I" in Rev 3:5c does not necessarily refer to the risen Christ as Son of Man.

The Vision of Harvest and Vintage

Between the seven trumpets (8:2–11:19) and the seven bowls (15:5–16:21), a series of visions is related, beginning with the woman clothed with the sun (ch. 12) and concluding with the conquerors singing the song of Moses in a heavenly setting (15:2–4). The fifth vision in this series[134] consists of the appearance of three angels, one by one, each with a verbal message (14:6–11). To this vision is appended an editorial comment (vs. 12) and two beatitudes, one spoken by a voice from heaven, the other by the Spirit (vs. 13). The sixth vision is of a symbolic harvest and vintage carried out by "one like a son of man" and three (other) angels. It is generally agreed that this vision was inspired in large part by an oracle in Joel[135] (4:13; 3:13 RSV) which uses the images of harvest and vintage for divine judgment upon the nations on the Day of the Lord (cf. 4:12 and 14). That the symbolic vision in Revelation has to do with judgment is supported by the way in which the vision of vintage shifts into battle imagery (vs. 20).[136]

Whether or to what degree the vision is dependent on synoptic tradition is a debatable point. Charles believed that vss. 15–17 were an interpolation, so naturally he did not consider parallels in Matthew to be significant for the relation of the (original form of the) book of Revelation to Matthew.[137] Bousset denied any connection to the synoptics.[138] Although he did not claim literary dependence, Austin Farrer wrote that in this vision "St. John comes very close to a central image of the synoptic tradition, and we should be wise to interpret him by St. Mark and St. Matthew."[139] G. B. Caird takes a position on this issue similar to Farrer's. He argued that "Any Christian at the end of the first century would without a moment's hesitation recognize that the coming of the Son of Man with his angel reapers meant the gathering of God's people into the kingdom."[140]

Louis Vos classifies Rev 14:14–19 in his section, "The Apocalyptist's Indirect Employment of the Sayings of Jesus."[141] He argued that it is "important to recognize and discern the many contributions which gospel traditions make to this pericope, both in terms of the expressed allusions, and in terms

---

134. For the enumeration of the visions, see A. Yarbro Collins, *The Combat Myth in the Book of Revelation* (HDR 9; Missoula, Mont., 1976), pp. 13–19.

135. See, e.g., Charles, *The Revelation of St. John*, vol. 2, pp. 22–24.

136. Cf. 1En 100:3.

137. Charles, *The Revelation of St. John*, vol. 2, pp. 18–19; cf. vol. 1, pp. lxxxiii–lxxxvi.

138. Bousset, *Die Offenbarung Johannis*, p. 389.

139. A. Farrer, *A Rebirth of Images: The Making of St. John's Apocalypse* (Glasgow, 1949; repr. Albany, 1986), p. 151 (the reprint is cited here).

140. G. B. Caird, *A Commentary on the Revelation of St. John the Divine* (New York, 1966), p. 194.

141. Vos, *The Synoptic Traditions in the Apocalypse*, p. x.

of the underlying formative thought." [142] He recognizes Dan 7:13 as the ultimate source of the expression ὅμοιον υἱὸν ἀνθρώπου. He doubts, however, that the apocalyptist was directly dependent on Dan 7:13 for this expression, holding rather that the gospel tradition was its immediate source. [143] The evidence for this conclusion is (1) that the son of man is portrayed as sitting in Rev 14:14, as in Mk 14:62/Mt 26:64, a portrayal different from Dan 7:13; (2) the son of man in Rev 14:14 is associated with a single cloud, as in Lk 21:27; this motif differs from the plural "clouds" in Dan 7:13; (3) the son of man of Rev 14:14 is portrayed as having authority and power to judge; this power and authority is symbolized by the crown and the sickle. These elements are not reminiscent of Dan 7:13 or Joel 4:13, but they are similar to the statement that Christ will come with "power and great glory" (Mt 24:30 par.). (4) The activity of the son of man, harvest and vintage, is symbolic of the judgment at the end of time, the gathering of the saved and the lost. Joel 4:13 uses the harvest as an image for judgment, but it is not the final judgment. (5) The final judgment is portrayed as a harvest in the sayings of Jesus; the similarities between Rev 14:14–19 and the parable of the tares, together with its explanation, are particularly close. (6) There is no instance in Jewish literature of angels playing a role similar to the one in both the synoptic sayings and Rev 14:14b. (7) The command which the angel coming from the temple gives to the son of man is related to the statement of Jesus in the synoptic apocalypse that only the Father, not even the Son, knows the time of the end; the angel in Rev 14:15 is an agent of God, informing the son of man (= the Son) that the time has arrived; (8) The twofold ingathering is explained by the synoptic tradition as meaning that there will be a great separation between the elect and the nonelect; Joel 4:13 probably refers to a vintage only; (9) the angel who has power over fire (Rev 14:18) is reminiscent of the fire into which the weeds/sons of the evil one are thrown in the parable of the tares. [144]

In spite of its apparent strength, Vos's argument is not compelling. The similarities between Rev 14:14–20 and various synoptic sayings can be explained without the assumption that this passage is dependent either on one or more of the gospels or on any specific saying used by a gospel. Vos's arguments will be examined one by one.

The portrayal of the son of man as sitting in Rev 14:14 does not necessarily derive from Mk 14:62 par. Although Vos is correct in remarking that the son of man is not portrayed as sitting in Daniel 7 or 4 Ezra 13, he is so portrayed in the Similitudes of Enoch (1En 37–71). Although J. T. Milik has argued that the Similitudes is a Christian work of the second or third century C.E., [145]

---

142. Ibid., p. 145.
143. Ibid., p. 146.
144. Ibid., pp. 146–52.

his thesis has been severely criticized.[146] Most scholars now agree that the work is Jewish and is to be dated to the first century C.E. The latest datable historical allusions in the work are the references to the invasion of Palestine by the Parthians in 40 B.C.E. (56:5–7) and to Herod's use of the waters of Callirhoe (67:7–9). Thus the Similitudes should be dated to the early first century C.E.[147] In this work the Son of Man is portrayed as sitting on the throne of his glory (1En 69:27).[148] It is explicitly said that he is seated on the throne for the purpose of judgment (1En 69:27).[149] Although the literary dependence of Revelation on the Similitudes of Enoch may not be demonstrable, it is likely that the author of Revelation was familiar with the apocalyptic traditions reflected in that text.[150]

Vos himself admits that the parallel between Rev 14:14 and Lk 21:27 (a single cloud) does not prove a connection between the two texts.[151] The author of Revelation may have employed the singular simply in order to convey a more vivid picture (cf. 10:1).

The crown of Rev 14:14 can readily be explained as a visual representation of the statement in Dan 7:13 that the one like a son of man was given "dominion and glory and kingdom." The sickle can be explained as derived from Joel 4:13.

Vos's argument that Joel 4:13 does not describe the final judgment of the end time, whereas Rev 14:14–20 does, is misleading. It is to be granted that the perspective of Joel 4:13 and its context is national, but it is also eschatological.[152] Furthermore, the author of Revelation did not need to refer to the saying preserved in Mt 13:36–43 or to any specific saying of Jesus to interpret the passage in Joel in terms of apocalyptic eschatology. The community

145. J. T. Milik, "Problèmes de la littérature Hénochique à la lumière des fragments araméens de Qumrân," HTR 64 (1971); idem, The Books of Enoch (Oxford, 1976).

146. D. W. Suter, "Weighed in the Balance: The Similitudes of Enoch in Recent Discussion," Religious Studies Review 7 (1981) 217–21.

147. J. C. Greenfield, "Prolegomenon," to H. Odeberg, 3 Enoch or the Hebrew Book of Enoch (New York, 1973), p. xvii. See also J. C. Greenfield and M. E. Stone, "The Enochic Pentateuch and the Date of the Similitudes," HTR 70 (1977) 51–65; D. W. Suter, Tradition and Composition in the Parables of Enoch (SBLDS 47; Missoula, Mont., 1979), p. 32. A date in the early part of the first century C.E. is accepted also by G. W. E. Nickelsburg, Jewish Literature Between the Bible and the Mishnah (Philadelphia, 1981), p. 223; and J. J. Collins, The Apocalyptic Imagination (New York, 1984), pp. 142–43.

148. Cf. 1En 45:3, 51:3; 55:4; 61:8; 62:1–2, 5–7. In 62:2 all the manuscripts read "the Lord of Spirits sat." Most commentators emend to "the Lord of Spirits set him" because the context requires some such emendation. These passages describe "the Chosen One" as seated on the throne of glory. In the present form of the work at least, the Chosen One and the son of Man are identical.

149. Cf. 1En 55:4, 61:8, 62:3.

150. The Similitudes most likely originated in the land of Israel/Palestine. See Yarbro Collins, Crisis and Catharsis, pp. 46–49, for an argument that the author of Revelation was a native or resident of Palestine before traveling to the Roman province of Asia.

151. Vos, The Synoptic Traditions in the Apocalypse, pp. 146–47 and n. 173.

152. Cf. H. W. Wolff, Joel and Amos (Hermeneia; Philadelphia, 1977), pp. 84–85.

at Qumran and some early Christians interpreted even noneschatological passages of the Jewish Bible in an eschatological way.[153] Although many commentators so assume, the harvest of Rev 14:14–16 does not necessarily refer to the ingathering of the elect. Rev 14:1–5 is indeed a vision of salvation and the 144,000 are called "first fruits for God and the Lamb" (vs. 4). In 15:2–4 another vision of salvation appears, depicting the conquerors in a heavenly setting. Neither vision, however, implies that 14:14–16 represents a gathering of all the faithful to Christ or to heaven. The harvest in vss. 14–16 is best understood as a visual representation of Joel 4:13a. The fact that the Heb. קָצִיר is translated as τρύγητος in the OG does not necessarily mean that the author of Revelation read the passage as a description of a single event, namely, vintage. קָצִיר often means a harvest of grain.[154] The author of Revelation may have recalled the Hebrew word or been familiar with a Greek recension which read θερισμός for קָצִיר.[155] Thus the author of Revelation probably presented a vision of judgment in 14:14–20 with the double image of harvest and vintage, as he understood the text of Joel to do. Finally it should be pointed out that it is misleading to describe this vision as referring to the *final* judgment. Verse 20 suggests, as noted above, that judgment here takes the form of a battle, for which harvest and vintage are metaphors. This battle is probably the same as the one described in 19:11–21.[156] This battle is analogous to that of Joel 4, namely, it is a battle of the champion of God's people against their enemies, epitomized in Revelation by Rome. The *final* judgment in Revelation takes place in 20:11–15.

In Mt 13:36–43 we have an allegorical interpretation of an older parable, which originally had a different application.[157] Jeremias attributed the interpretation to the work of the author of Matthew.[158] The elements of Matthew 13 pointed out by Vos as similar to Rev 14:14–19 are all in this later interpretation. Vos was incorrect in arguing that these elements are unique to the tradition associated with Jesus. In the Similitudes of Enoch, angels have a major role in the activities related to judgment. According to 1En 54:1–2, "they" will throw the kings and the mighty into a deep valley with burning fire. This is most probably an allusion to the eschatological, final judgment.[159] "They" are probably angels. This eschatological judgment is an antitype of the judgment executed by the angels Michael, Gabriel, Raphael, and Phanuel upon the fallen angels just prior to the flood. This judgment con-

153. See e.g. 1Cor 10:11.
154. See BDB, p. 894.
155. Compare Hatch-Redpath, vol. 1, p. 649.
156. Yarbro Collins, *Combat Myth*, p. 37.
157. J. Jeremias, *The Parables of Jesus* (rev. ed.; New York, 1963), pp. 81–85, 223–27; E. P. Sanders, *Jesus and Judaism* (Philadelphia, 1985), pp. 114–15.
158. Jeremias, *The Parables of Jesus*, pp. 84–85.
159. Note that the wicked and the adversaries of the faithful are sometimes described in similar terms in Rev (6:15, 19:18).

sisted of throwing "them on that day into the furnace of burning fire" (vss. 5–6). In 1En 55:3–4, the final judgment is described in terms of the Lord of Spirits laying hold of the wicked "by the hand of the angels on the day of distress and pain." At the time of the final judgment, "the angels of punishment" will take the wicked ("the mighty kings, and the exalted, and those who rule the dry ground") and repay them for the wrong they did to the chosen ones of the Lord of Spirits (1En 62:9–11). This repayment is referred to in some manuscripts as "the flames of the torment of Sheol" (1En 63:1, 10).[160] As the author of Matthew interpreted an older parable in light of Jewish apocalyptic traditions known to him, so the author of Revelation, independently of Matthew, interpreted an older text, Joel 4:13, in light of the same apocalyptic traditions, including Daniel 7.

Vos is correct that the angel of Rev 14:15 should be understood as an agent of God, announcing the arrival of the time for the judgment against the nations. It is not necessary, however, to connect this incident in the vision with the saying of Jesus in Mk 13:32 par. Such a "subordination" of the one like a son of man to God through his agents is perfectly compatible with an early christology in which the conception of the risen Christ is analogous to a high angel (Daniel 7) or the Son of Man in the Similitudes of Enoch.

The angel who has power over fire (vs. 18) need not be explained as an allusion to Mt 13:40–42. The association of angels of punishment with fire in the Similitudes of Enoch was pointed out above. Further, the notion of angels appointed over certain elements occurs in this document as well. According to 1 Enoch 60, there is a spirit appointed over the thunder and lightning (vs. 14). Likewise there is a spirit of the sea (vs. 16), of the hoarfrost (vs. 17), of the hail (vs. 18), of the mist (vs. 19), of the dew (vs. 20), and of the rain (vs. 21). In Rev 16:15, "the angel of the waters" is mentioned. It may be that the traditional schema of the four elements (earth, fire, water, and air) is reflected in 16:15 and 14:18.[161] The angel of 14:18 may be associated both with the heavenly altar and with the created element fire; cf. 8:3–5. The appearance of the angel here recalls both the vision of 8:3–5 and that of 6:9–11 and thus suggests that the judgment/battle of 14:14–20 is divine vengeance upon those who have persecuted the faithful.

A comment remains to be made on the expression ὅμοιον υἱὸν ἀνθρώπου, which appears in Rev 14:14 and 1:13. The word ὅμοιον does not appear in any manuscript or citation of the OG of Dan 7:13 or in Theodotion. It is likely that the author of Revelation used it in these two passages as a

---

160. Cf. 1En 67:9.
161. H. D. Betz, "Zum Problem des religionsgeschichtlichen Verständnisses der Apokalyptik," *ZTK* 63 (1966) 391–409; ET, "On the Problem of the Religio-Historical Understanding of Apocalypticism," in R. W. Funk, ed., *Apocalypticism* (*JThC* 6; New York, 1969), pp. 140–42; cf. A. Yarbro Collins, "The History-of-Religions Approach to Apocalypticism and the 'Angel of the Waters' (Rev 16:4–7)," *CBQ* 39 (1977) 374–79.

translation of כ in the Aramaic text of Dan 7:13 known to him. It is likely that he knew of the translation ὡς for כ and used ὅμοιος here as its equivalent. This conclusion is supported by the fact that he uses ὅμοιος here similarly to ὡς both in meaning and construction.[162]

Conclusion

The writer has argued elsewhere that the historical Jesus referred in his teaching to Dan 7:13 as an eschatological prophecy about to be fulfilled. In referring to the figure "one like a son of man" in that passage, Jesus used a definite form ("the one like a son of man" or "that son of man") in order to point to the text already known to his audience. He understood that figure as a heavenly being, perhaps an angel, and associated his own teaching and activity with that being, although he probably did not identify himself with the "one like a son of man." The sayings which refer to a heavenly son of man and which are likely to go back in some form to the historical Jesus are Mt 24:44 par., Mt 24:37–39 par., and Mt 24:27 par. After Jesus' death, some of his followers, presuming his exaltation to heaven, identified him with the heavenly figure of Dan 7:13, as other Jews, possibly in the same century, had identified that son of man with their patron, Enoch.[163] The writer has also argued in another context that sayings regarding the heavenly Son of Man in an eschatological role are characteristic of the Synoptic Sayings Source (Q) at all the stages of its compositional history which can reasonably be differentiated, including the earliest stage.[164]

The discussion above of various passages in Revelation related to the son of man tradition suggests the following conclusions. The author of Revelation used the expression υἱὸς ἀνθρώπου only allusively; i.e. when the phrase appears (1:13 and 14:14), other elements from Daniel 7 or even the wider context of Daniel 7–12 appear also. The phrase is not used in a titular or even quasi-titular manner. It is indefinite in both occurrences. It is clear, however, that the author of Revelation identified the one like a son of man in Dan 7:13 with the risen Christ. This is implied by the conflation of Dan 7:13 with Zechariah 12 in Rev 1:7 and by the saying in Rev 1:18 which clarifies 1:12–16. Thus the author of Revelation uses the phrase from Dan 7:13 in a way similar to that posited for the historical Jesus above. It is assumed that the phrase refers to a particular heavenly being, but the phrase itself is allusive to a text and not titular.

The author of Revelation, nevertheless, does not simply reproduce the

---

162. So Charles, *The Revelation of St. John*, vol. 1, pp. 36–37.

163. A. Yarbro Collins, "The Origin of the Designation of Jesus As 'Son of Man,'" *HTR* 80 (1987) 391–407.

164. A. Yarbro Collins, "The Son of Man Sayings in the Sayings Source," *To Touch the Text: Biblical and Related Studies in Honor of Joseph A. Fitzmyer, S.J.*, ed. M. P. Horgan and P. J. Kobelski (New York, 1989).

teaching of Jesus on the son of man. Revelation does not seem to contain a saying of Jesus on this topic in a form close to what Jesus plausibly may have said. Furthermore, the author of Revelation identifies the son of man with the risen Jesus, an identification which Jesus probably did not make. At the same time, the author of Revelation did not take the step of using the form ὁ υἱὸς τοῦ ἀνθρώπου as the Q tradition and the gospels did. The use of the quasi-titular definite form of the phrase is apparently unknown to the author of Revelation. This difference suggests that the tradition known to the author of Revelation, with regard to this topic at least, has its roots in Palestinian Christianity in the early period after the experiences of the resurrection, but in a context in which Q had not yet been formulated or in which that tradition was unknown. Likewise, the gospel of Mark and the other gospels seem to have been unknown to the author of Revelation. In the book of Revelation then, we seem to have an independent development of a very early christological tradition.

INDEXES

The indexes are organized according to the following categories:

I. Ancient Sources
   A. Old Testament/Hebrew Scriptures
   B. New Testament/Christian Scriptures
   C. Apocrypha and Pseudepigrapha (this section includes *both* OT *and* NT pseudepigrapha),
   D. Dead Sea Scrolls,
   E. Rabbinic Writings,
   F. Other Ancient Sources, including
      1. Ancient Near Eastern Texts,
      2. Classical Greek and Latin Sources,
      3. Josephus,
      4. Philo and Ps-Philo,
      5. Patristic Literature
II. Modern Authors.

As to the biblical references, when a discussion emphasizes text-critical issues, citations of scripture according to specific translation traditions, versions, recensions, or manuscripts are taken into account in the index. The abbreviations in these citations are largely standard, but it should be noted that while LXX^B = *Codex Vaticanus* and LXX^A = *Codex Alexandrinus*, LXX^{aq}, LXX^S, LXX^T, and LXX^L refer to Aquila, Symmachus, Theodotian, and Lucian, respectively. In addition, the designation LXX and OG (Old Greek) reflect the *author's* usage and what the author takes to constitute the LXX or OG must be determined on the basis of his or her discussion. All other citations without following abbreviations reflect the MT (Masoretic Text) of the Old Testament or the standard Greek text of the New Testament (Aland, et al.). For MSS abbreviations concerning the texts of *Revelation* and *Daniel,* these follow Kurt Aland, et al., *The Greek New Testament,* 3rd edition (Münster/Westphalia, 1975), pp. xiii–xli, and J. Ziegler, *Septuaginta 16:2: Susanna, Daniel, Bel et Draco* (Göttingen, 1954), pp. 7–68.

Thanks must go first to Jerry L. Gorham for the bulk of the data entry involved in the preparation of these indexes. Thanks are also due to Loren L. Johns for assistance with the formatting and with other technical matters relating to the indexes.

—Michael T. Davis

ANCIENT SOURCES

RABBINIC WRITINGS

MODERN AUTHORS